Dictionary Of The English Language

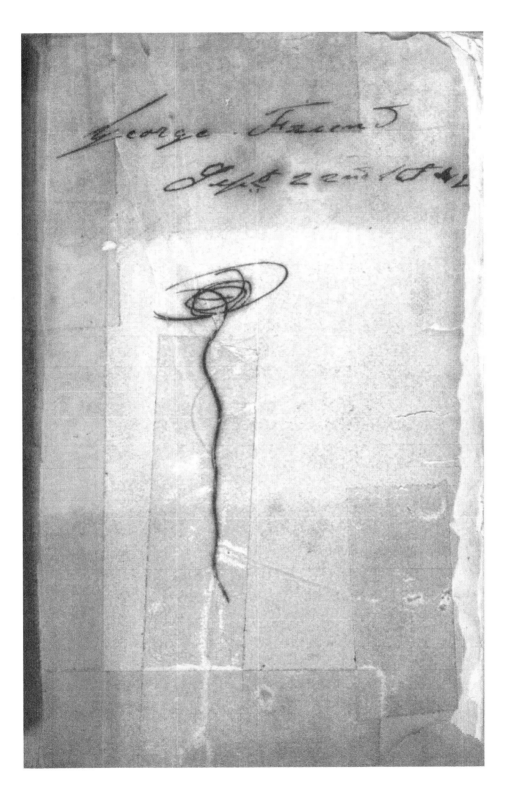

George Freund
September 1842

JOHNSON'S
DICTIONARY

OF THE

ENGLISH LANGUAGE:

CONTAINING

MANY ADDITIONAL WORDS

NOT TO BE MET WITH IN FORMER POCKET EDITIONS,

ACCENTED FOR PRONUNCIATION;

WITH

A LIST OF ABBREVIATIONS OF TITLES, &c. &c.

A COLLECTION OF FRENCH AND LATIN PHRASES,

An Alphabetical Account of the Heathen Deities,

SUCCINCT NOTICE OF MEN OF GENIUS AND LEARNING,

An accurate Table of the Imperial Weights and Measures,

A LIST OF THE CITIES, BOROUGHS, AND MARKET TOWNS IN ENGLAND AND

WALES, WITH THEIR MARKET DAYS AND DISTANCES FROM LONDON,

AND

A CHRONOLOGICAL TABLE

Of Remarkable Events, Discoveries, and Inventions, from the Creation of
the World.

———◆———

LONDON:

PRINTED FOR T. NOBLE, 79, FLEET STREET.

1819.

Pittsburgh. Loud satisfied exclamation of the reading of the last
clause!

ADVERTISEMENT.

THE excellence of DR. JOHNSON's DICTIONARY OF THE ENGLISH LAN-
GUAGE is now so fully proved, as to render any prefatory remarks
wholly unnecessary. In submitting, however, the present unique
edition of the great Lexicographer's Work to the Public, I trust I
may be permitted to point out the peculiar advantages by which it is
distinguished, and the grounds on which it rests its claim to public
support and approbation.

In this Edition will be found some thousand words which the desire
for compression and portability, or ignorance of their importance, has
expunged from numerous editions, which, by this practice, are rendered useless to the general reader, who refers to a Lexicon for a
definition of obsolete or seldom-used words, and not so much for those
which every-day employment renders familiar. I have laboured to
supply this hiatus by a selection from the Quarto Edition, and by the
addition of numerous modern terms, not hitherto collected and defined; thus giving to this Edition a distinguishing feature, which will
render it, I trust, of considerable utility in schools and for general reference. Whilst I have been thus careful in increasing the number of
Words, I have not neglected to attend to their correct pronunciation; and, by adhering to the principles laid down by Walker, in his
celebrated Treatise on English Pronunciation, I have accented each
Word in so clear a manner, that the Student, by observing the situation of the accent will be instantly enabled to ascertain the correct
pronunciation.

Appended to the Dictionary, will be found a Selection of Latin and
English Phrases and Quotations, which will prove of infinite service
to the unclassic reader; a List of Cities, &c. and their distances from
London, carefully compared with, and corrected by, the latest edition
of Gray's Book of Roads; a Table of Imperial Weights and Measures;
a copious Chronology of Remarkable Events; and a variety of important information on useful subjects.

THE EDITOR.

London, October, 1821.

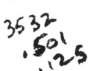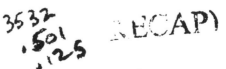

A CHRONOLOGICAL TABLE

OF

REMARKABLE EVENTS, DISCOVERIES, AND INVENTIONS.

[The whole comprehending, in one view, the Analysis or Outlines of General History, from the Creation to the present Time.]

	B.C.
THE creation of the world, and Adam and Eve	4004
The old world destroyed by a deluge, which continued 377 days	2348
The Tower of Babel built by Noah's posterity, upon which God miraculously confounds their language, and disperses them into different nations	2247
Noah supposed to have parted from his rebellious offspring, and to have founded the Chinese monarchy	2247
Celestial observations begun at Babylon	2233
Misraim, son of Ham, founds the kingdom of Egypt	2188
The covenant of God made with Abram, when he leaves Haran to go into Canaan	1921
Sodom and Gomorrah destroyed for their sins by fire from heaven	1697
Memnon, the Egyptian, invents the letters	1822
Prometheus first struck fire from flints	1715
Joseph dies in Egypt, which concludes the book of Genesis	1635
Cecrops brings a colony from Egypt, and begins the kingdom of Athens	1556
Scamander comes from Crete into Phrygia, and begins the kingdom of Troy	1546
Cadmus carries the Phœnician letters into Greece, and builds the citadel of Thebes	1493
Moses performs many miracles in Egypt, and departs from that kingdom, together with 600,000 Israelites, besides children	1491
The first ship that appeared in Greece was brought from Egypt by Danaus, who arrived at Rhodes, and brought with him his fifty daughters	1485
The first Olympic games celebrated at Olympia, in Greece	1453
The Pentateuch, or five first books of Moses, written in the land of Moab, where he died the year following, aged 110	1452
The Israelites, after sojourning in the wilderness forty years, are led under Joshua into the land of Canaan, and the period of the sabbatical year commences	1451
Iron found in Greece from the accidental burning of the woods	1406
The rape of Helen by Paris, which gave rise to the Trojan war	1193
David sole king of Israel	1018
The Temple solemnly dedicated by Solomon	1004
Elijah, the prophet, translated to heaven	896
Money first made of gold and silver at Argos	894
The city of Carthage, in Africa, founded by queen Dido	869
The kingdom of Macedon begins	814
Æra of the building of Rome, in Italy, by Romulus, first king of Rome	753
Samaria taken after a three years' siege, and the kingdom of Israel finished by Salmanasar, king of Assyria, who carries the ten tribes into captivity	720
The first eclipse of the moon on record	720
Byzantium (now Constantinople) built by a colony of Athenians	658
By order of Necho, king of Egypt, some Phœnicians sail from the Red Sea round Africa, and return by the Mediterranean	604
Thales, of Miletus, travels into Egypt, consults the priests of Memphis, acquires the knowledge of geometry, astronomy, and philosophy; returns to Greece, calculates eclipses, and gives general notions of the universe	600
The city of Jerusalem taken, after a siege of 18 months	587
The first comedy at Athens acted upon a moveable scaffold	562
The kingdom of Babylon terminates	538
The first tragedy acted at Athens, on a waggon, by Thespis	534
Learning encouraged at Athens, and a public library first founded	526
Tarquin, the seventh and last king of the Romans, expelled	509
Xerxes the Great, king of Persia, begins the expedition against Greece	481
The Decemvirs created at Rome, and the laws of the twelve tables compiled	451
The history of the Old Testament finished, about	409
Socrates, the founder of moral philosophy, put to death by the Athenians	400
Alexander the Great conquers Persia, and other nations of Asia. 331. Dies at Babylon, and his empire divided by his generals into four kingdoms	329
Dionysius of Alexandria, the first who found the exact solar year to consist of 365 days, 5 hours, and 49 minutes	

CHRONOLOGICAL TABLE.

A.D.

CHRONOLOGICAL TABLE.

A.D.

The princess royal of England married to the prince of Wirtemberg, May 18 1797
Lord Malmesbury returned a second time unsuccessful from a pacific negotiation .. 1797
Admiral Duncan defeated the Dutch fleet, of which he captured nine ships of the line,
    October 11, and was created a viscount... 1797
A general thanksgiving for the great naval victories of lords Howe, St. Vincent, and
    Duncan. December 19 1797
Treasonable and rebellious plans discovered to be on foot in Ireland, March 12.... 1798
Rebellion broke out in the south of Ireland, April 9 1798
Patriotic resolutions and associations formed in different counties of England for the
    defence of the country against invasion, April 16, &c............................... 1798
Habeas corpus act suspended, April 20 1798
Marquis Cornwallis appointed lord lieutenant of Ireland, June 13 1798
The glorious victory of the Nile achieved by admiral (afterwards baron) Nelson.... 1798
The French land in Kilala Bay, Ireland, August 24 1798
Battle of Austerlitz, in which the combined armies of Austria and Russia were de-
    feated by the French under Buonaparte, September................................ 1805
Battle of Jena, in which the Prussian army was complete y defeated by Buonaparte,
    September.. 1806
Buonaparte married by proxy to the archduchess Maria Louisa of Austria, at Vienna,
    March 11 1810
Sir F. Burdett committed to the Tower, April 9, and released June 21 1810
Princess Amelia died, November 2 1810
The empress of France, Maria Louisa, brought to bed of a son, March 20 1811
Christophe, a man of colour, crowned king of St. Domingo 1811
Russia declared war against France, March 19 1812
Mr. Percival, chancellor of the Exchequer, shot by Bellingham, May 11........... 1812
Lord Wellington took Salamanca, June 16 1812
The French entered Moscow, Sept. 14.—Abandoned it, Oct. 19 1812
Battle of Lutzen, between the allies and French, May 2 1813
Battle of Vittoria—French defeated, June 21 1813
Battle of Dresden—the allies defeated, general Moreau slain, Aug. 27 1813
British army from Spain enters France, Oct. 8 1813
The New Testament printed in the Chinese language 1814
The allied armies pass the Rhine, and occupy Coblentz, Jan. 2 1814
The custom-house of London burned down, with many adjoining warehouses,
    Feb 12 1814
Deputies from Bourdeaux invite Louis XVIII. to return to France, March 25 1814
Battle at the barriers of Paris—Marmont evacuates the city, March 30............. 1814
The allies enter Paris, March 31 1814
The senate of France declares N. Buonaparte and his family to have forfeited the
    imperial crown, April 2 1814
Buonaparte signed his abdication of the crown of France and Italy, April 4 1814
Buonaparte embarked for the Isle of Elba, April 28................................. 1814
Public entry of Louis XVIII. into Paris, May 3 1814
Peace proclaimed in London. June 20 1814
Napoleon Buonaparte quits Elba, meets with a favourable reception in France, and
    enters Paris, March 20... 1815
A confederation signed at Vienna, called the Holy Alliance, June 8 1815
Battle of Waterloo, June 18... 1815
Buonaparte gave himself up to the British government, July 15; and arrived at St.
    Helena. Oct. 16 1815
Princess Charlotte of Wales married to Leopold, prince of Saxe Coburg, May 12.... 1816
Algiers bombarded by lord Exmouth, and Christian slavery abolished 1816
Popular and riotous meetings in Spa-fields, December 1816
The Congress of the United States resolved to abolish the Slave Trade 1817
The princess Charlotte of Wales died, after being delivered of a still-born male
    child, Nov. 6... 1817
The duke of Clarence married to the princess of Saxe Meiningen; and the duke of
    Kent to a princess of Saxe Coburg, July 13 1818
Congress held at Aix-la-Chapelle, Sept. 29.. 1818
Queen Charlotte died at Kew, in her 75th year, Nov. 17 1818
Many distressed persons embarked, under the sanction of government, to establish
    a new colony at the cape of Good Hope.. 1819
Kotzebue assassinated at Manheim, by a student named Sandt, April 2............. 1819
Madame Blanchard ascended in a balloon surrounded by fire-works; the balloon
    took fire, and she was precipitated and killed, July 6 1819
20,000 Spanish soldiers, destined for South America, mutinied and deserted, July 13 1819
Congress on the affairs of Europe held at Carlsbad, August 1 1819
A popular meeting at Manchester to petition for reform dispersed by the Manchester
    yeomanry cavalry August 16.. 1819

JOHNSON'S
DICTIONARY.

ABBREVIATIONS.

a. Adjective—*s.* Substantive—*pron.* Pronoun—*v. a.* Verb Active—*v. n.* Verb Neuter—*ad.* Adverb—*prep.* Preposition—*conj.* Conjunction—*intj.* Interjection—*part.* Participle—*part. a.* Participial Adjective.

A, *s.* the first letter in the alphabet; a note in music; the indefinite article placed before substantives
Aback', *ad.* backward; back; a sea term
A 'acot, *s.* an ancient kind of a crown
Ab'acus, *s.* a counting table; in architecture, the uppermost member of a column
Abaf't, or Aft, *ad.* towards the stern from the ship's head; a sea term
Abai'sance, *s.* a bow; a mark of respect
Abal'ienate, *v. a.* to make over to another
Aban'don, *v. a.* to resign, to forsake, desert
Aban'doned, *a.* deserted; given up; wicked
Aban'donment, *s.* the act of abandoning
Aba'se, *v. a.* to cast down, to bring low, debase
Aba'sed, *part.* brought low, humbled [press
Aba'sement, *s.* the state of being brought low
Abash', *v. a.* to confuse, to make ashamed
Abash'ment, *s.* astonishment, confusion
Aba'te, *v. a.* to lessen; to lower in price; in common law, to *abate* a writ is, by some exception, to defeat or overthrow it
Aba'tement, *s.* the act of diminishing; the quantity abated, extenuation
Abb, *s.* the yarn on a weaver's warp
Ab'ba, *s.* a Syriac word signifying father
Ab'bacy, *s.* the rights, possessions, or privileges of an abbot
Ab'be, Ab'bey, Ab'by, *s.* a monastery for religious persons, whether men or women
Ab'bess, *s.* the governess of a nunnery
Ab'bot, *s.* the chief of a convent of men
Abbre'viate, *v. a.* to abridge, to shorten
Abbrevia'tion, *s.* the act of shortening
Abbrevia'tor, *s.* one who shortens or abridges
Abbre'viature, *s.* a mark used for the sake of shortening; a compendium or abridgement
Ab'dicate, *v. a.* to resign an office, to give up
Abdica'tion, *s.* resignation; act of giving up
Ab'dicative, *a.* that which implies resignation
Ab'ditive, *a.* hiding or concealing
Abdo'men, *s.* the lower part of the belly
Abdom'inal, *a.* relating to the abdomen
Abdom'inous, *a.* paunch-bellied; unwieldy
Abdu'ce, *v. a.* to separate; to draw away
Abdu'cent, *a.* drawing or pulling back
Abduc'tion, *s.* the act of drawing back or away
Abduc'tor, *s.* any muscle that contracts
Abeceda'rian, *s.* a teacher of the alphabet
Abece'dary, *a.* relating to the alphabet
Abed', *ad.* in bed, on the bed [way
Aber'rance, *s.* a wandering from the right

Aber'rant, *a.* wandering from the right way
Aberra'tion, *s.* the act of wandering
Abet', *v. a.* to aid, to encourage, to set on
Abet'ment, *s.* act of aiding, or encouraging
Abet'tor, *s.* he that aids; an accomplice
Abey'ance, *s.* in law, goods in reversion, but not in possession; dormancy
Abgrega'tion, *s.* seldom used, the act of separating from the flock
Abhor', *v. a.* to detest; to hate with acrimony
Abhor'rence, *s.* the act of hating; aversion
Abhor'rent, *a.* struck with abhorrence, foreign; contrary to; inconsistent with
Abi'de, *v. n.* to dwell in a place; to attend; to support; to persevere in any thing
Ab'ject, *a.* mean, base, vile, contemptible
Abjec'tedness, Abjec'tion, Ab'jectness, *s.* meanness of mind, servility, baseness
Ab'jectly, *ad.* in a servile manner, meanly
Abil'ity, *s.* power, skill, capacity, qualification
Abinfes'tate, *s.* the heir of an intestate person
Ab'jugate, *v. a.* to set free, to unyoke
Abjura'tion, *s.* the act of abjuring; a renouncing on oath
Abju're, *v. a.* to retract, or recant solemnly, to renounce an opinion; forsake the realm
Ablac'tate, *v. a.* to wean from the breast
Ablacta'tion, *s.* weaning; a method of grafting
Ablaquea'tion, *s.* the opening of the ground round roots of trees, to admit air or water
Abla'tion, *s.* the act of taking away
Ab'lative, *a.* that takes away; the sixth case of the Latin nouns
A'ble, *a.* having power; skilful
Able-bod'ied, *a.* strong of body, robust
Ab'legate, *v. a.* to send abroad on some public business or employment
A'bleness, *s.* strength of mind or body
Ab'lepsy, *s.* want of sight; inadvertence
Ab'ligate, *v. a.* to bind or tie up from
Ab'locate, *v. a.* to let out to hire
Ab'luent, *a.* that has the power of cleansing
Ablu'tion, *s.* act or cleansing; a religious purification
A'bly, *ad.* with ability
Ab'negate, *v. a.* to deny, to renounce, reject
Abnega'tion, *s.* denial; resignation
Abnor'mous, *a.* out of rule; vast, huge
Aboa'rd, *ad.* in, or on board a ship
Abo'de, *s.* an habitation, a dwelling place
Abo'de, *v. a.* to foretel, to prognosticate
Abo'dement, *s.* a secret anticipation; omen

Abol'ish, v. a. to repeal, to make void
Abol'ishable, a. that which may be abolished
Aboli'tion, s. the act of abolishing
Abom'inable, a. detestable, hateful; unclean
Abom'inableness, s. hatefulness, odiousness
Abom'inably, ad. extremely; excessively; exceedingly: in the ill sense
Abom'inate, v. a. to abhor, to detest, to hate
Abomina'tion, s. detestation, hatred; pollution, or defilement
Aborig'ines, s. the earliest inhabitants of a country
Abor'tion, s. a miscarriage; untimely birth
Abor'tive, a. untimely; premature
Above, prep. higher in place; superior to—ad. the regions of heaven
Above'board, ad. openly, fairly
Abou'nd, v. n. to have or be in great plenty
Abou't, prep. round; encircling, near to; engaged in; relating to—ad. every way
Abracadab'ra, s. a superstitious charm
Abra'de, v. a. to waste by degrees; to rub off
Abra'sion, s. the act of rubbing off
Abreas't, ad. close together, side by side
Abri'dge, v. a. to contract; to shorten minute parts, keeping still the substance
Abridg'ement, s. a summary; a larger work contracted into a smaller compass
Abroa'ch, ad. in a state to run; in a situation ready to yield the liquor contained
Abroa'd, ad. without doors; in foreign countries, widely spread
Ab'rogate, v. a. to annul, abolish, repeal
Abroga'tion, s. the act of annulling
Abrup't, a. sudden; rough; unconnected
Abrup'tly, ad. unseasonably; hastily
Abrup'tness, an abrupt manner, suddenness
Abscess', s. a tumour containing matter
Abscin'd, v. a. to cut off
Abscis'sa, s. part of the diameter of a conic section intercepted between the vertex and a semi-ordinate
Abscis'sion, s. the act of cutting or lopping off
Abscon'd, v. a. to hide one's self
Abscon'der, s. the person who absconds
Ab'sence, s. being absent; inattention
Ab'sent, a. not present; inattentive
Absen't, v. a. to keep away, to withdraw
Absentee', s. one who is absent from his employment, station, or country
Absin'thiated, part. impregnated with bitter
Absis't, v. n. to cease or leave off
Absol've, v. a. to set free; to acquit; to pardon
Ab'solute, a. complete; not relative; arbitrary; not limited; unconditional
Ab'solutely, ad. unconditionally, positively
Absolu'tion, s. acquittal; the remission of sins, or penance
Absol'utory, a. that which absolves or acquits
Ab'sonant, a. contrary to reason; absurd
Ab'sonate, v. a. to shun; to avoid; to hate
Absor'b, v. a. to suck up, to swallow up
Absor'bent, s. a medicine that draws away superfluous moisture in the body
Absor'pt, part. swallowed up
Absor'ption, s. the act of swallowing up
Abstai'n, v. n. to forbear, to refrain from
Abste'mious, a. temperate, abstinent, sober
Abste'miously, ad. temperately, soberly
Abste'miousness, s. sobriety, temperance
Absten'tion, s. the act of keeping off

Abster'ge, v. a. to cleanse; to wipe off
Abster'gent, a. having a cleansing quality
Abster'sion, s. the act of cleansing
Abstersive, a. that has the quality of cleansing
Ab'stinence, s. a refraining from; temperance
Abstrac't, v. a. to separate ideas; to abridge
Ab'struct, s. an abridgement, an epitome
Abstrac'ted, part. separated; refined, abstruse
Abstrac'tedly, ad. simply; separately
Abstrac'tion, s. the act of abstracting, &c.
Abstrac'tive, a. having the power to abstract
Abstrac'tly, ad. absolutely; simply
Abstru'se, a. hidden, obscure, difficult
Abstru'sely, ad. obscurely, not plainly
Abstru'seness, s. difficulty; obscurity
Absu'me, v. a. to waste by degrees
Absur'd, a. unreasonable; inconsistent
Absur'dity, s. not consistent with reason; folly
Absur'dly, ad. unreasonably, foolishly
Abun'dance, s. great plenty, exuberance
Abun'dant, a. plentiful; exuberant
Abun'dantly, ad. in plenty; amply; liberally
Abu'se, v. a. to reproach; to impose on; ill use
Abu'se, s. corrupt practice; unjust censure
Abu'ser, s. he that uses ill, or reproaches
Abu'sive, a. containing abuse
Abu'sively, ad. rudely; reproachfully
Abut', v. n. to join or border upon; to meet
Abut'tal, Abut'ment, s. that which joins to, or borders upon another thing
Abys'm, Abyss', s. hell; a fathomless gulf or pit
Academ'ical, a. belonging to an academy
Acade'mician, Academ'ic, Academi'cian, Academ'ist, s. a student at an academy
Acad'emy, s. a school where the arts and sciences are taught; an university
Acan'thus, s. the herb bear's foot
Acatalec'tic, s. a verse exactly perfect, having the complete number of syllables
Acatalep'tic, a. incomprehensible, obscure
Acce'de, v. n. to comply with or agree to
Accel'erate, v. a. to increase motion
Accel'erated, part. quickened, hastened
Accelera'tion, s. a quickening, hastening
Accen'd, v. a. to kindle; to set on fire
Accen'sion, s. the state of being kindled
Ac'cent, s. manner of pronunciation, a mark to direct the modulation of the voice
Accen't, v. a. to note the accent or mark
Accen'tuate, v. a. to place an accent properly
Accentua'tion, s. due placing of the accent
Accep't, v. a. to receive, to take, to admit
Accep'table, a. agreeable, reasonable
Accep'tably, ad. in an acceptable manner
Accep'tance, s. reception with approbation
Accepta'tion, s. reception, either agreeably or not; the received meaning of a word
Accep'ter, s. the person who accepts
Acceptila'tion, s. remission of a debt by an acquittance from a creditor
Access', s. admission to a place or person
Ac'cessary, s. an abettor; an accomplice
Acces'sible, a. that which may be approached
Acces'sion, s. addition; arriving at
Ac'cessory, a. additional; superadded;—s. an accomplice, not a principal
Ac'cidence, s. a little book containing the first rudiments of grammar
Ac'cident, s. property or quality of a word or being, separable from it, at least in thought; casualty; unforeseen event

Acciden'tal, a. happening by chance, casual
Acciden'tally, ad. fortuitously, casually
Accip'ient, s. a receiver—a. receiving
Accl'te, v. a. to call for or upon; to summon
Accla'im, Acclama'tion, s. a shout of applause; praise; exultation
Accliv'ity, s. the ascent of a hill
Accliv'ous, a. rising with a slope
Accloy', v. a. to cloy; to satiate; to surfeit
Accoi'l, v. n. to crowd; to hustle about
Accom'modable, a. that which may be fitted
Accom'modate, v. a. to supply; to reconcile
Accommoda'tion, s. reconciliation of a difference, provision of conveniences
Accom'panied, part. attended by
Accom'paniment, s. something added to another; harmonious union of parts
Accom'pany, v. a. to join; to associate with
Accom'plice, s. a partner, an associate
Accom'plish, v. a. to complete; to obtain; to adorn the body or improve the mind
Accom'plished, part. a. completed; elegant
Accom'plishment, s. completion; elegance; ornament of mind or body
Accom'pt, s. an account; a reckoning
Accom'ptant, s. a reckoner, a computer
Accor'd, v. a. to adjust; unite; agree with
Accor'd, s. a compact; harmony; union
Accor'dance, s. agreement; conformity
Accor'dant, a. willing; consenting
Accor'ding, prep. agreeably to; in proportion
Accor'dingly, ad. agreeably; conformably
Accor'porate, v. a. to unite
Accos't, v. a. to address, to salute
Acces'table, a. easy of access; familiar
Accou'cheur, s. a man-midwife
Accou'nt, v. a. to compute; to esteem; to answer for; to assign to; to give an account
Accou'nt, s. a computation; examination; narration; explanation; estimation
Accou'ntable, a. subject to an account
Accou'nted, part. valued, reckoned, esteemed
Accou'ple, v. a. to join or link together
Accou'tre, v. a. to attire, to dress, to furnish
Accou'trement, s. equipage, trappings
Accred'it, v. a. to countenance
Accre'tion, s. the act of growing to another
Accre'tive, a. that which by growth is added
Accru'e, v. n. to arise by profit; to he ad ed to
Accuba'tion, s. the ancient posture of leaning at meals
Accum'bent, a. leaning
Accu'mulate, v. a. to pile up, to heap together
Accumula'tion, s. an heaping up; a heap
Accu'mulative, a. that which increases ther
Accu'mulator, s. a gatherer or heaper together
Ac'curacy, s. exactness, nicety, correctness
Accur'se, v. a. to doom to misery
Accur'sed, part. a. that which is doomed to misery; execrable, hateful, detestable
Accu'sable, a. culpable; that may be censured
Accusa'tion, s. charge, imputation of blame
Accu'sative, s. the fourth case of a noun
Accu'se, v. a. to blame, to impeach, to censure; to charge with a crime
Accu'ser, s. a censor; one who prefers a complaint against another
Accus'tom, v. a. to use one's self to; to inure
Accus'tomable, a. habitual, customal
Accus'tomably, Accus'tomarily, ad. customarily long practised

Accus'tomary, a. common, usually done
Accus'tomed, part. a. frequent, usual
Ace, s. an unit on cards or dice; a trifle
Aceph'alous, a. without a head
Acer'b, a. acid, rough, bitter; severe
Acer'bate, v. a. to make bitter or sour
Acer'bity, s. severity of temper; a sour tast.
Acer'vate, v. a. to heap together, pile up
Acerva'tion, s. the act of heaping together
Aces'cent, a. tending to sourness, sharp, tar
Aceto'se, Ace'tous, a. sour, tart, as vinega
Ache, s. a continued pain
Ache, v. n. to be in continued pain
Achie've, v. a. to perform; to finish
Achie'vement, s. a deed; a performance; the escutcheons, or ensigns armorial
Achie'ver, s. he who accomplishes his ends
A'chor, s. a kind of shingles
Achromat'ic, a. remedying aberrations and colours in telescopes
Aci'cular, a. shaped like a small needle
Ac'id, a. sour, sharp, as vinegar
Acid'ity, A'cidness, s. sourness, sharpness
Acid'ulæ, s. medicinal springs impregnated with certain sharp particles
Acid'ulate, v. a. to tinge slightly with acids
Acina'ciform, a. resembling the shape of a sabre, fauchion, or scymetar
Acknowl'edge, v. a. to confess as a fault; to own as a benefit
Acknowl'edging, a. grateful for; confessing
Acknowl'edgment, s. concession; gratitude
Ac'me, s. the height or crisis of any thing
Acol'othist, s. a servitor in the Romish church
Ac'onite, s. wolf's bane; poison in general
A'corn, s. the seed or fruit of the oak
Acou'stica, s. the doctrine of sounds; medicines or instruments used to assist the hearing
Acquai'nt, v. a. to inform; make known [ing
Acqua'intance, s. familiarity; fellowship; a person with whom we are acquainted
Acqua'inted, a. well known to; familiar
Acques't, or Acquis't, s. a thing gained
Acquies'ce, v. n. to submit, yield, comply with
Acquies'cence, s. compliance; silent consent
Acqui'rable, a. that may be had; attainable
Acqui're, v. a. to gain by industry, or power
Acqui'rement, Acquisi'tion, s. that which is gained; the act of gaining; attainment
Acquis'itive, a. that which is acquired
Acquit't, v. a. to absolve; set free; discharge
Acquit'ment, s. the act of acquitting
Acquit'tal, s. deliverance from an offence
Acquit'tance, s. a writing testifying the receipt of a debt, a release
A'cre, s. a proportion of land containing 4810 square yards
Ac'rid, a. having a hot biting taste; bitter
Acrimo'nious, a. corrosive; sha p; severe
Ac'rimony, s. sharpness; ill nature; severity of temper or language; corrosiveness
Ac'ritude, Acri'ity, s. an acrid taste; a biting heat on the palate
Acroamat'ical, a. pertaining to deep learning
Acron'ical, a. te m of as' onomy applied to stars when they appear above or sink below the horizon at the time of sunset
Across', ad. laid over any thing, athwart
Acros'tic, s. a poem in which the name of the person or thing described is found on reading the first letters of every line

Act, v. n. to do, to perform ;—v. a. to imitate
Act, s. a deed, an exploit ; a part in a play
Ac'tion, s. opposite to rest ; a deed ; a battle ;
    a law suit ; gesture in speaking   [law
Ac'tionable, a. that which is punishable by
    ac'tionary, s. a holder of public stock
Ac'tive, a. nimble, agile, quick, busy
Ac'tively, ad. nimbly, quickly, briskly
Ac'tiveness, Activ'ity, s. nimbleness
Ac'tor, s. a stage player ; one that performs
Ac'tress, s. a female stage player
Ac'tual, a. certain ; real ; not speculative
ac'tually, ad. in act, in effect, really
Ac'tualness, s. the quality of being actual
Ac'tuary, s. a register, or clerk of a court
Ac'tuate, v. a. to move ; to put into action
Ac'tuate, a. Ac'tuated, part. put into action
Ac'tuate, v. a. to make sharp ; to point
Ac'uleate, a. having a sting or sharp point
Acu'men, s. a sharp point ; figuratively,
    quickness or sharpness of intellect
Acu'minated, part. ending in a sharp point
Acu'te, a. ingenious, sharp, keen, subtle
Acu'te, s. an accent marked thus (') to show
    when the voice should be raised
Acu'tely, ad. ingeniously, sharply, keenly
Acu'teness, s. sharpness, subtleness
Adac'ted, part. a. driven by force
Ad'age, s. a common saying ; a maxim
Ada'gio, s. in music, a term for slow time
Ad'amant, s. a loadstone ; a diamond
Adamante'an, a. impenetrable, very hard
Adaman'tine, a. hard ; made of adamant
Adap't, v. a. to proportion, to fit, to suit
Adapta'tion, Adap'tion, s. the fitness, or the
    act of fitting one thing to another
Add, v. a. to increase, to join to, number up
Addec'imate, v. a. to take or value tithes
Addee'm, v. a. to esteem ; reckon ; account
Ad'der, s. a viper ; a poisonous serpent
Ad'der's-grass, s. the name of a plant
Ad'der's-tongue, s. the name of an herb
Ad'dible, a. that which may be added
Ad'dice, Adze, s. an axe ; a cooper's tool
Addic't, v. a. to dedicate, to devote
Addic'ted, part. fond of, devoted to
Addic'tament, s. addition, the thing added
Addit'ion, s. a rule for adding sums together;
    an adding to ; in law, the residence, occu-
    pation, or rank of any person
Addit'ional, a. that which is added
Ad'dle, a. barren, empty ; originally applied
    to such eggs as are rotten—s. dry lees
Ad'dle-pated, a. weak ; empty headed
Address', v. n. to direct to ; to speak or apply
    to ; to prepare one's self for any action
Address, s. direction ; skill ; dexterity ; mode
    of behaviour ; a petition
Addu'ce, v. a. to bring in ; allere ; assign
Addu'cent, s. any muscle that contracts
Addul'ce, v. a. to sweeten ; to make pleasant
Adem'ption, s. privation, revocation
Adenog'raphy, s. a treatise of the glands
Ad'ept, s. one well versed in his art
Ad'equate, a. equal to, proportionate
Ad'equately, ad. duly, in exact proportion
Ad'equateness, s. exact proportion; equality
Adfec'ted, a. compounded, or affected
Adhe're, v. n. to rema n fixed to a party,
    person, or opinion ; to stick close to
Adhe'rence, s. tenacity ; attachment

Adhe'rent, a. sticking to ; uniting with
Adhe'rent, Adhe'rer, s. a follower ; pa tisan
Adhe'sion, s. the act of sticking to something
Adhe'sive, a. tenacious, sticking
Adhib'it, v. a. to make use of ; to apply
Adhibit'ion, s. use ; application
Adja'cency, s. state of being close or near to
Adja'cent, a. bordering upon, lying close to
Adiaph'orous, a. indifferent, neutral
Adiaph'ory, s. neutrality, indifference
Adjec't, v. a. to put to, to add to
Adjec'tion, s. the thing added, the act of ad i-
Adjectit'ious, a. thrown in, added   [ing
Ad'jective, s. a word added to a noun, to de-
    note its quality, as, bad, good, &c.
Adieu', ad. farewell
Adjoi'n, v.a. to put or unite to, to join to
Adjoi'ning, part. being near to, close to
Adjour'n, v. a. to defer, to put off
Adjour'nment, s. putting off to another day
Adipo'se, Ad'ipous, a. greasy, fat
Ad'it, s. a passage under ground for miners
Adjud'ge, v. a. to pass sentence, to decree
Adju'dicate, v. a. to determine by law
Ad'jugate, v. a. to yoke or couple to
Ad'junct, s. something adherent to another
Adjunc'tion, s. thing joined ; act of joining
Adjura'tion, s. the oath proposed ; a solemn
    proposing of an oath to another
Adju're, v. a. to impose an oath on one, pre-
    scribing the form in which he shall swear
Adjus't, v. a. to settle ; put in order ; regulate
Adjus'ting, Adjus'tment, s. the act of regulat-
    ing, or putting in method
Ad'jutant, s. a military officer, whose duty
    is to assist the major, by distributing pay,
    and superintending punishments
Adju'tor, s. an assistant, a helper
Adju'trix, s. she who helps
Ad'juvate, v. a. to forward, to help
Admeas'urement, s. the act of measuring
Admin'ister, v.a. to supply; to act as an agent
Administra'tion, s. act of administering
Administra'tor, s. one who manages the af-
    fairs of a person dying without a will
Administra'trix, s. a woman who administers
Ad'mirable, a. to be admired ; good, rare
Ad'mirably, ad. excellently, wonderfully
Ad'miral, s. the chief commander of a fleet
Ad'miralship, s. the office of an admiral
Ad'miralty, s. the supreme office for the su-
    perintendence of naval affairs
Admira'tion, s. wonder ; act of admiring
Admi're, v. a. to esteem ; to be surprised at
Admi'rer, s. a lover ; one that admires
Admis'sible, a. that which may be admitted
Admis'sion, s. the act of admitting ; the al-
    lowing of a position not fully proved
Admit', v. a. to grant entrance ; to grant in
    general ; to allow an argument or position
Admit'table, a. that which may be admitted
Admit'tance, s. the act of admitting ; custom
Admix', v. n. to mingle with something else
Admix'tion, s. the uniting or blending one
    substance with another
Admix'ture, s. the substance of bodies mixed
Admon'ish, v. a. to reprove, caution gently
Admon'isher, s. a reprover, an adviser
Admonit'ion, s. reproof, advice. counsel [ing
Admon'itory, a. warning gently, admonish
Ado', s. trouble, confusion, bustle, tumult

Adoles'cence, s. the flower or prime of youth
Adopt', v. a. to take a son or daughter by choice, who was not so by birth ; to embrace any particular method or manner
Adop'tion, s. the act or state of adopting
Ado'rable, a. divine ; worthy of adoration
Adora'tion, s. homage ; divine worship
Ado're, v. a. to honour highly ; to worship
Ador'n, v. a. to dress, decorate, embellish
Ador'nment, s. embellishment, ornament
Adow'n, prep. down ; towards the ground
Adrif't, ad. floating at random
Adroi't, a. dexterous, skilful, nimble
Adroi'tly, ad. dexterously, nimbly, skilfully
Adroi'tness, s. activity, skill, dexterity
Adry', a. athirst, desirous of drink, thirsty
Adscitit'ious, a. added, borrowed
Adstric'tion, s. the act of binding together
Advan'ce, v. a. to lend money ; to improve ; to aggrandise ; to grace ; to propose ; to bring forward
Advan'ce, s. a progression ; an improvement
Advan'ced, part. asserted ; forwarded
Advan'cement, s. progression, preferment
Advan'tage, s. favourable circumstance; convenience ; gain ; benefit ; superiority
Advan'tage, v. a. to promote ; to improve
Advanta'geous, Advan'tageable, a. profitable; gainful ; useful ; convenient
Advanta'geously, ad. profitably ; opportunely, conveniently
Advanta'geousness, s. convenience, usefulness
Adve'ne, v. n. to be superadded to [ness
Adve'nient, a. advening, superadding
Ad'vent, s. a coming; the time appointed as a preparation for the celebration of Christ's nativity, being four weeks before Christmas
Adven'tine, Adventit'ious, Adven'tive, a. accidental ; additional, extrinsically added
Adven'ture, v. n. to dare ; to try the chance
Adven'ture. s. an enterprise ; an accident
Adven'turer, s. one who hazards any chance, an unsettled person
Adven'turous, Adven'turesome, a. daring, courageous ; full of hazard, dangerous
Adven'turously, ad. hazardously, boldly
Ad'verb, s. in grammar, a word joined to a verb or adjective, to restrain or increase the latitude of their signification
Adver'bial, a. that which relates to adverbs
Adver'bially, ad. in the manner of an adverb
Advers'able, a. not in use ; contrary to
Adversa'ria, s. a common-place book
Ad'versary, s. an enemy, antagonist, foe
Ad'verse, a. calamitous ; contrary
Ad'versely, ad. unfortunately ; oppositely
Adver'sity, s. affliction, calamity, distress
Adver't, v. n. to attend to, to heed, to regard
Adver'tence, Adver'tency, s. attention to
Adverti'se, v. a. to give public notice, inform
Adver'tisement, s. notice in a public paper ; intelligence, information, admonition
Adverti'ser, s. one who gives information
Adverti'sing, part. giving intelligence
Adves'perate, v. n. to draw towards evening
Advi'ce, s. instruction; counsel; deliberation
Advi'sable, a. fit to be advised ; prudent
Advi'sableness, s. propriety ; fitness
Advi'se, v. to counsel, to inform, to deliberate
Advi'sedly, ad. deliberately ; prudently
Advi'ser, s. one who advises ; a counsellor

Adula'tion, s. high compliment ; flattery
Adula'tor, s. a parasite, a flatterer
Ad'ulatory, a. flattering; full of compliments
Ad'ult, a. past the age of infancy
Adul't, s. a person arrived at maturity
Adul'terate, a. Adul'terated, part. sullied by foreign mixture ; tainted with adultery
Adultera'tion, s. act of debasing by foreign mixture ; state of being contaminated
Adul'terer, s. a man guilty of adultery
Adul'teress, s. a woman guilty of adultery
Adul'terous, a. guilty of adultery
Adul'tery. s. violating the marriage bed
Adum'brate, v. a. to shadow out faintly
Adumbra'tion, s. a faint sketch ; the act of exhibiting imperfect representation
Aduna'tion, s. union; the state of being joined
Adun'city, s. a bend inwards ; crookedness
Ad'vocate, s. a pleader in a court of judicature ; the pleader of any cause as a controvertist or vindicator ; an intercessor
Advoca'tion, Ad'vocacy, s. the act of pleading ; plea ; apology ; excuse ; defence
Advowee', s. he that possesses the right of advowson, or presentation
Advow'son, s. a right to present to a benefice
Adu're, v. a. to burn up, to parch, to scorch
Adust', Adus'ted, a. burnt up, scorched
Adus'tible, a. that which may be burnt up
Adus'tion, s. act of burning, or drying
Ae'rial, a. belonging to the air ; high ; lofty
Ae'rie, s. a nest of eagles, or birds of prey
Aerol'ogy, s. the theory of the air
A'eromancy, s. the art of divining by the air
Aerom'etry, s. the art of measuring the air
A'eronaut, s. one who sails through the air
Aeros'copy, s. the observation of the air
Aerostat'ic, a. belonging to aerostation
Aerosta'tion, s. traversing the air in balloon
Aestiva'tion, s. in botany, the disposition of the petals within the floral gem or bud
Afar', ad. from a great distance, remotely
Afea'rd, a. afraid, daunted, terrified
Affabil'ity, s. condescension ; courteousness
Af'fable, a. easy of manners, courteous, mild
Af'fableness, s. condescension ; civility
Af'fably, ad. kindly, civilly, courteously
Affai'r, s. concern, transaction, business
Affec't, s. affection ; quality ; sensation
Affec't, v. a. to move the passions ; to imitate in a constrained manner ; to aim at
Affecta'tion, s. constrained imitation
Affec'ted, part. a. conceited, moved, afflicted
Affec'tedly, ad. conceitedly, hypocritically
Affec'tedness, s. silly pride, conceit
Affec'ting, part. moving ; imitating
Affec'tion, s. love, zeal ; passions in general
Affec'tionate, a. warm, tender, benevolent
Affec'tionately, ad. benevolently, tenderly
Affec'tive, a. that which affects ; moving
Affi'ance, s. a contract ; reliance, hope, confidence ; trust in the divine promises
Affi'ance, v. a. to bind by promise, to betroth
Affida'vit, s. a deposition on oath
Affi'ed, part. a. joined by contract
Affilia'tion, s. the adoption of a son
Affi'nage, s. the act of refining metals
Affi'ned, a. related to another
Affin'ity, s. relation by marriage, opposed consanguinity, connexion with
Affir'm, v. a. to tell confidently, to declare

Affir'mable, a. that may be affirmed ; true
Affirma'tion, s. declaration, confirmation
Affir'mative, a. that affirms or declares
Affir'matively, ad. absolutely, positively
Affix'. v. a. to subjoin, to fasten, to unite
Affia'tion, s. the act of breathing upon
Afflic't, v. a. to trouble, torment, grieve
Afflic'tion, s. calamity, misery, sorrow
Afflic'tive, a. tormenting, painful
Af'fluence, s. plenty, abundance ; concourse
Af'fluent, a. abundant, exuberant, wealthy
Af'flux, Afflux'ion, s. the act of flowing to any
   place ; that which flows
Affo'rd, v. a. to be able to bear expenses ; to
   be able to sell ; to produce ; to grant
Affran'chise, v. a. to make free
Affray', s. a disturbance, tumult, quarrel
Affri'ght, v. a. to alarm, confuse, terrify
Affri'ght, Affri'ghtment, s. fear, terror
Affron't, s. insult, outrage, disgrace
Affron't, v. a. to insult, to offend, to provoke
Affron'tive, a. abusive, injurious
Affu'se, v. a. to pour one thing on another
Affu'sion, s. the act of affusing
Affy', v. a. to trust in, to confide, to betroth
Afie'ld, ad. to or in the field, out of doors
Afloa't, ad. floating ; borne up by the water
Afoot', ad. on foot ; in motion ; in action
Afo're, prep. sooner in time ; in time past
Afo'rehand, ad. previously prepared, or fitted
Afo'resaid, a. named before, said before
Afrai'd, part. a. terrified, struck with fear
Afresh', ad. again, once more, anew
Af'ter, prep. in pursuit of ; in imitation of ;
   behind—ad. in succeeding time ; following
   another
Af'termath, s. the second crop of grass
Af'ternoon, s. time from noon to evening
Af'terthought, s. reflections formed after the
   act ; expedients formed too late
Af'terwards, ad. in succeeding time
A'ga, s. a Turkish military officer of rank
Again', ad. once more ; a second time ; in
   return ; on the other hand ; moreover
Again'st, prep. in opposition to; in contradic-
   tion to ; to the hurt of another
Aga'pe, ad. staring eagerly, or with surprise
Agas't, or Aghas't, a. staring with amazement,
   struck with terror, amazed
Ag'ate, s. the lowest sort of precious stone
Ag'aty, a. partaking of the nature of agate
Age, s. generation of men ; any period of
   time ; an hundred years ; maturity ; de-
   cline of life
A'ged, a. advanced in years, ancient, old
A'gency, s. managing another's affairs; action
A'gent, s. a substitute ; a factor ; an actor ;
   that which affects another thing
Agela'tion, s. a concretion of ice
Ag enera'tion, s. a growing to another body
Agglom'erate, v. a. to gather up in a ball
Agglu'tinate, v. n. to unite together
Agglutina'tion, s. cohesion, union
Ag'g andize, v. a. to advance in power, rank,
   or honour ; to exalt, to enlarge [ferred
Ag'grandizement, s. being exalted or pre-
Ag'gravate, v. a. to provoke ; to make worse
Aggrava'tion, s. the act of enlarging to enor-
   mity ; a provocation
Ag'gregate, a. framed by the collection of
   particular parts into one body or mass

Ag'gregate, v. a. to add or heap together
Ag'gregate, s. the collection of many parti-
   culars into one whole
Aggrega'tion, s. the state of being collected
Aggress', v. a. to assault or injure first
Aggres'sion, s. the first act of injury
Ag'ressor, s. one who first assaults another
Aggrie'vance, s. injury, wrong, hardship
Aggrie've, v. a. to injure, to harass, to vex
Aggrie'ved, part. injured, afflicted
Aggrou'p, v. a. to bring into one view
Ag'ile, a. ready, active, brisk, nimble
Ag'ileness, s. nimbleness, quickness
Agil'ity, s. speedy readiness, activity
A'gio, s. difference of exchange between
   bank notes and current money
Agis't, v. a. to let cattle feed in pasture
   grounds at so much per week
Ag'itable, a. that may be put in motion
Ag'itate, v. a. to shake ; revolve in the mind ;
   to affect with perturbation
Agita'tion, s. the act of shaking any thing ;
   perturbation of the mind ; controversial
   examination ; the state of being shaken
Ag'itative, a. having the power to agitate
Agna'tion, s. descent from the same father
Agni'tion, s. an acknowledgment
Agni'ze, v. a. to acknowledge ; to confess
Ago', ad. a long time since ; as, long ago
Agoe', ad. in a state of desire ; a low word
Ago'ing, part. a. moving, in action
Agonis'tes, s. a prize-fighter, a gladiator
Ag'onize, v. n. to be in extreme pain
Ag'ony, s. anguish ; pangs of death
Agra'rian, a. relating to fields or grounds
Agree', v. n. to concur, to settle, to accord
Agree'able, a. conformable to ; pleasing
Agree'ableness, s. consistency with ; resem-
   blance ; the quality of pleasing
Agree'ably, ad. consistently ; pleasingly
Agree'd, part. a. settled by mutual consent
Agree'ment, s. compact ; bargain ; concord
Ag'riculture, s. husbandry, tillage
Agricul'turist, s. a farmer, a husbandman
Ag'rimony, s. a name for the plant liver-
   wort
Agrou'nd, ad. stranded ; run ashore
A'gue, s. an intermitting fever with cold fits
Ah, interj. denoting contempt, or pity
Aha', interj. a word intimating triumph and
   contempt
Ahead', ad. farther on ; precipitantly
Aid, v. a. to assist, to support, to succour
Aid, Aid'ance, s. support, assistance, help
Ai'dant, Aid'ing, a. assisting, helping
Aid-de-camp, s. a military officer attendant
   on a general, to convey orders, &c.
Ai'dless, a. unsupported, friendless
Ail, v. n. to be in pain, or suffer sickness
Ai'ling, part. a. sickly, disordered
Ai'lment, s. disease, affliction, pain
Aim, v. a. to direct towards a mark ; to guess ;
   to tend toward ; to try to reach
Aim, s. endeavour, design, direction
Air, s. the element in which we breathe ;
   gentle wind ; vapour, scent ; the mien of
   a person ; tune or melody
Air, v. a. to expose to the air ; to warm
Ai'rily, ad. briskly, gaily, merrily
Ai'riness, s. exposure to the air ; gaiety
A'iring, s. a short excursion to enjoy the air

Ai'riess, a. wanting air; close

Ai'rpump, s. a machine by which the air is exhausted out of certain vessels

Ai'ry, a. gay, sprightly; belonging to the air

Aisle, Aile, s. a walk in a church

Ait, s. a small island in a river

Akin', a. related to; resembling; alike

Al'abaster, s. a kind of soft white marble

Alac' iously, ad. cheerfully

Alac'rity, s. readiness, briskness, willingness

A-la-mo'de, ad. according to the fashion

Alar'm, v. a. to surprise; to call to arms

Alar'm, s. su 'den terror; a notice of danger

Alar'ming, part. giving alarm; frightful

Alar'm-post, s. the spot to which each regiment is to repair in case of alarm

Alar'um, s. an alarm bell; a clock

Alas', Alack', interj. denoting pity or grief

Albe'it, ad. notwithstanding, although

Al'bion, s. the ancient name of Britain

Albu'men, s. the white about an egg. In botany, the substance of the lobes of the seed

Alcai'd, s. the name of a civil officer in Spain

Alchym'ical, a. relating to alchymy

Al'chymist, s. a professor of alchymy

Al'chymy, s. occult chemistry; a metal

Al'cohol, s. the substance of any body reduced into a fine impalpable powder; a pure rectified spirit; brandy

Al'coran, s. the book which contains the precepts of the Turkish religion, as instituted by their prophet Mahomet

Alco've, s. a recess to sit or lie in

A'lder, s. a tree resembling the hazel

A'lderman, s. an incorporated magistrate

A'ldern, a. made of alder wood

Ale, s. a liquor made by infusing malt and hops in hot water

A'leconner, s. an officer whose duty is to inspect the measures of public houses

Ale'gar, s. sour ale which has lost its spirit

A'lehoof, s. g oundivy; once used for hops

A'lehouse, s. a house where malt liquor is sold

Alem'bic, s. a vessel used in distilling

A'er't, a. vigilant, brisk, watchful. petulant

Aler'tness, s. briskness, sprightliness

Al'etude, s. fatness; bulkiness; heaviness

Alexan'drine, s. a verse of twelve syllables

Alexiphar'mic, Alexiter'ic, a. that which acts as an antidote to poison, or infection

Al'gebra, s. a literal arithmetic

Algebra'ic, Algebra'ical, a. pertaining to algebra

Algebra'ist, s. one well versed in algebra

Al'gid, a. chill, cold

Algid'ity, Al'gor, s. coldness, chilliness

Algi'fick, a. that wh ch produces cold

Al'gorithm, s. the science of numbers

Alguazi'l, s. a Spanish bailiff or constable

A'lias, ad. otherwise—s. in law, a writ

Al'ibi, s. elsewhere

Al'ible, a. nourishing; nutritive

A'lien, s. a stranger; a foreigner

A'lienable, a. that may be transferred

A'lienate, v. a. to withdraw the heart or affections; to transfer to another

A'lienate, a. estranged or withdrawn from

Aliena'tion, s. the act of transferring; mental derangement; change of affection

Ali'ght, v. a. to d smount, to descend

Ali'ke, ad. equally; with resemblance

Al'in ent, s. nutriment, food, support

Alim n'tal, a. nutritive, nourishing

Alimen'tary, a. that which belongs to aliment

Alimo'nious, a. that which nourishes

Al'imony, s. legal proportion of an estate allowed to support a wife, unless criminally separated from her husband

Al'iquant, a. parts of a given number, which, however repeated, will never make up the number exactly, as 3 is an aliquant ... 10, thrice 3 being 9, four times 3 making 12

Al'iquot, s. any portion of a given number which, being multiplied, will amount to that given number exactly

Ali've, a. active, sprightly; not dead

Alkales'cent, a. tending to the qualities of alkali

Al'kahest, s. a liquor, an universal dissolvent

Al'kali, s. the fixed salt of any body

Al'kaline, a. having the quality of alkali

Alkal'izate, v. a. to make alkaline

Al'kanet, s. the name of a plant

Alker'mes, s. a confection made of the scarlet grains called kermes

All, a. the whole number or quantity; every one. All is much used in composition

Allay', v. a. to temper one metal with another for coining, in this sense alloy is generally used; to compose, to pacify

Allay', s. any baser metal mixed with a superior kind to harden it; any thing which being added abates the predominant qualities of that with which it is mingled

Allecta'tion, s. an enticing; an alluring

Allega'tion, s. an affirmation, plea, excuse

Alleg'e, v. a. to maintain, to declare, to plead

Alleg'eable, a. that which may be alleged

Alleg'ed, part. asserted, given, pleaded

Alle'giance, s. the duty of a subject

Alle'giant, a. conformable to allegiance, loyal

Allegor'ical, Allegor'ic, a. after the manner of an allego y; not real; not literal

Al'legory, s. in rhetoric, a figurative manner of speech, in which something other is intended than the words literally taken

Alle'gro, s. a sprightly motion in music; ray

Allema'nde, s. a grave or slow piece of music

Alle'viate, v. a. to soften, to ease

Allevia'tion, s. that by which any pain is eased or any fault extenuated

Al'ley, s. any narrow passage, or walk

Alli'ance, s. a league or contract with foreign powers; relation by marria e, or kindred; similarity of qualities

Alli'ciency, s. the power of enticing

Alli'es, s. states who have entered into a league for their mutual defence

Alliga'tion, s. that rule of arithmetic which teaches to adjust the price of articles compounded of ingredients of different value; the act of tying together

Alliga'tor, s. a kind of pear, a crocodile

Allis'ion, s. the act of striking together

Allitera'tion, s. the beginning two or more words with the same letter

Alloca'tion, s. the act of placing or adding to

Allocu'tion, s. the act of speaking to another

Allo'dial, Allo'dian, a. independent; held without acknowledgment of superiority

Allon'ge, s. in fencing, a pass or thrust

Allot', v. a. to parcel out, distribute; grant

Allot'ment, *s.* the part given to any one

Allow', *v. a.* to permit, yield, or grant; to make an abatement in selling; to admit or acknowledge any position

Allow'able, *a.* that may be permitted, lawful

Allow'ance, *s.* abatement from a demand; a rate or appointment for any use; pension; indulgence; sanction; licence

Alloy', *s.* baser metal mixed in coinage

Allu'de, *v. a.* to insinuate, to hint at, refer to

Allu'minate, *v.a.* to decorate or adorn

Allu're, *v.a.* to decoy, to wheedle, to entice

Allu're, *s.* something set up to entice birds

Allu'rement, *s.* temptation, enticement

Allu'ringly, *ad.* in an enticing manner

Allu'sion, *s.* a reference, hint, implication

Allu'sive, *a.* hinting at something

Ally', *s.* a confederate, a friend, a relation

Al'manac, *s.* an annual calendar

Al'mandine, *s.* a kind of inferior ruby

A mi'ghty, *a.* of unlimited power, omnipotent—*s.* the Divine Being; God

A'mond, *s.* the fruit of the almond-tree

A'monds of the throat, *s.* two small glands on the sides of the basis of the tongue

Al'moner, *s.* the officer of a prince employed in the distribution of charity

Al'monry, *s.* the place where alms are given

A'lmost, *ad.* nearly, near, well nigh

A'ms, *s.* what is given to relieve the poor

Al'mshouse, *s.* a house built gratuitously for the poor

A'loes, *s.* a medicinal gum extracted from a tree of that name

Aloet'ic, Aloet'ical, *a.* consisting of aloes

Aloft', *ad.* above; on high; in the air

Al'ogy, *s.* unreasonableness, absurdity

Alo'ne, *a.* solitary; without company

Alon'g, *ad.* forward; onward; at length

Alon'gside, *ad.* by the side of the ship

Aloo'f, *ad.* remotely; at a distance

Alo'pecy, *s.* the falling off of the hair

Alou'd, *ad.* with much noise, loudly

Al'pha, *s.* the first letter in the Greek alphabet; signifying the *first* or *highest*

Al'phabet, *s.* the letters of any language

Alphabet'ical,*a.* according to the order of the alphabet

Alread'y, *ad.* now, at this time; so soon

A'lso, *ad.* in the same manner; likewise

A'ltar, *s.* the place where offerings to heaven are laid; the table in Christian churches where the communion is administered

A'lter, *v.a.* to reform, to change, to vary

A'lterable, *a.* that which may be changed

A'lterant, *a.* that which produces a change

Altera'tion, *s.* the change made; the act of altering or changing

A'lterative, *a.* medicines which affect the constitution by imperceptible gradations

Alterca'tion,*s.* controversy, wrangle, debate

Alter'nancy, *s.* action by turns

Alter'nate, *a.* one after another, by turns

Alter'nately, *ad.* mutually, by turns

Alterna'tion, *s.* reciprocal succession

Alter'native,*s.* the choice given of one of two things, so that if one is rejected the other must be taken

Althe'a, *s.* a flowering shrub

Althou'gh, *ad.* however, notwithstanding

Altim'etry, *s.* the art of measuring heights

Altis'onant, *a.* pompous; high-sounding

Al'titude, *s.* height of a place; elevation of a heavenly body above the horizon

Alt'o, *s.* the upper or counter-tenor—*a.* high

Altogeth'er, *ad.* entirely, completely

Alve'olate, *a.* divided into open cells, like honey-comb

Al'um, *s.* a mineral salt of an acid taste

Alu'minous, *a.* consisting of alum

A'lways, *ad.* constantly; perpetually

Amabil'ity, *s.* power of pleasing; loveliness

Amai'n, *ad.* fiercely, with vehemence

Amal'gam, *s.* a mixture of metals

Amal'gamate, *v.a.* to mix or unite metals

Aman'd, *v.* to send away, remove

Amanda'tion, *s.* the act of sending away

Amanuen'sis, *s.* a clerk or secretary, who writes what another dictates

Am'aranth, *s.* the name of a plant; in poetry, an imaginary flower that never fades

Amaran'thine, *a.* consisting of amaranths

Amar'itude, Amar'ulence, *s.* bitterness

Amass', *v.a.* to heap up, to collect together

Amass'ment, *s.* a heap, an accumulation

Amateur', *s.* a lover of the arts; a virtuoso

Am'atory, *a.* relating to or causing love

Amauro'sis, *s.* a dimness of sight occasioning the appearance of flies or dust floating before the eyes

Ama'ze, *v.a.* to surpass, astonish, to confuse

Ama'ze, *s.* confusion; astonishment

Ama'zedly, *ad.* confusedly, with amazement

Ama'zement,*s.* confused apprehension; fear, wonder at any event; admiration

Ama'zing, *part. a.* astonishing, wonderful

Ama'zingly, *ad.* wonderfully, astonishingly

Am'azon, *s.* the Amazons were a race of women famous for valour; a virago

Amba'ges, *s.* multiplicity of words

Ambas'sador, Embas'sador, *s.* a representative of a prince or state sent on any public business to a foreign power

Ambas'sadress, *s.* the lady of an ambassador

Am'bassage, Am'bassade, *s.* a mission

Am'ber, *s.* a yellow transparent gum, of a resinous taste; a kind of pale ale

A'mbergris, *s.* a fragrant drug used as a perfume and a cordial

Ambidex'ter, *s.* a person that can use both hands alike; a knave who plays on both sides; in law, a juror who receives a bribe from both parties for his verdict

Ambidex'trous, *a.* deceitful, double-dealing

Am'bient,*a.*compassing; surrounding, particularly applied to the air which surrounds all bodies; investing

Ambifa'rious, *a.* having a double meaning

Ambig'uity,*s.*doubtful meaning; uncertainty of signification; obscurity of words

Ambig'uous,*a.* mysterious, hidden, doubtful

Ambig'uously, *ad.* in a doubtful manner

Ambig'uousness, *s.* doubtfulness of meaning

Ambil'oquy, *s.* use of doubtful expressions

Ambil'oquous, *a.* using doubtful expressions

Am'bit, *s.* the circuit of any thing

Ambi'tion, *s.* great pride; an earnest desire of preferment, honour, or power

Ambiti'ous, *a.* desirous of honour; aspiring

Am'ble, *v. n.* to pace, to trip, to move easy

Ambro'sia, *s.* the name of a plant; in poetical language, the supposed food of the gods

Ambro'sial, a. possessing the qualities of ambrosia ; fragrant, delicious

Ambula'tion, s. the act of walking

Ambusca'de, Ambusca'do, Am'bush, s. a private post in which men lie to surprise an enemy ; the act of lying in wait to surprise an enemy

Am'el, s. the matter used for enamelling

Ame'liorate, v. a. to improve

A'men, ad. may it be so ; verily

Ame'nable, a. answerable to, responsible

Ame'nance, s. behaviour, conduct, mien

Amen'd, v.a. to reform, correct, grow better

Amen'dment, s. a reformation of life ; recovery of health ; a change for the better

Amen'ds. s. satisfaction ; recompence

Amen'ity, s. agreableness of situation

Amer'ce, v. a. to punish by fine or penalty

Amer'cement, Amer'ciament, s. a pecuniary fine or penalty

Am'ethyst, s. a precious stone, of a violet colour, supposed to hinder drunkenness

A'miable, a. pleasing, charming, lovely

A'miableness, s. loveliness, agreableness

Am'icable, a. kind, obliging, friendly

Am'icableness, s. good will, friendliness

Am'icably, ad. in a friendly way

Am'ice, s. the undermost part of a Romish priest's shoulder-cloth, or alb

Amid', Amid'st, ad. amongst, in the middle

Amiss', ad. criminally, wrong, faultily

Amis'sion, s. deprivation, dismission, loss

Amit', v. a. to drop, to dismiss, to lose

Am'ity, s. love, friendship ; harmony

Ammo'niac, s. the name of an Indian gum

Ammuni'tion, s. military stores

Am'nesty, s. an act of oblivion

Amon'g, Among'st, prep. mingled with

An'orist, Amoro'so, s. a lover, a gallant

Am'orous, a. enamoured, disposed to love

Am'orously, ad. fondly, kindly, lovingly

Amor't, a. dejected, spiritless, dull, heavy

Amo'tion, s. the act of putting away

Amou'nt, v. n. to increase, to rise in value

Amou'nt, s. whole result, the sum total

Amo'r. s. an affair of gallantry

Amphib'ious, a. that which partakes of two natures, so as to live in air or water

Amphibol'ogy, s. a doubtful discourse

Amphib'olous, a. doubtful ; tossed about

Am'phiscii, s. those people who inhabit the torrid zone, whose shadows fall both ways

Amphithe'atre, s. a circular or oval building, for public amusement, with seats one above another, and an area in the middle

Am'ple, a. liberal, diffusive, large, wide

Am'pleness, s. extent, liberality, largeness

Am'pliate, v. a. to extend, to enlarge

Amplia'tion, s. enlargement, diffuseness

Amplif'icate, v. a. to spread out, to enlarge

Amplifica'tion, s. extension, enlargement

Am'plify, v. a. to exaggerate, to enlarge

Am'plitude, s. extent, largeness, capacity ; in astronomy, an arch of the horizon

Am'ply, ad. liberally, copiously, largely

Ampu'tate, v. a. to cut off a limb

Amputa'tion, s. the act of cutting off a limb, or other part of the body

Am'ulet, s. an appendant remedy or preventive worn about the neck

Amu'se, v. a. to entertain with tranquillity, to divert, to deceive

Amu'sement, s. pastime, entertainment

Amu'sing, part. entertaining, pleasant

Amyg'dalate, a. made of almonds

A'na, ad. equally, in the same quantity

Anabap'tist, s. one of a religious sect who assert that baptism is improper till the person is of an age to answer for himself

Anac'mptic, a. reflecting, or reflected

Anac'horete, Anac'horite, s. an hermit

Anac'bronism, s. an error in computing time

Anaclat'ica, s. the science or doctrine of refracted lights ; dioptrics

Anacreon'tic, a. relating to the ancient poet Anacreon

Anadip'o'sis, s. reduplication ; a figure in rhetoric

Anagoget'ical, a. religiously mysterious

An'ag am, s. a conceit arising from a transposition of the letters of a sentence or a word, so as to form other words

Anagram'matist, s. a composer of anagrams

An'alect, s. fragments collected from authors

Analep'tic, a. comforting, restorative

Anal'ogical, a. used by way of comparison

Anal'ogous, a. having something similar

Anal'ogy, s. resemblance, proportion, similarity of one thing to another

Anal'ysis, s. a separation of any compound body into the parts of which it is formed , the solution of any thing, whether corporeal, or mental, to its first elements

Analyt'ic, a. belonging to an analysis

An'alyze, v.a. to resolve into first principles, to reduce to primitive parts

Anamorpho'sis, s. perspective projection. so that in one point of view an object shall appear deformed, and in another an exact representation

Ana'nas, s. the pine-apple

Anaph'ora, s. deformation; in rhetoric, when several clauses of a sentence are begun with the same word

An'arch, s. an author of confusion

An'archy, s. confusion, disorder, tumult ; a want of government

Anasar'ca, s. a kind of dropsy

Anastomo'sis, s. the inosculation of vessels

Anas'trophe, s. a figure whereby words that should have been precedent are postponed

Anath'ema, s. an ecclesiastical curse

Anath'ematize, v. a. to pronounce accursed by ecclesiastical authority

Anat'omist, s. one skilled in anatomy

Anat'omy, s. the art of dissecting any animal body to discover exactly its structure

An'cestors, s. forefathers, predecessors

An'cestry, s. descent, birth, lineage

An'chor, s. an iron instrument, which, being fixed in the ground, by means of the cable keeps the ship from driving

An'chor. v. a. to drop the anchor ; to fix on

An'chorage, s. duty paid for leave to anchor ; ground for anchoring in

An'choret, An'chorite, s. see Anachorete

Ancho'vy, s. a small sea fish pickled

An'cient, a. old, of old time, long since

A'ncient, s. the bearer of a flag, an ensign

A'nciently, ad. formerly in old times

A'ncientry, s. high lineage, dignity of birth

A'ncients, *s.* men who lived in old times; certain flags in a ship

Anci'pital, *a.* two-edged, or double-edged

And, *conj.* the particle by which sentences or terms are joined

Andan'te, *ad.* in music, moderately

An'd.ron, *s.* irons fixed to the end of a fire-grate, in which the spit turns

Androg'inal, *a.* partaking of both sexes

An'ecdote, *s.* a biographical incident

Ane'le, *v. a.* to give extreme unction

Anem'one, *s.* the wind flower

An'eurism, *s.* a disease of, or wound in, an artery, by which it becomes dilated

Anew', *ad.* over again, repeatedly

Anfrac'tuous, *a.* intricate, winding, mazy

A'ngel, *s.* a celestial spirit; a heavenly being; a gold coin worth about ten shillings

Angel'ica, *s.* the name of a plant

Angel'ical, Angel'ic, *a.* like angels, heavenly

An'ger, *s.* rage, resentment; pain of a sore

An'ger, *v. a.* to provoke, to enrage

Angi'na, *s.* a disorder called the quinsy

Ang og'raphy, *s.* a description of vessels in the human body; the nerves, arteries, &c.

An'gle, *s.* an instrument to take fish; a point where two lines meet

An'gle, *v. n.* to fish with a fishing-rod

An'glicism, *s.* an English idiom, or expression

An'gling, *s.* the art of fishing with a rod

An'gry, *a.* enraged, provoked; inflamed

An'guish, *s.* excessive pain of body or mind

An'gular, *a.* having corners or angles

Anhela'tion, *s.* the act of panting

Animadver'sion, *s.* reproof, blame, remark, observation, severe censure

Animadver't, *v. a.* to examine into, to reprove, to remark or criticise

An'imal, *s.* a body endued with life, motion, and sense—*a.* not spiritual

Anima'cule, *s.* a very small animal

An'imate, *v. a.* to give life to, to quicken

An'imate, *a.* possessing life; living

An'imated, *part.* brisk, vigorous, lively

Anima'tion, *s.* the act of animating; the state of being enlivened, that which animates

An'imative, *a.* brisk; tending to animate

Animos'ity, *s.* hatred, malignity, aversion

An'ise, *s.* a species of parsley

An'ker, *s.* a liquid measure of ten gallons

An'kle, *s.* the joint between the foot and leg

An'nalist, *s.* a writer of annals

An'nals, *s.* histories digested into years

An'nats, *s.* first fruits; annual masses

Annea'l, *v. a.* to temper glass; to bake

Annex', *v. a.* to unite, to connect, to subjoin

Annex', *s.* the thing annexed, or subjoined

Anni'hilate, *v. a.* to annul, to destroy

Annihila'tion, *s.* the act of destroying

Anniver'sary, *s.* a day celebrated as it returns in the course of the year—*a.* annual

An'no Dom'ini, *s.* the year of our Lord

Annota'tion, *s.* a note, an explanation

Annota'tor, *s.* a commentator, a critic

Annou'nce, *v. a.* to declare, to publish

Annoy', *v. a.* to harass, to vex, to injure

Annoy'ance, *s.* that which annoys or vexes

Annoy'er, *s.* one who injures or molests

An'nual, *a.* that which comes once a year

An'nually, *ad.* yearly; year by year

Annu'itant, *s.* one who has an annuity

Annu'ity, *s.* a yearly allowance for life

Annul', *v. a.* to abolish, to repeal, to abro

An'nular, *a.* having the form of a ring (gar

An'nulet, *s.* a little ring; a mark in heraldry in architecture, the small square members in the Doric capital, under the quarter round, are called *annulets*

Annu'merate, *v. a.* to include, to add to

Annumera'tion, *s.* addition to a number

Annun'ciate, *v. a.* to bring tidings, to declare

Annuncia'tion-day, *s.* the day celebrated by the church in commemoration of the angel's salutation of the Virgin Mary, solemnized on the 25th of March

An'odyne, *a.* having the power to ease pain

Anoi'nt, *v. a.* to rub with oil, to consecrate

Anom'alism, Anom'aly, *s.* irregularity

Anom'alous, *a.* irregular, deviating from rule

Anon', *ad.* soon, shortly, quickly

Anon'ymous, *a.* without a name

Anoth'er, *a.* not the same, one more

An'swer, *v. a.* to solve, to reply to

An'swer, *s.* a confutation, a reply, a solution

An'swerable, *a.* admitting of reply, accountable; proportionate; suitable

Ant, *s.* a pismire, an emmet

Antag'onist, *s.* an adversary, an opponent

Antarc'tic, *a.* relating to the southern pole

An'te, a Latin particle signifying before

Antece'de, *v. n.* to precede, to go before

Antece'dence, *s.* the act of going before

Antece'dent, *a.* preceding, going before

Antece'dent, *s.* that which goes before; the noun to which the relative is subjoined

Ante'chamber, *s.* the chamber adjoining, or leading to the chief apartments

An'tedate, *v. a.* to date before the real time

Antedi'luvian, *a.* existing before the deluge

An'telope, *s.* a kind of goat, with wreathed or curled horns

Antemerid'ian, *s.* morning, before noon

Anteme'tic, *a.* powerful, to prevent vomiting

Antemun'dane, *a.* that which was before the creation of the world; eternal

An'tepast, *s.* foretaste, anticipation

Antepenult', *s.* the last syllable but two in any word, as *te* in *antepenult*

Antepilep'tic, *s.* a medicinal preparation against convulsions

Ante'rior, *a.* previous, prior, going before

Anterior'ity, *s.* priority in time or situation

An'them, *s.* a holy song, or divine hymn

An'ther, *s.* summit, or tip of a flower

Anthol'ogy, *s.* a collection of flowers, poems, or devotions

Anthropomor'phite, *a.* holding a human form in the deity

Anthropoph'agi, *s.* eaters of human flesh

An'tic, *a.* odd, ridiculously wild, whimsical

An'tic, *s.* he that uses antics; a buffoon

An'tichrist, *s.* an adversary to Christ

Anti'christian, *a.* opposite to Christianity

Antic'ipate, *v. a.* to prevent, to foretaste

Anticipa'tion, *s.* the act of taking up something before its time; prevention

Antic'ly, *ad.* drolly, with odd gestures

Anticli'max, *s.* a sentence in which the last part is lower than the first

Anticonvul'sive, *a.* good against convulsion

Anticour'tier, *s.* one that opposes the court

Antido'tal, *a.* that which counteracts poison

An'tidote, *s.* a medicine to expel poison

Antifeb'rile, *a.* good against fevers

Antimonar'chical, *a.* against monarchy

Antimo'nial, *a.* made of antimony

An'timony, *s.* a mineral substance, which destroys all metals fused with it but gold

Antino'mians, *s.* a religious sect who prefer faith to practical morality

An'tinomy, *s.* contradiction between two laws, or two clauses in the same law

Antipathet'ical, *a.* having a natural contrariety to any thing

Antip'athy, *s.* a natural contrariety to any thing so as to shun it involuntarily

An'tiphone, *s.* a hymn of praise

Antiph'rasis, *s.* the use of words in a sense opposite to their proper meaning

Antip'odal, *a.* relating to the antipodes

Antip'odes, *s.* those people who, living exactly on the opposite part of the globe, have their feet directly opposite to ours

An'tipope, *s.* one that usurps the popedom

Antiqua'rian, An'tiquary, *s.* one who studies antiquity; a collector of ancient things

An'tiquate, *v.a.* to make obsolete

Anti'que, *a.* odd, old fashioned, ancient

Anti'que, *s.* a relic, a piece of antiquity

Antiq'uity, *s.* time past, long ago, ancientness; the people of old times

Antis'cii, *s.* people who live under the same meridian, equally distant from the equator and on opposite sides, so that they have noon and midnight at the same time, and while the one has summer, the other has winter

Antiscorbu'tic, *a.* good against the scurvy

Antisep'tic, *s.* a medicine to prevent putrefaction

Antis'trophe, *s.* the second stanza of an ode

Antith'esis, *s.* opposition of words or sentences; contrast

Antitrinita'rian, *s.* one who denies the doctrine of the Christian Trinity

An'titype, *s.* the original, which is represented by the type

Antityp'ical, *a.* that which explains the type

An'tler, *s.* the branch of a stag's horn

Antoe'ci, *s.* those inhabitants of the globe who live under the same latitude and longitude, but in different hemispheres

Antonoma'sia, *s.* a form of speech, in which, instead of a proper name, the dignity is used, as a king is called his *majesty*

An'tre, *s.* a cave, a den, a cavern

An'vil, *s.* an iron block which smiths use

Anxi'ety, Anx'iousness, *s.* perplexity; trouble of mind about some future event; depression of spirits, uneasiness

Anx'ious, *a.* solicitous; much concerned

An'y, *a.* every, either, whosoever

An'ywise, *ad.* in any manner

Ao'nian *Mount*, *s.* the fabled residence of the muses; the hill Parnassus

A'orist, *s.* indefinite, indeterminate

Aor'ta, *s.* the great artery which rises immediately out of the left ventricle of the heart

Apa'ce, *ad.* quickly, speedily, with haste

Apar't, *ad.* separately, privately, at a distance

Apar'tment, *s.* a part of a house, a room

Apathet'ic, *a.* without feeling

Ap'athy, *s.* a want of feeling, coldness, indolence, exemption from passion

Ape, *s.* a kind of monkey, a mimic

Ape, *v.a.* to imitate ludicrously, to mimic

Ape'rient, *a.* having the quality of opening; gently purgative

Aper'tion, *s.* an opening, a passage, a gap

Ap'erture, *s.* an open place, a gap

Ap'etalous, *a.* without flower leaves

A'pex, *s.* the tip or angular point of a thing

Aphe'lion, or Aphe'lium, *s.* that part of a planet in which it is at the point remotest from the sun

Aph'orism, *s.* a maxim, precept, general rule

A'piary, *s.* a place where bees are kept

Apie'ce, *ad.* to each one share, separately

A'pish, *a.* foppish, silly, insignificant

Apoc'alypse, *s.* a revelation, a vision

Apocalyp'tical, *a.* containing revelation

Apoc'ope, *s.* cutting off the last syllable

Apoc'rypha, *s.* books appended to the cred writings, of doubtful authors

Apoc'ryphal, *a.* not canonical, uncertain

Apoc'ryphally, *ad.* uncertainly, doubtfully

Apodic'tical, *a.* evident, demonstrative

Ap'ogee, Apoge'on, Apoge'um, *s.* that point in the heavens in which the sun or any planet is at its greatest possible distance from the earth during its whole revolution

Apolo'getical, *a.* defending, excusing

Apol'ogize, *v.a.* to plead for, to excuse

Ap'ologue, *s.* a moral tale, a fable

Apol'ogy, *s.* a defence, an excuse

Ap'ophthegm, *s.* a remarkable saying

Apoplec'tic, *a.* relating to an apoplexy

Ap'oplexy, *s.* a sudden deprivation of all sensation and motion by disease

Apos'tacy, *s.* departure from what a man has professed; dereliction

Apos'tate, *s.* one who renounces his religion

Apos'tatize, *v.n.* to change one's religion, to forsake one's principles

Apos'tle, *s.* a person sent to preach the gospel, particularly those despatched by our Saviour for that purpose

Apos'trophe, *s.* in grammar, a mark thus ('), signifying the contraction of any word, as can't, don't; a sudden turn in a discourse

Apos'trophize, *v.a.* to address by apostrophe

Apoth'ecary, *s.* a person whose business is to prepare medicines for sale

Ap'othegm, *s.* see Apophthegm

Apothe'osis, *s.* the consecrating or deifying any person after death

Ap'ozem, *s.* a decoction or infusion of herbs

Appa'l, *v. a.* to fright, to daunt, to terrify

Ap'panage, *s.* lands for younger children

Appara'tus, *s.* tools, furniture, equipage

Appar'el, *s.* dress, clothing, vestments

Appar'el, *v.a.* to dress, to deck, to cover

Appa'rent, *a.* plain, evident, certain

Appa'rently, *ad.* evidently, visibly, openly

Appari'tion, *s.* appearance, a spectre

Appar'itor, *s.* a low ecclesiastical officer

Appea'ch, *v. a.* to impeach, to censure, to reproach, to accuse

Appea'chment, *s.* an accusation, a charge

Appea'l, *s.* an application for justice

Appea'l, *v. n.* to refer to another as judge

Appea'r, *v. a.* to become visible, to be in sight, to be evident

Appea'rance, *s.* the act of coming into sight; semblance, not reality; show, probability

Appea'se, *v. a.* to pacify, to calm, to reconcile, to put in a state of peace

Appea'sement, *s.* the state of being at peace

Appel'lant, *s.* a challenger at arms; one who appeals to a superior court

Appella'tion, *s.* a name, address, term, title

Appel'latives, *s.* names for the whole rank of beings are called *appellatives*

Appel'latory, *a.* containing an appeal

Appen'd, *v. a.* to hang or join to, to add to

Appen'dage, *s.* something added

Appen'dant, *s.* an adventitious part

A, pen'dant, Appen'ded, *a.* hanging to something else, concomitant, annexed

Appen'dicate, *v. a.* to append, to join to

Appen'dix, *s.* addition made, supplement

Apperta'in, *v. n.* to depend upon, to belong to

Apper'tinent, *a.* relating or belonging to

Ap'petence, Ap'petency, *s.* carnal desire

Appetibil'ity, *s.* the state of being desirable

Ap'petible, *a.* desirable, good, engaging

Ap'petite, *s.* hunger, desire of sensual pleasure; violent longing

Applau'd, *v. a.* to praise, commend, extol

Applau'se, *s.* approbation, praise, laud

Ap'ple, *s.* a common fruit; pupil of the eye

Ap'plicable, *a.* fit to be applied, suitable

Applica'tion, *s.* the act of applying; the thing applied; intense study, great industry

Ap'plicative, Ap'plicatory, *a.* that applies

Appli'er, Ap'plicant, *s.* a student

Apply', *v. a.* to study; to address to; to suit to; to agree; to put one thing to another

Appoi'nt, *v. a.* to settle, determine, equip

Appoi'nted, *part.* agreed on, settled, chosen

Appoi'ntment, *s.* salary, post, stipulation

Appor'tion, *v. a.* to divide into just portions

Appo'se, *v. a.* to examine, puzzle, question

Ap'posite, *a.* well adapted to, fit, proper

Ap'positely, *ad.* fitly, suitably, properly

Apposi'tion, *s.* addition of new matter

Apprai'se, *v. a.* to set a price upon goods

Apprai'sement, *s.* the act of setting a price on

Apprai'ser, *s.* one who values or appraises

Appre'ciate, *v. a.* to reckon, to estimate

Apprehen'd, *v. a.* to seize on, to arrest; to comprehend or understand; to fear

Apprehen'sion, *s.* seizure; fear; conception

Apprehen'sive, *a.* fearful; jealous; sensible

Appren'tice, *s.* one bound by a written contract to a tradesman or artificer, who engages to instruct him fully in his art

Appren'ticeship, *s.* the term limited for the service of an apprentice [laid to

Ap'pressed, *a.* pressed or squeezed close;

Appri'ze, *v. a.* to acquaint, to inform

Appri'zed, *part.* instructed, informed

Appro'ach, *s.* the act of drawing near to

Appro'ach, *v. a.* to draw or bring near to

Approba'tion, *s.* the act of approving

Appro'priate, *v. a.* to set apart; consign to any particular use; annex to

Appropria'tion, *s.* the destination of something to a particular use or purpose

Appro'vable, *a.* worthy of approbation

Appro'val, Appro'vement, *s.* approbation

Appro've, *v. a.* to commend, to like; to allow of—*v.* to render one's self agreeable

Appro'ved, *part.* tried, examined, liked

Appro'ximate, *a.* going to, near to

Approxima'tion, *s.* approach to any thing

Appul'se, *s.* the act of striking against

Appur'tenance, *s.* that which appertains to something else

A'pricot, A'pricock, *s.* a wall fruit

A'pril, *s.* the fourth month of the year

A'prou, *s.* part of a woman's dress; a piece of lead which covers the touch-hole of a cannon to keep off the wet

Apropo's, *ad.* opportunely; to the purpose

Apt, *a.* quick, fit, ready, inclined, qualified

Ap'titude, *s.* tendency, fitness, disposition

Ap'tly, *ad.* acutely, readily, properly, justly

Ap'tness, *s.* quickness of apprehension; fitness, tendency, suitableness, readiness

Aquafor'tis, *s.* a corrosive liquor made by distilling nitre with calcined vitriol

Aquat'ic, *a.* growing or living in the water

Aquatin'ta, *s.* engraving which imitates Indian ink drawing

Aq'ueduct, *s.* a conveyance for carrying water, used by the ancients

A'queous, *a.* like water, watery, thin

Aq'uiline, *a.* resembling an eagle; applied to the nose, curved or hooked

Ar'abic, *s.* the language of the Arabians

Ar'able, *a.* fit for tilling or ploughing

Ara'neous, *a.* resembling a cobweb

Ara'tion, Ar'ature, *s.* the act of ploughing

Ar'atory, *a.* that which contributes to tillage

Ar'balat, Ar'balist, *s.* a cross-bow

Ar'biter, *s.* an umpire to settle a dispute

Arbit'rament, *s.* will, choice, decision

Ar'bitrarily, *ad.* without control, absolutely

Ar'bitrariness, *s.* despotism, tyranny

Ar'bitrary, *a.* despotic, unlimited, absolute

Ar'bitrate, *v. a.* to determine, decide, judge

Arbitra'tion, *s.* the decision of a cause; the termination of any dispute by persons mutually agreed on by the parties

Ar'bitrator, *s.* an umpire, a president, a judge

Ar'borary, *a.* of or belonging to trees

Arbo'reous, *a.* belonging to trees

Arbores'cent, *a.* growing like trees

Ar'toret, *s.* a small tree or shrub

Ar'borist, *s.* a naturalist who studies trees

Ar'bour, *s.* a bower, a seat shaded with trees

Ar'buscle, *s.* any small tree or shrub

Ar'bute, *s.* the strawberry tree

Arca'de, *s.* a continuation of arches

Arca'num, *s.* a secret, a mystery

Arch, Arc, *s.* part of a circle; the sky

Arch, *a.* chief, mirthful; lively, waggish

Arch, *v. a.* to build or cover with arches

Ar'chaism, *s.* an ancient phrase

Arch'angel, *s.* a chief angel; a plant

Archangel'ic, *a.* belonging to archangels

Archbish'op, *s.* the principal of the bishops

Archdea'con, *s.* a bishop's deputy

Archdea'conry, Archdea'conship, *s.* the office or jurisdiction of an archdeacon

Arch'duch'ess, *s.* the wife of an archduke

Archdu'ke, *s.* a sovereign prince, grand duke

Ar'ched, *part.* formed like an arch, vaulted

Ar'cher, *s.* one who fights with a bow

Ar'chery, *s.* the art of using a bow

Archety'pal, *a.* belonging to the original

Ar'chetype, *s.* the original, model, pattern

Archiepis'copal, *a.* belonging to an arch bishop

Archipel'aco, s. any sea which abounds with small islands; the most celebrated is situated between Asia, Macedon, and Greece

Architect, s. a professor of the art of building; a surveyor, the contriver of any thing

Ar chitecive, a. that performs the work of architecture

Ar'chitecture. s. the science of building

Ar'chitrave, s. the main beam of a building; ornamental part of a pillar

Ar'chives, s. records; a place for records

Archprel'ate, s. a leading or chief prelate

Archpres'byter, s. a chief presbyter

Ar'ctic, a. towards the north, northern

Ar'ctic circle, s. the circle at which the northern frigid zone commences, being 23 min. 30' from the North Pole

Arc'uate, v.a. to bend like an arch

Arcua'tion, s. an incurvation, an arching

Ar'dency. Ar'dentness, s. zeal, eagerness

Ar'dent, a. zealous, affectionate; fierce

Ar'dently, ad. affectionately, fervently, eagerly, zealously

Ar'dour, s. warm affection, fervency, zeal

Ar'duous, a. laborious, difficult

Are, the plural of the present tense of the verb to be

A'rea, s. the superficial content of any thing; any open surface

Arefac'ion, s. the state of growing dry

Arena'cious, Areno'se, a. full of sand, sandy

Ar'gent, a. shining like silver, white, silvery

Ar'gil, s. potter's clay, fat, soft earth

Argilla'ceous, Ar il'lous, a. consisting of clay

Ar'gol, s. the tartar or salt from wine lees

Ar' onauts, s. the companions of Jason in the ship Argo, on the voyage to Colchis

Ar'gosy, s. a large merchant ship

Ar'gue, v. a. to dispute, to reason, to debate

Ar'gument, s. a controversy, the subject of any discourse or writing; a reason alleged for or against a thing

Argument'al, a. belonging to argument

Argumenta'tion, s. the act of reasoning

Argumen'tative, a. consisting of argument, replete with argument, disputatious

Argu'te, a. witty, sharp, subtile, shrill

A'rianism, s. the doctrine of A. ius, who denied the divinity of Christ

Ar'id, a. parched up, dry

Arid'ity, s. dryness; insensibility in devotion

A'ries, s. the ram; a sign of the zodiac

Arie'tate, v. n. to butt like a ram

Ar'ight, ad. without mistake, rightly

A'ril, s. in botany, the outer coat of a seed

Ari'se, v. n. to mount up, to rise up

Aristoc'racy, s. a form of government which lodges the supreme power in the nobles

Aristocrat'ical, a. relating to aristocracy

Arith'metic, s. the science of computation

Arithmet'ical, a. according to the method or rule of arithmetic

Arithmetic'ian, s. one who professes the knowledge of arithmetic

Ark, s. the name generally applied to that vessel in which Noah was preserved from the deluge

Arm, s. the limb which reaches from the hand to the shoulder; inlet of the sea; a branch of a tree; power, as the secular arm

Arm, v. a. to provide with or take up arms

Arma'da, s. a large fleet of ships

Armadil'lo, s. a small animal like a hog

Ar'mament, s. a naval force; a storehouse

Armil'lary, a. surrounded with rings

Ar'millated, ad. wearing bracelets

Armin'ian:sm, s. a doctrine so called from its founder Arminius, who contended for free-will and universal redemption

Armip'otent, a. mighty in war

Ar'mistice, s. a short cessation of hostilities

Arm'let, s. a small arm of the sea, a bracelet

Armo'rial, a. belonging to the escutcheons or arms of a family

Ar'mory, s. a place in which arms are deposited for use; ensigns armorial

Ar'mour, Ar'mor, s. defensive arms to cover and defend the body

Ar'mourer, s. one who makes or sells arms

Ar'ms, s. warlike weapons; war in general; the ensigns armorial of a family

Ar'my, s. a large body of armed men

Aromat'ic, Aromat'ical, a. fragrant, spicy

Ar'omatize, v. a. to perfume, to scent

Around', ad. prep. around, encompassing

Arou'se, v. a. to raise up, to awake, to excite

A'row, ad. in a straight line, in a row

Aroy'nt, ad. begone, go away, depart

Ar'quebuse, s. a fuse, a hand-gun

Arrack', s. a spirit procured by distillation from a vegetable juice called toddy, which flows by incision out of the cocoa-nut tree

Arraign, v.a. to indict, to accuse, to charge

Arraign'ment, s. the act of accusing; a charge

Arra'nge, v. a. to set in order or place

Arra'ngement, s. the act of putting in order

Ar'rant, a. notorious, very bad, real

Ar'ras, s. rich tapestry or hangings

Array', s. in order of battle; dress

Array', v.a. to put in order, to dress, to deck

Arrea'r, Arrea'rage, s. that part of a debt which remains unpaid, though due

Arrest', v.a. to seize on; to obstruct—s. a legal caption or restraint of a man's person

Arret', s. the decision of a sovereign court

Arrie're, s. the last body of an army

Arri'val, s. the act of coming to a place

Arri've, v. n. to come to a place, to reach to

Ar'rogance, s. presumption, haughtiness

Ar'rogant, a. presumptuous, haughty

Ar'rogantly, ad. saucily, proudly, haughtily

Ar'rogate, v. a. to exhibit unjust claims, to claim in a proud manner; to assume

Ar'row, s. a pointed weapon shot from a bow

Ar'senal, s. a repository or magazine for all kinds of military stores

Ar'senic, s. a poisonous mineral

Art, s. science, dexterity, skill, cunning

Ar'tery, s. a canal or tube which conveys the blood from the heart to all parts of the body

Ar'tful, a. dexterous, cunning, artificial

Ar'tfully, ad. slily, with art, cunningly

Ar'tfulness, s. cunning; skill

Arthrit'ic, a. gouty, relating to the joints

Ar'tichoke, s. an esculent plant

Ar'ticle, v. to make terms; to stipulate

Ar'ticle, s. one of the parts of speech; a condition of a covenant; a stipulation

Artic'ulate, a. plain, distinct, divided

Artic'ulately, ad. clearly; in a distinct voice

Articula'tion, s. the act of pronouncing words; a joint or knot

c

Ar'tifice, s. fraud, trick; art or trade
Artif'icer, s. an artist or manufacturer
Artific'ial, a. not natural, made by art
Artil'lery, s. cannon, weapons of war
Artisan', s. an artist, an inferior tradesman
Ar'tist, s. a skilful man, a professor of an art
Ar'tless, a. without art or fraud, unskilful
Ar'tlessly, ad. naturally, without art
As, conj. in the same manner, because
Asafœt'ida, s. a gum of an offensive smell
Ashes'tos, s. a kind of fossil stone which may
   be split into threads and filaments, and
   which cannot be consumed by fire
Ascen'd, v. to mount upwards, to move high-
   er, to advance in excellence; to stand
   higher in genealogy
Ascen'dant, s. height, elevation; the part of
   the ecliptic above the horizon, supposed by
   astrologers to have great influence—a. pre-
   dominant, overpowering, superior
Ascen'dancy, s. superiority, influence
Ascen'sion, s. the act of ascending or rising
Ascen'sion-day, s. a festival ten days before
   Whitsuntide, in commemoration of our
   Saviour's ascension into heaven
Ascen't, s. a height, the rising of a hill
Ascertain, v.a. to establish, to make certain
Ascerta'inment, s. a fixed rule or standard
Ascet'ic, s. a hermit, a devout person—a. em-
   ployed in exercises of devotion and penance
Ascitit'ious, a. additional, supplemental
Ascri'be, v. a. to impute to, to attribute to
Ash, s. a well-known tree so called
Asha'med, a. confounded, abashed
Ash'es, s. the dust of any thing burnt, as of
   wood, coals,&c. the remains of a dead body
Asho're, ad. on shore, on the land, in safety
Ash-Wednesday, s. the first day of Lent
Ash'y, a. pale, a whitish grey like ash colour
Asi'de, ad. apart from the rest, to one side
As'inary, As'inine, a. belong ng to an ass
Ask, v.a. to beg, to seek, to claim, to require
Aska'nce, Aska'nt, ad. on one side, obliquely
Ask'er, s. an inquirer, an eft; a water newt
Askew', ad. sideways, contemptuously
Asla'nt, ad. on one side, obliquely
Aslee'p, ad. at rest, sleeping
Aslo pe, ad. with declivity, obliquely
Asp, s. a venomous serpent; a tree
Aspar'agus, s. an esculent plant
As'pect, s. look, appearance, air, view
As'pen, s. a kind of poplar tree, the leaves of
   which always tremble
As'perate, v. a. to make rough or uneven
Asper'ity, s. roughness, harshness of speech
Asper'se, v. a. to censure, to slander
Asper'sion, s. a sprinkling; calumny, censure
Asphal'tic, a. bituminous, gummy
As'phodel, s. a kind of plant, a da ily
As'pic, s. a very venomous serp·
As'pirate, v.a. to pronounce with ill breath
Aspira'tion, s. an ardent wish or desire; the
   act of pronouncing with full breath
Aspi're, v. n. to desire eagerly, to aim at
Asquin't, ad. obliquely, not in the straight
   line of vision
Ass, s. an animal of burden; a stupid fellow
Assail', v.a. to attack; to assault; to address
Assai'lant, s. one who attacks or invades
Assas'sin, Assas'sinator, s. a secret murderer
Assas'sinate, v. a. to murder to waylay

Assault, s. hostile onset, attack, storm
Assau'lt, v. a. to attack, to invade
Assay', s. trial, examination—r. a. to try
Assay'er, s. one who assays metals, &c.
Assem'blage, s. a collection of things
Assem'ble, v. a. to meet or call together
Assem'bly, s. a company assembled, a ball
Assen't, v. n. to agree to, to yield—s. consent
Asser't, v. a. to affirm, to maintain, to claim
Asser'tion, s. a positive affirmation
Assess', v. a. to charge with any certain sum
Assess'ment, s. the act of assessing or taxing
As'sets, s. effects left by a deceased person
   with which his executor is to pay his debts
Assevera'tion, s. a solemn protestation
Ass'head, s. a blockhead, a dunce
Assidu'ity, s. close application, diligence
Assid'uous, a. constant in application
Assi'gn, v.n. to make over a right to another,
   to mark out, to appoint
Assi'gnable, a. that may be transferred
Assigna'tion, s. an appointment, the transfer
   ring any thing to another
Assignee', s. one who is deputed to do any
   thing on behalf of others
Assi'gnment, s. a transfer, an appointment
Assim'ilate, v.a. to convert to the same nature
   or use with another thing; to bring to a
   resemblance or likeness
Assis't, v. a. to help, to aid, to succour
Assis'tance, s. help, relief, aid, support
Assis'tant, s. a person engaged in an affair, not
   as principal, but as an auxiliary
Assi'ze, s. the sitting of judges to determine
   causes; an order respecting the price,
   weight, &c. of sundry commodities
Asso'ciate, v. a. to join with, to unite
Asso'ciate, s. partner, companion, or sharer
Associa'tion, s. an entering into an agree
   ment with others, in order to perform some
   act; a partnership, a confederacy
Asso'nance, s. resemblance of sound
Assor't, v. a. to class, to range in order
Assor'tment, s. a quantity properly arranged
Assot', v. a. to infatuate
Assua'ge, v.a. to ease, to soften, to pacify
Assua'gement, s. what softens or mitigates
Assua'ger, s. one who appeases or pacifies
Assua'sive, a. mitigating, softening, mild
Assub'jugate, v. a. to subject to
As'suetude, s. custom, use, habit
Assu'me, v.a. to claim, to take, to arrogate
Assu'ming, a. haughty, arrogant
Assump'tion, s. the taking any thing to one's
   self; the thing supposed; a post late
Assump'tive, a. that which is assumed
Assu'rance, s. confidence; certainty; want of
   modesty; a contract; security; firmness
Assu're, v. a. to assert positively, to secure
As'terisk, s. a little star (*) serving as a refer
   ence to a note
As'terism, s. a constellation of fixed stars
Aster'n, ad. a sea term signifying behind
As'thma, s. a disease in the lungs
Asthmat'ic, Asthmat'ical, a. troubled with a
   disease in the lungs
Aston'ish, v. a. to confound, to amaze
Aston'ishment, s. surprise, amazement
As'tragal, s. an ornament in architecture
As'tral, a. relating to the stars, bright
Astray', ad. out of the right way, wrong

Astric'tion, s. the act of contracting parts
Astri'de, ad. with legs open, across
Astrin'ge, v. a. to draw together, to bind
Astrin'gent, a. contracting, binding [stars
Astrog'raphy, s. the science of describing
As'trolabe, s. an instrument used to take the
  altitude of the pole, the sun or stars, at sea
Astrol'oger, s. one who pretends to foretel
  events by observations of the stars
Astrol'ogy, s. the science of foretelling events
  by the knowledge of the stars
Astronom'ical, a. belonging to astronomy
Astron'omy, s. a science that teaches the
  knowledge of the heavenly bodies, their
  magnitude, motions, distances, &c.
As'tro-theol'ogy, s. divinity founded on the
  observation of the celestial bodies
Asun'der, ad. in two parts, separately
Asy'lum, s. a place of protection, a refuge
A'theism, s. the disbelief of a God
A'theist, s. one who disbelieves the existence
  of a God
Atheis'tical, a. belonging to atheism, impious
Athir'st, ad. thirsty, dry, in want of drink
Athlet'ic, a. vigorous, strong, bony, lusty
Athwart', ad. across, through; wrong
Atlan'tes, s. in architecture, the figures of
  men or beasts supporting an edifice
At'las, s. a collection of maps ; a mountain in
  Africa ; a rich kind of silk or stuff
At'mosphere, s. the air that encompasses the
  solid earth on all sides
At'om, At'omy, s. an extreme small particle
Atom'ical, a. belonging to atoms, minute
At'omist, s. one who maintains the doctrine
  of the atomical philosophy
Ato'ne, v. to expiate, to satisfy, to agree ; to
  stand as an equivalent for something
Ato'nement, s. expiation, concord, agree-
  ment
Atrabila'rian, Atrabila'rious, a. melancholy
Atramen'tal, Atramen'tous, a. black, inky
Atro'cious, a. wicked, heinous, enormous
Atro'ciously, ad. heinously, very wickedly
Atroc'ity, s. horrible wickedness
At'rophy, s. a disease in which what is taken
  for food cannot act as nourishment
Attach', v. a. to seize or lay hold on ; to win
  or gain over ; to fix to one's interest
Attach'ment, s. fidelity, regard, adherence
Attack', s. an assault on an enemy, an onset
Attack', v. a. to encounter, to assault, to im-
  pugn in any manner
Attai'n, v. a. to gain, to arrive at, to overtake
Attai'nable, a. that which may be attained
Attai'nder, s. the act of attainting in law; soil,
  taint, disgrace
Attai'nment, s. an acquisition ; a quality
Attai'nt, v. a. to corrupt, to dishonour
Attem'per, Attem'perate, v. a. to mingle, to
  proportion, to soften, to regulate
Attem'pt, v. a. to endeavour, to try, to essay
Atten'd, v. to wait for, or give attendance to,
  to accompany ; to regard with attention
Atten'dance, s. the act of waiting on another
Atten'dant, s. one who attends another—a.
  accompanying as subordinate
Atten'tion, s. close application of the mind to
  any thing ; the act of attending
Atten'tive, a. heedful, intent, regardful
Atten'uant a. making slender or thin

Atten'uate, v. a. to make slender, dilute
Attes't, v. a. to invoke, to bear witness of
Attesta'tion, s. witness, evidence, testimony
At'tic, a. elevated, just, elegant, fine
Atti're, s. clothes, habits, dress; a stag's horns
Atti're, v. a. to habit, to dress, to array
At'titude, s. gesture, posture, action
Attor'ney, s. one who is deputed to act and
  be responsible for another, particularly in
  affairs of law
Attrac't, v. a. to allure, to entice, to draw to
Attrac'tion, s. the power of drawing
Attrac'tive, s. alluring, inviting, enticing
Attrib'utable, a. that which may be ascribed
  or imputed
At'tribute, s. a quality inherent in a person
  or thing
Attrib'ute, v. a. to impute or ascribe to
Attri'tion, s. the act of wearing things by rub-
  bing one against another ; slight grief for
  sin : the lowest degree of repentance
Attu'ne, v. a. to make musical, to tune
Ava'il, v. a. to profit, to assist, to promote
Ava'ilable, a. advantageous, profitable, valid
Avail'ment, s. advantage, profit
Avan't-guard, s. the van or front of an army
Av'arice, s. niggardliness, covetousness
Avaric'ious, a. greedy, covetous, mean
Avas't, ad. stop, stay, hold, enough
Avau'nt, interj. begone; word of abhorrence
Au'burn, a. brown, of a fine tan colour
Auc'tion, s. a public sale of goods by bidding
Auctionee'r, s. the manager of an auction
Aucupa'tion, s. the act of bird-catching
Auda'cious, a. bold, impudent, saucy, daring
Auda'ciousness, Audac'ity, s. boldness, spirit,
  rashness, impudence
Au'dible, a. loud enough to be heard
Au'dience, s. an assemblage of persons to
  hear any thing; an interview, the reception
  of any man delivering a solemn message
Au'dit, s. a final account—v. to take a final
  account ; to scrutinize, to examine
Au'ditors of the Exchequer, s. officers who
  settle the Exchequer accounts
Au'ditory, s. an assembly of hearers; a place
  where lectures, &c. are heard
Aven'ge, v. a. to punish, to revenge
Av'enue, s. an entrance to a place ; an alley
  or walk of trees leading to a house
Aver', v. a. to affirm, to declare, to assent
Av'erage, s. the mean proportion or medium;
  a duty paid by merchants
Aver'ment, s. establishment by evidence
Avern'ant, s. a sort of grape
Aver'se, a. not favourable to, contrary to
Aver'sion, s. dislike, hatred, antipathy
Aver't, v. a. to keep off, to turn aside
Au'ger, s. a carpenter's tool to bore holes
Aught, pron. any thing [with
Augmen't, v. a. to add, to enlarge, to increase
Augmenta'tion, s. the act of increasing
Au'gur, s. a soothsayer, a diviner—v. to guess,
  to conjecture by signs
Au'gury, s. the art of foretelling events to
  come, by the flight, feeding, &c. of birds
Augus't, a. grand, noble, magnificent, holy
Au'gust, s. the eighth month in the year
A'viary, s. a place enclosed to keep birds
Avid'ity, s. eagerness, greediness
Au'lic, a. belonging to a court, royal

Anin, *s.* a French measure containing 48 gallons; likewise in length an ell

Aunt, *s.* a father or mother's sister

Avocate, *v. a.* to call away, to call from

Avoca'tion, *s.* the act of calling off or aside

Avoi'd, *v. a.* to shun, to retire, to escape

Avo rdupol's, *s.* a weight most commonly in use, containing 16 ounces to the pound

Avola'tion, *s.* the act of flying away

Avou'ch, *v. a.* to affirm, to justify, to assert—*s.* evidence, declaration

Avow', *v. a.* to assert, to declare, to profess

Avow'al, *s.* a positive or open declaration

Aure'lia, *s.* a term used for the first change of a maggot before it becomes a fly; chrysalis

Au'ricle, *s.* the external ear; two appendages of the heart covering its two ventricles

Auric'ula, *s.* a very beautiful flower

Auric'ular, *a.* within hearing; told in secret

Aurif'erous, *a.* having or producing gold

Auro'ra, *s.* poetically, the morning; an herb

Auro'ra Boreal'is, *s.* a luminous meteor, frequently visible in the northern hemisphere, generally called northern lights

Au'spice, *s.* an omen; influence, protection

Auspic'ious, *a.* fortunate, prosperous, happy

Auste're, *a.* rigid, harsh, severe, sourness of taste

Auster'ity, *s.* cruelty, severity; mortified life, harsh discipline, sourness of temper

Au'stral, *a.* southern, tending to the south

Authen'tic, *a.* original, genuine, proveable

Authen'ticate, *v. a.* to establish by proof

Authentic'ity, *s.* genuineness, authority

Au'thor, *s.* the writer of a book, opposed to a compiler; the first beginner of a thing

Author'itative, *a.* positive, having authority

Author'ity, *s.* legal power, rule, influence

Au'thorize, *v. a.* to justify, to give authority

Autog'ra hy, *s.* an original writing

Autom'aton, *s.* a machine which has the power of motion within itself, as a clock, watch, &c.

Autom'atous, *a.* having the power of motion in itself

Au op'sy, *s.* ocular demonstration

Autop'tica, *a.* perceived by one's own eyes

Autum'nal, *a.* belonging to autumn

Au'tumn, *s.* the season of the year between summer and winter

Avul'sion, *s.* pulling one thing from another

Auxil'iar, Auxil'iary, *s.* assistant, helper—*a.* aiding, helping, assisting

Auxilia'tion, *s.* aid, help

Awa'it, *v. a.* to wait for, to expect, to attend

Awa'ke. *v.* to rouse from sleep, to put into new action—*a.* not sleeping, without sleep

Awar'd, *v. a.* to determine, to adjudge, to give

Awar'd, *s.* a determination, a sentence

Awa're, *a.* attentive, vigilant, careful

Away', *ad.* ab ent; begone; let us go

Awe, *s.* fear, dread, reverence, respect

Aw'ful, *a.* that which strikes with awe, or fills with reverence; timorous, worshipful

Aw'fulness, *s.* quality of striking with awe

Awha'pe, *v. a.* to confound, to strike

Awhi'le, *ad.* for some space of time

Awk'ward, *a.* clumsy, unhandy, unpolite

Awk'wardly, *ad.* clumsily; inelegantly

Awl, *s.* a sharp instrument to make holes

Aw'less, *a.* wanting reverence

Awn, *s.* a slender sharp process issuing from the glume or chaff, in corn and grasses; the heard

Aw'ning, *s.* any covering spread over a ship or boat to keep off the heat or wet

Awo'ke, the *preterite* of *to awake*

Awry', *ad.* unevenly, obliquely, asquint

Axe, *s.* an instrument used to chop wood

Ax'il, *s.* the angle formed by a branch with the stem, or by a leaf with the branch

Ax'iom, *s.* a maxim or proposition, which being self-evident, cannot be made plainer by demonstration

Ax'is, *s.* a real or imaginary line, which passes directly through the centre of any thing that revolves on it

Ax'le, Ax'letree, *s.* the pin which passes through a wheel, and on which it turns

Ay. *ad.* yes, used to affirm the truth

Aye, *ad.* always, once more, for ever

Az'imuth, *s.* the azimuth of the s n or any wa is an arch between the meridian of the place and any given vertical line; an astronomical instrument

A'zure, *a.* sky-coloured; faint or light blue

B.

B, the second letter in the alphabet; a note in

Baa', *v. n.* to bleat or cry like a sheep [music

Ba'al, *s.* a Canaanitish idol

Bab'ble, *v. n.* to tell secrets, to talk idly

Bab'bler, *s.* a prattler, an idle talkative person

Babe, Ba'by, *s.* a young child of either sex

Baboon, *s.* a monkey of the largest kind

Bac'cated, *a.* beset with pearls having berries

Bacchana'lian, *s.* a drunken riotous person

Bac'chanals, *s.* drunken revels or riots

Bach'elor, *s.* an unmarried man; a knight of the lowest order; one who takes his first degree at the university

Back, *s.* the hinder part of a thing

Back, *v. a.* to mount a horse; to second, to strengthen, to maintain, to justify

Back'bite, *v. a.* to censure an absent person

Back'biter, *s.* one who slanders secretly

Back'ed, *part.* supported, seconded; mounted

Backgam'mon, *s.* a game with dice and tables

Backsli'der, *s.* an apostate

Back'stays, *s.* ropes to keep the masts from pitching forward

Back'sword, *s.* a sword with one sharp edge

Back'ward, *a.* unwilling, sluggishly

Ba'con, *s.* the fle h of a hog salted and dried

Bad, *a.* wicked, ill, vicious, sick, hurtful

Bade, *pret.* of *to bid*

Badge, *s.* a mark or token of distinction

Bad'ger, *s.* an animal resembling a hog and dog

Baf'fle, *v. a.* to deceive, to elude, to confound

Bag, *s.* a sack; a purse; an adder; an ornament; a purse of silk tied to men's hair

Bagatell'e, s. a trifle, a thing of no import
Bag'gage, s. the luggage of an army; a term for a worthless woman
Bagn'io, s. a warm bath; house of ill fame
Bag pipe, s. a Scotch musical instrument
Bail, s. surety given for another's appearance
Bail, v. a. to admit to bail, to give bail
Bai'lable, a. that may be set at liberty by bail
Bai'liff, s. an officer who puts in force an arrest; a land steward; a magistrate
Bai'liwick, s. the jurisdiction of a bailiff
Bait, s. a refreshment; a lure; a temptation
Bait, v. to bait the hook in angling; to set dogs upon; to take refreshment on a journey
Baize, s. a coarse kind of open cloth
Bake, v. to dress victuals in an oven; to harden by fire
Bal'ance, s. the difference of an account; a pair of scales; the beating part of a watch; in astronomy, one of the signs
Bal'ance, v. to make equal, to settle; to hesitate; to fluctuate
Balco'ny, s. a small gallery of wood or stone on the outside of a house
Bald, a. without hair, unadorned, inelegant
Bal'derdash, s. a rude mixture; confused or illiterate discourse
Ba'ldness, s. want of hair; nakedness
Ba'ldric, s. a belt; a girdle; the zodiac
Bale, s. goods packed for carriage; misery
Ba'leful, a. sorrowful, sad, full of misery
Balk, s. disappointment; a ridge of unploughed land; a great beam or rafter
Balk, Baulk, v. to disappoint of, to frustrate
Ball, s. any thing round; a globe; an entertainment of dancing
Bal'lad, s. a common or trifling song; an air
Bal'last, s. weight placed in the bottom of a ship, to prevent its oversetting—v. a. to keep any thing steady
Bal'latry, s. a song; a jig
Bal'let, s. an historical dance
Balloo'n, s. a globe made of silk, &c. which, being inflated with gas, rises into the air with any weight attached to it, proportionate to its size; a large vessel used in chemistry; a ball placed on a pillar
Bal'lot, s. a ball or ticket used in giving votes privately—v. a. to choose by ballot
Balm, s. the name of a plant—v. a. to sooth
Ba'lmy, a. having the qualities of balm; soft, soothing; odoriferous, fragrant
Bal'neary, s. a bathing room, bath
Ba'lsam, s. a shrub; an ointment
Balsam'ic, a. softening, mitigating, healing
Bal'uster, s. a small pillar or column
Balustra'de, s. a row of small pillars
Bamboo', s. an Indian cane, or measure
Bamboo'zle, v. a. to trick; a low word
Ban, s. a public notice; a curse, interdiction
Bana'na tree, s. a kind of plantain
Band, s. a bandage or tie; an ornament worn round the neck; a company
Ban'dage, s. a roller for a wound; a fillet
Ban'dbox, s. a thin slight box
Ban'delet, s. in architecture, any flat moulding or fillet
Bandit'ti, s. robbers, plunderers, outlaws
Bandolee'rs, s. small wooden cases, each of them containing powder that is a sufficient charge for a musket

Bando're, s. a musical three-stringed instrument
Ban'dy, v. a. to toss to and fro, to give and take reciprocally; to contend at a game
Ban'dy, a. crooked—s. a crooked stick
Ban'dy-legged, a. having crooked legs
Bane, s. ruin, poison, mischief—v. a. to poison
Ba'neful, a. hurtful, poisonous
Bang, s. a thump, a blow—v. a. to beat
Ban'ians, s. a particular sect in India, who hold a metempsychosis, and abstain from animal food
Ban'ish, v. a. to send from his own country
Ban'ishment, s. exile, transportation
Bank, s. a little hill; the side of a river; shoal in the sea; a repository where money is occasionally lodged
Ban'k-bill, s. a note for money in the bank
Ban'ker, s. one who receives money in trust
Ban'krupt, s. one who being unable to pay his debts, surrenders his effects
Ban'kruptcy, s. the state of a bankrupt
Ban'ner, s. a military standard or flag; also, in botany, the upper petal of a papillonaceous corolla
Ban'neret, s. a knight created in the field of battle
Bannian', s. a light undress, a morning gown
Ban'nock, s. a loaf or cake of oatmeal
Ban'quet, s. a sumptuous feast
Bans, s. publication of marriage at church
Ban'sticle, s. a very small prickly fish
Ban'ter, v. a. to rally, ridicule, jeer, play upon
Ban'tling, s. an infant, a young child
Bap'tism, s. the first sacrament of the Christian church, by which we are admitted to partake of all its privileges
Baptis'mal, a. relating to baptism
Bap'tist, Bapti'zer, s. one who christens
Bap'tistry, s. a font, or place for baptizing at
Bar, v. to secure, to fasten any thing with a bar; to obstruct or hinder
Bar, s. a long piece of wood or iron; a place assigned for lawyers to plead; a partition at which criminals are placed during trial; a hinderance; a small room in a tavern; a bank or rock at the entrance of a harbour; in music, a perpendicular line through the note lines, &c.
Barb, s. a Barbary horse; a beard; the points which stand backward in an arrow or fishing hook
Barb, v. a. to furnish horses with armour; to point an arrow; to shave the beard
Bar'bacan, s. a fortification before the walls of a town, an opening in the wall for guns
Bar'bacue, s. a hog dressed whole with spices
Barba'rian, s. a savage, a person without pity, a rude, uncivilized person; a foreigner
Barbar'ic, a. far-fetched, foreign
Bar'barism, s. inhumanity, ignorance; an uncouth manner of speaking or writing
Barbar'ity, s. savageness, cruelty
Bar'barous, a. uncivilized, ignorant, inhuman, rude, cruel; unacquainted with arts
Bar'bed, part. furnished with armour; jagged or bearded with hooks
Bar'bel, s. a large fish; superfluous fleshy knots growing in the mouth of a horse
Bar'ber, s. one whose trade is to shave
Bar'berry-tree, s. the name of a prickly shrub

C 3

Bard, *s.* a poet

Bare, *a.* naked, unadorned, lean, poor

Ba'refaced, *a.* impudent, shameless

Ba'rely, *ad.* naked'y ; merely ; openly

Bar'gain, *s. a* thing bought or sold ; a contract or agreement ; stipulation ; an event

Bar'gain, *v. a.* to make a contract for the purchase or sale of any thing

Barge, *s.* a large boat for trade or pleasure

Barll'la, *s.* potashes used in making glass

Bark, *s.* a small ship ; the rind of a tree

Bark, *v.* to make a noise like a dog or wolf ; to clamour at ; to strip trees of their bark

Bar'ker, *s.* a snarler, one that clamours

Bar'ley, *s.* corn used in making beer

Bar'ley-corn, *s.* a grain of barley ; in measurement, the third part of an inch

Barm, *s.* yeast, used to make drink ferment

Barn, *s.* a storehouse for corn, &c.

Bar'nacle, *s.* a sort of shellfish, which adheres to wood, &c. in the waters ; an iron instrument to hold a horse by the nose during an operation of farriery ; a bird like a goose

Barom'eter, *s.* an instrument to measure the weight of the atmosphere and the variations in it, in order chiefly to determine the changes of the weather

Baromet'rical, *a.* relating to a barometer

Bar'on, *s.* a rank in nobility next to a viscount ; two sirloins of beef

Bar'oness, *s.* a baron's lady

Bar'onet, *s.* the lowest title that is hereditary, next in rank to a baron

Bar'ony, *s.* the lordship whence a baron derives his title

Bar'oscope, *s.* an instrument to show the weight of the atmosphere

Bar'racan, *s.* a strong thick kind of camelot

Bar'rack, *s.* a building to quarter soldiers in

Bar'rator, *s.* an encourager of law suits ; a wrangler

Bar'ratry, *s.* foul practice in law ; a fraud committed by seamen on merchant's goods

Bar'rel, *s.* the hollow tube of a gun ; a round wooden vessel ; a cylinder

Bar'ren, *a.* unfruitful, steril, not prolific, uninventive, dull, unmeaning

Bar'renness, *s.* want of invention, sterility

Barrica'de, *v. a.* to fortify, to secure a place

Barrica'de, Barrica'do, *s. a* fortification, a bar to prevent admittance, an obstruction

Bar'rier, *s.* a defence, a boundary ; a bar to mark the limits of a place

Bar'rister, *s.* a pleader at the bar, an advocate

Bar'row, *s.* a small hand carriage to convey herbs, fruit, &c. ; a hog ; a small mount of earth under which bodies were anciently deposited

Bar'ter, *v. a.* to give any thing in exchange

Bar'ter, *s.* the act or practice of trafficking

Basal'tes, *s.* a kind of stone like iron

Basal'tic, *a.* relating to basaltes

Base, *s.* the foundation of any thing ; the pedestal of a statue ; a rustic play

Base, *a.* mean, vile, low ; metal below the standard ; in music, grave, deep

Ba'seness, *s.* meanness, vileness, bastardy

Bashaw', *s.* a governor or viceroy under the grand seignior ; a proud imperious person

Bash'ful, *a.* modest, timid, shamefaced, coy

Bas'il, *v. a.* to grind the edge of a tool

Bas'il, *s.* the name of a plant ; a kind of leather ; the edge of a joiner's tool

Basil'icon, *s.* a kind of ointment

Bas'ilisk, *s.* a kind of serpent, a cockatrice, said to kill by looking ; a piece of ordnance

Ba'sin, Ba'son, *s.* a small vessel to hold water ; a small pond ; a dock where ships may float in safety

Ba'sis, *s.* the foundation of any thing ; that on which any thing is raised ; the lowest of the three principal parts of a column ; the pedestal, the foot

Bask, *v.* to lie in the heat of the sun, or fire

Bas'ket, *s.* a vessel made of twigs or rushes

Bass, *s.* a mat used to kneel on in churches ; —*a.* in music, grave, deep

Bas'set, *s.* a certain game at cards

Bassoon', *s.* a musical wind instrument

Bass-relie'f, or Bas'so-relie'vo, *s.* raised work

Bass-vi'ol, *s.* a fiddle for the bass

Bas'tard, *s.* a child born out of wedlock

Bas'tardize, *v.* to declare a child illegitimate ; to beget a bastard

Baste, *v. a.* to beat with a stick ; to drip butter on meat whilst on the spit ; to sew in a slight manner

Bas'tile, *s.* formerly a state prison in France

Bastina'de, Bastina'do, *v. a.* to punish a person by beating him on the soles of his feet— *s.* the act of beating with a cudgel

Bas'tion, *s.* a huge mass of earth standing from a rampart ; a fortress ; a bulwark

Bat, *s.* a flattened club to strike a ball with ; an animal resembling a mouse, which flies with a sort of skin distended like wings

Batch, *s.* a quantity of any thing baked at one time ; any quantity made at once

Bate, *v. a.* to lower a price, to lessen, to remit

Bat-fowling, *s.* bird-catching in the night time

Bath, *s.* a place to bathe in ; the name of a city ; a measure

Bathe, *v. a.* to wash in a bath, to soften

But'let, *s.* a square piece of wood used for beating linen

Batoon, *s.* a staff or club ; a truncheon borne by a marshal in an army

Batta'lia, *s.* order of battle, battle array

Batta'lion, *s.* a body of foot soldiers, from 500 to 800 men ; a division of an army

Bat'ten, *s.* a scantling ; a narrow board

Bat'ten, *v. a.* to fatten, to grow fat, to fertilize

Bat'ter, *s.* a mixture of flour, milk, eggs, and salt—*v. a.* to beat down, to beat

Bat'tering-ram, *s.* a military engine, formerly used to batter down walls, having a head resembling a ram's

Bat'tery, *s.* raised work on which cannons are mounted ; in law, a violent assault

Bat'tle, *s.* a fight between armies or fleets

Bat'tle-array, *s.* a form or order of battle

Bat'tleaxe, *s.* a weapon like an axe ; a bill

Bat'tledoor, *s.* a flat instrument used to strike shuttlecocks with

Bat'tlement, *s.* a wall indented on the top of buildings ; a breastwork

Bauhee', *s.* in Scotland, a halfpenny [gots

Bav'in, *s.* a stick like those bound up in faggots

Bau'ble, *s.* a trifle, a plaything, a trinket

Bawl, *v.* to speak aloud, to call out, cry out

Baw'rel, *s.* a kind of hawk

Bay, *v. a.* to bark as a dog ; to surround

Bay, s. a tree; a road where ships can anchor; a term in architecture—a. a chesnut colour

Bay-salt, s. salt made from sea water exposed to the sun, so named from its colour

Bay-tree, s. the female laurel

Bayonet, s. a dagger fixed to a musket

Bays, s. an honorary crown or garland

Bay'window, s. a window jutting outward

Baza'ar, s. a constant market

Bdel'lium, s. an aromatic gum

Be, v. n. to exist, to have existence

Beach, s. the strand, the coast, the shore

Bea'con, s. an edifice on an eminence, where signs are made to direct seamen

Bead, s. a small glass ornament, with which necklaces, and monkish rosaries are made; any globular body

Bea'dle, s. an inferior officer in a parish, university, or trading company

Bea'gle, s. a small hound to hunt hares

Beak, s. the bill of a bird; a promontory

Be'aker, s. a cup with a spout formed like the beak of a bird

Beam, s. the principal piece of timber which supports a building; a ray of light; the balance of a pair of scales; the pole of a chariot; the horn of a stag

Beam, v. n. to emit beams or rays

Bean, s. a well-known kind of pulse

Bear, s. a rough, savage animal; a rude unpolished man; the name of two constellations, called the greater and lesser bear

Bear, v.a. to carry a load, to support, to keep from falling; to carry in remembrance; to be fruitful; to press; to endure; to be patient; to tend, to be directed to any point

Beard, s. hair which grows on the chin and lips; the barb of an arrow or hook

Bea'rdless, a. having no beard; youthful

Bea'rer, s. a supporter, a carrier of any thing

Bea'rgarden, s. any place of tumult

Bea'ring, s. the situation of any place, both as to distance and direction; gesture

Beast, s. an irrational animal; a brutal man

Bea'stly, a. filthy, nasty, obscene

Beat, v. a. to conquer; to strike; to throb

Beatif'ic, Beatif'ical, a. blissful, the making happy or blessed; belonging to the happy

Beatifica'tion, s. an acknowledgment made by the Pope and his consistory, that the person beatified is in heaven, and may be reverenced as blessed

Beat'ify, v. to bless with celestial enjoyment

Bea'ting, s. correction by blows

Beat'itude, s. happiness, blessedness, felicity

Beau, s. a fop, a man of dress, a coxcomb

Bea'ver, s. an animal, otherwise named the Castor, amphibious, and remarkable for his art in building his habitation; a hat made of its fur; the part of a helmet which covers the face

Beau'teous, Beau'tiful, a. lovely, elegant, fair

Beau'tifully, ad. in a beautiful manner

Beau'tify, v. a. to embellish, to adorn

Beau'ty, s. a beautiful person; that assemblage of graces which pleases the eye

Becaffi'co, s. a small bird, the fig-eater

Beca'lm, v. a. to quiet the mind, to still

Beca'me, the preterite of to become

Becau'se, conj. on this account that, for this reason that

Beck, s. a sign with the hand or head, a nod

Beck'on, v. n. to make a sign with the hand

Becom'e, v. a. to enter into some state; to befit, to be suitable to the person

Becom'ing, a. pleasing, elegant, graceful

Becom'ingness, s. elegant congruity

Bed, s. a place to sleep on; the channel of a river; a division in a garden in which seeds are sown; a layer, a stratum

Bedab'ble, v. a. to wet, to besprinkle

Bedag'gle, Bedrag'gle, v.a. to trail in the dirt

Bedau'b, v. a. to besmear, to daub

Bed'ding, s. the materials belonging to a bed

Bedeck', v.a. to adorn, to deck

Bedew', v. a. to moisten gently as with dew

Be'dehouse, s. an hospital or alms-house

Bed'fellow, s. one that lies in the same bed

Bed'lam, s. an hospital for lunatics

Bed'lamite, s. a madman, a noisy person

Bed'id, a. confined to bed by violent sickness or extreme old age

Bed'stead, s. the frame which supports a bed

Bee, s. an insect which produces honey; an industrious and careful person

Beech, s. the name of a large tree

Bee'chen, a. consisting of the wood of beech

Beef, s. the flesh of an ox, cow, or bull

Bee'f-eater, s. a yeoman of the guards

Beer, s. a liquor made of malt and hops

Beet, s. the name of a garden plant

Bee'tle, s. an insect; a large heavy mallet

Beeves, s. black cattle, oxen

Befa'll, v. n. to come to pass, to happen

Befit', v. a. to suit, to be suitable

Befo're, prep. further onward, not behind, in the presence of; prior to, sooner

Befo'rehand, ad. in a state of anticipation, first, previously

Befou'l, v. a. to dirty, to make foul, to so

Befrien'd, v. a. to be kind to, to favour

Beg, v. a. to ask alms, to petition, to entreat

Beget', v. a. to generate, to produce

Beg'gar, s. one who lives by begging

Beg'garly, a. stingy, in want—ad. meanly

Beg'gary, s. great want, poverty, indigence

Begin', v. a. to commence, to enter upon

Begin'ning, s. the first original or cause, the first part, the rudiments or first grounds

Begir'd, v. a. to gird, shut up, bind round

Begon'e, interj. go hence! get away!

Begot', Begot'ten, part. pass. of to beget

Begri'me, v. a. to dirty with soot, to soil

Begui'le, v. a. to impose on, to cheat, to deceive pleasingly, to amuse, to evade

Begun', part. pass. of to begin

Beha'lf, s. vindication, favour, support

Beha've, v. n. to demean, to conduct, to act

Beha'viour, s. conduct, course of life

Behea'd, v. a. to kill by cutting off the head

Behel'd, part. pass. of to behold

Behe'moth, s. the river horse; hippopotamus

Behes't, s. a command, precept, order

Behi'nd, prep. at the back of another, following another, remaining after another's departure; inferior to another

Behi'ndhand, ad. in arrears, late in time

Beho'ld, v. a. to look upon, to see, to view—interj. lo! see!

Beho'lden, part. a. obliged in gratitude

Behoo'f, s. advantage, profit

Behoo've, Beho've, v. n. to become, to be fit

Be'ing, s. existence; the person existing; a particular state or condition

Bela'bour, v. a. to thump, to beat soundly

Bela'ted, a. benighted, too late

Belay', v.a. to lay wait for; with seamen, to make fast a rope

Belch, v. n. to eject wind from the stomach

Bel'dam, s. a hag; a scolding woman

Belea'guer, v. a. to block up, to besiege

Bel'fry, s. a place where bells hang

Beli'e, v. n. to calumniate, to slander

Belie'f, s. creed, form containing the articles of faith; persuasion, opinion

Belie've, v.a. to think true, to trust, to credit

Belie'ver, s. a professor of Christianity

Beli'ke, ad. likely, probably, perhaps

Bell, s. a hollow sounding vessel

Belle, s. a gay, dressy young woman

Belles-le'ttres, s. polite literature

Bellig'erent, a. engaged in war

Bell-metal, s.a mixture of copper and pewter

Bel'low, v. n. to roar like a bull, or the sea; to make any violent outcry, to clamour

Bel'lows, s. an instrument to blow the fire

Bel'ly, s. the lower part of the body

Bell'man, s. he whose business it is to proclaim any thing in towns, and to gain attention by ringing his bell

Belon'g, v. n. to be the property of, to have relation to, to appertain to

Belov'ed, a. dear to, loved, valued much

Belo'w, ad. inferior, lower in place

Belt, s. a sash, a girdle, a cincture

Bel'wether, s. a sheep which leads the flock with a bell on his neck

Bemi're, v.a. to daub with mire, to soil

Bemo'an, v. a. to bewail, to lament, grieve

Bench, s. a seat to sit on; a tribunal of justice; justices sitting on the bench

Ben'cher, s. a senior in the inns of court

Bend, v. a. to bend, to crook; to subdue

Ben'dable, a. that which may be incurvated

Benea'th, prep. lower in place, under, lower in excellence; unworthy of

Benedict'ine, s. a monk of that order, named after its founder, St. Benedict

Benedic'tion, s. a blessing; an acknowledgment for blessings received

Benefac'tion, s. a benefice, a charitable gift

Benefac'tor, Benefac'tress, s. a man or woman who does acts of kindness; a patron

Ben'efice, s. a church living

Benef'icence, s. active kindness, generosity

Benef'icent, a. obliging, kind, doing good

Benefi'cial, a. helpful, advantageous

Benefi'ciary, s. he who possesses a benefice

Ben'efit, s. advantage, kindness, use

Benev'olence, s. charity; disposition to good

Benev'olent, a. having good will, kind

Benga'l, s. a sort of thin Indian cotton

Beni'ghted, part. overtaken by the night

Beni'gn, a. generous, kind, wholesome

Benig'nity, s. kindness, graciousness

Ben'ison, s. a benediction, a blessing

Bent, s. the state of being bent; declivity; fixed purpose, inclination, disposition

Benum'b, v. a. to make torpid, to stupify

Ben'zoin, s. a medicinal kind of resin, vulgarly called be-jamin

Bequea'th, v. a. to leave by will

Beque'st, s. something left by will

Berea've, v. a. to deprive of; to take away

Ber'gamot, s. a kind of pear; an essence or perfume; a sort of scented snuff

Ber'gmote, s. a court held to determine matters relative to mines and miners

Berlin', s. a coach of a particular construction, first used at Berlin

Ber'nardines, s. an order of monks, so named from their founder, St. Bernard

Ber'ry, s. a small fruit of several kinds

Ber'yl, s. a precious stone of a greenish cast

Besee'ch, v. a. to implore, to beg, to entreat

Besee'm, v. n. to befit, to become

Beset', v. a. to waylay, to harass, to perplex

Beshrew', v. a. to curse, to happen ill to

Besi'de, Besi'des, pr. over and above, near

Besie'ge, v. a. to lay siege to, to surround

Besmea'r, v. a. to daub, or smear over, to soil

Besmut', v. a. to blacken with smut

Be'som, s. a broom to sweep with

Besot', v.a. to infatuate, stupefy with liquor

Bespan'gle, v. a. to decorate with spangles

Bespat'ter, v. a. to splash with dirt; to asperse with reproach, to slander

Bespea'k, v. a. to order, to address, to show

Bespot', v.a. to mark with spots, to variegate

Besprin'kle, v. a. to sprinkle over

Bes', a. most preferable, most good

Bes'tial, a. like a beast, carnal, brutish

Bestir', v. a. to hasten, to move quickly

Bestow', v. a. to confer upon, to apply

Bestrew', v. a. to strew or scatter about

Bestri'de, v. a. to get across any thing

Bet, s. a wager—v. a. to lay a wager

Beta'ke, v. a. to have recourse to, to take

Be'tel, s. an Indian plant called water pepper

Bethin'k, v. n. to reflect, to recollect

Beti'de, v. n. to befal, to happen, to come

Beti'mes, ad. soon, early, seasonably

Beto'ken, v. a. to foreshow, to signify

Bet'ony, s. the name of a plant

Betray', v.a. to deliver up treacherously; to divulge a secret, to discover; to shew

Betroth', v. a. to give or receive a contract of marriage, to affiance

Bet'ter, a. superior, excelling, improved

Betwee'n, Betwix't, prep. in the middle

Bev'el, s. in masonry, a kind of square rul

Bev'erage, s. a drink, liquor to be drunk

Bev'y, s. a flock of birds; a company

Bewai'l, v. a. to lament, to bemoan

Bewar'e, v. n. to take care of, to be cautious

Bewil'der, v. a. to puzzle, to mislead

Bewit'ch, v. a. to injure by witchcraft, to fascinate, to charm, to please irresistibly

Bewray', v. a. to betray, to discover

Bey, s. a Turkish viceroy or governor

Beyon'd, prep. further onward than, on the further side of, remote from, above

Bez'el, Bez'il, s. that part of a ring in which the diamond or stone is fixed

Bez'oar, s. a medicinal stone from the East

Bezoar'dic, a. compounded with bezoar

Bian'gulous a. having two angles or corners

Bi'as, s. inclination; a weight in a bowl that turns it from a straight line

Bi'as, v. a. to incline partially, to prejudice

Bib, s. a piece of linen to pin before a child

Bib'acious, a. much addicted to drinking

Bib'ber, s. a toper, a tippler, a sot

Bi'ble, s. the sacred volume in which are contained the revelations of God

Bib'lical, a. relating to the bible or divinity

Bib'ulous, a. spungy, drinking moisture

Bice, s. a blue colour used in painting

Bick'er, v. n. to quarrel; to wrangle

Bid, v. a. to offer a price; to command

Bid'den, part. commanded, invited

Bid'd r.s. one who offers or preposes a price

Bid'ding, s. a command, charge, order

Bide, v. a. to dwell, to endure, to continue

Biden'tal, a. having two teeth

Bi'ding, s. an abode, residence, stop, stay

Bien'nial, a. continuing for two years

Bier, s. a carriage for the dead

Bie'stings, s. the first milk after calving

Bifa'rious, s. double, twofold; doubtful

Bif'erous, a. bearing fruit twice a year

Bif'id, Bif'idated, a. opening with a cleft

Bif'lorous, a. bearing two flowers

Bif'ormed, a. compounded of two forms

Big, a. great, large, swoln, pregnant

Big'amy, s. having two wives at once

Big'gin, s. a kind of cap for a child

Big'ot, s. one blindly devoted to a party

Big'otry, s. blind zeal, superstition

Bil'ander, s. a small vessel, broad and flat, used for the carriage of goods

Bil'berries, s. small purple-coloured berries

Bil'boes, s. a sort of stocks on board a ship

Bile, s. a thick bitter liquor collected in the gall bladder; a painful swelling

Bilge, s. the breadth of a ship's bottom

Bil'lingsgate, s. foul language; a scold

Bil'ious, a. full of bile; choleric

Bilk, v. a. to cheat, to defraud, to swindle

Bill, s. an account of money; the beak of a bird; an advertisement; an act of parliament; a kind of hatchet

Bill of exchange, s. a note which authorizes the bearer to demand a sum of money at a certain place

Bill of parcels, s. an account delivered by the seller to the buyer of goods

Bill, v. a. to kiss as doves; to caress; to publish

Bil'let, s. a small log of wood; a letter, a note, a small paper

Bil'let, v. a. to quarter soldiers

Bil'let-doux, s. a short love-letter, a card

Bil'liards, s. a game with balls and sticks

Bil'low, s. a large rolling wave

Bil'ocular, a. two-celled

Bin, s. a repository for corn, wine, &c.

Bi'nary, a. two and two; double

Bind, v. a. to confine with bonds; to oblige by stipulation, to contract; to make costive

Bind, s. a species of hops; a quantity

Bind'ing, s. a bandage; a fastening

Bin'ocle, s. a telescope with two tubes, so that an object may be seen with both eyes

Binoc'ular, a. having two eyes

Biog'rapher, s. a writer of lives

Biog'raphy, s. a writing or history of lives

Bipa'rous, a. bringing forth two at a birth

Bip'artite, a. cleft or divided in two parts

Bipartit'ion, s. the act of dividing in two

Bi'ped, s. an animal having only two feet

Bip'edal, a. two feet in length

Bipen'nated, a. having two wings

Bipe'talous, a. consisting of two flower leaves

Bird, s. a tree common in England; a rod

Bird, s. a name applied to all fowls

Bird'lime, s. a viscous substance used to entangle the feet of small birds

Bir'gander, s. a fowl of the goose kind

Birt, s. a fish resembling a turbot

Birth, s. the act of coming into life; lineage; rank inherited by descent; extraction

Bir'thright, s. the rights and privileges to which a person is born

Bir'thwort, s. the name of a plant

Bis'cuit, s. a kind of hard flat bread, &c.

Bisect', v. a. to divide into two equal parts

Bish'op, s. one of the head order of the clergy who has the charge of a diocese; a liquor composed of wines, oranges, sugar, &c.

Bish'opric, s. the diocese of a bishop

Bis'muth, s. a hard white brittle mineral

Bissex'tile, s. leap year; every fourth year

Bis'son, a. blind, deprived of sight

Bis'toury, s. chirurgical incision knife

Bisul'cous, a. cloven footed

Bit, s. a small piece of any thing; the iron mouth-piece of a bridle; a Spanish silver coin, value seven-pence halfpenny

Bite, s. se zure by the teeth; the act of a fish that takes the bait; a cheat, trick; a sharper

Bite, v. a. to separate or pierce with the teeth; to cut, to wound; to trick; to cheat

Bit'tacle, Bin'nacle, s. a frame of timber in the steerage, where the compass is placed

Bit'ter, a. of a hot, acrid, and biting taste; calamitous, severe, sharp, keen, satirical

Bit'tern, s. a bird of the heron kind

Bit'terness, s. a bitter taste; malice; grief

Bitu'men, s. a fat unctuous matter

Bitu'minous, a. compounded of bitumen

Bi'valve, Bival'vular, a. having two valves or shutters, said of two-shelled fish

Biv'ouac, v. n. to continue under arms all night

Blab, v. a. to tell a secret, to tell tales, to tattle

Blab, Blab'ber, s. a tell-tale

Black, a. cloudy, dark; wicked; mournful

Black, s. a dark colour; a negro; mourning

Black'amoor, s. a man by nature of a black complexion; a negro

Black'bird, s. the name of a bird

Black'-cattle, s. oxen, bulls, and cows

Black'cock, s. the heathcock

Black'en, v. a. to make black; to defame

Black'guard, s. a scoundrel, a dirty fellow

Black'ness, s. black colour

Black'rod, s. the usher belonging to the Order of the Garter; he is usher of Parliament

Black'smith, s. a smith who works in iron

Blad'der, s. urinary vessel; a pustule; a bag

Blade, s. the spire of grass before it seeds; the green shoots of corn; the sharp or cutting part of an instrument; a gay man

Blain, s. a blister, a pustule

Blame, s. imputation of a fault, offence

Blame, v. a. to censure, to reproach

Bla'meable, a. deserving censure, faulty

Bla'meableness, s. faultiness, guiltiness

Bla'meless, a. innocent, guiltless

Blanch, v. a. to whiten; to peel almonds; evade, to shift; to omit, to obliterate

Bland, a. gentle, soft, mild, kind

Blan'dish, v. a. to smooth, to soften

Blan dishment, s. soft words, flattery

Blank, s. a void space; a disappointment

Blank, *a.* unwritten, white; dull, confused
Blank verse, *s.* verse without rhyme
Blan'ket,*s.*a woollen cover for a bed ; a pear
Blasphe'me, *v. a.* to speak impiously of God
Blas'phemous, *a.* very wicked, very impious
Blas'phemously, *ad.* impiously, irreverently
Blas'phemy, *s.* indignity offered to God
Blast, *s.* a gust of wind ; the sound made by a wind instrument of music ; a blight which damages corn, trees, &c.
Blast, *v. a.* to injure, to blight, to wither
Bla'tant, *a.* bellowing as a calf noisy
Blaze, *s.* a flame, the light of a flame; a white mark on a horse ; a publication
Blaze, *v. a.* to flame, to declare. to publish
Bla'zon, Bla'zoury, *s.* the art of heraldry
Bla'zon,*v. a.*to explain figures on ensigns armorial ; to embellish ; to deck ; to make public ; to celebrate
Bleach, *v. a.* to grow white, to whiten
Blea'ched, *part.* made white, whitened
Bleak, *a.* chilly, cold, pale—*s.* a fish
Blear, *a.* watery, obscure, weak, dim
Blear'eyed, *a.* having so e eyes; inflamed
Bleat, *v. n.* to cry like a sheep
Bleed, *v. a.* to let blood ; to lose blood
Blem'ish, *s.* a deformity ; a spot or stain
Blem'ish, *v. a.* to injure, to defame
Bench, *v. n.* to shrink or fly off ; to obstruct
Blend, *v. a.* to mingle, to mix, to confound
Bless, *v. a.* to wish happiness to another
Bless'ed, Blest, *part.* happy, tasting felicity
Bless'ing, *s.* a good wish, divine favour
Bligh, *s.* a mildew—*v. a.* to blast ; to spoil ; to hinder from fertility
Blind, *a.* deprived of sight, obscure, dark
Blind, *s.* any thing which is placed to intercept the sight ; a false screen
Blind'fold, *a.* having the eyes covered
Blind'ne-s, *s.* a want of sight ; ignorance
Bli'ndworm, *s.* a small viper, not venomous
Blink, *v. n.* to see obscurely ; to wink
Blin'kard, *s.* one who has weak eyes
Bliss, *s.* the highest degree of happiness ; felicity ; happiness of blessed souls
Bliss'ful, *a.* full of joy ; very happy ; glad
Blis'ter, *s.* rising in the skin ; a plaster
Blis'ter.*v. a.*to apply a blister; rise in blisters
Blithe, Bli'thsome, *a.* sprightly, merry, gay
Bloat, *v. a.* to grow puffy ; to swell
Bloa'tedness, *s.* swelling, turgidness
Block,*s.*a large heavy piece of wood; a piece of marble ; a pulley ; a stupid fellow
Block, *v. a.* to inclose ; to shut up
Blocka'de, *s.* a siege carried on by shutting up a place to prevent any relief
Block'head, *s.* a dunce ; a stupid person
Block'-tin, *s.* the best tin ; unadulterated tin
Blood,*s.* the red fluid that circulates through the body ; lineage ; kindred ; a rake
Blood'hound,*s.*a hound of an exquisite scent
Blood'shed,*s.*slaughter, the crime of murder
Blood'shot, *a.* filled with blood ; red
Blood'y, *a.* stained with blood ; sanguinary
Bloom, *s.* the blossom or flower of a tree; the blue that appears on some fruit ; a native flush on the cheek ; the prime of life
Bloom, Blos'som. *v. n.* to produce blossoms
Bloo'ming, Bloo'my, *a.* flowry ; youthful
Blos'som, *s.* the flowers of trees or plants
Blot,*s.*a spot, a blur—*v. a.*to stain,to disgrace

Blotch, *s.* a pustule on the skin, a pimple
Blow, *s.* a stroke ; a sudden event ; the act of a fly, by which she lodges eggs in meat
Blow,*v. a.*to pant or breathe hard; to ut form flowers ; to drive by the force of wind ; to sound a musical instrument ; to swell
Blowze, *s.* a slattern, a ruddy fat wench
Blow'zy, *a.* ruddy-faced, sun-burnt
Blub'ber, *s.* the fat of a whale, &c.
Blub'ber,*v. n.*to swell the cheeks by weeping
Blud'geon, *s.* a short thick stick, a weapon
Blue, *a.* sky-coloured—*s.* an original colour
Blue'ness, *s.* the quality of being blue
Buff, *a.* blustering, stern, fierce ; large
Blun'der, *s.* a gross oversight, a mistake
Blun'der, *v. n.* to err ; to mistake grossly
Blun'derbuss,*s.*a short wi e gun discharged with many bullets at a time
Blunt,*a.*rough, rude. unpolite, dull, abrupt; obtuse, opposed to sharp or acute
Blunt, *v. a.* to dull the point or edge
Blun'tly, *ad.* roughly, rudely, plainly
Blun'tness, *s.* a want of edge ; rudeness
Blur, *s.* a spot. stain, imperfection
Blurt, *v. a.* to let fly without thinking
Blush, *v.* to betray shame or confusion by a red colour in the cheeks ; to colour
Blush,*s.*colour of the cheek raised by shame, &c. red or purple colour ; sudden appearance [ance
Blush'et, *s.* a young modest girl
Blus'ter, *v. n.* to bully, to roar, to puff
Blus'terer, *s.* a swagge er, a noisy person
Blus'trous, *a.* tumultuous, noisy
Boar, *s.* the male of all so ts of swine
Board, *s.* a flat piece of wood; a court held
Board.*v.a.*to pave with boards; to live where a certain rate is paid for eating ; to enter a ship by force
Boa'rder,*s.*one who pays to diet with another
Boardwa'ges, *s.* an allowance for victuals
Boar'ish, *a.* swinish, rude, cruel, brutish
Boast, *s.* a proud speech, cause of boasting
Boast, *v. n.* to glory in, to brag, to exult
Boa'ster, *s.* a braggart, a puffer, a swaggerer
Boa'stful, *a.* haughty, proud, vain
Boa's ingly, *ad.* vainly, ostentatiously
Boat, *s.* a small vessel used on rivers, &c.
Boa'tman, *s.* a manager of a boat
Boa'tswain, *s.* an inferior officer who superintends a ship's rigging. anchors, &c. and overlooks the sailors in their sundry duties
Bob. *v. a.* to cheat, to dodge, to dangle
Bob'bin, *s.* a small wooden instrument with which lace is made
Bob'tailed, *a.* having the tail cut short
Bode, *v. a.* to foreshow, portend
Bo'dement, *s.* an omen, foreboding
Bod'ice, *s.* a sort of stays for women
Bod'iless, *a.* without a body
Bod'ily, *a.* relating to the body ; real, actual
Bod'kin, *s.* a small iron instrument with a sharp point to pierce holes
Bod'y, *s.* matter as opposed to spirit ; a person ; a collective mass ; a corporation
Bod'y-clothes, *s.* clothing for horses
Bog, *s.* a marsh, a morass, a fen, a swamp
Bog'gle, *v. n.* to start, to waver, to hesitate
Bog'gler, *s.* a doubter, a timorous man
Bohe'a, *s.* a tea more astringent than green
Boil, *v. a.* to be agitated by heat ; to dress
Bo'iled. *part.* dressed in boiling water

Bot'her, s. a vessel for boiling water, &c.
Bois'terous, a. furious, stormy, turbulent
Bois'terously, ad. very loudly; violently
Bold, a. daring, stout, impudent, licentious
Bol'den, v. a. to make bold or confident
Bold'ly, ad. bravely, in a bold manner
Bold'ness, s. courage, confidence, impudence
Bole, s. earth; a corn measure of six bushels
Boll, s. round stalk or stem; a bowl
Boll, v. n. to rise in a stalk; to swell out
Bol'ster, s. a large pillow; a long cushion
Bol'ster, v. a. to support; to pad, compress
Bolt, s. the bar of a door; an arrow
Bolt, v. a. to fasten; to spring out; to sift
Bol'ter, s. a sieve to separate meal from bran
Bo'lus, s. a large pill, a kind of earth
Bomb, s. a globe of iron containing combustibles, &c. to be discharged from a mortar
Bom'bard, s. a great gun; a barrel for wine
Bombar'd, v. a. to attack with bombs
Bombardie'r, s. a bomb engineer
Bombar'dment, s. an attack made with bombs
Bombasi'n, s. a slight black silken stuff
Bombas't, a. high sounding—s. big words
Bombas'tic, a. of great sound but little mean-
Bombula'tion, s. a high sound. a hum [ing
Bom'bketch, s. a ship for bombs
Bona'sus, s. a kind of buffalo
Bond, s. a written obligation, cords, captivity
Bond, a. in a servile state; captive, enslaved
Bon'dage, s. slavery, captivity, imprisonment
Bon'dman, Bon'dmaid, s. a male or female
Bon'dsman, s. one bound for another [slave
Bone, s. the most solic part of the body
Bo'nelace, s. a coarse kind of lace; flaxen lace
Bo'neless, a. without bones; tender soft
Bon'fire, s. a fire made for triumph
Bon'net, s. a covering for the head, a cap
Bon'nily, ad. gaily, handsomely, prettily
Bon'ny, a. beautiful, merry, handsome, gay
Bo'num Mag'num, s. a great plum
Bo'ny, a. full of bone, stout, strong
Boo'by, s. a dull stupid fellow; a large bird
Book, s. a volume in which we read or write;
a particular part or division of a work
Book'binder, s. one who binds books
Book'keeper, s. one who keeps accounts
Book'keepin, s. the art of keeping accounts
Book'mate, s. a school-fellow [sion
Book'seller, s. a vender of books by profes-
Book'worm, s. a mite; a close student
Boom, s. a long pole used to spread the clue
of the studding-sail; a bar of wood or iron
laid across the mouth of a harbour
Boon, s. a present, a gift, a grant; a prayer
Boon, a. merry, pleasant, cheerful, gay
Boor, s. a lout, a clown, a rude man
Boo'rish a. clownish, rustic, rude
Boo'rishness, s. coarseness of manners
Booze, s. a stall for a cow or ox to feed in
Boot, v. a. to put on boots; to gain, to profit
Boot, s. covering for the legs; part of a coach;
booty, advantage, profit
Booth, s. a tent or stall erected in a fair
Boo'tjack, s. an utensil for pulling off boots
Boo'tless, a. useless, vain, unavailing
Boo'ty, s. spoil, pilla e. plunder
Bora'chio, s. a drunkard; a leathern bottle
Bora'mez, s. the vegetable lamp, generally
known by the name of Agnus Scythicus
Bo'rax, s. an artificial salt

Bor'der, s. an edging; a boundary, a side
Bor'derer, s. an inhabitant near the borders
Bore, s. the hollow of a gun or pipe
Bore, v. a. to pierce, to make a hole
Bo'real, a. northern, tending to the north
Bo'reas, s. the north wind
Bo'rer, s. one who bores; a gimlet
Born, part. brought into the world, bre
Borne, part. brought, supported, carried
Bor'ough, s. a corporation town
Bor'row, v. a. to ask a loan; take on credit
Bor'rower, s. one who borrows from another
Bos'cage, s. a grove, a wood, woodlands
Bos'ky, a. woody, rough
Bo'som, s. the breast; the heart; an enclosure
Bo'som, v. a. to enclose in the bosom
Boss, s. a knob, a stud, a raised work
Botan'ic, Botan'ical, a. relating to herbs
Bot'anist, s. a person skilled in herbs
Bot'any, s. the knowledge of plants; that part
of natural history relating to vegetables
Botch, s. an ulcerous swelling; a part in any
work clumsily ad ed
Botch, v. a. to patch, to mend clumsily
Bot'cher, s. one who mends old clothes
Both, a. the two, of two—ad. as well
Bot'tle, s. a glass vessel with a narrow mouth
Bot'tom, s. the lowest part of any thing; the
foundation; a valley; a dale
Bot'tomless, a. wanting a bottom, fathomless
Bot'tomry, s. money borrowed on a ship
Boud, s. an insect which breeds in malt
Bough, s. an arm of a tree, a branch
Bought, pret. of to buy—s. a flexure, a knot
Bougie, s. a wax taper; an instrument
Bounce, v. n. to leap, to spring; to bully
Boun'cer, s. a boaster; a bully; a lie
Bound, Boun'dary, s. an end, a limit, a mark
Bound, v. to jump, fly back, spring; to limit
Bound, a. destined for, going to
Boun'dless, a. infinite, unconfined, unlimited
Boun'dstone, s. a stone to play with
Boun'teous, Boun'tiful, a. generous, liberal
Boun'teously, Boun'tifully, ad. liberally
Boun'ty, s. munificence, generosity
Bour'geon, v. n. to sprout, to shoot, to bud
Bourn, s. a bound, a limit; torrent, brook
Bouse, or Boose, v. n. to drink to excess
Bou'sy, a. drunk, muddled with liquor
Bout, s. an essay, a trial, an attempt
Bouta'de, s. a start of fancy, a whim
Boute'feu, s. a disturber; an incendiary
Bow, s. an instrument to shoot arrows; a knot
made with a ribbon; an inclination of the
body in token of respect
Bow, v. a. to stoop, to bend, to crush
Bow'elless, a. cruel, merciless, unfeeling
Bow'els, s. the intestinal parts of the body;
tenderness, compassion
Bow'er, s. an arbour in a garden; an anchor
Bow'ery, a. cool, shady, retired
Bowl, s. a vessel to make punch in; a wooden
ball; the hollow of a cup or glass
Bowl, v. a. to play at bowls; to trundle, to roll
Bow'legged, a. having crooked legs
Bow'ler, s. one who bowls, or plays at bowls
Bow'line, s. the name of a ship's rope
Bow'ling-green, s. a level green for bowlers
Bow'man, s. an archer; shooter with bows
Bow'sprit, s. the mast which projects in a
sloping direction from a ship's head

Bow'string, *s.* the string used for a bow
Bow'yer, *s.* a maker of bows; an archer
Box, *s.* a case made of wood; a blow
Box, *v. a.* to pack in a box; to s'rike
Box'er, *s.* one who fights with the fist
Boy, *s.* a male child, a youth
Boy'ish, *a.* like a boy, trifling, childish
Boy'ishness, Boy'ism, *s.* play, childishness
Brub'ble, *s.* a broil, a clamour—*v. n.* to contest
Brace, *s.* a bandage; pair; tightness; a line
Brace, *v. a.* to bind, to strain up, to tighten
Bra'ced, *part.* bound, strained up, made tight
Bra'celets, *s.* ornaments for the wrists
Bra'cer, *s.* a bandage; any thing that tightens
Bra'chial, *a.* belonging to the arm
Brachy'graphy, *s.* the art or practice of writing in a small compass
Brack, *s.* a crack, a breach—*v. a.* to salt
Brack'et, *s.* a small support made of wood
Brack'ish, *a.* saltish, like sea water
Brad, *s.* a thin sort of nail used in floors
Brag, *s.* a boast; a game at cards
Brag, *v. n.* to boast, to display ostentatiously
braggado'cio, *s.* a swaggerer, a boaster
Brag'gart, Brag'ger, *s.* a vain puffing fellow
Braid, *v. a.* to weave together, to plait
Braid, *s.* a sort of lace; a knot; false hair
Brails, *s.* ropes used to draw up a ship's sails
Brain, *s.* the collection of vessels and organs within the skull, from which sense and motion arise; understanding, affections
Brain, *v. a.* to kill by beating out the brains
Brai'nless, *a.* foolish, silly, thoughtless, weak
Brai'npan, *s.* the skull containing the brains
Brai'nsick, *a.* diseased in the understanding
Brait, *s.* a rough, unpolished diamond
Brake, *s.* a thicket of brambles; a kneading-trough; an instrument for dressing flax
Bra'ky, *a.* thorny, prickly, thick, foul
Bram'ble, *s.* a prickly, or thorny bush
Bra'min, *s.* a Gentoo priest
Bran, *s.* the husks of ground corn
Branch, *s.* a small bough, a shoot; offspring
Branch, *v. a.* to spread in branches, to adorn
Bran'chery, *s.* the vascular parts of fruit
Bran'chless, *a.* without shoots or boughs
Bran'chy, *a.* full of branches, spreading
Brand, *v. a.* to mark with a brand, to burn
Brand, *s.* a lighted stick; a mark of infamy
Bran'ded, *part.* burnt with an iron, disgraced
Bran'dish, *v. a.* to wave, to flourish, to shake
Bran'dling, *s.* a small worm; the dew worm
Bran'dy, *s.* a strong distilled liquor
Bran'gle, *s.* a quarrel, a squabble, a dispute
Brank, *s.* a sort of grain called buck-wheat
Bran'ny, *a.* consisting of bran; foul, dry
Bra'zier, *s.* one who works in brass
Brasil', *s.* an American wood for dying red
Brass, *s.* a yellow metal made by mixing copper and lapis calliminaris; impudence
Brass'y, *a.* made of brass; hard as brass; bold
Brat, *s.* a child, by way of contempt
Brava'do, *s.* a brag, a boast, a threat
Brave, *s.* gallant, courageous, excellent
Brave, *v. a.* to challenge, to hector, to defy
Bra'vely, *ad.* gallantly, generously, nobly
Bra'very, *s.* courage, show, magnanimity
Bra'vo, *s.* one who murders for hire
Brawl, *v. a.* to speak loudly, to quarrel
Brawl'r, *s.* a quarrelsome person, a wrangler.

Brawn, *s.* the hard flesh of a boar; calf of the leg [new
Braw'niness, *s.* strength, robustness, hardness
Braw'ny, *a.* fleshy, muscular, strong, firm
Bray, *s.* the noise of an ass, harsh cry
Bray, *v. a.* to cry like an ass; to make a harsh noise; to bruise or pound in a mortar
Bray'er, *s.* one who brays like an ass
Braze, *v. a.* to solder with brass
Bra'zen, *a.* made of brass; daring, bold
Bra'zenface, *s.* a bold, impudent person
Bra'zenness, *s.* appearing like brass; impudence
Breach, *s.* a gap, an opening; a quarrel
Bread, *s.* food made of ground corn; support
Bread'corn, *s.* corn of which bread is made
Breadth, *s.* the measure from side to side
Break, *v. a.* to part or burst with violence; to train to obedience; to tame; to become a bankrupt; to dismiss from office, to fail out
Break, *s.* a breach, an opening, a failure
Brea'kers, *s.* waves which break, the water being too shallow to allow them to roll
Break'fast, *s.* the first meal—*v. n.* to eat
Bream, *s.* the name of a fish—*v. a.* to burn filth from a ship's bottom
Breast, *s.* that part of the body which contains the heart and lungs; the bosom; the heart; the conscience; the passions
Breas'thigh, *a.* as high as the breast
Breas'tknot, *s.* ribbons worn on the breast
Breas'twork, *s.* a guard raised breast high
Breath, *s.* life; air drawn in and discharged by the lungs; moving air; an instant
Breathe, *v. n.* to draw breath; to live; to rest
Brea'thing, *s.* a vent; secret prayer; respite
Breath'less, *a.* out of breath, hurried; dead
Breech, *s.* the hinder part of a gun, &c.
Breech'es, *s.* part of a man's apparel
Breed, *v. a.* to hatch, to plot; to cause
B eed, *s.* a cast, offspring, sort, number
Breed'ing, *s.* manners, education; nature
Breeze, *s.* a gentle gale, a stinging fly
Breez'y, *a.* fanned with gentle gales, cool
Bret, Brit, *s.* a fish of the turbot kind
Breth'ren, *s.* the plural of brother
Breve, *s.* a note in music; a summons
Bre'viary, *s.* a Romish priest's office book
Bre'viat, *s.* a short compendium
Brevi'r, *s.* a small size of printing letter
Brev'ity, Brie'fness, *s.* shortness, conciseness
Brew, *v. a.* to make liquors; to plot, contrive
Brew'er, *s.* one who brews; one who contrives [ing
Brew'house, *s.* a house appropriated to brew-
Brew'is, *s.* bread lightly boiled in pottage
Bribe, *s.* a reward given to pervert judgment
Bribe, *v. a.* to gain by gifts; to hire
Bri'bery, *s.* the act or crime of bribing; hire
Brick, *s.* a piece of burnt clay; a small loaf
Brick'bat, *s.* a piece of a brick
Brick'dust, *s.* dust made by pounding bricks
Brick'kiln, *s.* a place to burn bricks in
Brick'layer, *s.* a brick mason
Bri'dal, *a.* belonging to a wedding, nuptial
Bride, *s.* a woman newly married
Bri'de-cake, *s.* cake distributed at a wedding
Bri'degroom, *s.* a man newly married
Bri'demaid, *s.* a woman who attends the bride at the marriage ceremony
Bri'dewell, *s.* a house of correction

Bridge, *s.* a building over water, for the convenience of passing ; the upper part of the nose ; supporter of the strings to a violin

Bri'dle, *s.* the head reins of a horse, a check

Bri'dle, *v. a.* to restrain, to check, to guide

Bri'dle-hand, *s.* the hand which holds the bridle

Brief, *s.* an epitome ; short extract ; letters patent for charitable collections—*a.* short

Brie'fness, *s.* shortness, conciseness

Brie'fly, *ad.* shortly, concisely, in a few words

Bri'er, *s.* a prickly bush, a species of rose t. ee

Bri'ery, *a.* full of briers, prickly, rough

Briga'de, *s.* a party or division of soldiers

Brigadie'r-gen'eral, *s.* an officer next in rank to a major-general

Brig'and, *s.* a freebooter, a thief, a plunderer

Brig'antine, *s.* a small vessel ; a coat of mail

Bright, *a.* shining, clear, witty ; famous

Bri'ghten, *v. a.* to make bright, to polish

Bri'ghtness, *s.* acuteness ; wit ; evidence

Brigo'se, *a.* quarrelsome, contentious

Bril'liancy, *s.* splendour, lustre

Bril'liant, *a.* sparkling—*s.* a fine diamond

Brim, *s.* the edge ; bank of a fountain ; lip

Brim'mer, *s.* a glass full to the brim

Brim'stone, *s.* a yellow mineral, sulphur

Brin'ded, or Brin'dled, *a.* spotted, streaked

Brine, *s.* dissolved salt ; tears ; the sea

Bring, *v. a.* to fetch, prevail on, conduct

Bri'nish, Bri'ny, *a.* like brine, saltish

Brink, *s.* the edge of a place ; a recipice

Brisk, *a.* lively, quick, active, strong

Bris'ket, *s.* the breast of an animal

Bris'kly, *ad.* quickly, actively, nimbly

Bris'kness, *s.* quickness, liveliness, gaiety

Bris'tle, *s.* the hair on a swine's back

Bris'tle, *v. n.* to stand erect as bristles

Bris'tly, *a.* set with bristles ; angry, rough

Bris'tolstone, *s.* a kind of soft diamond

Brit, *s.* the name of a fish

Brit'ish, *a.* belonging to, or made in, Britain

Brit'on, *s.* a native of Great Britain

Brit'tle, *a.* apt to break, frail, weak

Brit'tleness, *s.* aptness to break, tenderness

Brize, *s.* the gad fly

Broach, *v. a.* to tap a vessel ; to give out

Broa'ched, *part.* tapped, uttered, pierced

Broa'cher, *s.* a teller of a thing ; a spit

Broad, *a.* wide, extended ; coarse ; vulgar

Broa'dcloth, *s.* a fine kind of woollen cloth

Broa'dness, *s.* breadth ; extent from side to side ; fulsomeness ; coarseness

Broa'dside, *s.* a volley of all the guns from one side of a ship at once ; the side of a ship ; a large single sheet of paper

Broa'dsword, *s.* a sword with a broad blade

Broca'de, *s.* a kind of fine flowered silk

Bro'cage, *s.* profit gained by promoting bargains ; dealing in old things ; hire

Brock, *s.* a badger

Brock'et, *s.* a red deer two years old

Broc'coli, *s.* a species of cabbage

Brogue, *s.* corrupt dialect ; a kind of shoe

Broi'dery, *s.* embroidery

Broil, *s.* a disturbance, quarrel, tumult

Broil, *v. a.* to roast on the fire, to be hot

Bro'ken, *part.* destroyed, reduced, shivered

Bro'er, *s.* one who does business for others

Bro'kerage, *s.* the pay or reward of a broker

Bron'chial, *a.* belonging to the throat

Bron'chocele, *s.* a tumour of that part of the aspera arteria, called the bronchos

Bronze, *s.* brass, brass colour ; a metal—*v. a.* to harden as brass

Brooch, *s.* a jewel, an ornament of jewels

Brood, *s.* offspring ; production, generation ; the number of chickens hatched at once

Brood, *v. n.* to sit on eggs ; to watch anxiously

Brook, *s.* a rivulet, a little river

Brook, *v. a.* to endure, to suffer, to bear

Broom, *s.* a besom to sweep with, a shrub

Broom'y, *a.* full of or like broom

Broth, *s.* liquor in which flesh is boiled

Broth'er, *s.* a male born of the same parents

Broth'erhood, *s.* society, union, class

Broth'erly, *a.* like brothers, very fond

Brow, *s.* the forehead ; edge of a place

Brow'beat, *v. a.* to bear down, to humble, to depress with stern looks or angry words

Brown, *s.* the name of a colour

Brow'nish, *a.* inclined to brown, reddish

Brown'ness, *s.* a brown colour

Brownstud'y, *s.* deep meditation or thought

Browse, *s.* underwood ; sprouts of trees

Browse, *v. n.* to feed on browse, to feed

Bruise, *v. a.* to hurt with blows, to crush

Bruise, *s.* a hurt from a blow, a spot

Bru'ising, *s.* a crushing ; the art of boxing

Bruit, *s.* a report, a noise—*v. a.* to noise about

Bru'mal, *a.* cold, belonging to winter

Brunet'te, *s.* a brown complexioned woman

Brunt, *s.* a shock, violence, an onset

Brush, *s.* an instrument for sweeping ; a fox's tail ; a rude assault ; a shock

Brush, *v. a.* to rub with a brush, to skin lightly

Brush'wood, *s.* rough, shrubby thickets

Brusk, *a.* harsh, uncivil, rude

Bru'tal, *a.* cruel, savage, inhuman, churlish

Brutal'ity, *s.* inhumanity, savageness

Bru'talize, *v. a.* to make savage or brutal

Bru'tally, *ad.* inhumanly, churlishly

Brute, *s.* a creature without reason

Brute, *a.* savage, senseless, ferocious, wild

Bru'tish, *a.* resembling a beast ; savage

Bry'ony, *s.* the name of a plant

Bub, *s.* a strong malt liquor ; any strong liquor—*v. n.* to throw out in bubbles

Bub'ble, *s.* a water bladder ; a cully ; a cheat —*v. a.* to cheat

Buc'caniers, *s.* pirates in America

Buck, *s.* the male of deer, rabbits, &c. ; water to wash clothes

Buck'bean, *s.* a plant ; a sort of trefoil

Buck'et, *s.* a vessel to draw up water in

Buc'kle, *s.* a fastening—*v. a.* to fasten with a buckle ; to engage ; to condescend

Buck'ler, *s.* a shield—*v. a.* to defend

Buck'ram, *s.* cloth stiffened with gum

Buck'skin, *s.* leather made with buck's skin

Buck'thorn, *s.* a thorn, a prickly bush

Bucol'ics, *s.* pastoral songs, rural dialogues

Bud, *s.* the first shoot of a plant, a germ

Bud, *v. a.* to put forth buds ; graft ; inoculate

Budge, *v. n.* to stir, to move off, to go

Bud'get, *s.* a pouch, a bag, store ; proposal

Buff, *s.* colour resembling yellow ; leather made of a buffalo's skin ; a military coat

Buff, Buf'fet, *v. a.* to box, to strike, to beat

Buf'falo, *s.* a kind of wild bull

Buffet', *s.* a kind of cupboard to hold china

Buf'fet, *s.* a blow with the fist ; a stroke

D

Buffoo'n, s. a low jester, an arch fellow
Buffoo'ne.y, s. mimicry, low jest
Bug, s. a disagreeable insect bred in beds
Bug'bear, s. a frightful object; false fear
Bu'gle, s. a small bead of glass, a plant
Bu'glehorn. s. a hunting horn
Build. r. to raise a building; to depend on
Buil'der, s. one who builds houses
Buil'ding, s. an edifice or fabric built
Bulb, s. a round root, such as onions, &c.
Bul'bous, a. having round roots
Bulge, v. n. to let in water; to jut out
Bu'limy, s. an enormous appetite
Bulk, s. size, magnitude; the mass; a bench
Bul'khead, s. a partition made in a ship
Bul'kiness, s. greatness of stature, or size
Bul'ky, a. large, lusty, of great size, heavy
Bull, s. the male of black cattle; a blunder;
   an edict of the Pope; a sign of the zo-
   diac
Bul'lace, s. a wild sour plum
Bul'late, a. blistered
Bull'baiting, s. a fight of dogs with a bull
Bull'dog, s. a strong dog of great courage
Bul'let, s. a round ball of lead or iron
Bul'letin, s. official account of public news
Bull'finch, s. the name of a small bird
Bull'head, s. a heavy stupid fellow; a fish
Bul'lion, s. gold or silver in the mass
Bullit'ion, s. the act or state of boiling
Bul'lock, s. a young bull or steer
Bully, s. a very noisy, quarrelsome person
Bully, v. a. to hector, to be noisy, to brawl
Bul'rush, s. a large rush growing by rivers
Bul'wark, s. a defence, a fortification
Bumbai'liff, s. a bailiff of the lowest rank
Bum'boat, s. a small boat, in which fruit,&c.
   are carried on shipboard for sale
Bump, s. a swelling, a thump, a blow
Bump, v. n. to make a noise as the bittern
Bum'per, s. a glass full of liquor to the brim
Bum'pkin, s. a clown, a rustic, a lout
Bun, s. a small kind of light cake
Bunch, s. a cluster, hard lump, knot
Bunch, v. n. to grow out in protuberances
Bun'chy, a. growing in, or full of bunches
Bun'dle, s. a parcel of things bound together
Bun'dle, v. a. to tie up, to put up together
Bung, s. a stopper for a barrel
Bun'gle, v. a. to perform any thing clumsily
Bun'gle, s. an awkwardness, a botch
Bun'gled, part. done in a clumsy manner
Bun'gler, s. a clumsy, awkward workman
Bun'ter, s. a dirty, low, vulgar woman
Bun'ting, s. a thin woolen cloth; a bird
Buoy, s. a body of wood or cork fastened with
   a rope to an anchor to discover where it
   lies, or to mark shoals, sunk rocks, &c.
Buoy, v. a. to keep afloat, support, uphold
Buoy'ancy, s. the quality of floating
Buoy'ant, a. that which will not sink; light
Buoy'ed, part. kept from sinking, supported
Bur, s. the prickly head of the burdock
Bur'bot, s. a fish full of prickles
Bur'den, s. a load; uneasiness; birth; the
   verse repeated in a song
Bur'den, v. a. to load, oppress, incumber
Bur'densome, a. troublesome, grievous
Bur'densomeness, s. weight, uneasiness
Bur'dock, s. a broad-leaved prickly plant
Bureau', s. a set of drawers with a desk

Burg'age, s. tenure proper to cities and towns
   conferring the privileges of a burgess
Bur'amot, s. a species of pear; a perfume
Bur'ganet, s. an ancient kind of helmet
Bur'geois, s. a citizen; a sort of printing letter
Bur'gess, s. a citizen, a freeman of a city; a
   representative
Burgh, s. a burgh town, a corporation
Bur'gher, s. a freeman; one who has a right
   to vote, and possesses other privileges
Bur'glary, s. the crime of housebreaking by
   night, or breaking in with intent to steal
Bur'gomaster, s. a principal citizen in Hol
Bu'rial, s. the act of interring the dead [land
Bu'rine, s. a tool for engraving, a graver
Burles'que, v. a. to lampoon, to ridicule
Burles'que, s. a jest, ludicrous language
Burles'que, a. jocular, droll, merry, laughable
Burlet'ta, s. a ludicrous musical farce
Bur'ly, a. blustering, swoln, falsely great
Burn, v. a. to consume by fire, to be inflamed
Burn, s. a hurt caused by fire
Bur'net, s. the name of a plant
Bur'ning, s. a state of inflammation
Burn'ish, v. a. to polish, to make bright
Bur'nisher, s. a person that burnishes or po
   lishes; an instrument used for polishing
Burr, s. the lobe or lap of the ear
Bur'rel, s. a sort of pear; a bee; an insect
Bur'relshot, s. nails, &c. shot from a cannon
Bur'row, v. n. to make holes, to mine
Bur'row, s. a corporate town; a rabbit hol
Bur'sar, s. the treasurer of a college
Burse, s. an exchange where merchants meet
Burst, v. a. to fly open, to break asunder
Burst, s. a sudden breaking, an eruption
Bur'stness, s. a tumour, a rupture
Bur'stwort, s. an herb good against ruptures
Bur'then, s. see Burden
Burt, s. a flat fish of the turbot kind
Bur'y, v. a. to put into a grave, to hide
Bush, s. a thick shrub, a bough
Bush'el, s. a dry measure containing 4 pecks
Bush'y, a. thick, full of small branches, &c.
Bus'ily, ad. very actively, with a hurry
Bus'iness, s. an employment, affair, trade
Busk, s. a piece of whalebone, or steel, worn
   by women to strengthen their stays
Bus'kin, s. a kind of half boot, a high shoe
   which comes to the middle of the leg
Buss, s. a small vessel, a fishing boat; a kiss
Bust, s. a half statue; a funeral pile
Bus'tard, s. a large bird of the turkey kind
Bus'tle, s. a hurry, a great stir, a tumult
Bus'tle, v. n. to hurry, to be busy, to stir
Bus'tler, s. an active person, a busybody
Bus'y, a. employed, officious, active
Bus'ybod, s. a meddling officious person
But, conj. nevertheless, except, however, &c.
But, s. end of a thing, limit, boundary
But'cher, s. one who kills animals to sell
But'cher, v. a. to slay, to kill, to murder
But'chered, part. killed, murdered, dead
But'cherly, a. cruel, bloody, barbarous, brutal
But'chery, s. cruelty, murder; the trade of a
   butcher; a slaughter-house
But'-end, s. the blunt or greater end of any
   thing
But'ler, s. he who is entrusted with a gentle-
   man's liquors and plate; an upper servant
But'ment, s. the support of an arch

Butt, s. a vessel containing 126 gallons; a mark; object of ridicule [animals
Butt, v. a. to strike with the head as horned
But'ter,s.an unctuous food made from cream
But'ter, v. a. to moisten with butter
But'terflower, s. a bright yellow May flower
But'terfly, s. a beautiful winged insect
But'teris, s. a farrier's paring instrument
But'termilk, s. the whey of churned cream
But'terpump, s. a fowl; the bittern
But'tertooth, s. one of the broad foreteeth
But'tery,s.a place where provisions are kept
But'tock, s. the thick part of the thigh
But'ton, v. a. to fasten with buttons
But'ton, s. a knob or ball used for the fastening the clothes; bud of a plant
But'tonhole, s. a hole to fasten a button
But'tress, s. a prop, a shore—v. a. to prop

Bux'om, a. brisk, lively, wanton, jolly
Bux'omness, s. amorousness, wantonness
Buy, v. a. to pay a price for, to treat for
Buy'er, s. one who buys, a purchaser
Buzz, s. a hum, a whisper, low talk
Buzz, v. a. to hum, like bees; to whisper spread secretly; to prate
Buz'zard, s. a hawk; blockhead, dunce
Buz'zer, s. a secret whisperer
Buz'zing, s. humming noise; low talk
By, pr. denoting the agent, means, way
By-and-by', ad. presently, in a short time
By-law, s. private rule or order in a society
By-path, s. a private or obscure path
By-room, s. a retired private room
By-stander, s. one unconcerned, a looker or
By-street, s. a private or obscure street
By-word, s. a cant word, a taunt

C.

C, the third letter of the alphabet, has two sounds, one like k, as call; the other like s, as cessation; a note in music
Cab, s. a Jewish measure of three pints
Cabal', s. private junto, an intrigue
Cabal', Cab'ala, s. the Jewish tradition
Cabal', v. n. to intrigue privately, to plot
Cab'alist, s. one skilled in Jewish traditions
Caballs'tical, a. secret, mysterious
Cabal'ler, s. an intriguer, contriver, plotter
Cabal'line, s. a coarse kind of aloes, used by farriers to physic cattle
Cab'bage, s. a well known vegetable
Cab'bage, v. a. to steal in cutting clothes
Cab'in, s. an apartment in a ship; a cottage
Cab'inet,s. a set of drawers; a room in which state consultations are held
Ca'ble, s. a rope to hold a ship at anchor
Cachec'tical, a. of a bad habit of body
Ca'chet, s. a seal, a private state letter
Cachex'y, s. a disordered habit of body
Cac'kle, v. n. to make a noise like a hen, &c.
Ca'cochymy, s. a diseased state of the blood
Cacode'mon, s. an evil spirit, a demon
Cadav'erous, a. having the appearance of a dead body
Cad'bate, s. a worm, good bait for trout
Cad'dis, s. a kind of tape; a warm or grub
Cade, a. soft, tame, tender, delicate
Ca'dence, s. a fall of the voice, a sound
Cadet', s. a volunteer, a younger brother
Ca'dew, s. the straw worm; an Irish mantle
Cad'ger, s. a huckster
Ca'di, s. a chief magistrate among the Turks
Cadu'ceus, s. Mercury's snaky staff
Cadu'cous, a. falling off, decaying
Caf'tan, s. a kind of habit, Persian garment
Cag, s. a small cask, a small barrel
Cage, s. a place of confinement
Cajo'le, v.a. to flatter, to deceive, to beguile
Cajo'ler, s. a flatterer, deceiver, parasite
Caisso'n, Caisso'n, s. a chest of bombs or powder; hollow fabric of timber
Cal'tiff, s. a base fellow, a knave, a wretch
Cake, s. sweet bread—v. a. to harden, unite
Calaman'co, s. a kind of woollen stuff
Cal'amine, s. a kind of earth; ore of tin

Calam'itous, a. wretched, miserable
Calam'ity, s. affliction, misery, loss
Cal'amus, s. a kind of sweet-scented wood
Calash', s. an open carriage; a head dress
Calca'reous, a. relating to calx
Calcina'tion, s. the act of pulverizing by fire
Calci'ne, v. a. to burn to a powder
Calcog'raphy. See Chalcography
Cal'culate, v. a. to reckon, to compute
Calcula'tion, s. a reckoning, computation
Cal'culator, s. a reckoner, a computer
Cal'culous, a. gravelly, stony, hard, gritty
Cal'dron,s.a very large kettle, a boiler, &c.
Caledo'nia, s. a name of Scotland
Calefac'tory, a. tending to warm, heating
Cal'efy, v. a. to make hot, to be heated
Cal'endar, s. a yearly register, an almanac
Cal'ender, v. a. to glaze linen, to smooth
Cal'ender,s. an engine to calender, hot press
Cal'enderer, s. the person who calenders
Cal'ends, s. the first day of every month
Cal'enture, s. a sun fever, frequent at sea
Calf, s. young of a cow; thick part of the leg
Cal'iber,s.the bore; diameter of a gun barrel
Cal'ico, s. an Indian stuff made of cotton
Cal'id, a. very hot, scorching, burning
Calid'ity, Cal'idness, s. of great heat
Caliga'tion, s. cloudiness, darkness
Calig'inous, a. dark, dusky, dim, obscure
Calig'raphy, s. very fair, beautiful writing
Ca'liph, s. the chief priest of the Saracens
Cal'iver, s. a hand gun, an arquebuse
Cal'ix, s. a cup
Calk, v. a. to stop the seams of a ship
Calk'er, s. one who calks a ship's seams
Call, v.a. to name, to summons, to invite; to summon judicially; to convoke
Call, s. a demand, summons, address
Cal'lat, Cal'let, s. a trull, worthless woman
Callid'ity, Cal'lidness, s. craftiness, art
Cal'ling, s. an employment, trade, &c.
Cal'lipers,s.compasses having bowed shanks
Callos'ity, s. a hard swelling without pain
Cal'lous, a. hardened, insensible, brawny
Cal'lousness, s. induration of the fibres
Cal'low, a. wanting feathers, bare
Calm, v. a. to quiet, still, pacify, compose

Calm, *s.* repose, rest, peace, serenity, quiet
Calm, *a.* unruffled, easy, undisturbed
Ca'lmly, *ad.* quietly, without passion, coolly
Ca'lmness, *s.* tranquillity, freedom from pas-
Ca'omel, *s.* mercury six times sublimed[sion
Calorif'ic, *a.* heating, causing heat
Calot'te, *s.* a cap or coif, a circular cavity
Cal'trop, *s.* an instrument of war with four
 spikes, thrown on the ground to annoy
 the enemies' horse; a plant
Calve, *v.n.* to bring forth or bear a calf
Cal'vinism, *s.* the doctrine of predestina-
 tion, &c. taught by Calvin
Cal'vinist, *s.* a follower of Calvin
Calum'niate, *v.a.* to accuse falsely, to revile
Calum'niator, *s.* a slander r, false accuser
Cal'umny, *s.* slander, false charge, aspersion
Calx, *s.* a powder made by fire, lime, &c.
Cal'ycle, *s.* a small bud of a plant
Cal'yx, *s.* the outer covering of the flower
Cam'bering, *a.* rising like an arch
Cam'bric, *s.* fine linen from Cambray
Cam'el, *s.* a large animal, common in Arabia
Cam'elots, *s.* stuff of silk and camel's hair
Came'o, *s.* a picture of only one colour
Cam'era-obscu'ra, *s.* an optical machine
 used in a darkened chamber, so that the
 light passing through a double convex
 g ass, represents objects inverted
Cam'let, *s.* a stuff made of wool and silk
Cam'omile, *s.* a fine physical herb
Ca'moys, *a.* flat of the nose, depressed
Camp, *s.* the order of tents for soldiers
Campai'gn, *s.* the time an army keeps the
 field in one year; a large open country
Campai'gner, *s.* an old experienced soldier
Campes'tral, *a.* growing in the fields, wild
Cam'phor, Cam'phire, *s.* a white gum
Cam'phorate, *a.* impregnated with camphor
Can, *v. n.* to be able to—*s.* a cup, a vessel
Cana'ille, *s.* the lowest of the people
Canal', *s.* a bason or course of water, a duct
Canal'-coal, *s.* a very fine kind of coal
Canalic'ulated, *a.* made like a pipe or gutter
Cana'ries, *s.* a cluster of islands in the Atlan-
 tic ocean, near the Barbary coast
Cana'ry, *s.* a wine brought from the Cana-
 ries; a dance—*v. n.* to dance, to frolic
Cana'ry-bird, *s.* an excellent singing bird
Can'cel, *v. a.* to blot out, make void, destroy
Can'cellated, *a.* crossed by lines; cross-barred
Can'celled, *part.* blotted out, made void
Can'cer, *s.* a crab fish; virulent sore, bad ul-
 cer, one of the twelve signs of the zodiac
Can'cerate, *v. n.* to grow cancerous
Can'cerous, *a.* inclining to or like a cancer
Can'crine, *a.* having the qualities of a crab
Can'dent, *a.* hot, fiery, burning, glowing
Can'did, *a.* open, honest, kind, fair, white
Can'didate, *s.* one who sues for a place
Can'didly, *ad.* uprightly, openly, fairly
Can'dify, *v. a.* to make white
Can'dle, *s.* a light made of tallow, wax, &c.
Can'dlemas, *s.* the feast of the Purification
 of the blessed Virgin Mary
Can'dlestick, *s.* an instrument to hold candles
Can'dour, *s.* an open temper, integrity
Can'dy, *v. a.* to conserve with sugar, congeal
Cane, *s.* a reed from which sugar is extracted;
 a walking stick—*v. a.* to beat with a cane
Candes'cen', *a.* growing white or old, hoary

Canic'ular, *a.* belonging to the dog star; ho
Cani'ne, *a.* having the properties of a dog
Can'ister, *s.* a box to hold 'ea; a small basket
Can'ker, *s.* a worm; disease; eating humour
Can'ker, *v.a.* to grow corrupt: pollute, corrode
Can'kerworm, *s.* a worm that destroys fruit
Can'nibal, *s.* a man eater, vile wretch
Can'non, *s.* a great gun for cannonading
Cannona'de, *v. a.* to batter with cannon
Cannonie'r, *s.* one who manages cannon
Canoe', *s.* an Indian boat
Can'on, *s.* a law, a rule; a dignitary in cathe
 drals; the book of holy scripture
Canon'ical, *a.* ecclesiastical, regular
Canon'ically, *ad.* agreeably to the canons
Canon'icals, *s.* established dress of the clergy
Can'onist, *s.* a doctor of canon law
Canoniza'tion, *s.* the act of making a saint
Can'onry, Can'onship, *s.* benefice of a canon
Can'opy, *s.* a cloth of state spread over the
 head; a tester; the sky—*v.a.* to cover with
 a canopy
Cano'rous, *a.* musical, loud, tuneful
Cant, *s.* obscure, corrupt words; wheedling
Cant, *v. a.* to flatter, to wheedle; to toss
Canta'ta, *s.* an air; a grave piece of music
Canta'tion, *s.* the act of singing
Cantee'n, *s.* a public-house attached to a
 barrack; a tin vessel to contain liquor
Can'ter, *s.* the gallop of an ambling horse;
 an hypocrite
Canthar'ides, *s.* Spanish flies for blisters
Can'thus, *s.* the corner of the eye
Can'ticle, *s.* a song of Solomon, pious song
Can'tle, *v. a.* to cut in pieces
Can'tlet, Can'tlet, *s.* a piece with corners
Can'to, *s.* part of a poem, section, division
Can'ton, *s.* the division of a country; a clan
Can'ton, Can'tonize, *v. a.* to divide land
Can'tred, *s.* an hundred in Wales, a division
Can'vass, *s.* a coarse stiff cloth; a soliciting
Can'vass, *v. a.* to solicit votes, to sue for ho
 nours, to debate, to sift, to examine
Can'zonet, *s.* a short song or air
Cap, *s.* a covering for the head, a reverence
Cap, *v. a.* to cover the top; to puzzle
Cap-a-pie', *ad.* from head to foot
Capabil'ity, *s.* capacity, adequateness, fine s
Ca'pable, *a.* equal to, qualified, intelligent
Capa'cious, *a.* large, wide, extended, vast
Capa'ciousness, *s.* largeness, a space, width
Capac'itate, *v. a.* to qualify, enable, make fit
Capac'ity, *s.* ability, se se; s ace, state
Capar'ison, *s.* a superb dress for a horse
Capar'ison, *v. a.* to dress pompously
Cape, *s.* the neckpiece of a coat; a headland
Ca'per, *s.* a jump, a leap; a berry, pickle
Ca'per, *v. n.* to dance, frisk about, skip
Ca'per-bush, *s.* a plant growing in the south
 of France; the buds are pickled for ea ing
Ca'pering, *part.* jumping about, skipping
Caph, *s.* a liquid measure of five wine pints
Ca'pias, *s.* a writ of execution
Capilla're, *s.* syrup of maidenhair
Capil'lary, Capil'laceous, *a.* small, minute,
 like a hair
Cap'ital, *a.* principal, chief, fine; criminal in
 the highest degree, deserving death
Cap'ital, *s.* a principal sum; ch ef city; large
 letter; stock; upper part of a pillar
Capita'tion, *s.* a numeration of heads

Capit'ular, *s.* a body of statutes in a chapter
Capit'ulate, *v. n.* to yield on certain terms
Capitula'tion, *s.* the surrendering a town upon certain terms; conditions, stipulations
Ca pon, *s.* a castrated cock
Capri'ce, *s.* fancy, humour, whim
Capri'cious, *a.* fanciful, whimsical, odd
Cap'ricorn, *s.* a sign of the zodiac, the goat, the winter solstice, a fly
Cap'stan, Cap'stern, *s.* an engine to draw up great weights, as anchors, &c.
Cap'sular, Cap'sulary, *a.* hollow as a chest
Cap'sulate, Cap'sulated, *a.* enclosed in a box
Cap'sole, *s.* a little chest or casket
Cap'tain, *s.* the commander of a troop of horse, a company of foot, or ship of war
Capta'tion, *s.* the art of catching favour
Cap'tivate, *v. a.* to charm, to subdue
Cap'tive. *s.* one taken in war, a slave
Captiv'ity, *s.* slavery, subjection, thrall
Cap'tion, *s.* the act of taking any person
Cap'tious, *a.* snarling, cross, peevish, surly
Cap'tor. *s.* he who takes a prisoner or a prize
Cap'ture, *s.* a prize, the act of taking a prize —*v. a.* to take as a prize
Capu'ched, *a.* covered over, as with a hood
Capuchi'n, *s.* a friar; a woman's cloak
Car, *s.* a chariot, a cart, Charles's wain
Ca'rac, *s.* a Spanish galleon, a large ship
Car'at, *s.* a weight of four grains
Caravan', *s.* a large carriage; a body of travelling merchants, or pilgrims
Caravan'sary. *s.* a public building erected for the convenience of eastern travellers, where they may repose, &c.
Ca'ravel, Car'vel, *s.* a light old-fashioned ship
Car'away, *s.* a plant producing a warm seed used in medicine and confectionary
Carbona'de. *v. a.* to cut or hack, and prepare meat for broiling or frying
Car'bine, Cara'bine, *s.* a small musket
Carbinie'r, Carabinie'r, *s.* a light horseman
Car'buncle, *s.* a precious stone; a red pimple
Car'case, *s.* the dead body of an animal; a bomb
Card, *s.* a painted paper used for games; the paper on which the points of the compass are marked; a complimentary note; an instrument with iron teeth
Card, *v. a.* to play at cards; to comb wool
Car'damoms, *s.* medicinal seeds
Car'diac, *a.* strengthening, cordial, cheering
Car'dinal, *a.* chief, principal, eminent
Car'dinal, *s.* a dignitary of the Romish church; a woman's cloak
Car'dinal-points, *s.* north, south, east, west
Car'dinal-virtues, *s.* temperance, prudence, justice, and fortitude
Care, *s.* anxiety, solicitude, charge
Care, *v. n.* to be anxious, to be affected with
Caree'n, *v. a.* to stop leaks, to calk, to be laid up
Caree'r, *s.* a course, race, swift motion
Ca'reful, *a.* full of concern, anxious, diligent
Ca'refulness, *s.* great care, vigilance
Ca'reless, *a.* heedless, negligent, unmindful
Ca'relessness, *s.* inattention, heedlessness
Caress', *v. a.* to endear, to fondle
Ca'ret, *s.* a note which shews where something interlined or written on the margin should be read
Car'go, *s.* a ship's lading, freight, great load

Caricatu're, *s.* a ludicrous, droll likeness
Ca'ries. Carios'ity, *s.* rottenness of the bones
Ca'rious, *a.* decayed, rotten, putrified
Cark, *s.* anxiety, care—*v. n.* to be anxious
Car'king, *part. a.* perplexing, distressing
Carle, *s.* a mean, rude man; a churl, a clown
Car'lings, *s.* timber lying fore and aft in a ship
Car'man. *s.* one who drives or keeps carts
Car'melite, *s.* a begging friar; a pear
Carmin'ative, *a.* that which expels wind
Carmi'ne, *s.* a bright red or crimson colour
Car'nage, *s.* slaughter, devastation, havoc
Car'nal, *a.* fleshly, sensual, lustful
Car'nally. *ad.* according to the flesh
Carna'tion, *s.* a flesh colour; a fine flower
Car'neous, Car'nous, *a.* fleshy, fat, plump
Car'nival, *s.* shrovetide, a Popish feast
Carniv'orous, *a.* eating of flesh, greedy
Carnos'ity, *s.* a fleshy excrescence
Car'ol, *s.* a song of exultation or praise
Car'ol, *v. a.* to praise, to sing, to celebrate
Carou'sal, *s.* a feast, festival, drinking bout
Carou'se, *v. n.* to drink hard, to tope
Carp, *v. n.* to cavil, to censure—*s.* a fish
Car'penter, *s.* an artificer in wood, a builder
Car'pet, *s.* a covering for the floor or table
Car'ping, *s.* cavil, abuse—*part. a.* censorious
Car'riage, *s.* a vehicle; manners, behaviour
Car'rer, *s.* one who carries; a sort of pigeon
Car'rion, *s.* any flesh not fit for food
Car'rot, *s.* a common garden root
Car'roty, *a.* red-haired, very red
Car'ry, *v. a.* to bear, convey; gain; behave
Cart, *s.* a carriage for luggage—*v. a.* to carry
Cartebla'nche, *s.* a blank paper to be filled with conditions entirely at the option of the person to whom it is sent
Cartel', *s.* an agreement between nations at war, relative to exchange of prisoners
Car'ter, *s.* one who drives a cart
Car'tilage, *s.* a gristle, tough substance
Cartilag'inous, *a.* consisting of gristles
Cartoo'n, *s.* a painting on large paper
Cartou'ch, *s.* a case to hold balls
Car'tridge, *s.* a paper case to hold powder
Car'tridge-box, *s.* a box containing cartridges
Car'twright, *s.* a maker or seller of carts
Carve, *v. a.* to cut meat, wood, or stone
Car'ving, *s.* sculpture, figures carved
Casca'de, *s.* a cataract, a waterfall
Case, *s.* a covering, sheath; outer part of a house; the state of things; a circumstance; variation of nouns
Case, *v. a.* to cover, to draw up, to strip off
Ca'seharden, *v. a.* to harden the outside
Ca'seknife, *s.* a large table or kitchen knife
Ca'semate, *s.* a kind of vault or arch of stone
Ca'sement, *s.* a window opening upon hinges
Cash, *s.* any money, properly ready money
Cashie'r, *s.* a cash keeper—*v. a.* to discard
Ca'shoo, *s.* the gum of an East-Indian tree
Cask, Casque, *s.* a head-piece, a helmet
Cask, *s.* a wooden vessel, a barrel
Cas'ket, *s.* a small box or chest for jewels
Cass'ate, *v. a.* to make void, to annul
Cas'sia, *s.* a very fragrant aromatic spice
Cas'sowary, *s.* a large bird of prey
Cas'sock, *s.* the long under garment of a priest
Cast, *s.* a throw; mould; shade; squint
Cast, *v. a.* to throw; model; contrive; condemn

D 3

Cas'tanet, s. small shells of ivory or hard wood, which dance, s rattle in their hands
Cas'taway, s. an abandoned or lost person
Cas'tellany, s. the lordship of a castle
Cas'tellated, a. enclosed within a building
Cas'tigate, v.a. to chastise, to beat, to punish
Castiga'tion, s. discipline, punishment
Cas'ting-net, s. a net thrown by the hand
Cas'tle, s. a fortified house; a project
Cas'tor, s. the name of a star; the beaver
Castrameta'tion, s. the art of encamping
Cas'trate, v. a. to geld, make imperfect
Castra'tion, s. act of gelding, curtailing, &c.
Cas'ual, a. accidental, fortuitous, uncertain
Cas'ualty, s. accident, what happens by chance   [of conscience
Cas'uist, s. one who studies and settles cases
Cas'uistry, s. the science or skill of a casuist
Cat, s. a domestic animal; kind of ship
Catachres'tical, a. far-fe'ched, forced
Cat'aclysm, s. an inundation, a deluge
Cat'acombs, s. caverns for burial of the dead
Catacou'stic, a. relating to reflected sounds
Cat'alogue, s. a list of articles, names, &c.
Cat'aphract, s. a horseman in complete ar-
Cat'aplasm, s. a poultice, soft plaster [mour
Cat'apult, s. an engine to throw stones, &c.
Cat'aract, s. a waterfall; disease in the eyes
Catarr'h, s. a disease of the head and throat
Catar'rhal, a. relating to the catarrh
Catas'trophe, s. a final event generally unhappy; the change or revolution which produces the final event of a dramatic piece
Cat'cal, s. a small squeaking instrument
Catch,v.a.to lay hold on,stop,ensnare,please
Catch, s. the act of seizing; any thing that catches; a contagion; a song in succession
Cat'ching, part. a. apt to catch, infectious
Cat'chpoll, s. a bailiff's follower, a serjeant
Cat'chup, Cat'sup, s. a kind of pickle usually made from mushrooms and walnuts
Cat'echetical, a. consisting of questions and answers
Cat'echise, v. a. to instruct by questions
Cat'echism, s. a form of instruction by questions and answers, concerning religion
Cat'echist, s. one who teaches the catechism
Catechu'men, s. one who is yet in the first rudiments of Christianity
Cate or'ical, a. positive, absolute, express
Cat'egory, s. a class, an order of ideas
Catena'rian, a. belonging to a chain
Catena'tion, s. a regular connexion, a link
Ca'ter, v. . to lay in victuals, to provide
Ca'ter, Ca'terer, s. a provider of victuals
Ca'teress, s. a woman that provides food
Cat'erpillar, s. an insect, a grub, a plant
Cat'erwaul, v. n. to cry like a cat
Cates, s. cakes, viands, dainties, nice foo l
Cat'gut, s. a kind of canvass; fiddle-strings
Cathar'tic, a. purging, cleansing
Cathedral, s. an episcopal or head church
Cathe'dral, a. episcopal, venerable, antique
Cath'olic, a. universal—s. a papist
Cathol'icon, s. an universal medicine
Cat'ling, s. a surgeon's knife; fiddle-string
Catop'trical, a. relating to reflected visions
Cat'tle, s. beasts of pasture, that are not wild
Cavalca'de, s. a procession on horseback
Cavalie'r, s. a knight, partisan, royalist
Cavalie'r, a. brave, gay, haughty, proud

Cavalie'rly, ad. arrogantly, haughtily
Cav'alry, s. horse soldiers, horse troops
Cava'zion, s. hollowing of the earth for cellarage
Cau'dle, s. a mixture of gruel or ale with spice, sugar, &c. for women in childbed
Cave, s. a cell, den, hollow place
Ca'veat, s. a law term to prevent further proceedings; an admonition; caution
Cav'ern, s. a den, cave, hollow place
Cav'erned, Cav'ernous, a. full of caverns
Cav'esson,s. in horsemanship, a sort of nose band put into the nose of a horse
Cauf, s. a chest with holes to keep fish in
Cavia're, s. the spawn of sturgeons pickled
Cav'il, v. n. to wrangle, to raise objections
Cavilla'tion, s. captious objection
Cav'iller, s. a captious disputant
Cav'ity, s. a hollow place, a cavern
Cauk, s. a coarse kind of spar found in mines
Caul, s. a part of a woman's cap; the integument inclosing the guts; net work of a wig
Cau'le'scent, a. having a stalk or stem
Caul'iflower, s. a sort of cabbage
Cau'sal, a. relating to or implying causes
Cause, s. a reason, party, motive, source
Cause, v. a. to effect, to occasion, to produce
Cau'seless,a. having no just reason; original
Cau'sey,Cau'seway,s.a raised and paved way
Cau'stic, s. a burning application
Cau'telous, a. cautious, wily, cunning
Cau'terize, v. a. to sear; to burn with irons
Cau'tery, s. an iron for burning, a caustic
Cau'tion, s. care, prudence, warning
Cau'tion, v. a. to give notice, warn, tell
Cau'tionary,a. given as a pledge, or security
Cau'tious, a. watchful, prudent, wary
Cau'tiously, ad. in a prudent, wary manner
Cau'tiousness, s. circumspection, vigilance
Caw, v. n. to cry as a crow or rook
Cease, v.a. to leave off; to stop; to be extinct; to fall; to put a stop to
Cea'seless, a. never ceasing, perpetual
Cec'ity, s. blindness. loss or want of sight
Ce'dar, s. a large evergreen tree
Cede, v. a. to yield or surrender
Ceil, v. a. to overlay or cover the inner roof
Cei'ling, s. the inner roof, the upper part
Cel'ature, s. the art of engraving
Cel'ebrate, v. a. to praise, commend; to distinguish by solemn rites
Celebra'tion,s.solemn remembrance; praise
Cele'brious, a. renowned, famous, noted
Celeb'rity, s. celebration, fame, renown
Celer'ity, s. velocity, swiftness, speed, haste
Cel'ery, s. the name of a salad herb
Celes'tial, s. inhabitant of heaven—a. heavenly
Cel'ibacy, Cel'ibate, s. a single life [venly
Cell, s. a small close room, cave; the part of a capsule in which the seeds are lodged
Cel'lar, Cel'larage, s. a room under ground where liquors or stores are deposited
Cel'lular, a. made up of cavities, hollow
Cemen't, s. that which unites; mortar
Cemen't, v. a. to join together, to solder
Cem'etery, s. a burying place, a churchyard
Cen'otaph, s. an empty or honorary tomb
Cen'ser, s. a perfuming or incense pan
Cen'sor, s. a magistrate of Rome who had the power of correcting manners; one addicted to censuring others

Censo'rian, *a.* belonging to a censor
Censo rious, *a.* addicted to censure, severe
Cen'surable, *a.* deserving censure, culpable
Cen'sure, *s.* reproach, blame ; judgment
Cen'sure, *v. a.* to reproach, blame, condemn
Cen'sus, *s.* an estimate of the population of any particular place
Cent, *s.* an abbreviation of the Latin word *centum*, a hundred
Cen'taur, *s.* a poetical being, supposed to be composed of a man and a horse ; a sign in the zodiac, Sagittarius ; a monster
Cen'tenary, *s.* the number of a hundred
Centen'nial, *a.* of a hundred years
Centes'imal, *a.* the hundredth
Centifi'dous, *a.* divided into a hundred parts
Centifo'lious, *a.* having a hundred leaves
Cen'tipede, *s.* a poisonous insect with a considerable number of feet
Cen'to, *s.* a composition consisting of scraps and fragments from various authors
Cen'tral, *a.* relating to the centre
Cen'tre, *s.* the middle, the chief place
Cen'tre, *v. a.* to place on a centre, to rest on
Cen'tric, *a.* placed in the centre
Centrif'ugal, *a.* flying from the centre
Cen'rip'etal, *a.* tending to the centre
Cen'tuple, *a.* an hundred fold
Centu'riate, *v. a.* to divide into hundreds
Centuria'tor, *s.* a name applied to historians who distinguish time by centuries
Centu'rion, *s.* a Roman military officer who commanded a hundred men
Cen'tury, *s.* a hundred years
Cephal'ic, *s.* any medicinal for the head
Ceras'tes, *s.* a horned serpent
Ce'rate, *s.* a salve made of wax
Cere, *v. a.* to cover or smear over with wax
Ce'recloth, Ce'rement, *s.* cloth dipped in melted wax, in which dead bodies were wrapped
Ceremo'nial, Ceremo'nious, *a.* formal
Cer'emony, *s.* outward rite; forms of civility; external form in religion
Cer'tain, *a.* sure, unfailing, resolved ; some
Cer'tainly, *ad.* without fail, indubitably
Cer'tainty, Cer'titude, *s.* a fulness of assurance, exemption from doubt
Certif'icate, *s* a testimony in writing
Cer'tify, *v. a.* to give certain information of
Certiorar'i, *s.* a writ issued from the court of Chancery to call up the records of a cause therein depending
Cer'vical, *a.* belonging to the neck
Ceru'lean, Ceru'leous, *a.* blue, sky-coloured
Cerulif'ic, *a.* producing a blue colour
Ceru'men, *s.* the wax of the ear
Ce'ruse, *s.* white lead reduced to calx
Cesa'rian, *a.* the Cesarian operation is the act of cutting the child out of the womb
Cess, *s.* a tax or rate, limit or bound
Cessa'tion, *s.* a rest, stop, respite, intermission of hostilities
Cess'ible, *a.* liable to give way, yielding
Ces'sion, *s.* the act of giving way, retreat
Ces'tus, *s.* the girdle or zone of Venus
Ceta'ceous, *a.* of the whale kind
Chafe, *v. a.* to fret, rage, make angry, fume
Chafe, *s.* passion, rage, violence, fume
Chaff, *s.* the husks of corn ; a worthless thing
Chaf'fer, *v. a.* to bargain, haggle, exchange

Chaf'ferer, *s.* a dealer, hard bargainer
Chaf'finch, *s.* a small common bird
Chaf'fy, *a.* full of chaff ; light, foul, bad
Cha'fingdish, *s.* a portable grate for coals
Chagri'n, *s.* vexation, ill humour
Chagri'n, *v. a.* to vex, to tease, to hurt
Chagri'ned, *part.* vexed, provoked, fretted
Chain, *s.* a line of links ; a fetter, a series
Chain, *v. a.* to fasten with a chain, enslave
Chai'nshot, *s.* bullets fastened by a chain
Chair, *s.* a moveable seat, a sedan
Chai'rman, *s.* one who carries a sedan ; the president of any public meeting
Chaise, *s.* a kind of light carriage
Chalcog'raphy, *s.* art of engraving on brass
Chal'dron, *s.* a measure of 36 bushels
Chal'ice, *s.* a cup standing on a foot
Chalk, *s.* a kind of white fossil
Chalk, *v. a.* to mark or manure with chalk
Chal'kcutter, *s.* one who digs chalk
Chal'kpit, *s.* a place where chalk is dug
Chal'ky, *a.* consisting of chalk, white
Cha'lenge, *v. a.* to call to fight, to claim, to accuse, to claim as due
Chal'lenge, *s.* a summons to combat ; demand
Chalyb'eate, *a.* impregnated with steel
Cham, Chan, *s.* the sovereign of Tartary
Chama'de, *s.* the beat of a drum, denoting a desire of the besieged to parley
Cha'mber, *s.* an apartment in a house
Cha'mberlain, *s.* one who takes care of chambers ; the sixth officer of the crown
Cha'mbermaid, *s.* a servant who has the care of rooms, or dresses a lady
Cha'mblet, *v. a.* to variegate, to streak
Chame'lion, *s.* an animal that is said to take the colour of whatever it is applied to, and, erroneously, to live on the air
Cham'fer, *s.* the fluting in a column
Chamoi's, *s.* an animal of the goat kind ; leather made of the goat's skin
Champ, *v. a.* to bite, to gnaw, to devour
Cham'paign, *s.* a wine , a flat open country
Champign'on, *s.* a small kind of mushroom
Cham'pion, *s.* a hero, a single combatant
Chance, *s.* event, fortune, luck, misfortune
Chan'cel, *s.* the east end of a church
Chan'cellor, *s.* a great officer of state
Chan'cery, *s.* a court of equity and conscience
Chan'cre, *s.* a bad sore, an ulcer
Chandelie'r, *s.* a branch to hold candles
Chan'dler, *s.* a person who sells candles, &c.
Change, *v. a.* to amend, to alter, exchange
Change, *s.* novelty, alteration ; small money
Cha'ngeable, Cha'ngeful, *a.* inconstant, fickle
Cha'ngeling, *s.* a child changed for another, a natural, an idiot , a waverer
Chan'nel, *s.* the bed of running waters, a narrow sea ; a furrow in a pillar
Chant, *s.* a melody, a song; cathedral service
Chant, *v. a.* to sing cathedral service
Chan'ter, *s.* a singer in a cathedral, a songster
Chan'ticleer, *s.* the cock ; a clear singer
Chan'tress, *s.* a woman singer
Chan'try, *s.* a chapel for priests to sing mass
Cha'os, *s.* a confusion ; an irregular mixture
Chaot'ic, *a.* confused, mixed, indigested
Chap, *s.* an opening, a cleft ; a beast's jaw
Chap, *v. a.* to crack, to open, to divide
Chape, *s.* a thin plate of metal at the point of a scabbard ; part of a buckle

Chap'el, s. a place of worship
Chap'elry, s. the bounds of a chapel
Chapero'n, s. a kind of cap or hood worn by the knights of the garter
Chap'fallen, a. having the mouth shrunk
Chap'iter, s. the capital of a pillar
Chap'lain, s. a clergyman who performs divine service in the army or navy, or in a nobleman's or a private family
Chap'less, a. without flesh about the mouth
Chap'let, s. a wreath or garland for the head
Chap'man, s. a dealer in goods; a cheapener
Chap'ped, Chapt, part. pass. cracked, cleft
Chap'ter, s. a division of a book; an assembly of the clergy of a cathedral
Char, s. a small fish; work done by the day
Char'acter, s. a representation of personal qualities; reputation; mark: letter
Characteris'tic, a. peculiar to, distinguishing
Charac'terize, v. a. to give a character of a person; to mark with a stamp; to imprint
Char'coal, s. coal made by burning wood under turf
Charge, v. a. to impute as a debt; to entrust; to accuse; to command; to load a gun
Charge, s. expence; trust; onset; command
Char'geable, a. costly, expensive; accusable
Char'ger, s. a war horse; a large dish
Cha'riness, s. care, caution, diligence, nicety
Char'iot, s. a carriage of pleasure or state
Chariotee'r, s. a chariot driver, a coachman
Char'itable, a. beautiful, kind, candid
Char'itably, ad. liberally, kindly
Char'ity, s. love, good-will, tenderness; alms
Chark, v. a. to burn wood to a black cinder
Char'latan, s. a mountebank, quack, cheat
Charlatan'ical, a. ignorant, quackish
Charles's-wain, s. the northern constellation; called Ursa Major, or the Great Bear
Char'lock, s. a weed which grows among corn, with a yellow flower
Charm, v. a. to bewitch, appease, delight
Charm, s. a spell or enchantment, a philter
Char'mer, s. one who charms or enchants
Char'ming, part. a. delightful, very pleasing
Char'nel-house, s. a receptacle for the bones of the dead, a vault for dead bodies
Chart, s. a delineation of coasts, &c.; a map
Char'ter, s. a privilege, immunity, or exemption, by royal grant, in writing
Char'tered, a. privileged; granted by charter
Char'ter-party, s. a paper relating to a contract of which each party has a copy
Char'woman, s. a woman hired by the day
Cha'ry, a. careful, diligent, cautious
Chase, v. a. to pursue, to hunt, to drive
Chase, s. pursuit of an enemy; a piece of ground larger than a park; bore of a gun
Chasm, s. a cleft, a vacuity, an opening
Chas'sy, s. a window frame, a fastening
Chaste, a. pure, uncorrupted, honest
Cha'sten, Chasti'se, v. a. to punish, correct
Chas'ti-ement, s. punishment, correction
Chas'tity, Chas'teness, s. purity of the body
Chat, v. n. to prate, to prattle, to talk idly
Chat, s. prattle, idle talk, conversation
Char'ellany, s. the district under a castle
Chat'tel, s. any moveable property
Chat'ter, v. n. to make a noise like birds, or with the teeth; to talk idly or carelessly
Chat'ender, Chev'in, s. the chub, a fish

Chaw'dron, s. the entrails of a beast
Cheap, a. to be had at a low rate—s. a bargain
Chea'pen, v. a. to lessen the value; to attempt to purchase, to bid for any thing
Chea'pness, s. lowness of price
Cheat, s. a trick, a fraud; a deceiver
Cheat, v. a. to impose, to gull, to deceive
Check, v. a. to curb, repress, chide, control
Check, s. a stop, restraint, curb, dislike, reproof; a kind of linen
Check'er, Cheq'uer, v. a. to diversify, to vary
Cheek, s. the side of the face below the eye; a name with mechanics for those parts of their machines that are double
Chee'ktooth, s. the hinder tooth or tusk
Cheer, s. entertainment, jollity, gaiety
Cheer, v. a. to comfort, to incite, to grow gay
Chee'rer, s. one who gives mirth, a gladdener
Chee'rful, a. full of life, gay, brisk, merry
Chee'rfulness, s. liveliness, mirth, alacrity
Chee'rless, a. gloomy, sad, without comfort
Chee'rly, Chee'ry, a. sprightly, merry, gay
Cheese, s. food made from milk curds
Chee'secake, s. cake made of curds, sugar, &c.
Chee'semonger, s. one who sells cheese
Chee'sevat, s. the wooden case in which the curds are pressed into cheese
Che'ly, s. the claw of a shell fish
Che'riff, s. the high priest of the Moors
Cher'ish, v. a. to nurse up, support, shelter
Cher'isher, s. a supporter, encourager
Cher'ry, s. a fruit—a. ruddy, blooming
Cher'ry-cheeked, a. having blooming cheeks
Chert, s. a kind of flint, flint in strata
Cher'ub, Cher'ubin, s. a celestial spirit
Cheru'bic, Cheru'bical, a. angelical
Cher'up, v. n. to chirp; to use a lively voice
Ches'nut, Chest'nut, s. a sort of fruit
Chess, s. a difficult game, in which two sets of men are moved in opposition
Chess'board, s. a board to play chess on
Ches'som, s. mellow earth
Chest, s. a large box or coffer; the breast
Chevalie'r, s. a knight, a gallant man
Che'vaux-de-frise, s. a military fence of spikes, pointed with iron; a kind of trimming
Chev'en, s. a river fish, the same with chub
Chev'eril, s. a kid; kid leather
Chew, v. a. to grind with the teeth; to masticate; to ruminate, to meditate on
Chica'ne, Chica'nery, s. sophistry, wrangling
Chick, Chick'en, s. the young of hens
Chick'enhearted, a. timorous, fearful
Chide, v. a. to reprove, to reproach, to blame
Chi'ding, part. reproving, scolding, rebuking
Chief, a. principal, eminent—s. a leader
Chie'fless, a. having no leader, weak
Chie'fly, ad. principally, above all, eminently
Chie'ftain, s. a commander, a leader
Chil'blain, s. a sore made by cold and frost
Child, s. an infant; male or female offspring
Chil'dbearing, s. the act of bearing children
Chil'dbed, Chil'dbirth, s. the state of a woman bringing a child; labour; travail
Chil'dermass-day, s. the day of the week throughout the year answering to the day on which the feast of the Holy Innocents is solemnized
Chil'dhood, s. infancy, the state of a child
Chil'dish, a. puerile, frivial, like a child

Chi' dishness, s. triflingness, puerility
Chi'kless, a. having no children, barren
Chil'dren, s. the plural of child
Chil'lad, s. a thousand
Chiliaed'ron, s. a figure of a thousand sides
Chil'iarch, s. a commander of a thousand men
Chill, a. cold, depressed—s. cold, chilness
Chill, v.a. to make cold, blast, discourage
Chil'liness,Chil'ness, s. a sensation of shivering, cold; want of warmth
Chil'ly, a. somewhat cold, frosty, raw
Chim'ar, s. part of a bishop's vesiment
Chime, s. a sound of bells, concord of sound
Chime, v.n. to sound in harmony, to agree
Chime'ra, s. an odd fancy; a feigned monster
Chimer'ical, a. whimsical, imaginary
Chim'inage, s. toll for passing through a forest
Chim'ney, s. a passage made for smoke [rest
Chim'ney-piece, s. an ornamental frame of marble, stone, &c. round a fire-place
Chin, s. the lowest part of the human face
Chi'na, s. a country; china ware, porcelain
Chin'cough, s. a violent disease of children
Chine, s. the backbone—v.a. to cut in chines
Chink, s. a small aperture longwise; money in burlesque—v. a. to jingle like money
Chin'ky, a. full of chinks, gaping, open
Chintz, s. Indian printed calico
Chip, v. a. to cut into small pieces, to hack
Chip, Chip'ping, s. a fragment cut off
Chirog'rapher, s. an officer in the Common Pleas who engrosses fines in that court
Chirog'raphy, s. the act of writing
Chirol'ogy, s. talking by the hand
Chir'omancy, s. divination by the hand
Chirp, v. n. to imitate the noise of birds
Chirp, s. the noise of birds or insects
Chir'ping, s. the gentle noise of birds
Chirur'geon, s. a surgeon; an operator
Chirur'gical, a. relating to surgery
Chis'el, s. a carpenter's tool to pare with
Chit, s. a baby, a child; sprout of corn
Chit'chat, s. common trifling talk, prattle
Chit'terlings, s. the guts; the bowels
Chiv'alry, s. military dignity, knighthood
Chives, s. the threads or filaments rising in flowers with seeds at the end; a species of small onion
Choc'olate, s. a preparation of the Indian cocoa nut shell; the liquor made from it
Choice, s. a thing chosen; power of choosing; plenty, variety; best part of any thing
Choice, a. of great value, select; careful
Choi'ceness, s. nicety, of particular value
Choir, s. a part of a church; a body of singers
Choke, v. a. to suffocate, block up, suppress
Choke, s. internal part of an artichoke
Cho'kepear, s. a rough, harsh, unpalatable pear; any sarcasm that stops the mouth
Chol'er, s. the bile; rage, anger, irascibility
Chol'eric, a. full of choler, offensive, angry
Choose, Chuse, v. a. to pick out, to select
Chop, v. a. to cut with a blow, to mince; to devour; to change; to break into chinks
Chop, s. a small piece of meat; a cleft
Chop'house, s. a house to eat provisions at
Chop'in, s. a Scotch quart, in wine measure
Chop'ping, a. lusty, large, jolly, healthy
Chop'ping, s. a sort of high-heeled shoe
Chop'py, a. full of holes or cracks
Cho'ral, a. belonging to or singing in a choir

Chord, s. the string of a musical instrument
Chord, v. a. to furnish or fasten with strings
Cho'rister, Cho'rist, s. a singer in cathedrals
Chorog'raphy, s. the art of describing particular places; teaching geography
Cho'ir s, s. a number of singers; a concert
Cho'sen, part. selected, made choice of
Chough, s. a sea bird which frequents rocks
Choule, s. the stomach of a bird; a jowl
Chouse, v. a. to cheat, to trick—s. a fool
Chrism, s. an holy unguent or oil
Chris'om, s. a child that dies within a month after its birth; a cloth
Chris'ten, v. a. to baptize, to name
Chris'tendom, s. the whole collective body of Christians
Chris'tening, s. the act of baptizing infants
Chris'tian, s. a disciple of Christ
Christian'ity, s. the religion taught by Christ
Chris'tianize, v. a. to make Christian
Chris'tian-name, s. the name given at baptism
Chris'tmas, s. the festival of the Nativity of Christ, the 25th of December
Chromat'ic, a. relating to colours or music
Chron'ic, Chron'ical, a. of long continuance
Chron'icle, s. a history, record, register
Chron'icle, v.a. to record in history [events
Chron'icler, s. an historian, recorder of
Chron'ogram, s. a kind of verse or description, the numeral letters of which make up the date of the action mentioned
Chronol'oger, s. an explainer of past time
Chronolog'ical, a. relating to chronology
Chronol'ogy, s. the art of computing time
Chrys'alis, s. aurelia, or the first apparent change of any species of insect
Chrys'olite, s. a precious stone of a dusky green, with a yellow cast
Chub, s. the name of a fish, the chevin
Chub'bed, a. big-headed, like a chub; stupid
Chuck, s. the voice of a hen; a kind word
Chuc'kle, v. a. to laugh much, to fondle
Churl, s. a blunt clownish person—a. surly
Chum, s. a messmate; a chamber fellow
Chump, s. a thick heavy piece of wood
Church, s. a place of divine worship; congregation; the collective body of Christians
Church, v.a. solemnly to return thanks in the church after child-birth
Chur'ching, s. the act of giving thanks in the church after child-birth
Chur'chman, s. a clergyman; a member of the church of England
Churchwar'den, s. a parish officer chosen by the minister and parishioners
Chur'chyard, s. the ground adjoining the church, where the dead are buried
Churl, s. a niggard; a rude person; a rustic
Chur'lish, a. untractable, selfish, provoking
Chur'lishly, ad. surlily, rudely, brutally
Chur'lishness, s. rudeness, ill nature
Churme, s. a confused sound, a noise
Churn, v. a. to make butter; to agitate
Churn, s. a vessel used to coagulate cream in
Chyla'ceous, a. belonging to chyle
Chyle, s. white juice of the stomach
Chym'ical, a. relating to chymistry
Chym'ist, s. a professor of chymistry
Chym'istry, s. the art of separating natural bodies by fire; preparing chymicals
Cic'atrice, s. a scar left by a wound

Cicatrize, v.a. to heal a wound, to skin over
Cicero'nian, a. like Cicero ; elegant, pure
Cicis'beo, s. a gallant attending a lady
Cic'urate, v. a. to tame, to make mild
Ci'der, s. a liquor made from apple juice
Ci'derkin, s. an inferior kind of cider
Cil'iary, a. relating to the eye-lids
Cilic'ious, a. made of hair, hairy, rough
Cim'eter, s. a Turkish hanger; a sort of sword, short and recurvated
Cimme'rian, a. extremely dark
Cin'cture, s. a belt, sash, ring, gird'e
Cin'der, s. coal burnt till the sulphur is gone
Cine'rous, a. of the colour of wood ashes
Cinerit'ious, a. having the form of ashes
Cin'gle, s. a girth used for a horse
Cin'nabar, s. vermilion ; red mineral
Cin'namon, s. the spicy bark of a tree
Cinque, s. five, the number of five on dice
Cinque-foil, s. a kind of five-leaved clove
Cinque-pace, s. a grave kind of dance
Cinque-ports, s. five havens on the eastern coast of England, viz. Hastings, S·lwich, Dover, Hithe, and Romney
Ci'on, s. a sprout ; the root of a plant
Ci'pher, s. the character (0) in numbers ; the initials of a person's name interwoven ; a secret manner of writing—v. n. to cast accounts
Ci'phering, s. the act of casting accounts
Circle, v. a. to make a circle; make round
Cir'cle, s. an orb, a round body : a company
Cir'cle, v. a. to move round any thing ; to confine ; to inclose ; to move circularly
Cir'clet, s. a small circle or orb
Cir'cuit, s. extent, space, act of moving round a y thing ; visitation of the judges
Cir'cuit, v. n. to move in a circle
Circu'itous, a. going round in a circuit
Cir'cular, a. like a circle, round
Circular'ity, s. a circular form
Cir'culate, v. a. to move round, to put about
Circula'tion, s. a circular motion, a return
Circumam'bient, a. surrounding
Circumam'bulate, v.n. to walk round about
Cir'cumcise, v. a. to cut off the fore-skin
Circumcis'ion, s. the act of cutting off the fore-skin, practised by the Jews, &c.
Circumduc't, v.a. to nullify, to contravene ; to carry or convey round
Circum'ference, s. a circle ; a compass ; the periphery or limit of a circle
Circumferen'tor, s. an instrument used in surveying to measure angles
Cir'cumflex, s. an accent used to regulate the pronunciation of syllables, including the acute and grave, marked (ʌ)
Circum'fluent, a. flowing round any thing
Circum'fluous, a. environing with waters
Circumfora'neous, a. wandering from house to house
Circumfu'se, v.a. to spread round, to diffuse
Circumfu'sion, s. the act of pouring round
Circumgy'rate, v. a. to wheel or roll round
Circumgyra'tion, s. the act of running round
Circumit'ion, s. the act of going round
Circumja'cent, a. lying round any thing
Circumliga'tion, s. the act of binding round
Circumlocu'tion, s. the use of indirect expressions, a circuit of words
Circummu'red, a. fenced or walled round

Circumnav'igate, v. a. to sail round
Circumnavi'a'tion, s. the act of sailing round
Circumnaviga'tor, s. one who sails round
Circumrota'tion, s. the act of whirling round
Circumscri'be, v.a. to inclose, confine, limit
Circumscrip'tion, s. a limitation; determination of form or magnitude
Cir'cumspect, a. watchful, cautious, wary
Circumspec'tion, s. caution, watchfulness
Circumspec'tive, a. watchful, attentive
Cir'cumspectly, ad. vigilantly, watchfully
Cir'cumstance, s. an accident, incident, event
Cir'cumstanced, a. placed or situated
Circumstan'tial, a. minute, particular
Circumstan'tiate, v. a. to describe exactly
Circumvalla'tion, s. a fortification surrounding a besieged place
Circumvec'tion, s. the act of carrying round
Circumven't, v. a. to over-reach, to deceive
Circumven'tion, s. deceit, fraud, prevention
Circumvest', v. a. to put or garnish round
Circumvol've, v. a. to roll round about
Circumvolu'tion, s. a turning round
Cir'cus, s. area for sports, with circular seats
Cisal'pine, a. lying on this side the Alps
Cist, s. a coat ; a case ; an angry tumour
Cis'tern, s. a vessel to catch or hold water
Cit'adel, s. a castle, a fortress, a place of arms
Cita'tion, s. reproof, impeachment, a summons to appear before a judge ; a quotation from another author; enumeration
Cite, v. a. to summon, to quote, to enjoin
Citess', s. a woman residing in a city
Cith'ern, s. an ancient kind of harp
Cit'izen, s. a freeman ; one inhabiting a city—a. having quali ies of a citizen
Cit'rine, a. like a citron ; of a lemon colour
Cit'rine, s. a species of chrystal extremely pure, out of which jewellers cut stones for rings, &c. frequently mistaken for the topaz
Cit'ron, s. a fruit resembling a lemon
Cit'y, s. an episcopal town
Civ'et, s. a perfume got from the civet cat
Civ'ic, a. relating to civil honours, &c.
Civ'il, a. civilized, political ; polite, kind
Civil'ian, s. a professor of civil law
Civil'ity, s. politeness, kindness ; freedom from barbarity
Civ'ilize, v.a. to polish, to instruct, to reclaim
Civ'ilized, part. improved, polished, civil
Civ'il-law, s. the national law of a country
Civ'il-war, s. an intestine war
Cize, s. the surface of any thing
Clack, s. a continued noise ; part of a mill
Clack, v.n. to talk fast, to let the tongue run
Clad, pret. and part. of to clothe
Claim, s. a demand of any thing due, a title
Claim, v. a. to demand of right, to require
Clai'mable, a. that which may be claimed
Clai'mant, s. one who owns or demands
Clai'med, part. demanded, owned
Clam'ber, v. n. to climb with difficulty
Clamm, v. a. to clog, to glue ; to sarve
Clam'miness, s. stickiness, ropiness
Clam'my, a. sticky, moist, ropy, viscous
Clam'our, s. outcry, vociferation, noise
Clam'orous, a. noisy, importunate, loud
Clamp, s. a piece of wood joined to another
Clan, s. a race ; a family ; sect of persons
Clan'cular, a. clandestine, hidden, private
Clandes'tine, a. secret, sly, hidden

Clandes'tinely, *ad.* secretly, craftily
Clang, Clan'gour, Clank, *s.* a sharp noise
Clan'gous, *a.* making a shrill noise
Clank, *v. a.* to make a loud noise; to clatter
Clap, *v. a.* to strike together; to applaud
Clap, *s.* an act of applause; an explosion of thunder; a loud noise
Clap'per, *s.* the tongue of a bell, &c.
Clap'perclaw, *v. a.* to scold, chide, beat
Clarencieu'x, *s.* the second king at arms
Clar'et, *s.* a light French wine
Clarifica'tion, *s.* the act of making clear
Clar'ify, *v. a.* to make clear, to illuminate
Clar'inet, *s.* a kind of hautboy
Clar'ion, *s.* a martial instrument, a trumpet
Clar'itude, Clar'ity, *s.* clearness, brightness
Cla'ro-obscuro, *s.* light and shade in painting
Clash, *v. n.* to contradict, to wrangle, to oppose
Clash, *s.* a noisy collision of two bodies
Clasp, *v. a.* to embrace, to hold fast, to hug
Clasp, *s.* a kind of hook; a holdfast
Clas'per, *s.* the thread of creeping plants
Class, *v. a.* to range or set in order
Class, Class'is, *s.* a rank, order, set, degree
Class'ic, *s.* a writer of the first rank
Class'ical, *a.* relating to authors of the first order or rank; elegant, learned
Clat'ter, *s.* a rattling confused noise, clamour
Clat'ter, *v. n.* to make a confused noise, to jar
Clause, *s.* a sentence, a stipulation, provision.
Clau'sure, *s.* a shutting up, a hedge
Cla'vated, Cla'vatous, *a.* club-shaped
Claw, *s.* the foot of a beast, bird, or fish
Claw, *v. a.* to tear with claws, to scratch
Clay, *s.* a common sort of earth
Clay'cold, *a.* cold as earth, dead, lifeless
Clean, *a.* free from dirt; pure, innocent
Clean, *v. a.* to free from dirt; to purify
Clean, *ad.* perfectly, quite, fully
Clean'liness, Clea'nness, *s.* purity, neatness
Clean'ly, *a.* free from dirt; pure, neat
Cleanse, *v. a.* to free from dirt; to purify
Clear, *ad.* clean, fully, quite, completely
Clear, *v. a.* to brighten, to remove, to gain
Clear, *a.* bright, guiltless; plain, not obscure
Clea'rance, *s.* the act of clearing; acquittal
Clea'rer, *s.* brightener, enlightener, purifier
Clea'rly, *ad.* brightly, plainly, evidently
Clea'rness, *s.* perspicuity, transparency
Clea'rsighted, *a.* discerning, judicious
Clea'rstarch, *v. a.* to stiffen with starch
leave, *v.* to stick to; unite aptly; split
Clea'ver, *s.* a butcher's instrument
Clef, *s.* a mark for the key in music
Cleft, *s.* a crack—*part. pass.* from *to cleave*
Clem'ency, *s.* mercy, tenderness, humanity
Clem'ent, *a.* mild, gentle, merciful, kind
Clench, *v. a.* to fasten, to bend, to pin down
Clepe, *v. a.* to name, to call
Clepsy'dra, *s.* an instrument used by the ancients to measure time by water
Cler'gy, *s.* the whole body or order of divines
Cler'gyman, *s.* a person in holy orders
Cler'ical, *a.* relating to the clergy, orthodox
Clerk, *s.* a clergyman; a scholar; a secretary or book-keeper; man of letters
Cler'kship, *s.* employ of a clerk; scholarship
Clev'er, *a.* dexterous, skilful, fit, ready
Clev'erness, *s.* knowledge, skill, art
Clew, *s.* a ball of thread, &c.; a guide
Clew, *v. a.* to draw up the sails to be furle

Click, *v. n.* to make a sharp noise
Click'er, *s.* a caller-in at a shop; a servant
Click'et, *s.* the knocker of a door
Cli'ent, *s.* an employer of an attorney, &c.
Cliff, or Clift, *s.* a precipice, a steep rock
Climac'ter, *s.* every seventh or ninth year
Climacter'ic, *a.* containing a number of years, at the end of which some great change is supposed to befal the body
Cli'mate, Clime, *s.* the air; a tract of land
Cli'max, *s.* rhetorical figure; ascent; gradation
Climb, *v. a.* to ascend up any place
Cli'mber, *s.* one that climbs; a plant
Clinch, *v. a.* to hold fast; to contract; bend
Clinch, *s.* a pun, a witty saying, part of a cable
Clin'cher, *s.* a cramp, holdfast; full answer
Cling, *v. n.* to twine round; to dry up
Clin'ic, *s.* a person confined in bed by disease
Clin'ical, *a.* bedrid, disordered, sick
Clink, *v. n.* to sound like metal
Clin'ker, *s.* a paving brick; bad cinders
Clin'quant, *s.* spangles, embroidery
Clip, *v. a.* to cut short, to confine, to embrace
Clip'per, *s.* a debaser of coin by clipping it
Clip'ping, *s.* the part cut off—*part.* cutting
Cloak, *v. a.* to hide, conceal, cover over
Cloak, *s.* an outer garment, cover; blind
Clock, *s.* an instrument to mark time; a beetle
Clock'work, *s.* movement by weights or springs
Clod, *s.* a lump of clay or earth; a clown, dolt
Clod'pate, Clod'pole, *s.* a stupid fellow, dolt
Clog, *s.* a sort of shoe; an obstruction
Clog, *v. a.* to hinder, load, burden, adhere
Clois'ter, *s.* a place of religious retirement; a peristyle; a square with piazzas
Clois'ter, *v. a.* to confine in a cloister
Close, *v.* to shut, join, enclose, confine
Close, *s.* a small field inclosed; end, pause
Close, *a.* private; shut fast; sly; cloudy
Clo'sebodied, *a.* sitting close to the body
Clo'sely, *ad.* slily, secretly, without deviation
Clo'seness, *s.* nearness, heat, privacy
Clos'et, *s.* a small private room
Clos'et, *v. a.* to shut in a closet; to conceal
Clo'sure, *s.* an enclosure, period, conclusion
Clot, *v. n.* to form clots, to coagulate
Clot, *s.* any thing clotted; a hard lump
Cloth, *s.* woollen or linen woven for garments; the covering for a table
Clothe, *v. a.* to cover with garments; dress
Clo'thier, *s.* a maker of woollen cloth
Clo'thing, Clothes, *s.* dress; garments
Cloud, *s.* body of vapours in the air, stain
Cloud, *v. a.* to darken with clouds
Clou'dcapt, *part.* topped with clouds
Clou'dless, *a.* free from clouds, pure, clear
Clou'dy, *a.* obscure, dark, gloomy, sullen
Clove, *s.* a spice, root or grain of garlick
Clo'ven, *part.* cleft, separated, divided
Clo'ver, *s.* a species of trefoil, kind of grass
Clo'vered, *a.* covered with clover
Clough, *s.* an allowance in weight; a cliff
Clout, *s.* a cloth for any mean use, a patch
Clou'ted, *part.* patched, congealed
Clown, *s.* a rustic, ill-bred man; a churl
Clow'nish, *a.* awkward, uncivil, rude
Cloy, *v. a.* to glut, surfeit, sate; to nail up
Cloy'less, *a.* that cannot glut or surfeit
Cloy'ment, *s.* a cloyed state, fulness
Club, *s.* a society; a heavy stick; suit of cards

Club, v. n. to join in common expense
Club'law, s. the law of arms, law of force
Club'room, s. the room a club meets in
Cluck, v. n. to call chickens, as a hen
Clumps, s. a blockhead, a stupid fellow
Clum'siness, s. heaviness, awkwardness
Clum'sy, a. awkward, thick, heavy
Clung, pret. and part. of to cling—a. dried
    up, worn down with leanness
Clus'ter, s. a bunch, collection, body, herd
Clutch, s. a grasp, talon, paw, hand
Clutch, v. a. to gripe, clinch, hold fast
Clut'ter, s. noise, hurry, bustle, clamour
Clys'ter, s. an injection into the anus
Coacer'vate, v. a. to heap together, to add
Coach, s. a carriage of state or pleasure
Coact, v. n. to act together, or in concert
Coac'tion, s. restraint, compulsion
Coac'tive, a. having the force to impel
Coad'jutant, a. co-operating, helping
Coadju'tor, s. an assistant, ally, helper
Coa'gent, s. one acting with another
Coagment', v. a. to cement, to heap together
Coag'ulate, v. a. to run into clots
Coagula'tion, s. the act of, or body formed by,
    coagulation; concretion
Coal, s. a fossil used for firing
Coa'lery, s. the place where coals are dug
Coales'ce, v. n. to join together, unite, to close
Coales'cence, s. act of uniting; concretion
Coali'tion, s. an union in one mass; junction
Coa'ly, a. containing coal, like coal
Coapta'tion, s. the adjustment of parts to
    each other
Coarct', v. a. to confine, to straighten, press
Coarse, a. gross, rough, rude, vile, large
Coa'rseness, s. roughness, meanness, rude-
Coast, s. a shore, bank, edge, side   [ness
Coast, v. n. to sail near to or along the coast
Coa'sting, s. sailing in sight of the land
Coat, s. a man's upper garment; a petticoat;
    the upper covering of all animals
Coax, v. a. to wheedle, entice, fawn upon
Co'balt, s. a kind of marcasite; a mineral
Cob'ble, v. a. to mend clumsily or coarsely
Cob'bler, s. a mender of shoes; a botcher
Cob'cal, s. a sandal worn by ladies in eastern
    countries; an open slipper
Cob'iron, s. an iron with a knob at one end
Cob'swan, s. the head or leading swan
Cob'web, s. a spider's web—a. weak, trifling
Coch'ineal, s. an insect used to dye scarlet
Coch'leated, a. formed like a screw
Cock, v. a. to cock a gun; to set up the hat
Cock, s. the male of small birds; a spout to let
    out liquids; part of a gun; form of a hat;
    the needle of a balance; heap of hay
Cocka'de, s. a ribbon worn on a hat
Cock'ahoop, ad. in high jollity and mirth
Cock'atrice, s. a sort of serpent
Cock'er, v. a. to fondle, indulge, pamper
Cock'er, s. a person who fights cocks
Cock'erel, s. a small cock; a young cock
Cock'et, s. a ticket from the custom-house
Cock'horse, a. on horseback; triumphant
Cock'ing, Cock'fight, s. a match of cocks
Cock'le, s. a shell fish; the weed cornrose
Cock'le, v. a. to shrink up into wrinkles
Cock'lestairs, s. winding or spiral stairs
Cock'loft, s. a room over a garret
Cock'match, s. a battle of cocks for money

Cock'ney, s. a Londoner, a mean citizen
Cock'pit, s. a place where cocks fight
Cock'scomb, s. the upper part of a cock's
    head; a plant; lobeswort
Cock'sure, a. very confident, quite certain
Co'coa, s. a kind of nut; liquor made from it
Coc'tion, s. the act of boiling; digestio
Cod, s. a sea fish; the bag of seeds
Code, s. a book of the civil law; a book
Cod'icil, s. appendage to a will
Codill'e, s. a term in playing at ombre
Cod'le, v. a. to dress badly, to parboil
Cod'ling, s. a sort of early apple
Coef'ficacy, Coeffic'iency, s. co-operation;
    the united power of several things
Coemp'tion, s. the act of buying up the whole
Coe'qual, a. equal with, in the same state
Coer'ce, v. a. to restrain by force, to check
Coer'cible, a. that is capable of being checked
Coer'cion, s. restrain', check, force
Coer'cive, a. serving to restrain, forcible
Coessen'tial, a. partaking of the same essence
Coeta'neous, a coeval, of the same age
Coeter'nal, a. equally eternal with another
Coe'val, s. a cotemporary
Coe'val, Coe'vous, a. being of the same age
Coexis't, v. n. to exist at the same time
Coexis'tent, a. existing at the same time
Cof'fee, s. the berry of an Arabian tree; the
    liquor extracted from that berry
Cof'feehouse, s. a house where coffee, &c. is
Cof'fer, s. a money chest, a treasure   [sold
Cof'ferer, s. a principal court officer
Cof'fin, s. a chest for dead bodies
Cog, v. a. to flatter, to cheat, to wheedle, to lie
Cog, s. tooth of a wheel by which it acts, &c.
Co'gency, s. strength, force, power
Co'gent, a. resistless, forcible, convincing
Cogita'tion, s. meditation, thought, care
Cog'nate, a. born together, allied, alike
Cogna'tion, s. relationship, kindred
Cognisee', s. one to whom a fine is made
Cognisor', s. one who acknowledge a fine
Cognit'ion, s. conviction, knowledge, trial
Cog'nizable, a. proper to be judged of
Cog'nizance, s. a judicial notice; a crest
Cogue, s. a small wooden vessel; a dram
Cohab'it, v. n. to live together
Cohab'itant, s. one living in the same place
Cohei'r, s. a joint heir with another person
Cohei'ress, s. a woman who is a joint heiress
Cohe're, v. n. to stick together, to agree,
    to fit
Cohe'rence, Cohe'rency, s. connexion
Cohe'rent, a. connected, sticking together
Cohe'sion, s. a state of union, connexion
Cohe'sive, a. having a sticking quality
Cohobate, v. a. to distil a second time
Cohoba'tion, s. repeated distillation
Co'hort, s. a troop of soldiers, in number 500
Coif, s. a head-dress, a woman's cap
Coil, v. a. to roll up a rope; to wind in a ring
Coil, s. noise, tumult; rope wound in a ring
Coil'ed, part. bent or twisted like a rope
Coin, s. money stampt with a legal impression
Coin, v. a. to make money; to stamp; invent
Coi'nage, s. the act of coining; money
Coinci'de, v. n. to concur, to agree with
Coin cidence, s. a concurrence, agreement
Coin cident, a. agreeing with, united
Col'ner, s. a maker of money; an inventor

Coit'ion, s. the act by which two bodies come together, the act of generation

Coke, s. cinder made from pit-coal

Col'ander, s. a kitchen sieve, drainer

Cola'tion, Col'ature, s. the act of straining

Colberti'ne, s. a kind of lace for women

Co d, a. not hot; not hasty; coy; chaste

Cold, s. cold weather; chilness; a disorder

Co'ldish, a. rather cold; reserved; shy

Co'ldly, ad. carelessly, indifferently

Co'ldness, s. want of heat; indifference

Co'lewort, s. a sort of cabbage

Col'ic, s. a distemper affecting the bowels

Collap'se, v. n. to fall close, or together

Col'lar, s. something round the neck; a band

Col'lar, v. a. to seize by the collar

Colla'te, v. a. to compare things similar; to examine books, if they be complete; to place in an ecclesiastical benefice

Collat'eral, a. side by side; not direct

Colla'tion, s. a gift; treat; comparison

Colla'tor, s. one who compares copies

Collea'gue, s. a partner in employment or office—v. n. to unite with

Collec't, v. a. to gather together, to infer

Col'lect, s. a short comprehensive prayer

Collec'tion, s. things gathered; an inference

Collec'tive, a. accumulative, apt to gather

Collec'tively, ad. in a body; wholly

Collec'tor, s. a gatherer; a tax gatherer

Col'lege, s. a house or school for learning

Colle'gian, s. a member of a college

Colle'giate, a. containing a college

Col'let, s. the part of a ring in which the stone is set; something round the neck

Col'lier, s. a coal-ship; a digger of coals

Colliga'tion, s. the act of binding together

Col'liquate, v. a. to melt, to soften, to liquify

Colli'quative, a. tending to dissolve or melt

Colliquefac'tion, s. the act of melting together

Collis'ion, s. act of striking together, a clash

Col'locate, v. a. to place, set in order, fix

Colloca'tion, s. the act of placing

Col'lop, s. a small cut or slice of meat

Collo'quial, a. relating to conversation

Col'loquy, s. a conversation, conference, talk

Collu'sion, s. a deceitful compact

Collu'sive, a. deceitful, fraudulent, bad

Col'ly, v. a. to grime with coal, to soil

Co'lon, s. this point (:) used to mark a pause greater than that of a semicolon, and less than that of a period; the greatest and widest of all the intestines

Col'onel, s. the commander of a regiment

Colo'nial, a. relating to a colony

Col'onise, v. a. to settle with inhabitants

Colonna'de, s. a range of columns or pillars

Col'ony, s. a body of people sent from the mother country to inhabit another place; the country so planted

Col'ophony, s. turpentine, rosin, pitch

Col'orate, a. coloured, tinged, stained, dyed

Colorif'ic, a. that is able to produce colour

Colos'sus, Colos'se, s. a very large statue

Col'our, s. hue, dye; a pretence

Col'our, v. a. to dye; blush; tinge; palliate

Col'ourable, a. plausible, specious, likely

Col'ouring, s. an art in painting, an excuse

Col'ourist, s. one who excels in colouring

Co'lours, s. a banner, streamer, flag

Colt, s. a young horse, inexperienced person

Col'umbary, s. a dove or pigeon house

Col'umn, s. a round pillar; part of a page

Colum'nar, a. formed in columns

Co'mate, s. an associate, a companion

Comb, s. an instrument to separate and adjust the hair; the cavities in which bees lodge their honey, the crest of a cock

Comb, v. a. to divide, to smooth, to dress

Com'bat, s. a battle, duel, contest, dispute

Com'bat, v. a. to fight, to resist, to oppose

Com'batant, s. one who fights with another; a champion; an antagonist

Combi'nate, a. betrothed, fixed, promised

Combina'tion, s. an association, a conspiracy

Combi'ne, v. to unite, agree, join, link

Combi'ned, part. united or joined together

Combus'tible, a. that which easily takes fire

Combus'tion, s. a burning, confusion, hurry

Come, v. n. to draw near, proceed, happen

Come'dian, s. an actor or writer of comedies

Com'edy, s. a humorous dramatic piece

Com'eliness, s. beauty, grace, dignity

Com'ely, a. decent, graceful, handsome

Com'ely, ad. gracefully, handsomely

Com'et, s. a blazing star

Com'fit, s. a kind of dry sweetmeat

Com'fort, v. a. to make glad, ease, revive

Com'fort, s. joy, ease, support, assistance

Com'fortable, a. giving comfort, pleasing

Com'fortless, a. without comfort, forlorn

Com'ic, a. relating to comedy, raising mirth

Com'ical, a. merry, diverting, arch, queer

Com'ing, s. a drawing near, an arrival

Com'ing, part. ready to come; fit ure; fond

Com'ma, s. a point marked thus (,)

Comman'd, v. a. to order, govern, overlook

Comman'd, s. act of commanding; order

Comman'der, s. a chief; a paving beetle

Comman'dress, s. a woman of chief power

Commem'orate, v. a. to celebrate, record

Commemora'tion, s. a public celebration

Commen'ce, v. n. to assume, to begin

Commen'cement, s. a beginning, date

Commen'd, v. a. to praise, to instruct

Commen'dable, a. deserving praise, worthy

Commen'dam, s. a void benefice held by some person till a pastor is provided

Commenda'tion, s. praise, message of love

Commen'datory, a. containing praise

Commen'surable, a. reducible to some common measure

Commen'surate, v. a. to reduce to some common measure—a. proportionable, equal

Commensura'tion, s. a reduction of some things to common measure

Com'ment, v. n. to write notes, to expound

Com'mentary, s. an exposition, annotation

Commenta'tor, s. expounder, explainer

Commenti'tious, a. invented, feigned

Com'merce, v. n. to hold intercourse

Com'merce, s. trade, barter; a game

Commer'cial, a. relating to trade, trading

Commere, s. a common mother

Commina'tion, s. a threat of punishment

Commin'gle, v. a. to mix together; to join

Commin'ute, v. a. to grind to powder

Comminu'tion, s. the act of grinding to small parts, pulverization

Commis'erable, a. wretched, deserving pity

Commisera'tion, s. sympathy, pity

E

Commissa'riat, s. persons attending an army, to regulate the procuration and conveyance of ammunition or provisions

Com'missary, s. a deputy or delegate

Commis'sion, s. a warrant, charge, trust

Commis'sion, v. a. to empower, to intrust

Commis'sioner, s. one empowered to act

Commis'sure, s. a joint, a mould, a seam

Commit', v. a. to do a fault; to give in trust; to intrust; to send to prison

Commit'tee, s. a select number of men chosen to examine or manage any matter

Commix', v. a. to mingle, to unite, to blend

Commix'ion, Commix'ture, s. a compound

Commo'de, s. a woman's head-dress

Commo'dious, a. convenient, useful, suitable

Commo'diousness, s. convenience, use

Commod'ity, s. merchandize, profit, interest

Com'modore, s. the captain who commands a squadron of ships of war

Com'mon, a. vulgar, equal, public, usual

Com'mon, s. an open country, public ground

Com'moner, s. a member of the house of commons; a man not noble; a student of the second rank at the university

Commonit'ion, s. advice, warning

Com'monly, ad. usually, frequently

Com'monness, s. frequency, an equal share

Commonpla'ce, v. a. to reduce to general heads

Commonpla'ce-book, s. a book where things to be remembered are put under general heads

Com'mons, s. the lower house of parliament; the common people; fare, food, diet

Com'monwealth, s. a republic, the public

Commo'tion, s. a disturbance, a tumult

Commo've, v. a. to disturb, to unsettle

Commu'ne, v. n. to converse, to impart sentiments mutually

Commu'nicant, s. one who participates in the sacrament of the Lord's Supper

Commu'nicate, v. a. to reveal, to impart; to receive the Lord's Supper

Communica'tion, s. the act of imparting or exchanging; conference; conversation; common boundary or inlet

Commu'nicative, a. ready to impart, free

Commu'nion, s. taking of the Lord's Supper; union, fellowship, intercourse

Commu'nity, s. the commonwealth, the body politic, a common possession

Commu'table, a. that may be exchanged

Commuta'tion, s. change of one thing for another, ransom, alteration

Commu'te, v. a. to exchange, to buy off

Com'pact, s. a contract, mutual agreement

Compac't, a. firm, solid, close, exact

Compac'tness, s. firmness, closeness

Compan'ion, s. associate, partner, mate

Com'pany, s. a number of persons assembled together; fellowship; body of merchants, a corporation; small body of foot soldiers

Com'pany, v. to accompany, associate with

Com'parable, a. of equal value or regard

Compar'ative, a. esteemed by comparison

Compar'atively, ad. in a state of comparison

Compa're, v. a. to make one thing the measure of another, to estimate

Compa're, s. similitude, comparison

Compar'ison, s. the act of comparing, state of being compared, simile in writing

Compar't, v. a. to divide, separate; arrange

Compart'iment, s. division of a picture, &c.

Compartit'ion, s. act of dividing; separate part

Com'pass, v. a. to surround, grasp, obtain

Com'pass, s. a circle, limits, space, power of the voice; an instrument composed of a needle and card, whereby mariners steer

Com'passes, s. an instrument for dividing, measuring, or drawing circles [pathy

Compas'sion, s. commiseration, pity, sympathy

Compas'sionate, a. merciful, kind, tender

Compas'sionately, ad. mercifully, tenderly

Compatibil'ity, s. suitableness, consistency

Compat'ible, a. consistent with, suitable to

Compa'triot, s. one of the same country

Compe'er, s. an equal, colleague, companion

Compe'er, v. n. to be equal with, to match

Compel', v. a. to force, constrain, oblige, &c.

Compella'tion, s. the style of address

Compen'dious, a. brief, short, summary

Compen'sate, Compen'se, v. a. to recompense, to make amends, to counterbalance

Compensa'tion, s. a recompence, amends

Com'petence, Com'petency, s. sufficiency

Com'petent, a. adequate, fit, consistent with

Com'petently, ad. reasonably, properly

Compet'ible, a. consistent with, suitable to

Competit'ion, s. a rivalship, contest, strife

Compet'itor, s. a rival, a foe, an opponent

Compila'tion, s. an assemblage, a collection

Compi'le, v. a. to collect from various authore

Compi'ler, s. a collector from various authors

Compla'cency, s. pleasure, civility, joy

Compla'cent, a. affable, civil, kind

Complai'nt, v. n. to murmur, bewail, inform

Complai'nant, s. a plaintiff in a lawsuit

Complai'nt, s. an accusation, a lamentation; a malady or disease

Complaisan'ce, s. obliging behaviour, civility

Complaisan't, a. desirous to please, civil

Compla'nate, Compla'ne, v. a. to smooth

Com'plement, s. the full quantity, &c.

Complemen'tal, a. completing, filling up

Comple'te, a. perfect, finished, full, ended

Comple'te, v. a. to finish, to perfect

Comple'tion, s. perfect state, accomplishment

Com'plex, a. composite; not simple

Complex'ion, s. the colour of the face, &c.

Complex'ly, ad. obscurely, intricately

Compli'ance, s. act of yielding, submission

Compli'ant, a. bending, yielding, civil

Com'plicate, a. compounded of many parts— v. a. to entangle, to join

Complica'tion, s. a mixture of many things

Com'pliment, s. an act of civility—v. to flatter

Complimen'tal, a. expressive of respect

Com'pline, s. evening service, vespers

Com'plot, s. a conspiracy, combination

Complot', v. a. to plot, join in, conspire

Complot'ter, s. a joint conspirator

Comply', v. n. to yield, to agree, to submit

Compo'nent, a. forming, constituting

Compor't, v. a. to bear, to behave, to endure

Com'port, Compor'tment, s. behaviour

Compor'table, a. suitable, consistent, fit

Compo'se, v. a. to quiet, settle, put togef

Compo'sed, part. a. calm, serious, sedate

Compo'ser, s. a writer, an author

Compos'te, a. in architecture, the *composite* order is the last of the five orders of columns so named, because its capital is composed out of those of the other orders

Composit'ion, s. a mixture ; a written work ; an agreement or compact ; the act of discharging a debt by paying part

Compos'itor, s. one who arranges the letters for printing

Com'post, Compos'ture, s. dung, manure

Compo'st, v. a. to manure, to enrich earth

Compo'sure, s. form, order ; tranquillity

Compota'tion, s. a drinking match

Compou'nd, v. to intermix, to mingle ; to come to terms with a debtor

Com'pound, s. a mass of ingredients ; a word formed from two or more words

Compou'nder, s. one who brings to terms, &c.

Comprehend', v. a. to conceive, to include

Comprehen'sible, a. conceivable, intelligible

Comprehen'sion, s. capacity, knowledge

Comprehen'sive, a. comprising much, understanding ; significant, full

Compress', v. a. to squeeze, to embrace

Com'press, s. a bolster of linen rags

Compres'sible, a. yielding to pressure

Compres'sion, s. act of bringing parts near

Compres'sure, s. the act of pressing against

Comprin't, v. a. to print another's copy

Compri'se, v. a. to contain, to include

Comproba'tion, s. attestation, a full proof

Com'promise, s. a bargain or compact—v. a. to settle a dispute by mutual concession

Compt, s. account, computation

Comptro'l, v. a. to control, to oppose

Comptro'ller, s. a director, a supervisor

Compul'satively, ad. by constraint

Compul'satory, a. forcing, compelling

Compul'sion, s. the act of compelling ; force

Compul'sive, Compul'sory, a. forcing

Compunc'tion, s. remorse, repentance

Compurga'tion, s. a vouching for another

Compu'table, a. that may be numbered up

Computa'tion, s. a calculation, an estimate

Compu'te, v. a. to reckon, to calculate

Compu'ted, part. estimated, calculated

Com'rade, s. an associate, a companion

Con, abbrev. for contra—v. a. to study

Concam'erate, v. a. to arch over, to vault

Concat'enate, v. a. to join or link together

Concatena'tion, s. a regular series of links

Con'cave, a. hollow ; the opposite of convex

Concav'ity, s. the inside cavity, hollowness of a round body

Con'cause, s. a mutual or joint cause

Concea'l, v. a. to hide, cover, keep secret

Concea'lable, a. capable of being concealed

Concea'lment, s. the act of hiding, shelter

Conce'de, v. a. to grant, to admit, to yield

Conce'it, s. an idea, fancy, opinion ; pride

Conce'it, v. a. to fancy, to imagine, to believe

Conce'ited, part. a. affected, fond of himself,

Conce'ivable, a. that may be thought [proud

Conce'ive, v. to form in the womb ; to comprehend, to think, to understand

Conce'iver, s. one who comprehends

Concen't, s. consistency, harmony

Concen'trate, v. a. to collect into a narrower compass round the centre

Concen'tre, v. n. to bring to one point

Concen'tric, a. having one common centre

Concen'tua., a. harmon.ous

Concep'tible, a. intelligible, conceivable

Concep'tion, s. the act of conceiving in the womb ; a notion, sentiment, idea, &c.

Concer'n, v. a. to interest, to affect, belong to

Concer'n, s. a business, an affair ; care

Concer'ning, prep. relating to or about

Concer'nment, s. a business, concern, care

Concer't, v. a. to settle privately, to contrive

Con'cert, s. music in several parts, harmony

Conces'sion, s. a grant, a thing yielded

Conch, s. a name of a fish, a shell

Concil'iate, v. a. to reconcile, to gain, to win

Concilia'tion, s. the act of gaining or winning

Concilia'tor, s. a friend, a peace-maker

Concin'nity, s. .tness, neatness, decency

Conci'se, a. short, brief, contracted

Conci'sely, ad. shortly, briefly

Conci'seness, s. brevity, shortness, force

Concis'ion, s. cutting off, excision

Concita'tion, s. a stirring up, disturbance

Con'clave, s. an assembly of cardinals, &c.

Conclu'de, v. a. to close, decide, determine

Conclu'dent, a. decisive, convincing

Concoag'ulate, v. a. to curdle ; to congeal

Concoc't, v. a. to digest by the stomach

Concoc'tion, s. digestion in the stomach

Concom'itance, s. a subsisting together

Concom'itant, a. accompanying, joining to

Concom'itant, s. a companion, attendant

Con'cord, s. agreement, union, harmony

Concor'dance, s. an index to the scriptures

Concor'dant, a. suitable, agreeable, fit

Concor'date, s. a compact, a convention

Concor'porate, v. a. to unite in one mass

Con'course, s. the confluence of many persons or things, a meeting

Concre'te, v. a. to form into one mass

Con'crete, a. formed by coalition of separate particles

Concre'tion, s. a union of parts, a mass

Con'cubine, s. a woman kept in fornication

Concu'piscence, s. irregular desire, sensuali-

Concu'piscen', a. lecherous ; libidinous [lity

Concur', v. n. to agree in one opinion

Concur'rence, s. union, just claim, help

Concur'rent, a. acting in conjunction

Concus'sion, s. the act of shaking, agitation

Condem'n, v. a. to pass sentence on, to blame

Condemna'tion, s. a sentence of punishment

Condem'n tory, a. passing condemnation

Conden'sate, v. a. to make thicker

Conden'sate, a. compressed into less space

Condensa'tion, s. the act of thickening

Conden'se, v. to grow close or thick—a. thick

Conden'ser, s. a vessel for condensing air

Conden'sity, s. the state of being condensed

Con'ders, s. those who direct herring fishers

Condescen'd, v. n. to yield, bend, stoop

Condescen'sion, s. submission, courtesy

Condi'gn, a. merited, deserved, suitable

Con'diment, s. sauce, seasoning, zest

Condi'te, v. a. to season, preserve by salt

Condi'tion, s. quality, rank, circumstance, tribute, stipulation, disposition

Condit'ional, a. by way of stipulation

Condit'ionary, a. agreed on, stipulated

Condo'le, v. to partake of another's sorrow

Condo'lence, s. grief for another's loss

Condona'tion, s. a forgiving, a pardoning

Con'dor, s. a large ravenous bird

Conduce', v. n. to promo e, to help, to conduct
Condu'cible, a. having the power of conduct-ing, accelerating, or promoting
Condu'cive, a. promoting any end
Con'duct, s. behaviour, economy
Conduc't, v. a. to guide, to order, manage
Conduc'tor, s. a leader, chief, director
Con'duit, s. a wate pipe, a duct, a canal
Cone, s. a solid body, in form of a sugar-loaf
Confab'ula'e, v. n. to converse, to chat
Confabula'tion, s. ea y conversation, chat
Confec'tion, s. a sweetmeat, a mixture
Confec'tioner, s. one who makes sweetmeats
Confed'eracy, s. a league, an engagement
Confed'erate, v. a. to combine, to unite
Confed'erate, s. an accomplice, an ally
Confedera'tion, s. close a liance, union
Confer', v. to bestow, to d scourse with
Con'ference, s. a discourse, a compar on
Confess', v. a. to acknowledge, own, g aut
Confess'edly, ad. avowedly, indisputably
Confes'sion, s. acknowledgment, profession
Con'fessor, s. one who hears confessions
Confest', a. known, evident, apparent
Confida'nt, Con'fident, s. a person trusted with a secret, a bosom friend
Confi'de, v. n. to trust in, to re y upon
Con'fidence, s. assurance, firmness, boldness
Con'fident, a. positive, impudent, bold
Confiden'tial, a. admitted to confidence, trusty
Configura'tion, s. the form of various parts adapted to each other
Config'ure, v. a. to fashion, dispose into form
Con'fine, s. limit, boundary, border
Confi'ne, v. to border upon, shut up, bound
Confi'nement, s. imprisonment, restraint
Confir'm, v. a. to establish, settle; to complete, to fix, to strengthen ; to administer the rite of ecclesiastical confirmation
Confir'mable, a. capable of being confirmed
Confirma'tion, s. proof, con incing tes imo-ny ; ecclesiastical r te by which baptized persons a e confirmed in the f ith
Confir'mative, a. having power to confirm
Confis'cate, v. a. to transfer private property to the public by way of penalty
Confisca'tion, s. the act of seizing private pro-perty when forfeited by crime, &c.
Con'fiture, s. a mixture of sweetmeats
Confix', v. a. to fix down, to fasten down
Confla'grant, a. burning together
Confla;ra'tion, s. a general fire or burning
Confla'tion, s. the act of blowing many instru-ments together ; a melting of metal
Conflic't, v. n. to fight, to strive, to contest
Con'flict, s. struggle, agony, contest
Con'fluence, s. a concourse of people ; union of several streams
Con'fluent, a. running into one channel
Con'flux, s. a joining of currents, a crowd
Confor'm, v. to comply with, to yie d, to suit
Confor'mable, a. suitable, agreeable, like
Conforma'tion, s. the form of things as relat-ing to each other
Confor'mist, s. one who complies with the rites of the established church   [blance
Confor'mity, s. a compliance with, resem-
Conforta'tion, s. the act of strengthening
Confou'nd, v. a. to amaze, to mix, to disturb
Confound'edly, ad. shamefully, hatefully
Confou'nder, s. one who amazes or perplexes

Confrater'nity, s. a religious b o herhood
Confrou't, v. a. to oppose, to face, to compare
Confron'ted, part. brought face to face
Confu'se, v. a. to perplex, confound, mix
Confu'sion, s. disorder, astonishment, hurry
Confu'table, a. that which may be disp r ved
Confuta'tion, s. act of confuting, disproof
Confu'te, v. a. to disprove, baffle, convict
Congee', Conge', s. a bow ; act of reverence
Conge'-d'elire, s. the king's permission to a dean and chap'er to choose a bishop
Congea'l, v. to freeze, grow stiff, harden
Congea'lab e, a. that which may be frozen
Congea'lment, s. a mass formed by frost
Conge'nial, a. partaking of the same nature
Con'geon, s. a dwarf, a little mean person
Con'ger, s. a fine kind of large eel, a sea eel
Conge'ries, s. a mass of small bodies
Conges't, v. a. to heap or lay up, to collect
Conges'tion, s. a collec ion of matter
Congla'ciate, v. a. to turn into ice, freeze
Conglo'bate, v. a. to gather into a hard ball
Congloba'tion, s. a round hard body
Conglob'ulate, v. n. to gather together into a little round mass
Conglom'erate, v. a. to make round, to wind up, to collect into one mass
Conglomera'tion, s. a heap, mixture
Conglutina'tion, s. act of glueing together
Con'gou, s. a finer sort of bohea tea
Congrat'ulant, a. rejoicing in participation
Congrat'ulate, v. to compliment on any happy event, to wish joy to ; to felicitate
Congratula'tion, s. a wishing of joy   [tary
Congrat'ulatory, a. wishing joy, complimen
Congree', v. n. to agree, to suit, to join
Congree't, v. n. to salute mutually
Con'gregate, a. collected, close, firm
Congrega'tion, s. an assembly, a collection
Con'gress, s. an assembly, a meeting; combat
Congres'sive, a. meeting, encountering
Congrue', v. n. to agree, to conform, to suit
Con'gruence Congru'ity, s. agreement, fituess
Con'gruen', a. suitable, agreeing
Con'gruious, a. meet, fit, agreeable, suitable
Cou'ic, Con'ical, a. in form of a cone
Con'ics, s. the doctrine of conic sections
Conjec'tor, Conjec'turer, s. a guesser
Conjec'tural, a. depending on a conjecture
Conjec'ture, s. a supposition, guess, idea
Conjec'ture, v. n. to suppose, to guess
Conjoi'n, v. a. to join, to connect, to league
Conjoi'ned, part. connected, united, near
Conjoi' tly, ad. in union, jointly, together
Con'jugal, a. belonging to marriage
Con'jugate, a. that springs from one original
Con'jugate, v. a. to join, to unite in marriage to vary a verb according to its tenses, &c.
Conjuga'tion, s. a pair, a couple; assemblage, union ; the form of inflecting verbs
Conjun'ct, a. conjoined, connected, united
Conjun'ction, s. an union, meeting together; a word connecting the clauses of a period
Conjun'ctive, a. closely joined together ; the mood of a verb
Conjun'cture, s. a peculiar or critical time
Conjura'tion, s. a plot, enchantment
Conju're, v. n. to enjoin solemnly, to conspire
Con'jure, v. a. to practise enchantments, &c.
Conju'red, part. bound by an oath
Con'jurer, s. an enchanter, a fortune-teller

Conlu'rement, *s.* a serious injunction
Connas'cence, *s.* community of birth
Conna'te, *a.* born with another
Connat'ural, *a.* suitable to nature
Connat'urally, *ad.* by nature, originally
Connec't, *v. a.* to unite, to join, to cement
Connec'ted, *part.* united, joined together
Connex', *v. a.* to unite together, to join
Connex'ion, *s.* an union, a relation
Conni'vance, *s.* the act of winking at a fault
Conni've, *v. n.* to wink at a fault, pass by
Connoisseu'r, *s.* a critic, a judge of letters
Connu'bial, *a.* relating to marriage, conjugal
Connutrit'ious, *a.* nourished together
Co'noid, *s.* a figure like a cone
Conquas'sate, *v. a.* to shake, to disorder
Con'quer, *v. a.* to overcome, to vanquish
Con'querable, *a.* possible to be vanquished
Con'queror, *s.* one who overcomes, a victor
Con'quest, *s.* victory, the thing gained
Consanguin'eous, *a.* near of kin, related
Consanguin'ity, *s.* relation by blood
Con'science, *s.* the faculty by which we judge of the goodness or wickedness of our own actions; veracity, reason; consciousness
Conscien'tious, *a.* scrupulous, just, exact
Con'scionable, *a.* reasonable, proper
Con'scious, *a.* inwardly persuaded, privy to
Con'sciously, *ad.* with inward persuasion
Con'sciousness, *s.* internal perception; internal sense of guilt or innocence
Con'script, *v.* written, registered, enrolled
Con'secrate, *v. a.* to make sacred, &c.
Consecra'tion, *s.* the act of making sacred
Consecta'neous, *a.* following of course
Consec'tary, *s.* a deduction—*a.* consequential
Consecu'tion, *s.* a train of consequences
Consec'utive, *a.* following in order, consequent
Consem'inate, *v. a.* to sow different seeds
Consen'sion, Consen't, *s.* concord, union
Consen't, *v. n.* to be of the same mind
Consenta'neous, *a.* agreeable to, consistent
Consen'tient, *a.* of the same opinion
Con'sequence, *s.* an effect; influence
Con'sequent, *a.* following naturally
Consequen'tial, *a.* conclusive; important
Con'sequently, *ad.* in or by consequence, necessarily, inevitably, pursuantly
Conser'tion, *s.* adaptation, junction
Conser'vancy, *s.* courts held for the preservation of the fishery on the river Thames
Conserva'tion, *s.* act of preserving
Conser'vative, *a.* having power to preserve
Conser'vatory, *s.* a place where any thing is preserved
Con'serve, *s.* a sweetmeat, preserved fruit
Conser've, *v. a.* to preserve or candy fruit
Conser'ver, *s.* one who lays up or preserves
Consid'er, *v.* to examine, to regard, to doubt
Consid'erable, *a.* worthy of regard, great
Consid'erably, *ad.* importantly, tolerably
Consid'erate, *a.* thoughtful, prudent
Consid'erately, *ad.* calmly, prudently, well
Considera'tion, *s.* regard, serious thought, prudence, reason, recompence
Consi'gn, *v. a.* to make over to another
Consi'gnment, *s.* the act of consigning
Consimil'ity, *s.* a joint likeness
Consis't, *v. n.* to subsist, to be made of

Consis'tence, Consis'tency, *s.* the natural state of bodies; agreement, substance
Consis'tent, *a.* conformable, firm
Consis'tently, *ad.* agreeably, properly
Consisto'rial, *a.* relating to a consistory
Con'sistory, *s.* spiritual court
Conso'ciate, *s.* an accomplice, an ally
Conso'ciate, *v. a.* to unite, to join, to cement
Consocia'tion, *s.* alliance, confederacy
Conso'lable, *a.* that which admits comfort
Consola'tion, *s.* alleviation of misery
Consol'atory, *a.* tending to give comfort
Conso'le, *v. a.* to cheer, to revive, to comfort
Conso'ler, *s.* one who gives comfort
Consol'idate, *v.* to harden, to combine
Consolida'tion, *s.* uniting in a solid mass
Con'sonance, *s.* an accord of sound, consistency, agreement; friendship, concord
Con'sonant, *a.* agreeable, suitable, fit
Con'sonant, *s.* a letter not sounded by itself
Con'sonous, *a.* harmonious, musical
Consopia'tion, *s.* the act of laying to sleep
Con'sort, *s.* a wife or husband, a companion
Consor't, *v.* to associate with, to marry
Conspectu'ity, *s.* sense of seeing, view
Conspicu'ity, *s.* brightness, clearness
Conspic'uous, *a.* easy to be seen, eminent
Conspic'uously, *ad.* remarkably, eminently
Conspic'uousness, *s.* clearness, renown
Conspir'acy, *s.* a plot, a lawless combination
Conspir'ator, Conspi'rer, *s.* a plotter
Conspi're, *v. n.* to plot, to agree, to concert
Conspurca'tion, *s.* defilement, pollution
Con'stable, *s.* a common peace officer
Con'stableship, *s.* the office of a constable
Con'stancy, *s.* firmness, continuance
Con'stant, *a.* firm, unchangeable, fixed
Con'stantly, *ad.* certainly, invariably, steadily
Constella'tion, *s.* a cluster of fixed stars
Consterna'tion, *s.* fear, astonishment, wonder
Con'stipate, *v. a.* to crowd, to thicken
Constipa'tion, *s.* the act of crowding together
Constit'uent, *a.* essential, composing
Constit'uent, *s.* one who deputes, an elector
Con'stitute, *v. a.* to make, depute, to set up
Constitu'tion, *s.* the frame of body or mind; law of a country, form of government
Constitu'tional, *a.* legal, according to the established government; radical
Con'stitutive, *a.* essential, able to establish
Constrai'n, *v. a.* to compel, to force, to press
Constrai'nable, *a.* liable to constraint
Constrai'nt, *s.* compulsion, confinement
Constric'tion, *s.* contraction, force
Constrin'ge, *v. a.* to compress, to bind
Constrin'gent, *a.* of a binding quality
Constru'ct, *v. a.* to build, to form, compile
Construc'tion, *s.* act of building, fabrication; meaning, interpretation; syntax
Construc'tive, *a.* capable of construction
Construc'ture, *s.* an edifice, a pile, a building
Con'strue, *v. a.* to translate, to interpret
Con'stuprate, *v. a.* to deflower, to debauch
Consubstan'tial, *a.* of the same substance
Consubstantial'ity, *s.* existence of two bodies in the same substance
Consubstan'tiate, *v. a.* to unite two bodies into one common substance or nature
Consubstantia'tion, *s.* the union of the body of our Saviour with the sacramental bread ment

E 3

Con'sul, s. the chief magistrate at Rome ; an officer appointed to superintend the trade of his nation in foreign countries

Con'sular, a. belonging to a consul

Con'sulate, Con'sulship, s. office of consul

Consult', v. a. to ask advice, to debate, plan

Consulta'tion, s. the act of consulting

Consu'mable, a. that may be destroyed

Consu'me, v. a. to waste, to spend, lessen

Consu'med, part. wasted away, lessened

Consu'mer, s. one who consumes

Consum'mate, v.a. to perfect, to complete

Consumma'tion, s. completion, perfection

Consump'tion, s. the act of wasting away or destroying ; a disease

Consum'ptive, a. wasting, destructive

Contab'ulate, v. a. to floor with boards

Con'tact, s. a touch, close union, juncture

Contac'tion, s. the act of touching, juncture

Conta'gion, s. an infection, a pestilence

Conta'gious, a. catching, infectious

Contain', v. a. to comprise, hold, restrain

Contai'nable, a. that may be contained

Contam'inate, v. a. to corrupt, to pollute

Contam'inate, a. polluted, corrupted

Contamina'tion, s. pollution, defilement

Contem'n, v. a. to scorn, neglect, despise

Contem'per, Contem'perate, v.a. to moderate by mixture ; to temper

Contem'perament, s. a degree of any quality

Contempera'tion, s. the act of tempering, a proportionate mixture of parts

Contem'plate, v. to meditate, study, muse

Contempla'tion, s. reflection, thought

Contem'plative, a. meditative, thoughtful

Contem'plator, s. one employed in study

Contem'porary, s. one who lives in the same age with another

Contem'porary, Contempora'neous, a. living at the same time, born in the same age

Contem'porise, v. a. to make contemporary

Contem'pt, s. disdain, scorn, vileness, hate

Contem'ptible, a. deserving scorn, vile

Contem'ptibly, ad. meanly, basely, vilely

Contem'ptuous, a. insolent, scornful, proud

Conten'd, v. to vie with, to strive, to contest

Conten'der, s. a combatant, hero, champion

Conten't, a. satisfied, willing, easy

Conten't, s. moderate happiness, satisfaction, extent—v. a. to gratify, to satisfy

Contenta'tion, s, satisfaction, easiness

Conten'ted, part. satisfied, not repining

Conten'tion, s. strife, quarrel, debate, zeal

Conten'tious, a. quarrelsome, cross, perverse

Conten'tless, a. discontented, uneasy

Content'ment, s. satisfaction, gratification

Conten'ts, s. the heads of a book, an index ; what is contained in any thing, amount

Conter'minous, a. bordering upon, near

Con'test, s. a dispute, quarrel, debate

Contes't, v. to wrangle, debate, vie with

Contes'table, a. disputable, doubtful

Context', v. a. to weave together

Con'text, s. series of a discourse—a. united

Con'texture, s. the disposition of parts one among another ; the constitution

Contigu'ity, s. actual contact

Contig'uous, a. meeting so as to touch

Con'tinence, or Con'tinency, s. chastity, moderation, forbearance ; continuity

Con'tinent, a. chaste, sober, abstemious

Con'tinent, s. land not disjoined by the sea from other land ; what contains any thing

Contin'gent, s. casual, uncertain

Contin'gent, s. chance, proportion, quota

Contin'ual, a. uninterrupted, incessant

Contin'ually, ad. without ceasing, ever

Contin'uance, s. permanence, duration ; abode

Contin'uate, a. continual, uninterrupted

Continua'tion, s. a constant succession

Contin'ue, v. to remain in the same state ; to persevere, to dwell, to last, to protract

Continu'ity, s. uninterrupted connexion

Contor't, v. a. to twist, to torture, to writhe

Contor'tion, s. a strain, a twist, a flexure

Contou'r, s. the outline of a figure

Con'traband, a. unlawful, illegal, prohibited

Con'tract, s. an agreement, a bargain

Contrac't, v. to bargain; to betroth; to shrink up ; to shorten ; to bring, to procure

Contrac'tible, a. that may be contracted

Contrac'tile, a. able to contract itself

Contrac'tion, s. an abbreviation, the act of shortening, the state of being contracted

Contrac'tor, s. one who makes bargains

Contradic't, v.a. to deny, to oppose verbally

Contradic'ter, s. a denier, an opposer

Contradic'tion, s. opposition, inconsistency

Contradic'tory, a. inconsistent with[qualities

Contradistin'ction, s. distinction by opposite

Contraregular'ity, s. contrariety to rule

Contra'riant, a. inconsistent, cross

Con'traries, s. propositions that oppose

Contrari'ety, s. inconsistency, opposition

Con'trarily, ad. in a different manner

Con'trariwise, ad. on the contrary

Con'trary, a. disagreeing, opposite, adverse

Con'trast, s. an opposition ; dissimilitude

Contras't, v. a. to place in opposition

Contras'ted, part. set in opposition to

Contravalla'tion, s. an opposite fortification

Contrave'ne, v. a. to oppose, to hinder

Contrave'ner, s. he who opposes another

Contraven'tion, s. opposition, obstruction

Contrib'utary, a. paying tribute to the same sovereign

Contrib'ute, v. to bear a part, to give

Contrib'uting, part. helping, assisting

Contribu'tion, s. the act of contributing ; levy, a military exaction

Contrib'utory, a. promoting the same end

Contris'tate, v. a. to make sorrowful

Con'trite, a. truly penitent, very sorrowful

Contri'tion, s. penitence ; act of grinding

Contri'vance, s. a scheme, an art, a plot

Contri've, v. a. to invent, plan, project

Contri'ver, s. an inventor, a schemer

Contro'l, s. authority, power, restraint, check

Contro'l, v. a. to govern, confute, restrain

Contro'llable, a. subject to control

Contro'ller, s. one who has power to control

Contro'llership, s. the office of a controller

Contro'lment, s. restraint, opposition

Controver'sial, a. relating to disputes

Con'troversy, s. a quarrel, dispute, enmity

Controver't, v.a. to dispute, debate, quarrel

Controver'tible, a. disputable, uncertain

Con'trovertist, s. a disputant, a reasoner

Contuma'cious, a. perverse, obstinate

Contuma'ciously, ad. perversely, obstinate

Contuma'ciousness, or Con'tumacy, s. obstinacy, perverseness, stubbornness

Contume'lious, *a.* reproachful, brutal, rude
Con'tumely, *s.* reproach, rudeness
Contn'se, *v. a.* to bruise, to beat together
Coutu'sion, *s.* a bruise, act of bruising
Convales'cence, *s.* a renewal of health
Convales'cent, *a.* recovering, &c.
Conve'nable, *a.* consistent with, fit
Conve'ne, *v.* to call together, to assemble
Conve'nience, *s.* propriety, fitness, ease
Conve'nient, *a.* well adapted, suitable, fit
Conve'niently, *ad.* fitly, commodiously
Con'vent, *s.* a religious house, a nunnery
Conven'ticle, *s.* an assembly for worship, a meeting house, a secret assembly
Conven'tion, *s.* an assembly; an agreement or contract for a limited time
Conven'tional, *a.* done by contract; stipulated
Conven'tionary, *a.* settled by contract
Conven'tual, *a.* belonging to a convent
Conver'ge, *v. n.* to tend to one point
Conver'gent, *a.* tending to one point
Conver'sable, *a.* fit for conversation, sociable
Con'versant, *a.* acquainted with, skilled in
Conversa'tion, *s.* familiar discourse, chat
Conver'sative, *a.* relating to public life
Con'verse, *s.* manner of discoursing in familiar life, acquaintance, familiarity
Conver'se, *v. n.* to discourse, to cohabit with
Con'verse, *a.* contrary, directly opposite
Conver'sely, *ad.* by a change of order or place
Conver'sion, *s.* change from one state into another; transmutation; change from one religion to another
Con'vert, *s.* one whose opinion is changed
Conver'it, *v. a.* to change, turn, appropriate
Conver'ter, *s.* one who makes converts
Conver'tible, *a.* susceptible of change
Con'vex, *a.* rising in a circular form, as the outside of a globe; opposite to concave
Con'vex, *s.* a convex or spherical body
Convex'ity, *s.* a spherical form, rotundity
Convey', *v. a.* to carry, send, make over
Convey'ance, *s.* act of removing any thing; a deed or writing, by which property is transferred; secret management, &c.
Convey'ancer, *s.* a lawyer who draws up writings by which property is transferred
Convey'er, *s.* one who carries or transmits
Convic'it, *v. a.* to prove guilty, to detect
Con'vict, *s.* one convicted or detected
Convic'tion, *s.* detection of guilt, full proof
Convic'tive, *a.* tending to convince
Convin'ce, *a.* to make one sensible of, to prove one guilty of, to prove
Convin'cible, *a.* capable of conviction
Convin'cingly, *ad.* without room to doubt
Convi've, *v. a.* to entertain, to revel, to feast
Conviv'ial, *a.* gay, social, festive, pleasing
Conun'drum, *s.* a quibble, low jest, quirk
Con'vocate, *v. a.* to summon or call together
Convoca'tion, *s.* an ecclesiastical assembly
Convo'ke, *v. a.* to call or summon together
Convol've, *v. a.* to roll together, wind, turn
Convolu'ted, *a.* rolled upon itself, twisted
Convolu'tion, *s.* a rolling together
Convoy', *v. a.* to accompany for defence
Con'voy, *s.* an attendance for defence
Con'usance, *s.* cognisance; notice
Convul'se, *v. a.* to give a violent motion
Convul'sion, *s.* an involuntary and irregular contraction of the muscles, fibres, &c.

Convul'sive, *a.* affected with convulsions
Con'ey, *s.* a rabbit, an animal that burrows in the ground
Coo, *v. n.* to cry as a dove or pigeon
Cook, *s.* one who dresses victuals, &c.
Cook, *v. a.* to dress or prepare victuals, &c.
Coo'kery, *s.* the art of dressing victuals
Cool, *v.* to make or grow cool, to quiet
Cool, *a.* somewhat cold, not fond
Coo'ler, *s.* a brewing vessel used to cool beer in; what cools the body
Coo'lly, *ad.* without heat or passion
Coo'lness, *s.* gentle cold; want of affection, freedom from passion, indifference
Coom, *s.* soot, dust, grease from wheels
Coomb, *s.* a corn measure of four bushels
Coop, *s.* a wooden cage for poultry; a barrel
Coop, *v. a.* to shut up, confine, cage, restrain
Coopee', *s.* a motion in dancing
Coo'per, *s.* a maker of coops or barrels
Co-op'erate, *v. n.* to labour for the same end
Co-opera'tion, *s.* the act of jointly contributing or concurring to the same end; election, choice, assumption
Co-opera'tive, *a.* promoting the same end
Co-opta'tion, *s.* adoption, assumption
Co-or'dinate, *a.* holding the same rank
Coot, *s.* a small black water fowl
Cop, *s.* the top of any thing, the head
Co'pal, *s.* the Mexican term for a gum
Copar'cenary, Copar'ceny, *s.* joint succession to any inheritance
Copar'tner, *s.* a joint partner in business
Copar'tnership, *s.* the having an equal share
Cope, *s.* a priest's cloak; a concave arch
Cope, *v.* to contend with, to oppose, struggle
Co'pesmate, *s.* a companion, friend, associate
Cop'ier, Cop'yist, *s.* a copier; an imitator
Co'ping, *s.* the covering of a wall
Co'pious, *a.* plentiful, abundant, full
Co'piously, *ad.* plentifully; without brevity
Co'piousness, *s.* plenty; exuberance of style
Cop'ped, Cop'pled, *a.* rising in a conic form
Cop'pel, *s.* an instrument used in chemistry. Its use is to try and purify gold and silver
Cop'per, *s.* a metal; a large boiler
Cop'peras, *s.* a sort of mineral, or vitriol
Cop'per-plate, *s.* an impression from a figure engraved on copper; the plate on which any thing is engraved for printing
Cop'persmith, *s.* a manufacturer of copper
Cop'pery, *a.* tasting of, or mixed with, copper
Cop'pice, Copse, *s.* a wood of small low trees
Cop'pledust, *s.* a powder for purifying metals
Cop'ulate, *v.* to mix, conjoin, unite
Copula'tion, *s.* the congress of the two sexes
Cop'ulative, *a.* mixing or joining together
Cop'y, *s.* a transcript from an original, a pattern, an imitation; a picture drawn from another picture
Cop'y, *v.* to transcribe, write from, imitate
Cop'y-book, *s.* a book in which copies are written for learners to imitate
Cop'yhold, *s.* a tenure under the lord of manor, held by the copy of a court roll
Cop'yholder, *s.* one possessed of copyhold land
Copyright, *s.* the sole right to print a book
Coquet', *v. a.* to deceive in love, jilt
Coqu'try, *s.* deceit in love; affectation

Coquet'te, *s.* a gay, airy girl, who by various arts endeavours to gain admirers
Cor'al, *s.* a sea plant, a child's ornament
Cor'alline, *a.* consisting of coral
Cora'nt, *s.* a nimble sprightly dance
Corb, *s.* a basket used in coaleries
Cor'ban, *s.* an alms-basket, a gift, an alms
Cord, *s.* a rope; a sinew; a measure of wood
Cord, *v. a.* to fasten or tie with cords
Cor'dage, *s.* the ropes for a ship
Cor'date, *a.* heart shaped
Cordelier', *s.* a Franciscan friar
Cor'dial, *s.* a cherishing, reviving draught
Cor'dial, *a.* reviving, hearty, sincere
Cordial'ity, *s.* affection, sincerity, esteem
Cor'dially, *ad.* sincerely, truly, heartily
Cor'dwain, *s.* a fine Spanish leather
Cor'dwainer, Cor'diner, *s.* a shoemaker
Cor'dwood, *s.* wood tied up for firing
Core, *s.* the heart or inner part of a thing
Coria'ceous, *a.* consisting of or like leather
Corian'der, *s.* a plant, a hot seed
Cor'inth, *s.* the fruit usually called currant
Corinth'ian-*order*. *s.* the name of the fourth order in architecture
Cork, *s.* a tree resembling the ilex; its bark, the stopple of a bottle—*v. a.* to stop up
Cor'kscrew, *s.* a screw to draw corks with
Cor'morant, *s.* a bird of prey; a glutton
Corn, *s.* a grain; seeds which grow in ears, not in pods; an excrescence on the feet
Corn, *v. a.* to salt, to granulate
Cor'nchandler, *s.* a retailer of corn
Cor'nel, *s.* a plant, the cornelian cherry
Corne'lian, *s.* a precious stone
Cor'neous, *a.* horny, resembling horn
Cor'ner, *s.* an angle; a secret or remote place; the utmost limit, or extremity
Cor'net, *s.* a musical instrument; the officer who bears the standard of a troop of horse
Cor'neter, *s.* one who plays on a cornet
Cor'nice, *s.* the uppermost ornament of a wall or wainscot, the top of a column
Cor'nicle, *s.* a small horn
Cornig'erous, *a.* horned, having horns
Cornuco'pia, *s.* the horn of plenty
Cornu'te, *v. a.* to bestow horns; to cuckold
Cornu'te, *a.* shaped like a horn
Cornu'ted, *part.* having horns, cuckolded
Cornu'to, *s.* a cuckold; a man horned
Cor'ollary, *s.* an inference, surplus, deduction
Cor'ollated, *a.* having flowers like a crown
Cor'onal, *s.* a garland, a chaplet—*a.* relating to the top of the head
Cor'onary, *a.* relating to a crown
Corona'tion, *s.* act or solemnity of crowning
Cor'oner, *s.* a civil officer, who, with a jury, inquires into casual or violent deaths
Cor'onet, *s.* a crown worn by nobility
Cor'poral, *s.* the lowest officer of the infantry
Corpo'real, Cor'poral, *a.* bodily, material
Corporal'ity, *s.* state of being embodied
Corpora'lly, *ad.* bodily
Cor'porate, *a.* united in a body
Corpora'tion, *s.* a body politic, authorised by common consent to grant in law any thing within the compass of their charter
Corps, *s.* a body of soldiers, a regiment
Corpse, *s.* a dead body, a corse, a carcase
Cor'pulence, *s.* bulkiness of body, fleshiness
Cor'pulent, *a.* fleshy, fat, bulky

Cor'puscle, *s.* a small body, an atom
Corru'de, *v. a.* to rub off, to scrape together
Corradia'tion, *s.* an union of rays in a point
Correc't, *v. a.* to mend faults, to punish
Correc't, *a.* finished with exactness
Correc'tion, *s.* amendment, punishment
Correc'tive, *a.* able to correct or alter, good
Correc'tly, *ad.* exactly, accurately, neatly
Correc'tness, *s.* exactness, accuracy, nicety
Corre'gidor, *s.* a chief magistrate in Spain
Cor'relate, *s.* what stands in opposite rela.
Correl'ative, *a.* having a reciprocal relati.
Correp'tion, *s.* reproof, blame, chiding
Correspon'd, *v. n.* to agree, to suit, to fit, to keep up a commerce with another by letters
Correspon'dence, *s.* friendship, intercourse, interchange of civilities; agreement, fitness
Correspon'dent, *a.* answerable, suitable
Correspon'dent, *s.* one with whom correspondence is kept up by mutual letters
Cor'rigible, *a.* corrective, punishable
Corrob'orant, *a.* confirming, strengthening
Corrob'orate, *v. a.* to confirm, to establish
Corrobora'tion, *s.* the act of strengthening
Corro'de, *v. a.* to eat by degrees
Corro'dible, *a.* that which may be corroded
Corro'sible, *a.* possible to be consumed by a menstruum
Corro'sion, *s.* the act of eating away
Corro'sive, *s.* a corroding medicine
Corro'sive, *a.* able to consume or corrode
Corro'siveness, *s.* the quality of corroding
Cor'rugate, *v. a.* to wrinkle or purse up
Corrup't, *v.* to defile, to taint, to bribe
Corrup't, *a.* debauched, vicious, rotten
Corrup'ter, *s.* one who corrupts or taints
Corrup'tible, *a.* that which may be corrupted
Corrup'tion, *s.* wickedness, matter or pus
Corrup'tive, *a.* able to corrupt or taint [cence
Corrup'tness, *s.* badness of morals, putres-
Cor'sair, *s.* a plunderer on the seas, a pirate
Corse, *s.* a dead or putrid body, a carcase
Cor'selet, or Cor'slet, *s.* a light armour for the fore part of the body
Cortes, *s.* representatives of the Spanish states
Cor'tical, *a.* barky, belonging to the bark
Cor'ticated, *a.* resembling the bark of a tree
Cor'vet, Corvet'to, *s.* the curvet, a frolic
Corus'cant, *a.* glittering, flashing, bright
Corusca'tion, *s.* a quick vibration of light
Cosmet'ic, *s.* a wash to improve the skin
Cos'mical, *a.* relating to the world; rising or setting with the sun
Cosmog'ony, *s.* the creation of the world
Cosmog'rapher, *s.* one who writes a description of the world
Cosmog'raphy, *s.* the science of the general system of the world
Cosmop'olite, *s.* a citizen of the world
Cos'set, *s.* a lamb brought up by the hand
Cost, *s.* expense, price, charge, luxury, loss
Cost, *v. n.* to be bought for, had at a price
Cos'tal, *a.* relating or belonging to the ribs
Cos'tard, *s.* a head, a sort of large apple
Cos'tive, *a.* bound in the body, restringe
Cos'tliness, *s.* expensiveness, extravagance
Cos'tly, *a.* dear, expensive; of great price
Cot, Cot'tage, *s.* a hut, a very small house
Cotem'porary, *see* Contem'porary
Coterie', *s.* an assembly, society, club
Cotil'lion, *s.* a light French dance

Cot'quean, s. a man who busies himself with women's affairs

Cot'tager, s. one who lives in a hut

Cot'ton, s. a plant; the down of the cotton tree; stuff or cloth made of cotton

Couch, v. to lie down; to fix; to hide

Couch, s. a seat of repose; a layer

Cou'chant, a. lying down, squatting

Cou'cher, s. he that possesseth cataracts

Cove, s. a small bay or creek; a shelter

Cov'enant, v. to contract, bargain, agree

Cov'enant, s. a contract, bargain, deed

Covenantee', s. a stipulator, a bargainer

Cov'enous, a. fraudulent, treacherous, base

Cov'er, v. a. to overspread; hide; conceal

Cov'er, s. concealment, pretence, screen

Cov'ering, s. dress; any thing that covers

Cov'erlet, Cov'erlid, s. the outermost covering of a bed, the counterpane or quilt

Cov'ert, s. a retreat, a thicket, a hiding place

Cov'ert, a. sheltered, secret; state of a woman sheltered by marriage

Cov'et, v. a. to desire earnestly; to long for

Cov'etable, a. that which may be longed for

Cov'etous, a. desirous of saving, greedy

Cov'ey, s. an old bird with her young; a hatch; a company; a number of birds together

Cough, s. a convulsion of the lungs

Cov'in, s. a deceitful agreement, a collusion

Coul'ter, s. a ploughshare

Coun'cil, s. an assembly for consultation

Coun'sel, s. advice, direction; a pleader

Coun'sel, v. a. to direct, to advise

Coun'sellor, s. one who gives advice

Count, s. reckoning, number; a foreign title

Count, v. a. to cast up, to number, to account

Coun'tenance, s. form of the face; look; aspect of assurance; patronage

Coun'tenance, v. a. to patronise, to support

Coun'ter, s. a shop table; base money

Coun'ter, ad. contrary to; in a wrong way

Counteract', v. a. to act contrary to; hinder

Counterbal'ance, s. an opposite weight

Counterbal'ance, v. a. to act against with an opposite weight

Counterbuff', v. a. to repel, to strike back

Coun'terchange, s. a mutual exchange

Coun'tercharm, s. that by which a charm is broke—v. a. to destroy an enchantment

Coun'tercheck, s. a stop; reproof, rebuke

Counterev'idence, s. opposite testimony

Coun'terfeit, a. forged, deceitful, seditious

Coun'terfeit, v. a. to forge, to imitate

Countermand', v. a. to contradict an order

Coun'termarch, s. a march backward

Coun'termine, s. a mine made to frustrate the use of one made by the enemy

Countermine', v. a. to defeat secretly

Coun'termotion, s. a contrary motion

Coun'terpane, s. the upper covering of a bed

Coun'terpart, s. a correspondent part

Coun'terplea, s. a replication in law

Coun'terplead, v. a. to contradict, to deny

Coun'terplot, s. an artifice opposed to an artifice; plot against plot

Coun'terpoint, s. a coverlet woven in squares

Coun'terpoise, s. an equivalence of weight

Counterpoise', v. a. to counterbalance

Counterpro'ject, s. correspondent scheme

Coun'terscarp, s. a ditch next a camp

Countersign', v. a. to undersign; to confirm

Counterten'or, s. a middle part in music

Counterti'de, s. a contrary tide

Coun'terturn, s. the height of a play

Countervail', v. a. to be equivalent to; to have equal value or force—s. equal weight

Coun'terview, s. a contrast, an opposition

Coun'tess, s. the lady of a count or earl

Coun'tless, a. infinite, innumerable

Coun'try, s. a tract of land; one's native soil; a region; rural parts; not cities

Coun'try, a. rural, rustic; unpolite

Coun'tryman, s. a rustic; a husbandman; one born in the same country

Coun'ty, s. a shire; an earldom; a count

Coun'ty, a. belonging to a county or shire

Coupee', s. a motion in dancing; a caper

Coup'le, s. a brace, a pair; man and wife

Coup'le, v. a. to join together; to marry

Coup'let, s. two verses, a pair

Cour'age, s. bravery, active fortitude

Coura'geously, ad. bravely, nobly, stoutly

Couran'to, s. a nimble, sprightly dance; series of consequences

Cou'rier, s. a messenger sent in haste

Course, s. a career; a race; a race-ground; track in which a ship sails; service of meat; order of succession; method of life; settled rule; natural bent; empty form

Course, v. to pursue, to hunt, to rove about

Cour'ser, s. a horse-racer, a race-horse

Cours'ing, s. pursuit of hares with hounds

Court, s. the residence of a prince; a narrow street; seat of justice; jurisdiction

Court, v. a. to make love to, to woo a woman

Cour'teous, a. elegant of manners, kind

Court'eousness, s. complaisance, civility

Courtesan', s. a lewd woman, a prostitute

Cour'tesy, s. complaisance, civility, favour

Cour'tier, s. an attendant on a court; a lover

Courtleet', s. court of the lord of the manor for regulating copyhold tenures, &c.

Court'like, a. polite, elegant, well-bred

Court'liness, s. civility, complaisance

Court'ly, a. soft, elegant, flattering

Court'ship, s. the act of wooing a woman

Cous'in, s. any one collaterally related more remotely than brothers or sisters

Cow, s. the female of the bull—v. to deject

Cow'ard, s. he who wants courage; a poltroon

Cow'ardice, s. pusillanimity, fear

Cow'ardly, a. fearful, timorous, mean

Cow'er, v. n. to sink by bending the knees

Cow'herd, s. one who keeps or tends cows

Cowl, s. a monk's hood; a vessel for water

Cow'led, part. rolled up conically

Cow'slip, s. a small early yellow flower

Cox'comb, s. a cock's topping, a beau, a fop

Coxcom'ical, a. foppish, conceited, pert

Coy, a. modest, reserved, decent, shy

Coy'ish, a. rather shy, chaste, modest

Coy'ness, s. reserve, modesty, shyness

Coz'en, v. a. to cheat, to defraud, to trick

Coz'enage, s. fraud, cheat, deceit, trick

Coz'ener, s. a cheater, a knave

Crab, s. a fish; a wild apple; a peevish person

Crab'bed, a. peevish, morose, cynical

Crab'bedly, ad. peevishly, morosely

Crab'bedness, s. sourness of taste; asperity

Crack, s. a chink; a sudden noise; a boaster

Crack, v. a. to break into chinks; to split

Crack'brained, a. crazy, wanting reason
Crack'er, s. a kind of squib; a boaster
Crack'le, v. a. to make slight cracks, &c.
Crack'ling, s. a noise made by slight cracks
Crack'nel, s. a kind of hard brittle cake
Cra'dle, s. a moveable bed on which children are agitated; a frame of wood for launching a ship; a case for a broken bone
Craft, s. art; cunning; small sailing ships
Craf'tily, ad. artfully, cunningly
Craf'tiness, s. cunning, craft, deceit, fraud
Craf'tsman, s. a mechanic, an artificer
Craf'ty, a. cunning, deceitful, artful
Crag, s. a steep rock; nape of the neck
Crag'ged, Crag'gy, a. rugged, rough
Crag'gedness, Crag'giness, s. roughness
Cram, v. n. to stuff; to eat greedily
Cram'bo, s. a play at which one gives a word and another finds a rhyme
Cramp, s. a contraction of the limbs; a piece of iron bent at one end; restriction
Cramp, v. a. to restrain, obstruct, confine
Cramp, a. difficult, troublesome, hard
Cram'piron, s. an iron to fasten together
Crane, s. a bird; a crooked pipe; a machine
Cra'nium, s. the skull
Crank, s. end of an iron axis; a conceit
Crank, a. lusty, healthy, easily overset
Cran'kle, v. a. to run into angles; to break into unequal surfaces
Cran'nied, a. full of or having chinks
Cran'ny, s. a chink; a little crack; a cleft
Crape, s. a thin stuff used in mourning
Crap'ulence, s. sickness from drunkenness
Crap'ulous, a. sick with intemperance
Crash, v. a. to break, to bruise, to make a noise
Crash, s. a loud mixed noise by a fall
Cras'situde, s. grossness, heaviness, coarseness
Cratch, s. a rack for hay or straw [ness]
Crate, s. a hamper to pack earthenware in
Cravat', s. a neckcloth
Crave, v. a. to ask earnestly, beg; to long for
Cra'ven, s. a conquered cock, a coward
Craunch, v. a. to crash with the teeth
Craw, s. the crop or first stomach of birds
Craw'fish, Cray'fish, s. the river lobster
Crawl, v. n. to creep; move slowly; cringe
Cray'on, s. a paste; a drawing, a pencil
Craze, v. a. to break, to crack the brain
Cra'ziness, s. weakness, feebleness of body
Cra'zy, a. feeble, weak, broken; sickly
Creak, v. n. to make a harsh noise
Cream, s. the oily part of milk
Crea'mfaced, a. looking pale, cowardly, wan
Crea'my, a. full of cream; rich, luscious
Crease, s. a plait or fold—v. a. to mark by folding
Crea'te, v. a. to produce, to cause, to form
Crea'tion, s. act of creating; the world
Crea'tive, a. having the power to produce
Crea'tor, s. the Being who bestows existence
Crea'ture, s. a being created; an animal not human; a dependant; general term for man; a word of tenderness or contempt
Cre'dence, s. credit, belief, reputation
Creden'da, s. articles of faith or belief
Cre'dent, a. easy of belief; having credit
Creden'tials, s. letters of recommendation
Credibil'ity, Cred'ibleness, s. a just claim to credit; worthiness of belief, probability

Cred'ible, a. worthy of credit; probable
Cred'it, s. belief; influence; trust reposed
Cred'it, v. a. to believe, repose confidence
Cred'itable, a. reputable, worthy of esteem
Cred'itably, ad. reputably, with honour
Cred'itor, s. one who trusts or gives credit
Credu'lity, s. easiness of belief
Cred'ulous, a. apt to believe, unsuspecting
Creed, s. a confession of faith, a belief
Creek, s. a small bay; a corner, a nook
Creep, v. n. to move slowly; bend, fawn, &c.
Creep'er, s. a plant; an iron instrumen
Crema'tion, s. the act of burning
Cre'mor, s. a creamy or milky substance
Cre'nated, a. indented, notched, rough
Crepita'tion, s. a low, crackling noise
Crepus'cule, s. twilight; glimmering light
Crepus'culous, a. glimmering, faint light, dim
Cres'cent, s. an increasing moon, half moon
Cres'cent, Cres'cive, a. increasing, growing
Cress, s. the name of a water herb
Cres'set, s. a light set on a beacon; an herb
Crest, s. a plume of feathers on the top of a helmet; ornament of the helmet in heraldry; spirit; pride; any tuft on the head
Cres'ted, a. ornamented with a crest
Cres't-fallen, a. dejected, spiritless, low
Cres'tless, a. without armour; poor, mean
Creta'ceous, a. chalky, having chalk
Crev'ice, s. a cleft, a crack; a fish
Crew, s. a ship's company; mean assembly
Crew'el, s. a ball of worsted yarn, &c.
Crib, s. a stall, a manger; a cottage
Crib, v. a. to steal privately; to shut up
Crib'bage, s. the name of a game at cards
Crib'ble, s. a sieve used for cleaning corn
Cribra'tion, s. the act of cleansing or sifting
Crick, s. noise of a hinge; pain in the neck
Crick'et, s. a game with bats and balls; an insect that chirps about ovens, &c.; a stool
Cri'er, s. one who cries goods for sale
Crime, s. an offence, sin, wickedness
Cri'meless, a. innocent, pure from guilt
Crim'inal, Crim'inous, a. faulty, wicked
Crim'inal, s. a person accused or guilty
Crimina'tion, s. accusation, charge, censure
Crim'inatory, a. tending to accuse or censure
Crim'inous, a. guilty, iniquitous, wicked
Crim'osin, s. a species of red colour
Crimp, a. crisp, brittle, easily crumbled
Crim'ple, v. a. to contract, to curl up
Crim'son, s. a very deep red colour
Crin'cum, s. a whimsy, a contradiction
Cringe, s. servility, mean reverence
Crink, Crin'kle, s. a wrinkle; fold, winding
Crin'kle, v. to run in wrinkles or folds
Cri'nose, Crinig'erous, a. hairy, wild, rough
Crip'ple, s. a lame person—v. a. to make lame
Cri'sis, s. a critical time or turn
Crisp, v. a. to indent, to curl; make brittle
Crisp, Cris'py, a. brittle, curled, winding
Crispa'tion, s. the act of curling; curled state
Crisp'ness, Cris'pitude, s. crispy state
Crite'rion, s. a mark by which any thing is judged of, as to its goodness or badness
Crit'ic, s. one versed in criticism, a censor
Crit'ical, a. accurate, judicious; captious
Crit'icise, v. a. to judge, to censure, to blame
Crit'icism, s. art of judging, remark
Criti'que, s. act of criticising; a criticism
Croak, s. the cry of a frog, crow, or raven

Cro'ceous, a. yellow, like saffron
Crecita'tion, s. the croaking of ravens or frogs
Crock, s. an earthen vessel, an earthen pot
Crock'ery, s. all kinds of earthen ware
Croc'odile, s. a large, voracious, amphibious animal, in shape resembling a lizard
Cro'cus, s. an early flower; saffron
Croft, s. a small home field, a close
Crone, s. an old ewe; an old woman
Cro'ny, s. a friend, an acquaintance
Crook, s. a sheep-hook, a hooked stick
Crook, v. a. to bend, to pervert
Crook'ed, a. bent, perverse, winding
Crop, s. the produce; a bird's stomach
Crop, v. a. to lop, cut short; to reap, to mow
Crop'ful, a. quite full, crammed, satisfied
Cro'sier, s. the pastoral staff of a bishop
Cros'let, s. a small cross; a head cloth
Cross, s. one straight body laid at right angles over another; a misfortune; vexation
Cross, a. thwart, oblique; fretful, captious
Cross, v. a. to lay athwart; to cancel; to pass over; to vex; to sign with the cross
Cross'bite, s. a deception—v. a. to cheat
Cross'bow, s. a weapon for shooting
Cross'grained, a. ill-natured, troublesome
Cross'ness, s. peevishness, perverseness
Crotch, s. a hook; the fork of a tree
Crot'chet, s. one of the notes in music, equal to half a minum; a mark in printing formed thus []; a conceit, whim, fancy
Crouch, v. to stoop low, to cringe, fawn
Croupa'de, s. a high leap; a summerset
Crow, s. a bird; an iron lever—v. to make the noise of a cock; to vapour, to boast
Crowd, s. a confused multitude; the populace
Crowd, v. to press close, to swarm
Crown, s. a diadem worn on the head denoting royal dignity; a silver coin; the top of the head; regal power; a garland
Crown, v. a. to invest with a crown; to adorn; to complete; to reward
Cru'cial, a. transverse, running across
Cru'ciate, v. a. to torment, to torture, to pain
Cru'cible, s. a pot used to melt metals
Cru'cifix, s. a representation in painting, statuary, &c. of our Saviour's passion
Crucifix'ion, s. the act of nailing to the cross
Cru'ciform, a. shaped like a cross
Cru'cify, v. a. to nail or fasten to a cross
Crude, Cru'dy, a. unripe, raw, undigested
Cru'deness, Cru'dity, s. indigestion, harshness
Cru'die, v. a. to congeal, to turn to curds
Cru'el, a. hard-hearted, fierce, inhuman
Cru'elty, s. inhumanity, want of feeling
Cru'et, s. a phial for oil or vinegar
Cruise, v. n. to sail in quest of an enemy
Crui'ser, s. a ship that sails in quest of an enemy, or of plunder
Crumb, s. the soft part of bread; a small fragment or piece of bread
Crum'ble, v. a. to break or fall into pieces
Crum'my, a. full of crumbs, soft, plump
Crum'ple, v. a. to wrinkle, disorder, ruffle
Crum'pling, s. a small green codling
Crup'per, s. a leather to keep a saddle right
Cru'ral, a. relating or belonging to the leg
Crusa'de, Croisa'de, s. an expedition against infidels; a Portugal coin, value 2s. 6d.
Cru'set, s. a goldsmith's melting pot
Crush, v. a. to bruise, to squeeze; to ruin

Crush, s. a falling down, a crash, a collision
Crust, s. any shell or external coat; case of a pye baked; outward part of bread
Crusta'ceous, a. shelly, with joints
Crus'ty, a. snappish, morose, captious, surly
Crutch, s. a support used by cripples
Cry, v. to weep, to call, proclaim, exclaim
Cry, s. a weeping, outcry, shriekin
Cryp'tic, Cryp'tical, a. secret, hidden
Cryptog'raphy, s. secret kind of writing
Crys'tal, s. a mineral, transparent stone
Crys'talline, a. transparent, bright, clear
Crystalliza'tion, s. congelation into crystals
Crys'tallize, v. a. to form salts into small transparent bodies; to freeze, to congeal
Cub, s. the young of a beast, generally of a fox or bear—v. a. to bring forth
Cu'batory, a. recumbent, easy, lying down
Cu'bature, s. the solid contents of a body
Cube, s. a square solid body; a die
Cu'bic, Cu'bical, a. formed like a cube
Cu'bit, s. a measure of eighteen inches
Cu'bital, a. as long as a cubit
Cuck'ing-stool, s. an engine invented for the punishment of scolds, and unquiet women
Cuck'old, s. the husband of an adultress
Cuck'old, v. a. to commit adultery
Cuck'oldy, a. mean, poor, despicable, base
Cuck'oo, s. a bird; a word of contempt
Cu'cumber, s. name of a plant, and its fruit
Cud, s. food reposited in the first stomach of an animal, to be chewed
Cud'den, Cud'dy, s. a blockhead, a clown
Cud'dle, v. n. to lie close or low, to hug
Cud'gel, s. a fighting-stick—v. a. to fight or beat with sticks
Cue, s. the end of a thing; intimation, hint
Cuff, s. a blow, a box; part of a sleeve
Cuirass, s. a breastplate of leather or steel
Cuirassie'r, s. a soldier in armour
Cuish, s. armour that covers the thighs
Cu'linary, a. belonging to the kitchen
Cul'leader, s. a draining vessel
Cul'ly, s. a man duped by a woman
Culm, s. a kind of small coal, soot, &c.
Cul'minate, v. n. to be in the meridian
Cul'pable, a. criminal, guilty, blameable
Cul'prit, s. a man arraigned before a judge
Cul'tivate, v. a. to manure, till, improve
Cultiva'tion, s. act of improving soils, &c.
Cul'ture, s. act of cultivation, improvement, melioration—v. a. to till, to manure
Cul'ver, s. a pigeon, a wood-pigeon
Cul'verin, s. a species of ordnance
Cum'ber, v. a. to embarrass, to entangle
Cum'bersome, Cum'brous, a. burthensome, embarrassing, vexatious, oppressive
Cum'bersomeness, s. hindrance
Cu'mulate, v. a. to heap or pile up, to amass
Cumula'tion, s. the act of heaping up
Cund, v. a. to give notice, to inform, show
Cu'neated, Cu'neal, Cune'iform, a. relating to a wedge; having the form of a wedge
Cun'ning, a. artful, skilful, subtle, crafty
Cun'ning, Cun'ningness, s. artifice, slyness
Cun'ningly, ad. artfully, craftily, slily
Cup, s. a drinking vessel; a part of a flower
Cup, v. a. to draw blood by scarification
Cup'bearer, s. an officer of the household
Cup'board, s. a case where victuals, &c. are
Cu'pel, Cup'pel, s. a refining vessel [pu

Cupid'ity, s. sensual desire, concupiscence
Cu'pola, s. a dome, an arched roof
Cur, s. a dog; a snappish or mean man
Cu'rable, a. that which admits of a remedy
Cu'racy, s. the employment of a curate
Cu'rate, s. a parish priest; one who officiates in the room of the beneficiary
Curb, v. a. to restrain, to bridle, to check
Curb, s. part of a bridle; restraint, inhibition
Curd, s. the coagulation of milk
Curd, Cur'dle, v. to coagulate, concrete
Cure, s. a remedy, restorative; act of healing; employment or benefice of a curate
Cure, v. a. to restore to health; to salt
Cu'red, part. restored, healed, preserved
Cu'reless, a. having no remedy, incurable
Cur'few, s. eight o'clock bell; a fire plate
Curios'ity, s. a rarity; inquisitiveness
Cu'rious, a. rare, accurate, nice, inquisitive
Curl, s. a ringlet of hair; a wave
Curl, v. a. to turn into ringlets, to twist
Cur'lew, s. a kind of land and water fowl
Curmud'geon, s. an avaricious fellow, a miser, a griper, a niggard, a churl
Cur'rant, s. the name of a tree and its fruit
Cur'rency, s. circulation, general reception; general esteem; readiness of utterance; fluency; paper established as, and passing for, the current money of the realm
Cur'rent, a. circulatory, popular, general
Cur'rent, s. a running stream
Cur'rently, ad. with a constant motion, popularly
Cur'ricle, s. a chaise on two wheels, calculated for expedition, drawn by two horses
Cur'rier, s. a dresser of tanned leather
Cur'rish, a. quarrelsome, sour, brutal
Cur'ry, v. a. to dress leather; to beat
Cur'rycomb, s. an iron comb for horses
Curse, s. a bad wish; torment, vexation
Curse, v. a. to wish evil to; to afflict
Cur'sedly, ad. shamefully, miserably
Cur'sitor, s. a clerk in Chancery
Cur'sorary, a. hasty, careless
Cur'sorily, ad. hastily, without care
Curso'riness, s. slight attention
Cur'sory, a. quick, careless, inattentive
Curt, a. concise, short, abridged
Curtail', v. a. to cut short, cut off, abridge
Cur'tain, s. furniture of a bed or window, fortification—v. a. to inclose with curtains
Curta'tion, s. the distance of a star from the ecliptic; a term in astronomy

Curva'tion, s the act of bending or crooking
Cur'vature, s. crookedness, bent form
Curve, v. a. to crook, to bend—a. crooked
Curvet', a. a leap, a frolic, a bound
Curvet', v. a. to leap, prance, bound, frisk
Curvilin'ear, a. consisting of crooked lines
Cush'ion, s. a soft seat for a chair
Cusp, s. the horns of the moon; a point
Cus'pated, a. terminating in a point, pointed
Cus'pidate, v. a. to sharpen, to point
Cus'tard, s. a sweet food made of milk, &c.
Cus'tody, s. security, imprisonment, care
Cus'tom, s. habitual practice, usage, fashion; king's duties on exports and imports
Cus'tomary, Cus'tomable, a. conformable to established usage, habitual, frequent, general, wonted, common
Customar'ily, ad. commonly, generally
Cus'tomer, s. one who buys any thing
Cus'tom-house, s. a house where duties are received on exports and imports
Cut, v. a. to carve, divide, hew, shape
Cut, s. a cleft or wound made with an edged tool; a printed picture; shape, fashion
Cuta'neous, a. relating to the skin
Cu'ticle, s. a thin skin; the scarf skin
Cutic'ular, a. belonging to the skin
Cut'lass, s. a broad cutting sword
Cut'ler, s. one who makes knives, &c.
Cut'lery, s. ware made by cutlers
Cut'ter, s. a fast sailing vessel; one who cuts
Cut'throat, s. an assassin, a murderer
Cut'ting, s. a piece cut off, a branch
Cut'tle, s. a fish; a foul-mouthed fellow
Cya'thiform, a. shaped like a drinking glass
Cy'cle, s. a circle; a periodical space of time
Cy'cloid, s. a figure of the circular kind
Cyclopæ'dia, s. a circle of knowledge; a course of the sciences
Cyg'net, s. a young swan
Cyl'inder, s. a long round body; a roller
Cylin'drical, a. resembling a cylinder
Cymar', s. a slight covering; a scarf
Cym'bal, s. a musical instrument
Cym'biform, a. boat-shaped
Cynan'thropy, s. canine madness
Cyn'ic, Cyn'ical, a. satirical, churlish
Cy'nosure, s. the north polar star
Cy'press, s. a tree; an emblem of mourning
Cy'prus, s. a thin silky gauze; a rush
Cyst, s. a bag containing morbid matter
Czar, s. the title of the Emperor of Russia
Czari'na, s. the title of the Empress of Russia

D.

D, s. the fourth letter of the alphabet; a note in music
Dab, v. a. to moisten; to strike gently
Dab, s. a flat fish; a gentle blow; an artist
Dab'ble, v. to play in water; to meddle
Dab'bler, s. a superficial meddler in science; one that plays in water
Dab'chick, s. a water fowl; a chicken
Dace, s. a small river fish resembling a roach
Dac'tyle, s. a kind of poetical foot, consisting of one long syllable and two short ones
Dæ'dal, Dæda'lian, a. cunning, intricate

Daf'fodil, Daf'fodilly, s. a flower, a lily
Daft, v. a. to throw away, to toss aside
Dag'ger, s. a kind of short sword, a poniard
Dag'gle, v. to trail in the mire or water
Dag'gletail, a. bemired—s. a slattern
Dai'ly, a. and ad. happening every day, often
Dain'tily, ad. delicately, nicely, deliciously
Dain'ty, a. nice, delicate—s. a delicacy
Dai'ry, s. a milk farm; a house where milk manufactured; pasturage
Dai'ry-maid, s. the woman servant who superintends the dairy

Dai'sied, a. full of or adorned with daisies
Dai'sy, s. a small common spring flower
Da'ker, s. a dicker, a number of ten hides
Dale, s. a valley, a space between two hills
Dal'liance, s. mutual caresses, love, delay
Da'lop, s. a turf, heap, quantity, clump
Dal'ly, v. a. to toy with, trifle, amuse, delay
Dam, s. a mother of brutes; a floodgate; a
 mole or bank to confine water
Dam, v. a. to shut up, to obstruct, to confine
Dam'age, s. mischief, loss, retribution
Dam'age, v. to injure, to impair, to hurt
Dam'ageable, a. that which may be hurt
Dam'ask, s. silk or linen woven into regular
 figures—v. a. to weave in flowers
Damaskee'n, v. a. to inlay iron with gold
Dame, s. a lady, mistress of a family; title of
 honour for women; women in general
Damn, v. a. to doom to torments in a future
 state; to curse; to condemn, to censure
Dam'nable, a. most wicked; destructive
Damna'tion, s. exclusion from Divine mercy,
 condemnation to eternal punishment
Dam'ned, part. a. cursed, detestable
Dam'nify, v. a. to hurt, to injure, to impair
Damp, a. wet, moist, foggy; dejected
Damp, s. a moist air, fog; dejection
Damp, v. a. to wet, to moisten; to deject
Dam'sel, s. a young maid, a country lass
Dam'son, Dam'ascene, s. a small black plum
Dance, v. n. to move in measure—s. a lively
 motion of one or many in concert
Dan'cing, s. a motion of the feet to music
Dandeli'on, s. the name of a plant
Dan'dle, v. a. to fondle a child, to play
Dan'druff, s. scurf, &c. on the head
Da'newort, s. the dwarf-elder, wall-wort
Dan'ger, s. peril, hazard—v. a. to endanger
Da'ngerless, a. very safe, without hazard
Da'ngerous, a. unsafe, hazardous
Dan'gle, v. to hang loose, to follow humbly
Dan'gler, s. one who hangs about women
Dank, a. very damp, wet, moist, humid
Dapat'ical, a. sumptuous in cheer, costly
Dap'per, a. little and active, tight, neat
Dap'perling, s. a little person, a dwarf
Dap'ple, a. of various colours, streaked
Dare, v. a. to defy, to challenge
Da'ring, a. bold, fearless, adventurous
Dark, a. wanting light, not plain, blind
Dar'ken, v. to make dark, cloud, perplex
Dar'kness, s. absence of light; wickedness
Dark'some, a. not luminous, gloomy, obscure
Dar'ling, s. a favourite—a. beloved, dear
Darn, or Dearn, v. a. to repair holes
Dar'nel, s. a weed growing in the fields
Dar'rain, v. a. to range troops for battle
Dart, s. a weapon thrown by the hand
Dar'tingly, ad. very swiftly, like a dart
Dash, v. to strike against; to mingle; to cross
 or blot out; to besprinkle; to confound
Dash, s. a mark in writing, thus —; a blow
Das'tard, s. a coward, a poltroon
Das'tardly, a. cowardly, timorous, mean
Data, s. truths admitted
Date, v. a. to note the precise time
Date, s. the time when any event happened,
 or at which a letter is written; a fruit
Da'teless, a. without any fixed date or term
Da'tive, s. in grammar, the case that signifies
 the person to whom the thing is given

Daub, v. a. to smear, paint coarsely, flatter
Dau'ber, s. a coarse, low painter
Daugh'ter, s. a female descendant, a woman
Daunt, v. a. to frighten, to discourage
Daun'ted, part. intimidated, dispirited
Daun'tless, a. fearless, not easily dejected
Dau'phin, s. the French heir apparent
Daw, s. the name of a bird, a jackdaw
Dawn, v. n. to grow light, glimmer
Dawn, s. the break of day, beginning
Day, s. the time between the rising and setting
 of the sun; sunshine, light; the time from
 noon to noon
Day'-book, s. a tradesman's journal
Day'break, s. first appearance of day, dawn
Day'light, s. the light of the day
Day'star, s. the morning star; Venus
Daz'zle, v. a. to overpower with light
Dea'con, s. one of the lowest of the clergy
Dea'conry, s. dignity or office of deacon
Dead, a. deprived of life, motionless, dull
Dead'en, v. a. to deprive of sensation
Dead'ly, a. destructive, mortal, cruel
Dead'ly, ad. mortally, irreconcileably
Dead'ness, s. want of warmth
Deaf, a. wanting the sense of hearing
Deaf'en, v. a. to deprive one of hearing
Deaf'ness, s. want of the power of hearing
Deal, s. fir wood; quantity, part
Deal, v. to distribute; to give each his due
Dealba'tion, s. the art of bleaching
Deal'er, s. a trader; one who deals cards
Dea'ling, s. business, intercourse, practice
Dealt, part. used, given out, handled
Deambula'tion, s. the act of walking abroad
Dean, s. the second dignitary of a diocese
Dea'nery, s. the office or house of a dean
Dear, a. beloved; costly, valuable, scarce
Dea'rly, ad. with fondness; at a high price
Dearth, s. scarcity, need, want; barrenness
Dear'ticulate, v. a. to dismember, to disjoint
Death, s. the extinction of life, mortality
Death'less, a. immortal, never dying
Death'like, a. resembling death, still
Death'watch, s. a small insect that makes a
 tinkling noise, superstitiously imagined to
 prognosticate death
Deaura'tion, s. the act of gilding
Debar', v. a. to exclude, prevent, preclude
Debark', v. a. to leave the ship, to go on shore
Debase, v. a. to degrade, adulterate, lower
Deba'sement, s. act of degrading or debasing
Deba'te, s. a dispute, a quarrel, a contest
Debate, v. to dispute, to deliberate, to argue
Debauch, s. lewdness, excess, luxury
Debauch, v. a. to corrupt, to vitiate
Debauchee', s. a drunkard; a lecher
Debau'chery, s. lewdness, intemperance
Debel, Debel'late, v. a. to conquer in war
Deben'ture, s. a writ, or written instrument
 by which a debt is claimed
Deb'ile, a. weak, feeble, faint, languid
Debil'itate, v. a. to enfeeble, to weaken
Debil'ity, s. weakness, faintness, languor
Deb'it, v. a. to charge as debtor
Debonair', a. elegant, well-bred, civil, gay
Debt, s. that which one man owes to another
Debt'ed, a. indebted to, obliged to
Debt'or, s. one who owes money, &c.
Dec'ade, s. the sum or number of ten
Dec'agon, s. a plain figure of ten equal sides

Dec'alogue, *s.* the ten commandments
Decam'p, *v. n.* to shift a camp; to move on
Decan't, *v. a.* to pour gently by inclination
Decan'ter, *s.* a glass vessel for liquor
Decap'itate, *v. a.* to behead, to cut or lop off
Decay', *s.* a consuming away, a decline
Decay', *v. n.* to consume, to decline, to rot
Decea'se, *s.* death, departure from life
Decea'se, *v. n.* to die, to depart from life
Decea'sed, *part.* departed from life, dead
Deceit', *s.* cheat, fraud, pretence, artifice
Deceit'ful, *a.* full of deceit, fraudulent
Deceive, *v. a.* to delude, to impose upon
Deceiver, *s.* one who leads into error
Decem'ber, *s.* the last month of the year
Decem'virate, *s.* a government by ten rulers
De'cency, *s.* modesty, propriety, not ribaldry
Decen'nial, *a.* what continues for ten years
De'cent, *a.* modest, becoming, suitable, fit
De'cently, *ad.* modestly, in a proper manner
Decep'tible, *a.* capable of being deceived
Decep'tion, *s.* a fraud, a cheat, a beguiling
Decep'tive, *a.* having the power of deceiving, false
Decerp't, *a.* plucked away, taken off
Decerta'tion, *s.* a contention, a contest
Dechar'm, *v. a.* to counteract a charm
Decide, *v. a.* to determine, conclude, settle
Deci'dedly, *ad.* positively, absolutely, really
Deci'der, *s.* one who determines quarrels
Decid'uous, *a.* falling off, not perennial
Dec'imal, *a.* numbered by tens
Decima'tion, *s.* a selection of every tenth
Deci'pher, *v. a.* to explain, unravel, unfold
Deci'sion, *s.* the termination of a difference
Deci'sive, *a.* final, terminating, dogmatic
Deci'sively, *ad.* in a conclusive manner
Deck, *v. a.* to dress, to cover, to array
Deck, *s.* the floor of a ship, a pile of cards
Declai'm, *v. n.* to harangue, to rhetoricate
Declai'mer, *s.* one who declaims
Declama'tion, *s.* a discourse addressed to the passions, an harangue
Declam'atory, *a.* pertaining to declamation
Decla'rable, *a.* capable of illustration, real
Declara'tion, *s.* an affirmation, publication
Declar'ative, *a.* explanatory, proclaiming
Declar'atory, *a.* affirmative, expressive, clear
Decla're, *v. a.* to tell openly, to proclaim
Decla'red, *part.* affirmed, made known
Declen'sion, *s.* descent; variation of nouns; decline from a state of perfection
Decli'nable, *a.* capable of being declined
Declina'tion, *s.* descent; the act of bending
Declina'tor, *s.* an instrument for dialling
Decli'ne, *v.* to lean, to bend downwards, to decay; to refuse; to shun; to vary words
Decli'ne, *s.* a decay; a tendency to worse
Decliv'ity, *s.* an oblique or gradual descent
Decoc't, *v. a.* to boil; strengthen; digest
Decoc'tion, *s.* a preparation by boiling
Decoc'ture, *s.* what is drawn by decoction
Decolla'tion, *s.* the act of beheading
Decompose', *v. a.* to dissolve or resolve a mixed body
Decompou'nd, *v. a.* to compose of things already compounded, to separate compounds
Dec'orate, *v. a.* to beautify, to adorn
Decora'tion, *s.* an ornament, added beauty
Deco'rous, *a.* decent, becoming, suitable
Decor'ticate, *v. a.* to divest of bark, to peel

Deco'rum, *s.* decency, seemliness, order
Decoy', *v. a.* to allure, to entrap, to ensnare
Decoy', *s.* a place to catch wild fowl, a lure
Decoy'-duck, *s.* a duck that leads others
Decrea'se, *v.* to make less, to be diminished
Decrea'se, *s.* state of growing less, a decay
Decree', *v. a.* to appoint by edict, to sentence
Decree', *s.* an edict, established rule, law
Decrep'it, *a.* wasted and worn by age
Decrepita'te, *s.* a crackling noise
Decrep'itude, *s.* the last efforts of old age
Decres'cent, *a.* growing less, decreasing
Decre'tal, *a.* containing a decree
Decre'tal, *s.* a book of decrees or edicts
Dec'retory, *a.* judicial, definitive, critical
Decry', *v. a.* to clamour against, to censure
Decum'bence, *s.* the act of lying down
Decum'bent, *a.* lying on the ground; low
Dec'uple, *a.* tenfold; repeated ten times
Decu'rion, *s.* a commander of ten men
Decur'rent, *a.* extending downwards
Decur'sion, *s.* the act of running down
Decurta'tion, *s.* the act of cutting down
Decus'sate, *v. a.* to intersect at acute angles
Dedec'orate, *v. a.* to disgrace, to reproach
Dedenti'tion, *s.* a loss or shedding of teeth
Ded'icate, *v. a.* to inscribe, to devote to
Ded'icated, *part.* inscribed, consecrated
Dedica'tion, *s.* a complimentary address at the beginning of a book; a consecration
Dedi'tion, *s.* the act of yielding up any thing
Dedu'ce, *v. a.* to conclude or infer from
Dedu'cement, *s.* the thing deduced
Dedu'cible, *a.* that which may be inferred
Dedu'ct, *v. a.* to subtract, to separate
Deduc'tion, *s.* an abatement, an inference
Deduc'tive, *a.* that which may be deduced
Deed, *s.* an exploit, an action, a writing
Deed'less, *a.* inactive, sluggish, indolent
Deem, *v. n.* to judge; to think; to conclude
Deep, *a.* far to the bottom, sagacious
Deep, *s.* the sea; the most solemn or still part
Dee'ply, *ad.* to a great depth, sorrowfully
Deer, *s.* a forest animal hunted for venison
Defa'ce, *v. a.* to destroy, to disfigure, to raze
Defa'cement, *s.* violation, destruction, injury
Defai'lance, *s.* failure, miscarriage
Defal'cate, *v. a.* to cut or lop off, to abridge
Defalca'tion, *s.* a diminution, amputation
Defama'tion, *s.* slander, reproach, calumny
Defam'atory, *a.* scandalizing, calumnious
Defa'me, *v. a.* to censure falsely, to slander
Defat'igate, *v. a.* to fatigue, to weary
Defau't, *s.* omission, failure, defect, crime
Defau'lter, *s.* one who fails in payment
Defea'sance, *s.* act of annulling; defeat
Defea'sible, *a.* that which may be annulled
Defea't, *v. a.* to overthrow, rout, frustrate
Defea't, *s.* an overthrow, a deprivation
Defea'ted, *part.* routed, disappointed
Defea'ture, *s.* an alteration of countenance
Def'ecate, *v. a.* to cleanse, brighten, purify
Def'ecate, *a.* purged from, cleansing from lees
Defeca'tion, *s.* purification
Defec't, *s.* a fault, an imperfection, a blemish
Defec'tible, *a.* imperfect, deficient, wanting
Defec'tion, *s.* failure, revolt, apostacy
Defec'tive, *a.* full of defects; not sufficient
Defen'ce, *s.* a guard, resistance, vindication
Defen'celess, *a.* unguarded, naked, impotent
Defen'd, *v. a.* to protect, prohibit, vindicate

Defen'dant, *s.* the person prosecuted
Defen'der, *s.* a protector, a vindicator
Defen'sible, *a.* that may be defended, right
Defen'sive, *a.* state of defence, safeguard
Defer', *v.* to delay, to put off; to refer to
Def'erence, *s.* regard, submission, respect
Def'erent, *a.* that which carries or conveys
Defi'ance, *s.* a challenge; an expression of contempt or abhorrence
Defic'iency, *s.* a defect, imperfection, want
Defic'ient, *a.* defective, wanting, failing
Defi'le, *v. a.* to make foul, violate, pollute
Defi'le, *s.* a narrow passage, a lane
Defi'led, *part.* corrupted, polluted, tainted
Defi'lement, *s.* corruption, pollution
Defi'ler, *s.* one that violates; a corrupter
Defi'nable, *a.* that which may be ascertained
Defi'ne, *v.* to explain; decide, mark limits
Defi'ner, *s.* one who describes
Def'inite, *a.* certain, precise, limited
Defi'nite, *s.* a thing defined or explained
Def'initeness, *s.* certainty, limitedness
Defini'tion, *s.* a short description of a thing by its properties; a decision
Defin'itive, *a.* positive, determinate, express
Defin'itively, *ad.* positively, expressly
Deflagrabil'ity, *s.* an aptness to take fire
Deflagra'tion, *s.* act of consuming by fire
Deflect', *v. n.* to turn aside, to deviate
Deflec'tion, *s.* a turning aside, deviation
Deflex'ure, *s.* a bending down, a deflection
Deflora'tion, *s.* a selection of what is best; rape
Deflou'r, *v. n.* to deprive a maiden of her virginity, to ravish; to take away the beauty and grace of any thing
Def'luous, *a.* that flows down, or falls off
Defluxion, *s.* flow of humours downward
Defoeda'tion, *s.* a defilement; pollution
Defo'rcement, *s.* withholding of lands, &c. by force from the right owner
Defor'm, *v. a.* to disfigure, to dishonour
Defor'med, Defor'm, *a.* ugly, disfigured
Defor'mity, *s.* ugliness, crookedness
Defrau'd, *v. a.* to rob by a trick; to cozen
Defrau'der, *s.* one who cheats or defrauds
Defray', *v. a.* to bear expenses or charges
Deft, *a.* handsome, neat, proper, ready
Defun'ct, *a.* extinct, dead—*n.* a dead man
Defunc'tion, *s.* a decease, extinction
Defy', *v. a.* to challenge, to slight
Degen'eracy, *s.* departure from virtue; vice
Degen'erate, *v. n.* to decay in virtue or kind
Degen'erate, *a.* unlike ancestors, base
Degenera'tion, *s.* the act of degenerating
Degen'erous, *a.* degenerated, base, vile
Deglu'tinate, *v. a.* to unglue; slacken, undo
Deglu'tition, *s.* the act of swallowing
Degrada'tion, *s.* a placing lower; baseness
Degra'de, *v. a.* to place lower; to lessen
Degree', *s.* quality, station, class; on the earth or miles; the 360th part of a circle
Dehort', *v. a.* to dissuade, to discourage
Dehorta'tion, *s.* dissuasion
Dei'cide, *s.* the death of our Saviour
Deject', *v. a.* to cast down, grieve, afflict
Dejec'tion, *s.* lowness of spirits; weakness
Dejec'ture, *s.* excrement; refuse
Deifica'tion, *s.* the act of making a god
Dei'fy, *v. a.* to make a god of, to adore
Deign, *v. a.* to vouchsafe, to permit, to grant

De'ism, *s.* the opinion of those who acknowledge one God, but deny revealed religion
De'ist, *s.* one who believes in the existence of God, but follows no particular religion
Deis'tical, *a.* belonging to deism
De'ity, *s.* the Divine Being; God
Delacta'tion, *s.* a weaning from the breast
Delap'sed, *a.* bearing or falling down
Dela'te, *v. a.* to carry, to accuse, to convey
Dela'tion, *s.* a conveyance; an accusation
Delay', *v.* to put off, to stop, to frustrate
Delay', *s.* a deferring; a hindrance, a stop
Delec'table, *a.* pleasing, delightful
Delecta'tion, *s.* pleasure, delight
Del'egate, *v. a.* to intrust; to send away
Del'egate, *s.* a deputy, a vicar, a commissioner
Del'egates, *s. pl.* a court of appeal
Delega'tion, *s.* commission, trust
Delete'rious, *s.* deadly, destructive
Dele'tion, *s.* act of blotting out; destruction
Dele'te, *v. a.* to blot out
Delf, Delfe, Delph, *s.* a mine; a quarry; a kind of counterfeit China ware
Delibra'tion, *s.* an attempt, an essay; taste
Delib'erate, *v. n.* to think, muse, hesitate
Delib'erate, *a.* circumspect, slow, wary
Delibera'tion, *s.* thought, circumspection
Delib'erative, *a.* apt to consider
Del'icacy, *s.* nicety, politeness, daintiness
Del'icate, *a.* fine, pure, polite, nice, dainty
Del'icateness, *s.* tenderness, effeminacy
Delic'ious, *a.* sweet, agreeable, pleasant
Deliga'tion, *s.* the act of binding up
Delight', *s.* joy, satisfaction, pleasure
Delight', *v.* to please, to content, to satisfy
Delight'ful, *a.* charming, pleasant
Delight'some, *a.* delightful, pleasant
Delin'eate, *v. a.* to design, paint, sketch
Delinea'tion, *s.* the first draught of a thing
Delin'quency, *s.* a failure in duty; a fault
Delin'quent, *s.* a criminal, an offender
Del'iquate, *v. a.* to melt, clarify, dissolve
Delir'ious, *a.* light-headed, doating, raving
Delir'ium, *s.* alienation of mind; dotage
Deliv'er, *v. a.* to resign; to rescue; pronounce
Deliv'erance, *s.* freedom from; utterance
Deliv'erer, *s.* a preserver, relater
Deliv'ery, *s.* rescue; release; childbirth
Dell, *s.* a cavity, a pit, a shady covert
Delu'de, *v. a.* to deceive, cheat, disappoint
Delve, *v. n.* to dig, to sift, to fathom
Delve, *s.* a ditch, a cave, a den, a pitfal
Del'ver, *s.* one who digs with a spade
Del'uge, *s.* a general inundation
Del'uge, *v. a.* to drown, to overwhelm
Delu'sion, *s.* a cheat, an error, a deception
Delu'sive, Delu'sory, *a.* apt to deceive
Dem'agogue, *s.* the ringleader of a faction
Deman'd, *s.* a claim; a call; a question
Deman'd, *v. a.* to claim, ask with authority
Deman'dant, *s.* the plaintiff in an action
Deman'der, *s.* one who asks with authority
Demea'n, *v. a.* to behave; to undervalue
Demea'nour, *s.* behaviour, carriage
Dement'ate, *v. n.* to grow mad
Dementa'tion, *s.* madness, delirious state
Demer'it, *s.* the opposite to merit; ill deserving—*v. n.* to deserve punishment
Deme'sne, *s.* a patrimonial estate
Dem'i, *a.* half; at Oxford, a half fellow
Dem'i-devil, *s.* half a devil; a wicked wretch

Dem'i-god, s. half a god ; a great hero
Demig a'tion, s. a removing from place to place, changing the habitation
Dem'irep, s. a woman of light fame
Demi'-e, s. decease, death ; will
Demi'se, v. a. to bequeath at one's death
Demis'sion, s. degradation, depression
Demit', v. a. to depress, to degrade
Democ'racy, s. the government of the people
Democrat'ical, a. relating to democracy
Demol'ish, v. a. to destroy. ruin, raze
Demol'isher, s. a destroyer, a layer waste
Demoli'tion, s. act of overthrowing buildings
De'mon, s. a spirit, generally evil
Demo'niac, s. one possessed with a devil
Demonol'ogy, s. a treatise on evil spirits
Demon'strable, a. that which may be proved
Demon'strate, v. a. to prove with certainty
Demon stra'tion, s. deducible evidence
Demon'strative, a. invincibly conclusive
Demoraliza'tion, s. destruction of morals
Demul'cent, a. mollifying, softening
Demur', v. to delay. to doubt of, to pause
Demur', s. doubt, hesitation
Demu're, a. grave, sober, affectedly modest
Demu'rely, ad. gravely, solemnly. affectedly
Demur'rage, s. allowance for delaying ships
Demur'rer, s. a pause in a law suit
Den, s. a cave for wild beasts ; a cavern
Den'ary, a. belonging to, or containing ten
Denay', s. a refusal, a rejection, a denial
Deni'able, a that which may be denied
Deni'al, s. a refusal. abjuration, negation
Deni'e , s. a contradictor ; a French coin
Deni'grate, v. a. to blacken, to render black
Deniza'tion, s. the act of infranchising
Den'izen, s. a freeman, a citizen
Denom'inate, v.a. to give a name to, to name
Denomina'tion, s. a name given to a thing
Denom'inative, a. that which gives a name
De ota'tion, s. the act of marking
Deno'te, v. a. to mark, to be a sign of
Denou'nce, v. a. to threaten, inform against
Dense, a. compact, close, almost solid
Den'sity, s. closeness, compactness
Dent, v. a. to indent, to mark with notches
Den'tal, a. belonging to the teeth
Denter'il, s. modillions in architecture
Dentic'ulated, a. set with small teeth
Den'tifrice, s. a powder to cleanse the teeth
Den'tist, s. a tooth doctor
Den'tition, s. the act of breeding the teeth
Denu'date, Denu'de, v. a. to strip, to divest
Denuncia'tion, s. a public menace
Deny', v. a. to contradict ; to disown, refuse
Deob'struent, a. removing obstructions
Deodand', s. so feiture made to God
Deop'pilate, v. a. to clear a passage
Depa'nt, v. a. to picture, to describe
Depar't, v. to go away; to die; to apostatize
Depar't, Depar'ture, s. a going away ; death
Depar'tment, s. a separate office ; duty
Depau'perate, v. a. to make poor
Depec'tible, a. tough, tenacious, clammy
Depen'd, v. n. to rely on ; to hang from
Depen'dance, s. reliance, connexion, trust
Depen'dant, a. in the power of another
Depen'dant, Depen'dent, Depen'der, s. one who lives in subjection to another
Depen dent, a. hanging from or down
Dephlegm', v. a. to clear from phlegm

Depic't, v.a. to paint, to pourtray, to describe
Depic'ted, part. painted, told, described
Depi'lous, a. without hair, smooth
Deple'tion, s. act of emptying out or from
Deplo'rable, a. sad, lamentable, hopeless
Deplo're, v.a. to lament, bemoan, bewail
Deplu'med, a. stripped of the feathers
Depo'nent, s. a witness on oath ; in grammar such verbs as have no active sound
Depop'ulate, v. a. to unpeople, to lay waste
Depopula'tion, s. act of unpeopling ; waste
Depor't, v. n. to behave, to demean, to carry
Depor't, Depor'tment, s. behaviour, conduct
Deporta'tion, s. exportation, exile
Depo'se, v. a. to divest, to degrade ; to attest
Depos'it, v.a. to lay up as a pledge—s. a pawn, a pledge, thing given in security
Deposi'tion, s. the act of giving public testimony ; degrading one from dignity
Depos'itory, s. the place wher any thing is lodged ; a storehouse ; a warehouse
Dep ava'tion, s. depravity, defamation
Deprave', v. a. to corrupt, to vitiate
Deprave'ment, Deprav'ity, s. vitiated state
Dep'reca e, v.a. to pray deliverance from; to implore mercy ; to avert by prayer
Depreca'tion, s prayer against evil
Depre'ciate, v. a. to lessen in value
Dep'reda e, v. a. to pilla e, to rob, to spoil
Depreda'tion, s. a robbing. a spoiling
Depreda'tor, s. a plunderer, a robber
Deprehen'd, v.a. to catch unawares, discover
Depress', v. a. to deject. to humble, to sink
Depres'sion, s. the act of humbling; act of pressing down ; abasement ; lowness of spirit
Depres'sor, s. he that presses or keeps down
Depriva'tion, s. the act of taking from
Depri've, v. a. to take from, bereave, debar
Depth, s. deepness ; abstruseness ; the abyss
Depu'celate, v. a. to deflour ; to violate
Dep'urate, a. cleansed, free from dregs, pure
Depura'tion, s. making clear or pure
Dep'uratory, a. tending to purify, to cleanse
Depu'tation, s. act of deputing ; vicegerency
Depu'te, v. a. to empower to act, to appoint
Dep'uty, s. any one who transacts business for another, a viceroy, a substitute
Derac'inate, v. a. to pluck up by the roots
Derai'gn, v.a. to justify; to prove, to disorder
Dera'nge. v. a. to confuse, to disorder
Derelic'tion, s. an utter forsaking or leaving
Deri'de, v. a. to ridicule, to laugh at, to mock
Deri'sion, s. scorn, contempt, laughing stock
Deri'sive, a. ridiculing, mocking, scoffing
Deri'vable, a. attainable by right or descent
Deriva'tion, s. tracing from its original
Deriv'ative, a. derived from another
Deri've, v. a. to deduce from its original; to owe its origin to ; to descend from
Dernier', a. the last, the only remaining
Der'ogate, v. to disparage, lessen, detract
Der'ogate, a. lessened in value, damaged
Deroga'tion, s. a defamation ; detraction
Derog'atory, Derog'ative, a. detractory; that lessens the value of; dishonourable
Der'vis, Der'vise, s. a Turkish priest
Des'cant, s. a song ; disputation ; discourse
Des'cant, v. n. to discourse at large, to sing
Descend', v. n. to come down ; to sink
Descen'dant, s. the offspring of an ancestor
Descen'dent, a. proceeding from

Descen'sion, *s.* the act of sinking or falling ; a degradation ; a declension

Descen't, *s.* a declivity ; birth ; invasion

Descri'be, *v. a.* to represent by words, &c.

Descrip'tion, *s.* the act of describing; delineation ; representation ; a lax definition

Descrip'tive, *a.* tending to describe, full

Descry',*v.a.* to spy out, to detect, to discover

Desecra'tion, *s.* the abolition of consecration

Des'rt, *s.* worth, merit, claim to reward

Des'ert, *s.* a wilderness ; waste ; solitude

Deser't, *v.a.* to abandon, to forsake, to quit

Deser'ter, *s.* he who quits his regiment clandestinely ; he who forsakes his cause

Deser'tion,*s.* act of abandoning or forsaking

Desert'less, *a.* without merit, worthless

Deser've, *v. n.* to be worthy of good or ill

Deser've dly,*ad.* worthily,according to desert

Deser'ving, *part.* worthy of ; kind ; good

Desic'cant, *s.* an application to dry sores

Desic'ca'e, *v. a.* to dry up, to exhale

Desid'era e, *v. a.* to want, to miss

Desidera'tum, *s.* something wanted

Desi'gn, *v. a.* to purpose, to plan, to project

Desi'gn, *s.* an intention, a scheme, a plan

Designa'tion, *s.* intention ; appointment

Desi'gnedly, *ad.* purposely, intentionally

Desi'gner, *s.* a contriver ; an architect [ous

Designing, *a.* insidious, deceitful, treacher-

Desi'rable, *a.* worthy of desire, pleasing

Desi're,*s.*wish ; eagerness to enjoy or obtain

Desi're, *v. a.* to wish, to entreat, to covet

Desi'rous, *a.* full of desire, anxious, eager

Desi'rously, *ad.* eagerly, with desire

Desis't, *v. n.* to cease from any thing, to stop

Desis'tive, *a.* ending, final, conclusive

Desk, *s.* an inclining table to write on

Des'olate, *v.a.* to make desert, to lay waste

Des'olate,*ad.*laid waste,solitary,uninhabited

Desola'tion, *s.* destruction, gloominess

Despai'r, *s.* hopelessness, despondency

Despai'r,*v.n.* to be without hope, to despond

Despat'ch, *v. a.* to send away hastily ; to kill

Despat'ch, *s.* hasty messenger ; speed

Despera'do, *s.* a desperate person

Des'perate, *a.* having no hope ; mad, rash

Des'perately, *ad.* furiously, madly, rashly

Despera'tion, *s.* hopelessness, rashness

Des'picable, *a.* contemptible, worthless, vile

Despi'sable, *a.* mean, contemptible

Despi'se, *v. a.* to scorn, to slight, to contemn

Despi'te, *s.* malignity, malice ; defiance

Despi'te, *v. a.* to vex, to distress, to affront

Despi'teful, *a.* malicious, full of spleen

Despoi'l, *v. a.* to rob, to deprive, to plunder

Despolia'tion, *s.* the act of plundering

Despon'd, *v. n.* to lose hope, to despair

Despon'dency, *s.* hopelessness, despair

Despon'dent, *a.* despairing, hopeless

Despon'sate, *v. a.* to betroth, to affiance

Des'pot, *s.* an absolute prince ; one that governs with unlimited authority

Despot'ic, *a.* absolute in power

Des'potism, *s.* absolute authority, tyranny

Despuma'tion, *s.* the act of scumming

Desser't, *s.* the last course at a feast ; fruit

Des'tinate, *v. a.* to design for any end

Destina'tion, *s.* the purpose intended

Des'tine, *v. a.* to doom, to devote, to appoint

Des'tiny, *s.* doom, fate ; invincible necessity

Des'titute, *a.* forsaken, unfriended, [ous use

Destitu'tion, *s.* poverty, want, indigence

Destroy', *v. a.* to lay waste ; overturn ; kill

Destroy'er, *s.* the person who destroys

Destruc'tible, *a.* liable to destruction

Destruc'tion, *s.* ruin ; demolition ; murder

Destruc'tive,*a.*that which destroys; wasteful

Desue'tude, *s.* disuse of a custom

Des'ultorily, *ad.* in a desultory manner

Des'ultory, *a.* unsettled, immethodical

Desu'me, *v. a.* to take from any thing

Detach', *v. a.* to send off a party, to separate

Detach'ment, *s.* a body of troops sent off

Detai'l, *s.* a minute and particular relation

Detai'n, *v. a.* to withhold ; keep in custody

Detai'nder, *s.* a writ to detain in custody

Detai'ner, *s.* one who detains, or holds back

Detec't, *v. a.* to discover, to find out

Detec'tion, *s.* discovery of fraud or guilt

Deten'tion, *s.* the act of detaining ; restraint

Deter', *v. a.* to discourage, to dishearten

Deter'ge, *v. a.* to cleanse a wound

Deter'gent, *a.* that which cleanses

Deteriora'tion, *s.* the act of making worse

Deter'ment, *s.* cause of discouragement

Deter'minable, *a.* that which can be decided

Deter'minate, *v. a.* to limit, to fix

Deter'minate, *a.* limited, fixed, decisive

Deter'minately, *ad.* decisively, resolutely

Determina'tion, *s.* a resolution ; a decision

Deter'mine,*v.a.* to resolve, to decide, to fix

Deter'mined, *part.* decided, resolved

Deter'sion, *s.* the act of cleansing a sore

Detes't, *v. a.* to hate, dislike greatly, abhor

Detes'table, *a.* hateful, abominable, odious

Detesta'tion, *s.* abhorrence, abomination

Dethro'ne, *v.a.* to depose from a throne

Detona'tion, *s.* the noise which happens or mixing fluids that ferment with violence

Detrac't, *v. a.* to derogate, defame, slander

Detrac'tion, *s.* defamation, calumny, slander

Detrac'tive, *a.* tending to detract

Detrac'tory, *a.* derogatory, defamatory

Det'riment, *s.* loss, mischief, damage

Detrimen'tal, *a.* mischievous, harmful

Detri'tion, *s.* the act of wearing away

Detru'de, *v. a.* to thrust down, to lower

Detrun'cate, *v.a.* to lop, to cut

Detru'sion, *s.* the act of thrusting down

Devasta'tion, *s.* waste, destruction, havoc

Deuce, *s.* the two in cards or dice ; the devil

Devel'op,*v.a.* to unfold, to unravel, to detect

Deves't, *v. a.* to strip, free from, take away

Devi'ate, *v. n.* to wander, to err, to go astray

Devia'tion, *s.* quitting the right way ; offence

Devi'ce, *s.* contrivance, stratagem, emblem

Dev'il, *s.* a fallen angel ; a wicked person

Dev'ilish, *a.* having the qualities of the devil

De'vious,*a.*out of the common track ; erring

Devi'se,*v.a.*to contrive,to invent,to consider

Devi'sed, *part.* contrived ; given by will

Devisee', *s.* one to whom a thing is devised

Devoi'd, *a.* vacant, empty, in want of

Devoi'r,*s.* service ; an act of obsequiousness

Devol've, *v.* to fall by succession ; roll down

Devo'te, *v. a.* to dedicate ; to give up

Devotee', *s.* a bigot, a superstitious person

Devo'tion, *s.* worship ; piety ; zeal ; ardour

Devou'r,*v.a.* to eat ravenously, to consume

Devou't, *a.* religious, pious, holy, sincere

Devou'tly,*ad.* piously; with fervent devotion

Dew, *s.* a thin cold vapour—*v. a.* to wet

F 3

Dew'berry, s. a fruit; a kind of raspberry
Dew'drop, s. a drop of dew, a spangle of dew
Dew'lap, s. the flesh that hangs down from the throats of oxen; the lip flaccid with age
Dew'y, a. resembling or moist with dew
Dexter'ity, s. activity of limbs, expertness
Dex'terous, a. expert, subtile, active [ner
Dex'terously, ad. expertly, in an artful man-
Dex'tral, Dex'ter, a. on the r ght hand side
Dey, s. the title of a Moorish prince
Diabe'tes, s. an involuntary discharge of
Diabol'ical, a. impious, like the devil [urine
Diaco'dium, s. the syrup of poppies
Diacous'tics, s. the science of sounds
Di'adem, s. a crown, a mark of royalty
Diær'esis, s. the separation of syllables
Diagnos'tic, s. a distinguishing symptom
Diag'onal, s. reaching from angle to angle
Di'agram, s. a mathematical scheme
Di'al, s. a plate on which a hand marks the hour of the day by the progress of the sun
Di'alect, s.subdivision of a language, manner of expression; particular style
Dialec'tic, s. logic; the art of reasoning
Di'alling, s. the art of constructing dials
Dial'ogist, s. a speaker in a dialogue
Di'alogue, s. a conference; a conversation between two or more persons
Diam'eter, s. a line, which, passing throu gh a circle, divides it into two equal parts
Diamet'rical, a. describing a diameter
Diamet'rically, ad. in a diametrical direction; in direct opposition
Di'amond, s. the most valuable of all gems
Diapa'son, s. a term in music; an octave
Di'aper, s. a sort of fine flowered linen
Diaph'anous, a. transparent, pellucid, clear
Diaphoret'ic, a. promoting perspiration
Di'aphragm, s. the midriff; a partition
Diarrhœ'a, s. a flux of the belly, looseness
Di'ary, s. a daily account; journal
Dias'tole, s. the making a short syllable long; the dilation of the heart
Dib'ble, s. a gardener's planting tool; a spade
Dice, s. pl. of Die—v. n. to game with dice
Di'cer, s. a player at dice, a gamester
Dic'tate, v. a. to tell what to write; instruct
Dic'tate, s. a precept, an admonition
Dicta'tor, s. a ruler; a Roman magistrate
Dictato'rial, a. authoritative, dogmatical
Dicta'torship, s. the office of a dictator
Dic'tion, s. style, expression, language
Dic'tionary, s. a book containing the words of any language alphabetically; word-book
Didac'tic, Didac'tical, a. doctrinal; giving precepts or directions for some art
Didac'tically, ad. in a didactic manner
Die, v. to lose life, expire; to tinge, colour
Die, s. a small marked cube for gaming; stamp used in coinage; tincture, colour
Di'er, s. one whose trade is to die cloth, &c.
Di'et, s. food; a convocation of princes
Di'et, v. to supply with food; to eat by rule
Dif'fer, v. n. to be unlike, to contend, to vary
Dif'ference, s. dissimilitude; a dispute
Dif'ferent, a. unlike, distinct, not the same
Dif'ferently, ad. in a different manner
Dif'ficult, a. troublesome, not easy, peevish
Dif'ficulty, s. perplexity, distress; opposition
Dif'fidence, s. distrust, want of confidence
Dif'fident, a. not

Dif'fluent, a. flowing every way, not fixed
Dif'form, a. not uniform, irregular
Diffor'mity, s. irregularity of form
Diffu'se, v. a. to pour out, to spread, to scatter
Diffu'se, a. scattered, not concise, copious
Diffu'sed, Diffu'sedly, ad. widely, copiously
Diffu's'veness, s. dispersion
Diffu'sive, a. dispersed, extended, scattered
Dig, v. a. to turn up or cultivate land
Diges't, v. to dissolve; to range in order
Di'gest, s. the pandect of the civil law
Diges'tible, a. capable of being digested
Diges'tion, s. the operation of dissolving food in the stomach; reduction to a regular plan; preparation of matter by heat
Dig'ger, s. one who digs or turns up earth
Dight, v. a. to deck, to adorn, to dress
Dig'it, s. the twelfth part of the diameter of the sun or moon; three quarters of an inch; any number under ten
Dig'ital, a. relating to a digit, or the finger
Dig'nified, part. invested with honours
Dig'nify, v. a. to advance, to honour, to exalt
Dig'nitary, s. a clergyman advanced to some rank above that of a parochial priest
Dig'nity, s. grandeur, honour, rank
Digress', v. n. to turn aside, to expatiate
Digres'sion, s. a deviation from the subject
Dike, s. a ditch, a bank, a channel, a mound
Dilac'erate, v. a. to tear, to rend in two
Dilap'idate, v. n. to fall to ruin
Dilapida'tion, s. buildings fallen into decay
Dila'table, a. capable of extension, elastic
Dila'te, v. to widen; to relate copiously
Dila'tor, s. that which widens or extends
Dil'atoriness, s. slowness, sluggishness
Dil'atory, a. slow, loitering, tardy, sluggish
Dilem'ma, s. difficulty, vexatious alternative
Dil'igence, s. industry, constant application
Dil'igence, a. persevering, not idle, assiduous
Dilu'cid, a. plain, clear, not obscure
Dilu'cidate, v. a. to explain, to make clear
Dilu'te, v. a. to make weak or thin
Dilu'tion, s. the act of making weak or thin
Dilu'vian, a. relating to the deluge
Dim, a. not clear in sight, not clearly discern
Dimen'sion, s. extent, bulk, capacity [ea
Dimin'ish, v. to lessen, to impair, to degrade
Diminu'tion, s. the act of making less
Dimin'utive, a. little, small, contracted
Dim'ity, s. a fine fustian, or cloth of cotton
Dim'ness, s. dulness of sight; stupidity
Dim'ple, s. a hollow in the chin or cheek
Dim'ply, a. full of dimples
Din, s. a continued sound, a loud noise
Dine, v. to eat, to give a dinner, to feed
Dinet'ical, a. whirling round, vertiginous
Ding, v. to dash violently; huff, bluster
Din'gle, s. a hollow between hills
Din'gy, a. dirty, dark, foul, soiled
Din'ner, s. the meal eaten about mid-day
Dint, s. a mark; a blow; force, violence
Dinumera'tion, s. act of numbering out singly
Di'nus, s. a whirlwind; a giddiness
Dioce'san, s. a bishop or head of a diocese
Di'ocese, s. the jurisdiction of a bishop
Diop'trics, s. the science of refracted lights
Dip, v. to immerge; to engage; to mois en
Diph'thong, s. two vowels joined together
Diplo'ma, s. a deed or privilege of degree

Dip tote, *s.* a noun of two cases only

Dire, Di'reful, *a.* dreadful, horrible, dismal

Direc't, *a.* straight, plain, open, express

Direc't, *v. a.* to command; adjust, regulate

Direc'tion, *s.* a superscription; an aim

Direc'tly, *ad.* immediately, apparently; in a straight line; rectilinearly

Direc'tor, *s. a* ruler, a guide, a superintendant

Direc'tory, *s.* a form of prayer; a rule

Di'reness, *s.* dismalness, hideousness, horror

Direp'tion, *s.* the act of robbing or plundering

Dirge, *s.* a funeral or mournful ditty

Dirk, *s.* a kind of dagger or short sword

Dirt, *s.* mud, mire, filth; meanness

Dir'tiness, *s.* nastiness, filthiness, sordidness

Dir'ty, *a.* nasty, foul, sullied; mean, base

Dir'ty, *v. a.* to foul, to soil; to scandalize

Dirup'tion, *s.* the act or state of bursting

Disabil'ity, *s.* want of power, weakness

Disa'ble, *v. a.* to render incapable, to impair

Disabu'se, *v. a.* to set right, to undeceive

Disadvan'tage, *s.* loss; injury to interest

Disadvanta'geous, *a.* hurtful, prejudicial

Disadvanta'geously, *ad.* in a hurtful manner

Disaffec't, *v. a.* to fill with discontent

Disaffec'ted, *part.* not wishing well to

Disaffec'tion, *s.* want of loyalty or zeal

Disaffirm'ance, *s.* a confutation; a negation

Disagree', *v. n.* to differ in opinion, to quarrel

Disagree'able, *a.* unpleasing, odious, offensive

Disagree'ment, *s.* difference, unsuitableness

Disallow', *v.* to deny; to reject; to censure

Disallow'able, *a.* not allowable, improper

Disan'imate, *v. a.* to deprive of life; reject

Disanima'tion, *s.* privation of life

Disannul', *v. a.* to make void, to annul

Disappea'r, *v. n.* to vanish, to be lost to view

Disappoi'nt, *v. a.* to defeat expectation

Disappoi'ntment, *s.* defeat of hopes; a balk

Disap proba'tion, *s.* a dislike, a censure, hate

Disappro've, *v. a.* to dislike, to censure

Disar'm, *v. a.* to take away or divest of arms

Disa'rmed, *part.* deprived of arms, stript

Disarray', *s.* disorder, confusion; undress

Disas'ter, *s.* misfortune, mishap, grief

Disas'trous, *a.* unlucky, dismal, calamitous

Disavou'ch, Disavow', *v. a.* to deny, disown

Disavow'al, Disavow'ment, *s.* a denial

Disban'd, *v. a.* to dismiss from military service; to break up, to separate, to scatter

Dishar'k, *v. a.* to land from a ship, to unload

Disbelie'f, *s.* a refusal of belief; discredit

Disbelie've, *v. a.* not to believe; to deny

Disbelie'ver, *s.* one who refuses belief

Disbranch', *v. a.* to separate or lop off

Disbur'den, *v. a.* to discharge, to unload

Disbur'se, *v. a.* to lay out or spend money

Disbur'sement, *s.* a disbursing of money

Discan'dy, *v. n.* to melt, dissolve, soften

Discar'd, *v. a.* to dismiss or reject from service

Discar'nate, *a.* stripped of flesh   [vice

Discer'n, *v. n.* to descry, distinguish, judge

Discer'nible, *a.* perceptible, discoverable

Discer'ning, *part. a.* knowing, judicious

Discer'nment, *s.* judgment, acuteness, skill

Discer'pible, *a.* separable, frangible

Dischar'ge, *v. a.* to dismiss; to pay; to emit

Dischar'ge, *s.* an acquittance; a dismission

Discin'ct, *a.* loosely dressed; ungirded

Discin'd, *v. a.* to cut in pieces; to divide

Disci'ple, *s.* a follower; a scholar

Disci'pleship, *s.* the state of a disciple

Dis'cipline, *s.* a military regulation; order

Dis'cipline, *v. a.* to educate; to keep in order; to regulate; to reform; to punish

Disclai'm, *v. a.* to disown, renounce, deny

Disclo'se, *v. a.* to reveal, to discover, to tell

Disclo'sure, *s.* revealing a secret; discovery

Discol'our, *v. a.* to stain or change colour

Discom'fit, *v. a.* to conquer, to defeat

Discom'fiture, *s.* loss of battle; overthrow

Discom'fort, *v. a.* to grieve, sadden, deject

Discom'fort, *s.* melancholy, uneasiness

Discommen'd, *v. a.* to censure, to blame

Discommen'dable, *a.* censurable, blameable

Discommo'de, *v. a.* to put to inconvenience

Discommo'dious, *a.* troublesome, inconvenient

Discompo'se, *v. a.* to displace, to vex, to fret

Disconcer't, *v. a.* to discompose, to unsettle

Disconfor'mity, *s.* want of agreement

Disconcru'ity, *s.* disagreement, inconsistency

Discon'solate, *a.* wanting comfort; sorrowful

Discon'tent, *s.* a want of content

Disconten'ted, *part. a.* dissatisfied; uneasy

Disconten'tedness, Discontent'ment, *s.* the state of being discontented; uneasiness

Discontin'uance, Discontinua'tion, *s.* a cessation; intermission; separation of parts

Discontin'ue, *v.* to leave off; to interrupt

Discontinu'ity, *s.* disunion of parts

Dis'cord, *s.* opposition; disagreement

Discor'dance, *s.* inconsistency, disagreement

Discor'dant, *a.* incongruous, inconsistent

Discor'dantly, *ad.* inconsistently, peevishly

Discov'er, *v. a.* to disclose, to spy, to detect

Discov'ered, *part.* betrayed, found out

Discov'ery, *s.* the act of finding; invention

Discou'nt, *v. a.* to pay back, to count back

Dis'count, *s.* an allowance, a drawback

Discou'ntenance, *v. a.* to abash, to discourage

Discou'ntenance, *s.* cold treatment

Discou'rage, *v. a.* to deter, dissuade, depress

Discou'ragement, *s.* cause of fear, determent

Discou'rse, *s.* conversation; a treatise

Discou'rteous, *a.* uncivil, unpolite, rude

Dis'cous, *a.* broad, wide, flat

Discred'it, *s.* disgrace, reproach, ignominy

Discred'it, *v. a.* not to believe; to disgrace

Discree't, *a.* prudent, not forward, cautious

Discrep'ance, *s.* a difference, contrariety

Discre'te, *a.* distinct, separated, disjointed

Discre'tion, *s.* prudence; liberty of acting

Discre'tionary, *a.* left at large, unrestrained

Discrim'inate, *v. a.* to mark; separate; select

Discrimina'tion, *s.* act of distinguishing one from another; a distinction; a mark

Discrim'inous, *a.* perilous, dangerous

Discu'bitory, *a.* fitted to a leaning posture

Discum'bency, *s.* the act of leaning at meat

Discum'ber, *v. a.* to disengage, to disburthen

Discur'sion, *s.* the act of running to and fro

Discur'sive, *a.* argumentative, progressive

Discur'sory, *a.* rational, argumentative

Dis'cus, *s.* quoit; a round iron for play

Discuss', *v. a.* to argue, to examine

Discus'sion, *s.* disquisition of a question

Discu'tient, *s.* a repelling medicine

Disdai'n, *s.* scorn, contempt, indignation

Disdai'n, *v. a.* to scorn, to slight, to

Disdai'nful, *a.* haughty, contemptuous

Disea'se, *s.* distemper, malady,

Disea'se, v. a. to afflict, to pain, to torment
Disea'sed, part. afflicted with a distemper
Disembar'k, v. to put on shore, to land
Disembit'ter, v. a. to free from bitterness
Disembod'ied, a. divested of the body
Disembo'gue, v. to discharge into the sea
Disembroi'l, v.a. to disentangle, to clear up
Disenchan't, v.a. to free from enchantment
Disencum'ber,v.a.to disburden;to exonerate
Disenga'ge, v. to extricate, free from, quit
Disenga'ged, part. a. clear from; at leisure
Disen'an'gle, v. a. to unravel, to disengage
Disenthra'l, v. a. to rescue, to set free
Disenthro'ne, v.a. to depose a sovereign
Disentran'ce, v. a. to awake from a trance
Disespou'se, v. a. to divorce, to separate
Disestee'm, s. dislike, slight regard
Disfa'vour, v. a. to discountenance
Disfigura'tion, s.act of disfiguring; deformity
Disfig'ure, v. a. to deform, mangle, deface
Disfig'urement, s. defacement of beauty
Disfran'chise, v. a. to deprive cities of their
  charters, immunities, or privileges
Disgorge', v.a. to vomit, pour out with force
Disgra'ce, v. a. to dishonour, to dismiss
Disgra'ce, s. loss of favour, dishonour
Disgra'ceful, a. ignominious, shameful
Disgra'cious, a. unfavourable, unpleasing
Disgui'se, s. a dress to deceive; a pretence
Disgui'se, v.a. to conceal; deform, disfigure
Disgus't, s. a dislike, an aversion; offence
Disgus't,v.a.to provoke, to offend; to distaste
Disgus'tful, a. causing aversion, nauseous
Dish, s. a vessel used to serve up meat in
Dish, v. a. to put or serve up meat in a dish
Dishabill'e, s. a loose dress, an undress
Dishab'it, v. a. to throw out of place; expel
Dishear'ten, v. a. to terrify, to depress
Disher'it, v. a. to cut off from inheritance
Dishev'el, v. a. to spread the hair loosely
Dishon'est, a. void of probity, faithless
Dishon'esty, s. knavery; incontinence
Dishon'our, v. a. to violate, to disgrace
Dishon'our, s. disgrace, reproach, censure
Dishon'ourable, a. reproachful, shameful
Dishor'n, v. a. to strip or deprive of horns
Disinclina'tion, s. dislike, want of affection
Disincli'ne, v. a. to produce dislike to
Disincor'porate, v.a. to dissolve, to separate
Disingenu'ity, s. unfairness, insincerity
Disingen'uous, a. illiberal, mean, unfair
Disinher'it, v. a. to deprive of inheritance
Disinter', v. a. to take out of a grave
Disin'terested, a. superior to selfish views
Disjoi'n, v. a. to disunite, separate, sunder
Disjoi'nt,v.to put out of joint;to fall in pieces;
  to crumble; to make incoherent
Disjoi'nted, part. divided, separated
Disjudica'tion, s. the act of settling
Disjun'ct, a. divided, disjoined, separate
Disjun'ction, s. a separation, a disunion
Disk, s. the face of the sun, a quoit
Disli'ke, s. aversion, hatred, disapprobation
Disli'ke, v. a. to hate, to disapprove
Disli'ken, v. a. to make unlike
Disli'mn, v. a. to strip out of a picture
Dis'locate, v.a. to put out of joint, to displace
Disloca'tion, s. act of displacing; a luxation
Dislod'ge, v. to drive out; to move away
Disloy'al, a. not true to allegiance; faithless
Dis'loyally, ad. not faithfully; disobediently

Disloy'alty, s. want of allegiance
Dis'mal, a. uncomfortable, sorrowful; dark
Dis'mally, ad. horribly, sorrowfully
Disman'tle, v.a. to strip; destroy; overthrow
Dismas'k, v.a. to divest of a mask; uncover
Dismas't, v. a. to deprive a ship of her masts
Dismay', v.a. to affright, to terrify, to deject
Dismay', s. a fall of courage; fright, terror
Di'sme, s. a tenth part, a tithe
Dismem'ber, v. a. to cut off a limb, &c.
Dismiss', v. a. to discard, to send away
Dismiss'ed, part. discarded, sent away
Dismis'sion, s. a sending away; deprivation
Dismor'tgage, v.a. to redeem from mortgage
Dismou'nt,v. to throw or alight from a horse
Disobe'dience, s. a breach of duty
Disobe'dient, a. undutiful, froward
Disobey', v. a. not to obey, to transgress
Disobli'ge, v. a. to offend, provoke, disgust
Disobli'ging, part. a. offensive, disgusting
Disor'der, s. irregularity, tumult; sickness
Disor'der, v.a. to disturb, ruffle; make sick
Disor'derly, a. irregular, confused; lawless
Disor'dinate, a. living irregularly; vicious
Disor'ganize, v. a. to break in pieces
Disow'n,v.a. to deny, renounce, not to allow
Dispan'd, v.a. to spread abroad, to display
Dispar'age, v. a. to treat with contempt
Dispar'agement, s. a reproach, a disgrace
Dispar'ity, s. dissimilitude, inequality
Dispar'k, v.a. to throw open a park
Dispar't, v.a. to divide in two, to separate
Dispas'sion, s. composure, coolness of temper
Dispas'sionate, a. cool, impartial, moderate
Dispat'ch. See Despat'ch.
Dispel', v. a. to dissipate; to drive away
Dispen'd, v. a. to spend, expend, consume
Dispen'sary, s. a place where medicines are
  dispensed to the public
Dispensa'tion, s.a distribution;an exemption:
  an indulgence from the Pope
Dispen'satory, s. the directory for making
  medicines; a pharmacopeia
Dispen'se, v. to distribute; to excuse
Dispeo'ple, v. a. to depopulate, to lay waste
Disper'ge, v. a. to sprinkle, to scatter
Disper'se, v. a. to drive away, to scatter
Disper'sion, s. the act of spreading abroad
Dispir'it, v. a. to discourage, deject, damp
Displa'ce, v.a. to put out of place, to remove
Displa'cency, s. incivility, offence, disgust
Displan't, v. a. to remove a plant; to drive
  away a people from their residence
Displanta'tion, s. the removal of a people
Display', v. a. to exhibit; to spread wide
Display', s. exhibition, grandeur
Displeas'ant, a. unpleasing, bad, offensive
Displea'se, v. a. to offend, vex, disgust
Displeas'ure, s. offence, hate, anger
Displo'de, v. a. to vent with violence
Displo'sion, s. a bursting with violence
Dispor't, s. play, pastime, merriment, sport
Dispo'sal, s. conduct; regulation
Dispo'se,v.to set in order; to adjust; to regu-
  late; to incline; to sell
Dispo'sed, part. sold; inclined; placed
Disposi'tion, s. temper of mind; order, me-
  thod; quality; tendency; situation
Dispossess', v. a. to deprive; to dismiss
Disposses'sion, s. the act of putting out
Dispo'sure, s. disposal; posture; state; power

Disprai'se, s. disgrace, b'ame, censure
Disprai'se, v.a. to censure, blame, condemn
Dispread', v. a. to spread different ways
Disprof'it, s. dama e, loss—v. a. to injure
Dis roo'f, s. a refutation, a confutation
Dispropor'tion, v. a. to mismatch
Dispropor'tion, s. want of symmetry; unsuitableness; inequality, disparity
Dispropor'tionate.Dispropor'tionate. a. unsuitable in quan'ity; unfit; unequal
Dispro've, r.a. to refu e, to confute
Dispun'i hable, a. fre from penal restraint
Dis'putable, a. liable to be contes ed
Dis'putant, s. a reasoner, a con'rovertist
Disputa'tion, s. argumental contest
Disputa'tious.Dispu' ative, s. inclined to dispute; argumenta ive; captious
Dispu'te, v. a. to debate, contend, wrangle
Dispu' e, s. controversy, contes, heat
Dispu'teless, a. undeniable, undisputed
Disqualifica'tion, s. that which disqualifies
Disqual'ify, v. a. to disable, to make unfit
Disqui'et, v.a. to disturb, harass, fret, vex
Disqui'et, Disqui'etude, s. uneasiness
Disqui'etly, ad. without rest, anxiously
Disquisi'tion, s. a disputative inquiry
Disregar'd,s. silght notice, contempt, neglect
Disregar'd, v. a. to neglect, slight, despise
Disregar'dful, a. neg igent, contemptuous
Disrel'ish, s. bad taste, nauseousness, dislike
Disrel'ish, v. a. to make nauseous, &c.
Disrep'utable, a. u becoming, disgraceful
Disreputa'tion, Disrepu'te, s. dishonour
Disrespec't, s. want of reverence, rudeness
Disro'be, v.a. to undress, to strip, to uncover
Disrup'tion, s. a breaking assunder, a rent
Dissat sfac'tion, s. discontent, disgust
Dissatisfac'tory, a. not giving content
Dissat'isfy, v.a. to displea e, to offend
Dissec't, v.a. to divide nicely; to cut in pieces
Dissec'tion, s. anatomy; nice examination
Dissei'se, v. a. to deprive, to dispossess
Disseisee', s. one deprived of his lands
Dis-sei'sin, s. an unlawful ejectment
Dissei'sor, s. he that dispossesses another
Dissem'blance, s. want of resemblance
Dissem'ble. v. to play the hypocrite
Dissem'bled. part. not real
Dissem'bler, s. a pretender, an hypocrite
Dissem'inate, v. a. to scatter, spread, sow
Dissemina'tion, s. he act of scattering
Dissem na'tor,s. one who spreads or scatters
Dissen'sion, s. strife, disagreement, discord
Dis en't, v.n. to differ in opinion; to differ
Dissen't.s.disagreement,differenceofopinion
Di-sen'ter,s.one who dissents, one who does not conform to the established church
Di-sen' tious, a. qua relsome, contentious
Disserta'tion, s. a treatise, a discourse
Disser've, r. a. to do an injury to, to hurt
Disser'vice, s. mischief, injury, ill turn
Disser' iceable, a. mischievous, injurious
Dissev'er, r. a to part in two to disunite
Dissi'i'ion, s. the act of bursting in two
Dissim'ilar, a. unlike, heterogeneous
Dissimilar'ity, Dissimi'litude, s. unlikeness
Dissimula'tion, s. a dissembling; hypocrisy
Dis'sipate, v.a. to spend lavishly, to d sperse
Dissipa'tion, s. extravagant spending, waste
Disso'ciate, v. a. to separate, to disunite
Dis'soluble, a. capable of separation

Dissol've, r. to melt; separate, disunite
Dissol'vent, a. having the power of melting
Dissol'vable, a. liable to be dissolved
Dis'solute, a. loose, debauched, unrestrained
Dis'soluteness, s. debauchery, looseness
Dissolu'tion, s. death, a dissolving; destruction, act of break ing up an assembly
Dis'sonance, s. harshness, discord
Dis'sonant, a. harsh, unharmonious
Dissua'de, r. a. to advise to the contrary
Dissua'sive,a. tending to dissua e—s. dehortation, argument tending to dissuade
Dissyl'lable, s. a word of two sy lables
Dis'taff, s. a staff used in spinning
Dista'n. v. a. to tinge, to stain; to defame
Dis'tance, s. intervening time or space; distant behaviour; respect; reserve
Dis'tance, r. a. to leave behind in a race
Dis'tant, a. remote in place or time; shy
Dista'-te, s. dislike, aversion, disgust
Dista'steful, a. nauseous, malignant
Distem'per, s. a malady, disease; uneasiness
Distem', er. v. a. to disease; dis'urb, ruffle
Distem'perature, s. intemperateness; noise
Distem'pered, part. diseased; disturbed
Disten'd, v. a. to stretch out in breadth
Disten'ded, part. widened, swelled
Disten't, s. length or space of extension
Disten'tion, s. act of stretching; breadth
Dis'tich, s. a couple of lines; a couplet
Distil', v. to draw by distillation; to drop
Distilla'tion, s. the act of distilling by fire
Distil'ler, s. one who distils spirits
Distin'ct, a. s parate, different, unconfused
Distin'ction, s. difference; mark of honour
Distin'ctive, a. able to distinguish, judicious
Distin'ctively,Distin'ctly, ad. not confusedly
Distin'ctness, s. plainness, clearness
Distin'guish, v.a. to discern, ma k; honour
Distin'guishable, a. capable of distinction
Distin'guished,part.a.eminent,transcendent
Distor't, v. a. to writhe, misrepresent, twist
Distor'tion, s. grimace; misrepresentation
Distrac't, v. a. to vex, to make mad, to divide
Distrac'ted, part. a. wild, perplexed; divided
Distrac'tedly, ad. franticly, madly
Distrac'tion, s. madness; discord, confusion
Distrai'n, v.a. to seize goods or chattels
Distrain't, s. a seizure of goods, &c.
Distress', r. a. to make miserable, to harass
Distress'. s. want, misery; a distraining
Distress'ed, a. full of trouble, miserable
Distrib'ute, v. a. to divide among many
Distribu'tion, s. the act of distributing
Distrib'utive,a.what assigns each his portion
Dis'trict, s. a circuit; province, region
Distrus't, v. a. not to trust, to disbelieve
Distrus't, s. want of confidence; suspicion
Distrus'tful, a. apt to distrust; timorous
Disturb'.v.a.to perplex, interrupt, confound
Distur'bance,s.perplexity, tumult,confusion
Distur'ber, s. a violator of peace
Disvalua'tion, s. loss of reputation, disgrace
Disval'ue, v. a. to undervalue, to slight
Disu'n ion,s.a separation; breach of concord
Disuni'te, v. a. to divide; to separate friends
Disu'nity, s. state of actual separation
Disu'se, v. a. to leave off, to disaccustom
Disu'se, Disu'sage, s. want of practice or use
Disvouch,v.a. to destroy the credit of; deny
Ditch. s. a moat in fortification; a trench

Dit'cher, s. a man who makes ditches
Dithyram'bic, s. a song in honour of Bacchus
Dit'tied, a. sung; adapted to music
Dit'to, s. the aforesaid, the same repeated
Dit'ty, s. a song; a musical poem
Divan', s. the Ottoman grand council
Divar'icate, v. a. to divide into two
Divarica'tion, s. a division of opinions
Dive, v. n. to sink voluntarily under water; to enter deeply into any matter or business
Di'ver, s. one who dives; a water fowl
Diver'ge, v. n. to depart from one point
Diver'gent, a. going farther asunder
Di'vers, a. sundry, several. more than one
Di'verse, a. unlike, different, contrary
Diversifica'tion, s. variation, change
Diver'sify, v. a. to variegate, to distinguish
Diver'sion, s. a turning aside; game, pastime
Diver'sity, s. unlikeness, difference
Di'versely, ad. variously, differently
Diver't, v. a. to turn aside; to amuse
Diver'ting, part. pleasing, merry, agreeable
Diver'tingly, ad. in an amusing manner
Diver'tise. v. a. to divert, please, exhilarate
Diver'tisement, s. recreation, pleasure
Divest', v. a. to dispossess; to strip
Divest'ure, s. the act of stripping off
Divi'dable, Divi'dant, a. divisable, different
Divi'de, v. to separate, to part; give in shares
Div'idend, s. a share; part allotted in division
Divi'ders, s. a pair of compasses
Divid'ual, a. divided, shared with others
Divina'tion. s. a prediction of future events
Divi'ne, v. to foretel, to foreknow, to guess
Divi'ne, a. heavenly, godlike, not human
Divi'ne, s. a minister of the gospel, a priest
Divi'nely, ad. in a godlike manner
Divi'ner, s. one who professes divination
Divin'ity, s. the Supreme Being; godhead; science of divine things; theology
Divis'ible, a. that can be divided
Divis'ion, s. the act of dividing; part of a discourse; partition; discord, disunion
Divi'sor, s. the number that divides
Divo'rce, v. a. to separate; to force asunder
Divo'rce, Divo'rcement, s. the legal separation of husband and wife; disunion
Diuret'ic, Diuret'ical, a. provoking urine
Diur'nal, a. performed in a day, daily
Diur'nal, s. a journal, a day-book
Diur'nally, ad. daily, day by day, every day
Diuturn'ity, s. length of duration
Divul'ge, v. a. to publish, proclaim, declare
Di'zen, v. a. to dress or deck gaudily
Diz'ziness, s. thoughtlessness, giddiness
Diz'zy, a. giddy, thoughtless
Do, v. to act any thing, either good or bad
Doc'ible, Doc'ile, a. easily taught, tractable
Docil'ity, Doc'ibleness, s. aptness to be taught
Dock, s. a ship-builder's yard; an herb
Dock, v. a. to lay in a dock; to cut short
Dock'et, s. a direction tied upon goods
Dock'yard, s. a yard for naval stores, &c.
Doc'tor, s. a title in divinity, physic, law, &c.
Doc'torship, s. the highest academical degree
Doc'trinal, a. relating to doctrine; pertaining to the means or act of teaching
Doc'trine, s. maxim, precept, act of teaching
Doc'ument, s. a precept, direction, instruction; a precept magisterially dogmatical
Documen'tal, a. relating to instruction

Dodec'agon, s. a figure of twelve equal sides
Dodge, v. a. to use craft; to follow unperceived; to use mean artifices; to quibble
Doe, s. the female of a buck
Doff, v. a. to strip, to put off dress; to delay
Dog, s. a domestic animal; a lump of iron
Dog, v. a. to follow slily and continually
Dog'days. s. days from July 21 to August 28
Doge, s. the chief magistrate of Venice
Dog'ged, a. obstinately sullen, gloomy
Dog'ger, s. a small ship with one mast
Dog'gerel, s. despicable vers e—a. mean, vile
Dog'gish. a. brutal, snappish, currish
Dog'ma, s. an established principle; a notion
Dogmat'ical. a. authoritative, magisterial
Dog'matism, s. an authoritative assertion
Do'matist, s. a positive assertor or teacher
Dog'star, s. a certain star, from which the dog-days derive their appellation
Doi'ly, s. a small napkin used after dinner
Do'ings, s. pl. actions, feats, stir, bustle
Doit, s. a small piece of Dutch money
Dole, s. a part, share; misery, grief
Dole, v. a. to distribute, to deal
Dole'ful, a. sorrowful, feeling grief, dismal
Dole'fully, ad. in a sad or dismal manner
Dole'some, a. melancholy, gloomy, heavy
Doll, s. a little girl's baby or puppet
Dol'lar, s. a foreign coin of different value, from about 2s. 6d. to 4s. 6d.; a counter
Dolorif'ic, a. causing grief or pain
Dol'orous, a. sorrowful, dismal, painful
Do'lour, s. lamentation, grief, pain, pang
Dol'phin. s. a kind of beautiful sea-fish
Dolt, s. a heavy stupid fellow, a thickscull
Dol'tish, a. mean, stupid, blockish, dull
Domain, s. dominion; estate, empire
Dome, s. a building; arched roof; cupola
Domes'tic, a. belonging to the house; not foreign, private; intestine
Domes'tic, s. a dependant, a servant
Domes'ticate, v. a. to render domestic
Dom'icil, s. a mansion-house, habitation
Dom'inate, v. a. to prevail over; to govern
Domina'tion, s. power; insolent authority
Dominee'r, v. a. to rule with insolence; to act without control; to swell
Domin'ical, a. denoting the Lord's day
Domin'ion, s. sovereign authority; power; district, territory; an order of angels
Dom'ino. s. kind of hood or long dress
Don, s. a Spanish title for a gentleman
Dona'tion. s. a gift, a bounty, a present
Don'ative, s. a gift, a benefice, a largess
Done, part. pass. of the verb to do
Donee interj. a word used to confirm a wager
Do'nor, s. a benefactor, a giver, a bestower
Doom, v. a. to judge; to destine; to condemn
Doom, s. a judicial sentence; final judgment; condemnation; destiny; ruin
Doo'med, part. condemned, fated, destined
Doo'msday, s. the day of judgment
Doo'msday-hook, s. a book made by order of William the Conqueror, in which all the estates in England were registered
Door, s. the gate of a house, a passage
Doq'uet, s. a paper containing a warrant
Dor'ic, a. relating to the Doric architecture
Dor'mant, a. sleeping; concealed, private
Dor'mitory, s. a place to sleep in; a female vault; a burial-place

Dor'mouse, *s.* a small animal which passes a large part of the winter in sleep

Dorr, *s.* a flying insect; the hedge chafer

Dor'ture, *s.* a dormitory; a place to sleep in

Dose, *s.* so much of any medicine as is taken at one time; what falls to a man's lot

Dot, *s.* a small point or spot in writing, &c.

Dot, *v. n.* to make points or spots

Do'tage, *s.* silly fondness; weakness of mind

Do'tal, *a.* relating to a dowry or portion

Do'tard. Do'ter, *s.* a fond lover; one whose age has impaired his intellects

Dote, *v. n.* to love with excessive fondness

Do'ted, *a.* gifted. endowed. possessed of

Do'tingly, *ad.* lovingly, fondly

Dor'tard, *s.* a tree kept low by cutting

Doub'le, *a.* twice as much, twofold

Doub'le, *v.* to make twice as much; to fold; to sail round a headland; to play tricks

Doub'le, *s.* a plait or fold; an artifice, trick

Doubledea'ler, *s.* a deceitful, subtle fellow

Doubledea'ling, *s.* cunning, dissimulation

Doublemind'ed, *a.* deceitful, perfidious

Doub'let, *s.* a waistcoat; two; a pair

Doubleton'gued. *a.* false, deceitful, hollow

Doubloo'n, *s.* a Spanish coin, value two pistoles

Doub'ly, *ad.* twice the quantity; twice

Doubt, *v.* to question, to distrust, to scruple

Doubt, *s.* suspicion, suspense difficulty

Doub'tful, *a.* uncertain, not determined

Doub'tfully. Doub'tingly. *ad.* uncertainly

Doub'tfulness, *s.* instability of opinion

Doub'tless, *a.* and *ad.* without doubt or fear

Douce'ur, *s.* a conciliating bribe; a sweetener

Dove, *s.* a sort of pigeon, a wild pigeon

Dov'ecot, Dov'ehouse, *s.* a house for pigeons

Dov'elike, *a.* meek, harmless. gentle

Dov'etail, *s.* a term used by joiners

Dough, *s.* unbaked paste, kneaded flour

Dou'ghty, *a.* eminent, brave, illustrious

Dou'ghy, *a.* not quite baked, soft, pale

Douse, *v.* to plunge suddenly into water

Dow'ager, *s.* a widow with a jointure

Dow'dy. *s.* an awkward, ill-dressed woman

Dow'er, or Dow'ery. *s.* a wife's portion; a widow's jointure; gift, endowment

Dow'eriess, *a.* without fortune, unportioned

Dow'las, *s.* a kind of coarse strong linen

Down, *s.* a large open plain; the finest, softest feathers; soft hair or wool

Down, *prep.* along a descent—*ad.* on the ground; into declining reputation

Dow'ncast, *a.* bent down, dejected

Dow'nfal, *s.* calamity, ruin, sudden change

Dow'nhill, *s.* a descent—*a.* descending

Downly'ing, *part.* near the time of childbirth

Downri'ght, *a.* plain, undisguised, apparent

Downri'ght, *ad.* honestly, plainly, completely

Downs, *s.* a hilly, open country

Dow'nward, *a.* bending down, dejected

Dow'nward, Dow'nwards. *ad.* from a higher situation to a lower; toward the centre

Dow'ny, *a.* covered with a nap; tender, soft

Dowse, *s.* a slap on the face—*v. a.* to strike

Doxol'ogy. *s.* a form of giving glory to God

Dox'y, *s.* a strumpet, a loose wench

Doze, *v.* to slumber, to dull, to stupify

Doz'en, *s.* the number of twelve

Do'ziness, *s.* drowsiness, inclination to sleep

Drab, *s.* a thick woollen cloth; a prostitute

Drachm, *s.* an old Roman coin; the eighth part of an ounce

Draff. *s.* refuse; any thing thrown away

Draft, *s.* a bill drawn on another for money

Drag, *v.* to pull along by force, to trail

Drag, *s.* a net or hook; a hand cart

Drag'gle, *v. a.* to trail in the dirt

Drag'gled, *part.* made dirty by walking

Drag'net, *s.* a net drawn along the bottom

Drag'on, *s.* a winged serpent; a constellation

Drag'onlike. *a.* furious, fierce, fiery

Dragoo'n, *s.* a horse soldier; a bully

Dragoo'n, *v. a.* to force one against his will

Drain, *s.* a channel to carry off water

Drain, *v.* to draw off, to make quite dry

Drake, *s.* the male of a duck; a small piece of artillery

Dram, *s.* in troy weight, the eighth part of an ounce; a glass of spirituous liquor

Dra'ma, *s.* the action of a play; a poem

Dramat'ic, *a.* represented by action; theatric

Dram'atist, *s.* a writer of plays

Dra'per, *s.* one who sells or deals in cloth

Dra'pery, *s.* clothwork; the dress of a picture

Dras'tic, *a.* powerful, efficacious, vigorous

Draught, *s.* the act of drinking; the quantity of liquor drank at once; quantity drawn; a sketch, or delineation; a drain; a sink; act of pulling carriages

Draught, Draft, *a.* used in or for drawing

Draughts, *s.* a kind of play on chequers

Draw, *v.* to pull forcibly; to attract; to represent by picture; to win, allure; to unsheath

Draw'back, *s.* money paid back on exports

Draw'bridge, *s.* a bridge made to draw up

Draw'er, *s.* a sliding box; one who draws

Draw'ers, *s.* a kind of light under-breeches

Draw'ing, *s.* a representation, a delineation

Draw'ing-room, *s.* the room in which company assemble at court

Drawl, *v. n.* to speak slowly or clownishly

Draw'-well, *s.* a deep well to draw water from

Dray, *s.* a sort of carriage used by brewers

Draz'el, *s.* a mean low wretch; a drab

Dread, *s.* great fear, awe, terror, affright

Dread, *v.* to fear greatly, to stand in awe

Dread, *a.* mighty, great, awful, venerable

Dread'ful, *a.* terrible, horrid, frightful

Dread'fully, *ad.* terribly, frightfully

Dread'less, *a.* fearless, daring, undaunted

Dream, *s.* thoughts in sleep, an idle fancy

Dream, *v.* to think in sleep; to be sluggish

Dream'er, *s.* one who dreams; a mope

Dream'less, *a.* free from dreams

Drear, Drea'ry, *a.* dismal, gloomy, mournful

Drea'riness, *s.* gloominess, dulness

Dredge, *s.* an oyster net; mixture of grain

Dredge, *v. a.* to besprinkle flour on meat while roasting; to catch with a net

Dreg'giness, *s.* fulness of lees, feculence

Dreg'gy, *a.* containing dregs, not clear

Dregs. *s.* the sediment of liquors, lees

Drench, *v. a.* to steep, soak, fill with drink

Drench. *s.* a horse's physical draught

Dress, *s.* clothes, finery, ornaments

Dress, *v. a.* to clothe, to adorn, to deck; to cook; to adjust; to cover a wound

Dress'er, *s.* he who dresses; a kitchen table

Dress'ing, *s.* the act of clothing, &c.

Dress'ing-room, *s.* a place used to dress in

Drib, *v. a.* to cut short, to crop, to lop off

Drib'ble, v. n. to drop slowly; drivel, slaver
Drib'let, s. a small part of a large sum
Dri'er, s. that which absorbs moisture
Drift, s. any thing driven at random; a design, a tendency; a heap; a storm
Drift, v. a. to urge along; to throw on heaps
Drill, s. a small dribbling brook; an instrument to bore holes with; a baboon, an ape
Drill, v.a. to train to arms; to bore; to delay
Drink, s. a liquor to be swallowed
Drink, v. to quench thirst, to swallow liquors
Drin'kable, a. what may be drank
Drin'ker, s. one who drinks to excess
Drip, v. n. to drop—s. what drops
Drip'ping, s. the fat that drops from meat while it is roasting or baking
Drip'ple, a. weak, unusual, rare
Drive, v. to force along; to guide a carriage; to urge in any direction; to carry on
Driv'el, v. a. to slaver; to dote; to be weak
Driv'el, s. spittle, slaver; an idiot, a fool
Driv'eller, s. a slaverer, a fool, an idiot
Driv'en, Dro'ven, part. of to drive
Dri'ver, s. one who drives or urges on
Driz'zle, v. to fall in short slow drops
Driz'zly, a. shedding small rain
Drock, s. a piece of wood in a plough
Droll, v. n. to work slowly, &c.—s. a drone
Droll, s. a jester, a buffoon, a farce
Droll, v. n. to jest, to play the buffoon
Droll, a. comical, merry, humorous, laughing
Dro'llery, s. buffoonery, idle jokes [able
Drom'edary, s. a very swift kind of camel
Dro'mo, s. a swift sailing vessel; a fish
Drone, s. the bee which collects no honey; a sluggard, an idler; a slow humming
Drone, v. n. to live in idleness, to dream
Dro'nish, a. sluggish, idle, inactive, dull
Droop, v. n. to pine away, faint, languish
Droo'ping, part. fainting, languishing
Drop, s. a small quantity, or globule, of any liquid; a diamond hanging on the ear
Drop, v. to fall in drops, to let fall; to cease; to die, to come to nothing; to utter slightly
Drop'let, s. a small drop; a small ear-ring
Drop'pings, s. that which falls in drops
Drop'sical, a. diseased with a dropsy
Drop'sy, s. collection of water in the body
Dross, s. the scum of metals; dregs, refuse
Dross'iness, s. foulness, rust, feculence
Dross'y, a. full of dross, foul, worthless
Drove, s. a herd of cattle; a tumult, a crowd
Dro'ver, s. one who drives cattle to market
Drought, Drouth, s. dry weather; thirst
Drou'ghty, a. wanting rain; sultry, thirsty
Drown, v. to suffocate in water, to overwhelm in water; to bury in an inundation, to immerge, to deluge, to overflow
Drow'sily, ad. sleepily, lazily, idly, heavily
Drow'siness, s. sleepiness, idleness
Drow'sy, a. sleepy, stupid, heavy, dull
Drub, s. a thump, a blow, a knock
Drub, v. a. to thresh, to bang, to beat
Drub'bing, s. a threshing, a chastisement
Drudge, v. n. to labour in mean offices
Drudge, s. one employed in mean labour
Drud'gery, s. hard, mean labour; slavery
Drud'gingly, ad. toilsomely, laboriously
Drug, s. a medicinal simple; a thing of little value or worth; a drudge
Drug'get, s. a slight kind of woollen stuff

Drug'gist, s. a person who sells physical drugs
Dru'id, s. an ancient British priest and bard
Drum, s. an instrument of military music; the tympanum of the ear
Drum, v. n. to beat a drum
Drum-ma'jor, s. chief drummer of a regiment
Drum'mer, s. one who beats a drum
Drum'stick, s. the stick for beating a drum
Drunk, a. intoxicated with strong liquors
Drun'kard, s. one given to excess in drinking
Drun'kenness, s. intoxication, inebriety
Dry, a. arid; thirsty; barren; not rainy
Dry, v. to free from moisture, to drain
Dry'ly, ad. frigidly, coldly; oddly
Dry'ness, s. want of moisture
Dry'nurse, s. a woman who brings up and feeds a child without the breast
Du'al, a. expressing the number two
Dub, v. a. to confer any kind of dignity
Du'bious, a. doubtful, not clear, uncertain
Du'bitable, a. doubtful, very uncertain
Du'cal, a. pertaining to a duke
Duca'pe, s. a kind of rich silk
Du'cat, s. a foreign coin in silver, valued at about 4s. 6d.—in gold, 9s. 6d.
Duck, s. a water fowl, female of the drake; declination of the head; word of fondness
Duck, v. to dive under water as a duck
Duck'ing, s. the act of putting under water
Duck'ing-stool, s. a chair to duck scolds in
Duck'-legged, a. having legs like a duck
Duck'ling, s. a young or small duck
Duct, s. a channel or passage; a guidance
Duc'tile, a. flexible, complying, pliable
Ductil'ity, s. flexibility, compliance
Dud'geon, s. a small dagger; ill-will, malice
Due, a. owed; proper, appropriate, exact, fit
Due, ad. exactly, duly, nicely
Due, s. a debt; just title; right; tribute
Du'el, s. a fight between two persons
Du'ellist, s. one who fights a duel
Du'enna, s. an old governante
Duet', s. a song or air in two parts
Dug, s. the pap or teat of a beast
Duke, s. the dignity next below a prince
Duke'dom, s. the territories, possessions, quality, or title of a duke
Dul'cet, a. sweet, harmonious, luscious
Dul'cify, Dul'corate, v. a. to sweeten
Dul'cimer, s. a kind of musical instrument
Dull, a. melancholy, stupid, slow, blunt
Dull, v. a. to stupify, to blunt; to sadden
Dul'ness, s. stupidity, indocility; dimness
Duloc'racy, s. a predominance of slaves
Du'ly, ad. properly, exactly, regularly
Du'mal, Du'mose, a. full of bushes; rough
Dumb, a. silent, mute; incapable of speech
Dumb'ness, s. an incapacity to speak; silence
Dump'ling, s. a small boiled pudding
Dumps, s. melancholy, sullenness
Dun, a. colour between brown and black
Dun, s. a clamorous, troublesome creditor
Dun, v. a. to press, to ask often for a debt
Dunce, s. a thickscull, a dullard, a dolt
Dung, s. soil; the excrement of animals
Dung, v.a. to fatten land with dung
Dun'geon, s. a dark prison under ground
Dung'hill, s. a heap of dung; a mean person
Dun'ner, s. one employed to get in debts
Duode'cimo, a. a book printed in duodecimo has twelve leaves to a sheet

Dupe, *v. a.* to trick, to impose on, to cheat
Dupe, *s.* a credulous, simple man
Du'ple, *a.* double; one repeated
Du'plicate, *s.* an exact copy of any thing
Du'plicate, *v. a.* to double, to fo d together
Duplica'tion, *s.* the act of doubling; a fold
Duplic'ity, *s.* deceit; doubleness of tongue
Du rable, *a.* strong, lasting, hard, firm
Durabil'ity, *s.* the power of lasting
Du'rably, *ad.* in a firm and lasting manner
Du'rance, *s.* imprisonment, continuance
Dura'tion, *s.* length of time, continuance
Dure, *v. n.* to last, to remain, to continue
Du'ring, *prep.* for the time of continuance
Durst, *pret.* of *to dare*
Dusk, *a.* tending to darkness, dark-coloured
Dus'kish, Dus'ky, *a.* inclining to darkness; tending to obscurity; sad, gloomy
Dust, *v. a.* to clear or free from dust; to sprinkle with dust; to clean furniture

Dust, *s.* earth dried to a powder; the grave
Dus'ty, *a.* clouded or covered with dust
Dut'chess, *s.* the lady of a duke
Dut'chy, *s.* a territory giving title to a duke
Du'teous, Du'tiful, *a.* obedient, reverential, submissive, expressive of respect
Du'tifully, *ad.* obediently, reverently
Du'ty, *s.* to whatever we are bound by nature, law, or reason; service; a tax, impost
Dwarf, *s.* a man below the middle size
Dwar'fish, *a.* small, low, stinted in size
Dwell, *v. n.* to inhabit; to continue long
Dwel'ling, *s.* place of residence, habitation
Dwin'dle, *v. n.* to shrink, to grow feeble
Dy'ing, *part.* expiring; giving a colour to
Dy'nasty, *s.* government; sovereignty
Dys'crasy, *s.* a distemper in the blood
Dys'entery, *s.* a looseness, a flux
Dys'ury, *s.* a difficulty in making urine

E.

e, *s.* the fifth letter of the alphabet; a note in music
Each, *pron.* either of the two; every one of any number
Ea'ger, *a.* zealous, ardent, vehement, keen
Ea'gerly, *ad.* ardently, keenly, hotly
Ea'gerness, *s.* earnestness, impetuosity
Ea'gle, *s.* a bird of prey; the Roman standard
Ea'gle-eyed, *a.* sharp sighted as an eagle
Ea'gle-speed, *s.* swiftness like an eagle
Eag'let, *s.* a young eagle
Ear, *s.* the whole organ of hearing; power of judging of harmony; spike of corn
Earl, *s.* the title of nobility next to a marquis
Earl'dom, *s.* the seigniory of an earl
Ear'less, *a.* wanting ears
Ear'liness, *s.* the state of being very early
Ear'ly, *ad.* betimes, soon—*a.* soon
Earlmar'shal, *s.* the officer that has the chief care of military solemnities
Earn, *v. a.* to gain by labour, to obtain
Earn'ed, *part.* gotten by labour, acquired
Earn'est, *a.* ardent, eager, zealous, warm
Earn'est, *s.* seriousness; money advanced
Earn'estly, *ad.* eagerly, zealously, warmly
Ear'ring, *s.* an ornament for the ear
Earsh, *s.* a field that is ploughed
Ear'shot, *s.* within hearing; space heard in
Earth, *s.* land, mould; the terraqueous globe
Ear'then, *a.* made of earth or clay
Earth'ly, *a.* not heavenly, corporeal, vile
Earth'quake, *s.* a tremor of the earth
Earth'worm, *s.* a worm; a mean sordid wretch
Earth'y, *a.* consisting of earth; foul, gross
Ear'wax, *s.* wax that gathers in the ear
Ear'wig, *s.* an insect; a whisperer
Ease, *s.* quiet, rest after labour; facility
Ease, *v. a.* to free from pain, slacken, relieve
Ea'sel, *s.* a painter's frame for canvas
Ease'ment, *s.* assistance, refreshment, ease
Ea'sily, *ad.* without difficulty, gently
Ea'siness, *s.* quiet; liberty; readiness
East, *s.* the quarter where the sun rises
Eas'ter, *s.* the festival in commemoration of the resurrection of our Saviour

Eas'terly, *a.* and *ad.* towards the east
Eas'tern, *a.* belonging to the east; oriental
East'ward, *ad.* towards the east
Fa'sy, *a.* not difficult; credulous; quiet
Eat, *v.* to take food, to consume, to swallow
Ea'table, *a.* that which may be eaten
Fa'ten, *part.* devoured, swallowed, consumed
Eaves, *s.* the edges of the roof which overhang the house
Eaves'dropper, *s.* a listener under windows
Ebb, *v. n.* to flow back to the sea; to decay
Ebb, *s.* a flowing back to the sea; was e
Eb'on, Eb'ony, *s.* a hard black valuable wood
Ebri'ety, *s.* intoxication, drunkenness
Ebulli'tion, *s.* act of boiling, or bubbling up
Eccen'tric, *a.* deviating from the centre; incoherent, irregular, anomalous
Eccentric'ity, *s.* deviation from a centre
Ecclesias'tic, *s.* a priest, a clergyman
Ecclesias'tical, *a.* relating to the church
Ec'ho, *s.* the reverberation of a sound
Eclair'cissement, *s.* an explanation
Ecla't, *s.* splendour, lustre, show, renown
Eclec'tic, *s.* selecting, choosing at will
Eclipse, *s.* an obscuration of the sun, moon, &c. from the intervention of some other body—*v. a.* to disgrace; to cloud
Eclip'tic, *s.* the apparent orbit of the earth, so called because eclipses take place there
Ec'logue, *s.* a pastoral or rural poem, so called because Virgil named his pastorals eclogues
Econom'ical, *a.* frugal, saving, thrifty
Econ'omist, *s.* one that is frugal or thrifty
Econ'omize, *v. n.* to save, to retrench
Econ'omy, *s.* frugality; disposition of things
Ec'stasy, *s.* excessive joy, enthusiasm, rapture
Ecstat'ic, *a.* transporting, enrapturing
Edac'ity, *s.* voracity, ravenousness
Ed'der, *s.* wood on the tops of fences
Ed'dy, *s.* a turn of water, a whirlpool
Ed'dy, *a.* whirling, moving circularly
Eden'tated, *a.* deprived of teeth
Edge, *s.* the sharp part of a blade; a brink
Ed'ging, *s.* a fringe; an ornamental border
Edge'less, *a.* unable to cut, obtuse, blunt

a

Edge'tool, s. a tool made sharp to cut
Edge'wise, ad. in a direction of the edge
Ed'ible, a. fit to be eaten, eatable
E'dict, s. a proclamation, an ordinance
Edifica'tion, s. improvement, instruction
Ed'ifice, s. a fabric, a building
Ed'ify, v. a. to improve, instruct, persuade
E'dile, s. the title of a Roman magistrate
Edit'ion, s. the impression of a book
Ed'itor, s. one who prepares or revises any
  literary work for publication
Ed'ucate, v. a. to instruct, to bring up
Educa'tion, s. the instruction of children
Edu'ce, v. a. to bring out, to extract
Educ'tion, s. the act of bringing into view
Edulcora'tion, s. the act of sweetening
Eel, s. a serpentine slimy fish
Ef'fable, a. that may be spoken; expressive
Effa'ce, v. a. to blot out, to destroy
Effect', s. event produced, issue; reality
Effect', v. a. to bring to pass, to produce
Effec'tion, s. a deduced construction, problem
Effec'tive, a. operative, serviceable, active
Effec'tively, ad. powerfully, with effect
Effect'less, a. useless, without effect
Effec'ts, s. goods, furniture, moveables
Effec'tual, a. efficacious, powerful
Effec'tuate, v. a. to bring to pass, to fulfil
Effem'inacy, s. unmanly delicacy
Effem'inate, a. womanish, tender, voluptuous
Efferves'cence, s. the act of growing hot; pro-
  duction of heat by intestine motion
Effica'cious, a. productive of effects; power-
  ful to produce the consequences intended
Ef'ficacy, s. power or ability to effect
Effi'cience, s. a producing of effects; agency
Effi'cient, a. causing or producing effects
Ef'figy, s. representation in painting, &c.
Efflores'cence, s. production of flowers
Efflores'cent, a. shooting out in flowers
Ef'fluence, s. that which issues or derives it-
  self from some other principle
Ef'fluent, a. flowing from, issuing out of
Efflu'via, s. those small particles which are
  continually flying off from bodies
Efflu'x, v. n. to run out—s. an effusion
Ef'fort, s. a laborious endeavour, a struggle
Effra'ible, a. dreadful, terrible, frightful
Effron'tery, s. impudence, shamelessness
Efful'gence, s. lustre, splendour, brightness
Efful'gent, a. shining, luminous, bright
Effu'se, v. a. to pour out; to shed; to spill
Effu'sion, s. the act of pouring out; waste
Eft, s. an evet, a newt—ad. soon, quickly
Egg, s. that which is laid by feathered animals
  and various kinds of insects, &c. from which
  their young are produced; spawn
Egg, v. a. to incite, to spur on, to instigate
Eg'lantine, s. a species of rose; sweetbriar
E'gotism, s. frequent mention of one's self
E'gotist, s. he who talks much of himself
E'gotize, v. n. to talk much of one's self
Egre'gious, a. extraordinary, eminently bad
Egre'giously, ad. eminently; shamefully
E'gress, Egres'sion, s. the act of going out of
  any place; departure
E'gret, s. a fowl of the heron kind
E'griot, s. a species of sour cherry
Ejac'ulate, v. a. to throw out, to shoot out
Ejacula'tion, s. a short fervent prayer
Ejac'ulatory, a. hasty; suddenly darted out

Eject', v. a. to expel, throw out, cast away
Ejec'tion, s. the act of casting out, expulsion
Eject'ment, s. a legal writ, by which any inha-
  bitant of a house, or tenant of an estate
  is commanded to depart
Fi'ht, s. twice four
Eigh'teen, a. ten and eight united
Eight'fo d, a. eight times the number, &c.
Eighth'ly, ad. in the eighth place
Eight'score, a. eight times twenty
Eigh'ty, a. eight times ten
Ei'sel, s. vinegar; any thing very acid
Ei'ther, pron. whether the one or the other
Ejula'tion, s. a lamentation, wailing
Eke, or Eek, v. a. to protract; to supply
Eke, ad. likewise, also, besides, further
Elab'orate, a. finished with great diligence
  and exactness; any thing studied
Elab'orately, ad. laboriously, with much stu-
Elan'ce, v. n. to throw out, to dart out [dy
Elap'se, v. a. to glide away, to pass away
Flas'tic, a. springing back, recovering
Elastic'ity, s. a property in bodies by which,
  on being bent or compressed, they spring
  back to their original form and tension
Ela'te, a. flushed with success; haughty
Ela'te, v. a. to exalt, to puff up, to heighten
Ela'tion, s. haughtiness arising from success
El'bow, s. the bending of the arm; an angle
El'bow-chair, s. a chair with arms
Eld, s. old people, old times, old age
El'der, a. exceeding another in years
El'der, s. the name of a well-known tree
El'derly, a. rather old, advanced in years
El'ders, s. ancestors; ancient rulers
El'dership, s. seniority; primogeniture
El'dest, a. the first born, the oldest
Elecampa'ne, s. the plant named starwort
Elec't, v. a. to choose for any office or use,
  to select as an object of eternal mercy
Elec't, Elec'ted, part. a. chosen, preferred
Elec'tion, s. the power or act of selecting
Elec'tive, a. exerting the power of a choice
Elec'tor, s. he that has a vote in the election
  of any office; a prince who has a voice in
  the choice of the German emperor
Elec'toral, a. of or belonging to an elector
E ec'torate, s. the territory, &c. of an elector
Elec'tre, s. amber; a mixed metal
Elec'trical, a. power of producing electricity
Electric'ity, s. that property in bodies where-
  by, when rubbed, they attract or repel light
  bodies, emit flame, and produce other sin-
  gular and extraordinary phenomena
Elec'tuary, s. a soft compound medicine
Eleemos'ynary, a. living on charity
El'egance, s. beauty without grandeur
El'egant, a. beautiful, pleasing; not coarse
El'egantly, ad. in a pleasing manner; neatly
Ele'giac, a. used in elegies; sorrowful
El'egy, s. a mournful, pathetic poem; a dirge
El'ement, s. constituent principle of any
  thing; the four elements are earth, water,
  fire, air, of which our world is formed;
  rudiments of literature or science; proper
  habitation, &c.
Elemen'tal, a. produced by the elements
Elemen'tary, a. not compound, simple
El'ephant, s. the largest of quadrupeds; ivory
Elephan'tine, a. relating to the elephant
El'evate, v. a. to dignify, exalt; make glad

El'evate, El'evated, *part. a.* exalted, elated

Eleva'tion, *s.* a raising up, height, dignity

Elev'en, *a.* ten and one

Elf, *s.* a fairy, a devil, a wandering spirit

Elf'lock, *s.* a knot of hair twisted by elves

Elic'ite, *v. a.* to strike out, to fetch out

Elic'it, *a.* brought into act, drawn out

Elicita'tion, *s.* the will drawn into action

Eli'de, *v. a.* to break in pieces or destroy

Eli'gible, *a.* fit to be chosen; preferable

Eli'gibleness, *s.* worthiness to be chosen

Elim'inate, *v. n.* to turn out of doors, reject

Elimina'tion, *s.* act of banishing; rejection

Elin'guid, *a.* tonguetied; speechless, dumb

Eliqua'tion, *s.* act of separating by fusion

Eli'sion, *s.* act of cutting off; separation

Elix'ation, *s.* the act of boiling

Elix'ir, *s.* any medicine or cordial; a medicine made by strong infusion

Elk, *a* large wild animal of the stag kind

Ell, *a* measure of one yard and a quarter

Ellip'sis, *s.* an oval figure; a chasm, a defect

Ellip'tical, *a.* formed like an ellipsis

Elm, *s.* the name of a tall tree

Elocu'tion, *s.* eloquence, flow of language

Elloge, E'logy, Eu'logy, *s.* praise, panegyric

El'ogist, Eu'logist, *s.* one who pronounces a panegyric

Eloi'gne, *v. a.* to remove, to put at a distance

Elon'gate, *v.* to lengthen, draw out; go off

Elonga'tion, *s.* the act of lengthening

Elo'pe, *v. a.* to run away; to go off clandestinely; to break loose from confinement

Elo'pement, *s.* a departure from just confinement

E'lops, *s.* a fish; a kind of serpent

Eloquence, *s.* the power of speaking with fluency and elegance

El'oquent, *a.* having the power of an orator

Else *pron.* other; one besides—*ad.* otherwise

Elsewhere, *ad.* in a different place

El'vish, *a.* relating to elves or fairies

Elu'cidate, *v. a.* to explain, to clear up

Elucida'tion, *s.* an explanation, a clearing up

Elucida'tor, *s.* an explainer, an expositor

Elu'de, *v. a.* to escape by stratagem; to shun

Elu'dible, *a.* possible to be defeated

Elum'bated, *a.* weakened in the loins

Elu'sion, *s.* escape from examination, artifice

Elu'sive, Elu'sory, *a.* tending to elude

Elu'te, *v. a.* to wash off, to clean, to cleanse

Elu'triate, *v. a.* to decant or strain out

Elux'ate, *v. a.* to strain or put out of joint

Elys'ian, *a.* pleasant, exceedingly delightful

Elys'ium, *s.* the place assigned by the heathens to happy souls after death; any place excellently pleasant

Ema'ciate. *v. a.* to lose flesh; to waste; to pine

Emacia'tion, *s.* the state of growing lean

Emacula'tion, *s.* the act of freeing any thing from spots or foulness

Em'anant, *a.* flowing from something else

Em'anate. *v. n.* to flow or issue from

Emana'tion, *s.* the act of issuing or flowing from any other substance; that which flows

Em'anative, *a.* issuing from another

Eman'cipate, *v. a.* to free from slavery

Emancipa'tion, *s.* a deliverance from slavery

Emas'culate, *v. a.* to deprive of virility

Emba'le, *v. a.* to bind or pack up; to enclose

Embal'm, *v. a.* to impregnate a body with aromatics, that it may resist putrefaction

Embar', *v. a.* to shut in, to stop, to hinder

Embar'go, *s.* a prohibition to sail

Embar'k, *v.* to go on shipboard; to engage in any affair

Embarka'tion, *s.* a going or putting on shipboard; engaging in any affair

Embar'rass, *v. a.* to perplex, to distress

Embar'rassment, *s.* perplexity, trouble

Emba'se, *v. a.* to vitiate, vilify; impair

Em'bassage, Em'bassy, *s.* a public message

Embat'tle, *v. a.* to range in order of battle

Embay', *v. a.* to enclose in a bay, to bathe

Embel'lish, *v. a.* to beautify, to adorn

Embel'lishment, *s.* decoration, ornament

Em'bers, *s.* hot ashes or cinders

Embez'zle, *v. a.* to steal privately; to waste

Embez'zlement, *s.* a misapplying of a trust

Embla'ze, *v. a.* to blazon, to paint, to adorn

Embla'zon, *v. a.* to adorn with figures of heraldry; to set off pompously

Em'blem, *s.* a moral device; an allusive picture; an occult representation; enamel

Emblemat'ical, *a.* allusive, using emblems

Emblemat'ically, *ad.* in the manner of emblems

Emboss', *v. a.* to engrave, with relief or rising work; to enclose; to hunt hard

Emboss'ing, *s.* the art of making figures in relief

Emboss'ment, *s.* relief, rising work [levo

Embow'el, *v. a.* to take out the entrails, gut

Embra'ce, *v. a.* to hold fondly in the arms; to contain, to comprise, to include

Embra'ce, *s.* a clasp; fond pressure in the arms

Embra'sure, *s.* a battlement; an aperture in fortifications for cannon

Em'brocate, *v. a.* to rub a part diseased

Embroca'tion, *s.* a fomentation, a lotion

Embroi'der, *v. a.* to adorn with figure-work

Embroi'derer, *s.* one who works embroidery

Embroi'dery, *s.* variegated needle-work

Embroi'l, *v. a.* to disturb, distract, confuse

Embru'ted, *a.* reduced to brutality, depraved

Em'bryo, *s.* the child in the womb indistinctly formed; any thing unfinished

Embur'se, *v. a.* to restore money owing

Emenda'tion, *s.* an alteration, a correction

Em'erald, *s.* a kind of green precious stone

Emer'ge, *v. a.* to rise out of; to issue from

Emer'gency, *s.* a rising out of; any sudden occasion, or unexpected casualty

Emer'gent, *a.* rising into view again

Em'erods, Em'eroids, *s.* painful swellings of the hæmorrhoidal veins; piles

Emer'sion, *s.* act of coming into view again

Em'ery, *s.* an iron ore; a glazier's diamond

Emet'ic, *a.* causing vomits—*s.* a vomit

Emica'tion, *s.* a sparkling or glittering

Em'igrant, *s.* one who changes his place of abode—*a.* going from place to place

Em'igrate, *v. n.* to remove from one's abode

Emigra'tion, *s.* the change of habitation

Em'inence, *s.* summit; loftiness; a conspicuous situation; a part rising above the rest a title given to cardinals; distinction

Em'inent, *a.* nigh, dignified, exalted

Em'inently, *ad.* highly, conspicuously

Em'issary, *s.* a secret agent, a spy

Emis'sion, *s.* act of shooting or throwing out

Emit', *v. a.* to send forth, to dart out

Em'met, *s.* a pismire, an ant

Emmew', *v. a.* to mew or coop up, to confine

Emol'lien', a. softening, relaxing, suppling

Emollit'ion, s. the act of softening

Emol'ument, s. profit, gain, advantage

Emo'tion, s. disturbance of mind; a sudden motion; vehemence of passion

Empa'le, v.n. to ence with pales; to enclose; to put to death by spitting on a stake

Empan'nel, v. a. to swear a jury

Empar'lance, s. a petition, conference, motion

Empas'sion, v. a. to affect with passion

Em'peror, s. a monarch superior to a king

Em'phasis, s. a remarkable stress laid by the voice on a word or sentence

Emphat'ic, Emphat'ical, a. forcible, striking

Emphat'ically, ad. forcibly, strongly

Em'pire, s. imperial power, command

Empir'ic, s. a pretended physician, a quack

Empir'ic, Empir'ical, a. practised only by rote; versed in experiments

Empir'icism, s. dependance on experience, without the rules of art; quackery

Emplas'tic, a. viscous, glutinous

Emplea'd, v. a. to indict, to prefer a charge

Employ', v. a. to keep at work; to use

Employ',Employ'ment, s. object of industry; business; office; business intrusted

Employ'er, s. one who sets others to work

Empo'rium, s. a place of merchandise, a principal mart; a commercial city

Empov'erish, v. a. to make poor, to exhaust

Empow'er, v. a. to authorise, to commission

Em'press, s. the wife of an emperor; a female invested with imperial dignity

Empri'se, s. a hazardous undertaking

Emp'tiness, s. a void space, vacuity; want of knowledge, want of substance

Emp'ty, a. not full, unfurnished; ignorant

Emp'ty, v. a. to evacuate; to exhaust

Empur'ple, v. a. to make of a purple colour

Empuz'zle, v. a. to puzzle, to perplex

Empyre'al, a. refined, heavenly, aerial

Empyre'an, s. the highest heaven, where the pure element of fire is supposed to subsist

Empyr'eum, Empyreu'ma, s. the burning of any matter in boiling or distillation

Empyro'sis, s. conflagration, or general fire

Em'ulate, v. a. to rival; to equal; to imitate

Emula'tion, s. rivalry; contention; envy

Em'ulative, a. inclined to rivalry

Emula'tor, s. a competitor, a rival

Emul'ge, v. a. to milk out; empty, drain

Emul'gent, a. milking or draining out

Em'ulous, a. rivalling, desirous to excel

Emul'sion, s. an oily, lubricating medicine

Ena'ble, v. a. to make able, to empower

Enac't, v. a. to decree, represent, establish

Enac'ted, part. decreed, established

Enam'el, v. a. to inlay, variegate with colours

Enam'el, s. substance used in enamelling

Enam'eller, s. one who enamels or inlays

Enam'our, v. a. to inspire with love

Enca'ge, v. a. to shut in a cage, to coop up

Encam'p, v. to form a camp, to pitch tents

Encam'pment, s. a camp; tents pitched in order

Encha'fe, v. a. to enrage, provoke, irritate

Enchai'n, v. a. to fasten with a chain; to bind

Enchan't, v. a. to bewitch, to delight highly

Enchan'ter, s. a magician, a sorcerer

Enchan'tment, s. magical charms, spells; high delight; irresistible influence

Enchan'tress, s. a sorceress, a woman whose excellence or beauty is irresistible

Encha'se, v. a. to infix; to adorn; set in gold

Enchirid'ion, s. a small pocket volume

Encir'cle, v. a. to environ, to surround

Enclit'ics, s. particles which throw back the accent upon the foregoing syllable

Enclo'se, v. a. to fence in; to surround

Enclo'sure, s. ground enclosed or fenced in

Enco'mium, s. a panegyric, eulogy, praise

Encom'pass, v. a. to encircle, to surround, to shut in; to include, to contain, to environ

Enco're, ad. once more, again; yet

Encoun'ter, s. a battle; a duel; engagement, accidental meeting; casual incident

Encou'nter, v. to attack, fight; to meet

Encour'age, v. a. to animate, to embolden

Encour'agement, s. incitement, support

Encroa'ch, v. a. to invade; advance by stealth

Encroa'chment, s. an unlawful intrusion

Encum'ber, v. a. to clog, to load, to embarrass

Encum'brance, s. a clog, an impediment

Encyclope'dia, s. the whole circle of sciences

End, s. a conclusion, design, point; death

Endam'age, v. a. to prejudice, to hurt

Enda'nger, v. a. to bring into peril, hazard

Endea'r, v. a. to render dear, or beloved

Endea'rment, s. the state and cause of love

Endeav'our, s. labour directed to some end

Endeav'our, v. to strive, labour, attempt

Ende'mial, Endem'ic, a. used of such diseases as arise from some causes peculiar to the country where they reign

Ende'w, v. n. to disgorge; to cleanse

Endi'te, Endi'te, v. a. to charge with some crime; to compose; to draw up, to write

Endic'tment, s. a legal accusatory declaration

En'ding, part. finishing—s. the conclusion

En'dive, s. a common sallad herb; succory

En'dless, a. without end, continual, infinite

Endor'se, v. a. to superscribe; to accept a bill

Endor'sed, part. signed upon the back

Endor'sement, s. superscription; acceptance

Endow', v. a. to give a portion; to endue

Endow'ment, s. wealth given; a natural or acquired accomplishment

Endue', v. a. to supply with grace; to invest

Endu'rance, s. continuance, sufferance

Endu're, v. to bear, sustain, last; brook

En'emy, s. a foe, an opponent, an antagonist

Energet'ic, a. forcible, active, strong

En'ergy, s. power, efficacy, force

Ener'vate, Ener've, v. a. to weaken; to crush

Enfee'ble, v. a. to weaken, deprive of force

Enfeoff', v. a. to invest with possessions

Enfet'ter, v. a. to bind in fetters, to confine

Enfila'de, s. a straight passage—v. a. to pierce in a straight line

Enfo'rce, v. to give force; to instigate

Enfo'rcement, s. compulsion, sanction

Enfran'chise, v. a. to make free, to liberate

Enfran'chisement, s. the act of making free, release from slavery or imprisonment

Enga'ge, v. to enter in an affair; to persuade; to induce; to gain; to employ; to bind; to encounter, to fight

Enga'gement, s. a battle; an obligation by contract; employment of the attention

Engar'rison, v. a. to protect by a garrison

Engen'der, v. a. to beget; excite; produce

En'gine, s. a military machine; an agent

Enginee'r, s. one who manages engines; one who directs the artillery of an army

Engir'd, v. a. to surround; to encircle

En'glish, a. whatever belongs to England

Englut', v. a. to swallow up; to pamper

Engor'ge, v. t. gorge, to swallow, to devour

Engra'il, v. a. to indent in curve lines

Engrai'n, v. a. to die in grain, to die deep

Engrap'ple, v. n. to close with; to contend

Engra'sp, v. a. to hold fast in the hand

Engra've, v. a. to cut characters or figures

Engra'ver, s. one who cuts on metals, &c.

Engra'ving, s. a picture engraved

Engro'ss, v.a. to purchase the whole of any commodity, to sell it at a high price; to fatten; to thicken, to copy in a large hand

Enhan'ce, v.a. to raise the price; to raise in esteem; to aggravate; to lift up

Enig'ma, s. a riddle, an obscure question

Enigmat'ical, a. obscure, darkly expressed

Enjoi'n, v.a. to direct, to prescribe, to order

Enjoi'nment. s. a direction. a command

Enjoy', v.a.to obtain possession of; to delight in; to please; to exhilarate

Enjoy'ment, s. happiness, pleasure, fruition

Enkin'dle, v. a. to set on fire, to inflame

Enlar'ge, v. to increase; to expatiate

Enlar'gement, s. an increase; a release

Enli'ghten, v. a. to illuminate; to instruct

Enlin'k, v.a. to chain together, to bind

Enlis't, v. a. to enrol or register

Enli'ven, v. a. to make lively, to animate

Enmesh', v. a. to net, to entangle

En'mity, s. malevolence, ill will, malice

Enno'ble, v. a. to elevate, to dignify

En'nui, s. heaviness, weariness

Enoda'tion, s. the act of untying a knot

Enor'mity, s. villany, great wickedness

Enor'mous, a. wicked in a high degree; irregular, disordered; very large, out of rule

Enor'mously, ad. beyond measure

Enough', ad. sufficiently—s. a sufficiency

Enow', a. the plural of Enough

Enra'ge, v.a. to make furious, to irritate

Enra'nge, v. a. to place regularly, to range

Enra'nk, v. a. to place in orderly ranks

Enrap'ture, v. a. to transport with pleasure

Enri'ch, v. a. to make rich; to fertilize

Enri'dge, v. a. to form with ridges

Enri'ng, v. a. to bind round, to encircle

Enri'pen, v. a. to ripen, to mature

Enro'be, v. a. to dress, to clothe

Enro'l, v.a. to record, to register. to inwrap

Enrol'ment, s. a record, a register

Enro'ot, v. a. to fix by the root

Ens, s. any being or existence

Ensam'ple, s. an example, a pattern

Ensan'guine, v. a. to smear with gore

Ensched'ule, v. a. to insert in a schedule

Ensea'm, v. a. to sew up, to close up

Ensea'r, v. a. to stanch or stop with fire

Enshie'ld, v.a. to cover; to protect, to defend

Enshri'ne, v. a. to preserve as a holy relic

En'siform, a. shaped like a sword

En'sign, s. a flag or standard of a regiment; the officer who carries it; a signal

Ensla've, v. a. to reduce to slavery

Ensla'vement, s. state of slavery, bondage

Enstee'p, v. to put under water, to soak

Ensue', v. to follow, to pursue; to succeed

Ensu'rance, s. exemption from hazard

Ensu're, v. to indemnify. to ascertain

Entab'lature, Entab'lement, s. the architrave, frieze, and cornice of a pillar

Enta'il, s. an estate settled with regard to the rule of its descent; engraver's work

Enta'il, v.a. to settle an estate so that it cannot be bequeathed at pleasure by any subsequent possessor

Enta'me, v. a. to tame, to subjugate

Entan'gle, v. a. to twist, to ensnare, to confuse

En'ter, v. to go or come into; to set down in writing; to be initiated in; to be engaged in

En'tering, s. a passage into a place, entrance

Enterla'ce, v. a. to interweave, to intermix

Enterpar'lance, s. mutual talk; parley

Enterple'ad, v. n. to discuss a point incidentally falling out, before the principal cause

En'terprise, s. a hazardous attempt

Enterta'in, v. a. to treat at table; to talk with, to amuse; to foster in the mind

Enterta'ining, part. a. pleasing, amusing

Enterta'inment, s. treatment at table; conversation; hospitable reception; amusement, dramatic performance

Enthro'ne, v. a. to set on a throne, to exalt

Enthu'siasm, s. heat of imagination

Enthu'siast, s. one of a hot, credulous imagination; one of exalted ideas, or elevated fancy; one who thinks himself inspired

Enthusias'tic, a. over-zealous in any thing

En'thymeme, s. an imperfect syllogism, wanting the major or minor proposition

Enti'ce, v. a. to allure, to invite, to attract

Enti'cement, s. an allurement, a bait

Enti're, a. undivided, whole, in full strength

Enti'rely, ad. wholly, completely, fully

Enti'tle, v. a. to give a title or right to

Enti'tled, part. having a right to; named

En'tity, s. something which really exists

Entoi'l, v. a. to ensnare, to take, to perplex

Ento'mb, v. a. to put in a tomb, to bury

Entomol'ogy, s. natural history of insects

En'trails, s. the bowels, the intestines

En'trance, s. a passage; the act of entering

Entran'ce, v. a. to put into a trance

Entrap', v. a. to catch in a trap, to ensnare

Entrea't, v. a. to importune, to beg earnestly

Entrea'ty, s. a petition, a solicitation

En'try, s. the act of entrance; a passage

Enu'bilous, a. free from clouds, fair

Enu'cleate, v. a. to solve, disentangle, clear

Envel'op, v. a. to cover, to hide, to surround

Enven'om, v.a. to taint with poison; to enrage

En'viable, a. deserving envy; excellent

En'vious, a. full of envy, spiteful, malicious

En'viously, ad. with envy, with malignity

Envi'ron, v. a. to encompass, surround, involve

Envi'rons, s. places adjacent, neighbourhood

Enu'merate, v. a. to count up singly

Enumera'tion, s. the act of reckoning over

Enun'ciate, v. a. to proclaim, to declare

Enuncia'tion, s. declaration, information

Enun'ciative, a. declarative, expressive

En'voy, s. a minister sent from one power to another; a public messenger, in dignity below an ambassador; a messenger

En'vy, v. a. to grieve at the happiness of others; to hate another for excellence or success; to impart unwillingly

En'vy s. vexation at another's good; malice

E'pact, *s.* eleven days of the solar above the lunar year; a Hebrew measure

Ep'aulet, *s.* a shoulder-knot, of lace, &c.

Epaul'ment, *s.* in fortification, a side-work of earth thrown up, or bags of earth, gabions, or of fascines and earth

Ephem'era, *a.* a fever that terminates in one day; an insect that lives but a day

Ephem'eral, *a.* diurnal, done in a day

Ephem'eris, *s.* an account of the daily motions and situations of the planets

Ephem'erist, *s.* one who studies astrology

E'phod, *s.* an ornament worn by Jewish priests

Ep'ic, *a.* comprising narrative; heroic

Epice'dium, *s.* an elegy, poem on a funeral

Ep'icene, *a.* common to both sexes

Ep'icure, *s.* a man wholly given to luxury

Epicure'an, *a.* luxurious, contributing to luxury—*s.* a follower of Epicurus

Epidem'ic, Epidem'ical, *a.* general, universal

Epider'mis, *s.* the outer skin of the body

Ep'igram, *s.* a short pointed poem

Epigrammat'ic, *a.* dealing in epigrams

Epigram'matist, *s.* a writer of epigrams

Ep'ilepsy, *s.* a convulsion of the whole body or of its parts, with loss of sense

Epilep'tic, *a.* convulsed, affected with epilepsy

Ep'ilogue, *s.* a speech at the end of a play

Epiph'any, *s.* a festival in commemoration of our Saviour's being manifested to the world by a star, the twelfth day after Christmas

Epis'copacy, *s.* a government by bishops

Epis'copal, *a.* relating to a bishop

Episcopa'lian, *s.* an advocate for episcopacy

Ep'isode, *s.* an incidental narrative in a poem separable from the main subject

Episod'ical, *a.* contained in an episode

Epis'tle, *s.* a message under cover; a letter

Epis'tolary, *a.* suitable to letters

Ep'itaph, *s.* an inscription on a tomb

Epithala'mium, *s.* a nuptial song

Ep'ithet, *s.* an adjective denoting a quality

Epit'ome, *s.* an abridgement, an abstract

Ep'och, Ep'ocha, *s.* the time at which a new computation began

Ep'ode, *s.* the stanza following the strophe and antistrophe in an ode

Epopee', *s.* an epic or heroic poem

Ep'ulary, *a.* belonging to a banquet, jolly

Epula'tion, *s.* a banquet, a feast, jollity

Epulot'ic, *s.* a healing medicament

Equabil'ity, *s.* evenness; equality to itself

E'quable, *a.* equal to itself, uniform, even

E'quably, *ad.* evenly, uniformly

E'qual, *s.* one of the same rank and age

E'qual, *a.* like another; uniform, even, just

E'qual, E'qualize, *v. a.* to make equal

Equal'ity, *s.* uniformity, likeness

E'qually, *ad.* in the same degree, impartially

Equanim'ity, *s.* evenness of mind, composure

Equa'tion, *s.* bringing things to an equality

Equa'tor, *s.* a great circle, whose poles are the poles of the world, dividing the globe into the northern and southern hemispheres

Equato'rial, *a.* pertaining to the equator

Equer'ry, *s.* master of horse to a king

Eques'trian, *a.* pertaining to a horseman or knight; belonging to the 2d rank in Rome

Equidis'tant, *a.* being at the same distance

Equifor'mity, *s.* uniform quality

Equilat'eral, *a.* having all sides equal

Equili'brate, *v. a.* to balance equally

Equilib'rium, *s.* equality of weight, equipoise

Equinoc'tial, *a.* pertaining to the equinox

Equinoc'tial, *s.* an imaginary circle in the heavens, under which the equator moves in its diurnal motion; when the sun crosses this line, he makes equal days and nights all over the world

E'quinoxes, *s.* the precise times when the sun enters into the first point of Aries and Libra, making equal days and nights; even measure; equality

Equinu'merant, *a.* having the same number

Equip', *v. a.* to dress or fit out, to provide

Eq'uipage, *s.* attendance, horses and carriages; furniture for a horseman

Equip'ment, *s.* the thing equipped or fitted

E'quipoise, *s.* an equality of weight [out

Equipol'lent, *a.* having equal power or force

Equipon'derant, *a.* being of the same weight

Equipon'derate, *v. n.* to weigh equally

Eq'uitable, *a.* just, fair, impartial, candid

Eq'uitably, *ad.* impartially, justly

Eq'uity, *s.* justice, right, impartiality, honesty

Equiv'alence, *s.* equality of worth or power

Equiv'alent, *s.* a thing of the same value

Equiv'alent, *a.* equal in value or force

Equiv'ocal, *a.* uncertain, ambiguous, doubtful

Equiv'ocally, *ad.* uncertainly, doubtfully

Equiv'ocate, *v. n.* to use doubtful expressions

Equivoca'tion, *s.* ambiguity of speech; double or doubtful meaning, delusive words

Equiv'ocator, *s.* one who equivocates

E'ra, *s.* an epoch; a point of time

Eradia'tion, *s.* emission of radiance

Erad'icate, *v. a.* to pull up by the roots

Eradica'tion, *s.* act of tearing up by the roots

Era'se, *v. a.* to efface, to rub out, to destroy

Era'sed, *part.* expunged, rubbed out

Ere, *ad.* before, sooner than

Erec't, *v. a.* to build, exalt, elevate

Erec't, *a.* upright; not depressed, bold

Erec'tion, *s.* a building or raising up

Erect'ness, *s.* uprightness of posture

Erelong', *ad.* before a long time passes

Er'emite, *s.* a hermit; a retired person

Eremit'ical, *a.* religious; retired, solitary

Erenow', *ad.* before this time

Erewhi'le, *ad.* some time ago, heretofore

Frin'go, *s.* a sea-holly, a plant

Er'meline, Er'mine, *s.* a beast, or its skin

Er'mined, *a.* clothed with ermine

Ero'de, *v. a.* to canker, to eat away

Eroga'tion, *s.* the act of bestowing or giving

Ero'sion, *s.* the act of eating away

Err, *v. n.* to miss the right way; to mistake

Er'rand, *s.* what one is sent about; a message

Er'rant, *a.* wandering; completely bad, vile

Er'rantness, Er'rantry, *s.* an errant state

Erra'ta, *s. pl.* faults made in printing a book

Errat'ic, *a.* wandering, changeable, irregular

Er'rhine, *a.* occasioning sneezing

Erro'neous, *a.* subject to error, wandering

Erro'neously, *ad.* by mistake; not rightly

Er'ror, *s.* a mistake, a blunder; offence, sin

Erst, *ad.* when time was; formerly, first

Erubes'cence, *s.* redness; a blush

Eructa'tion, *s.* a belch, a sudden burst of wind

Erudi'tion, *s.* knowledge, learning

Eru'ginous, *a.* copperish, brassy, rusty

Erup'tion, s. the act of bursting forth with violence ; a humour, a pustule

Erup'tive, a. bursting, or tending to burst

Escala'de, s. the act of scaling walls

Escal'op, s. a shell-fish ; oysters broiled

Esca'pe, v. to get out of danger ; to fly

Esca'pe, s. act of shunning; subterfuge; mistake ; flight ; danger ; excuse, evasion

Escar'gatoire, s. a nursery for snails

Es'char, s. a scar made by hot applications

Escharot'ic, a. burning, searing ; caustic

Eschea't, s. whatever falls to the lord of the manor as a forfeit, or on the death of a tenant dying without heir

Eschew', v. a. to fly, to shun, to avoid

Es'cort, s. a guard to a place ; a convoy

Escort', v. a. to guard to a place ; to convoy

Escot', v. a. to pay a reckoning ; to support

Escout', s. a scout ; a spy ; a listener

Escritoi'r, s. a kind of desk upon drawers

Es'culent, a. eatable ; fit for food

Escut'cheon, s. the shield of the family

Espal'ier, s. a dwarf tree planted in rails

Espec'ial, a. principal, leading, chief

Espe'cially, ad. principally, chiefly

Espi'al, s. one sent out to spy ; a scout

Espou'sal, a. relating to espousals

Espou'sals, s. pl. the act of contracting or affiancing a man and woman to each other

Espou'se, v. a. to engage for marriage ; to marry ; to defend ; to maintain

Espy', v. to see at a distance ; to watch

Esqui're, s. a title next below a knight

Essay', v.a. to endeavour, to try, to attempt

Es'say, s. a trial, experiment, endeavour

Es'sence, s. the substance, nature, or being of any thing ; existence ; a smell ; a perfume

Es'sence, v. a. to scent, to perfume

Essen'tial, a. necessary, very important

Essen'tial, s. existence ; a chief point

Essen'tially, ad. necessarily, constitutionally, by the constitution of nature

Esso'ine, s. an excuse for non-appearance

Estab'lish, v. a. to make firm ; to settle

Estab'lished, part. settled, firmly fixed

Estab'lishment, s. a settlement, a salary

Esta'te, s. a fortune ; condition of life, rank

Esteem', v. a. to value, think well of, prize

Esteem', s. high value ; reverential regard

Es'timable, a. deserving esteem

Es'timableness, s. the being worthy of esteem

Es'timate, v. a. to set a value on, to rate

Es'timate, s. a calculation ; a set price or value ; assignment of value ; computation

Estima'tion, s. esteem, opinion, a valuing

Es'tival, a. pertaining to the summer

Estra'de, s. a level place ; a public road

Estra'nge, v. to become strange ; to alienate

Estra'ngement, s. distance ; a removal

Estre'at, s. a true copy of an original writing

Es'tuary, s. an arm of the sea ; a frith

Es'ture, s. violence, commotion

Es'urine, a. corroding, consuming, eating

Et'ching, s. a way of engraving on copper by eating in the figures with aqua-fortis

Eter'nal, a. perpetual, constant, endless

Eter'nalize, Eter'nize, v. a. to perpetuate

Eter'nity, s. endless duration

E'ther, s. pure air, a pure element

Ethe'real, a. heavenly ; pure, refined

Eth'ic, Eth'ical a. moral, treating on morals

Eth'ics, s. pl. the doctrine of morality

Eth'nic, a. heathenish—s. a pagan, a heathen

E tiol'ogy, s. account of the causes of any thing

Etiquett'e, s. the polite form or manner of doing any thing

Etui', s. a case for tweezers, scissors, &c.

Etymolog'ical, a. relating to etymology

Etymol'ogy, s. radical derivation of words

Et'ymon, s. an origin ; a primitive word

Evac'uate, v. a. to make void, empty ; quit

Evacua'tion, s. a discharge, an emptying, an abolition, nullification ; an ejectment

Eva'de, v. to elude, to avoid, to shift off

Evanes'cent, a. vanishing, imperceptible

Evangel'ical, a. agreeable to the gospel

Evan'gelist, s. a writer or preacher of the gospel ; a bringer of good tidings

Evan'gelize, v. n. to instruct in the gospel

Evan'id, a. faint, evanescent, weak

Evap'orate, v. to fly away in vapours or fumes

Evapora'tion, s. a flying away in fumes

Eva'sion, s. an excuse, artifice, subterfuge

Eva'sive, a. equivocating, elusive, shuffling

Eu'charist, s. the act of thanksgiving ; the sacrament of the Lord's Supper

Eucharis'tical, a. relating to the Eucharist

Eu'crasy, s. a good habit of body

Eve, E'ven, s. close of the day ; the vigil or fast to be observed before a holiday

E'ven, a. level, parallel ; uniform, calm

Evenhand'ed, a. impartial, equitable, just

E'vening, s. the close of the day

E'venly, ad. levelly, impartially, uniformly

E'venness, s. uniformity, regularity, calmness

E'ven-song, s. the evening worship

Even't, s. an end, issue, incident, consequence

Even'tful, a. full of changes or incidents

E'ventide, s. the time of the evening

Even'tilate, v. a. to winnow, to sift out ; to discuss ; to examine ; to investigate

Even'tual, a. consequential ; accidental

Even'tually, ad. in the last result, in the end

Ev'er, ad. at any time ; always, eternally

Ev'ergreen, s. a plant all the year green

Everlas'ting, a. without end, perpetual

Everlas'ting, Everlas'tingness, s. eternity

Everliv'ing, a. living always, immortal

Evermo're, ad. without end, eternally

Ever'sion, s. the act of overthrowing

Ever't, v. a. to destroy, to overthrow

Ev'ery, a. each one of all, belonging to all

Ev'erywhere, ad. in every place

Evic't, v. a. to take away ; to dispossess

Evic'ted, part. taken away ; proved

Evic'tion, s. a proof, conviction, evidence

Ev'idence, s. proof, testimony

Ev'ident, a. apparent, plain ; well known

Ev'idently, ad. plainly, apparently, certainly

E'vil, a. bad, wicked, corrupt ; unhappy

E'vil, E'vilness, s. wickedness ; calamity

Evilmind'ed, a. mischievous, malicious

Evilspea'king, s. calumny, defamation

Evin'ce, v. a. to make clear, to prove

Evis'cerate, v. a. to embowel ; to search

Ev'itable, a. that may be avoided

Ev'itate, v. a. to shun, to avoid ; to escape

Eu'logy, s. encomium, praise

Eu'nuch, s. one who is castrated

Evoca'tion, s. a calling out or from

Evo'ke, v. a. to call out, invoke, summon

Evola'tion, s. the act of flying away

Evol've, v. a. to unfold, to disentangle
Evolu'tion, s. act of unfolding ; a displaying ;
 doubling ; wheeling ; extracting
Evomi'tion, s. the act of vomiting out
Eu'phony, s. an agreeable, pleasing sound
Eu'phrasy, s. the herb eyebright
Euroc'lydon, s. a tempestuous NE wind
Evul'sion, s. the act of plucking out or away
Ewe, s. a female sheep
Ew'er, s. a vessel in which water is brought
 for washing the hands
Exacerba'tion, s. increased malignity
Exac't, a. accurate, nice, methodical
Exac't, v.a. to extort ; to summon ; to enjoin
Exac'ted, part. imposed, demanded
Exac'tion, s. extortion ; a severe tribute
Exact'ly, ad. accurately, fitly, nicely
Exact'ness, s. accurateness, regularity, nicety
Exag'gerate, v.a. to heighten by representa-
 tion ; to amplify or enlarge
Exaggera'tion, s. the act of heaping up ; an
 enlarging ; aggravation ; amplification
Exag'itate, v. a. to stir up, to disquiet
Exa'lt, v. a. to lift up, to magnify, to extol
Exalta'tion, s. the act of raising up
Examina'tion, Exa'men, s. critical disquisi-
 tion ; a trial or proof ; a questioning
Exam'ine, v.a. to ask questions ; to consider
Exam'iner, s. one who examines
Exam'plary, a. serving for a pattern
Exam'ple, s. a model, pattern, precedent
Exan'imate, a. lifeless, depressed, spiritless
Exant'iate, v. a. to draw out ; to exhaust
Exas'perate, v.a. to vex, enrage, provoke
Exaspera'tion, s. a strong provocation
Exauc'torate, v. a. to deprive of a benefice
Excar'nate, v. a. to clear from flesh
Ex'cavate, v. a. to make hollow, or cut into
Excee'd, v. to surpass, to go beyond, to exceed
Excee'ding, part. a. great in quantity, &c.
Excee'dingly, ad. to a great degree
Excel', v. to surpass, outdo ; to be eminent
Ex'cellence, s. dignity ; goodness, purity; that
 wherein one excels ; a title of honour
Ex'cellent, a. being of great virtue
Ex'cellently, ad. to an eminent degree ; well
Excep't, v. to leave out, to object to, to exempt
Excep't, Excep'ting, prep. with exception of ;
 in exclusion of ; unless
Excep'tion, s. an exclusion ; objection, cavil
Excep'tionable, a. liable to be objected to
Excep'tious, a. peevish, froward
Excep'tive, a. including an exception
Except'less, a. neglecting all exceptions
Excep'tor, s. one who objects ; objector
Excer'n, v.a. to separate by straining out
Excerp't, a. plucked off ; culled out, chosen
Excerp'tion, s. act of gleaning, selecting
Excess', s. intemperance, superfluity
Excess'ive, a. beyond due bounds
Excess'ively, ad. exceedingly ; in a great de-
 gree ; eminently
Excha'nge, v.a. to give one thing for the sake
 of another ; to truck ; to barter
Excha'nge, s. the act of bartering; the balance
 of money of different nations ; the place
 where merchants meet ; barter, traffic
Exchequ'er, s. the court where the public
 revenues are received and paid
Exci'se, s. a tax levied upon commodities
Exci'seable, a. liable to the excise

Exci'seman, s. an inspector of excised goods
Excis'ion, s. extirpation ; destruction
Excita'tion, s. the act of stirring up
Exci'te, v.a. to encourage, to rouse, stir up
Exci'tement, s. the motive which excites
Exclai'm, v.n. to make an outcry, to cry out
Exclama'tion, s. an outcry, a clamour; a note
 thus [!] that marks a pathetical sentence
Exclam'atory, a. pertaining to exclamation
Exclu'de, v.a. to shut out ; prohibit ; debar
Exclu'sion, s. a rejection ; act of shutting out
Exclu'sive, a. excepting, excluding, debarring
Exclu'sively, ad. to the exclusion of all others
Excog'itate, v.a. to invent ; to hit off
Excogita'tion, s. an expedient, an invention
Excommu'nicate, v.a. to exclude ; to censure
Excommunica'tion, s. an ecclesiastical inter-
 dict, or exclusion from the fellowship of
 the church ; an anathema
Exco'riate, v. a. to strip off the skin ; to flay
Excoria'tion, s. loss of skin ; spoil, plunder
Excortica'tion, s. stripping off the bark
Ex'crement, s. human soil, dung, &c.
Excremen'tal, a. voided as excrement
Excremen'titious, a. containing excrement
Excres'cence, s. superfluous flesh growing
 on any part of the body ; a tumour ; a wart
Excre'tion, s. ejection of animal substance
Ex'cretive, a. able to eject excrements
Excru'ciate, v.a. to torment, to torture
Excru'ciate, Excru'ciated, part. tormented
Excuba'tion, s. act of watching all night
Excul'pate, v. a. to clear from imputation
Excur'sion, s. a digression ; ramble, inroad
Excur'sive, a. rambling, wandering, deviating
Excu'sable, a. pardonable
Excu'se, v. a. to extenuate, pardon, remit
Excu'se, s. a plea ; an apology ; a pardon
Excu'seless, a. without excuse, inexcusable
Excuss', v. a. to seise and detain by law
Ex'ecrable, a. abominable, detestable
Ex'ecrably, ad. hatefully, cursedly
Ex'ecrate, v. a. to wish ill to, to curse
Execra'tion, s. a curse ; a wishing of evil
Exec't, v.a. to cut out ; to cut away
Ex'ecute, v. a. to perform, to put to death
Ex'ecuter, s. one who executes or performs
Execu'tion, s. a performance ; death inflicted
 by forms of law ; a seizure
Execu'tioner, s. he that inflicts punishments
Exec'utive, a. having power to act ; active
Exec'utor, s. he that is intrusted to execute
 the will of the testator
Exec'utrix, s. a female executer
Exem'plar, s. a pattern, copy to be imitated
Ex'emplary, a. worthy of imitation
Exem'plify, v. a. to illustrate by example
Exem'pt, v. a. to free from, to privilege
Exem'ption, s. privilege, immunity
Exen'terate, v.a. to take out the bowels
Ex'equies, s. ceremony of burying the dead
Exer'cent, a. practising, following a calling
Ex'ercise, v. to perform, to employ, to exert
Ex'ercise, s. labour ; performance, exertion
Exercita'tion, s. exercise, use, practice
Exer't, v. a. to use an effort ; perform
Exer'tion, s. the act of exerting ; an effort
Exe'sion, s. the act of eating through
Exestua'tion, s. a state of boiling, effervescence
Exfo'liate, v. n. to shell off, to peel off
Exhala'tion, s. evaporation, vapour fum

Exha'le, v. a. to send or draw out fumes
Exha'lement, s. matter exhaled, a vapour
Exhau'st, v. a. to draw out totally, to waste
Exhaust'less, a. never to be emptied
Exhib'it, v.a. to display, offer to view, show
Exhib'ited, part. displayed, shown, produced
Exhib'iter, s. he that displays any thing
Exhibit'ion, s. display; pension, allowance
Exhil'arate, v. a. to make cheerful
Exhilara'tion, s. the state of being enlivened
Exhor't, v. a. to incite to any good action
Exhorta'tion, s. an incitement to good
Exhor'tative, Exhor'tatory, a. encouraging
   to good; tending to exhort
Exhuma'tion, s. the digging a corpse out of
   the ground
Ex'igence, s. necessity, want, demand
Ex'igent, s. a pressing business; a writ
Exig'uous, a. small, slender, diminutive
Ex'ile, v. a. to transport, to banish
Ex'ile, s. a person banished, banishment
Exis't, v. n. to have a being, to be
Exis'tence, Exis'tency, s. a state of being
Exis'tent, a. in being, possessed of existence
Ex'it, s. a going out; a departure; death
Ex'odus, s. a journey from a place; the second
   book of Moses, so called from its contents
Exon'erate, v. a. to disburden, to unload
Exonera'tion, s. the act of disburdening
Exopta'tion, s. an earnest desire or wish
Ex'orable, a. that which may be persuaded
Exor'bitance, s. enormity, great depravity
Exor'bitant, a. enormous, excessive
Ex'orcise, v. a. to cast out malignant spirits
Ex'orcist, s. a caster out of malignant spirits
Exor'dium, s. introduction to a discourse
Exot'ic, a. foreign—s. a foreign plant
Expan'd, v. a. to spread, to enlarge, to dilate
Expan'se, s. a body widely extended
Expansibil'ity, s. capacity of extension
Expan'sion, s. act of spreading out, extent
Expan'sive, a. spreading, extensive
Expa'tiate, v.n. to enlarge on; range at large
Expa'triated, part. banished from home
Expec't, v.n. to wait for, to stay, to attend for
Expec'tancy, s. something expected; hope
Expec'tant, a. waiting in expectation
Expecta'tion, s. the act of expecting
Expec'torate, v. a. to eject from the breast
Expectora'tion, s. a discharge by coughing
Expe'dience, Expe'diency, s. propriety, fitness
Expe'dient, a. convenient, proper; quick
Expe'dient, s. a method, a device, a way
Expe'diently, ad. suitably, fitly, quickly
Ex'pedite, v.a. to facilitate, to hasten
Ex'pedite, a. quick, nimble, agile, ready
Expedit'ion, s. speed; warlike enterprise
Expedit'ious, a. quick, nimble, speedy, alert
Expedit'iously, ad. speedily, quickly, nimbly
Expel', v. a. to drive out, to eject, to banish
Expen'd, v. a. to lay out, disburse, spend
Expen'se, s. cost, charges, money paid out
Expen'seless, a. without charge or cost
Expen'sive, a. costly, given to expense
Expen'siveness, s. addition to expense
Expe'rience, s. knowledge gained by practice
Expe'rience, v.a. to try, to know by practice
Expe'rienced, part. a. skilful by experience
Exper'iment, v.a. to try; to search out by trial
Exper'iment, s. trial, essay, proof of any thing
Experimen'tal, a. relating to experiment

Experimen'tally, ad. by experience; by trial
Ex'pert, a. skilful, dexterous, ready
Expert'ly, ad. skilfully, dexterously, readily
Expert'ness, s. skill, readiness, art
Ex'piable, a. that which may be atoned for
Ex'piate, v. a. to atone for a crime
Expia'tion, s. the act of atoning for a crime
Ex'piatory, a. having the power of expiation
Expira'tion, s. an end; respiration; death
Expi're, v. to breathe out; to die; to exhale
Explai'n, v. a. to expound, to illustrate
Expla'nate, a. spread out
Explana'tion, s. act of explaining, a note
Explan'atory, a. containing explanation
Ex'pletive, s. a word or syllable used merely
   to take up room
Ex'plicable, a. that which may be explained
Ex'plicate, v.a. to explain, unfold, expand
Explica'tion, s. act of explaining or opening
Explic'it, a. unfolded, distinct, plain, clear
Explic'itly, ad. plainly, clearly, directly
Explo'de, v.a. to treat with scorn and disdain
Exploit', s. a great action, an achievement
Explo're, v. a. to search into, to examine
Explo'sion, s. the act of driving out any thing
   with noise and violence
Explo'sive, a. driving out with noise [ket
Ex'port, s. a commodity sent to a foreign mar
Expo'rt, v. a. to send out of a country
Exporta'tion, s. sending of goods abroad
Expo'se, v.a. to lay open, make bare; put in
   danger; cast out to chance
Expo'sed, part. laid open, cast out to chance
Exposit'ion, s. explanation, interpretation
Expos'itor, s. an explainer, an interpreter
Expos'tulate, v. n. to argue, to altercate
Expostula'tion, s. discussion of an affair; al-
   tercation, debate; accusation, charge
Expo'sure, s. an exposing to sight; a situation
Expou'nd, v. a. to explain, lay open, unfold
Expou'nder, s. an explainer, an interpreter
Express', v. a. to utter, pronounce, declare,
   denote, represent; to squeeze out
Express', a. plain, direct, manifest, clear
Express', s. a courier; a message sent
Express'ible, a. that may be uttered
Expres'sion, s. act of representing any thing;
   mode of speech; a phrase; act of squeez-
   ing or forcing out any thing, as by a press
Expres'sive, a. adapted to express; strong
Express'ly, ad. in direct terms, clearly
Expres'sure, s. expression, utterance
Exprobra'tion, s. reproachful accusation
Expro'priate, v.a. to make no longer our own
Expu'gn, v. a. to conquer, to take by assault
Expul'tion, s. a discharge by spitting
Expul'se, v. a. to drive out, to force away
Expul'sion, s. act of driving out or expelling
Expul'sive, a. having the power of expulsion
Expun'ge, v. a. to blot out, to efface
Expur'gatory, a. used in purging or purifying
Ex'quisite, a. choice; consummately bad
Ex'quisitely, ad. completely, perfectly
Ex'quisiteness, s. perfection, nicety
Ex'script, s. a writing copied from another
Exsibila'tion, s. act of hissing off the stage
Exsic'cant, a. drying, having power to dry
Exsic'cate, v. a. to dry, to dry up
Exsicca'tion, s. the act of drying up
Exsic'cative, a. having the power of drying
Exsuc'culent, a. without juice, juiceless

Exsuc'tion, *s.* the act of sucking out
Exsus'citate, *v. a.* to stir up; to rouse up
Exsuda'tion, *s.* a sweating, an exfiltration
Ex'tancy, *s.* parts rising up above the rest
Ex'tant, *a.* now in being, standing in view
Extem'poraneous, *a.* unpremeditated, sudden
Extem'porary, *a.* not premeditated
Extem'pore, *ad.* without premeditation
Extem'porise, *v. n.* to speak extempore
Exten'd, *v. a.* to stretch out, enlarge, widen
Exten'sible, *a.* capable of extension
Exten'sion, *s.* the state of being extended
Exten'sive, *a.* large, wild, comprehensive
Exten'sively, *ad.* largely, widely, capaciously
Exten'siveness, *s.* largeness, diffusiveness
Exten't, *s.* the circumference of any thing; in law, an execution, seizure
Exten'uate, *v.a.* to lessen, diminish, palliate
Extenua'tion, *s.* mitigation, palliation
Exte'rior, *a.* external, outward; not intrinsic
Exter'minate, *v. a.* to root out, drive away
Extermina'tion, *s.* destruction; excision
Exter'n, Exter'nal, *a.* outward, visible
Exter'nally, Exte'riorly, *ad.* outwardly
Exter'sion, *s.* the act of rubbing off
Extil', *v. n.* to drop from, to distil from
Extilla'tion, *s.* the act of falling in drops
Extim'ulate, *v. a.* to incite by stimulation
Extimula'tion, *s.* power of exciting sensation
Extin'ct, *a.* put out, extinguished; dead
Extinc'tion, *s.* act of extinguishing or quenching; suppression, destruction
Extin'guish, *v.a.* to put out, to quench, to suppress, to obscure, to cloud, to destroy
Extin'guishable, *a.* that may be quenched
Extin'guisher, *s.* a hollow cone placed on a burning candle to extinguish it
Extin'guishment, *s.* act of quenching
Extir'pate, *v. a.* to eradicate, to destroy
Extirpa'tion, *s.* act of rooting out, excision
Extol', *v. a.* to praise, celebrate, magnify
Extor't, *v. a.* to draw by force, to wring or wrest from one, to gain by violence
Extor'tion, *s.* an unlawful exaction of more than is due; act of gaining by rapacity
Extor'tioner, *s.* one who practices extortion
Extrac't, *v. a.* to draw out of, to select
Ex'tract, *s.* the substance extracted; the chief heads of a book; a quotation; an abstract
Extrac'tion, *s.* act of drawing out; descent
Extrajudic'ial, *a.* out of the course of law
Extramis'sion, *s.* act of emitting outwards
Extramun'dane, *a.* beyond the verge of the material world; in the infinite void space
Extra'neous, *a.* foreign, not belonging to
Extraor'dinarily, *ad.* eminently, remarkably
Extraor'dinariness, *s.* uncommonness
Extraor'dinary, *a.* remarkable, eminent
Extraparo'chial, *a.* out of the parish bounds
Extraprovin'cial, *a.* not in the same province
Extrareg'ular, *a.* not subject to rule
Extrav'agant, *a.* wasteful, irregular, wild

Extrav agance, Extrav'agancy, *s.* prodigality irregularity; bombast; outrage
Extrav'agantly, *ad.* wastefully, luxuriously, wildly; in an unreasonable degree
Extrav'agate, *v.n.* to wander out of limits
Extrav'asated, *a.* out of its proper vessel
Extrav'enate, *a.* let out of the veins
Extre'me, *a.* utmost, greatest, last; pressing, immoderate, of the highest degree
Extre'me, *s.* the utmost point, highest degree of any thing, extremity, end
Extre'mely, *ad.* in the utmost degree, greatly
Extrem'ity, *s.* utmost point; utmost distress, necessity; rigour; violence of passion
Ex'tricate, *v.a.* to clear, to disembarrass
Extrica'tion, *s.* the act of disentangling
Extrin'sic, Extrin'sical, *a.* outward, external
Extrin'sically, *ad.* from without
Extruc't, *v.a.* to build, to form, to raise
Extru'de, *v. a.* to throw out, to thrust off
Extru'sion, *s.* act of thrusting from or out
Exu'berance, *s.* a swelling or bunching out, a knob or protuberant part
Exu'berance, *s.* overgrowth, luxuriance
Exu'berant, *a.* overabundant, luxuriant
Exu'berantly, *ad.* abundantly, luxuriantly
Exuc'cous, *a.* without moisture, dry
Exuda'tion, *s.* a sweating out, perspiration
Exu'date, Exu'de, *v.n.* to discharge by sweat
Exul'cerate, *v.a.* to make sore with an ulcer, to irritate with virulence; to corrode
Exul't, *v. n.* to rejoice above measure
Exul'tance, Exulta'tion, *s.* joy, transport
Exu'ndate, *v. a.* to overflow
Exunda'tion, *s.* overflow, abundance
Exu'perable, *a.* that may be overcome
Exu'perant, *a.* overbalancing, exceeding
Exus'citate, *v.a.* to rouse from sleep, stir up
Exus'tion, *s.* consumption by fire
Exu'viæ, *s.* the cast shells or skins of animals; whatever is thrown off, or shed; the refuse, the scum
Ey'as, *s.* a young hawk taken from a nest
Eye, *s.* the organ of sight; attention, notice; an external mark or scar in some seeds
Eye, *v. a.* to keep in view, to watch
Eye'ball, *s.* the pupil or apple of the eye
Eye'brow, *s.* the hairy arch over the eye
Eye'lash, *s.* hair on the edge of the eyelid
Eye'less, *a.* without eyes, blind, sightless
Eye'let, *s.* a small hole for the light, &c.
Eye'lid, *s.* the membrane covering the eye
Eye'shot, *s.* a glance, a sight, transient view
Eye'sight, *s.* the sight of the eye
Eye'sore, *s.* something offensive to the sight
Eye'tooth, *s.* the tooth next the grinders
Eyewit'ness, *s.* an ocular evidence; one who gives testimony of a fact seen with his own eyes
Eyre, *s.* the court of justices itinerants
Ey'ry, *s.* a place where birds of prey build their nests and hatch

F.

F. *s.* the sixth letter of the alphabet; a note in music
Faba'ceous, *a.* having the nature of a bean

Fa'ble, *s.* an instructive fiction; a falsehood
Fa'ble, *v.* to feign, to tell falsehoods
Fa'bled, *part.* celebrated in tables

Fab'ric, s. an edifice, a building; a system
Fab'ricate, v. a. to build, construct, form
Fab'ulist, s. a writer of fables
Fab'ulous, a. full of fables, feigned, forged
Fab'ulously, ad. in fiction
Face, s. the visage; front; appearance; superficies of any thing; resemblance
Face, v. a. to meet in front; to oppose boldly; to cover with an additional boldness; to stand opposite to
Fa'cet, s. a small irregular surface
Face'tious, a. gay, witty, cheerful, lively
Face'tiously, ad. gaily; wittily, cheerfully
Face'tiousness, s. cheerful wit, mirth
Fac'ile, a. not difficult; easy; flexible, pliant
Facil'itate, v. a. to make easy clear
Facil'ity, s. readiness, easiness, affability
Fa'cing, part. fronting, set over against
Fa'cing, s. an ornamental covering
Facin'orous, a. wicked, detestably bad
Fact, s. a deed or action; reality; thing done
Fac'tion, s. a party in a state; discord
Fac'tious, a. given to faction, seditious
Fac'tiously, ad. criminally dissensious
Facti'tious, a. made by art, artificial
Fac'tor, s. an agent for another, a deputy
Fac'tory, s. a district inhabited by traders in a foreign country; mercantile agents
Facto'tum, s. a servant employed alike in all kinds of business
Fac'ulty, s. power of mind; ability; dexterity
Facun'dity, s. easiness of speech, eloquence
Fad'dle, v. n. to trifle, to play, to toy
Fade, v. to wither, reduce to languor
Fadge, v. n. to fit, to suit; not to quarrel
Fæ'ces, s. excrements; dross, dregs
Fag, v. a. to labour, to grow weary
Fag, Fag'end, s. the worst end of a thing
Fag'ot, s. a bundle of wood for fuel, &c.
Fail, v. to become a bankrupt; to omit; to neglect; to desert; to perish, decay, die
Fai'ling, Fai'lure, s. a deficiency, a becoming insolvent; ship; omission
Fain, a. glad, obliged, forced—ad. gladly
Faint, a. weak, languid, cowardly
Faint, v. n. to sink motionless; to decay
Faint-heart'ed, a. timorous, cowardly
Fai'nting, s. temporary loss of animal motion
Fal'ntish, a. rather faint or low
Faint'ishness, s. weakness in a slight degree
Faint'ly, ad. languidly, feebly, timorously
Faint'ness, s. feebleness, langour, dejection
Fair, a. clear; beautiful; just; favourable
Fair, ad. civilly, gently; complaisantly
Fair, s. a free market; the female sex
Fai'ring, s. a present given at a fair
Fair'ly, ad. honestly, plainly, beautifully
Fair'ness, s. candour, honesty; beauty
Fai'ry, s. an enchantress, a fay, an elf
Fai'ry, a. given by or belonging to fairies
Faith, s. belief, sincerity, fidelity; tenet held
Faith'ful, a. firm to the truth, loyal, sincere
Faith'fully, ad. sincerely, honestly
Faith'fulness, s. honesty, loyalty, veracity
Faith'less, a. unbelieving; perfidious
Faith'lessness, s. perfidy, treachery
Fal'cated, a. hooked, bent like a scythe
Fal'chion, s. a kind of crooked sword
Fal'con, s. a small hawk trained for sport
Fal'coner, s. a breeder and trainer of falcons
Fal'conet, s. a small piece of ordnance

Fal'conry, s. the art of training up or fowling with hawks
Fall, v. n. to drop down; decrease; happen
Fall, s. act of falling; downfall, ruin
Falla'cious, a. producing mistake; sophistica
Fal'lacy, s. deceitful argument, sophism
Fallabil'ity, s. liableness to error
Fal'lible, a. liable to be deceived, frail
Fa'lling, s. a sinking; an indenting; sin
Fa'lling-sickness, s. the epilepsy
Fal'low, v. n. to plough in order to replough
Fal'low, a. uncultivated, unploughed, neglec-
False, a. not true, counterfeit, not just [ed
Falseheart'ed, a. deceitful, treacherous
Fal'sely, ad. not truly, erroneously
Fal'sehood, Fal'sity, s. an untruth, a lie
Fal'sific, a. making false, dealing falsely
Fal'sify, v. to tell lies, to forge, to counterfeit
Fal'ter, v. n. to hesitate in speech; stumble
Fal'tering, part. a. stammering; stumbling
Fame, s. celebrity, glory, renown, report
Fa'med, a. celebrated, renowned, famous
Fa'meless, a. without fame, mean, obscure
Famil'iar, a. domestic, unceremonious, affa-
Famil'iar, s. an intimate; a demon [ble
Familiar'ity, s. intimate correspondence, easy intercourse, acquaintance
Famil'iarize, v. a. to make easy by habit
Famil'iarly, ad. without formality, easily
Fam'ily, s. household; generation, race
Fam'ine, s. scarcity of food, dearth
Fam'ish, v. to starve, to kill with hunger
Fa'mous, a. celebrated, renowned
Fa'mously, ad. renownedly, with celebrity
Fan, s. an instrument made of silk, paper, &c. used by ladies to move the air and cool themselves; an utensil to winnow corn
Fan, v. a. to cool by a fan; to winnow corn
Fanat'ic, a. an enthusiast, a visionary
Fanat'ic, Fanat'ical, a. enthusiastic
Fanat'icism, s. a religious frenzy, enthusiasm
Fan'ciful, a. imaginative, whimsical
Fan'cifully, ad. imaginarily, capriciously
Fan'cy, s. imagination, thought; caprice, frolic, taste; idle scheme, vagary
Fan'cy, v. to imagine; to be pleased with, to like; to pourtray in the mind
Fane, s. a temple; a weathercock
Fan'faron, s. a bully, a blusterer, a hector
Fanfarona'de, s. a bluster; a boast, a puff
Fang, s. the long tusk of an animal, a talon
Fang'ed, part. furnished with fangs
Fan'gle, s. a silly attempt, a trifling scheme
Fan'nel, s. a sort of scarf worn about the left arm of a mass priest when he officiates
Fantas'tic, Fantas'tical, a. imaginary, irrational, whimsical, capricious, unsteady
Fan'tasy, s. imagination, humour, idea
Far, a. a great way off, remote—ad. distantly
Farce, s. a ludicrous dramatic representation
Far'cical, a. belonging to a farce; droll
Far'cey, s. the leprosy of horses
Far'del, s. a bundle, a burden, a pack
Fare, s. provisions; hire of carriages, &c.
Fare, v. n. to go, to travel; to feed, to eat; to happen to any one well or ill
Fa'rewell, ad. the parting compliment, adieu
Far'fetched, a. brought from places distant, unnatural, elaborately strained
Farina'ceous, a. mealy, tasting like meal
Farm, s. land occupied by a farmer

Far'mer, s. one who cultivates hired ground
Far'most, a. most distant
Farrag'inous,a.formed of different materials
Farra'go, s. a medley, a confused mass
Far'rier, s. a horse doctor; a shoer of horses
Far'row,s.a litter of pigs—v.a. to bring forth
Far'ther, a. more remote, longer [pigs
Far'ther, v. a. to promote, to facilitate
Far'thermore, ad. besides, moreover
Far'thest, a. at or to the greatest distance
Far'thing, s. the fourth part of a penny
Far'thingale,s. a hoop to spread the petticoat
Fas'ces, s. a bundle of rods anciently carried
before the Roman consuls
Fascia'tion, s. a bandage, a tying up
Fascic'ular, a. of or belonging to a bundle
Fas'cinate, v. a. to enchant, to bewitch
Fascina'tion, s. enchantment, witchcraft
Fasci'ne, s. a faggot or havin
Fas'cinous, a. caused by enchantment
Fash'ion, s. form, custom, mode, manner
Fash'ion, v. a. to form, fit, adapt, mould
Fash'ionable,a.approved by custom, modish
Fash'ionableness, s. modish elegance
Fash'ionably, ad. with modish elegance
Fash'ioned, part. formed, adapted, framed
Fast, v. n. to abstain from food
Fast, s. an abstinence from food
Fast, a. swift, firm—ad. firmly, swiftly
Fas'ten, v. a. to make fast, to cement
Fas'tener, s. one that makes fast or firm
Fas'thanded, a. niggardly, avaricious
Fastid'ious, a. disdainful, squeamish
Fas'tness,s.firmness,strength; a strong place
Fas'tuous, a. proud, disdainful, haughty
Fat, a. full-fed, fleshy, plump, coarse; rich
Fat, s. an oily and sulphureous part of the
blood; a vessel in which any thing is put to
ferment; commonly written vat
Fat, v. to make fat, to grow fat, to fatten
Fa'tal, a. destructive, deadly, inevitable
Fa'talist, s. one who maintains that all things
happen by invincible necessity
Fatal'ity, s. predestination, a decree of fate
Fa'tally, ad. mortally, destructively
Fate, s. destiny; death; cause of death
Fa'ted, a. decreed by fate; determined
Fa'ther, s. one who has a child
Fa'ther, v. a. to adopt a child; to ascribe
Fa'therhood, s. the character of a father
Fa'ther-in-law,s.father of one's husband,&c.
Fa'therless, a. without a father
Fa'therly, a. like a father, careful, tender
Fath'om, s. a measure containing six feet
Fath'om, v. a. to penetrate into, to sound
Fath'omless, a. bottomless; impenetrable
Fatid'ical, a. having the power to foretel
Fatif'erous, a. mortal, deadly
Fat'igable, a. easily wearied
Fati'gue, s. weariness, lassitude, labour
Fati'gue,Fat'igate,v.a. to weary,tire, fatigue
Fat'ling, s. a young animal for slaughter
Fat'ness, s. plumpness, fertility; sliminess
Fat'ten, v. to grow fat; to be pampered
Fatu'ity, s. foolishness, weakness of mind
Fat'uous, a. foolish, stupid, impotent, feeble
Favil'lous, a. consisting of ashes
Fault, s. a slight crime, an offense; a defect
Faul'ter, s. he who commits a fault, an offen-
Faul'tily, ad. not rightly, improperly [der
Faul'tless,a. without fault,blameless,perfect

Fau'lty, a. guilty of a fault, bad, wrong
Faun, s. a rural deity; a satyr
Fau'nic, a. rustic, wild, artless, rude, plain
Fa'vour, v.a. to support, conduce to, assist
Fa'vour, s. kindness, lenity, support; good-
will; a knot of ribbons; countenance, fea-
ture
Fa'vourable, a. kind, tender, propitious
Fa'vourably, ad. with favour, kindly
Fa'voured,part.a.regarded with kindness;
partiality; featured, with well or ill
Fa'vourite, s. a person or thing beloved
Fa'vouritism, s. use of power for favourites
Fau'cet, s. a small tube for a cask
Fawn, s. a young deer—v. n. to flatter
Faw'ning, part. flattering, cringing
Fay, s. a fairy, an elf; faith
Fe'alty, s. loyalty, homage, submission
Fear, s. terror, dread, awe, anxiety
Fear, v. to be afraid of, to dread, to frighten
Fea'rful, a. afraid, timorous, awful, terrible
Fea'rfully, ad. timorously, terribly; in fear
Fea'rfulness, s. timorousness, dread; terror
Fea'rless, a. free from fear, intrepid
Fea'rlessness,s.freedom from fear,intrepidi-
Feasibil'ity,s.the practicability of a thing [ty
Fea'sible, a. practicable, that may be done
Feast, s. a sumptuous treat, a festival
Feast,v.a. to entertain sumptuously, pamper
Feat, s. a deed, an act; trick or slight
Feat, a. neat, ready, quick
Feath'er, s. the plume of birds; an ornament
Feath'er, v. a. to dress or fit with feathers
Feath'er-bed, s. a bed stuffed with feathers
Feath'ered, a. clothed with feathers
Feath'erless, a. without feathers, naked
Fea'tly, ad. neatly, readily, niiably
Fea'ture, s. the cast or make of the face; any
lineament or single part of the face
Feaze, v. a. to untwist a rope; to beat
Feb'rifuge, s. a medicine to cure fevers
Fe'brile, a. relating or belonging to a fever
Feb'ruary, s. the second month of the year
Februa'tion, a sacrifice, &c. for the dead
Fec'ulence, s. muddiness, sediment, lees
Fec'ulent, a. dreggy, excrementitious, foul
Fec'und, a. prolific, fruitful, rich
Fecunda'tion, s. the act of making fruitful
Fecun'dity, s. fruitfulness, fertility
Fecun'dify, v.a. to make fruitful
Fed, prep. and part. of to feed
Fed'ary, s. a partner, or a dependant
Fed'eral, a. relating to a league or contract
Fed'erary, s. a confederate; an accomplice
Fee, v.a. to reward; to hire; to pay; to bribe
Fee, s. a reward; perpetual right, perquisite
Fee'ble, a. weak, debilitated, sickly
Fee'bled, part. made weak, enfeebled
Fee'bleness, s. weakness, infirmity
Feed, v. to supply with food, to cherish
Feed, s. pasture for cattle; food
Fee'der, s. one who gives or eats food
Feel,v.to perceive by the touch,to be affec-
by; to try; to sound; to know
Feel, s. the sense of feeling, the touch
Fee'ling, s.sensibility,perception, tenderness
Fee'lingly, ad. with great sensibility
Feet, s. the plural of Foot
Fee'tless, a. without feet
Feign, v. to dissemble, invent, relate falsely
Fei'gned, part. dissembled, pretended

feign'edly, ad. in fiction, not truly
feint, s. false appearance, a mock assault
felic'itate, v.a. to make happy; congratulate
felicita'tion, s. congratulation
felic'itous, s. happiness blissfulness, prosperity
felic'itous, a. happy, prosperous
Fe'line, a. like or pertaining to a cat
Fell, a. savage, cruel, bloody—s. a skin
Fell, v. a. to cut down, to knock down
Fell'monger, s. a dealer in skins or hides
Fel'loe, s. the circumference of a wheel
Fel'low, s. an equal, associate; a mean person
Fel'low, v. a. to pair with, to suit with
Fel'lowship, s. society, companionship, equality; establishment in a college
Fe'lo-de-se, s. a self-murderer, a suicide
Fel'on, s. one guilty of a capital crime
Felo'nious, a. wicked, malign, villanous
Felo'niously, ad. in a felonious manner
Fel'ony, s. a capital crime or offence
Felt, v. a. to unite stuff without weaving
Felt, s. stuff used in making hats; a skin
Felt, pret. of to feel
Fel'tre, v. a. to clot together like felt
Feluc'ca, s. a small open boat with six oars
Fe'male, Fem'inine, a. not masculine, effeminate, tender, soft, delicate, emasculated
Fe'male, Fem'inine, s. one of that sex that brings forth young
Feminal'ity, s. female nature
Fem'oral, a. belonging to the thigh
Fen, s. a moor, a marsh, low moist ground
Fence, s. a guard, enclosure, hedge, mound
Fence, v. to guard, to enclose; to act on the defensive, to guard against
Fen'celess, a. without enclosure, open
Fen'cer, s. one who teaches or practises fencing
Fen'cible, a. capable of defence
Fen'cing, s. the art of defence by weapons
Fend, v. to keep off, to shut out; to dispute
Fen'der, s. a fence to keep in the cinders
Fenera'tion, s. usury, interest
Fen'ny, a. marshy, inhabiting the marsh
Feo'dal, a. held from another
Feo'dary, s. one who holds from another
Feoff, v. a. to put in possession, to invest
Feoff'ee, s. one put in possession
Feoff'er, s. one who gives possession
Feoff'ment, s. the act of granting possession
Fera'cious, a. abundant, fertile, fruitful
Ferac'ity, s. fertility, fruitfulness
Fe'ral, a. funeral, mournful, deadly
Feria'tion, s. the act of keeping holiday
Feri'ne, a. savage, wild, fierce, barbarous
Feri'neness, Fer'ity, s. wildness, barbarity
Ferment', v.a. to exalt or rarify by intestine motion of its parts
Fer'ment, s. internal motion, riot, tumult
Fermenta'tion, s. the act of fermenting
Fermen'tative, a. causing fermentation
Fern, s. a plant growing on heaths, &c.
Fer'ny, a. overgrown with fern
Fero'cious, a. fierce, savage, ravenous
Feroc'ity, s. savageness, fierceness, wildness
Fer'reous, a. irony, partaking of iron
Fer'ret, s. a small animal; a kind of tape
Fer'ret, v. a. to vex or tease one; drive out
Ferru'ginous, a. partaking of iron
Fer'rule, s. an iron ring at the end of a stick
Fer'ry, v. to carry over in a boat

Fer'ryboat, Fer'ry, s. a boat for passage; the passage over which the boat passes
Fer'ryman, s. one who ferries or keeps a ferry
Fer'tile, a. fruitful, plenteous, abundant
Fertil'ity, s. fruitfulness, abundance
Fer'tilize, v. a. to make plenteous, to fecun.
Fer'vency, s. ardour, zeal, eagerness, heat
Fer'vent, a. ardent, hot, zealous, vehement
Fer'vently, ad. eagerly; with pious ardour
Ferves'cent, a. growing fervent
Fer'vid, a. vehement, ardent, zealous
Fer'vidness, Fer'vour, s. heat of mind, warmth, zeal
Fer'ula, s. an instrument of correction [ers
Fes'cue, s. a wire to point out letters to learn-
Fes'tal, a. relating to feasts, joyous, gay
Fes'ter, v.n. to corrupt, grow virulent, rankle
Fes'tival, s. a day of civil or religious joy
Fes'tive, a. gay, joyous, pertaining to feasts
Festiv'ity, s. a festival, a time of rejoicing
Festoo'n, s. an ornament of twisted flowers
Festu'cous, a. formed of straw
Fetch, v.a. to go and bring a thing, to draw
Fetch, s. a stratagem, a trick, an artifice
Fet'id, a. stinking, having an offensive smell
Fetif'erous, a. bringing forth fruit or young
Fet'lock, s. a tuft of hair that grows behind a horse's pastern, or ankle joint
Fe'tor, s. a stink, a stench
Fet'ter, v. a. to enchain; to tie, to shackle
Fet'ters, s. chains for the feet
Fet'tle, v. n. to do trifling business
Fe'tus, Fœ'tus, s. any animal in embryo
Feud, s. a quarrel, opposition, contention
Feu'dal, a. dependant, held by tenure
Feu'datory, s. one who holds of a lord or chief
Fe'ver, s. a disease attended with thirst and a quickened pulse
Fe'verish, Fe'verous, Fe'very, a. troubled with a fever, tending to a fever, burning, hot
Fe'verishness, s. a feverish disorder
Feu'illage, s. a bunch or row of leaves
Few, a. a small number, not many
Few'ness, s. smallness of number, brevity
Fi'at, s. a sentence, judgment, decree
Fib, s. a falsehood—v. n. to tell lies, to lie
Fib'ber, s. a teller of lies
Fi'bre, s. a small thread or string
Fi'brous, a. full of, or composed of, fibres
Fic'kle, a. changeable, unfixed, inconstant
Fic'kleness, s. inconstancy, unsteadiness
Fic'tion, s. a story invented; a falsehood
Fic'tious, Ficti'tious, a. imaginary, counterfeit, false, not true, not real, allegorical
Ficti'tiously, ad. falsely, counterfeitly
Fid'dle, s. a musical instrument, a violin
Fid'dle, v. n. to play upon the fiddle, to trifle
Fid'dlefaddle, s. a trifler, a trifle
Fid'dler, s. one who plays upon the fiddle
Fid'dle-string, s. the string of a fiddle
Fidel'ity, s. honesty, faithfulness, veracity
Fid'get, v. n. to move nimbly or irregularly
Fidu'cial, a. confident, undoubting
Fidu'ciary, s. one who holds in trust
Fief, s. a manor; possession held by tenure
Field, s. a cultivated tract of ground; place of battle; a battle; a wide expanse; extent, space
Field'book, s. a book used by surveyors
Field'fare, s. a bird; a kind of thrush
Field'-piece, s. a small cannon used in battle

Fiend, _s._ an infernal being; an enemy

Fierce, _a._ furious, outrageous, ravenous

Fie'rcely, _ad._ furiously, violently, vehemently

Fie'rceness, _s._ ferocity, violence, fury

Fi'ery, _a._ consisting of fire; hot, passionate

Fife, _s._ a small pipe blown to the drum

Fi'fer, _s._ one who plays on a fife

Fif'teen, _a._ five and ten added

Fif'ty, _a._ five tens added

Fig, _s._ a tree that bears figs; its fruit

Fight, _v._ to contend in battle, to combat

Fight, _s._ a battle, a duel, an engagement

Fi'ghter, _s._ a warrior, a duellist

Fig'ment, _s._ a fiction, device, invention

Fig'ulate, _a._ made of potter's earth or clay

Fig'urable, _a._ capable of being formed

Fig'ural, Fig'urate, _a._ of a certain form

Fig'urative, _a._ not literal, metaphorical

Fig'uratively, _ad._ by a figure, not literally

Fig'ure, _s._ a character denoting a number, an image; shape; external form; eminence

Fig'ure, _v. a._ to form into any shape

Fig'ured, _part. a._ represented; adorned

Fila'ceous, _a._ consisting of threads

Fil'ament, _s._ a slender thread; a fibre

Fil'bert, _s._ a fine hazel nut with a thin shell

Filch, _v. a._ to steal, to rob, to pilfer, to cheat

Fil'cher, _s._ a petty thief, a robber

File, _s._ a steel tool to polish iron, &c. with; a line of soldiers; a wire for papers

Fil'emot, _s._ a brown or yellow-brown colour

Fil'ial, _a._ pertaining to or beseeming a son

Fil'iform, _a._ shaped like a thread

Fil'igree, _s._ a kind of delicate work on gold or silver in manner of grains or threads

Fi'lings, _s._ particles rubbed off by a file

Fill, _v. a._ to make full, to surfeit, to satisfy

Fill, _s._ fulness, satiety; part of a carriage

Fil'let, _s._ a band tied round the head, &c.; a bandage; the fleshy part of the thigh

Fil'lip, _v. a._ to jerk or hit with the finger

Fil'lip, _s._ a jerk of the finger from the thumb

Fil'ly, _s._ a young mare; opposed to a colt

Film, _s._ a thin skin or pellicle

Fil'my, _a._ composed of thin membranes

Fil'ter, _v. a._ to strain, to percolate

Fil'ter, _s._ a strainer, a source

Filth, _s._ pollution, grossness; nastiness, dirt

Fil'thiness, _s._ dirtiness; corruption, impurity

Fil'thy, _a._ nasty, dirty; polluted, obscene

Fil'trate, _v. a._ to filter, to strain, to percolate

Fin, _s._ the wing of a fish, by which he swims

Fi'nable, _a._ that which may be fined

Fi'nal, _a._ decisive, ultimate; mortal

Fi'nally, _ad._ conclusively, ultimately, fully

Finan'ce, _s._ income, revenue, profit

Financie'r, _s._ one who collects or farms the public revenue

Find, _v. a._ to discover, to detect; to remark

Fine, _a._ not coarse, thin, pure, clear; elegant

Fine, _s._ a pecuniary forfeit, penalty, mulct

Fine, _v. a._ to refine; inflict a pecuniary penalty

Fi'nely, _ad._ elegantly; subtilely, keenly

Fi'neness, _s._ elegance, purity, show, splendour

Fi'ner, _s._ one who refines metals

Fi'nery, _s._ show, splendour, gaiety in attire

Finesse'e, _s._ an artifice, a stratagem

Fin'ewed, _a._ mouldy, dirty, muddy, nasty

Fin'ger, _s._ a part of the hand; breadth of the finger

Fin'ger, _v. a._ to touch lightly; to pilfer

Fin'ical, _a._ nice, affected, foppish, conceited

Fin'ically, _ad._ foppishly, superfluously nice

Fi'ning-pot, _s._ a pot for refining metals

Fi'nis, _s._ the conclusion, the end

Fin'ish, _v. a._ to perfect, to complete, to end

Fin'isher, _s._ one who perfects or completes

Fi'nite, _a._ limited; opposed to infinite

Fi'niteness, _s._ limitation, confinement

Fin'less, _a._ wanting fins

Fin'ny, _a._ furnished with fins

Fir, _s._ the tree of which deal boards are made

Fire, _s._ that which has the power of burning; lustre; passion of love; ardour of temper

Fire, _v._ to discharge fire-arms; to kindle

Fi're-arms, _s._ arms discharged by fire

Fi'rebrand, _s._ a piece of wood kindled; one who inflames factions, an incendiary

Fi'redrake, _s._ a fiery serpent, or meteor

Fi'relock, _s._ a soldier's gun, a musket

Fi'reman, _s._ one who is employed to extinguish burning houses; a violent man

Fi'repan, _s._ a pan for holding fire

Fi'reship, _s._ a ship filled with combustibles

Fi'rework, _s._ an exhibition of fire

Fi'ring, _s._ fuel, something used for the fire

Fir'kin, _s._ a vessel containing nine gallons

Firm, _a._ strong, fast, hard, steady, constant

Firm, _s._ the name or names under which the business of any trading house is carried on

Fir'mament, _s._ the sky, the heavens

Firmamen'tal, _a._ celestial, belonging to the firmament; elementary; ethereal

Fir'man, _s._ a permission to trade, &c.

Fir'mly, _ad._ steadily, immoveably, constantly

Fir'mness, _s._ steadiness, solidity, stability

First, _a._ earliest in time; highest in dignity

Fir'stfruits, _s._ the first produce of any thing

Fir'stling, _s._ the first produce or offspring

Fis'cal, _s._ the exchequer, the revenue

Fish, _s._ an animal existing only in water

Fish, _v._ to catch fish; to catch by artifice

Fish'er, Fish'erman, _s._ one whose occupation is to catch fish with nets, or by angling

Fish'ery, _s._ employment or trade of fishing

Fish'hook, _s._ a hook to catch fish with

Fish'ify, _v. a._ to turn to fish

Fish'ing, _s._ the practice or art of catching fish

Fish'meal, _s._ a meal made of fish

Fish'monger, _s._ one who sells or deals in fish

Fish'y, _a._ consisting of, or like fish

Fis'sile, _a._ easy to be cleft

Fis'sure, _s._ a cleft, a small chasm, an opening

Fist, _s._ the hand closed or clenched

Fis'ticuffs, _s._ a battle with fists

Fis'tula, _s._ a sinuous ulcer callous within

Fis'tulous, _a._ pertaining to a fistula; hollow, like a reed or pipe

Fit, _s._ a paroxysm of any distemper; disorder of the animal spirits; distemperature

Fit, _a._ qualified, convenient, meet, suitable

Fit, _v. a._ to suit, to adapt, to accommodate

Fitch, _s._ a small kind of wild pea; a vetch

Fit'ful, _a._ varied by paroxysms

Fit'ly, _ad._ properly, aptly, commodiously

Fit'ness, _s._ propriety, meetness, convenience

Fi'vefold, _a._ five times as much

Fives, _s._ a game at balls; a disease of horses

Fix, _v. a._ to fasten; settle, determine; rest

Fixa'tion, Fix'edness, _s._ stability, solidity

Fix'ed, _part._ fastened, settled, determined

Fixid'ity Fix'ity, _s._ coherence of parts

Fix'ture, s. any article fixed to the premises, position; stable pressure

Fix'ure, s. position; pressure; firmness

Fiz'gig, s. a kind of harpoon to strike fish

Flab'biness, s. limberness, softness

Flab'by, a. soft, limber, not stiff, not firm

Fla'bile, a. subject to be blown by wind

Flac'cid, a. weak, limber, not tense, not stiff

Flaccid'ity, s. limberness; want of tension

Flag, v. a. to grow dejected, lose vigour, droop

Flag, s. the colours of a ship or land-forces; a flat stone for paving; a water plant

Flag'elet, s. a small flute, a musical pipe

Flagella'tion, s. the act of scourging

Flag'gy, a. weak, limber, not tense; insipid

Flagit'ious, a. wicked, vile, atrocious

Flagit'iousness, s. wickedness, atrocity

Flag'on, s. a drinking vessel of two quarts

Flag'officer, s. the commander of a squadron or part of a fleet of ships

Fla'grancy, s. burning heat, inflammation, fire

Fla'grant, a. glowing, ardent; notorious

Flag'ship, s. the admiral's ship

Flail, s. an instrument to thresh corn with

Flake, s. any thing that appears loosely put together; a layer, a stratum, a lamina

Fla'ky, a. broken into lamina or strata

Flam, s. a lie, a falsehood, an illusory pretext

Flam'beau, s. a lighted wax torch

Flame, s. a light emitted from fire; fire; the passion of love; brightness of fancy

Flame, v. n. to shine as fire, shine like flame

Fla'men, s. an ancient Pagan priest

Flammabil'ity, s. aptitude to take fire

Flamma'tion, s. the act of setting on flame

Flam'meous, a. consisting of flame

Flammif'erous, a. bringing flame

Fla'my, a. inflamed, flaming, burning

Flank, s. the side; part of a bastion—v. a. to attack the side of a battalion, or fleet

Flan'nel, s. a soft nappy stuff made of wool

Flap, s. any thing that hangs broad and loose; a blow with the hand; a disease in horses

Flap, v. to beat with a flap; to fall with flaps; to ply the wings with a noise

Flap'dragon, v. a. to devour—s. a game

Flare, v. n. to glitter offensively; to be in too much light; to flutter with splendid show

Flash, v. to glitter with a quick flame

Flash, s. a sudden blaze; a sudden burst of wit

Flash'y, a. showy, empty, insipid

Flask, s. a bottle, a vessel; a powder-horn

Flas'ket, s. a large basket; a kind of tray

Flat, s. a level; a shallow; even ground

Flat, a. level, smooth; dull, tasteless; not shrill

Flat, v. to make level, make vapid, depress

Flat'ly, ad. peremptorily; frigidly, dully

Flat'ness, s. evenness; dulness, deadness

Flat'ten, v. to make even; dispirit, deject

Flat'ter, v. a. to praise falsely; to please with blandishments; to raise false hopes

Flat'terer, s. a fawner, a cajoler [praise

Flat'tery, s. artful obsequiousness; false

Flat'tish, a. approaching to flatness; dull

Flat'ulency, s. windiness; airiness, vanity

Flat'ulent, Flat'uous, a. windy; vain, empty

Flaunt, v. n. to give one's self airs; to make a fluttering show in apparel

Flaunt, s. any thing loose and airy

Fla'vour, s. a taste, relish; fragrance, odour

Fla'vourous, a. fragrant, palatable, odorous

Flaw, s. a breach, a crack; a defect, a fault

Flax, s. a fibrous plant, of which the finest thread is made; the fibres of flax cleaned

Flax'-dresser, s. he who prepares flax

Flax'en, a. made of flax, like flax; fair

Flay, v. a. to strip off the skin

Flea, s. a small insect remarkable for agility

Flea'bitten, a. stung by fleas; worthless

Fleak, s. a small lock, thread, or twist

Fleam, s. an instrument used to bleed cattle

Fleck, v. a. to spot, to dapple, to streak

Fledge, v. a. to supply with feathers or wings

Flee, v. n. to run from danger, or for shelter

Fleece, s. the wool from one sheep

Fleece, v. a. to strip off the fleece; to plunder

Flee'ced, part. stripped of substance, plundered

Flee'cy, a. woolly, covered with wool

Fleer, v. n. to mock, to jest with insolence

Fleet, a. swift of pace, active, nimble

Fleet, s. a company of ships; a creek

Fleet, v. to fly swiftly, vanish; live merrily

Flee'ting, part. a. passing away continually

Fleet'ly, ad. with swift pace, nimbly

Fleet'ness, s. swiftness, celerity, nimbleness

Flesh, s. a part of the animal body

Flesh, v. a. to initiate; to glut; to harden

Flesh'fly, s. a fly that feeds upon flesh

Flesh'iness, s. fulness of flesh, plumpness

Flesh'liness, s. carnal appetites or passions

Flesh'ly, a. carnal, corporeal, human

Flesh'meat, s. animal food, flesh of animals

Flesh'y, a. full of flesh, plump, musculous

Flet, part. skimmed, deprived of the cream

Flet'cher, s. a maker of bows and arrows

Flew, pret. of to fly

Flew'ed, a. chapped; deep mouthed

Flexibil'ity, s. compliance, facility, ductility

Flex'ible, Flex'ile, a. pliant, manageable

Flex'ion, s. the act of bending; a turn, a joint

Flex'uous, a. winding, not steady, variable

Flex'ure, s. the part bent, the joint

Flick'er, v. a. to flutter, to play the wings

Fli'er, s. a runaway, a fugitive; part of a jack

Flight, s. the act of flying or running away; a flock of birds; the stairs from one landing place to another; heat of imagination

Fli'ghty, a. wild, full of imagination; swift

Flim'sy, a. weak, spiritless, feeble, mean

Flinch, v. n. to shrink from suffering

Flin'cher, s. he who shrinks or fails

Fling, v. to throw, dart; flounce; scatter

Fling, s. a throw; a contemptuous remark

Flint, s. a hard kind of pebble

Flin'ty, a. made of flint; cruel, inexorable

Flip, s. a drink made of beer, spirits, and sugar; a liquor much used in ships

Flip'pancy, s. lightness, pertness

Flip'pant, a. pert, nimble, talkative

Flip'pantly, ad. in a flippant, pert manner

Flirt, v. to jeer; to run about idly

Flirt, s. a pert hussey; a sudden trick

Flirta'tion, s. a quick, sprightly motion

Flit, v. n. to fly away; to remove; to flutter

Flitch, s. the side of a hog salted and cured

Flit'ter, s. a rag or tatter, garment rent

Flix, s. fur, down, soft air; the fur of hares

Float, s. the quill or cork fastened to a fishing-line; large pieces of timber fastened together to convey goods with the stream; the flux; the act of flowing

Float, v. n. to swim on the surface of the water

Flock, s. a company of sheep, birds, &c.
Flock, v. n. to gather in crowds; to assemble
Flog, v. a. to scourge or whip, to chastise
Flood, s. a deluge, an inundation; influx of the tide; the sea; a body of water
Flood, v. a. to cover with water, to deluge
Flood'gate, s. a gate to stop or let out water
Flood'mark, s. a mark that is left by the flood
Flook, or Fluke, s. the broad part of an anchor
Floor, s. the bottom of a room; a story
Flop, v. a. to clap the wings with noise
Flo'ral, a. relating to Flora or to flowers
Flores'cence, s. the flowering of a plant
Flo'ret, s. a small imperfect flower
Flor'id, a. flushed with red, rosy, blooming
Flor'idness, s. freshness of colour; elegance
Florif'erous, a. productive of flowers
Flo'rin, s. a coin of different value, in Spain 4s. 4d. halfpenny, in Sicily and Palermo 2s.6d. in Germany2s.4d. and in Holland 2s.
Flo'rist, s. a cultivator of flowers
Flos'culous, a. composed or formed of flowers
Flot'son, s. goods casually drifting on the sea
Flounce, v. to deck with flounces; to move with violence in water; to be in anger
Flounce, s. a loose full trimming sewed to women's apparel, so as to swell and shake
Floun'der, v. n. to struggle with violence and irregular motion; to plunge in water
Floun'der, s. a small flat river fish
Flour, s. the fine part of ground wheat
Flour'ish, v. to be in vigour; adorn; boast
Flour'ish, s. ostentatious embellishment; a short musical overture; bravery
Flout, v. to mock, treat with mockery, insult
Flow, v. to run as water; to overflow
Flow, s. the rise of water; not the ebb
Flow'er, s. the blossom of a plant, the prime
Flow'er, v. n. to be in blossom, to be in flower
Flow'eret, Flow'ret, s. a small flower
Flow'ery, a. adorned with, or full of, flowers
Flow'ingly, ad. with plenty; with volubility
Flown, part. of to flee; gone away; elate
Fluc'tuant, a. wavering, uncertain
Fluc'tuate, v. n. to be uncertain or irresolute
Fluctua'tion, s. uncertainty, indetermination
Flue, s. pipe of a chimney; soft down or fur
Flu'ency, s. copiousness of speech, volubility
Flu'ent, a. eloquent, flowing; liquid
Flu'ently, ad. flowingly, volubly; copiously
Flu'id, s. any animal juice, a liquid
Flu'id, a. running as water, not solid
Fluid'ity, s. the quality of flowing easily
Flum'mery, s. a food made of flour, wheat, &c.
Flung, part. and pret. of to fling
Flu'or, s. a fluid state, catamenia
Flur'ry, s. flutter of spirits; gust of wind
Flush, v. a. to redden, to colour; to elate
Flush, s. violent flow; cards all of a suit
Flush'ed, part. elated, reddened, heated
Flus'ter, v. a. to put in confusion, &c.
Flute, s. a musical pipe; a furrow or channel in a pillar or column
Flu'ting, s. fluted work on a pillar, &c.
Flut'ter, v. to fly with agitation of the wings
Flut'ter, s. hurry, tumult; disorder of mind
Flux, a. unconstant; not durable
Flux, s. a dysentery; the tide or flowing of the sea; confluence; concourse
Flux'ion, s. act of flowing, matter that flows
Fly, s. a winged insect; balance of a jack

Fly, v. to move with wings; to shun; to run away; to pass swiftly; to spring suddenly
Fly'blow, v. a. to fill with maggots
Fly'fish, v. n. to angle with a fly upon a hook
Foal, v. a. to bring forth a foal
Foal, s. the offspring of a mare
Foam, v. n. to froth, to be violently agitated
Foam, s. froth, spume
Foa'my, a. covered with foam, frothy
Fob, s. a small pocket for a watch, &c.
Fob, v. n. to cheat, to trick, to defraud
Fo'cal, a. belonging to a focus
Fo'cus, s. the point to which rays converge
Fod'der, s. dry food for cattle—v. a. to feed
Foe, s. an enemy, an opponent, a persecutor
Fœ'tus, or Fe'tus, s. a child in the womb
Fog, s. thick mist, moist vapour; aftergrass
Fog'giness, s. state of being misty or dark
Fog'gy, a. misty, dark, cloudy, dull
Foi'ble, s. a failing, a weakness
Foil, v. a. to defeat, to put to the worst
Foil, s. a defeat; a blunt sword used in fencing; a glittering substance
Foi'son, s. abundance; plenty
Foist, v. a. to insert by forgery; to cram in
Foi'sty, a. fusty, mouldy, smelling bad
Fold, s. a pen for sheep; a double or plait
Fold, v. to double up; to shut, to enclose
Fo'liage, s. the leaves or tufts of trees
Fo'liate, a. leaved, or having leaves
Folia'tion, s. the leafing of a plant
Fo'lio, s. a large book, of which the pages are formed by a sheet of paper once doubled
Folk, s. people, mankind, nations
Fol'low, v. to go after, to obey, to attend
Fol'lower, s. attendant, copier; companion
Fol'ly, s. foolishness, weakness, simplicity
Foment', v. a. to bathe with warm lotions; to cherish with heat; to abet, to encourage
Fomenta'tion, s. the application of hot flannel to any part, dipped in medicated decoction
Fon, s. an idiot; a fool
Fond, a. tender, foolish, indiscreet, silly
Fond, Fon'd e, v. to caress, to be fond of
Fon'dling, s. one much caressed or doated on
Fond'ly, ad. with extreme tenderness
Fond'ness, s. tender passion; foolishness
Fout, s. a baptismal bason
Fon'tanel, s. an issue, a place of discharge
Food, s. victuals; any thing that nourishes
Fool, s. an idiot; a natural; a buffoon
Fool, v. to toy, to trifle, disappoint, deceive
Fool'ery, s. habitual folly; an act of folly
Foolhar'dy, a. madly adventurous, daring
Fool'ish, a. void of understanding, imprudent
Fool'ishness, s. want of reason, silliness
Foot, s. that on which any animal or thing is supported; a measure of twelve inches
Foot, v. to dance, tread, walk; kick, spurn
Foot'ball, s. a blown bladder cased with leather
Foot'boy, s. an attendant in livery, a menial
Foot'ed, a. shaped in the foot; trod, walked
Foot'ing, s. ground for the foot; basis, foundation; walk, tread; entrance; support
Foot'man, s. a servant in livery; a soldier
Foot'pad, s. a highwayman that robs on foot
Foot'path, s. a narrow way for passengers
Foot'step, s. a mark of a foot, a trace, a track
Foot'stool, s. a stool to put the feet on
Fop, s. a vain fellow, a simpleton, a coxcomb

Fop'pery, *s.* affectation of importance, folly
Fop'pish, *a.* foolishly ostentatious, vain, idle
Fop'pishness, *s.* ostentatious vanity
For, *prep.* because of—*conj.* on this account
For'age, *s.* provisions in general   [that
For'age, *v.* to wander in search of provisions;
   to feed on spoil, to ravage, to plunder
Forasmuch', *conj.* whereas, because, since
Forbea'r, *v.* to pause, to intermit, to abstain
Forbea'rance, *s.* lenity, command of temper
Forbid', *v.* to prohibit, to oppose, to interdict
Forbid'ding, *part. a.* causing aversion, aus-
Force, *v.* to compel; to urge; to violate [tere
Force, *s.* violence, strength; an armament
For'ceps, *s.* a surgical instrument
Fo'rcible, *a.* strong, efficacious, impetuous
Fo'rcibly, *ad.* with great strength, powerfully
Ford, *s.* the shallow part of a river; the
   current
Ford, *v. a.* to pass a river without swimming
Fo'rdable, *a.* passable without swimming
Fo'rded, *part.* passed over without swimming
Fore, *a.* anterior, not behind—*ad.* before
Forebo'de, *v. n.* to foretel, to prognosticate
Fo'recast, *v.* to scheme, to foresee, to contrive
Fo'recast, *s.* contrivance, antecedent policy
Fo'recastle, *s.* the foredeck of a ship
Fo'recited, *part.* quoted before or above
Foreclo'se, *v. a.* to shut up; to preclude
Fo'redock, *s.* the anterior part of a ship
Foredo', *v. a.* to ruin; to weary, to overdo
Foredo'om, *v. a.* to determine beforehand
Fo'refather, Fo'regoer, *s.* an ancestor
Forefen'd, *v. a.* to avert, to hinder; to secure
Fo'refront, *s.* the front; the forehead
Forego'. *v. a.* to give up; to lose; to go before
Fo'reground, *s.* that part of the ground of a
   picture which seems to lie before the figures
Fo'rehand, *a.* done too soon
Fore'head, *s.* the upper part of the face
For'eign, *a.* not domestic; not allied; alien
For'eigner, *s.* one of another country
Forejud'ge, *v. a.* to be prepossessed, to pre-
Foreknow'. *v. a.* to know beforehand [judge
Forek nowl'edge, *s.* prescience, knowledge of
   that which has not yet happened
Fo'reland, *s.* a promontory, a cape, a headland
Forelay', *v. a.* to lay wait for, to entrap
Fo'relock, *s.* the hair on the forehead
Fo'reman, *s.* the first or chief person
Fo'remast, *s.* the first or head-mast of a ship
Foremen'tioned, *a.* mentioned before
Fo'remost, *a.* first in place, first in dignity
Fo'renamed, *a.* nominated before
Fo'renoon, *s.* the time before mid-day [ture
Foren'sic, *a.* belonging to courts of judica-
Foreordai'n, *v.* to determine beforehand
Fo'repart, *s.* the anterior part in place or
Fo'rerank, *s.* the first rank, the front [name
Forerea'ch, *v. n.* to get first, to sail faster
Forerun', *v. a.* to come before, to precede
Forerun'ner, *s.* one sent before, a harbin-
   ger, a messenger; a presage, a prognostic
Foresay', *v. a.* to prophesy, to predict, foretel
Foresee', *v. a.* to see beforehand, to foreknow
Foreshow', *v. a.* to discover before it happens,
   to predict, to prognosticate
Fo'resight, *s.* foreknowledge, penetration
For'est, *s.* a woody, untilled tract of ground
Foresta'l, *v. a.* to purchase before others, in
   order to sell at a high price

Foresta'ller, *s.* one who forestals the market
For'ester, *s.* a keeper of a forest
Fo'retaste, *s.* a taste before, anticipation of
Foretel', *v.* to utter, to predict, to prophesy
Forethin'k, *v. a.* to anticipate in the mind
Fo'rethought, *s.* prescience, anticipation; cau-
   tion, provident care
Foreto'ken, *v. a.* to foreshow—*s.* omen, sign
Fo'retop, *s.* the front of a periwig, &c.
Forewarn', *v. a.* to admonish, caution against
Forewarn'ing, *s.* caution given beforehand
Forewish', *v. a.* to desire beforehand
For'feit, *s.* a fine for an offence; a penalty
For'feitable, *a.* liable to be forfeited
For'feiture, *s.* act of forfeiting; a fine, a mulct
Forfen'd, *v. a.* to forbid, to prevent
Forge, *s.* a place where metals are beaten into
   form, a furnace
Forge, *v. a.* to form by the hammer; to coun-
   terfeit, to invent, to falsify
For'gery, *s.* the crime of falsification
Forget', *v. a.* to lose memory of, to omit
Forget'ful, *a.* apt to forget, inattentive
Forget'fulness, *s.* loss of memory; neglect
Forgiv'e, *v. a.* to pardon, to excuse, to remit
Forgiv'eness, *s.* the act of forgiving; pardon
Fork, *v. n.* to shoot into blades or branches
Fork, *s.* an instrument with two or more
   prongs for various domestic or other uses
For'ked, For'ky, *a.* opening into two or more
   parts, like the prongs of a fork
Forlor'n, *a.* deserted, lost, helpless, desperate
Forlorn'ness, *s.* misery; solitude
Forlye', *v. n.* to lie across or athwart
Form, *s.* figure, shape; ceremony, empty
   show; order, elegance; a long seat; a class
Form, *v. a.* to fashion, to contrive, to adjust
For'mal, *a.* solemn, methodical, affected
For'malist, *s.* one who is fond of formality
Formal'ity, *s.* ceremony, stiffness, preciseness
For'mally, *ad.* solemnly, stiffly, precisely
Forma'tion, *s.* the act of forming
For'mative, *a.* having the power of forming
For'mer, *a.* before another in time; past
For'merly, *ad.* in past times
For'midable, *a.* terrible, tremendous, dread-
For'midably, *ad.* dreadfully, terrifically [ful
For'mless, *a.* having no form; shapeless
For'mula, *s.* a prescribed rule or pattern
For'mulary, *s.* a book of stated models, &c.
For'nicate, *v. n.* to commit lewdness
Fornica'tion, *s.* concubinage, unchastity be-
   tween single persons; the crime of idolatry
For'nicator, *s.* he who commits fornication
Fornica'tress, *s.* a woman who without mar-
   riage cohabits with a man
Forsa'ke, *v. a.* to abandon, to leave; neglect
Forsa'ken, *part.* deserted, neglected, left
Forsoo'th, *ad.* in truth, certainly, very well
Forswea'r, *v.* to renounce upon oath, to com-
   mit perjury, to swear falsely
Fort, *s.* a fortified house, a castle
For'ted, *a.* guarded by, or having forts
Forth, *ad.* forward, abroad, out of doors
Forthcom'ing, *part.* ready to appear
Forthri'ght, *ad.* straight forward, directly
Forthwith', *ad.* immediately, without delay
For'tieth, *a.* the tenth taken four times
Fortifica'tion, *s.* the science of military archi-
   tecture; a place built for strength
For'tify, *v. a.* to strengthen, to encoura

H 3

For'tilage, For'tin, For'tlet, s. a little fort
For'titude, s. bravery, courage, force of mind
For'tnight, s. the space of two weeks
For'tress, s. a fortified place, a strong hold
Fortu'itous, a. happening by chance, acciden-
Fortu'itously, ad. accidentally, by chance [tal
Fortu'itousness, s. accident
For'tunate, a. lucky, successful, happy
For'tunately, ad. prosperously, happily
For'tune, s. the good or ill that befals man-
kind ; estate, portion ; chance ; futurity
For'tune-hunter, s. a man who endeavours
to marry a woman only for her fortune
For'tune-teller, s. one who imposes on people
by a pretended knowledge of futurity
For'ty, a. four times ten
Fo'rum, s. any public place
For'ward, a. anterior ; ardent, warm, eager ;
confident, bold ; early ripe
For'ward, v. a. to hasten, accelerate, patronize
For'wardly, ad. hastily, eagerly, quickly
For'wardness, s. eagerness ; immodesty
Fosse, s. a moat, ditch, intrenchment
Fos'sil, s. a mineral—a. what is dug up
Fos'ter, v. a. to cherish, to nurse, to bring up
Fos'terage, s. the office or charge of nursing
Fos'terbrother, s. one bred at the same breast
Fos'terchild, Fos'terling, s. a child brought
up by those that are not its natural parents
Fought, pret. and part. of to fight
Foul, a. not clean, impure ; ugly ; coarse
Foul, v. a. to dirty, to bemire, to daub
Foul'faced, a. having an ugly, hateful face
Foul'ly, ad. nastily, filthily, not fairly
Foul'mouthed, a. using scurrilous language
Foul'ness, s. nastiness, odiousness, ugliness
Found, pret. and part. pass. of to find
Found, v. a. to establish, build ; cast metals
Founda'tion, s. the basis of an edifice; the first
principles or grounds ; establishment
Foun'der, s. an establisher, a builder; a caster
Foun'der, v. to sink to the bottom; grow lame
Foun'dery, Foun'dry, s. a casting house [er
Foun'dling, s. a child found without an own-
Fount, Foun'tain, s. a spring, a spout of water
Foun'tful, a. full of fountains or springs
Four'fold, a. four times as many
Four'footed, a. having four feet
Four'score, a. four times twenty ; eighty
Four'teen, a. four and ten ; twice seven
Fowl, s. a winged animal ; a bird
Fowl'er, s. a sportsman who pursues birds
Fowl'ingpiece, s. a gun for shooting birds
Fox, s. a wild animal of the canine kind, re-
markable for his cunning ; a knave
Fox'case, s. the skin of a fox
Fox'chase, s. pursuit of a fox with hounds
Fox'hunter, s. one who hunts foxes
Fox'trap, s. a snare or gin to catch foxes
Fract, v. a. to break, to infringe, to violate
Frac'tion, s. the act of breaking ; a broken
part of an integral
Frac'tional, a. belonging to a fraction
Frac'tious, a. cross, quarrelsome, captious
Frac'ture, v. a. to break a bone—s. a breach,
separation of continuous parts
Frag'ile, a. brittle, weak, easily broken
Fragil'ity, s. brittleness, frailty, weakness
Frag'ment, s. an imperfect piece, a part
Fra'grance, Fra'grancy, s. sweetness of smell,
pleasing scent, grateful odour

Fra'grant, a. odorous, sweet of smell
Fra'grantly, ad. with sweet scent
Frail, a. feeble, weak, liable to error
Frail, s. a basket made of rushes ; a rush
Frail'ty, s. weakness, infirmity of mind
Frame, v. a. to form, to compose, to fabricate;
to regulate ; to invent, plan, adjust
Frame, s. any thing constructed of various
parts or members; order, regularity; form,
shape ; contrivance, construction
Fran'chise, v. a. to make free—s. an exemp-
tion, immunity, privilege ; a district
Fran'gible, a. brittle, fragile, easily broken
Fran'ion, s. a paramour ; a boon companion
Frank, a. liberal, unreserved, ingenuous
Frank, s. a French coin ; a free letter
Frank, v. a. to exempt letters from postage
Fran'kincense, s. an odoriferous drug
Frank'ly, ad. freely, without reserve, plainly
Frank'ness, s. liberality, ingenuousness
Fran'tic, a. mad, turbulent, outrageous
Frater'nal, a. brotherly, becoming brothers
Frater'nity, s. a society, a corporation
Frat'ricide, s. the murder of a brother
Fraud, s. cheat, deceit, trick, artifice
Frau'dulence, Frau'dulency, s. deceitfulness,
proneness to artifice, trickishness
Frau'dulent, Frau'dful, a. deceitful, full of ar
tifice, performed by art, trickish
Frau'dulently, ad. by fraud, treacherously
Fraught, s. a cargo, a freight
Fraught, part. a. laden, filled, charged
Pray, s. a quarrel, a duel, a battle ; a defect
Pray'ed, part. worn by rubbing, terrified
Freak, s. a sudden fancy, a humour, a whim
Freak'ish, a. whimsical, capricious
Freck'le, s. a spot in the skin—n. a. to spot
Freck'led, a. full of freckles or spots
Free, a. at liberty ; open, liberal ; licentious
Free'booter, s. a plunderer, a robber
Free'born, a. inheriting liberty
Free'cost, s. free from expense or charge
Free'dom, s. liberty, unrestraint, privilege
Freehear'ted, a. liberal, unrestrained
Free'hold, s. land held in perpetual right
Free'holder, s. one who has a freehold
Free'ly, ad. at liberty ; spontaneously
Free'man, s. one not a slave; one partaking of
rights, immunities, and privileges
Free'minded, a. unconstrained, without care
Free'ness, s. liberality, ingenuousness
Freespo'ken, a. speaking without reserve
Free'stone, s. a stone so called, because it may
be cut in any direction, having no grain
Free'thinker, s. a disbeliever of revelation
Freeze, v. a. to be congealed with cold
Freight, s. that with which a ship is loaded ;
the money due for transportation of goods
Frenet'ic, a. distracted, mad, outrageous
Fren'zy, s. madness, distraction of mind
Fre'quency, s. state of being often done or
seen ; usualness ; a full assembly
Fre'quent, a. often done, seen, or occurring
Frequent', v. a. to visit often, to resort to
Fre'quently, ad. repeatedly, not rarely
Fres'co, s. coolness, shade, duskiness
Fresh, a. cool ; new; florid, brisk, vigorous
not stale ; not salt ; not vapid ; recent
Fresh'en, v. a. to make or grow fresh
Fresh'et, s. a pool of fresh water
Fresh'ly, ad. coolly ; ruddily ; newly

Fresh'ness, s. newness, bloom, spirit

Fret, s. commotion or agitation of the mind ; agitation of liquors by fermentation

Fret,v. to vex; to corrode; to rub, wear away

Fret'ful. a. peevish, dissatisfied, angry

Fret'fulness, s. peevishness, passion

Fret'work, s. raised work in masonry

Fri'able, a. easily reduced to powder

Fri'ar, s. a religious brother of some order

Fri'arlike,Fri'arly,fri'ary,a.unskilled in the world ; recluse, monastic

Fri'ary, s. a convent or monastery of friars

Frib'ble, s. a fop. a coxcomb, a trifler

Fricasse'e,s.a dish of chick-ns, &c. cut small and dressed with strong sauce

Fric'tion, s. the act of rubbing bodies toge-

Fri'day, s. the sixth day of the week   [ther

Friend,s.an intimate, a confidant, a favourer

Frien'ded, part. befriended, assisted, aided

Frien'dless, a. without friends, forlorn

Frien'dliness,s.a disposition to friendship or benevolence ; kind behaviour

Frien'dly, ad. kind, favourable, salutary

Frien'dship, s. highest degree of intimacy ; personal kindness; favour; help,assistance

Frieze,Frize, s. a warm coarse kind of cloth ; a term in ornamental architecture

Frig'ate, s. a small ship of war

Fright, s. a sudden terror, a panic

Fright, Fri'ghten, v. a. to terrify, to daunt

Fri'ghtful, a. causing fright, dreadful

Fri'ghtfully,ad.terribly,dreadfully, horribly

Frig'id, a. cold, unmoved, impotent, dull

Frigid'ity, s. coldness, dulness

Frig'idly, ad. coldly, dully, unfeelingly

Frigorif'ic, a. causing or producing cold

Frill, v. n. to quake—s. a kind of ruffle

Fringe,s. ornamental trimming—v.a. to trim

Frip'pery,s.paltry, ridiculous finery; dresses vamped up ; old clothes, tattered rags

Frisk, v. n. to leap. to dance, to skip

Fris'kiness, s. gaiety, liveliness

Fris'ky, a. gay, frolicsome, airy, wanton

Frit, s. ashes or salt to make glass with

Frith, s. a strait of the sea ; a kind of net

Frit'ter, v. a. to crumble away in small particles, &c.—s. a small pancake

Frit'tered, part. divided or cut into small pieces   [meanness

Frivol'ity, Friv'olousness, s. triflingness,

Friv'olous, a. trifling, slight, of no moment

Priv'olously, ad. insignificantly, vainly

Friz'zle, v. a. to curl in short curls

Fro, ad. contraction of from, to and fro

Frock,s. a gown for children ; a dress ; a coat

Frog, s. a small amphibious animal

Frol'ic, s. a wild prank ; a flight or whim— v. n. to play pranks, to be merry

Frol'ic, Frol'icsome, a. gay, wild, jocund

From, prep. away ; out of; noting privation

Frond, s. a twig of a tree with its leaves

Front, s. the face, the forehead ; fore part of any thing ; van of an army

Front, v. to stand foremost. to be opposite to

Fron'tier, s. a verge of territory ; a limit

Frontiniac', s. a luscious French wine

Fron'tispiece,s.an engraving to face the title page of a book ; that part of any building or other body that directly meets the eye

Fron'tless, a. not blushing, wanting shame

Fron'tlet, s. a bandage worn on the forehead

Frost, s. power or act of congelation; the last effect of cold producing ice

Fros'tbitten, part. withered by the frost

Fros'ty, a. excessive cold ; chilliness in affec-

Fro'h,s.foam; empty show of eloquence[tion

Froth'ily, ad. with foam; in a trifling manner

Froth'iness, s. lightness, vanity, emptiness

Froth'y, a. full of foam ; trifling, empty

Frou'zy, a. strong, fetid. musty ; dim

Fro'ward, a. ungovernable, peevish, angry

Fro'wardly, ad. peevishly. perversely

Fro'wardness, s. peevishness, perverseness

Frown, s. a wrinkled look ; look of displea

Frown. v. n. to knit the brows   [sure

Frow'ningly,ad.sternly:with a look of anger

Fro'zen, part. pass. of to freeze

Fructif'erous, a. bearing fruit

Fructifica'tion, s. the act of bearing fruit

Fruc'tify, v. a. to make fruitful, to fertilize

Fruc'tuous, a. fruitful, tending to fertilize

Fru'gal, a. thrifty. sparing, parsimonious

Frugal'ity, s. parsimony

Fru'gally, ad. parsimoniously, sparingly

Fruit, s. the produce of the earth, trees, and plants ; the offspring of the womb

Frui'tage, s. fruit collectively; various fruits

Frui'tbearing, part. producing fruit

Fruit'erer, s. one who trades in fruit

Fruit'tery, s. a fruit loft ; fruit collectively

Fruit'ful, a. prolific, fertile, plenteous

Fruit'fully, ad. plenteously, abundantly

Fruit'fulness,s.fertility, plentiful production

Fruit'ion, s. enjoyment, possession

Fru'itive, a. enjoying, possessing

Fruit'less, a. unprofitable ; without offspring

Fruit'lessly, ad. unprofitably, vainly, idly

Fruit'loft, s. a loft to preserve fruit in

Fruit't-tree, s. a tree that produces fruit

Frumenta'ceous, a. made of grain

Frumenta'rious, a. pertaining to corn

Fru'menty,Fur'menty,s. food made of wheat boiled in milk and sweetened

Frump, v. a. to mock, to browbeat

Frush, v. a. to break, crush, or bruise

Frustra'neous,a. useless, without advantage

Frus'trate, a. ineffectual, vain, void

Frus'trate, v. a. to disappoint, to defeat

Fry, s. a swarm of little fishes

Fry, v. a. to dress food in a frying-pan

Fub,v.a.to put off, to delay by false pretences

Fu'cus, s. a paint for the face

Fud'dle, v. to tipple, to make drunk

Fu'el, s. the matter or aliment of fire

Fuga'ciousness, s. uncertainty, volatility

Fu'gitive, a. flying, unsteady, volatile

Fu'gitive, s. a runaway, a deserter

Fu'gitiveness, s. instability, volatility

Ful'ciment, s. a prop whereon a body rests

Ful'crum, s. a prop or support

Fulfil', v. a. to accomplish, to perform

Fulfrau'ght, a. fully or completely stored

Ful'gency, s. splendour, lustre

Ful'gent, Ful'gid, a. shining, glittering

Fulig'inous, a. sooty, smoky

Fu'limart, s. a kind of stinking ferret

Full, a. stored, replete, perfect, saturated

Full, s. complete measure ; the total

Full, ad. without abatement; exactly

Fullblow'n, Fullsprea'd, a. spread to the ut-most extent, fully expanded

Fullbot'tomed, a. having a large bott

Ful'ler, s. he whose trade is to cleanse cloth
Ful'ler's-earth, s. a soft unctuous marl, used by fullers for whitening cloth
Fulley'ed, a. having large prominent eyes
Full'ed', a. fat, plump, corpulent, sated
Ful'ly, ad. completely, without vacuity
Ful'minant, a. making a noise like thunder
Ful'minate, v. to thunder, to make a loud noise; to issue out ecclesiastical censures
Fulmina'tion, s. the act of thundering, &c.
Ful'ness, s. completeness, repleteness, plenty
Ful'some, a. nauseous, offensive, rank
Fuma'do, s. a smoked or dried fish
Fum'ble, v. n. to attempt any thing awkward-
Fum'bler, s. one who acts awkwardly [ly
Fume, s. vapour, smoke; rage, conceit
Fume, v. n. to smoke; to be in a rage
Fu'mid, a. smoky, vaporous
Fu'migate, v. a. to smoke; to perfume
Fumiga'tion, s. a scent raised by fire
Fu'mingly, ad. angrily, in a rage
Fu'mous, Fu'my, a. producing fumes
Fun, s. sport, high merriment
Func'tion, s. an occupation, an employment
Fund, s. a repository of public money
Fun'dament, s. the hinder part of the body
Fundamen'tal, a. serving for the foundation; essential; not merely accidental
Fundamen'tally, ad. essentially; originally
Fu'neral, s. the solemnization of a burial
Fu'neral, a. used on interring the dead
Fune'real, a. suiting a funeral; dark, dismal
Fun'gous, a. spongy, excrescent
Funic'ular, a. consisting of small fibres
Fun'nel, s. a vessel for pouring liquor into a bottle; the hollow part of a chimney
Fun'ny, a. droll, laughable, comical, merry
Fur, s. the soft hairy skins of several beasts; a substance sticking to the sides of vessels
Furac'ity, s. a disposition to theft
Fur'below, s. fur or other ornamental stuff sewed on the lower part of a garment

Fur'bish, v. a. to burnish, to polish
Fu'rious, a. raging, mad, violent, passionate
Fu'riously, ad. violently, madly, vehemently
Furl, v. a. to draw up, to contract
Fur'long, s. eighth part of a mile; 220 yards
Fur'lough, s. a temporary leave of absence from military service
Fur'nace, s. an enclosed fireplace
Fur'nish, v. a. to supply, to equip, to adorn
Fur'niture, s. goods put into a house for use or ornament; appendages; equipage
Fur'rier, s. a dealer in furs
Fur'row, s. any long trench or hollow
Fur'ry, a. covered with or consisting of fur
Fur'ther, ad. to a greater distance
Fur'ther, v. a. to forward, to assist, to promote
Fur'thermore, ad. moreover, besides
Fur'thermost, Fur'thest, a. the most distant
Fu'ry, s. rage, passion, madness, frenzy
Furze, s. a prickly shrub used for fuel; gorse
Fur'zy, a. overgrown with furze
Fuse, v. to melt, put into fusion, be melted
Fusee', Fusil', s. a kind of light, neat musket; the match with which a bomb is set on fire
Fusibil'ity, s. the quality of growing liquid by heat
Fu'sible, Fu'sil, a. capable of being melted
Fusi'form, a. shaped like a spindle
Fusilie'r, s. a soldier armed with a fusil
Fu'sion, s. the state of being melted
Fuss, s. a bustle, a hurry, a noise, a tumult
Fus'tian, s. a cloth made of cotton and linen; a bombast style—a. ridiculously timid
Fustila'rian, s. a low fellow, a scoundrel
Fus'tiness, s. mustiness; a mouldy smell
Fus'ty, a. ill smelling, musty, mouldy
Fu'tile, a. talkative, worthless, trifling
Futil'ity, s. loquacity, vanity, silliness
Fu'ture, a. that which is to come hereafter.
Fu'ture, Futu'rity, s. the time to come
Fuzz, v. n. to fly out in small particles
Fy, or Fie, interj. a word of blame

G.

G, s. seventh letter of the alphabet; a note in music
Gab'ardine, s. a coarse frock
Gab'ble, Gab, v. n. to prate loudly and noisily
Gab'ble, s. loud talk without meaning
Gab'bler, s. a prater, a chattering fellow
Ga'bel, s. a tax, an excise
Ga'bion, s. in fortification, a wicker basket filled with earth, and placed upon bastions
Ga'ble, s. the sloping roof of a building
Gad, s. an ingot of steel; a graver; a stile
Gad, v. n. to ramble about without business
Gad'der, s. one that gads or rambles abroad
Gad'fly, s. a breeze fly that stings cattle
Gaff, s. a harpoon, or large hook
Gaf'fer, s. master, friend, neighbour
Gaf'fles, s. artificial spurs upon cocks
Gag, v. n. to stop the mouth
Gag, s. something applied to stop the mouth
Gage, s. a pledge, a pawn, a caution
Gage, v. a. to impawn, to wager, to measure
Gag'gle, v. n. to make a noise like a goose
Gai'ety, s. merriment; show, finery

Gai'ly, ad. cheerfully, airily, splendidly
Gain, s. profit, interest, advantage
Gain, v. to attain, to obtain, to procure
Gai'ner, s. one who receives advantage
Gai'nful, a. lucrative, advantageous
Gai'nly, ad. handily, readily
Gain'say, v. a. to controvert, to contradict
Gainstan'd, v. a. to withstand, to oppose
Gai'rish, a. gaudy, fine, splendid, flighty
Gai'rishness, s. finery, extravagant joy
Gait, s. manner and air of walking
Gai'ters, s. a kind of spatterdashes
Ga'la, s. a grand entertainment or procession
Gal'axy, s. a luminous tract, composed of the combined radiance of a number of stars
Gul'banum, s. a strong-scented gum or resin
Gale, s. a gentle wind; a stormy blast
Gal'eas, s. a low-built vessel, with oars and sail
Gal'eated, a. covered as with a helmet
Gal'iot, s. a small galley, or sort of brigantine
Gall, s. bile; rancour, malignity, anger
Gall, v. a. to rub off the skin; to tease, har
Gal'lant, a. brave, gay, fine, spacious

Gallan't, *s.* a gay, sprightly man ; a lover

Gal'lantly, *ad.* bravely, generously, nobly

Gal'lantry, *s.* bravery; courtship ; splendour

Galleo'n, *s.* a large Spanish ship

Gal'lery, *s.* a passage leading to several apartments ; a balcony round a building

Gal'ley, *s.* a small vessel both for sails and oars

Gal'leyslave, *s.* a person condemned for some crime to row in the galleys

Gal'liard, *s.* a gay, brisk man ; a lively dance

Gal'licism, *s.* a mode of speaking after the manner of the French ; a French idiom

Galligas'kins, *s.* large open hose

Gallimau'fry, *s.* a hotch-potch, a medley

Gal'lipot, *s.* a pot painted and glazed

Gal'lon, *s.* a liquid measure of four quarts

Gal'lop, *v. n.* to move by leaps, or very fast

Gal'lop, *s.* motion of a horse running at speed

Gal'low, *v. a.* to terrify, to frighten

Gal'loway, *s.* a horse not more than fourteen hands high, much used in the north

Gal'lows, *s.* a tree for executing malefactors

Galvan'ic, *a.* respecting galvanism

Gal'vanism, *s.* the action of metallic substances

Gamba'does, *s.* spatterdashes for riding

Gam'bler, *s.* a cheating gamester

Gambo'ge, *s.* a concreted vegetable juice

Gam'bol, *s.* a skip, a frolic, a hop, a prank

Gam'bol, *v. a.* to dance, leap, skip, frisk

Gam'brel, *s.* the leg of a horse

Game, *s.* sport of any kind ; field sport, as the chace; insolent merriment; mockery; contests exhibited to the people

same, *v. n.* to play extravagantly for money

Ga'mecock, *s.* a cock bred to fight

Ga'mekeeper, *s.* one who looks after game, and sees it is not destroyed

Ga'mesome, *a.* frolicsome, gay, sportive

Ga'mester, *s.* one viciously addicted to play

Gam'mon, *s.* the buttock of a hog salted and dried ; a kind of play with dice

Gam'ut, *s.* the scale of musical notes

Gan'der, *s.* the male of the goose

Gang, *s.* a number herding together ; a tribe

Gan'grene, *s.* a mortification, a putrefaction

Gan'grene, *v. a.* to corrupt to mortification

Gan'grenous, *a.* mortified, putrified

Gang'way, *s.* the passage in a ship

Gant'let, *s.* a military punishment, in which the criminal runs through the whole regiment, and receives a lash from each soidier

Gan'za, *s.* a kind of wild goose

Gaol, *s.* a place of confinement, a prison

Gao'ler, *s.* the keeper of a prison   [nue

Gap, *s.* an opening, a breach, a hole, an ave-

Gape, *v. n.* to yawn ; to stare ; to crave

Garb, *s.* dress, attire, exterior appearance

Gar'bage, Gar'bish, *s.* offals ; the entrails

Gar'ble, *v. a.* to sift, to separate, to part

Gar'boil, *s.* disorder, tumult, uproar

Gar'den, *v. n.* to cultivate a garden   [&c.

Gar'den, *s.* a place for growing herbs, fruit,

Gar'dener, *s.* one who attends a garden

Gar'dening, *s.* the act or art of planning out and cultivating gardens

Gar'garism, Gar'gle, *s.* a liquid medicine to wash the throat or mouth with

Gar'gle, *v. a.* to wash the throat ; to warble

Gar'got, *s.* a distemper common to hogs

Gar'land, *s.* a wreath of flowers or branches

Gar'lic, *s.* a well-known plant; a strong onion

Gar'ment, *s.* any covering for the body

Gar'ner, *s.* a place to put threshed corn in

Gar'ner, *v. a.* to store as in a granary

Gar'net, *s.* a red gem, of various sizes

Gar'nish, *v. a.* to decorate, to embellish

Gar'nish, Gar'niture, *s.* embellishment

Gar'ran, *s.* a small horse ; a hobby

Gar'ret, *s.* the uppermost room of a house

Garrettee'r, *s.* one that lives in a garret

Gar'rison, *s.* soldiers in a fortification

Gar'rison, *v. a.* to secure by fortresses, &c.

Garru'lity, *s.* talkativeness, loquacity

Gar'rulous, *a.* prattling, chattering, talkative

Gar'ter, *s.* a ribband or string to hold up the stocking ; mark of the order of the garter

Gas, *s.* a spirit not capable of coagulation

Gascona'de, *s.* a bravado, a boast—*v. n.* to brag

Gash, *s.* a deep and wide wound

Gas'kins, *s.* wide hose or breeches

Gasp, *s.* catch of breath in the last agonies

Gasp, *v. n.* to pant for breath

Gate, *s.* a large door, an avenue, an opening

Gath'er, *v.* to collect, assemble, pick up ; to crop ; to fester ; to thicken ; to select

Gath'erer, *s.* one who gathers ; a collector

Gath'ering, *s.* a collection ; a tumour

Gath'ers, *s.* plaits in a garment

Gaude, Gau'dery, *s.* an ornament, finery

Gaude, *v. n.* to exult, to rejoice at any thing

Gau'dily, *ad.* showily, splendidly, gaily

Gau'diness, *s.* showiness, tinsel appearance

Gau'dy, *a.* splendid, showy, pompous

Gau'dy, *s.* a festival in colleges

Gave, *pret.* of *to give*

Gav'elkind, *s.* equal division of a patrimony

Gav'eloc, *s.* an iron bar, a pick javelin

Gauge, *v. a.* to measure the contents of a vessel—*s.* a measure, a standard

Gau'ger, *s.* one who measures quantities

Gaunt, *a.* lean, thin, slender, meagre

Gaunt'let, *s.* an iron glove for defence, &c.

Gav'ot, *s.* a kind of brisk dance

Gauze, *s.* a thin transparent silk

Gawk'y, *a.* rustic, awkward, foolish

Gay, *a.* airy, merry, frolicsome, cheerful

Gaze, *v. n.* to look earnestly or intently

Gaz'ette, *s.* a paper of public intelligence

Gazettee'r, *s.* a writer of newspapers

Ga'zingstock, *s.* one gazed at with scorn

Gazo'n, *s.* pieces of fresh earth covered with grass, cut in form of a wedge

Gear, or Geer, *s.* furniture, harness, dress

Geese, *s. plural* of Goose

Gel'able, *a.* what may be congealed

Gel'atine, Gela'tinous, *a.* formed into a jelly

Geld, *v. a.* to cut, to castrate, to deprive

Gel'der, *s.* one who gelds or castrates

Gel'ding, *s.* a horse that has been gelded

Gel'id, *a.* extremely cold, frozen

Gem, *s.* a jewel, or precious stone ; first bud

Gemina'tion, *s.* repetition, reduplication

Gem'ini, *s.* twins ; a sign in the zodiac

Gem'inous, *a.* double, twofold

Gem'mary, *a.* pertaining to gems or jewels

Gen'der, *s.* a sex, a sort, a kind

Gen'der, *v.* to beget, to produce, to cause

Genealog'ical, *a.* pertaining to families

Geneal'ogist, *s.* one who traces descents

Geneal'ogy, *s.* history of family succession

Gen'eral, *a.* common, usual, extensive

Gen'eral, *s.* one who commands an army
Generalis'simo, *s.* the supreme commander
General'ity, *s.* the main body, the bulk
Gen'erally, *ad.* in general, frequently
Gen'erate, *v.a.* to beget, to cause, to produce
Genera'tion, *s.* offspring, progeny, race
Gen'erative, *a.* prolific, fruitful, productive
Gener'ical, *a.* what comprehends the genus
Gener'ically, *ad.* with regard to the genus
Generos'ity, Gen'erousness, *s.* liberality
Gen'ero *.s, a.* bountiful, noble, munificent
Gen'erously, *ad.* bountifully, liberally, nobly
Gene'sis, *s.* the first book of Moses, which
  treats of the formation of the world
Gen'et, *s.* a well-formed Spanish horse
Geno'va, *s.* the spirit of juniper
Ge'nial, *a.* tending to cheerfulness; contribu-
  ting to propagation; native; festive
Ge'nially, *ad.* naturally; cheerfully, gaily
Genic'ulated, *a.* knotted, jointed
Ge'nio, *s.* a man of peculiar mind
Gen'itals, *s.* the parts belonging to generation
Gen'iting, *s.* an early apple, in June
Gen'itive, *a.* in grammar, the case of nouns
  which denotes property or possession
Ge'nius, *s.* intellectual power; disposition;
  nature; a spirit either good or evil
Genteel', *a.* polite, graceful, elegant, civil
Genteel'ly, *ad.* gracefully, elegantly, politely
Genteel'ness, *s.* gracefulness, elegance, po-
  liteness; qualities befitting a man of rank
Gen'tian, *s.* felwort or baldmony; a plant
Gen'tile, *s.* one ignorant of the true God
Gentilesse', *s.* complaisance, civility
Gen'tilism, *s.* paganism, heathenism
Gentil'ity, *s.* good extraction; elegance of be-
  haviour; nicety of taste; heathenism
Gen'tle, *a.* well born; meek. mild, soft
Gen'tle, *s.* a worm used in fishing
Gen'tleman, *s.* a man of birth, not noble
Gen'tlemanlike, *a.* befitting a gentleman
Gen'tleness, *s.* meekness, kindness
Gen'tlewoman, *s.* a woman well descended; a
  word of civility or irony
Gen'tly, *ad.* meekly, softly, inoffensively
Gen'try, *s.* a class of people above the vulgar,
  a term of civility real or ironical
Genuflec'tion, *s.* the act of kneeling
Gen'uine, *a.* true, natural, real, not spurious
Gen'uineness, *s.* freedom from adulteration
Ge'nus, *s.* a class of being, comprehending
  under it many species
Geocen'tric, *a.* in astronomy, applied to a
  planet which has the earth for its centre
Geog'rapher, *s.* one who describes the earth
  according to its different parts
Geograph'ical, *a.* relating to geography
Geog'raphy, *s.* the knowledge of the earth
Ge'omancer, *s.* a fortune-teller
Ge'omancy, *s.* the act of foretelling by figures
Geoman'tic, *a.* pertaining to geomancy
Geom'eter, Geometric'ian, *s.* one skilled in the
  science of geometry
Geome'tral, Geomet'ric, Geomet'rical, *a.* per-
  taining to geometry; laid down in geometry
Geomet'rically, *ad.* according to geometry
Geom'etry, *s.* the science of quantity, exten-
  sion, or magnitude, abstractedly considered
George, *s.* a figure of St. George on horseback
  worn by knights of the garter; a brown
  loaf

Geor'gic, *s.* a rural poem; the science of hus-
  bandry set off with all the beauties of poetry
Gera'nium, *s.* a greenhouse plant
Ger'man, *s.* a brother, a near relation
Germe, Ger'min, *s.* a sprouting seed
Ger'minate, *v. n.* to sprout, to bud. to shoot
Ger'und, *s.* in Latin, a kind of verbal noun
Gest, *s.* an action, representation, show
Gesta'tion, *s.* the act of bearing young
Gestic'ulate, *v. n.* to play antic tricks, &c.
Gesticula'tion, *s.* antic tricks, various pos-
  tures; too much gesture in speaking
Ges'ture, *s.* posture, movement of the body
Get, *v.* to acquire, obtain, learn, win, seize
Gew'gaw, *s.* a toy, a bauble—*a.* trifling
Ghas'tliness, *s.* frightful aspect, paleness
Ghas'tly, *ad.* like a ghost, horrible, pale
Ghas'tness, *s.* ghastliness, horror of look
Gher'kin, *s.* a small cucumber for pickling
Ghost, *s.* the soul of man; a spirit
Gho'stliness, *s.* spiritual tendency
Gho'stly, *a.* spiritual, relating to the soul
Giam'beaux, *s.* armour for the legs; greaves
Gi'ant, *s.* one unnaturally large and tall
Gi'antlike, Gi'antly, *a.* gigantic, vast
Gibbe, *s.* an old worn-out animal
Gib'berish, *s.* unintelligible talk; cant words
Gib'bet, *s.* a gallows—*v. n.* to hang up
Gib'bier, *s.* game, wild fowl
Gibbos'ity, Gibbous'ness, *s.* convexity
Gib'bous, *a.* convex, crooked-backed
Gib'cat, *s.* an old worn-out cat
Gibe, *s.* a sneer, scoff, word of contempt
Gi'bingly, *ad.* scornfully, contemptuously
Gib'lets, *s.* the pinions, gizzard, &c. of a goose
Gid'dily, *ad.* unsteadily, carelessly, heedlessly
Gid'diness, *s.* state of being giddy; change-
  ableness, frolic, wantonness, quick rotation
Gid'dy, *a.* unsteady, whirling, changeful
Gid'dybrained, *a.* thoughtless, careless
Gift, *s.* a thing given; bribe; power
Gif'ted, *a.* endowed with eminent powers
Gig, *s.* any thing that is whirled round in
  play; a kind of chaise; a fiddle
Gigan'tic, *a.* giantlike, big, bulky, enormous
Gig'gle, *v. n.* to laugh idly, to titter
Gild, *v. a.* to overlay with gold; to adorn
Gil'der, *s.* one who lays gold on the surface of
  bodies; a coin from 1s. 6d. to 2s. value
Gil'ding, *s.* gold laid on a surface for orna-
  ment
Gill, *s.* a measure containing a quarter of a
  pint; the apertures at the side of a fish's
  head; the flesh under the chin; ground-ivy
Gil'lyflower, *s.* corrupted from July flower
Gilt, *s.* gold laid on the surface of any thing,
  golden show—the *participle* of *to gild*
Gim, Gim'my, *a.* neat, smart, spruce
Gim'crack, *s.* a slight or trivial mechanism
Gim'let, *s.* a borer with a screw at its point
Gimp, *s.* a kind of silk twist or lace
Gin, *s.* the spirit drawn from juniper; a snare
Gin'ger, *s.* an Indian root of a hot acrid taste
Gin'gerbread, *s.* a kind of bread made of trea-
  cle, ginger, flour, &c.
Gin'gerly, *ad.* cautiously, softly, nicely
Gin'gival, *a.* belonging to the gums
Gin'gle, *s.* a shrill resounding noise
Gin'gle, *v.* to make a sharp tinkling noise
Gip'sey, *s.* a vagabond who pretends to
  fortunes by palmistry or physiognomy

Girandole, s. a branched candlestick
Gird, v. to bind round, to dress; to sneer
Gir'der, s. the largest timber on a floor
Gir'dle, s. any thing bound round the waist
Girl, s. a female child, or young woman
Girl'ish, a. acting like a girl, youthful
Girt, Girth, s. a broad belt, by which the saddle is fixed upon the horse; a bandage
Give, v. a. to bestow, allow, yield, permit
Giv'er, s. one who gives, a granter, a donor
Giz'zard, s. the musculous stomach of a fowl
Gla'cial, a. icy, made of ice, frozen
Glacia'tion, s. act of freezing, ice formed
Gla'cis, s. in fortification, a sloping bank
Glad, a. elevated with joy, cheerful, gay
Glad, Glad'den, v. a. to make glad, to cheer
Glade, s. a lawn or opening in a wood
Gladia'tor, s. a prize-fighter, a sword-player
Glad'ly, ad. joyfully, with merriment
Glad'ness, s. exultation, joy, cheerfulness
Glad'some, a. delighted, pleased, causing joy
Glaire, s. the white of an egg; a halbert
Glaire, v. a. to smear with the white of eggs
Glance, s. a quick view, sudden shoot of light or splendour; a beam of light
Glance, v. n. to censure by oblique hints
Gland, s. a part of the human body
Glandif'erous, a. bearing acorns and mast
Glandulos'ity, s. a collection of glands
Glan'dulous, Glan'dular, a. relating to the glands
Glare, s. overpowering lustre, splendour
Glare, v. to shine so as to dazzle the eyes
Gla'ring, a. blazing out; barefaced
Glass, s. an artificial transparent substance
Glass, a. made of glass, vitreous
Glass, v. a. to cover with glass; see in a glass
Glass'furnace, s. a place for making glass in
Glass'grinder, s. one who polishes glass
Glass'house, s. a house where glass is made
Glass'man, s. one who sells glass
Glass'metal, s. glass in fusion
Glass'work, s. manufactory of glass
Glas'sy, a. made of glass, resembling glass
Glau'cous, a. having a light green colour
Glaive, s. a broad sword, a falchion
Glaze, v. a. to furnish or cover with glass
Gla'zier, s. one who glazes windows
Gleam, s. a sudden shoot of light; lustre
Glea'ming, a. flashing, darting, shining
Glea'my, a. darting sudden shoots of light
Glean, v. n. to gather any thing thinly scatter-
Glea'ner, s. one who gleans after reapers [ed
Glea'ning, s. the act of gleaning, the thing gleaned or picked up
Glebe, s. turf, soil; land possessed as part of the revenue of an ecclesiastical benefice
Glebos'ity, s. fulness of clods, turfiness
Gle'bous, Gle'by, a. turfy, cloddy
Glee, s. joy, merriment, cheerfulness, gaiety
Glee'ful, a. merry, gay, cheerful
Gleek, s. music; a musician—v. a. to sneer
Gleen, v. n. to shine with heat or polish
Gleet, s. a thin matter issuing from ulcers
Glen, s. a valley, a dale
Glib, a. smooth, slippery, voluble
Glib'ly, ad. smoothly, volubly
Glib'ness, s. smoothness, slipperiness
Glide, v. n. to flow gently, to move smoothly
Glike, s. a scoff, a sneer, a flout
Glim'mer, v. n. to shine or appear faintly

Glim'mer, Glim'mering, s. a weak, faint light
Glimpse, s. a faint light; a short view
Glis'ten, v. n. to shine, to sparkle with light
Glit'ter, v. n. to shine, gleam; to be specious
Glit'ter, Glit'tering, s. brightness, lustre
Gloar, v. n. to look askew, to squint [ver
Glout, v. n. to cast side glances as a timid lo-
Glo'bated, Glo'bed, a. formed like a globe
Globe, s. a sphere; the terraqueous ball
Globo'se, Glob'ular, Glob'ulous, a. spherical, round, in form of a small sphere
Globos'ity, s. roundness of form, sphericity
Glo'bule, s. a small particle of a round figure
Glom'erate, v. a. to gather into a ball
Gloom, s. imperfect darkness; obscurity; cloudiness of aspect; heaviness of mind
Gloo'miness, s. want of light; obscurity; heaviness of mind; want of cheerfulness
Gloo'mily, ad. dimly, dismally, sullenly
Gloo'my, a. obscure, cloudy, melancholy
Glo'ried, a. illustrious, honourable
Glorifica'tion, s. the act of giving glory
Glo'rify, v. a. to worship, to honour, to exalt
Glo'rious, a. illustrious, excellent, boastful
Glo'riously, ad. renownedly, nobly, splendid
Glo'ry, s. honour, renown, praise, fame [ly
Glo'ry, v. n. to boast in, to be proud of
Gloss, s. a superficial lustre; a specious representation; comment
Gloss, v. to explain, to comment, to palliate
Glos'sary, s. a dictionary explaining obscure or antiquated words
Glos'sing, s. an explanation by glosses
Glos'sy, a. shining, bright, smoothly polished
Glove, s. a cover for the hands
Glov'er, s. one who makes or sells gloves
Glout, v. n. to pout, to look sullen
Glow, v. to be heated; to feel activity of fancy
Glow, s. shining heat, vividness of colour
Glow'worm, s. a small creeping grub, whose tail being luminous shines in the dark
Gloze, s. flattery, gloss, specious show
Glue, s. a thick viscous cement, made by boiling the skin of animals to jelly
Glue, v. a. to join with viscous cement
Glum, a. sullen, stubbornly grave
Glut, v. a. to devour, to saturate, to cloy
Glut, s. overmuch, more than enough
Glutinos'ity, Glu'tinousness, s. tenacity
Glu'tinous, a. gluey, viscous, tenacious
Glut'ton, s. one who eats to excess
Glut'tonous, a. given to excessive feeding
Glut'tony, s. excess, luxury of the table
Gnar, Gnarl, v. n. to growl, to rumour
Gnar'led, a. knotty, rough
Gnash, v. to grind the teeth in a rage
Gnash'ing, s. a grinding of the teeth
Gnat, s. a small winged stinging insect
Gnaw, v. a. to pick with the teeth; to corrode
Gno'mon, s. the hand or pin of a dial
Gnomon'ics, s. the science or art of dialling
Go, v. n. to walk, to proceed, to travel, to pass
Goad, s. a pointed stick to drive oxen with
Goad, v. a. to prick, to stimulate, to incite
Goal, s. a starting-post; final purpose
Goar, s. an edging sewed upon cloth
Goat, s. a ruminant animal, that seems of a middle species between deer and sheep
Goat'herd, s. one who tends goats
Goat'ish, a. resembling a goat; lustful
Gob'bet, v. a. to swallow at a mouthful

Gob'ble, v. a. to eat voraciously and hastily
Gob'let, s. a bowl, or large cup
Gob'lin, s. an evil spirit, a fairy, an elf
Go'cart, s. a thing to teach children to walk
God, s. the Supreme Being   [sponsor
God'child, s. a child for whom one became
God'dess, s. a female divinity
God'dess-like, a. resembling a goddess
God'father, s. a male sponsor in baptism
God'head, s. the Deity, the divine nature
God'less, a. irreligious, wicked, atheistical
God'like, a. divinely, supremely excellent
God'liness, s. piety to God, sincere religion
God'ly, a. pious, religious, righteous
God'mother, s. a female sponsor in baptism
God'son, s. a boy for whom one was sponsor
Gog'gle, v. n. to look asquint
Gog'gle-eyed, a. having large eyes; squint-
   eyes; not looking straight
Go'ing, s. the act of walking, departure
Gold, s. the heaviest of all metals; money
Go'ldbeater, s. one who beats gold
Go'lden, a. made of gold; bright, happy
Go'ldfinch, s. a small singing bird
Go'ldsmith, s. one who manufactures gold
Gome, s. the black grease of a cart-wheel
Gon'dola, s. a boat much used at Venice
Gone, part. pret. from to go, past, dead, lost
Gon'falon, s. an ensign, a standard
Gonorrhœ'a, s. a morbid venereal discharge
Good, a. not evil, proper, sound, wholesome
Good, s. the contrary to evil; virtue
Good'liness, s. beauty, elegance, grace
Good'ly, a. graceful, beautiful, splendid, gay
Good'ness, s. desirable qualities
Goods, s. furniture, merchandise, freight
Good'y, s. a low term of civility
Goose, s. a large water-fowl; a tailor's iron
Goo'seberry, s. a small tree and its fruit
Gor'bellied, a. big-bellied, corpulent, fat
Gord, s. an instrument of gaming
Gor'dian-knot, s. an inextricable difficulty
Gore, s. clotted blood, congealed blood
Gore, v. a. to stab, to pierce with a horn
Gorge, s. the throat, the swallow
Gorge, v. n. to glut, to swallow, to satiate
Gor'geous, a. fine, glittering, splendid
Gor'geously, ad. magnificently, splendidly
Gor'get, s. a breast-plate worn by military
   officers; formerly, armour for the throat
Gor'gon, s. any thing ugly or horrid
Gor'mandize, v. n. to feed ravenously
Gor'mandizer, s. a voracious eater, a glutton
Gorse, s. furze, a thick prickly shrub
Go'ry, a. covered with blood; murderous
Gos'hawk, s. a hawk of a large kind
Gos'ling, s. a goose not yet full grown
Gos'pel, s. the holy book of the Christian reve-
   lation; God's word; theology, divinity
Gos'pel, v. n. to fill with religious thoughts
Gos'samer, s. the fine down of plants
Gos'sip, s. a sponsor in baptism; a tatler
Gos'sip, v. n. to chat, to prate; to be merry
Got, Got'ten, part. pass. of to get
Goth'ic, a. in manner of the Goths, antique
Gove, v. n. to mow, to put in a goff or mow
Gov'ern, v. to rule, to direct, to manage
Gov'ernable, a. submissive to authority
Gov'ernance, s. government, control, rule
Gov'erna'nte, Gov'erness, s. a woman that has
   the care of young ladies; a tutoress

Gov'ernment, s. an establishment of legal au-
   thority; executive power; manageableness
Gov'ernor, s. a ruler, a tutor, a commander
Gouge, s. a chisel with a round edge
Goula'rd, s. an extract of lead   [tle
Gourd, s. a plant resembling a melon; a bot-
Gour'dy, a. swelled in the legs, &c.
Gout, s. a periodical, painful disease; a drop
Gou'ty, a. diseased or afflicted with the gout
Gown, s. a long upper garment
Gow'nsman, s. a man devoted to the arts of
   peace; a student in divinity, law, &c.
Grab'ble, v. to grope; to lie prostrate
Grace, s. favour, kindness, pardon, privilege,
   virtue; beauty; a short prayer at meals
Grace, v. a. to dignify, to favour, to embellish
Gra'cecup, s. the cup of health after grace
Gra'ceful, a. beautified with dignity, comely
Gra'cefully, ad. elegantly, with dignity
Gra'cefulness, s. elegance of manner
Gra'celess, a. without grace, abandoned
Grac'ile, a. slender, lean, small
Gracil'ity, s. slenderness, thinness, smallness
Gra'cious, a. benevolent, graceful, virtuous
Gra'ciously, ad. kindly, in a pleasing manner
Gra'ciousness, s. kind condescension
Grada'tion, s. a regular advance, order
Grad'atory, s. a flight of steps
Gra'dient, a. walking, moving by steps
Grad'ual, a. done by degrees, step by step
Grad'uality, Gradua'tion, s. a regular pro-
   gression by succession of degrees
Grad'ually, ad. by degrees, step by step
Grad'uate, v. a. to mark with degrees; height-
   en; dignify with a degree in the university
Grad'uate, s. one dignified with an academi-
   cal degree, an academician
Gradua'tion, s. regular progression by suc-
   cession of degrees; conferring degrees
Graff, or Graft, s. a young scion, &c.
Graff, or Graft, v. a. to insert a scion or branch
   of one tree into the stock of another
Grain, s. all kinds of corn; the 24th part of a
   pennyweight; any minute particle; direc-
   tion of the fibres of wood or any fibrous
   matter; the form of the surface with re-
   gard to smoothness or roughness; temper
Grai'ned, a. rough, made less smooth
Grains, s. the husks of malt in brewing
Gramin'eal, Gramin'eous, a. grassy
Graminiv'orous, a. grass-eating
Gram'mar, s. the science of speaking or writ-
   ing a language correctly and with preci-
   sion; the book which teaches it
Gramma'rian, s. one who teaches grammar
Grammat'ical, a. belonging to grammar
Grammat'ically, ad. according to grammar
Gram'pus, s. a large fish of the whale kind
Gran'ary, s. a storehouse for threshed corn
Gran'ate, Gran'ite, s. a kind of fine speckled
   marble; a species of gem
Grand, a. splendid, great, high in power
Gran'dchild, s. the child of a son or daughter
Gran'daughter, s. the daughter of a son
Grandee', s. a man of high rank or power
Gran'deur, s. state, magnificence
Gran'dfather, s. father's or mother's father
Grandil'oquous, a. using a lofty style
Grand'inous, a. full of hail
Gran'dmother, s. father's or mother's mother
Gran'dsire, s. a grandfather, an ancestor

Gran'dson, s. the son of a son or daughter
Grange, s. a farm house, a lone house
Graniv'orous, a. eating or living on grain
Gran'nam, Gran'dam, s. a grandmother
Grant, v.a. to allow, to admit; to bestow
Grant, s. the thing granted; a gift, a boon
Grantee', s. he to whom a grant is made
Gran'tor, s. he by whom any grant is made
Gran'ulary, a. resembling grains or seeds
Granula'tion, s. a breaking into small masses
Gran'ule, s. a small compact particle
Gran'ulous, a. full of little grains
Grape, s. fruit of the vine growing in clusters
Graph'ical, a. well delineated
Graph'ically, ad. in a picturesque manner
Grap'nel, s. an iron hook to catch hold of and
   secure an enemy's ship; a small anchor
Grap'ple, v. to contest in close fight; to lay
   fast hold of, to seize, to fasten, to fix
Grasp, v. to hold in the hand, to seize
Grasp, s. seizure of the hand, possession
Grass, s. the common herbage of fields, &c.
Grass'hopper, s. a small chirping insect that
   hops in the summer grass
Gras'siness, s. the state of abounding in grass
Grass'y, a. covered with grass
Grate, s. an enclosure made with bars, the
   range of bars within which fires are made
Grate, v. to rub or wear away; to offend
Gra'teful, a. willing to acknowledge and re-
   pay benefits; acceptable, pleasing, delicious
Gra'tefully, ad. with gratitude, pleasingly
Gra'ter, s. a rough instrument to grate with
Gratifica'tion, s. pleasure, delight; reward
Grat'ify, v. a. to indulge, to please, to requite
Gra'ting, part. a. rubbing; disagreeable
Gra'tingly, ad. harshly, offensively
Gra'tis, ad. for nothing, without reward
Grat'itude, Gra'tefulness, s. a duty to bene-
   factors; a desire to return benefits
Gratu'itous, a. voluntary, bestowed without
   claim or merit, asserted without proof
Gratu'itously, ad. voluntarily, without claim
Gratu'ity, s. a recompence, a present
Grat'ulate, v. a. to congratulate, to wish joy
Gratula'tion, s. the act of rejoicing on behalf
   of another; expression of joy; salutation
Grat'ulatory, a. expressing congratulation
Grave, s. the place in which the dead are de-
   posited; the name of an accent
Grave, a. serious, solemn, sober, not showy
Grave, v. to carve in any hard substance
Gra'veclothes, s. the dress of the dead
Grav'el, s. hard sand; sandy matter concreted
   in the kidneys and bladder
Grav'el, v. a. to cover with gravel; puzzle
Grave'less, a. wanting a tomb; unburied
Grav'elly, a. abounding with gravel
Gra'vely, ad. seriously, without tawdry show
Gra'ver, s. one that engraves; a graving tool
Gra'vestone, s. a stone placed over the grave
Gravid'ity, s. state of being with child
Grav'itate, vn. to weigh or press downwards;
   to tend to the centre of attraction
Gravita'tion, s. act of tending to the centre
Grav'ity, Gra'veness, s. seriousness; weight
Gra'vy, s. the juice of dressed meat
Gray, a. white and black mixed; hoary
Gray'beard, s. an old man
Graze, v. to feed on grass; to touch lightly
Gra'zier, s. one who feeds cattle

Gra'zing, s. the act of feeding on grass
Grease, s. the soft part of the fat
Grease, v. a. to smear with fat; to bribe
Grea'siness, s. oiliness, fatness, unctuousness
Grea'sy, a. fat, oily, smeared with grease
Great, a. large, illustrious, eminent
Great-bel'lied, a. pregnant, teeming
Great'ly, ad. in a great degree, illustriously
Great'ness, s. largeness, dignity, power, state
Greaves, s. armour for the legs
Gre'cism, s. idiom of the Greek language
Greed'ily, ad. eagerly, voraciously, ravenous-
Greed'iness, s. ravenousness, voracity   [ly
Greed'y, a. ravenous, hungry, eager
Green, a. not ripe, fresh, young, new
Green, s. a colour; a grassy plain; leaves
Green-cloth, s. a board or court of justice
   held in the king's household
Gree'neyed, a. having greenish eyes
Green'finch, s. a small singing bird; a fish
Green'gage, s. a species of plum
Green'house, s. a conservatory for plants, &c
Green'ish, s. inclining to a green colour
Green'ness, s. a green colour; unripeness
Greensick'ness, s. a disease incident to vir
   gins, so called from the paleness it produces
Green'sward, s. a turf on which grass grows
Greet, v. to address, to congratulate
Gree'ting, s. a kind of salutation at meeting
Greeze, s. a flight of steps, a step
Grega'rious, a. going in flocks or herds
Grena'de, Grena'do, s. a little hollow ball of
   iron used in battle, which being fille i wi h
   powder and set on fire by a fusee, does
   mischief wherever it is thrown
Grenadier', s. a tall foot-soldier
Grey'hound, s. a tall, fleet, hunting dog
Grice, s. a little pig; a flight of steps
Grid'elin, s. a colour mixed of white and red
Grid'iron, s. grate to broil meat on
Grief, s. sorrow, trouble of mind, disease
Grie'vance, s. the state of uneasiness, hardship
Grieve, v. to afflict, mourn, lament, hurt
Grie'vous, a. afflictive, painful, atrocious
Grie'vously, ad. painfully, calamitously
Grif'fin, Grif'fon, s. a fabulous creature, hav
   ing the head and paws of a lion, and the
   body and wings of an eagle
Grig, s. a small eel; a merry creature
Grill, v. a. to broil on a gridiron
Grim, a. ill-looking, ugly, horrible, hideous
Grima'ce, s. a distortion of the countenance,
   from habit or contempt; air of affectation
Grimal'kin, s. an old cat, &c.
Grime, s. dirt—v. to dirty, to sully, to daub
Grim'ly, ad. horribly, sourly, crabbedly
Grim'ness, s. horror; frightfulness of visage
Grin, s. an affected laugh; a snarl; a trap
Grin, v. n. to show the teeth set together
Grind, v. to reduce any thing to powder; to
   sharpen, to oppress, to harass
Grin'der, s. one that grinds, the instrument of
   grinding; the back tooth
Gri'ndstone, s. a stone for grinding on
Gripe, v. to clutch, to pinch, to squeeze
Gripe, s. a grasp; oppression; the colic
Gri'per, s. an oppressor, an usurer
Gri'pingly, ad. with pain in the guts
Gris'amber, s. used by Milton for amberg
Gris'kin, s. the backbone of a hog
Gris'ly, a. dreadful, hideous, horrible

Grist, s. corn to be ground; provision, supply

Gris'tle, s. a cartilaginous substance

Gris'tly, a. full of gristles, cartilaginous

Grit, s. the coarse part of meal; sand

Grit'tiness, s. sandiness, abounding in grit

Grit'ty, a. full of hard particles

Griz'zle, s. a mixture of white and black

Griz'zled, Griz'zly, a. somewhat gray

Groan, v. n. to breathe with a hoarse noise

Groan, s. a deep sigh from sorrow or pain

Groat, s. four-pence—pl. hulled oats

Gro'cer, s. a dealer in teas, sugar, &c.

Gro'cery, s. wares which are sold by grocers

Grog, s. spirits and water without sugar

Gro'gram, s. a kind of silken stuff with pile

Groin, s. the part next the thigh

Groom, s. one who tends horses, a servant

Groom porter, s. an officer of the king's household who has the direction of games

Groom of the Stole, s. an officer who has the charge of the king's wardrobe

Groove, s. a hollow channel cut with a tool

Grope, v. n. to feel where one cannot see

Gross, a. thick, fat; palpable, stupid

Gross, s. the bulk, main body; twelve dozen

Gro'ssly, ad. coarsely; without delicacy

Gro'ssness, s. coarseness, want of delicacy

Grot, Grot'to, s. a cavern made for coolness

Grotes'que, a. distorted of figure, unnatural

Grove, s. a walk shaded by trees

Grov'el, v. n. to lie or creep on the ground; to be mean and low-minded

Grov'eller, s. an abject, mean wretch

Ground, s. land; floor; dregs; first principle

Ground, v. a. to lay on the ground, &c.

Ground, pret. and part. of to grind

Groundi'vy, s. the plant alehoof or tunhoof

Grou'ndless, a. void of truth

Grou'ndling, s. a fish; one of the vulgar

Grou'ndplot, s. the plot or space of ground on which a building is placed

Grou'ndrent, s. the rent paid for the ground on which a house is built, &c.

Grou'ndsel, Grun'sel, s. timber next the ground; lower part of a building; a plant

Grou'ndwork, s. the ground; first principle

Group, s. a crowd, a huddle, a cluster

Grouse, s. a kind of wild fowl; a moor cock

Grout, s. coarse meal, pollard; dregs

Grow, v. n. to vegetate, improve, increase

Growl, v. n. to snarl, to grumble, to murmur

Grow'ling, s. the act of snarling, grumbling

Growth, s. vegetation; thing produced; increase of stature; advancement

Grub, v. a. to destroy by digging, to dig out

Grub, s. a small destructive worm; a dwarf

Grub'ble, v. n. to feel in the dark

Grudge, v. to envy, give unwillingly, repine

Grudge, s. an old quarrel, ill will, envy

Grud'ging, s. reluctance, malignity

Grud'gingly, ad. unwillingly, malignantly

Gru'el, s. oatmeal boiled in water

Gruff, Grum. a. sour of aspect, surly, harsh

Gruff'ly, ad. harshly, ruggedly; sourly

Grum'ble, v. n. to murmur, to growl, to snarl

Grum'ble, s. one who grumbles, a murmurer

Grum'bling, s. a murmuring thro' discontent

Gru'mous, a. thick, clotted like blood

Grunt, s. the noise of a hog

Grunt, gruntle, v. n. to murmur like a hog; to make a grumbling noise

Grun'ter, s. he who grunts; a kind of fish

Guai'acum, s. a physical wood

Guarantee', s. a power who undertakes to see stipulations faithfully performed

Guar'anty, v. a. to answer for performance

Guard, s. a state of caution, vigilance, defence

Guard, v. a. to protect, to defend, to watch

Guard'ian, s. one who has the care of an orphan; a superintendant

Guard'ian, a. defending, superintending

Guard'ianship, s. the office of a guardian

Guard'less, a. without defence or care

Guard'ship, s. a ship that guards a coast

Guberna'tion, s. government, superintendency

Gud'geon, s. a fish; a man easily cheated

Guer'don, s. a reward, a recompence

Guess, v. to conjecture rightly, to find out

Guess, s. a supposition, a conjecture

Guest, s. one who is entertained by another

Gui'dage, s. the reward given to a guide

Gui'dance, s. direction, government

Guide, v. a. to direct, to regulate, to instruct

Guide, s. one who directs another, a regulator

Gui'deless, a. without a guide

Guild, s. a corporation, a fraternity, a society

Guile, s. deceitful, cunning, insidious artifice

Guile'ful, a. treacherous, insidious, artful

Guile'fully, ad. deceitfully, treacherously

Guile'less, a. free from deceit, innocent

Guilloti'ne, s. a machine for beheading

Guilt, s. an offence, a fault, a crime

Guil'tily, ad. without innocence, criminally

Guil'tiness, s. the state of being guilty

Guil'tless, a. free from crime, innocent

Guil'ty, a. not innocent, corrupt, wicked

Guin'ea, s. a gold coin, value 21 shillings

Guise, s. manner, custom, habit, dress

Guitar', s. a stringed musical instrument

Gules, a. in heraldry, a red colour

Gulf, s. a large bay, an abyss, a whirlpool

Gulf'y, a. full of gulfs or whirlpools

Gull, v. a. to cheat, to defraud, to trick

Gull, s. a sea bird; one easily cheated

Gul'let, s. the throat, the meat pipe

Gul'lyhole, s. the hole where the gutters empty themselves in the sewers

Gulos'ity, s. greediness, voracity, gluttony

Gulp, v. a. to swallow eagerly with noise

Gulp, s. as much as is swallowed at once

Gum, s. the viscous juice of trees; the fleshy covering that contains the teeth

Gum, v. a. to close or smear with gum

Gum'miness, s. the state of being gummy

Gummos'ity, s. the nature of gum

Gum'my, a. consisting of gum, full of gum

Gun, s. general name for fire-arms; a flagon

Gun'ner, s. a cannonier, whose employment is to manage the artillery of a ship in battle

Gun'nery, s. the science of artillery

Gun'powder, s. a composition of saltpetre, sulphur, and charcoal, which easily takes fire

Gun'shot, s. the reach or range of a gun

Gun'smith, s. a man who makes guns

Gun'stock, s. the wood for fixing a gun in

Gun'stone, s. the shot of a cannon

Gun'wale, Gun'nel, s. that piece of timber which on either side of a ship reaches from the half deck to the forecastle

Gurge, s. a gulf, a whirlpool

Gur'gle, v. n. to fall or gush with noise

Gur'net, Gur'nard, s. a kind of sea fish

Gush, v. n. to flow or rush out with violence
Gust, s. sudden blast of wind; taste, liking
Gus'set, s. a small square piece of cloth used in shirts and other garments
Gusta'tion, s. the act of tasting
Gust'ful, a. well tasted, tasteful, relishing
Gus'to, s. the relish of any thing; liking
Gus'ty, a. stormy, rough, tempestuous
Gut, s. the internal passage for food
Gut, v. a. to draw out the guts; to plunder
Gut'ter, s. a passage for water
Gut'tle, v. a. to gormandize, to eat greedily

Gut'tler, s. a greedy, ravenous eater
Gut'tulous, a. in the form of a small drop
Gut'tural, a. pronounced in the throat
Guy, s. a rope to hoist things into a ship
Guz'zle, v. to drink greedily
Guz'zler, s. a toper; a gormandizer
Gymnas'tic, a. relating to athletic exerci
Gymnas'tically, ad. athletically
Gynecoc'racy, a. petticoat government
Gyra'tion, s. the act of turning a thing round
Gyre, s. a ring, a circle
Gyves, s. chains for the legs, fetters

H.

H, s. the eighth letter of the alphabet
Ha! interj. an expression of wonder, surprise, sudden exertion, or laughter
Ha'beas-corpus, s. a writ, which a man indicted and imprisoned for some trespass may have out of the King's Bench, to remove himself at his own costs to the bar of that prison, to answer the cause there
Hab'erdasher, s. a dealer in small wares
Hab'erdashery, s. goods sold by a haberdasher, as pins, thread, laces, tape, &c.
Hab'erdine, s. a dried salt cod
Haber'geon, s. armour for neck and breast
Habit'ment, s. dress, apparel, clothes
Habil'itate, v. n. to qualify, to entitle, to fit
Habil'ity, s. faculty, power
Hab'it, s. state of any thing; custom; dress
Hab'itable, a. fit to be inhabited
Hab'itant, s. an inhabitant, a dweller
Habita'tion, s. place of abode, dwelling
Habit'ual, a. customary, accustomed
Habit'ually, ad. by habit, customarily
Habit'uate, v. a. to accustom to; to use often
Habit'uated, part. accustomed to, often used
Hab'itude, s. familiarity, habit, relation
Habna'b, ad. at random, by chance
Hack, v. a. to cut into small pieces, to chop
Hack, s. any thing used in common
Hack'le, v. a. to dress flax
Hack'ney, s. a hired horse, a hireling
Hack'neyed, part. used in common
Had'dock, s. a small sea fish of the cod kind
Ha'des, s. the place of departed spirits
Haft, s. a handle—v. a. to set in a haft
Hag, s. a witch, a fury, an ugly old woman
Hag'gard, s. any thing wild; a hawk
Hag'gard, Hag'gardly, a. deformed, ugly
Hag'gess, s. a sheep's maw filled with mince meat, spices, &c. a favourite Scotch dish
Hag'gish, a. deformed, horrid
Hag'gle, v. to beat down the price in buying; to carve awkwardly, to mangle
Hag'gler, s. one who is tardy in buying
Hagiog'rapher, s. a holy writer
Hail, s. frozen rain—interj. health be to you
Hail, v. n. to pour down hail; to call to
Hail'shot, s. small shot scattered like hail
Hail'stone, s. a particle or single ball of hail
Hair, s. one of the integuments of the body
Hair'brained, a. wild, giddy, irregular
Hair'bell, s. a flower; the hyacinth
Hair'breadth, s. a very small distance
Hair'cloth, s. a prickly stuff made of hair

Hair'iness, s. the state of being hairy
Hair'less, a. without hair, bald
Hair'y, a. covered with, or consisting of hair
Hal'berd, s. a soldier's battle-axe
Hal'cyon, a. placid, calm, quiet—s. a sea bird
Hale, a. healthy, robust, hearty, sound
Hale, v. a. to drag by force, to pull violently
Half, s. a moiety, an equal part—ad. equally
Half'blooded, a. mean, base, degenerate
Half'heard, a. imperfectly heard
Half'penny, s. a common copper coin
Half'sighted, a. having a weak discernment
Half'way, ad. in the middle
Half'wit, s. a foolish fellow, a blockhead
Hal'ibut, s. a large flat sea fish
Hal'lmass, s. the feast of All Saints, Nov. 1
Hall, s. a court of justice, a large room
Hallelu'jah, s. praise ye the Lord
Halloo', v. a. to incite by shouts, to shout to
Hal'low, v. a. to make holy, to consecrate
Hallucina'tion, s. a mistake, a blunder
Ha'lo, s. a circle round the sun or moon
Hal'ser, Haw'ser, s. a rope less than a cable
Halt, v. n. to stop in a march; to limp
Halt, s. a stop in a march; act of limping
Hal'ter, s. a rope to tie about the neck of a horse or malefactor: a strong string, a cord
Halve, v. a. to divide into two parts
Ham, s. a leg of pork cured; the thigh
Ha'mated, a. hooked, set with hooks
Ham'let, s. a small village
Ham'mer, s. an instrument to drive nails
Ham'mer, v. to beat or form with a hammer
Ham'mock, s. a swinging bed in a ship
Ham'per, s. a large basket for carriage
Hamper, v. a. to embarrass, perplex, entangle
Ham'string, s. the tendon of the ham
Ham'string, v. a. to cut the tendon of the ham
Han'aper, s. a treasury; an exchequer
Hand, s. the palm with the fingers; a measure of four inches; cards held at a game
Hand, v. a. to give, to deliver down; to guide
Hand'basket, s. a portable basket
Hand'bell, s. a bell rung by the hand
Hand'breadth, s. a measure of four inches
Hand'cuff, v. a. to confine the hands of prisoners with irons—s. the instrument
Hand'ed, a. with hands joined, using hands
Hand'ful, s. as much as the hand can grasp
Handgal'lop, s. a gentle, easy gallop
Han'dicraft, s. a manual occupation
Han'dily, ad. with skill, with dexterity
Han'diness, s. dexterity, readiness

Han'diwork, *s.* work done by the hand
Hand'kerchief,*s.* a piece of silk or linen used
  to wipe the face, or cover the neck
Han'dle, *v.a.* to touch, to treat of, to manage
Han'dle, *s.* that part of a thing held
Hand'maid, *s.* a maid that waits at hand
Hand'mill, *s.* a small mill for grinding
Hand'sel, *v.a.* to use a thing the first time
Hand'sel, or Han'sel, *s.* the first act of sale
Hand'some, *a.* graceful, beautiful, generous
Hand'somely, *ad.* beautifully, liberally
Hand'writing, *s.* a cast or form of writing
  peculiar to each hand
Hand'y, *a.* dexterous, ready, convenient
Hand'y-dandy, *s.* a childish play
Hang, *v.* to suspend ; to dangle ; to choke
Hang'er, *s.* a short broad sword
Hang'er-on, *s.* a dependant, a spunger
Hang'ings, *s.* ornaments of silk, stuff, paper,
  &c. hung against walls
Hang'man, *s.* the public executioner
Hank, *s.* a skein of thread, &c.; a ring
Hank'er, *v. n.* to long importunately
Hap,*s.* chance, casual event—*v. n.* to happen
Haphaz'ard, *s.* mere chance, accident
Hap'less, *a.* unhappy, luckless, unfortunate
Hap'ly, *ad.* peradventure, by accident
Hap'pen, *v. n.* to come to pass ; to fall out
Hap'pily, *ad.* prosperously, successfully
Hap'piness, *s.* felicity, good fortune
Hap'py, *a.* felicitous, lucky, addressful
Ha'ram, Ha'rem, *s.* a seraglio
Harang'ue, *s.* a speech, a public oration
Har'ass, *v. a.* to vex, to weary, to fatigue
Har'binger, *s.* a forerunner, a messenger
Har'bour, *v.* to shelter, entertain, sojourn
Har'bour, Har'bourage, *s.* a port or haven
Hard, *a.* firm, close ; difficult, severe
Hard, *ad.* laboriously ; diligently, nimbly
Hard'en, *v.a.* to make obdurate, to indurate
Hardfa'voured, *a.* coarse of feature
Hardheart'ed, *a.* inexorable,cruel,merciless
Har'diness, *s.* hardship, fatigue ; boldness
Har'dly, *ad.* with difficulty, oppressively
Hardmouth'ed, *a.* disobedient to the rein
Hard'ness, *s.* a hard quality ; obduracy
Hard'ship, *s.* fatigue, injury, oppression
Hard'ware, *s.* ware made of iron, steel, &c.
Hard'wareman, *s.* a maker of hardware
Har'dy, *a.* bold, daring, brave ; strong, firm
Hare, *s.* a well-known swift, timid animal
Ha'rebrained, *a.* wild, giddy, unsettled
Har'ier, *s.* a small dog for hunting hares
Hark ! *interj.* listen ! hear ! attend
Har'lequin, *s.* a merry-andrew, a buffoon
Har'lot, *s.* a prostitute, a strumpet
Har'lotry,*s.* the trade of a harlot; fornication
Harm,*s.* injury, mischief, crime, wickedness
Harm'ful, *a.* hurtful, mischievous, noxious
Harm'less, *a.* innocent, innoxious, unhurt
Harm'lessness, *s.* harmless disposition
Harmon'ic,Harmon'ical,*a.*pertaining to har-
  mony, adapted to each other
Harmon'ics, *s.* the doctrine of sounds
Harmo'nious, *a.* musical, well adapted
Harmo'niously, *ad.* musically, with concord
Har'monize, *v. a.* to adjust in fit proportions
Har'mony, *s.* concord, correspondent senti-
  ment, just in proportion of sound
Har'ness, *s.* armour ; furniture for horses
Harp, *s.* a lyre ; a constellation

Harp, *v. n.* to play on the harp ; to dwell on
Harp'er, *s.* one who plays on the harp
Harponee'r, *s.* he that throws the harpoon
Harpoo'n, *s.* a dart to strike whales with
Harp'sichord, *s.* a musical instrument with
Har'py, *s.* a bird ; a ravenous wretch [keys
Har'ridan, *s.* a decayed strumpet
Har'row, *s.* a frame of timber set with iron
  teeth, to break the clods of earth, &c.
Har'row, *v. a.* to break with the harrow ; to
  tear up, to lay waste, to disturb, to pillage
Harsh, *a.* austere, rough, rigorous, peevish
Harsh'ly, *ad.* austerely, morosely, violently
Harsh'ness,*s.*roughness to the ear, sourness
Hars'let, Has'let, *s.* the entrails of a hog
Hart, *s.* the male of the roe, a stag
Harts'horn, *s.* spirit drawn from the horn
Har'vest, *s.* the season of reaping,&c. a plant
Har'vest home,*s.*the feast or song at the end
  of harvest ; time of gathering in harvest
Hash, *v. a.* to mince, chop into small pieces
Hasp, *s.* a clasp for a staple—*v. a.* to shut
Has'sock, *s.* a mat or cushion to kneel on
Haste, Ha'sten, *v. n.* to hurry, to urge on
Haste, *s.* quickness ; passion
Ha'stily, *ad.* speedily, passionately, rashly
Ha'stiness, *s.* speed, hurry, angry testiness
Ha'stings, *s.* peas that come early
Ha'sty, *a.* quick, sudden. rash, vehement
Hastypud'ding, *s.* milk and flour boiled
Hat, *s.* covering for the head
Hatch,*v.*to produce young from eggs; to con
  trive, to plot, to form by meditation
Hatch, *s.* a sort of half door ; an opening in a
  ship's decks ; a brood of young birds ; dis
  covery, disclosure
Hat'chel, *v.a.* to beat flax—*s.* the instrument
Hat'chet, *s.* a small axe   [to beat flax
Hat'chet-face, *s.* an ugly, deformed face
Hat'chment, *s.* an escutcheon for the dead
Hat'chway, *s.* the place over the hatches
Hate, *v.a.* to detest, to abominate, to abhor
Hate, Ha'tred, *s.* great dislike, ill-will
Ha'teful, *a.* malignant, malevolent
Ha'tefully, *ad.* abominably, odiously
Hat'ter, *s.* a maker of hats
Have, *v. a.* to possess, hold, enjoy, receiv
Ha'ven, *s.* a harbour, port, shelter
Ha'vener, *s.* an overseer of a port
Hav'ing, *s.* possession, hold, fortune
Haugh, *s.* a little low meadow ; a close
Haugh'tily, *ad.* proudly, contemptuously
Hau'ghtiness, *s.* pride, arrogance
Hau'ghty, *a.* proud, arrogant, lofty
Haul, *v. a.* to pull, to drag by violence
Haum, *s.* straw
Haunch, *s.* the thigh, the hip, the hind part
Haunt, *v.* to frequent troublesomely, to ap-
  pear frequently—*s.* a place of resort
Hav'oc,*v.a.*to lay waste—*s.*devastation,spoil
Haut'boy, *s.* a wind instrument resembling a
  clarionet ; a kind of large strawberry
Haw, *s.* the berry of the hawthorn
Hawk, *s.* a voracious bird of prey
Hawk,*v.n.*to fly hawks at fowls;to cry goods;
  to force up phlegm with a noise
Hawk'ed, *part. a.* carried about for sale
Hawk'er, *s.* a pedlar, a newscarrier
Haw'thorn, *s.* the thorn that bears haws
Hay, *s.* grass dried in the sun ; a dance
Hay'maker, *s.* one employed in making hay

Hay'rick, Hay'stack, s. a quantity of hay stacked up and thatched

Haz'ard, s. chance, danger; a game at dice

Haz'ard, v. a. to expose to chance or danger

Haz'ardable, a. liable to chance or danger

Haz'ardous, a. dangerous, exposed to chance

Haze, s. a thick fog, a mist; a rime

Ha'zel, s. the nut tree

Ha'zel, Ha'zelly, a. light brown, like hazel

Ha'zy, a. foggy, misty, rimy, dark

Head, s. that part of the body which contains the brain; the top; a chief, a principal

Head, v. a. to command, influence; behead

Head'ache, s. a pain in the head

Head'band, s. a fillet for the head; a top-knot

Head'borough, s. a subordinate constable

Head'dress, s. the dress of a woman's head

Head'iness, s. strong quality in liquors; hurry

Head'land, s. a promontory, a cape

Head'less, a. without a head, inconsiderate

Head'long, a. rash, thoughtless, precipitate

Head'most, a. most advanced, first

Head'piece, s. armour; force of mind

Head'stone, s. the first or capital stone

Head'strong, a. ungovernable, unrestrained

Head'y, a. rash, violent, precipitate, strong

Heal, v. to cure a wound; to reconcile

Hea'ling, part. a. mild, gentle, sanative

Health, s. freedom from sickness or pain

Health'ful, Health'some, a. free from sickness, well-disposed, salutary, wholesome

Health'ily, ad. without sickness or pain

Health'iness, s. a state of health

Health'less, a. sickly, weak, infirm

Health'y, a. free from sickness, in health

Heap, s. a pile, a cluster, a confused tumble

Heap, v. a. to pile, to heap up, to accumulate

Hear, v. to perceive by the ear, to listen to

Hear'er, s. one who attends to any discourse

Hear'ing, s. the sense by which sounds are perceived; audience; judicial trial

Heark'en, v. n. to listen, to attend, to regard

Hear'say, s. rumour, report, common talk

Hearse, s. a close carriage to convey the dead

Heart, s. the seat of life in an animal body

Heart'ache, s. sorrow, anguish of mind

Heart'burning, s. a pain in the stomach

Heart'dear, a. sincerely beloved

Heart'easing, a. giving quiet

Heart'en, v. a. to encourage, to strengthen, to animate; to manure land

Heart'felt, a. felt in the conscience

Hearth, s. the place on which the fire is made

Heart'ily, ad. sincerely, fully from the heart

Heart'iness, s. sincerity, freedom from hypocrisy; strength, vigour, diligence

Heart'less, a. spiritless, wanting courage

Heart'sick, a. pained in mind; mortally ill

Heart'strings, s. the tendons or nerves supposed to brace and sustain the heart

Heart'whole, a. with the affections unfixed; with the vitals yet unimpaired

Heart'y, a. healthy, strong, sincere, cordial

Heat, s. the sensation caused by fire; hot weather; a course at a race; a flush in the face; party rage; violent passion

Heat, v. a. to make hot; to warm with passion

Hea'ter, s. an iron made hot and put into a box-iron, to smooth and plait linen

Heath, s. a plant; common ground

Heath'cock, s. a fowl that frequents heaths

Hea'then, s. a pagan, a gentile, an idolater

Hea'then, Hea'thenish, a. pagan, savage

Hea'thenism, s. paganism, gentilism; the principles or practices of heathens

Heave, s. a lift; an effort to vomit

Heave, v. to lift, to raise; to keck; to pant

Heav'en, s. the regions above; the residence of the blessed; the expanse of the sky

Heav'en-born, a. descended from heaven

Heav'enly, a. supremely excellent, celestial

Heav'ily, ad. sorrowfully, afflictively

Heav'iness, s. weight; depression of mind

Heav'y, a. weighty; sluggish, dejected

Heb'domad, s. a space of seven days, a week

Hebdom'adal, Hebdom'adary, a. weekly

Heb'etate, v. a. to dull, to stupefy, to blunt

Heb'etude, s. dulness, bluntness, obtuseness

He'braism, s. an Hebrew idiom

Hebric'ian, s. one skilled in Hebrew

He'brew, s. the Jewish language

Hec'atomb, s. a sacrifice of an hundred cattle

Hec'tic, Hec'tical, a. constitutional, habitual, troubled with morbid heat—s. a fever

Hec'tor, s. a bully, a noisy fellow—v. to vaunt

Hed'eral, a. made of or resembling ivy

Hedge, v. to make a hedge; enclose; shift

Hedge, s. a fence made of thorns, shrubs, &c.

Hedge'born, a. mean born, obscure, low

Hedge'hog, s. a quadruped set with prickles

Hedg'er, s. one who makes hedges

Hedg'ing-bill, s. a bill used in making hedges

Hedge'pig, s. a young hedgehog

Heed, v. a. to mind, to attend to, to regard

Heed, s. care, seriousness, caution

Heed'ful, a. careful, cautious, attentive

Heed'fulness, s. caution, vigilance

Heed'less, a. careless, negligent, inattentive

Heed'lessness, s. carelessness, negligence

Heel, s. the hind part of the foot

Heel'piece, v. a. to mend the heel of a shoe

Heft, s. a handle; a heave, an effort

He'gira, s. the epocha of the Turks, reckoned from the day Mahomet fled from Mecca

Heif'er, s. a young cow

Heigh'ho! interj. denoting languor, &c.

Height, s. elevation or extension upwards; utmost degree; elevation of rank

Height'en, v. a. to raise, to exalt, to improve

Hei'nous, a. very wicked, atrocious

Hei'nously, ad. wickedly, atrociously

Hei'nousness, s. great wickedness

Heir, s. one who inherits by law, a successor

Heir'ess, s. a female who inherits by law

Heir'less, a. having no heir

Heirloo'm, s. what descends with a freehold

Heir'ship, s. the state, &c. of an heir

Held, pret. of to hold

Hel'iacal, a. pertaining to the sun

Hel'ical, a. spiral, with many circumvolutions

Heliocen'tric, a. belonging to the sun

Heliog'raphy, s. a description of the sun

Hell, s. the residence of wicked spirits

Hell'doomed, a. consigned to hell

Hel'lebore, s. the Christmas flower; a plant

Hel'lenism, s. an idiom of the Greek

Hell'hound, s. an agent or dog of hell, a wretch

Hell'ish, a. wicked, infernal, sent from hell

Hell'ishly, ad. infernally, very wickedly

Hell'kite, s. a kite of infernal breed—hell prefixed to any word denotes detestation

Helm, s. the rudder; a headpiece

I A

Helm'ed, a. furnished with a headpiece
Hel'met, s. a covering for the head in war
Help, v. to assist, to aid, to support, to cure
Help,s. assistance, succour, support, remedy
Help'ful, a. useful, assisting, salutary
Help'less,a.destitute of help, wanting power
    to succour one's se f, irremediable
Hel'ter-skel'ter, ad. confusedly, in a hurry
Helve, s. the handle of an axe
Helvet'ic, a. of or relating to the Swiss
Hem, s. the edge of a garment folded down
    and sewed , a sudden expulsion of breath
Hem, v. a. to close with a hem ; to shut in
Hem'isphere, s. the half of a globe
Hemispher'ical, a. being half round
Hem'istic, s. half a verse
Hem'lock, s. a narcotic plant used in phys c
Hem'orrhage, s. a violent flux of blood
Hem'orrhoids, s. the piles, the emrods
Hemp, s. a plant of wh ch ropes are made
Hem'pen, s. made of hemp
Hen, s. the female of any land fowl
Hence ! interj. or ad. away, at a distance; for
    this reason, f om this cause
Hencefo'rth, Hencefor'ward, ad. from this
    time forward, from this time to futurity
Hend, v. a. to seize, to surround, to crowd
Hen'harm. Hen'harrier, s. a kind of haw .
Hen'pecked, a. governed by a wife
Hen'roost, s. a place where poultry rest
Hepat'ical, a. belonging to the liver
Hep'tagon, s. a figure of seven equal sides
Hep'tarchy, s. a sevenfold government
Her, pron. belonging to a female
Her'ald, s. an officer whose duty is to pro-
    claim peace, and denounce war, to be em-
    ployed in martial messages, and to judge
    and examine coats of arms ; a precursor
Her'aldry, s. the art or office of a herald
Herb, s. a plant, chiefly of the esculent kind
Herba'ceous, a. relating to herbs
Her'bage, s. pasture, grass, herbs in general
Her'bal, s. a treatise or book of plants
Her'balis , s. one skilled in herbs
Her'by, a. having the nature of herbs
Hercu'l an, a. very great or difficult
Herd, s. a flock, a drove, a company
Herd, v. to associate ; to put into a herd
Herds'man.s. one employed in tending herds
Here, ad. in this place or state
Hereabou'ts, ad. about this place
Hereaf'ter, ad. in a future state
H reby', ad. by this ; by these means
Hered'itable, a. whatever may be inherited
Heredit'ament, s. an inheritance
Hered'itary, a. descending by inheritance
Here'in, Hereinto', ad. in or into this
Hereof', ad. from this ; of this
Her on', Hereupon', ad. upon this
Here'siarch, s. a leader in heresy
Her'esy, s. a fundamental error in religion ;
    differing from the orthodox church
Her'etic,s.one who propagates heretical opi-
    nions in opposition to theChristian religion
Heret'ical a. re a ing to heresy
Hereto', Hereunto', ad. to this : unto this
Heretofo're, ad. formerly, anciently
Herewith', ad. with this
Her'iot, s. a fine to the lord of the manor
Her'itage,s.inheritance,estate by succession
Hermaph'rodite, s. animal uniting two sexes

Hermet'ic, Hermet'ical, a. chymical
Her'mit, s. a solitary devout person
Her'mitage, s. a hermit's cell
Hern, or Her'on, s. a large water fowl
He'ro, s. a brave man, a great warrior
Her'oess, Her'oine, s. a female hero
Hero'ic, Hero'ical, a. brave, noble
Hero'ically, ad. bravely, courageously
Her'oism, s. the qualities of a hero
Her'ring, s. a small sea fish
Herself't, pron. the female personal pronoun
Hes'itate, v. n. to delay, to pause, to doubt
Hesita'tion, s. doubt, intermission of speech
Hest, s. a command, precept, injunction
Het'erocolites, s. pl. in grammar, all nouns
    which vary in their gender or declension
Het'. rodox,a. deviating from the es ablished
    church opinion ; not orthodox
Heteroge'neal,Heteroge'neous, a. unlike; of
    a nature diametrically opposite
Heterop'tics, s. pl. false optics, deception
Hew, v.a. to cut with an axe, chop, labour
Hex'agon, s. a figure of six equal sides
Hexag'onal, a. having six sides or angles
Hexam'eter, s. a verse of six feet
Hey ! interj. a word expressive of joy
Hey'd y ! interj. expression of exultation
Hia'tus, s. an aperture, an opening, a breach
Hiber'nal, a. belonging to the winter
Hic'cius-doc'cius, s. a juggler
Hick'up, s. a convulsion of the stomach
Hid, Hid'den, part. pass. of to hide
Hide, v. to conceal, to cover, to lie hid
Hide, s. the skin of an animal, &c.
Hid'eous, a. horrible, frightful, dreadful
Hid'eously, ad. dreadfully, horribly
Hie, v. a. to hasten, to go quickly
Hi'erarch, s. the chief of a sacred order
H 'erarchy, s. an ecclesiastical government
Hieroglyph'ics, s. pl. the symbolical charac
    ters u ed by the ancient Egyptians
Hieroglyph'ical, a. emblematical, allusive
Hig'gle, v. n. to use many words in bargain
    ing ; to carry about ; to chaffer
Hig'gledy-pig'gledy, ad. confusedly
Hig'gler, s. one who hawks about provisions
High a. elevated, great, proud, exorbitant
High'blown, part. much swelled with wind
High'born, part. of noble extraction
High'flier, s. one extravagant in opinion
High'land, s. a mountainous country
High'lander, s. a mountaineer
High'ly, ad. in a great degree; arrogantly
High'mettled, a. proud or ardent of spirit
High'minded, a. haughty, proud
H go'nes , s. dignity of nature, a title
Highsea'soned, part. hot to the taste
Highspir'ited, part. a. bold, daring, insolent
High'ty-tigh'ty, a. giddy, thoughtless
Highwro'ught, part. splendidly finished
H ghwa'ter, s. the utmost flow of the tide
Highwa'y, s. a great road, a public path
High'wayman, s. a robber on the highway
Hilar'ity, s. gaiety, cheerfulness, mirth
Hil'ary, s. a ter m that begins in January
Hil'ding, s. a mean, cowardly wretch
Hill, s. elevation of ground, a high land
Hill'ock, s. a small hill
Hill'y, a. full of hills, unequal in surface
Hilt, s. the handle of a sword
H.m, pr m. the oblique case of he

Hind, s. a she stag; a peasant, a boor
Hin'der, v. a. to obstruct, to impede, to stop
Hin'derance, s. an impediment, a stop
Hind'ermost, Hind'most, a. the last
Hinge, s. a joint on which a door turns; a rule
Hint, v. n. to allude, to bring to mind
Hint, s. a remote suggestion, an intimation
Hip, s. a joint of the thigh; the fruit of the briar; lowness of spirits
Hip'pish, a. much dejected, low in spirits
Hip'pogriff, s. a winged or fabulous horse
Hippopot'amus, s. the river horse; an animal found in the Nile
Hip'shot, a. sprained in the hip
Hire, v. a. to engage for pay—s. wages
Hi'reling, s. one who serves for wages; a mercenary and unprincipled writer
Hiss, v. to cry like a serpent; to explode by hisses, to testify disapprobation
Hist! i. tj. exclamation commanding silence
Histo'rian, s. a writer of facts and events
Histor'ical, a. pertaining to history
Histor'ically, ad. in the manner of history
His'tory, s. a narration of facts
H.strion'ic, a. befitting a stage player
Hit, v. to strike, to clash, to reach, to succeed
Hit, s. a stroke, a lucky chance
Hitch, v. n. to catch, to move by jerks
Hitch, s. a kind of knot or noose
Hitch'el, s. a tool on which flax is combed
Hithe, s. a landing place for goods, &c.
Hith'er, ad. to this place—a. nearer
Hith'ermost, a. nearest to this side
Hith'erto, ad. to this time; till now; yet
Hive, s. a place for bees; a company
Hoard, v. to lay up privately
Hoard'ed, part. laid up in private
Hoa'rfrost, s. frozen dew; a white frost
Hoar'iness, s. state of being hoary or whitish
Hoarse, a. having a rough, harsh voice
Hoa'rsely, ad. with a rough harsh voice
Hoarse'ne-s, s. roughness of voice
Hoar'y, Hoar, a. grey with age, whitish
Hob'ble, v. n. to walk lamely or awkwardly
Hob'by, s. a species of hawk; a stupid fellow
Hob'byhorse, s. a small horse; a favourite thing or amusement; a plaything
Hob'goblin, s. a sprite, an apparition, a fairy
Hob'nail, s. a nail used in shoeing horses
Hock, s. the small end of a gammon of bacon; a sort of German wine
Hoc'kle, v. a. to hamstring, to lame
Ho'cus-po'cus, s. a juggler, a cheat
Hod, s. a bricklayer's trough
Hodge'podge, s. a confused mixture, a medley
Hodier'nal, a. of or relative to this day
Hoe, s. a garden tool for weeds, &c.
Hoe, v. a. to cut or dig with a hoe
Hog, s. the general name of swine
Hog'cote, Hog'sty, s. a house for hogs
Hog'geral, s. an ewe of two years old
Hog'gish, a. selfish, greedy, brutish
Hog'herd, s. a keeper of hogs
Ho'go, s. a mess of high relish; a stink
Hogs'head, s. a measure of 63 gallons
Hog'wash, s. draff which is given to swine
Hoi'den, s. an awkward country girl
Hoist, v. a. to raise up on high
Hold, v. to keep, to detain, to have within
Hold, s. a support; power, custody
Hold! interj. stop! forbear! be still

Hold'er, s. one who holds any thing
Hold'fast, s. an iron hook, a catch
Hole, s. a hollow place; a rent in a garment a mean habitation; a subterfuge
Ho'liday, Ho'lyday, s. a day of gaiety and mirth, an anniversary feast; a time of festivity
Ho'lily, ad. piously, religiously, inviolably
Ho'liness, s. piety; the Pope's title
Hol'la, Hol'lo, v. n. to call to any one
Hol'land, s. fine linen made in Holland
Hol'low, a. having a void within; deceitful
Hol'low, s. a cavity, a hole, an opening
Hol'lowness, s. the state of being hollow
Hol'ly, s. a tree; an evergreen shrub
Hol'lyhock, s. the rose mallow
Holme, s. a river island; the evergreen oak
Hol'ocaust, s. a burnt sacrifice
Holp, Hol'pen, part. pass. of to help
Hol'ster, s. a case for a horseman's pistols
Holt, s. a wood, particularly of willows
Ho'ly, a. pure, religious, sacred, immaculate
Hom'age, s. respect, duty, fealty, service
Home, s. place of constant residence; country
Ho'inebred, a. native, artless, plain
Ho'meliness, s. plainness, coarseness
Ho'mely, a. not elegant, coarse
Ho'menade, a. made at home; plain
Ho'mer, s. a measure of about three pints
Ho'mespun, a. made at home; inelegant
Ho'meward, ad. toward home
Hom'icide, s. murder; a murderer
Hom'ily, s. a discourse read in churches
Homoge'neous, a. of the same nature
Homon'ymous, a. equivocal, ambiguous
Homot'onous, a. equable, correspondent
Hone, s. a stone to whet razors, &c.
Hon'est, a. sincere, just, true, upright, chaste
Hon'estly, ad. justly, uprightly, sincerely
Hon'esty, s. justice, purity, truth, virtue
Hon'ey, s. the sweet concoction of bees, &c.
Hon'eybag, s. the stomach of a bee
Hon'eycomb, s. cells of wax for honey
Hon'eydew, s. a sweet dew on plants
Hon'eyed, part. a. covered with honey
Hon'eyless, a. without honey; empty
Hon'eymoon, s. first month after marriage
Hon'eysuckle, s. an odoriferous woodbine
Hon'orary, a. done or instituted in honour, conferring honour without gain
Hon'our, s. reputation, virtue, dignity
Hon'our, v. a. to reverence, exalt, dignify
Hon'ourable, a. equitable, illustrious, generous
Hon'ourably, ad. reputably, nobly
Hood, s. an upper covering for the head
Hood'wink, v. a. to blind, to deceive, to hide
Hoof, s. the horny part of a horse's foot
Hook, s. a bent piece of iron, wood, &c.
Hook, v. a. to catch, to fasten, to ensnare
Hook'ed, a. bent, curvated
Hoop, s. any thing circular
Hoop, v. to bind with hoops; to shoot
Hoop'ingcough, s. a convulsive cough
Hoot, s. a shout of contempt—v. n. to shout
Hop, s. a plant; a jump; a mean dance
Hop, v. to leap on one leg, walk lame, &c.
Hope, s. confidence in a future event
Hope, v. to expect with desire
Ho'peful, a. full of expectation, promising
Ho'peless, a. without hope; abandoned, left
Hop'ground, s. ground set apart for hops
Hop'per, s. a part of a mill; a basket

Hop'ple, v. n. to tie the feet together

Ho'ral, Hor'ary, a. relating to an hour

Horde, s. a clan, a migratory crew

Hore'hound, s. a medicinal herb

Hori'zon, s. a great imaginary line or circle, which divides the heavens and earth into two parts or hemispheres

Horizon'tal, a. near the horizon; level

Horn, s. defensive weapon of an ox; an instrument of wind music

Horn'book, s. the first book for children

Horn'ed, a. furnished with horns

Horn'er, s. one who deals in horns

Horn'et, s. a large strong stinging fly

Horn'pipe, s. a kind of single dance

Horn'y, a. made of horns, hard, callous

Hor'ologe, s. an instrument denoting time

Hor'oscope, s. the configuration of the planets at the hour of a person's birth

Hor'rible, a. dreadful, shocking, terrible

Hor'ribly, ad. dreadfully, hideously

Hor'rid, a. hideous, enormous

Hor'ridly, ad. shockingly, hideously

Horrif'ic, a. causing horror or dread

Hor'ror, s. terror mixed with detestation

Horse, s. an animal; a wooden machine

Hor'seback, s. the seat or state of riding

Hor'sebean, s. a small kind of bean

Hor'sebreaker, s. one who tames horses

Hor'sefly, s. a fly that stings horses

Hor'sehair, s. the hair of horses

Hor'selaugh, s. a loud, violent, rude laugh

Hor'seleech, s. a leech that bites horses

Hor'seman, s. one skilled in riding

Hor'semanship, s. the art of managing a horse

Hor'semarten, s. a large kind of bee

Hor'semeat, s. provender for horses

Hor'seplay, s. rough play, rudeness

Hor'sepond, s. a pond to water horses at

Horserad'ish, s. a root acrid and biting, a species of scurvy-grass

Hor'seshoe, s. a shoe for horses; an herb

Hor'seway, s. a broad open way

Horta'tion, s. the act of exhorting, advice

Horta'tive, a. tending to exhort, animating

Hor'ticulture, s. the act of cultivating gardens

Hor'tulan, a. belonging to a garden

Hosan'na, s. an exclamation of praise to God

Hose, s. stockings; breeches

Ho'sier, s. one who sells stockings, &c.

Hos'pitable, a. kind to strangers, friendly

Hos'pitably, ad. in a hospitable manner

Hos'pital, s. a receptacle for the sick and poor

Hospital'ity, s. the practice of entertaining strangers; liberality in entertainments

Host, s. a landlord; an army; a number

Hos'tage, s. a person left as a pledge for securing the performance of conditions

Host'ess, s. a female host, a landlady

Hos'tile, a. adverse, opposite; warlike

Hostil'ity, s. open war, a state of warfare

Hos'tler, s. the manager of horses at an inn

Hot, a. having heat, furious, lustful, eager

Hot'bed, s. a bed of earth made hot by the fermentation of dung and manure

Hot'cockle, s. a species of childish play

Hotel', s. a genteel public lodging house

Hot'headed, a. passionate, violent

Hot'house, s. a building contrived for ripening exotics, &c. by means of heat

Hot'spur, s. a violent, precipitate man; a pea

Hove, Ho'ven. part. pass. raised, swelled

Hov'el, s. a shed, a shelter for cattle

Hov'er, v. n. to hang overhead, to wander

Hough, s. the lower part of the thigh

Hough, v. a. to hamstring, to cut up

Hound, s. a dog used in the chase

Hour, s. the 24th part of a day

Hour'glass, s. a glass filled with sand, for the purpose of measuring time

Hour'ly, a. done every hour, frequent

House, s. a place of human abode

House, v. to put under shelter, to harbour

House'breaker, s. one who robs houses

House'breaking, s. robbing of houses

House'hold, s. a family living together

House'hold-stuff, s. furniture, utensils, goods

House'keeper, s. one who keeps a house; a superintending female servant

House'keeping, s. domestic management

House'less, a. destitute of abode

House'maid, s. a female menial servant

House'room, s. convenient apartments

House'warming, s. a feast usual on taking possession of a house

House'wife, s. a female economist

House'wifery, s. frugality in domestic affairs

How, ad. in what manner or degree

How'beit, ad. nevertheless, notwithstanding

Howev'er, ad. notwithstanding; yet, at least

How'itzer, s. a kind of bomb

Howl, v. n. to utter cries in distress, as a dog

Howl'ing, s. the noise of a dog, &c.

Howsoev'er, ad. in whatever manner

Hox, v. a. to hamstring, to hough

Hoy, s. a coasting vessel, a small ship

Hub'bub, s. tumult, confusion, great noise

Huck'aback, s. a kind of figured linen

Huck'lebone, s. the hip bone

Huck'ster, s. a retailer of small wares

Hud'dle, v. to do a thing in a flurry; to crowd together in a confused manner

Hudibras'tic, a. doggrel; like Hudibras

Hue, s. a shade of colour, tint; pursuit, clamour

Huff, v. to chide with insolence

Huff'ish, a. arrogant, hectoring, insolent

Hug, v. a. to embrace fondly, to hold fast

Huge, a. vast, large, immense, enormous

Huge'ly, ad. immensely, greatly, very much

Huge'ness, s. enormous bulk, greatness

Hug'ger-mug'ger, s. a by-place; secrecy

Hulk, s. the body of a ship; a clown

Hull, s. the body of a ship; a shell or husk

Hum, v. n. to sing low, to buzz; to deceive

Hum, s. a buzzing noise; a deception

Hu'man, a. having the qualities of a man

Huma'ne, a. kind, tender, benevolent

Huma'nely, ad. kindly; with good nature

Human'ity, s. compassion, benevolence, generosity; the nature of man

Hu'mankind, s. the race of man

Hum'ble, a. modest, submissive; not proud

Hum'ble, v. a. to condescend; to subdue

Hum'bles, s. pl. the entrails of a deer

Hum'bly, ad. without pride; with humility

Hum'drum, s. a stupid person—a. dull

Humecta'tion, s. a moistening or wetting

Hu'meral, a. belonging to the shoulder

Hu'mid, a. wet, watery, moist, damp

Humid'ity, s. moisture, dampness

Humilia'tion, s. the act of humility

Humil'ity, s. freedom from pride, modesty

Hum'mingbird, *s.* the smallest of all birds

Hu'mour, *s.* moisture; whim, jocularity

Hu'mour, *v. a.* to soothe, to qualify

Hu'morist, *s.* one who gratifies his humour

Hu'morous, *a.* jocular, pleasant, whimsical

Hump'back, *s.* a crooked back; high shoul-

Hunch, *v. n.* to jostle; to crook the back [ders

Hun'dred, *s.* ten multiplied by ten; part of a county or shire

Hung, *pret.* and *pass. part.* of *to hang*

Hun'ger, *s.* a desire of food; violent desire

Huu'gry, *a.* in want of food

Hunks, *s.* a covetous, sordid wretch, a miser

Hunt, *v.* to chase, to pursue, to search for

Hunt, *s.* a pack of hounds; a chase, a pursuit

Hunt'er, *s.* one who chases animals

Hunts'man, *s.* one who manages the dogs for, and one who delights in, hunting

Hur'dle, *s.* a grate; sticks wove together for various uses; a sort of sledge, &c.

Hurds, *s. pl.* the refuse of hemp or flax

Hurl, *v. a.* to throw with violence

Hurl'bat, *s.* whirlbat; a weapon

Hur'ly-bur'ly, *s.* bustle, confusion, tumult

Hur'ricane, *s.* a violent storm, a tempest

Hur'ry, *v.* to hasten, to move with haste

Hur'ry, *s.* haste, precipitation; a '*'' nit

Hurt, *s.* harm; mischief, bruise, wound

Hurt, *v. a.* to injure, to harm, to wound

Hurt'ful, *a.* mischievous, pernicious

Hurt'fully, *ad.* mischievously, perniciously

Hurt'fulness, *s.* mischievousness, pernici-
ousness

Hur'tle, *v.* to skirmish, to move violently

Hurt'less, *a.* harmless, innoxious, innocent

Hus'band, *s.* a married man; an economist

Hus'band, *v. a.* to manage frugally; to till

Hus'bandless, *a.* without a husband

Hus'bandman, *s.* one who works in tillage

Hus'bandry, *s.* tillage; thrift, parsimony

Hush. *v.* to still, quiet, appease; to forbid

Hush'money, *s.* a bribe to induce secresy

Husk, *s.* the outward integument of fruits

Husk'y, *a.* abounding in husks; dry

Hussa'r, *s.* a kind of horse soldier

Hus'sy, *s.* a sorry or bad woman; a hag

Hus'tings, *s. pl.* a council, a court held

Hus'tle, *v. a.* to shake together

Hus'wife, *v. a.* to manage with frugality

Hut, *s.* a poor cottage, a mean abode

Hutch, *s.* a corn chest; a rabbit-box

Hux, *v. n.* to catch pike with a bladder, &c.

Huzza! *interj.* a shout of joy or acclamation

Hy'acinth, *s.* a flower; a colour

Hyacin'thine, *a.* like hyacinths

Hy'ades, *s. pl.* the seven stars

Hy'aline, *a.* glassy, crystalline, clear

Hy'dra, *s.* a monster with several heads

Hy'dragogues, *s. pl.* medicinal preparations for the purgation of watery humours

Hydrau'lical, *a.* relating to hydraulics

Hydrau'lics, *s. pl.* the science which treats of the motion of fluids, and the art of conveying water

Hy'drocele, *s.* a watery rupture

Hydroceph'alus, *s.* dropsy in the head

Hy'drogen, *s.* inflammable air

Hydrog'rapher, *s.* one who draws maps of the sea; a teacher of hydrography

Hydrog'raphy, *s.* description of the watery part of the terraqueous globe

Hy'dromancy, *s.* a prediction by water

Hy'dromel, *s.* honey and water; mead

Hydrom'eter, or Hygrom'eter, *s.* an instrument to measure the degrees of moisture

Hydropho'bia, *s.* a distemper occasioned by the bite of a mad dog; dread of water

Hydrop'ical, *a.* dropsical, watery

Hydrostat'ical, *a.* relating to hydrostatics

Hydrostat'ics, *s. pl.* the science of the gravita-
tion of fluids; weighing fluids

Hy'emal, *a.* belonging to winter

Hye'na, *s.* a fierce animal like a wolf

Hym, *s.* a species of a very fierce dog

Hymene'al, *a.* pertaining to marriage

Hymn, *v. a.* to praise in songs of adoration

Hymn, *s.* a divine song, a song of praise

Hym'nic, *a.* relating to hymns

Hyp, *v. a.* to make melancholy, to dispirit

Hypal'lage, *s.* a change of cases, &c.

Hyper'bole, *s.* a rhetorical figure, which con sists in representing things much greater or less than they really are

Hyperbol'ical, *a.* exaggerating beyond fact

Hyperbo'lize, *v.* to exaggerate or extenuate

Hyperbo'rean, *a.* northern, cold

Hypercrit'ic, *s.* an unreasonable critic

Hypercrit'ical, *a.* critical beyond use

Hy'phen, *s.* a note of conjunction thus (-), put between two words or syllables, to show that they are to be joined together

Hypnot'ic, *s.* a medicine causing sleep

Hypochon'driac, *s.* one affected with melancholy, or disordered in the imagination—
a. melancholy, dispirited

Hyp'ocist, *s.* an astringent medicine

Hypoc'risy, *s.* dissimulation, a pretence

Hyp'ocrite, *s.* a dissembler in religion, &c.

Hypocrit'ical, *a.* dissembling, insincere, false

Hypos'tasis, *s.* a distinct substance; per-
sonality; a term more particularly used in the doctrine of the Holy Trinity

Hypostat'ical, *a.* constitutive; distinct

Hypoth'esis, *s.* a system upon supposition

Hypothet'ical, *a.* supposed, conditional

Hypothet'ically, *ad.* upon supposition

Hyrst, or Herst, *s.* a wood or thicket

Hys'sop, *s.* the name of a purgative plant

Hyster'ic, Hyster'ical. *a.* troubled with fits

Hyster'ics, *s.* fits peculiar to women

I.

I, or J, the ninth letter of the alphabet

I, *pron.* myself

Jab'ber, *v. n.* to talk much or idly, to chatter

Jab'berer, *s.* one who talks inarticulately

Ja'cent, *a.* lying at length, extended

Ja'cinth, *s.* a precious gem; the hyacinth

Jack, *s.* John; a young pike; an engine

Jack'al, *s.* a beast somewhat resembling a fox said to hunt or start prey for the lion

Jack'alent, *s.* a simple, sheepish fellow

Jack'anapes, s. a monkey; a coxcomb
Jack'daw, s. a black chattering bird
Jack'et, s. a short coat, a close waistcoat
Jac'obin, s. one of a faction in France
Jac'obite, s. a partisan of James II.
Jactita'tion, s. tossing motion, restlessness
Jacula'tion, s. the act of throwing or darting
Jade, s. a worthless horse; a sorry woman
Jade, v. a. to weary, to tire, to ride down
Ja'dish, a. unruly, vicious; unchaste
Jagg, v. a. to notch—s. a denticulation
Jag'gy, a. uneven, ragged, notched
Jal'ap, s. a purgative root from New Spain
Jam, s. a conserve of fruit; a child's frock
Jam, v. a. to confine between; to wedge in
Jamb, s. the upright post of a door
Iam'bic, s. verses which are composed of a
    long and short syllable alternately
Jan'gle, v. to quarrel, to be out of tune
Jan'izary, s. a Turkish soldier; a guard
Jan'ty, or Jaun'ty, a. showy, gay, giddy
Jan'uary, s. the first month of the year
Japa'n, s. a varnish made to work in colours
Japan'ner, s. one skilled in japan work
Jar, v. n. to clash, to differ, to disagree
Jar, s. an earthen vessel; a harsh sound
Jar'gon, s. gabble, gibberish, nonsensical talk
Jas'per, s. a precious green stone
Jav'elin, s. a spear or half pike
Jaun'dice, s. a distemper from obstructions
    of the glands of the liver
Jaun'diced, a. affected with the jaundice
Jaunt, v. n. to walk or travel about
Jaunt, s. an excursion, a ramble, a flight
Jau'ntiness, s. airiness, briskness, flutter
Jaw, s. the bone in which the teeth are fixed
Jay, s. a bird with gaudy feathers
Ja'zel, s. a precious azure or blue stone
Ice, s. frozen water; sugar concreted
Ice'house, s. a house where ice is reposited
Ichnog'raphy, s. a ground plot, a platform
I'chor, s. a humour arising from ulcers
I'chorous, a. sharp, thin, indigested
I'cicle, s. dripping water frozen, hanging
    from the eaves of a house, &c.
I'ciness, s. state of generating ice
I'con, s. a picture, a representation
Icter'ical, a. afflicted with the jaundice
I'cy, a. full of ice, cold; frigid, backward
Ide'a, s. mental imagination; a notion
Ide'al, a. mental, conceived, intellectual
Iden'tic, Iden'tical, a. the same
Iden'ticalness, Iden'tity, s. sameness
Ides, s. pl. a term of time amongst the an-
    cient Romans. It is the 13th day of each
    month, except March, May, July, and
    October, in which it is the 15th
Id'iom, s. a particular mode of speech
Id'iot, s. a fool, a natural, a changeling
Id'iotism, s. folly; natural imbecility of mind
I'dle, a. unemployed, lazy, worthless
I'dle, v. n. to spend time in inactivity
Idlehead'ed, a. foolish, unreasonable
I'dleness, s. sloth, laziness, folly
I'dler, s. a lazy person, a sluggard
I'dly, ad. lazily, carelessly, foolishly
I'dol, s. an image worshipped as a god
Idol'ater, s. a worshipper of idols
Idol'atrize, v. n. to worship idols
Idol'atrous, a. tending or given to idolatry
Idol'atry, s. the worship of images

I'dolize, v. n. to worship as a deity
I'dyl, s. a small short poem; an eclogue
Jeal'ous, a. suspicious, cautious, fearful
Jeal'ousy, s. suspicion, in love especially
Jeer, v. to treat with scorn, to flout, to scoff
Jeho'vah, s. the appropriate name of God
    in the Hebrew language
Jejune, a. hungry; unaffecting, trifling
Jeju'neness, s. poverty; want of matter
Jel'ly, s. a light transparent sizy broth; a
    sweetmeat of various species
Jen'net, s. a Spanish or Barbary horse
Jen'neting, s. a species of forward apple
Jeop'ard, v. a. to hazard, to put in danger
Jeop ardous, a. hazardous, dangerous
Jeop'ardy, s. danger, hazard, peril
Jerk, s. a quick smart lash; a quick jolt
Jerkin, s. a jacket; a kind of hawk
Jer'sey, s. a fine yarn of wool
Jes'samine, s. a fine fragrant flower
Jest, s. anything ludicrous; a laughing-stock
Jes'ting, s. talk to raise laughter
Jes'uit, s. one of a religious order
Jesuit'ical, a. shuffling, deceitful, equivocal
Jet, s. a curious black fossil; a spout of water
Jet, v. n. to shoot forward, to protrude
Jet'sam, s. goods cast on shore by shipwreck
Jet'ty, a. made of jet, black as jet
Jew'el, s. a precious stone, a gem
Jew'eller, s. one who deals in precious stones
Jews'-harp, s. a small musical instrument
If, conj. suppose it to be so; though
Ig'neous, a. containing or emitting fire
Ig'nis-fat'uus, s. a kind of fiery vapour,
    called Will-with-a-wisp; a delusion
Ignite, v. a. to set on fire; to kindle
Ignit'ion, s. the act of setting on fire
Igni'tible, a. inflammable, easily set on fire
Igno'ble, a. mean of birth; worthless
Igno'bly, ad. disgracefully, meanly
Ignomin'ious, a. disgraceful, shameful, mean
Ignomin'iously, ad. scandalously, meanly
Ig'nominy, s. disgrace, shame, reproach
Ignora'mus, s. a foolish fellow, vain preten-
Ig'norance, s. want of knowledge [der
Ig'norant, a. illiterate, without knowledge
Jig, s. a light careless dance or tune
Jilt, s. a deceiving woman—v. a. to deceive
Jin'gle, s. any thing sounding; a rattle
Ile, s. a walk or alley in a church
Il'iac, a. relating to the lower bowels
Il'iad, s. an heroic poem by Homer
Ill, a. sick, disordered, not in health
Ill, s. wickedness, misfortune, misery
Illab'orate, a. done without much labour
Illap'se, s. gradual entrance of one thing into
    another, casual coming, a sudden attack
Illa'queate, v. a. to ensnare, to entangle
Illa'tion, s. an inference, a conclusion
Il lative, a. that which may be inferred
Illau dable, a. not deserving praise
Illau'dably, ad. unworthily, meanly
Ille'gal, a. contrary to law, unjust
Illegal'ity, s. contrariety to law
Ille'gally, ad. in a manner contrary to law
Illeg'ible, a. what cannot be clearly read
Illegit'imacy, s. a state of bastardy
Illegit'imate, a. born out of wedlock
Illfa'voured, a. of a bad countenance
Illib'eral, a. not noble, disingenuous
Illib'erally, ad. disingenuously, &c.

Illic'it, a. unlawful, unfit ; contraband
Illim'itable, a. that which cannot be limited
Illit'erate, a. unlearned, untaught, ignorant
Illit'erateness, s. a want of learning
Illna'ture, s. malevolence, captiousness
Illna'tured, a. peevish, cross, untractable
Ill'ness, s. sickness, disorder, weakness
Illog'ical, a. contrary to rules of reasoning
Illu'de, v.a. to mock, to deceive, to play upon
Illume',Illu'mine,Illu'minate,v.a.to enlight-
en, to illustrate, to decorate
Illumina'tion,s.the act of giving light;bright-
ness ; lights displayed as a sign of joy
Illu'sion, s. a false show, error, mockery
Illu'sive, a. deceiving by false show
Illu'sory, a. deceiving, fraudulent
Illus'trate, v.a. to brighten with light, to ex-
plain, to elucidate, to clear
Illustra'tion, s. explanation, exposition
Illus'trative, a. able or tending to explain
Illus'trious, a. conspicuous, eminent, noble
Illus'triously, ad. eminently, conspicuously
Im'age,s.a statue, a picture, an idol ; an idea
Im'agery, s. sensible representation ; show
Imag'inable, a. possible to be conceived
Imag'inary, a. fancied, ideal, visionary
Imagina'tion, s. fancy, scheme, conception
Imag'ine, v. a. to fancy, scheme, contrive
Imbec'ile, v.a. to lessen a fortune privately
Imbe'cile. a. weak, feeble
Imbecil'ity, s. weakness, feebleness
Imbi'be, v.a. to drink in, to admit into
Imbit'ter, v. a. to make bitter ; to exasperate
Imbod'y, v.a. to condense to a body; inclose
Imbo'lden, v. a. to make bold, to encourage
Imbo'som, v. a. to hold in the bosom
Imbow', v. a. to arch, to vault
Imbow'er, v. a. to shelter with trees
Im'bricate, v. a. to cover with tiles
Imbrica'tion, s. a concave indenture
Imbrow'n, v.a. to make brown ; to obscure
Imbrue', v. a. to soak, to steep, to wet much
Imbru'te, v. a. to degrade by brutality
Imbue' v. a. to tincture deep, to tinge
Imbur'se, v. a. to stock with money
Im'itable,a.possible or worthy to be imitated
Im'itate,v.a.to follow the manner, action, or
way of another person ; to copy
Im'itative, a. inclined or tending to copy
Imita'tion, s. the act of copying ; an attempt
to make a resemblance ; a copy
Imita'tor, s. he who imitates or copies
Imita'trix, s. she who imitates, &c.
Immac'ulate,a. without stain,undefiled,pure
Imman'acle, v. a. to fetter, to confine
Imma'ne, a. cruel, wild ; prodigiously great
Im'manent, a. inherent, internal, intrinsic
Imman'ifest,a. not plain, uncertain,doubtful
Imman'ity,s.barbarity,brutality,savageness
Immarces'sible, a. perpetual, unfading
Immar'tial, a. not warlike, impotent, weak
Immate'rial, a. trifling ; incorporeal
Immatu're, a. not ripe, not perfect ; hasty
Immatu'rely, ad. too early, too soon
Immatu'rity, s. unripeness, incomplete
Immeas'urable, a. that cannot be measured
Imme'diate, a. instant ; acting by itself
Imme'diately, ad. instantly, presently
Immed'icable, a. not to be healed, past cure
Immemo'rial, z. past time of memory
Immen'se, a. unlimited, vast, infinite

Immensely, ad. without measure, infinitely
Immen'sity, s. unbounded greatness,infinity
Immer'ge, Immer'se, v.a. to sink or plunge
under water ; to dip in water
Immer'sion, s. dipping under water
Immethod'ical, a. irregular, confused
Immethod'ically, ad. without method
Im'minence, s. an impending danger
Im'minent, a. impending, threatening
Imminu'tion, s. a diminution, a decrease
Immis'sion, s. a sending in, an injection
Immix', Immin'gle, v. a. to blend, to unite
Immix'able, a. impossible to be mixed
Immobil'ity, s. incapacity of motion
Immod'erate,a.excessive,morethan enough,
exceeding the due means
Immod'erately, ad. in an excessive degree
Immodera'tion, s. want of moderation
Immod'est, a. shameless, impure, obscene
Immod'estly, ad. without modesty
Immod'esty, s. a want of modesty or purity
Im'molate, v. a. to sacrifice, to offer up
Immola'tion, s. the act of sacrificing
Immor'al, a. dishonest, vicious, irreligious
Immoral'ity, s. want of virtue ; vice
Immor'tal, a. never to die, perpetual
Immortal'ity, s. life never to end
Immor'talize,v.to make or become immortal
Immor'tally, ad. with exemption from death
Immo'veable, a. unshaken, stable, firm
Immo'veably, ad. in a state not to be shaken
Immu'nity, s. privilege, freedom, exemption
Immu're,v.a.to inclose, to confine, to shut in
Immu'sical. a. inharmonious, harsh
Immutabil'ity, s. invariableness, constancy
Immu'table, a. invariable, unalterable
Imp, s. an offspring ; a puny devil
Imp, v. a. to enlarge ; to lengthen
Impact', v. a. to drive close or hard
Impai'nt, v.a. to paint, to decorate, to adorn
Impai'r,v.to injure, to make worse, to lessen
Impal'pable, a. not to be perceived by touch
Impar'ity, s. inequality, disproportion
Impar'lance, s. dialogue, conference
Impart', v.a. to communicate ; to grant unto
Impar'tance, s. a communication ; a grant
Impar'tial, a. just, equitable, equal
Impartial'ity, s. equitableness, justice
Impar'tially, ad. equitably, without bias
Impass'able, a. that which cannot be passed
Impas'sible, a. exempt from pain
Impas'sioned, a. seized with passion
Impa'tience, s. uneasiness under sufferings ;
vehemence of temper, eagerness
Impa'tient, a. eager, not able to endure
Impa'tiently, ad. eagerly, passionately
Impaw'n, v. a. to pawn, to give as a pledge
Impea'ch, v.a. to accuse by public authority
Impea'chment, s. a legal accusation ; an im-
pediment, obstruction, hinderance
Impear'l, v. a. to form like pearls, to adorn
Impec'cable, a. not subject to sin, perfect
Impe'de, v. a. to hinder, to obstruct, to let
Imped'iment, s. hinderance, obstruction
Impel', v. a. to urge forwards, to press on
Impel'lent, s. a power to drive forward
Impen'd, v. n. to hang over, to be at hand
Impen'dent, a. hanging over, or near
Impen'ding, a. hanging ready to fall
Impen'etrable,a. that which cannot be pene-
trated or discovered ; not to be pierced

Impen'itence, *s.* a hardness of heart; want of remorse for crimes; obduracy
Impen'itent, *a.* remorseless, obdurate
Impen'itently, *ad.* without repentance
Im'perate, *a.* done with consciousness
Imper'ative, *a.* commanding, ordering
Imper'atively, *ad.* in a commanding manner
Impercep'tible, *a.* not to be perceived
Impercep'tibly, *ad.* in a manner not to be perceived; not subject to perception
Imper'fect, *a.* not complete, defective, frail
Imperfec'tion, *s.* a defect, a fault, a failure
Imper'fectly, *ad.* not completely, not fully
Imper'forate, *a.* not pierced through
Impe'rial, *a.* belonging to an emperor
Impe'rialist, *s.* one belonging to an emperor
Impe'rious, *a.* haughty, arrogant, lordly
Impe'riously, *ad.* arrogantly, insolently
Impe'riousness, *s.* air of command; authority
Imper'ishable, *a.* not to be destroyed
Imper'sonal, *a.* having no person
Imperspic'uous, *a.* not sufficiently clear
Impersua'sible, *a.* not to be persuaded
Imper'tinence, *s.* folly, intrusion; a trifle
Imper'tinent, *a.* intrusive, meddling
Imper'tinently, *ad.* intrusively, officiously
Imper'vious, *a.* impassable, inaccessible
Imper'viousness, *s.* the state of not admitting passage
Im'petrate, *v. a.* to obtain by treaty
Impetuos'ity, *s.* violence, vehemence, fury
Impet'uous, *a.* violent, fierce, forcible
Im'petus, *s.* a violent effort, stroke, force
Impi'ety, *s.* wickedness, irreverence
Impig'norate, *v. a.* to pledge, to pawn
Impin'ge, *v.* to fall or strike against, to clash
Impin'guate, *v. a.* to fatten, to make fat
Im'pious, *a.* wicked, irreligious, profane
Im'piously, *ad.* wickedly, profanely
Impla'cable, *a.* malicious, not to be pacified, inexorable, constant in enmity
Impla'cably, *ad.* with constant enmity
Implan't, *v. a.* to ingraft, to insert, to infix
Implau'sible, *a.* not specious, impersuasive
Implea'd, *v. a.* to prosecute, to sue at law
Im'plement, *s.* a tool, instrument; vessel
Imple'tion, *s.* the act of filling up
Im'plex, *a.* intricate, complicated, entangled
Im'plicate, *v. a.* to entangle, to embarrass
Implica'tion, *s.* involution, a tacit inference; a necessary consequence
Implic'it, *a.* tacitly understood; founded on the authority of others   volved
Implic'itly, *ad.* dependen   by inference
Implo're, *v. a.* to ask, beseech, beg, solicit
Imply', *v. a.* to comprise, to infold, suggest
Impoi'son, *v. a.* to kill or corrupt with poison
Impoli'te, *a.* unpolite, ungenteel, rude
Impol'itic, *a.* imprudent, indiscreet
Impon'derous, *a.* void of weight, light
Impo'rous, *a.* free from pores, compact
Impo'rt, *v. a.* to bring commodities from abroad; to signify or denote; to concern
Im'port, *s.* things imported; importance
Impor'tance, *s.* a matter, subject, moment
Impor'tant, *a.* momentous, of consequence
Importa'tion, *s.* act of bringing from abroad
Impo'rter, *s.* one who brings from abroad
Impo'rtless, *a.* trifling, of no consequence
Impor'tunate, *a.* incessant in solicitation
Importu'ne, *v. a.* to vex with solicitation

Importu'nely, *ad.* incessantly, unseaso
Importu'nity, *s.* incessant solicitation
Impor'tuous, *a.* having no harbour
Impo'se, *v. a.* to enjoin as a duty; to dece
Impo'seable, *a.* that may be laid by obligati
Impo'ser, *s.* one who imposes, or enjoins
Imposi'tion, *s.* a tax or tribute; an injunction; a cheat or fallacy; an oppression
Impositi'tious, *a.* primitive, radical
Impossibil'ity, *s.* that which cannot be done
Impos'sible, *a.* impracticable
Im'post, *s.* a tax, a custom to be paid
Impos'thumate, *v. n.* to form an abscess
Impos'thume, *s.* corrupt matter formed into an abscess; the act of forming an abscess
Impos'ter, *s.* a false pretender, a cheat
Im'potence, *s.* want of power, feebleness
Impu'nity, *s.* exemption from punishment
Im'potent, *a.* wanting power, weak, feeble
Im'potently, *ad.* without power, weakly
Impou'nd, *v. a.* to shut up in a pinfold
Imprac'ticable, *a.* impossible, unattainable
Im'precate, *v. a.* to invoke evil, to curse
Impreca'tion, *s.* an invocation of evil
Im'precatory, *a.* containing wishes of evil
Impreg'nable, *a.* not to be taken, unmoved
Impreg'nate, *v. a.* to make prolific
Impreju'dicate, *a.* unprejudiced, impartial
Imprepara'tion, *s.* a want of preparation
Impress', *v. a.* to print, to stamp; to force
Impress'ible, *a.* what may be impressed
Impres'sion, *s.* the print of a seal or stamp, an edition of a book; image fixed in the mind; influence, operation
Impres'sive, *a.* tending, or able, to impress
Impres'sure, *s.* a mark made by pressure
Impri'mis, *ad.* in the first place
Imprin't, *v. a.* to print, to fix on the mind
Impris'on, *v. a.* to shut up, to confine
Impris'onment, *s.* a confinement in prison
Improbabil'ity, *s.* difficulty to be believed
Improb'able, *a.* incredible, unlikely
Im'probate, *v. a.* to disapprove, to disallow
Improba'tion, *s.* the act of disallowing
Improb'ity, *s.* dishonesty, baseness
Improlif'icate, *v. a.* to make unfruitful
Improp'er, *a.* unqualified, unfit, not just
Improp'erly, *ad.* not fitly, not accurately
Impro'priate, *v. a.* to convert to private use
Impropria'tion, *s.* church lands in the immediate possession of a layman
Impropri'ety, *s.* unfitness, inaccuracy
Impros'perous, *a.* unsuccessful, unfortunate
Impro'vable, *a.* capable of improvement
Impro've, *v.* to raise from good to better
Improve'ment, *s.* progress from good to better, the act of improving; education
Improv'idence, *s.* a want of forethought
Improv'ident, *a.* wanting care to provide
Impru'dence, *s.* indiscretion, folly, negligence   [ous
Impru'dent, *a.* wanting prudence, injudici
Impru'dently, *ad.* indiscreetly, carelessly
Im'pudence, *s.* immodesty, shamelessness
Im'pudent, *a.* wanting modesty, shameless
Im'pudently, *ad.* saucily, shamelessly
Impu'gn, *v. a.* to assault, to attack   [bility
Impu'issance, *s.* weakness, feebleness, ina
Im'pulse, *s.* a communicated force; an inward indignation; idea, motive
Impul'sive, *a.* having power to impel

...re, a. unchaste; unholy; drossy
...rely, ad. in an impure manner
...u'rity s. filthiness, lewdness
...ur'ple, v. a. to colour as with purple
...pu'table, a. chargeable upon any one
...puta'tion, s. an accusation or charge
...pu'tative, a. that which may be imputed
...pu'te, v. a. to charge upon, to attribute
...putres'cible, a. that cannot be corrupted
...abil'ity, s. a want of power, impotence
...acces'sible, a. not to be come at
...ac'curacy, s. a want of exactness
...ac'curate, a. not exact, not accurate
...ac'tion, s. cessation from labour, idleness
...ac'tive, a. sluggish, indolent, not diligent
...ac'tively, ad. without labour, sluggishly
...activ'ity, s. idleness; sluggishness; rest
...ad'equate, a. defective, disproportionate
...ad'equately, ad. defectively, imperfectly
...adver'tence, s. inattention, carelessness
...adver'tent, a. careless, negligent
...adver'tently, ad. carelessly, negligently
...a'lienable, a. that cannot be alienated
...aliment'al, a. affording no nourishment
...amora'to, s. a lover, a fond person
...ane, a. empty, void, useless
...an'imate, a. void of life, without animation
...ani'tion, s. an emptiness of body
...ap'petence, s. want of stomach or appetite
...ap'plicable, a. not to be particularly applied
...applica'tion, s. inactivity, indolence
...ap'posite, a. unfit, improper, unsuitable
...arable, a. not capable of tillage
...artic'ulate, a. not uttered distinctly
...artic'ulately, ad. indistinctly, confusedly
...artific'ial, a. done contrarily to art
...artific'ially, ad. immethodically, badly
...atten'tion, s. disregard, carelessness
...atten'tive, a. regardless, careless
...atten'tively, ad. heedlessly, carelessly
...au'dible, a. not to be heard, void of sound
...au'gurate, v. a. to invest with solemnity
...augura'tion, s. investiture by solemn rites
...aura'tion, s. the act of covering with gold
...auspic'ious, a. unlucky, unfortunate
...be'ing, s. inherence, inseparableness
...born, a. innate; implanted by nature
...bred, a. bred or hatched within
...cales'cence, s. an increasing warmth
...canta'tion, s. an enchantment, a charm
...can'tatory, a. dealing by enchantment
...can'ton, v. a. to join to a canton
...capabil'ity, s. a disqualification, inability
...ca'pable, a. unable, unfit, disqualified
...capa'cious, a. narrow, of small content
...capac'itate, v. a. to disqualify, to disable
...capac'ity, s. inability, a want of power
...car'cerate, v. a. to imprison, to confine
...car'n. v. a. to cover with or breed flesh
...car'nadine, v. a. to die or tinge with red
...car'nate, a. clothed or embodied in flesh
...carna'tion, s. the act of assuming a body
...case, v. a. to cover, to inwrap, to inclose
...ca'vated, a. made hollow; bent in
...cau'tious, a. unwary, careless, negligent
...cau'tiously, ad. heedlessly, unwarily
...cen'diary, s. one who sets houses or towns
...on fire; a sower of sedition and strife
...cense, s. perfume offered to images
...cense, v. a. to provoke, exasperate, enrage
...cen'sory, s. a vessel for burning incense in

Incen'tive, s. an incitement or motive
Incen'tive, a. inciting, encouraging
Incep'tion, s. a commencing, a beginning
Incer'titude, s. uncertainty, doubtfulness
Inces'sant, a. continual, uninterrupted
Inces'santly, ad. without intermission
In'cest, s. unnatural and criminal conjunc-
    tion of persons too nearly related   [tion
Inces'tuous, a. guilty of unnatural cohabita-
Inch, s. a measure, the twelfth part of a foot
Inch'ipin, s. part of a deer's inside
Inch'meal, s. a piece of an inch long
Incho'ate, v. a. to begin, to commence
Inchoa'tion, s. a beginning of a work
Incide, v. a. to cut, to cut into, to divide
In'cidence, In'cident, s. an accidental cir-
    cumstance, a casualty, an event
In'cident, Inciden'tal, a. happening by
    chance, casual; fortuitous; occasional
Incin'erate, v. a. to burn to ashes
Incip'ient, a. beginning, arising
Incircumspec'tion, s. a want of caution
Incis'ed, a. cut, made by cutting
Incis'ion, Incis'ure, s. a cut, a wound made
Incis'ive, a. having the quality of cutting
Incis'or, s. a tooth so called, the cutter
Incita'tion, Incite'ment, s. an incentive
Incite, v. a. to stir up, to animate, to spur
Incivil'ity, s. rudeness, a want of courtesy
Inclem'ency, s. cruelty; harshness
Inclem'ent, a. unmerciful, harsh, rough
Incli'nable, a. favourably disposed, willing
Inclina'tion, s. tendency to a point; propen-
    sity of mind; affection; natural aptness
Incline, v. to lean, to bend; to be disposed
Inclip, v. a. to grasp, to surround, to enclose
Inclois'ter, v. a. to shut up in a cloister
Incloud, v. a. to darken, to obscure
Include, v. a. to comprise; to enclose, to shut
Inclu'sion, s. the act of including
Inclu'sive, a. comprehending, enclosing
Incoag'ulable, a. incapable of concretion
Incoexis'tence, s. the not existing together
Incog', Incog'nito, ad. in a state of con-
    cealment
Incog'itancy, s. a want of thought
Incog'itative, a. wanting power of thought
Incohe'rence, s. incongruity; want of cohe-
    sion; want of connexion; inconsequence
Incohe'rent, a. inconsistent, disagreeing
Incohe'rently, ad. inconsistently, loosely
Incombus'tible, a. not to be consumed by fire
In'come, s. revenue, rent, profit
Incommen'surable, a. not to be measured
Incommis'cible, a. not to be mixed
Incommo'de, v. a. to trouble, to embarrass
Incommo'dious, a. unsuitable, vexatious
Incommo'diously, ad. inconveniently, unfitly
Incommu'nicable, a. not communicable or
    impartible, not to be told
Incommu'table, a. not to be exchanged
Incompact', a. not joined, not cohering
Incom'parable, a. excellent above compare
Incom'parably, ad. beyond comparison
Incompas'sionate, a. void of pity, cruel
Incompatibil'ity, s. inconsistency with
Incompat'ible, a. inconsistent with another
Incom'petency, s. insufficiency, inability
Incom'petent, a. not adequate, unsuitable
Incom'petently, ad. unsuitably, unfitly
Incomple'te, a. not finished, not perfect

E

Incompli'ance, s. untractableness, refusal
Incompo'sed, a. disturbed, discomposed
Incompos'ite, a. uncompounded, simple
Incomprehensibil'ity, Incomprehen'sibleness, s. the quality of being inconceivable
Incomprehen'sible, a. not to be conceived
Incomprehen'sibly, ad. inconceivably
Incompress'ible, a. not capable of being forced into a less space, not to be pressed
Inconcea'lable, a. not to be hid or kept secret
Inconcei'vable, Inconcep'tible, a. not to be conceived or imagined, incomprehensible
Inconcei'vably, ad. beyond comprehension
Inconclu'dent, a. inferring no consequence
Inconclu'sive, a. not conclusive, not convincing, not exhibiting cogent evidence
Inconclu'siveness, s. want of rational conviction, want of proof or cogency
Inconcoc't, a. unripened, immature [ed
Inconcoc'tion, s. the state of being undigest-
Inconcur'ring, a. not agreeing or uniting
Inconcus'sible, a. not to be shaken
Incon'dite, a. irregular, unpolished, rude
Inconditi'onal, Incondi'tionate, a. unlimited, unrestrained; without condition
Inconfor'mity, s. incompliance with practice
Incon'gruence, Incongru'ity, s. inconsistency, disagreement, unsuitableness, absurdity
Incon'gruous, a. inconsistent, not fitting
Inconnex'edly, ad. without any connexion
Incon'sequence, s. inconclusiveness
Incon'sequent, a. without regular inference
Inconsid'erable, a. unworthy of notice
Inconsid'erableness, s. small importance
Inconsid'erate, a. thoughtless, careless
Inconsid'erately, ad. thoughtlessly
Inconsid'erateness, Inconsidera'tion, s. a want of thought; negligence, inattention
Inconsis'tency, s. unsteadiness, incongruity
Inconsis'tent, a. contrary, incompatible
Inconsis'tently, ad. abruptly, incongruously
Inconsis'ting, a. disagreeing with
Inconso'lable, a. not to be comforted
Incon'sonancy, s. disagreement with itself
Inconspic'uous, a. not discernible
Incon'stancy, s. unsteadiness, mutability
Incon'stant, a. not firm, variable, unsteady
Inconsu'mable, a. not to be wasted
Incontes'table, a. indisputable, certain
Incontes'tably, ad. indisputably
Incontig'uous, a. not joined together
Incon'tinence, s. unchastity, intemperance
Incon'tinent, a. unchaste, loose; immediate
Incon'tinently, ad. unchastely; directly
Incontrover'tible, a. indisputable, certain
Incontrover'tibly, ad. indisputably, certainly
Inconve'nience, s. unfitness, disadvantage
Inconve'nient, a. incommodious, unfit
Inconve'niently, ad. unfitly, unseasonably
Inconver'sable, a. incommunicative, unsociable
Inconver'tible, a. not to be changed [cial
Inconvin'cibly, ad. obstinately
Incor'poral, Incorpo'real, Incor'porate, a. immaterial, spiritual, distinct from body
Incor'porate, v. to form into one body, to mix, to associate, to unite, to embody
Incorpore'ity, s. immateriality
Incorrec't, a. not accurate, not exact
Incorrec'tly, ad. not in a correct manner
Incorrec'tness, s. inaccuracy, carelessness
Incor'rigible, a. bad beyond amendment

Incor'rigibleness, s. hopeless depravity
Incor'rigibly, ad. to a degree of depravity beyond all means of amendment
Incorrup't, a. free from corruption, honest
Incorruptibil'ity, s. incapacity of decay
Incorrup'tible, a. not admitting decay
Incorrup'tion, s. incapacity of corruption
Incorrup'tness, s. purity of conduct, integrity
Incras'sate, v. a. to thicken, to make thick
Incrassa'tion, s. the act of thickening
Incras'sative, a. that which thickens
Increa'se, v. to grow, to make more
In'crease, s. augmentation, produce, &c.
Incredibil'ity, s. quality of being incredible
Incred'ible, a. not to be believed
Incredu'lity, s. hardness of belief
Incred'ulous, a. hard of belief, refusing
Incre'mable, a. not consumable by fire
In'crement, s. an increase, a produce
Increpa'tion, s. the act of chiding, reproof
Incres'cent, Incres'sant, a. increasing
Incrim'inate, v. a. to accuse another
Incrus't, v. a. to cover with a hard crust
Incrusta'tion, s. something superinduced
In'cubate, v. n. to sit upon eggs, to hatch
Incuba'tion, s. the act of sitting upon eggs
In'cubus, s. a disorder; the night-mare
Incul'cate, v. a. to impress by admonition
Inculca'tion, s. the act of inculcating
Incul'pable, a. unblameable, upright, pure
Incul'pably, ad. unblameably
Incul't, a. uncultivated, untilled, rude
Incum'bency, s. the keeping of a benefice
Incum'bent, s. one who possesses a benefice
Incum'bent, a. imposed as a duty; necessary
of attention; lying or leaning upon
Incur', v. a. to become liable to, to deserve
Incu'rable, a. hopeless, irremediable
Incu'rably, ad. without remedy or cure
Incu'rious, a. inattentive, negligent
Incur'sion, s. an invasion, inroad, attack
Incur'vate, v. a. to bend, make crooked, bow
Incurva'tion, s. the act of bending; flexion,
the body in token of reverence
Incur'vity, s. crookedness; state of bent
In'dagate, v. a. to search diligently
Indaga'tion, s. a diligent search, an inquest
In'dagator, s. a searcher, an examiner
Indar't, v. a. to dart in, to strike in
Indebt'ed, a. in debt; obliged to or by
Inde'cency, Indeco'rum, s. any thing improper, unseemly, or unbecoming
Inde'cent, a. unfit to be known, unbecoming
Inde'cently, ad. without decency
Indecid'uous, a. not falling, not shed, not
Indeci'sion, s. want of determination
Indeci'sive, a. not determining
Indeclin'able, a. not varied by termination
Indeco'rous, a. indecent, unbecoming
Indee'd, ad. in truth, in verity, in real
Indefat'igable, a. unwearied with labour
exhausted by application or attention
Indefat'igably, ad. without weariness
Indetea'sible, a. not to be cut off; irrevocable
Indefec'tible, a. not subject to defect
Indefen'sible, a. what cannot be defended
Indefi'nable, a. not to be defined
Indefi'nite, a. unlimited, undetermined
Indef'initely, ad. in an unlimited
Indefin'itude, s. an unlimited quantity
Indelib'erate, a. unpremeditated, rash

del'ible, a. not to be erased, or annulled	Indis'solubly, ad. for ever o. ...atory
del'icacy, s. want of elegant decency	Indistin'ct, a. not plainly marked, confused
del'icate, a. wanting decency, rude	Indistinc'tly, ad. disorderly, uncertainly
demnifica'tion, s. reimbursement, security	Indistinc'tness, s. confusion, obscurity
dem'nify, v. a. to maintain unhurt	Indistur'bance, s. calmness, peace, quiet
dem'nity, s. exemption from punishment	Individ'ual, a. undivided; numerically one
demon'strable, a. not to be proved	Individ'ual, s. every single person
den't, v. to scollop; to make a compact	Individ'ually, ad. with distinct existence
den't, Indenta'tion, s. an inequality	Individual'ity, s. separate or distinct exist-
den'ture, s. a covenant or deed indented	Indivis'ible, a. what cannot be divided [ence
depen'dence, Indepen'dency, s. freedom;	Indivisibil'ity, s. impossibility of division
an exemption from reliance or control	Indo'cible, Indo'cile, a. unsusceptible of in-
depen'dent, a. free, not controllable	struction, untractable, stupid, dull
depen'dently, ad. without dependance	Indocil'ity, s. untractableness, dulness
depen'dents, s.pl. a sect of dissenters who	Indoc'trinate, v. a. to instruct, to teach
hold every congregation a complete church	In'dolence, s. laziness, inattention
deser't, s. a want of worth or merit	In'dolent, a. lazy, careless, inattentive
des'inently, ad. without cessation	In'dolently, ad. heedlessly, inattentively
destruc'tible, a. not to be destroyed	In'draught, s. an inlet, a passage inwards
deter'minable, a. not to be fixed or defined	Indren'ch, v. a. to soak, to drown
deter'minate, a. indefinite, not defined	Indu'bious, Indu'bitable, a. not doubtful
deter'mined, a. unfixed, unsettled	Indu'bitably, ad. unquestionably, certainly
devo'tion, s. a want of devotion, irreligion	Indu'bitate, a. undoubted, evident, certain
devou't, a. not devout, irreligious	Indu'ce, r. a. to persuade, bring on, influence
i'dex, s. table of contents to a book; a mark	Indu'cement, s. motive for doing a thing
or figure of a hand to direct to something	Induc't, v. a. to put into actual possession of
remarkable; the pointer out	an ecclesiastical benefice; to bring in
dexter'ity, s. awkwardness; inactivity	Induc'tion, s. taking possession, entrance
i'dicant, a. pointing out, showing	Induc'tive, a. capable to infer or produce
i'dicate, v. a. to point out, to show, to tell	Indue', v. a. to invest, to furnish with
idica'tion, s. a mark, a symptom, token	Indul'ge, v. a. to gratify, to humour, to fondle
ide'ative, a. pointing out, showing; a modi-	Indul'gence, s. favour granted, fondness, gen-
fication of a verb, expressing affirmation	tleness tenderness, kindness; forbearance
idic'tion, s. declaration, proclamation; a	Indul'gent, a. favouring, liberal, gentle
cycle of 15 years, appointed by Constantine	Indul'gently, ad. without severity or censure
dif'ference, s. negligence; impartiality	Indul't, Indul'to, s. privilege or exemption
dif'ferent, a. careless; tolerable; neutral;	In'durate, v. to make hard, to harden the mind
impartial, unbiassed; passable; regardless	Indura'tion, s. obduracy, hardness of heart
dif'ferently, ad. impartially, tolerably	Indus'trious, a. diligent, laborious; designed
i'digence, s. poverty, want, great need	Indus'triously, ad. diligently, laboriously
dig'enous, a. native to a country	In'dustry, s. diligence, assiduity
i'digent, a. poor, needy, in want; empty	Ine'briate, v. to intoxicate, to grow drunk
diges'ted, a. not formed, not concocted	Inebria'tion, s. intoxication, drunkenness
diges'tible, a. not to be digested	Ineffabil'ity, s. unspeakableness
diges'tion, s. the state of meats unconcoct-	Inef'fable, a. unspeakable, inexpressible
dig'itate, v. a. to point out, to show [ed	Inef'fably, ad. in a manner not to be expressed
digita'tion, s. the act of pointing out	Ineffec'tive, a. that which produces no effect
di'gn, a. unworthy, bringing indignity	Ineffec'tual, a. without power, weak
dig'nant, a. angry, raging, inflamed	Ineffec'tually, ad. without effect, vain
digna'tion, s. anger mixed with contempt	Ineffica'cious, a. ineffectual, weak, feeble
ig'nity, s. contumely, contemptuous insult	Inef'ficacy, s. want of effect, want of power
i'digo, s. a plant used for dyeing blue [ry	Inel'egance, s. want of elegance or beauty
direc't, a. not straight, not fair, not honest	Inel'egant, a. not becoming, despicable, mean
direc'tly, ad. obliquely, not in express terms	Inel'oquent, a. not oratorical, not persuasive
liscer'nible, a. that cannot be discerned	Inep't, a. unfit, useless, incapable, foolish
liscerp'tible, a. not to be separated	Inep'tly, ad. unfitly, triflingly, foolishly
liscree't, a. imprudent, injudicious	Inep'titude, s. unfitness, unsuitableness
liscree'tly, ad. imprudently, foolishly	Inequal'ity, s. unevenness, disproportion
liscret'ion, s. imprudence, inconsideration	Iner'rable, a. exempt from error
liscrim'inate, a. not separated, confused	Iner't, a. sluggish, motionless, dull
liscrim'inately, ad. without distinction	Iner'tly, ad. sluggishly, heavily, dully
lispen'sable, a. not to be remitted	Inesca'tion, s. the act of baiting
lispen'sably, ad. without remission	Ines'timable, a. above all price, invaluable
lispo'se, v. a. to disorder, to make unfit	Inev'ident, a. not plain, obscure
lispo'sed, part. disordered, disqualified	Inev'itable, a. unavoidable, not to be escaped
lisposit'ion, s. disorder of health; dislike	Inev'itably, ad. without possibility of escape
lis'putable, a. uncontrovertible	Inexcu'sable, a. not to be excused or palliated
lis'putably, ad. without controversy	Inexha'lable, a. that cannot evaporate
'ssol'vable, a. that cannot be dissolved	Inexhau'sted, a. unemptied, not spent
ssolubil'ity, s. firmness, stableness	Inexhau'stible, a. not to be drained
'soluble, a. binding for ever; stable, firm	Inexis'tent, a. not in being, not existent

Inex'orable, _a._ not to be moved by entreaty

Inexpe'dience, _s._ want of fitness or propriety

Inexpe'dient, _a._ improper, inconvenient

Inexpe'rience, _s._ a want of experience

Inexpe'rienced, _a._ not experienced

Inexper't, _a._ unskilful, unskilled, unhandy

Inex'piable, _a._ not to be atoned for

Inex'plicable, _a._ incapable of being explained

Inexpres'sible, _a._ not to be told; unutterable

Inexpres'sibly, _ad._ unutterably

Inexpug'nable, _a._ impregnable; not to be taken by assault; not to be subdued

Inextin'guishable, _a._ unquenchable

Inex'tricable, _a._ not to be disentangled

Ineye', _v. n._ to inoculate, to ingraft

Infallibil'ity, _s._ exemption from error

In'famous, _a._ notoriously bad, shameless

In'famously, _ad._ shamefully, scandalously

In'famy, _s._ notoriety of bad character

In'fancy, _s._ the first part of life; the beginning

In'fant, _s._ a child under seven years of age; in law, a person under twenty-one years

Infan'ta, _s._ a princess descended from the blood royal of Spain or Portugal

Infan'ticide, _s._ the murder of infants by Herod

In'fantile, In'fantine, _a._ pertaining to an infant

In'fantry, _s._ the foot soldiers of an army [fant

Infat'uate, _v. a._ to strike with folly; bewitch

Infatua'tion, _s._ the act of striking with folly

Infea'sible, _a._ impracticable; not to be done

Infec't, _v. a._ to taint, to pollute, to poison

Infec'tion, _s._ a contagion, a corrupt effluvium

Infec'tious, _a._ contagious, apt to infect

Infec'tive, _a._ having the quality of contagion

Infecun'dity, _s._ want of fertility

Infelic'ity, _s._ misery, unhappiness, calamity

Infer', _v. a._ to conclude from, to induce

In'ference, _s._ a conclusion from premises

Infer'rible, _a._ deducible from premised grounds

Infe'rior, _s._ one lower in rank or station

Infe'rior, _a._ lower in place, value, or station

Inferior'ity, _s._ lower state of dignity or value

Infer'nal, _a._ hellish, very bad, tartarean

Infer'tile, Infec'und, _a._ unfruitful, barren

Infertil'ity, _s._ unfruitfulness, barrenness

Infest', _v. a._ to annoy, plague, harass, disturb

In'fidel, _s._ an unbeliever, a miscreant, a pagan

Infidel'ity, _s._ a want of faith, treachery

In'finite, _a._ unbounded, immense, unlimited

In'finitely, _ad._ without limits, immensely

In'finiteness, Infin'itude, _s._ boundlessness

Infin'itive, _a._ in grammar, the _infinitive_ mood affirms, or intimates the intention of affirming, but does not do it absolutely

Infin'ity, _s._ immensity, endless number

Infir'm, _a._ weak of body or mind, not solid

Infir'mary, _s._ lodgings for the sick

Infir'mity, _s._ weakness, disease, failing

Infir'mness, _s._ weakness, feebleness

Infix', _v. a._ to drive in; to implant; to fasten

Inflame', _v. a._ to set on fire; to irritate

Inflam'mable, _a._ easy to be set on fire

Inflamma'tion, _s._ the state of being in a flame; an unnatural heat of the blood

Inflam'matory, _a._ having power to inflame

Infla'te, _v. a._ to swell or puff up with wind

Infla'tion, _s._ act of being swelled; flatulence

Inflec't, _v. a._ to bend, bow, vary, change

Inflec'tion, _s._ the act of bending; modulation of the voice; variation of a noun or verb

Inflexibil'ity, Inflex'ibleness, _s._ stiffness

Inflex'ible, _a._ not to be bent, immoveable

Inflex'ibly, _ad._ inexorably, invariably

Inflic't, _v. a._ to impose as a punishment

Inflic'tion, _s._ the act of using punishment

Inflic'tive, _a._ that which imposes punishment

In'fluence, _s._ an ascendant power

In'fluence, _v. a._ to have power over, to bias

In'fluent, _a._ flowing or running into

Influen'tial, _s._ exerting influence or power

Influen'za, _s._ an epidemic disease

In'flux, _s._ act of flowing into; infusion; power

Infold', _v. a._ to wrap up, to enclose

Info'liate, _v. a._ to cover with leaves

Infor'm, _v. a._ to tell, to instruct, to animate

Infor'mal, _a._ irregular, disorderly

Infor'mant, _s._ one who prefers an accusation

Informa'tion, _s._ intelligence given, charge of accusation preferred; instruction

Infor'mer, _s._ one who gives intelligence

Infor'midable, _a._ not to be dreaded

Infor'mity, _s._ want of shape

Infor'tunate, _a._ unhappy, unlucky

Infrac't, _v. a._ to break in pieces

Infrac'tion, _s._ the act of breaking; violation

Inframun'dane, _a._ below the world

Infran'gible, _a._ not to be broken

Infre'quency, _s._ rarity, uncommonness

Infre'quent, _a._ strange, uncommon, unusual

Infrig'idate, _v. a._ to chill, to make cold

Infrin'ge, _v. a._ to break a law or command

Infrin'gement, _s._ a violation, a breach [men

Infrugif'erous, _a._ not bearing fruit

Infu'mate, _v. a._ to dry with smoke

Infu'riate, _a._ enraged, raging

Infusca'tion, _s._ the act of blackening

Infu'se, _v. a._ to pour in, to instil, to inspire

Infu'sible, _a._ possible to be infused

Infu'sion, _s._ the act of pouring in or steeping

Infu'sive, _a._ having the power of infusion

Ingannua'tion, _s._ a delusion, deception

Ingath'ering, _s._ the getting in the harvest

Ingem'inate, _v. a._ to double; to repeat

Ingen'erate, Ingen'erated, _a._ unbegotten

Inge'nious, _a._ witty, acute, inventive

Inge'niously, _ad._ in an ingenious manner

In'genite, _a._ unborn, innate, native

Ingenu'ity, _s._ openness, candour; subtilty

Ingen'uous, _a._ fair, candid, generous, noble

Ingen'uously, _ad._ openly, fairly, candidly

Inges't, _v. a._ to throw into the stomach

Inglo'rious, _a._ void of honour, mean

Inglo'riously, _ad._ in an ignominious manner

In'got, _s._ a wedge of gold or silver, &c.

Ingraff', Ingraf't, _v. a._ to plant the sprig of one tree in the stock of another; to fix deep

Ingra'te, _s._ an ungrateful person

Ingra'tiate, _v. a._ to get into favour

Ingra'tiating, _s._ the act of getting favour

Ingrat'itude, _s._ return of evil for good

Ingre'dient, _s._ component part of any body

In'gress, _s._ entrance, power of entrance

Ingres'sion, _s._ the act of entering; entrance

In'guinal, _a._ relating to the groin

Ingulf', _v. a._ to cast into a gulf

Ingur'gitate, _v. a._ to swallow greedily

Ingus'table, _a._ not to be tasted, insipid

Inhab'it, _v._ to dwell, to occupy, to possess

Inhab'itable, _a._ fit to be inhabited

Inhab'itant, _s._ one who dwells in a place

Inha'le,   draw in with the air

rmo'nious, a. unmusical, not sweet
rence, s. quality of that which adheres
rent, a. existing in something else; in-
s, inborn; cleaving to
it, v. a. to possess by inheritance
itable, a. obtained by succession
itance, s. an hereditary possession
itor, s. one who receives by succession
ltress, Inher'itrix, s. an heiress
r'se, v. a. to inclose in a monument
it, v. a. to prohibit, to hinder, to repress
bit'ion, s. a prohibition, an embargo
'ld, v. a. to contain in itself
s'pitable, a. unkind to strangers
spital'ity, s. a want of hospitality
n'man, a. barbarous, savage, cruel
man'ity, s. cruelty, barbarity
manly, ad. cruelly, barbarously
u'mate, Inhu'me, v. a. to bury, to inter
uma'tion, s. the act of burying
ee't, v. n. to throw in or up; to dart in
jec'tion, s. the act of casting in
n'ical, a. unfriendly; adverse, unkind
m'itable, a. not to be copied
n'itably, ad. very excellently
u'itous, a. unjust, wicked, sinful
iq'uity, s. injustice, wickedness, crime
it'ial, a. placed at the beginning
it'iate, v. a. to admit, to instruct
itia'tion, s. the act of admitting a person
into any order or society
ju'dicable, a. not cognizable by a judge
judic'ial, a. not according to law
judi'cious, a. wanting judgment
junc'tion, s. command, precept, order
n'jure, v. a. to wrong, to hurt unjustly
ju'rious, a. unjust, hurtful, destructive
n'jury, s. mischief, outrage, annoyance
jus'tice, s. unfair dealing, iniquity
nk, s. a black liquid for writing, &c.
n'kle, s. a kind of narrow fillet, a tape
n'kling, s. a hint, a whisper, an intimation
n'ky, a. black as ink, resembling ink
n'land, a. remote from the sea, interior
nlaw, v. a. to clear of outlawry
nlay', v. a. to variegate by matter inlaid
In'let, s. an entrance, a passage into
In'ly, ad. internally, secretly, in the heart
In'mate, s. one living in the same house
In'most, In'nermost, a. deepest within
Inn, s. a house of entertainment for travel-
lers; a house where students are boarded
Inna'te, a. inborn, ingenerate, natural
Innav'igable, a. not to be passed by sailing
In'ner, a. interior, not outward
Inn'holder, Inn'keeper, s. one who keeps a
house of entertainment for travellers
In'nocence, s. purity, harmlessness, simpli-
Inno'cent, a. pure, harmless, unhurtful [city
In'nocently, ad. without guilt, harmlessly
Innoc'uous, a. harmless in effects
Innoc'uously, ad. without mischievous ef-
In'novate, v. a. to introduce novelties [fects
Innova'tion, s. the introduction of novelty
In'novator, s. an introducer of novelties
Innox'ious, a. not hurtful, harmless
Innuen'do, s. an oblique hint
Innu'merable, a. not to be numbered
Inobser'vable, a. unworthy of observation
Inoc'ulate, v. a. to propagate by insertion

Inocula'tion, s. a grafting in the bud; prac-
tice of transplanting the small-pox, by in-
fusing matter from ripened pustules into
the veins of the uninfected
Ino'dorous, a. not affecting the nose
Inoffen'sive, a. harmless, hurtless, innocent
Inoffen'sively, ad. innocently, harmlessly
Inoffen'siveness, s. harmlessness
Inop'inate, a. unexpected, sudden
Inopportu'ne, a. unseasonable, inconvenient
Inor'dinate, a. irregular, disorderly
Inor'dinately, ad. irregularly; not rightly
Inor'dinateness, s. irregularity; intempe-
Inorgan'ical, a. without proper organs [rance
Inos'culate, v. n. to unite by contact
Inoscula'tion, s. an union; a kiss
In'quest, s. a judicial inquiry or examination
Inqui'etude, s. uneasiness, disquiet
In'quinate, v. a. to pollute, corrupt, defile
Inquina'tion, s. a pollution, a corruption
Inqui're, v. a. to ask about, to seek out
Inqui'ry, s. interrogation, search
Inquisit'ion, s. a judicial inquiry; a court
established for the detection of heresy
Inquis'itive, a. prying, curious, &c.
Inquis'itor, s. a judge of the inquisition
In'road, s. an incursion, a sudden invasion
Insalu'brious, a. unhealthy, noxious to health
Insan'able, a. incurable, irremediable
Insa'ne, a. mad, making mad
Insa'neness, Insan'ity, s. madness
Insa'tiable, Insa'tiate, a. not to be satisfied
Insa'tiableness, s. greediness, not to be satis-
Insatisfac'tion, s. an unsatisfied state [fied
Insat'urable, a. that cannot be glutted
Inscri'be, v. a. to write upon; to dedicate
Inscrip'tion, s. a title, name, or character,
written or engraved upon any thing
Inscru'table, a. unsearchable, hidden
Insculp', v. a. to engrave, to cut on
Insculp'ture, s. any thing engraved
Insea'm, a. to mark by a seam or scar
In'sect, s. a small creeping or flying animal
Insec'tile, a. having the nature of insects
Insec'tion, s. the act of cutting into
Insecu're, a. not secure, not safe
Insecu'rity, s. want of safety, hazard, danger
Insen'sate, a. stupid, wanting thought
Insensibil'ity, s. stupidity, torpor
Insen'sible, a. imperceptible; slowly, gradual
Inseparabil'ity, Insep'arableness, s. the qua-
lity of being such as cannot be severed
Insep'arable, a. not to be disjointed
Insep'arably, ad. with indissoluble union
Insert', v. a. to place among other things
Inser'tion, s. the act of inserting
Inser'vient, a. conducive to some end
Inship', v. a. to stow or shut up in a ship
Inshri'ne, v. to inclose in a shrine
Insic'cation, s. the act of drying in
In'side, s. internal part; part within
Insid'ious, a. treacherous, diligent to entrap
Insid'iously, ad. treacherously, slily
Insid'iousness, s. craftiness, deceit
In'sight, s. an inspection; a deep view
Insignif'icance, s. a want of meaning
Insignif'icant, a. unimportant, trifling
Insignif'icantly, ad. without importance
Insince're, a. not hearty, unfaithful
Insincer'ity, s. dissimulation, want of truth
Instain'ew, v. a. to strengthen, to confirm
K 3

Insin'uant, *a.* able to gain favour
Insin'uate, *v.* to hint artfully, to wheedle
Insinua'tion, *s.* the act of insinuating
Insip'id, *a.* without taste; flat, dull
Insipid'ity, *s.* want of taste or spirit
Insip'ience, *s.* stillness; want of sense
Insis't, *v. n.* to persist in, to urge
Insis'tent, *a.* standing or resting upon
Insi'tiency, *s.* an exemption from thirst
Insi'tion, *s.* the act of grafting, a graft
Insi'tive, *a.* ingrafted, not natural
Insna're, *v. a.* to entrap, to inveigle
Insobri'ety, *s.* drunkenness, want of sobriety
Inso'ciable, *a.* averse from conversation
Insola'tion, *s.* exposition to the sun
In'solence, *s.* haughtiness, pride
In'solent, *a.* haughty, overbearing, proud
In'solently, *ad.* haughtily, rudely
Insol'vable, *a.* not to be solved or paid
Insol'uble, *a.* not to be dissolved or cleared
Insol'vency, *s.* an inability to pay debts
Insol'vent, *a.* not able to pay debts
Insomuch', *ad.* so that, to such a degree
Inspec't, *v. a.* to examine minutely
Inspec'tion, *s.* a close examination
Inspec'tor, *s.* a superintendant
Insper'sion, *s.* a sprinkling upon
Insphe're, *v. a.* to place in an orb
Inspira'tion, *s.* a drawing of the breath; an infusion of supernatural ideas
Inspi're, *v.* to breathe or infuse into
Inspir'it, *v. a.* to animate, to encourage
Inspis'sate, *v. a.* to thicken, to make thick
Inspissa'tion, *s.* the act of thickening liquids
Instabil'ity, *s.* inconstancy, mutability
Insta'ble, *a.* inconstant, changing
Instal'l, *v. a.* to put into possession, to invest
Installa'tion, *s.* a putting into possession
Instal'ment, *s.* the act of installing
In'stance, *s.* importunity, earnestness; motive; process of suit; example
In'stant, *s.* the present or current month
In'stant, *a.* urgent, immediate, quick
Instanta'neous, *a.* done in an instant
In'stantly, Instanta'neously, *ad.* immediately; in an indivisible point of time
Insta'te, *v. a.* to place in a certain rank
Instaura'tion, *s.* a restoration, a renewal
Instead', *ad.* in place of, equal to
Instee'p, *v. a.* to soak, to lay in water
In'step, *s.* the upper part of the foot
In'stigate, *v. a.* to tempt or incite to ill
Instiga'tion, *s.* an encouragement to a crime
Instiga'tor, *s.* he who incites to ill
Instil', *v. a.* to infuse by drops; to insinuate
Instilla'tion, *s.* the act of pouring in by drops; the act of infusing into the mind
Instimula'tion, *s.* an urging forward
Instin'ct, *a.* moved, animated
In'stinct, *s.* a natural desire or aversion
Instin'ctive, *a.* acting without the direction of choice or reason
Instin'ctively, *ad.* by the call of nature
In'stitute, *v. a.* to fix, to establish, to appoint
In'stitute, *s.* an established law, a maxim
Institu'tion, *s.* positive establishment, law
In'stitutor, *s.* an establisher, an instructor
Instruc't, *v. a.* to teach, to direct, to train up
In'structer, *s.* a teacher, an institutor
Instruc'tion, *s.* the act of teaching; information; mandate, precept

Instruc'tive, *a.* conveying knowledge
In'strument, *s.* a tool; a deed or contract
Instrument'al, *a.* conducive to some end
Insuf'ferable, *a.* insupportable, intolerable
Insuffic'iency, *s.* inadequateness, inability
Insuffic'iently, *ad.* without skill, unfitly
Insuffla'tion, *s.* the act of breathing upon
In'sular, *a.* belonging to an island
In'sulated, *a.* standing by itself
In'sult, *s.* act of insolence or contempt
Insul't, *v. a.* to treat with insolence
Insuperabil'ity, *s.* quality of being invincible
Insu'perable, *a.* insurmountable, invincible
Insuppor'table, *a.* not to be suffered
Insuppor'tableness, *s.* insufferableness
Insuppor'tably, *ad.* beyond endurance
Insurmount'able, *a.* unconquerable
Insurmount'ably, *ad.* unconquerably
Insurrec'tion, *s.* a rebellion, a sedition
Intac'tible, *a.* not perceptible to the touch
Intag'lio, *s.* what has figures engraven on it
Inta'stable, *a.* not to be tasted, insipid
In'teger, *s.* the whole of any thing
In'tegral, *a.* whole, not fractional, complete
In'tegrant, *a.* contributing to make a whole
Integ'rity, *s.* honesty, purity of mind
In'tegument, *s.* what covers another
In'tellect, *s.* perception, understanding
Intellec'tive, *a.* capable of understanding
Intellec'tual, *a.* relating to the understanding
Intel'ligence, *s.* notice; spirit, skill
Intel'ligent, *a.* knowing, instructed, skilful
Intel'ligible, *a.* easily conceived or understood
Intel'ligibly, *ad.* clearly, plainly, distinctly
Intem'perament, *s.* bad constitution
Intem'perance, *s.* excess, irregularity
Intem'perate, *a.* immoderate, ungovernable
Intem'perature, *s.* a disorder in the air, or of the body; excess of some quality
Inten'able, *a.* that which cannot be held
Inten'd, *v. a.* to mean, to design, to regard
Inten'dant, *s.* an officer who superintends
Inten'erate, *v. a.* to make tender, to soften
Intenera'tion, *s.* act of making tender
Inten'se, *a.* vehement, ardent, attentive
Inten'sely, *ad.* to a great or extreme degree
Inten'seness, *s.* eagerness, closeness
Inten'sion, *s.* the act of stretching or forcing
Inten'sive, *a.* intent, full of care
Inten't, *a.* fixed with close application
Inten't, *s.* a design, a purpose, drift, view
Inten'tion, *s.* a design, a purpose
Inten'tional, *a.* designed, done by design
Inten'tive, *a.* diligently applied, attentive
Inten'tively, Intent'ly, *ad.* closely
Intent'ness, *s.* close or anxious application
Inter', *v. a.* to bury, to put under ground
Interca'lary, *a.* inserted out of the common order to preserve the equation of time, as the 29th of February in a leap-year is an intercalary day
Intercala'tion, *s.* insertion of a day
Interce'de, *v. n.* to mediate, to pass between
Interce'dent, *a.* mediating, going between
Intercep't, *v. a.* to stop, to seize, to obstruct
Interces'sion, *s.* mediation, interposition
Interces'sor, *s.* a mediator, an agent
Intercha'in, *v. a.* to chain, to link together
Intercha'nge, *v. a.* to exchange
In'terchange, *s.* an exchange, a bargain

Interchangeable, *a.* given and taken mutual-
Intercip'ient, *a.* that which intercepts [ly
Interci'sion, *s.* interruption
Interclu'de, *v. a.* to shut out, to intercept
Intercolumnia'tion, *s.* the space or distance
between the pillars
Intercos'tal, *a.* placed between the ribs
In'tercourse, *s.* communication, exchange
In'tercur, *v. n.* to happen; to intervene
Intercur'rence, *s.* a passage between
Intercur'rent, *a.* running between
Interdic't, *v. a.* to prohibit, to forbid
Interdic'tion, *s.* a prohibition, a curse
Interdic'tory, *a.* belonging to an interdiction
In'terest, *v.* to concern, affect, influence
In'terest, *s.* a concern, influence; usu y
Interfe're, *v. n.* to interpose, to intermeddle
Interfe'rence, *s.* mediation, interposition
Inter'fluent, *a.* flowing between
Interful'gent, *a.* shining between
Interfu'sed, *a.* poured forth, in, or among
Interja'cent, *a.* intervening, lying between
Interjec'tion, *s.* a sudden exclamation
In'terim, *s.* mean time or while
Interjoi'n, *v. a.* to join together, intermarry
Inte'rior, *a.* inner, not outward
Interknow'ledge, *s.* a mutual knowledge
Interla'ce, *v. a.* to intermix, to put together
Interlap'se, *s.* the time between two events
Interlar'd, *v.a.* to insert between; to diversify
by mixture; to mix meat with bacon
Interlea've, *v. a.* to insert blank leaves
Interli'ne, *v. a.* to write between the lines
Interlinea'tion, *s.* a correction made by wri-
ting between the lines
Interlin'k, *v. a.* to connect chains together
Interlocu'tion, *s.* interchanging of speech
Interlocu'tor, *s.* one who talks with another
Interloc'utory, *a.* consisting of a dialogue
Interlo'pe, *v. n.* to intrude in or between
Interlo'per, *s.* one who runs into a business
to which he has no right; an intruder
Interlu'cent, *a.* shining between
In'terlude, *s.* a short prelude or farce
Interlu'nar, *a.* between old moon and new
Intermar'riage, *s.* a marriage in two families,
where each takes one, and gives another
Intermed'dle, *v. n.* to interpose officiously
Interme'diacy, *s.* interposition
Interme'dial, Interme'diate, *a.* intervening,
lying between, intervenient
Interme'dium, *s.* a distance between
Inter'ment, *s.* sepulchre, burial
Intermigra'tion, *s.* an exchange of place
Inter'minable, Inter'minate, *a.* unbounded
Intermin'gle, *v.a.* to mingle, to mix together
Intermis'sion, *s.* a cessation for a time
Intermis'sive, Intermit'tent, *a.* not conti-
nual; leaving off for a while
Intermit', *v.* to grow mild between fits
Intermix', *v.* to mingle, to join together
Intermix'ture, *s.* a mixture of ingredients
Intermun'dane, *a.* subsisting between worlds
or between orb and orb
Intermu'ral, *a.* lying between walls
Intermu'tual, *a.* mutual, interchanged
Inter'nal, *a.* inward, not external, intrinsic
Inter'nally, *ad.* inwardly, mentally
Interne'cine, *a.* endeavouring mutual de-
struction
Interne'cion, *s.* massacre, slaughter.

Interno'de, *s.* space between two knots of
joints
Internun'cio, *s.* a messenger passing and re-
passing between two parties
Interpella'tion, *s.* a summons, a call
Inter'polate, *v.a.* to insert words improperly
Interpola'tion, *s.* something foisted in, or
added to the original matter
Interpola'tor, *s.* one who falsifies a copy by
foisting in counterfeit passages
Interpo'sal, Interposit'ion, *s.* intervention,
agency between parties, mediation
Interpo'se, *v.* to mediate, to intervene
Inter'pret, *v. a.* to explain, to translate
Interpreta'tion, *s.* an explanation
Inter'preter, *s.* an expositor, a translator
Interreg'num, Interre'ign, *s.* the time in which
a throne is vacant between the death of
one prince and the accession of another
Interroga'tion, *s.* a question, an inquiry; a
point marked thus [?] denoting a question
Inter'rogate, *v.* to examine by questions
Interrog'ative, *s.* a pronoun used in asking
questions, as who? what? which?
Interrog'atory, *s.* a question, an inquiry
Interrup't, *v. a.* to hinder; divide; separate
Interrup'tion, *s.* hinderance, intervention
Interse'cant, *a.* dividing into parts
Intersec't, *v. n.* to cut, to cross each other
Intersec'tion, *s.* a point where lines cross
Intersem'inate, *v. a.* to sow between
Interser't, *v. a.* to put in between
Interser'tion, *s.* an insertion, a thing inserted
Intersper'se, *v. a.* to scatter here and there
Interstel'lar, *a.* placed between the stars
Inter'stice, *s.* a space between things
Intertex'ture, *s.* a weaving between
Intertwi'ne, *v. a.* to unite by twisting
In'terval, *s.* interstice, vacuity; time elapsing
between two assignable points; remission
of a distemper, or delirium
Interve'ne, *v.n.* to come between persons, &c.
Interve'nient, *a.* passing between, interven
Interven'tion, *s.* interposition, agency [ing
Interver't, *v. a.* to turn another way
In'terview, *s.* a sight of one another
Intervol've, *v. a.* to involve one in another
Interwea've, *v. a.* to mix one with another
Intes'table, *a.* disqualified to make a will
Intes'tate, *a.* dying without a will
Intes'tinal, *a.* belonging to the bowels
Intes'tine, *a.* internal, inward; domestic
Intes'tines, *s.* the bowels, the entrails
Inthral', *v. a.* to enslave, to shackle
Inthral'ment, *s.* servitude, slavery, difficulty
In'timacy, *s.* close familiarity
In'timate, *v. a.* to hint, to suggest
In'timate, *a.* inmost, inward, familiar
In'timate, *s.* a familiar friend, a confidant
In'timately, *ad.* closely, familiarly, nearly
Intima'tion, *s.* a hint; an obscure or indirect
declaration or direction
Intim'idate, *v. a.* to frighten, or dastardise
In'to, *prep.* noting entrance
Intol'erable, *a.* insufferable, very bad
Intol'erably, *ad.* to a degree beyond suffer-
Intol'erant, *a.* not able to endure [ance
Intona'tion, *s.* the act of thundering
Intor't, *v. a.* to twist, wreath, wring
Intox'icate, *v.a.* to make drunk, to inebriate
Intoxica'tion, *s.* inebriation, ebriety

Intrac'table, _a._ unmanageable, unruly
Intrac'tably, _ad._ ungovernably, stubbornly
Intran'sitive, _a._ not passing into another
Intransmu'table, _a._ impossible to be changed
Intreas'ure, _v. a._ to lay up; hoard, save
Intren'ch, _v. n._ to fortify with a trench, to encroach, to break with hollows
Inc'en'chant, _a._ not to be divided or hurt
Intren'chment, _s._ a fortification with a trench, to defend against an attack
Intrep'id, _a._ fearless, resolute, brave
Intrepid'ity, _s._ fearlessness, courage, boldness
Intrep'idly, _ad._ boldly, daringly, fearlessly
In'tricacy, _s._ perplexity, difficulty, involution
In'tricate, _a._ intangled, perplexed, obscure
Intri'gue, _s._ a plot, an amour; intricacy
Intri'gue, _v. n._ to carry on private designs
Intri'guingly, _ad._ with secret plotting
Intrin'sic, Intrin'sical, _a._ inward, natural, not accidental; closely familiar; intimate
Introdu'ce, _v. a._ to bring or usher in
Introduc'tion, _s._ a bringing in; a preface
Introduc'tive, Introduc'tory, _a._ previous, serving as conveyance to something else
Introgres'sion, _s._ entrance; act of entering
Intromis'sion, _s._ the act of sending in
Intromit', _v. a._ to send in; to allow to enter
Introspec'tion, _s._ a view of the inside
Introve'nient, _a._ entering, coming in
Intru'de, _v. n._ to intermeddle, to force in uncalled, to encroach
Intru'der, _s._ a person who intrudes
Intru'sion, _s._ the act of intruding
Intru'sive, _a._ intruding upon, encroaching
Intrust', _v. a._ to put in trust with
Intui'tion, _s._ immediate perception or sight
Intu'itive, _a._ seen by the mind immediately, without the aid of reasoning
Intu'itively, _ad._ without deduction of reason, by immediate perception
Intumes'cence, _s._ a swelling, a tumour
Inturges'cence, _s._ act or state of swelling
Intwi'ne, _v. a._ to twist or wreathe together
Inva'de, _v. a._ to make a hostile entrance
Inva'der, _s._ an assailant, intruder, encroacher
Invales'cence, _s._ health; strength; force
Inval'id, _a._ weak; of no force or weight
Invali'd, _s._ a soldier or other person disabled by sickness or wounds
Inval'idate, _v. a._ to weaken; to make void; to deprive of force or efficacy
Invalid'ity, _s._ weakness, want of power
Invalu'able, _a._ precious above estimation
Inva'riable, _a._ unchangeable, constant
Inva'riableness, _s._ unchangeableness, constancy
Inva'riably, _ad._ constantly, stedfastly
Inva'sion, _s._ a hostile entrance, an attack
Inva'sive, _a._ entering in a hostile manner
Invec'tive, _s._ railing, sharp expressions
Invec'tively, _ad._ satirically, abusively
Invel'gh, _v. a._ to rail at, declaim against
Invel'gle, _v. a._ to allure, to entice
Invel'gler, _s._ a deceiver, an allurer
Inven't, _v. d._ to discover, to forge, to feign
Inven'tion, _s._ a fiction, discovery, forgery
Inven'tive, _a._ apt to invent, ingenious
Inven'tor, _s._ a contriver, a finder out
In'ventory, _s._ a catalogue of moveables
Inver'se, _a._ inverted, opposed to _direct_
Inver'sely, _ad._ in an inverted order
Inver'sion, _s._ change of order, time, place, &c.

Inver't, _v. a._ to turn upside down; place the last first; turn into another channel
Inver'tedly, _ad._ in contrary or reversed order
Inves't, _v. a._ to confer; to clothe; to enclose
Inves'tigable, _a._ what may be searched out
Inves'tigate, _v. a._ to trace or search out
Investiga'tion, _s._ an examination
Inves'titure, _s._ the act of giving possession
Inves'tment, _s._ clothes, dress, habit, garment
Inver'eracy, _s._ long continuance of any thing bad, as diseases, &c.; obstinacy of mind
Invet'erate, _a._ long established, obstinate
Invet'erateness, _s._ continuance, obstinacy
Invetera'tion, _s._ the act of hardening or confirming by long continuance
Invid'ious, _a._ envious; malignant
Invid'iousness, _s._ quality of provoking envy
Invid'iously, _ad._ malignantly, enviously
Invig'orate, _v. a._ to strengthen, to animate
Invigora'tion, _s._ the act of invigorating
Invin'cible, _a._ unconquerable, insuperable
Invin'cibleness, _s._ an invincible state of quality
Invin'cibly, _ad._ insuperably, unconquerably
Invi'olable, _a._ not to be profaned or broken
Invi'olate, _a._ uninjured, unbroken, unprofaned [glutinous matter
Invis'cate, _v. a._ to slime; to entangle with
Invisibil'ity, _s._ imperceptibleness to the sight
Invis'ible, _a._ not to be seen, imperceptible
Invis'ibly, _ad._ imperceptibly to sight
Invita'tion, _s._ the act of inviting, a bidding
Invi'te, _v._ to bid, call, persuade, entice
Invi'ter, _s._ one who invites or allures others
Invi'tingly, _ad._ in an alluring manner
Inum'brate, _v. a._ to cover with shade
Innuc'tion, _s._ the act of anointing
Inun'date, _v._ to overflow a place with water
Inunda'tion, _s._ an overflow of water
In'vocate, _v. a._ to implore, to call upon
Invoca'tion, _s._ a calling upon in prayer
In'voice, _s._ a catalogue of a ship's freight
Invo'ke, _v. a._ to call upon, to pray to
Invol've, _v. a._ to inwrap, comprise, entangle
Invol'untarily, _ad._ not by choice
Invol'untary, _a._ not done willingly
Involu'tion, _s._ a complication, rolling up
Inurban'ity, _s._ incivility, rudeness
Inu're, _v. a._ to habituate, to accustom
Inu'rement, _s._ custom, use, frequency
Inur'n, _v. a._ to intomb, to bury
Inus'tion, _s._ the act of marking by fire
Inu'tile, _a._ useless, unprofitable
Inutil'ity, _s._ unprofitableness, uselessness
Invul'nerable, _a._ that cannot be wounded
In'ward, In'wardly, _ad._ within; privately
In'ward, _a._ placed within; reflecting
In'wardness, _s._ intimacy, familiarity
Inwe'ave, _v. a._ to mix in weaving, to entwine
Inwrap', _v. a._ to involve, perplex, puzzle
Inwrea'the, _v. a._ to surround with a wreath
Inwrou'ght, _a._ adorned with work
Job, _s._ a piece of chance work; petty work
Job, _v._ to buy and sell as a broker; to strike suddenly with a sharp instrument
Job'ber, _s._ one who does chance work
Job'bernowl, _s._ a loggerhead, a blockhead
Jobe, _v. a._ to rebuke, to reprimand
Jock'ey, _s._ one who rides or deals in horses
Jock'ey, _v. a._ to jostle, to cheat, to trick
Joco'se, Joc'ular, _a._ merry, waggish

Joco'seness, Jocos'ity, Jocular'ity, s. merriment; disposition to jest
Joco'sely, ad. waggishly, in jest, in game
Joc'und, a. merry, gay, lively, airy
Joc'undly, ad. merrily, sportfully, gaily
Jog, Jog'gle, v. to shake, to push
Jog'ger, s. one who moves heavily and dully
Join, v. to unite together, combine, close
Join'er, s. one who makes wooden utensils
Joint, s. the articulation where bones meet
Joint, v. a. to divide a joint; to join
Joint, a. shared among many, combined
Joint'ed, a. full of joints, knots, &c.
Joint'er, s. a kind of long plane
Joint'ly, ad. together, not separately
Joint'ress, s. one who has a jointure
Joint'u·e, s. an income settled on a wife, to be enjoyed after her husband's decease, in consideration of her dowry
Joist, s. the secondary beam of a floor
Joke, v. n. to jest, to be merry—s. a jest
Jo'ker, s. a jester, a merry fellow
Jole. s. the face or cheek; the head of a fish
Jol'lily, ad. in a disposition to noisy mirth
Jol'lity, s. merriment, festivity, gaiety
Jol'ly, a. gay, airy, brisk, merry, cheerful; plump, like one in high health
Jolt, v. to shake, to jostle as a carriage does
Jol'thead, s. a great head, a blockhead, a dolt
Ion'ic, a. an order in architecture
Jonquill'e, s. a species of daffodil
Jor'den, s. a pot, a chamber pot
Jos'tle, v. a. to justle; to rush against
Jot, Io'ta, s. a point, a tittle
Jo'vial, a. jolly, merry, airy, gay
Jo'vially, ad. merrily, gaily
Jo'vialness, Jo'vialty, s. gaiety, merriment
Jour'nal, s. a diary, a paper published daily
Jour'nalist, s. a writer of journals
Jour'ney, s. travel by land or by sea
Jour'neyman, s. a hired workman
Joust, s. a tilt, a tournament; mock fight
Joy, s. gaiety, mirth, happiness, festivity
Joy, v. to rejoice, gladden, exhilarate
Joy'ful, a. full of joy, glad, exulting
Joy'fully, ad. merrily, gladly, with joy
Joy'fulness, s. joy, gladness, exultation
Joy'less, a. void of joy; giving no pleasure
Joy'ous, a. glad, merry, giving joy
Ipecacuan'ha, s. an emetic Indian plant
Iras'cible, a. apt to be easily provoked
Iras'cibleness, s. aptness to be angry
Ire, s. anger, rage, passionate hatred
I'reful, a. very angry, raging, furious
I'ris, s. the rainbow; the circle round the pupil of the eye; the fleur-de-luce
Irk'some, a. tedious, wearisome, troublesome
I'ron, s. a common useful metal
I'ron, a. made of iron, harsh; hard
I'ron, v. a. to smooth with a hot iron
Iron'ical, a. expressing one thing and meaning another; speaking by contraries
Iron'ically, ad. by the use of irony
I'ronmonger, s. a dealer in iron
I'ronmould, s. a yellow stain in linen
I'rony, s. mode of speech in which the meaning is contrary to the words
Irra'diance, Irra'diancy, s. emission of rays or beams of light upon any subject
Irra'diate, v. a. to brighten, to illuminate
  s. an enlightening, &c.

Irra'tional, a. contrary to reason, absurd
Irrationali'ty, s. want of reason
Irra'tionally, ad. without reason, absurdly
Irreclaim'able, a. not to be reclaimed
Irreconci'lable, a. not to be reconciled
Irrecov'erable, a. not to be regained
Irrecov'erably, ad. beyond recovery
Irredu'cible, a. that which cannot be reduced
Irrefragibil'ity, s. strength of argument not to be refuted or denied
Irref'ragable, a. not to be confuted
Irref'ragably, ad. above confutation
Irrefu'table, a. that which cannot be refuted
Irreg'ular, a. immethodical, disorderly
Irregular'ity, s. neglect of method and order
Irreg'ularly, ad. without observation of method
Irreg'ulate, v. a. to make irregular
Irrel'ative, a. single, unconnected
Irrel'evant, a. inapplicable, not to the purpose
Irrelig'ion, s. contempt of religion, impiety
Irrelig'ious, a. ungodly; despising religion
Irrelig'iously, ad. impiously, with impiety
Irreme'able, a. admitting no return
Irreme'diable, a. admitting no cure, incurable
Irremis'sible, a. not to be pardoned
Irremo'veable, a. not to be changed
Irrep'arable, a. not to be repaired or recovered
Irrep'arably, ad. without recovery or amends
Irreplev'iable, a. not to be redeemed
Irreprehen'sible, a. exempt from blame
Irrepresent'able, a. not to be represented
Irreproach'able, a. free from reproach
Irrepro'vable, a. not to be blamed
Irresis'tible, a. that which cannot be resisted
Irresistibil'ity, s. power above opposition
Irresis'tibly, ad. in manner not to be opposed
Irres'oluble, a. not to be broken, or dissolved
Irres'olute, a. not determined, fickle
Irres'olutely, ad. without firmness of mind
Irresolu'tion, s. want of firmness of mind
Irrecov'erable, a. irrecoverable, irreparable
Irrev'erence, s. want of veneration
Irrev'erent, a. not paying due respect
Irrev'erently, ad. without due veneration
Irrever'sible, a. not to be changed or recalled
Irrev'ocable, a. not to be recalled, &c.
Irrev'ocably, ad. without recal
Ir'rigate, v. a. to moisten, to water, to wet
Irrig'uous, a. watery, dewy, moist, wet
Irri'sion, s. the act of laughing at another
Ir'ritable, a. easily provoked, fretful
Ir'ritate, v. a. to provoke, fret, agitate
Irrita'tion, s. provocation, stimulation
Irrup'tion, s. an inroad, entrance by force
Is, v. the third person singular of to be
Is'chury, s. stoppage of urine
I'singlass, s. a lightish, firm glue, prepared from the intestines of certain fish
I'sland, Isle, s. land surrounded by water
I'slander, s. an inhabitant of an island
Isoch'ronal, a. being of equal duration
I'solated, a. separated, like an island
Isos'celes, s. a triangle with two equal sides
Is'sue, s. an event; termination; offspring; a fontanel, a vent made in a muscle for the discharge of some humours
Is'sue, v. to send out, come out, arise
Is'sueless, a. having no offspring
Isth'mus, s. a neck or jut of land
Itch, s. a disease; a teasing desire
I'tem, s. a hint, innuendo, a new article

It'erant, *a.* repeating
It'era e, *v. a.* to repeat, to do over again
Itera'tion, *s.* a recital over again, repetition
Itin'erant, *a.* wandering, unsettled
Itin'erary, *s.* a diary or book of travels
Itself', *pron.* it and *self*
Ju'bilant, *a.* uttering songs of triumph
Jubila'tion, *s.* the act of declaring triumph
Ju'bilee, *s.* a public festivity, a season of joy
Jucun'dity, *s.* pleasantness, agreeableness
Juda'ical, *a.* of or relating to the Jews, Jewish
Ju'daism, *s.* the religion of the Jews
Ju'daize, *v. n.* to conform to Judaism
Judge, *s.* an officer who presides in a court
    of judicature ; one who has skill to decide
    upon the merit of any thing
Judge, *v. a.* to pass sentence, decide, discern
Judg'ment, *s.* an opinion, sentence, &c.
Ju'dicatory, *s.* a court of justice, &c.
Ju'dicature, *s.* a power to distribute justice
Judic'ial, Judic'iary, *a.* done in due form of
    justice, &c. passing judgment
Judic'ially, *ad.* in the forms of legal justice ;
    in a judiciary manner
Judic'ious, *a.* prudent, wise, skilful
Judic'iously, *ad.* skilfully, wisely
Jug, *s.* a large drinking vessel
Jug'gle, *v. n.* to play tricks by slight of hand
Jug'gle, *s.* a trick, imposture, deception
Jug'gler, *s.* a cheat, trickish fellow
Ju'gular, *a.* belonging to the throat
Ju'gulate, *v. a.* to cut the throat
Juice, *s.* sap in vegetables ; fluid in animals
Jui'celess, *a.* dry, without moisture
Jui'ciness, *s.* plenty of juice, succulence
Jui'cy, *a.* moist, full of juice, succulent
Juke, *v. n.* to perch upon any thing, as birds
Ju'lep, *s.* a medicine made of sweetened water
July', *s.* the seventh month of the year
Ju'mart, *s.* the mixture of a bull and a mare
Jum'ble, *v. a.* to mix confusedly together
Jum'ble, *s.* a violent and confused mixture
Ju'ment, *s.* a beast of burden
Jump, *v. n.* to leap, skip, joit, leap suddenly
Jump, *s.* a leap, a skip, a lucky chance
Jun'cate, *s.* a cheesecake ; an entertainment

Jun'cous, *a.* full of bulrushes
Junc'tion, *s.* an union ; a coalition
June, *s.* the sixth month from January
Ju'nior, *a.* one younger than another
Ju'niper, *s.* a plant which produces a berry
Junk, *s.* a small Chinese ship ; an old cable
Jun'ket, *s.* a sweetmeat—*v. n.* to feast secretly
Jun'to, *s.* a cabal, a faction
I'vory, *s.* the tooth of an elephant
Juppon', *s.* a short close coat
Ju'rat, *s.* a magistrate in some corporatio
Ju'ratory, *a.* giving an oath
Jurid'ical, *a.* used in courts of justice
Jurid'ically, *ad.* with legal authority or form
Juriscon'sult, *s.* one who gives law opinions
Jurisdic'tion, *s.* legal authority ; a district
Jurispru'dence, *s.* the science of law
Ju'rist, *s.* a professor of civil law, a civilian
Ju'ror, Ju'ryman, *s.* one serving on a jury
Ju'ry, *s.* a certain number of persons sworn
    to declare the truth upon such evidence as
    shall be given before them
Ju'rymast, *s.* a sea term for what is set up
    instead of a mast lost in storm or fight
Just, *a.* upright, honest, regular, virtuous
Just, *s.* a mock fight on horseback, a tilt
Just, *ad.* exactly, accurately, nearly
Jus'tice, *s.* equity, right law ; an officer
Jus'ticeship, *s.* rank or office of a justice
Justic'iary, *s.* one who administers justice
Jus'tifiable, *a.* defensible by law or reason
Jus'tifiableness, *s.* fitness to be justified
Jus'tifiably, *ad.* in a justifiable manner
Justifica'tion, *s.* a proof of innocence : vin-
Justifica'tor, *s.* one who justifies [dication
Jus'tifier, *s.* one who justifies or defends
Jus'tify, *v. a.* to clear from guilt, defend
Jus'tle, *v.* to encounter, to clash ; to push
Jus'tly, *ad.* uprightly, honestly, properly
Jus'tness, *s.* justice, reasonableness
Jut, *v. n.* to push or shoot out
Jut'ty, *v. a.* to shoot out beyond
Ju'venile, *a.* youthful, young
Juvenil'ity, *s.* youthfulness of temper, &c.
Juxtaposit'ion, *s.* a placing by each other
I'vy, *s.* a common plant

K.

K, the tenth letter of the alphabet
Kail, *s.* a kind of cabbage
Kal'endar, *s.* an account of time
Ka'li, *s.* a sea weed of which glass is made
Kam, *a.* crooked, thwart, awry
Kaw, *v.* to cry as a raven, crow, or rook
Kaw, *s.* the cry of a raven or crow
Kayle, *s.* ninepins, kettlepins, nine holes
Keck, *v. n.* to retch at vomiting, to heave
Kec'kle, *v. a.* to tie a rope round a cable
Kecks, Keck'sy, *s.* dry, hollow stalks
Kedg'er, *s.* a small anchor used in a river
Keel, *s.* the bottom of a ship
Keel'fat, *s.* a vessel for liquor to cool in
Keel'hale, *v. a.* to drag under the keel
Keen, *a.* sharp, eager, acrimonious
Keen'ly, *ad.* sharply, vehemently, bitterly
Keen'ness, *s.* sharpness, asperity, vehemence
Keep, *v. a.* to retain, preserve, continue

Keep, *s.* custody, restraint, guardianship
Keep'er, *s.* one who keeps or holds any thing
Keep'ing, *s.* custody, support
Keg, or Kag, *s.* a small barrel used for fish
Kell, *s.* a sort of pottage, the omentum
Kelp, *s.* a salt from calcined sea weed
Kel'son, Keel'son, *s.* the wood next the keel
Ken, *v. a.* to see at a distance, decry, know
Ken, *s.* view, the reach of sight
Ken'nel, *s.* a cot for dogs ; a water course
Kept, *pret.* and *part. pass.* of *to keep*
Ker'chief, *s.* a kind of head-dress
Kern, *s.* an Irish foot soldier ; a hand-mill
Kern, *v.* to form into grains ; to granulate
Ker'nel, *s.* the substance within a shell
Ker'nelly, *a.* full of kernels
Ker'sey, *s.* a kind of coarse stuff
Ketch, *s.* a heavy ship
Ket'tle, *s.* a vessel for boiling liquor

Ket'tle-drum, s. a drum with a body of brass
Key, s. an instrument to open a lock, &c., a tone in music; a wharf for goods
Key'age, s. money paid for wharfage
Key'hole, s. the hole to put a key in
Key'stone, s. the middle stone of an arch
Kibe, s. a chap in the heel, a chilblain
Kick, v. a. to strike with the foot
Kick, s. a blow with the foot
Kick'shaw, s. a fantastical dish of meat
Kid, s. the young of a goat; a bundle of furze
Kid, v. a. to bring forth kids
Kid'der, s. an ingrosser of corn   [ings
Kid'nap, v. a. to steal children or human be-
Kid'napper, s. one who steals human beings
Kid'neybean, s. a garden herb
Kid'neys, s. certain parts of an animal which separate the urine from the blood
Kil'derkin, s. a beer measure of 18 gallons
Kill, v. a. to deprive of life, to destroy
Kil'ler, s. one who deprives of life
Kil'low, s. a blackish kind of earth
Kiln, s. a stove for drying or burning in
Kim'bo, a. crooked, bent, arched
Kin, s. a relation, kindred, the same kin
Kind, a. benevolent, favourable, good
Kind, s. general class, particular nature
Kin'dle, v. to set on fire; to enrage
Kind'ly, ad. benevolently, with good will
Kind'ly, a. homogeneal, mild, softening
Kind'ness, s. benevolence, good will, love
Kin'dred, s. relation, affinity, relatives
Kin'dred, a. congenial, related, allied
Kine, s. the plural of cow
King, s. a monarch, a chief ruler
King'craft, s. the act or art of governing
King'dom, s. the dominion of a king
King'fisher, s. a beautiful small bird
King'ly, a. royal, august, noble, monarchical
Kingse'vil, s. a scrofulous disease
King'ship, s. royalty, monarchy
Kins'folk, s. relations, persons related
Kins'man, s. a man of the same family
Kins'woman, s. a female relation
Kirk, s. a church; the church of Scotland
Kir'tle, s. an upper garment, a gown
Kiss, v. a. to join the lips; to touch gently
Kiss, s. a salute given by joining lips
Kit, s. a small fiddle; a wooden vessel
Kitch'en, s. a room used for cookery
Kitch'en-gar'den, s. a garden for roots, &c.
Kitch'en-maid, s. an under cook maid
Kite, s. a bird of prey; a fictitious bird of paper, serving as a plaything for boys

Kit'ten, s. a young cat—v. n. to bring forth young cats
Klick, v. n. to make a small sharp noise
Knab, v. a. to bite with noise
Knack, s. dexterity, readiness; a toy
Knag, s. a hard knot in wood, a wart
Knag'gy, a. knotty, set with hard rough knots
Knap, s. a protuberance, a prominence
Knap, v. to bite, to break in sunder
Knap'sack, s. a soldier's bag
Knare, Knur, Knurle, s. a hard knot
Knave, s. a petty rascal, a scoundrel
Kna'very, s. dishonesty, craft, deceit
Kna'vish, a. dishonest, waggish, wicked
Kna'vishly, ad. fraudulently, mischievously
Knead, v. a. to work dough with the fist
Knead'ing-trough, s. a trough to knead in
Knee, s. a joint between the leg and thigh
Knee'deep, a. rising or sunk to the knees
Knee'pan, s. a small round bone at the knee, a little convex on both sides
Kneel, v. n. to bend or rest on the knee
Knell, s. the sound of a funeral bell
Knew, pret. of to know
Knife, s. a steel utensil to cut with
Knight, s. a title next in dignity to a baronet, a champion—v. a. to create a knight
Knighter'rant, s. a wandering knight
Knighter'rantry, s. the feats, character, or manner of wandering knights
Knight'hood, s. the dignity of a knight
Knight'ly, a. befitting a knight
Knit, v. a. to make stocking work; close
Knit'ter, s. one who knits or weaves
Knit'ting-nee'dle, s. a wire used in knitting
Knit'tle, s. a string that gathers a purse round
Knob, s. the protuberance of a tree, &c.
Knob'bed, Knob'by, a. full of knobs, hard
Knock, s. a sudden stroke, a blow
Knock, v. to clash, to strike with noise
Knock'er, s. a hammer hanging at the door
Knoll, v. to ring or sound as a bell
Knot, s. a part which is tied; a difficulty
Knot, v. to make knots, unite, perplex
Knot'ted, Knot'ty, a. full of knots; hard
Know, v. to understand, to recognise
Know'ing, a. skilful, intelligent, conscious
Know'ingly, ad. with skill, designedly
Know'ledge, s. skill, learning, perception
Knuc'kle, v. a. to beat with the knuckles
Knuc'kle, v. n. to submit, to bend
Knuc'kled, a. jointed; having knuckles
Knuc'kles, s. the joints of the fingers
Knuff, s. an awkward person, a lout

L.

L, s. the eleventh letter of the alphabet
La! interj. look, behold, see
Lab'danum, s. a resin of the softer kind
Labefac'tion, s. the act of weakening
Lab'efy, v. a. to weaken, to impair
La'bel, s. a short direction upon any thing
La'bent, a. sliding, gliding, slipping
La'bial, a. uttered by or relating to the lips
Lab'orant, s. a chymist
Lab'oratory, s. a chymist's work room

Labo'rious, a. diligent in work; tiresome
Labo'riously, ad. with labour or toil
La'bour, s. toil, work, childbirth
La'bour, v. to toil, to work; be in travail
La'bourer, s. one who toils or takes pains
La'bouring, a. striving with effort
Lab'yrinth, s. a maze full of windings
Lace, s. platted cord of gold, silver, or thread
Lace, v. n. to fasten with a lace; to adorn
La'ceman, s. one who deals in lace

Lac'erable, a. that may be rent or torn
Lac'erate, v. a. to tear in pieces, to rend
Lacera'tion, s. the act of tearing or rending
Lach'rymal, a. generating tears
Lach'rymary, a. containing tears
Lach'rymatory, s. a vessel to preserve tears
Lacin'iated, a. adorned with fringes
Lack, v. to want, to need, be without
Lack'brain, s. one that wants wit
Lack'er, s. a kind of yellow varnish
Lack'er, v. a. to cover with lacker
Lack'ey, s. a footboy, an attending servant
Lack'ey, v. a. to attend servilely
Lack'lustre, a. wanting brightness, dull
Lacon'ic, a. short, brief, concise
Lacon'ically, ad. briefly, concisely
La'conism, s. a concise, pithy style
Lac'tant, a. suckling, giving milk
Lac'tary, a. milky—s. a dairy house
Lacta'tion, s. the act of giving suck
Lac'teal, s. a vessel that conveys chyle
Lac'teal, Lac'teous, a. conveying chyle
Lactes'cent, Lactif'ic, a. producing milk
Lad, s. a boy, a stripling; a swain
Lad'der, s. a frame with steps for climbing
Lade, v. a. to load, freight; throw out
La'ding, s. a freight, cargo of a ship
La'dle, s. a large spoon; a vessel; a handle
La'dy, s. a female title of honour; a woman
La'dybird, La'dycow, s. a small red insect
Ladyday', s. the 25th of March, the Annunciation of the blessed Virgin Mary
La'dylike, a. soft, delicate, elegant
La'dyship, s. the title of a lady
Lag, a. coming behind, sluggish, last
Lag, v. n. to loiter, to stay behind
La'ic, La'ical, a. relating to the laity
Laid, pret. part. of to lay
Lain, pret. part. of to lie
Lair, s. the couch of a boar or wild beast
Laird, s. in Scotland, the lord of a manor
La'ity, s. the people, as distinguished from the clergy; the state of a layman
Lake, s. a large inland water; a colour
Lamb, s. the young of a sheep
Lam'bative, a. taken by licking
Lam'bent, a. playing about, gliding over
Lamb'kin, s. a little or young lamb
Lamb'like, a. meek, gentle, mild
Lamb'swool, s. ale and roasted apple
Lame, a. crippled, hobbling, imperfect
Lame, v. a. to make lame, to cripple
Lam'ellated, a. covered with films or plates
La'mely, ad. like a cripple, imperfectly
La'meness, s. the state of a cripple
Lament', v. to mourn, grieve, bewail
Lam'entable, a. mournful, sorrowful
Lam'entably, ad. mournfully, pitifully
Lamenta'tion, s. an expression of sorrow
Lament'er, s. he who mourns or laments
Lam'ina, s. a thin plate or scale
Lamina'ted, a. plated, covered with plates
Lam'mas, s. the first of August
Lamp, s. a light made with oil and a wick
Lamp'black, s. a black made by holding a lighted torch under a basin
Lampoo'n, s. a personal satire; abuse, censure
Lampoo'n, v. to abuse personally
Lampoo'ner, s. a writer of personal satire
Lam'prey, s. a fish much like an eel
Lana'rious, a. pertaining to wool

Lance, s. a long spear—v. a. to pierce, to cut
Lance'olate, a. shaped like the head of a lance
Lan'cet, s. a small pointed instrument
Lan'cinate, v. a. to tear, to rend
Land, s. a country, region, earth, estate
Land, v. to set or come on shore
Lan'ded, a. having a fortune in land
Land'fall, s. a sudden translation of property in land by the death of a rich man
Land'flood, s. inundation by rain
Land'grave, s. a German title of dominion
Land'holder, s. one whose fortune is in land
Land'ing, s. a place to land at; the stair top
Land'jobber, s. one who buys and sells land
Land'lady, s. the mistress of an inn
Land'locked, a. shut in or enclosed by land
Land'lord, s. the master of an inn
Land'mark, s. a mark of boundaries
Land'scape, s. the prospect of a country
Land'tax, s. a tax upon land and houses
Land'waiter, s. an officer of the customs, who is to watch what goods are landed
Lane, s. a narrow street or alley
Lan'guage, s. human speech in general
Lan'guet, s. any thing cut like a tongue
Lan'guid, a. weak, faint, dull, heartless
Lan'guidness, s. feebleness, weakness
Lan'guish, v. n. to grow feeble, to pine
Lan'guishingly, ad. weakly, tenderly, feebly
Lan'guishment, s. a softness of mien
Lan'guor, s. want of strength or spirit
Lan'ifice, s. a woollen manufacture
Lanig'erous, a. bearing wool
Lank, a. loose, not fat, slender, languid
Lank'ness, s. want of plumpness
Lan'squenet, s. a game at cards; a foot soldier
Lan'tern, s. a case for a candle; a lighthouse
Lap, s. that part of a person sitting which reaches from the waist to the knees
Lap, v. to wrap round, to lick up
Lap'dog, s. a little dog for the lap
Lap'ful, s. what is contained in the lap
Lap'idary, s. a polisher of stones and gems
Lap'idate, v. a. to stone, to kill by stoning
Lapida'tion, s. the act of battering with stones
Lapid'eous, a. stony, of the nature of stone
Lapides'cence, s. stony concretion
Lapidif'ic, a. forming stones
Lap'idist, s. a dealer in stones or gems
Lap'per, s. one who wraps up or laps
Lap'pet, s. the loose part of a head-dress
Lapse, s. a small error or mistake; fall
Lapse, v. n. to glide slowly; to fall from perfection, truth, or faith; to slip by mistake
Lap'wing, s. a clamorous bird with long wings
Lar'board, s. the left hand side of a ship
Lar'ceny, s. petty theft or robbery
Lard, s. the fat of swine melted
Lard, v. a. to stuff with bacon; to fatten
Lar'der, s. a room where meat is kept
Large, a. big, wide, copious, abundant
Large'ly, ad. extensively, liberally, widely
Large'ness, s. bulk, greatness, extension
Lar'gess, s. a present, bounty, gift
Lark, s. a small singing bird
Lar'um, s. an alarm; machine contrived to make a noise at a certain hour
Lasciv'ious, a. lewd, lustful, wanton, soft
Lasciv'iously, ad. lewdly, wantonly, loosely
Lasciv'iousness, s. wantonness
Lash, s. a part of a whip; a stroke

Lash, v. a. to scourge, to strike, or satirize
Lass, s. a girl, maid, young woman
Las'situde, s. fatigue, weariness, languor
Lass'lorn, a. forsaken by a mistress
Last, a. latest, hindmost, utmost
Last, s. the wooden mould on which shoes are formed; a certain measure or weight —ad. the last time; in conclusion
Last, v. n. to endure, continue, persevere
Las'tage, s. customs paid for freightage
Las'ting, part. a. durable, perpetual
Last'ly, ad. in the last time or place
Latch, s. fastening of a door, &c.
Lat'chet, s. a string that fastens the shoe
Late, a. slow, tardy; deceased
Late, ad. far in the day or night; lately
La'tely, Lat'terly, ad. not long ago
La'tency, s. obscurity, abstruseness
La'teness, s. time far advanced
La'tent, a. hidden, concealed, secret
Lat'eral, a. growing out on the side
Lat'erally, ad. by the side, sidewise
Lat'eran, s. the Pope's palace at Rome
Lath, s. a long thin slip of wood; a division of a country, usually containing three and sometimes more hundreds
Lath, v. a. to fit up with laths
Lathe, s. a turner's tool
Lath'er, s. the froth of water and soap
Lat'in, s. the language of the old Romans
Lat'inism, s. an idiom of the Latin tongue
Lat'inist, s. one skilled in Latin
Lat'inize, v. to make or use Latin
La'tion, s. removal of a body in a right line
La'tish, a. somewhat late
Lat'itancy, s. the state of lying hid
Lat'itant, a. concealed, lying hid
Lat'itude, s. breadth, width, extent, diffusion; a degree reckoned from the equator
Latitudina'rian, a. unlimited, not confined
La'trant, a. barking, snarling
La'tria, s. the highest kind of worship
Lat'ten, s. brass; iron tinned over
Lat'ter, a. modern; the latest of two
Lat'terly, ad. of late
Lat'termath, s. a second mowing
Lat'tice, s. a window formed of grate work
Lava'tion, s. the act of washing
Lava'tory, s. a wash; a bathing place
Laud, s. praise—v. a. to praise, to celebrate
Laud'able, a. commendable, salubrious
Laud'ably, ad. in a manner deserving praise
Laud'anum, s. the tincture of opium
Lave, v. to wash, to bathe, lade out
Lav'ender, s. a fragrant plant
La'ver, s. a washing vessel
Laugh, v. to make that noise which sudden merriment excites; to deride, to scorn
Laugh'able, a. proper to excite laughter, droll
Laugh'er, s. one who laughs much
Laugh'ing-stock, s. an object of ridicule
Laugh'ter, s. a convulsive merry noise
Lav'ish, v. a. to waste, to scatter profusely
Lav'ish, a. indiscreetly liberal, wild
Lav'ishly, ad. profusely, prodigally
Launch, v. to put to sea; to dart forward
Laun'dress, s. a washer-woman
Laun'dry, s. a room where clothes are washed
Lavol't, or Lavol'ta, s. an old brisk dance
Lau'reat, s. the royal poet
Lau'reate, a. decked with laurel

Lau'rel, s. an evergreen tree
Lau'reled, a. decorated with laurel
Law, s. a rule of action; a decree, edict, or statute; a judicial process
Law'ful, a. conformable to law, legal
Law'fully, ad. legally, agreeably to law
Law'fulness, s. the allowance of law
Law'giver, s. one who makes laws, legislator
Law'less, a. illegal, unrestrained by law
Lawn, s. a plain between woods; fine linen
Law'suit, s. a process in law, a litigation
Law'yer, s. professor of law, an advocate
Lax, a. loose, vague, slack; loose in body
Lax, s. a looseness, a diarrhœa; a fish
Lax'ative, a. relieving costiveness
Lax'ity, Lax'ness, s. looseness, openness
Lay, v. to place along; to beat down; to calm, to settle; to wager; to protrude eggs; impose
Lay, s. a row; a stratum; grassy ground; a meadow; a song or poem
Lay, a. not clerical; belonging to the people, as distinct from the clergy
Lay'er, s. a stratum; a sprig of a plant
Lay'man, s. one of the laity; an image
La'zar, s. one infected with filthy diseases
La'zarhouse, or Lazaret'to, s. a house to receive lazars in; an hospital
La'zily, ad. idly, sluggishly, heavily
La'ziness, s. idleness, slothfulness
La'zy, a. idle, sluggish, unwilling to work
Lea, Lee, Ley, s. ground enclosed
Lead, s. the heaviest metal except gold
Lead, v. to guide, to conduct, to induce
Lead'en, a. made of lead; heavy, dull
Lea'der, s. a conductor, a commander
Lea'ding, part. a. principal, going before
Leaf, s. the green parts of trees and plants; part of a book, one side, a door, or table
Lea'fless, a. naked, or stripped of leaves
League, s. a confederacy; three miles
League, v. n. to confederate, to unite
Leak, v. n. to let water in or out; to drop
Lea'kage, s. allowance for loss by leaks
Lea'ky, a. letting water in or out; loquacious
Lean, a. thin, meagre—s. meat without fat
Lean, v. n. to rest against, tend towards
Lean'ness, s. want of flesh, meagreness
Leap, v. to jump; to bound, to spring
Leap, s. a bound, jump, sudden transition
Leap'frog, s. a play of children
Leap'year, s. every fourth year
Learn, v. to gain knowledge, to teach
Learn'ed, a. versed in science, skilled
Lea'mer, s. one who is learning any thing
Learn'ing, s. skill in any thing, erudition
Lease, s. a temporary contract made for possession of houses or lands; tenure for years
Lease, v. to glean, to gather up
Lea'ser, s. a gatherer after the reaper
Leash, s. a leathern thong, a band to tie with
Lea'sing, s. lies, falsehood, deceit
Least, a. superlative of little, the smallest—ad. in the lowest degree
Leath'er, s. an animal's hide dressed
Leath'ercoat, s. an apple with a tough rind
Leath'er-dresser, s. he who dresses leather
Leath'ern, a. made of leather
Leath'er-seller, s. he who deals in leather
Leave, s. permission, licence, a farewell
Leave, v. to quit, forsake, bequeath
Leav'en, v. a. to ferment, taint, imbue

Leav'en, or Lev'en, s. ferment mixed with any body to make it light
Leaves, s. the plural of Leaf
Lea'vings, s. a remnant, relics, offal, refuse
Lech, v. a. to lick over
Lech'erous, a. lewd, lustful, wanton
Lech'erously, ad. lewdly, lustfully
Lech'ery, s. lewdness, lust, wantonness
Lec'tion, s. a reading; a variety in copies
Lec'tionary, s. the Romish service book
Lec'ture, v. to read lectures; to reprimand
Lec'ture, s. a discourse on any subject
Lec'turer, s. an instructor, a preacher
Led, part. pret. of to lead
Ledge, s. a small moulding on the edge
Led'ger, s. the chief book of accounts
Lee, s. dregs; the side opposite the wind
Leech, s. a small water bloodsucker
Leek, s. a common pot herb
Leer, s. an oblique cast of the eye
Leer, v. n. to look obliquely or archly
Lees, s. dregs, sediment
Leet, s. a court held by lords of manors
Lee'ward, a. opposed to windward, toward that side of a ship on which the wind does not blow
Lee'way, s. the lateral movement of a ship to leeward of her course
Left, part. pret. of to leave
Left, a. opposite to the right; sinister
Left'handed, a. using the left hand
Leg, s. the limb between the knee and foot
Leg'acy, s. a bequest made by will
Le'gal, a. conformable to law, lawful
Legal'ity, Le'galness, s. lawfulness
Le'galize, v. a. to make lawful, to authorize
Le'gally, ad. lawfully, according to law
Leg'ate, s. an ambassador from the Pope
Legatee', s. one who has a legacy left him
Leg'atine, a. belonging to a legate
Lega'tion, s. a deputation, an embassy
Lega'tor, s. one who makes a will
Le'gend, s. a chronicle, or register; a fabulous narrative; an inscription
Leg'endary, a. fabulous, unauthentic
Legerdemai'n, s. sleight of hand, a juggle
Leger'ity, s. lightness, nimbleness
Leg'ged, a. having legs, put on legs, prepared
Leg'ible, a. easy to be read, evident
Leg'ibly, ad. in a manner easy to be read
Le'gion, s. a body of Roman soldiers, consisting of about 5000; a military force; a great number
Leg'islate, v. n. to make or pass laws, to enact
Legisla'tion, s. the act of giving laws
Leg'islative, a. lawgiving, making laws
Leg'islator, s. one who makes laws
Leg'islature, s. the power that makes laws
Legit'imacy, s. a lawful birth, genuineness
Legit'imate, a. born in marriage
Legit'imately, ad. lawfully, genuinely
Leg'ume. Legu'men, s. seeds or pulse
Legu'minous, a. belonging to pulse
Lei'surable, a. done at or having leisure
Lei'surably, ad. without tumult or hurry
Lei'sure, s. freedom from business or hurry
Lei'surely, a. not hasty, deliberate, slow—ad. without tumult or hurry
Le'man, s. a sweetheart or gallant
Lem'ma, s. a proposition previously assumed
Lem'on, s. the name of an acid fruit

Lemona'de, s. water, sugar, and lemon juice
Lend, v. a. to grant the use of any thing
Lend'er, s. one who lends any thing
Length, s. extent from end to end; distance
Leng'then, v. to make longer
Le'nient, a. assuasive, mitigating emollient
Le'nient, s. an emollient application
Len'ify, v. a. to assuage, mitigate, soften
Len'itive, a. assuasive—s. a palliativ
Len'ity, s. mildness, mercy, tenderness
Lens, s. a glass spherically convex
Lent, s. the quadragesimal fast; time of abstinence from Ashwednesday to Easter
Lent'en, a. such as is used in Lent; sparing
Lentic'ular, a. doubly convex; like a lens
Len'til, s. a sort of pulse or pea
Len'titude, s. sluggishness, slowness
Len'tor, s. tenacity, viscosity; slowness, delay
Len'tous, a. viscous, tenacious, glutinous
Le'onine, a. having the nature of a lion
Leop'ard, s. a spotted beast of prey
Lep'er, s. one infected with a leprosy
Lep'erous, Lep'rous, a. having the leprosy
Lepo'rean. Lep'orine, a. belonging to a hare, having the nature of a hare
Lep'rosy, s. a distemper of white scales
Less, Les'ser, ad. in a smaller degree
Lessee', s. one who takes a lease of another
Les'sen, v. to grow less; degrade; shrink
Les'son, s. a task to learn or read; a precept
Les'sor, s. he who grants a lease to another
Lest, conj. that not, in case that
Let, v. a. to allow, to suffer, to hire out
Let, s. a hinderance, impediment, obstacle
Lethar'gic, a. sleepy, drowsy, heavy
Leth'argy, s. a morbid drowsiness, sleepiness
Le'the, s. oblivion, a draught of oblivion
Lethif'erous, a. deadly, fatal
Let'ter, s. a written message; a character in the alphabet; a printing type; one who lets or permits
Let'tercase, s. a case to put letters in
Let'ters, s. literature, learning
Let'tered, a. literate, educated to learning; marked with letters
Let'ter-foun'der, s. one who casts letters
Let'tuce, s. a common salad plant
Le'vant, a. eastern—s. the coast lying E in the Mediterranean
Lev'ee, s. a crowd of attendants; a toilet
Lev'el, s. a plane; standard; an instrument whereby masons adjust their work
Lev'el, a. even, plain, flat, smooth
Lev'el, v. to make even; to lay flat; to aim
Lev'eller, s. one who destroys superiority
Lev'elness, s. an equality of surface
Le'ver, s. the second mechanical power used to elevate a great weight
Lev'eret, s. a young hare
Lev'et, s. a blast on a trumpet
Lev'iable, a. that may be levied
Levi'athan, s. by some supposed to mean the crocodile, but, in general, the whale
Lev'igate, v. a. to rub, to grind, to smooth
Le'vite, s. one of the tribe of Levi
Levit'ical, a. belonging to the Levites
Lev'ity, s. lightness, inconstancy, vanity
Lev'y, v. a. to raise, collect, impose
Lev'y, s. the act of raising money or men
Lewd, a. wicked lustful, not clerical
Lewd'ness, s. lustful licentiousness

Lexicog'rapher, *s.* a writer of dictionaries
Lex'icon, *s.* a book for explaining words
Li'able, *a.* subject to, not exempt
Li'ar, *s.* one who tells falsehoods
Li'ard, *a.* roan—*s.* a French farthing
Liba'tion, *s.* an offering made of wine
Li'bel, *s.* a satire, defamatory writing
Li'beler, *s.* a defamatory writer, lampooner
Li'belous, *a.* defamatory, abusive, scurrilous
Lib'eral, *a.* free, bountiful, generous
Liberal'ity, *s.* munificence, bounty
Lib'erally, *ad.* bountifully, magnanimously
Lib'erate, *v. a.* to set free, to deliver
Lib'ertine, *s.* a dissolute liver, a rake
Lib'ertine, *a.* licentious, irreligious
Lib'ertinism, *s.* irreligion, licentiousness
Lib'erty, *s.* freedom, exemption, leave
Libid'inous, *a.* lewd, licentious, lustful
Li'bra, *s.* one of the signs of the zodiac
Libra'rian, *s.* one who has the care of books
Li'brary, *s.* a large collection of books
Li'brate, *v. a.* to balance, to hold in equipoise
Libra'tion, *s.* the state of being balanced
Lice, *s.* the *plural* of Louse
Li'cence, *s.* a permission, liberty
Li'cense, *v. a.* to grant leave ; to permit by a
  legal grant; to set at liberty
Licen'tiate, *s.* one who has a licence to prac-
  tise any art or faculty
Licen'tious, *a.* unrestrained, disorderly
Licen'tiousness, *s.* boundless liberty ; con
  tempt of just restraint
Lick, *v. a.* to touch with the tongue, to lap
Lick'erish, *a.* nice, delicate, greedy
Lic'orice, *s.* a root of a sweet taste
Lic'tor, *s.* the beadle among the Romans
Lid, *s.* a cover for a pan, box, &c.
Lie, *s.* a fiction, a falsehood : any thing im-
  pregnated with another body, as soap, &c.
Lie, *v. n.* to tell a lie ; to lean upon, to rest
Lief, Lieve, *ad.* willingly, soon
Liege, *s.* a sovereign—*a.* subject ; faithful
Lie'ger, *s.* a resident ambassador
Lieu, *s.* place, room, stead, behalf
Lieuten'ancy, *s.* the office of a lieutenant
Lieuten'ant, *s.* a deputy, a second in rank
Lieuten'antship, *s.* the rank of a lieutenant
Life, *s.* animal being, conduct, condition
Li'feguard, *s.* guard of a prince's person
Li'feless, *a.* dead ; without force or spirit
Li'fetime, *s.* the duration of life
Lift, *v. a.* to raise up, elevate, support
Lift, *s.* the act of lifting up; a struggle
Lig'ament, *s.* a band to tie parts together
Lig'ature, *s.* a bandage, any thing bound on;
  the act of binding
Light, *s.* the transparency of air caused by the
  rays of the sun, &c. ; mental knowledge ;
  situation ; a taper
Light, *a.* not heavy, active ; bright : not dark
Light, *v.* to kindle, to lighten ; to rest on
Light'en, *v.* to flash with lightning
Light'er, *s.* a boat for unloading ships
Light'erman, *s.* one who manages a lighter
Lightfin'gered, *a.* thievish, dishonest
Lightfoot'ed, *a.* ninble, swift, active
Lighthead'ed, *a.* delirious, thoughtless
Lightheart'ed, *a.* gay, merry, cheerful
Light'ly, *ad.* without reason ; nimbly
Light'ness, *s.* a want of weight; levity
Light'ning *s.* the flash before thunder

Lights, *s.* the lungs ; organs of breathing
Light'some, *a.* luminous, gay, airy
Lig'neous, *a.* made of wood, like woo.
Li'gure, *s.* a kind of precious stone
Like, *a.* resembling, equal, likely
Like, *ad.* in the same manner, probabl
Li'kelihood, *s.* appearance, probability
Li'kely, *ad.* probably—*a.* probable
Li'ken, *v. a.* to make like, to compare
Like'ness, *s.* resemblance, similitude, form
Like'wise, *ad.* in like manner, also
Li'king, *s.* plumpness ; state of trial
Lil'ied, *a.* embellished with lilies
Lil'y, *s.* a beautiful flower
Lil'ylivered, *a.* whitelivered, cowardly
Li'mature, *s.* the filings of any metal
Lima'tion, *s.* the act of filing or polishing
Limb, *s.* a member, bough, border, edge
Limb, *v. a.* to tear asunder, dismember
Lim'bec, *s.* a still ; a vessel to distil
Lim'bed, *a.* formed with regard to limbs
Lim'ber, *a.* flexible, easily bent, pliant
Lim'bo, *s.* a place of misery, a prison
Lime, *s.* a stone ; a fruit—*v. a.* to ensnare
Lime'kiln, *s.* kiln for burning stones to lime
Lim'it, *s.* bound, border, utmost reach
Lim'it, *v. a.* to restrain, keep within boun
Lim'itary, *a.* placed at the boundaries
Limita'tion, *s.* restriction ; a boundary
Limn, *v. n.* to draw, to paint any thing
Lim'ner, *s.* a painter, a picture-maker
Li'mous, *a.* muddy, slimy, miry
Limp, *v. n.* to halt, to walk lamely
Limp, *a.* vapid, weak ; easily bent
Lim'pet, *s.* a kind of shell-fish
Lim'pid, *a.* clear, pure, transparent
Lim'pidness, *s.* clearness, purity
Limp'ingly, *ad.* in a halting manner
Li'my, *a.* viscous ; containing lime
Linch'pin, *s.* the iron pin of an axletree
Linc'tus, *s.* a medicine to be licked up
Lin'den, *s.* the lime tree
Line, *v. a.* to guard within ; to cover
Line, *s.* a string ; an angler's string,
  equator ; extension ; limits ; progeny
  neaments ; tenth of an inch
Lin'eage, *s.* a family, race, progeny
Lin'eal, *a.* descending in a right line
Lin'eally, *ad.* in a direct line, duly
Lin'eament, *s.* a feature ; a discriminatin,
  mark in the form
Lin'ear, *a.* composed of lines, like lines
Linea'tion, *s.* a draught of a line or lines
Lin'en, *s.* cloth made of hemp or flax
Lin'en-dra'per, *s.* he who deals in linen
Ling, *s.* heath ; a kind of sea fish
Lin'ger, *v.* to remain long ; pine ; hesitate
Lin'geringly, *ad.* tediously, slowly, withou.
  delay
Lin'get, *s.* a small mass of metal ; a bird
Lin'go, *s.* a language, tongue, speech
Lingua'cious, *a.* full of tongue, talkative
Lin'guiform, *a.* tongue-shaped
Lin'guist, *s.* one skilful in languages
Lin'iment, *s.* an ointment, a balsam
Li'ning, *s.* that which is within any thing
Link, *s.* a ring of a chain ; a torch of pitch
Link, *v. a.* to unite, to join, to connect
Lin'net, *s.* a small singing bird
Lin'seed, *s.* the seed of flax
Lin'sey-wool'sev, *a.* made of linen and wool

Lin'stock, s. a staff with a match at the end
Lint, s. linen scraped soft; flax
Lin'tel, s. the upper part of a door frame
Li'on, s. the most magnanimous of beasts
Li'oness, s. a she-lion
Lip, s. the outer part of the mouth; the edge
  of any thing, &c.
Lipoth'ymous, a. swooning, fainting
Lipoth'ymy, s. a swoon, a fainting fit
Lip'pitude, s. blearedness of eyes
Liqua'tion, s. capacity of being melted
Liquefac'tion, s. state of being melted
Liq'uefiable, a. capable of being melted
Liq'uefy, v. to melt, to grow liquid
Liques'cent, a. melting, dissolving
Liq'uid, a. not solid, fluid, dissolved
Liq'uid, s. a fluid substance, a liquor
Liq'uidate, v. a. to lessen debts, to clear
Liq'uids, s. these four letters, l, m, n, r
Liq'uor, s. any thing liquid; any strong drink
Lisp, v. n. to clip words in pronunciation
List, v. to choose; to enlist soldiers; to listen
List, s. a roll; a catalogue; place for fight-
  ing; willingness; outer edge of cloth
List'ed, a. striped; party-coloured
Lis'ten, v. to hearken, hear, attend to
List'less, a. careless, heedless, indifferent
List'lessly, ad. without thought, heedlessly
List'lessness, s. inattention; want of desire
Lit, pret. of to light
Lit'any, s. a form of supplicatory prayer
Lit'eral, a. not figurative, exact
Lit'erary, a. respecting letters or learning
Litera'ti, s. men of learning
Lit'erature, s. learning, skill in letters
Lith'arge, s. lead vitrified, either a one or
  with a mixture of copper
Lithe, Li'thesome, a. limber, pliant
Lithog'raphy, s. art of engraving on stone
Lith'omancy, s. a prediction by stones
Lithot'omist, s. one who cuts for the stone
Lit'igant, s. one engaged in a lawsuit
Lit'igate, v. a. to contest in law, to debate
Litiga'tion, s. a judicial contest, lawsuit
Litig'ious, a. quarrelsome, disputable
Litig'iously, ad. wranglingly
Litig'iousness, s. a wrangling disposition
Lit'ter, s. a kind of vehiculary bed; a brood
  of young; a birth of animals; things thrown
  sluttishly about; straw laid under animals
Lit'ter, v. a. to bring forth; to scatter about
Lit'tle, a. small in quantity; diminutive
Lit'tle, s. a small space, not much
Lit'tle, ad. in a small quantity or degree
Lit'toral, a. belonging to the sea shore
Lit'urgy, s. the public form of prayer
Live, v. n. to be in a state of life; to feed
Live, a. quick, active; not extinguished
Li'velihood, s. the means of living, support
Li'veliness, s. sprightliness, vivacity
Liv'elong, a. tedious, lasting, durable
Li'vely, a. brisk, gay, strong, energetic
Liv'er, s. one of the entrails; one who lives
Liv'er-col'our, s. a very dark red
Liv'ergrown, a. having a great liver
Liv'ery, s. clothes with different trimmings
  worn by servants
Liv'eryman, s. one who wears a livery; a
  freeman of some standing in a company
Liv'ery-sta'ble, s. a public stable
Liv'id, a. discoloured, as with a blow

Livid'ity, s. discoloration, as by a blow
Liv'ing, s. maintenance, support, a benefice
Liv're, . the sum by which the French
  reckon their money, equal to 10d. sterling
Lixiv'ial, a. impregnated with salts
Lixivi'ate, a. making a lixivium
Lixiv'ium, s. ley made of ashes, water, &c.
Liz'ard, s. a small creeping animal, a serpent
Lo! interj. look! see! behold!
Load, s. a burden; weight; violence of blows
Load, v. a. to burden; freight; charge a gun
Load'stone, s. the magnet, a stone with an
  attracting and repelling power
Loaf, s. any thick mass of bread or sugar, &c.
Loam, s. a fat unctuous earth, marl
Loa'my, a. of the nature of loam, marly
Loan, s. any thing lent, interest
Loath, a. unwilling, disliking, not ready
Loathe, v. a. to hate, nauseate
Loath'ful, a. hating, abhorred, odious
Loath'ing, s. hatred, abhorrence, aversion
Loath'ingly, ad. in a fastidious manner
Loath'some, a. abhorred, causing dislike
Loath'someness, s. the quality of hatred
Loaves, s. plural of loaf
Lob, s. a clumsy person; a prison; a worm
Lob'by, s. an opening before a room
Lobe, s. a part of the lungs; a division
Lob'ster, s. a crustaceous shell-fish
Lo'cal, a. relating to or being of a place
Local'ity, s. existence or relation of place
Lo'cally, ad. with respect to place
Loca'tion, s. the act of placing; a situation
Lock, s. an instrument to fasten doors, &c.
Lock, v. to fasten with a lock, to close
Lock'er, s. a drawer, a cupboard, &c.
Lock'et, s. an ornamental lock, &c.
Lock'ram, s. a sort of coarse linen
Locomo'tion, s. power of changing place
Locomo'tive, a. able to change place
Lo'cust, s. a devouring insect
Lodge, v. to place, settle, reside; lie flat
Lodge, s. small house in a park; porter's room
Lodg'ment, s. an encampment; possession
  of the enemy's works; accumulation
Lodg'er, s. one who hires a lodging
Lodg'ing, s. a temporary abode; a room hired
Loft, s. a floor; the highest floor
Loft'ily, ad. on high, haughtily, sublimely
Loft'iness, s. local elevation, pride, sublimity
Loft'y, a. high, sublime, haughty, proud
Log, s. a piece of wood; a Hebrew measure
Log'arithms, s. the index of the ratios of
  numbers one to another
Log'book, s. journal of a ship's course, &c.
Log'gats, s. an old game, now called skittles
Log'gerhead, s. a dolt, thickskull, blockhead
Log'ic, s. the art of using reason well, in our
  inquiries after truth
Log'ical, a. of or pertaining to logic
Log'ically, ad. according to the laws of logic
Logic'ian, s. one skilled in logic
Logis'tic, a. relating to sexagesimals
Log'line, s. a line to measure a ship's way
Logom'achy, s. a contention about words
Log'wood, s. a wood used in dyeing
Loin, s. the reins, the back of an animal
Loi'ter, v. n. to linger, to spend time idly
Loi'terer, s. a lingerer, idler, a lazy wretch
Loll, v. to lean idly, to hang out
Lone, a. solitary, single, lonely

Lo'neliness, Lo'neness, *s.* solitude
Lo'nely, Lo'nesome, *a.* solitary, dismal
Long, *a.* having length; tedious, slow
Long, *v. n.* to wish or desire earnestly
Longanim'ity, *s.* forbearance, patience
Long'boat, *s.* the largest boat of a ship
Lounge, *s.* a thrust or push in fencing
Longev'ity, *s.* great length of life
Longe'vous, *a.* long-lived, living long
Longim'anous, *a.* having long hands
Longim'etry, *s.* art of measuring distances
Long'ing, *s.* earnest wish; continual desire
Long'ingly, *ad.* with incessant wishes
Lon'gitude, *s.* length; the distance of any part of the earth, east or west from London, or any other given place
Longitu'dinal, *a.* measured by the length, running in the longest direction
Long'some, *a.* tedious, tiresome, long
Long-suf'fering, *a.* patient, not easily provo-
Long-suf'fering, *s.* patience of offence [ked
Long'ways, Long'wise, *ad.* in length
Loug-wind'ed, *a.* long-breathed, tedious
Loo, *s.* the name of a game at cards
Loo'bily, *ad.* awkwardly—*a.* clumsy
Loo'by, *s.* a lubber, clumsy clown
Loof, *s.* a part of a ship
Look, *v.* to seek for, expect, behold
Look, *s.* the air of the face, mien
Look! *interj.* see! lo! behold! observe!
Look'ing-glass, *s.* glass which reflects images
Loom, *v. n.* to appear obscurely at sea
Loom, *s.* a weaver's frame for work; a bird
Loon, *s.* a sorry fellow, a scoundrel, a rascal
Loop, *s.* a noose in a rope, &c.
Loop'hole, *s.* an aperture; shift, evasion
Loose, *v.* to unbind, relax, set free
Loose, *a.* unbounded, wanton—*s.* liberty
Loose'ly, *ad.* not fast, irregularly, unchastely
Loo'sen, *v.* to relax any thing, to separate
Loo'seness, *s.* irregularity; unchastity; a flux
Lop, *v. a.* to cut the branches of trees
Loqua'cious, *a.* full of talk; inclined to blab
Loquac'ity, *s.* too much talk, prattle
Lord, *s.* a monarch; a supreme person; a ruler; a nobleman; a title of honour
Lord, *v. n.* to domineer, to rule despotically
Lor'ding, Lor'dling, *s.* a lord, in ridicule
Lord'liness, *s.* dignity, high station, pride
Lord'ly, *a.* proud, imperious, insolent
Lord'ship, *s.* dominion; a title given to lords
Lore, *s.* lesson, instruction, learning
Lor'icate, *v. a.* to place over
Lor'imer, Lor'iner, *s.* a bridle-cutter
Lorn, *a.* forsaken, lost, forlorn
Lose, *v.* to suffer loss, not to win; to fail
Los'el, *s.* a meanworthless fellow, a scoundrel
Lo'ser, *s.* one who has incurred loss
Loss, *s.* damage; forfeiture; puzzle
Lot, *s.* fortune; lucky chance; portion
Lote, *s.* a tree; a plant
Lo'tion, *s.* a medicine to wash any thing with
Lot'tery, *s.* a game of chance; a sortilege; a distribution of prizes by chance
Loud, *a.* noisy, clamorous, turbulent
Loud'ly, *ad.* noisily, clamorously
Loud'ness, *s.* noise, clamour, turbulence
Love, *v. a.* to regard with passionate affection
Love, *s.* the passion between the sexes; kindness; courtship; liking, fondness, concord
Lov'e-letter *s.* a letter of courtship

Lov'elily, *ad.* amiably, in a lovely manner
Lov'eliness, *s.* amiableness
Lov'elorn, *a.* forsaken by one's love
Lov'ely, *a.* amiable, exciting love
Lov'er, *s.* one who is in love; a friend
Lov'esick, *a.* disordered with love, languish.
Lov'esong, *s.* a song expressing love [ing
Lov'esuit, *s.* courtship
Lov'etale, *s.* narrative of love
Lov'etoy, *s.* small presents made by lovers
Lov'etrick, *s.* the art of expressing love
Lough, or Loch, *s.* a lake; standing water
Lov'ing, *part. a.* kind, affectionate
Lov'ing-kind'ness, *s.* tenderness, mercy
Lov'ingly, *ad.* affectionately, with kindness
Louis-d'or', *s.* a French gold coin
Lounge, *v. n.* to idle, or live lazily
Loun'ger, *s.* an idler, an indolent man
Louse, *s.* a small animal, of which different species live on the bodies of men, of beasts, and perhaps of all living creatures
Lou'sily, *ad.* in a paltry, mean, scurvy way
Lou'siness, *s.* the state of abounding with lice
Lou'sy, *a.* swarming with lice; mean
Lout, *s.* an awkward fellow, a clown
Lout'ish, *a.* clownish, bumkinly
Lou'ver, *s.* an opening for the smoke
Low, *a.* not high; humble, depressed, mean
Low, *v.* to sink, to make low; to bellow
Low, *ad.* not on high, with a low voice, abjectly; not a high price
Low'er, *s.* cloudiness of look, gloominess
Low'er, *v.* to humble, depress; to appear dark, stormy, and gloomy; to frown
Low'ering, *ad.* gloomily, cloudily
Low'ermost, *a.* lowest, deepest
Low'ing, *s.* the bellowing of oxen, &c.
Low'land, *s.* a low country, a marsh
Low'liness, *s.* meanness, want of dignity
Low'ly, *a.* humble, mean, wanting dignity
Low'ness, *s.* contrariety to height; meanness of character; want of rank; depression
Low-spir'ited, *a.* dejected, not lively
Loxodrom'ic, *s.* the art of oblique sailing by the rhomb, which always makes an equal angle with every meridian
Loy'al, *a.* true to a prince, a lady, or a lover
Loy'alist, *s.* one rigidly faithful to his king
Loy'ally, *ad.* with fidelity or adherence
Loy'alty, *s.* fidelity, adherence to a prince
Loz'enge, *s.* a medicine made in small pieces to be chewed in the mouth till it melts
Lub'ber, Lub'bard, *s.* a lazy sturdy fellow
Lub'berly, *ad.* awkwardly, clumsily
Lu'bric, Lu'bricous, *a.* slippery, unsteady
Lu'bricate, *v.* to make smooth or slippery
Lubric'ity, *s.* slipperiness; wantonness
Luce, *s.* a pike full grown
Lu'cent, *a.* shining, bright, splendid
Lu'cern, *s.* an herb growing with singular quickness
Lu'cid, *a.* shining, bright, pellucid, clear
Lucid'ity, *s.* splendour, brightness
Lu'cifer, *s.* the devil; the morning star
Lucif'erous, Lucif'ic, *a.* giving light
Luck, *s.* chance; fortune, good or bad
Luck'ily, *ad.* fortunately, by good hap
Luck'iness, *s.* good hap, casual happiness
Luck'less, *a.* unfortunate, unhappy
Luck'y, *a.* fortunate, happy by chance
Lu'crative, *a.* profitable, bringing money

L 3

Lu'cre, s. gain, profit, pecuniary advan'age
Lucta'tion, s. a struggle, effort, contest
Lu'cubrate, v. n. to watch, to study by night
Lucubra'tion, s. a nightly study or work
Lu'cubratory, a. composed by cand'e-light
Lu'culent, a. clear, lucid, certain. evi ent
Lu'dicrous, a. exciting laughter; burlesque
Lu'dicrously, ad. in burlesque, sportively
Ludifica'tion, s. the act of mocking
Luff, v. n. to keep close to the wind
Lug, v. to pull with violence, to drag
Lug, s. fish; a pole or perch; an ear
Lug'gage, s. any thing cumbrous or heavy
Lug sail, s. a k nd of square sail
Lu'kewarm, a. moderately warm; indifferent
Lu'kewarmness. s. moderate heat, &c.
Lull, v. a. to compose to sleep, put to rest
Lul'laby, s. a song to quiet infants
Lumba'go, s. pains about the loins
Lum'ber, s. old useless furniture, &c.
Lu'minary, s. any body that gives light
Lu'minous, a. shining, enlightened, bright
Lump, s. a shapeless mass; the gross
Lump'ing, Lump'ish, a. large, heavy, great
Lump'ishly, ad. with stupidity or heaviness
Lump'y, a. full of lumps; dull, heavy
Lu'nacy, s. madness, loss of reason
Lu'nar, Lu'nary, a. relating to the moon
Lu'nated, a. formed like a half moon
Lu'natic, s. a madman—a. mad
Luna'tion, s. a revolution of the moon
Lunch, Lun'cheon, s. a handful of food
Lunett'e, s. a half moon in fortification
Lungs, s. the parts for breathing
Lunt, s. a match cord to fire guns with
Lu'pine, s. a kind of pulse
Lurch, v. to shift, play tricks, lurk, devour
Lurch, s. a forlorn or deserted state
Lur'cher, s. a hunting dog; a glutton
Lure, s. an enticement—v. to entice, attract
Lu'rid, a. pale, gloomy, dismal
Lurk, v. n. to lie in wait, to lie hidden
Lur'ker, s. a thief that lies in wait
Lus'cious, a. sweet, pleasing, delightful

Lush, a. of a dark, deep colour
Lusk, a. idle, lazy, worthless
Lusk'ishness, s. a disposition to laziness
Luso'rious, Lu'sory, a. used in play. sportive
Lust, s. carnal desire—v. n. to long for
Lust'ful, a. having loose, irregular desires
Lus'tily, ad. stoutly. with vigour
Lus'tiness. s. stoutness. vigour of body
Lus'trate, v. a. to cleanse, to purify
Lustra'tion, s. purification by water
Lus're, s. brightness; renown; a sconce with
lights; the space of five years
Lus'tring, s. a kind of shining silk
Lus'trous, a. bright, shining, luminous
Lus'ty, a. stout, vigorous, able of body
Luta'rious, a. living in mud, like mud
Lute, s. a musical instrument; a clay with
which chymists close up their vessels
Lute, v. n. to close with lute or clay
Lu'theran, s. a follower of Luther
Lu'theranism, s. the doctrine of Luther
Lu'tulent, a. muddy, foul, turbid
Lux, Lux'ate, v. a. to put out of joint
Luxa'tion, s. a disjointing; thing disjointed
Luxu'riance, Luxu'riancy, s. exuberance;
abundant or wanton; plenty or growth
Luxu'riant, a. superfluously plenteous
Luxu'rious, a. enslaved by pleasure, softened
by pleasure; enervating; exuberant
Luxu'riously, ad. voluptuously, deliciously
Luxu'riousness, s. voluptuousness
Lux'ury, s. delicious fare; profuseness, ad
diciedness to pleasure; lewdness
Lycan'thropy, s. a species of madness
Lye, s. See lee and lie
Ly'ing, part. of to lie—s. the act of telling lie
Lymph, s. a pure transparent fluid
Lym'pheduct, s. a vessel to convey lymph
Lynx, s. a sharp-sighted spotted beast
Lyre, s. harp, a musical instrument
Lyr'ic, Lyr'ical, a. pertaining to a harp, o.
to odes or poetry sung to a harp
Lyr'ic, s. a poet who writes songs for the harp
Lyr'ist, s. one who plays on the harp

M.

M, s. the twelfth letter of the alphabet
Macaro'ni, s. a fop, a finical fellow
Macaron'ic, s. a confused mixture
Macaroo'n, s. a sweet cake or biscuit
Macaw', s. a West Indian bird
Mace, s. an ensign of authority; a spice
Ma'cebearer, s. one who carries the mace
Mac'erate, v. a. to make lean; to steep
Macera'tion, s. a making lean; a steeping
Mac'hinal, a. relating to machines
Mac'hinate, v. a. to plan, to contrive
Machina'tion, s. an artifice, malicious scheme
Machi'ne, s. any complicated work
Macki'nery, s. enginery; any complicated
workmanship; decoration in a poem
Machi'nist, s. a constructor, &c. of engines
Mac'ilent, a. lean, lank, thin
Mac'kerel, s. a small sea fish
Ma'crocosm, s. the world or visible system,
opposed to microcosm. the world of man
Macta'tion, s. the act of killing for sacrifice

Mac'ula, Macula'tion, s. a spot, a stain
Mac'ulate, Mac'kle, v. a. to stain, to spot
Mad, a. disordered in the mind; enraged
Mad, Mad'den, v. to make mad; to enrage
Mad'am, s. a term of address to a lady
Mad'brained, a. hotheaded, wild, disordered
Mad'cap, s. a wild, hotbrained fellow
Mad'der, s. a plant much used in dyeing
Made, part. pret. of to make
Mad'efy, v. a. to moisten, to make wet
Mad'house, s. a house for madmen
Mad'ly, ad. foolishly, furiously, rashly
Mad'man, s. a man deprived of his senses
Mad'ness, s. loss of understanding; insanity,
fury, rage, distraction, wildness
Mad'rigal, s. a pastoral air or song
Maf'fle, v. n. to stammer, to stutter
Magazi'ne, s. a repository of provisions, &c.
a miscellaneous pamphlet
Mag'got, s. a small grub; a whim, caprice
Mag'gotty, a. full of maggots; whimsical

Ma'gi, s. eastern astrologers or priests
Mag'ic, Mag'ical, a. done by secret powers
Mag'ic, s. sorcery, enchantment
Magic'ian, s. one skilled in magic
Magiste'rial, a. lofty, arrogant, haughty
Magiste'rially, ad. arrogantly, proudly
Mag'istracy, s. the office of a magistrate
Mag'istrate, s. a man vested with authority
Magnal'ity, s. something above the common
Magnanim'ity, s. elevation of the soul
Magnan'imous, a. great of mind, brave
Magne'sia, s. a powder gently purgative
Mag'net, s. the stone that attracts iron
Magnet'ic, Magnet'ical, a. attractive
Mag'netism, s. the power of the loadstone
Magnif'ic, Magnif'ical, a. illustrious ; grand
Magnif'icence, s. grandeur, splendour
Magnif'icent, a. fine, splendid, pompous
Magnif'ico, s. a grandee of Venice
Mag'nifier, s. a glass that increases the bulk
  of any object ; an extoller ; an encomiast
Mag'nify, v. a. to make great, to extol
Mag'nitude, s. greatness, comparative bulk
Mag'pie, s. a bird ; a talkative person
Mahog'any, s. a valuable brown wood
Maid, Mai'den, s. a virgin ; a woman servant
Mai'den, a. fresh, new, unpolluted
Mai'denhead, s. virginity ; freshness, newness
Mai'dhood. Mai'denhood, s. virginity
Maidma'rian, s. a kind of dance
Majes'tic, Majes'tical, a. august, grand
Majes'tically, ad. with dignity
Maj'esty, s. dignity, grandeur, elevation
Mail, s. armour ; a postman's bag
Maim, v. a. to hurt, to wound, to cripple
Maim, s. lameness, injury, defect
Main, a. principal, chief ; forcible ; important
Main, s. the gross, the whole ; the ocean
Main'land, s. a continent
Main'ly, ad. chiefly, powerfully, principally
Main'mast, s. the chief or middle mast
Main'prize, s. a bail, pledge, or surety
Main'sail, s. the sail of the mainmast
Maintain', v. to keep, defend, justify, support
Maintain'able, a. defensible, justifiable
Main'tenance, s. sustenance, protection
Main'top, s. the top of the mainmast
Main'yard, s. the yard of the mainmast
Ma'jor, a. greater, senior, elder
Ma'jor, s. the office above the captain ; in lo-
  gic, the first proposition of a syllogism
Majora'tion, s. enlargement, increase
Major'ity, s. the greater number ; the office
  of a major ; full age ; end of minority
Maize, s. a sort of Indian wheat
Make, v. to create, force, gain, reach, form
Make, s. form, structure, nature
Ma'ker, s. the Creator ; he who makes
Ma'kepeace, s. a peace-maker, reconciler
Ma'king, s. the act of forming
Mal'ady, s. a disease, a sickness
Mal'apert, a. saucy, impertinent, bold
Malapert'ness, s. quick impudence ; sauciness
Malax'ate, v. a. to make soft, to moisten
Male, s. the he of any species
Maladminstra'tion, s. bad conduct in any
  public employ ; bad management
Mal'content, a. discontented—s. a rebel
Maledic'ted, a. accursed or banned
Maledic'tion, s. a curse, an execration
Malefac'tion, s. a crime

Malefac'tor, s. an offender against law
Malef'ic, a. mischievous, hurtful
Malprac'tice, s. bad practice or behaviour
Malev'olence, s. ill will, malignity, spite
Malev'olent, a. illnatured, malignant
Mal'ice, s. badness of design, ill will
Malic'ious, a. intending ill, malignant
Malic'iously, ad. with intention of mischief
Malic'iousness, s. malice, ill will [ious
Mali'gn, a. unfavourable, pestilential, nox-
Malig'nancy, Malig'nity, s. malevolence
Malig'nant, a. noxious to life
Malig'nantly, ad. enviously, maliciously
Mal'kin, s. a dirty wench ; a mop
Mall, s. a public walk ; a beater or hammer
Mall, v. a. to beat or strike with a mall
Mal'lard, s. the drake of the wild duck
Malleabil'ity, s. the quality of enduring the
  hammer, and spreading without breaking
Mal'leable, a. capable of enduring the ham-
  mer, and spreading without breaking
Mal'leableness, s. malleability, ductility
Mal'leate, v. a. to beat with a hammer
Mal'let, s. a wooden hammer
Malm'sey, s. a sort of grape ; a kind of wine
Malt, s. barley steeped in water, and dried
Malt'floor, s. a floor for drying malt on
Malt'house, s. a house for malting in
Maltre'at, v. a. to treat ill or amiss
Ma'tster, s. one who deals in malt
Malversa'tion, s. misbehaviour in any office,
  mean artifices or shifts
Mam, Mamma', s. a fond word for mother
Mam'met, s. a puppet ; artificial figure
Mam'millary, a. belonging ● the paps
Mam'moc, v. to tear or pull in pieces
Mam'moc, s. a shapeless piece
Mam'mon, s. riches, wealth
Man, s. human being ; the male ; not a boy
Man, v. a. to furnish with men, &c.
Man'acles, s. chains for the hands ; shackles
Man'age, Man'agement, Man'agery, s. con-
  duct, frugality ; cunning practice ; discipline
Man'ageable, a. governable, tractable
Man'ager, s. a man of frugality ; a conductor
Mana'tion, s. the act of issuing from
Man'chet, s. a small loaf of fine bread
Man'cipate, v. a. to enslave, to bind to he
Man'ciple, s. the steward of a community
Manda'mus, s. a writ in the king's bench
Mandari'n, s. a Chinese magistrate or noble
Man'date, s. a command, a precept, a charge
Man'datory, a. preceptive, directory
Man'dible, s. the jaw—a. eatable
Mandib'ular, a. belonging to the jaw
Man'drake, s. a plant with singular roots
Man'ducate, v. a. to chew, to eat
Manduca'tion, s. eating, chewing
Mane, s. the hair on the neck of a horse
Man'eater, s. one who eats human flesh
Ma'nes, s. a ghost, shade, departed soul
Man'ful, a. bold, stout, daring, valiant
Man'fully, ad. boldly, stoutly, valiantly
Mange, s. a filthy disease in cattle
Ma'nger, s. a long wooden trough in which
  animals are fed
Man'gle, v. a. to lacerate ; to cut or tear in
  pieces ; to butcher ; to smooth linen
Man'gler, s. a hacker ; one who mangles
Man'go, s. an Indian fruit and pickle
Ma'ngy, a. infected with the mange

Man'hood, s. courage, bravery, virility
Ma'niac, s. a person mad
Mani'acal, a. affected with madness
Man'ifest, a. plain, open, detected
Man'ifest, v. a. to show plainly, make public
Manifesta'tion, s. discovery, publication
Man'ifestly, ad. plainly, evidently, clearly
Manifes'to, s. a public protestation
Man'ifold, a. many in number, divers
Man'ikin, s. a little man
Manti'le, s. a ring or bracelet; a card
Man'iple, s. handful; small band of soldiers
Man'kind, s. the human race
Man'like, Man'ly, a. firm, brave, stout
Man'liness, s. bravery, stoutness, dignity
Man'na, s. a physical drug, &c.
Man'ner, s. form, habit, mien, kind
Man'nerly, a. civil, complaisant
Man'ners, s. polite behaviour, morals
Manœu'vre, s. skilful management
Man'or, s. a lord's jurisdiction
Manse, s. a parsonage house
Man'sion, s. a dwelling-house, an abode
Man'slaughter, s. murder without malice
Man'tel, s. raised work over a chimney
Man'telet, s. a kind of short cloak; in fortification, a pent-house for shelter
Manti'ger, s. a large monkey, or baboon
Man'tle, s. a cloak—v. to ferment, to cover
Mantol'ogy, s. the gift of prophecy
Man'tua, s. a woman's gown
Man'tua-ma'ker, s. one who makes gowns
Man'ual, a. performed or paid by the hand
Man'ual, s. a small book of prayer, &c.
Manu'bial, a. taken as spoils in war
Manuduc'tion, s. guidance by the hand
Manufac'tory, s. a place where things are
  manufactured
Manufac'ture, s. any thing made by art
Manufac'ture, v. a. to make by art
Manufac'turer, s. an artificer, a workman
Manumis'sion, s. the act of freeing slaves
Manumit', v. a. to release from slavery
Manu'rable, a. capable of cultivation
Manu're, v. a. to dung—s. soil for land
Man'uscript, s. a book written, not printed
Man'y, a. numerous, several
Man'y-col'oured, a. having various colours
Man'y-cor'nered, a. having many corners
Man'y-head'ed, a. having many heads
Man'y-lan'guaged, a. having many languages
Map, s. a delineation of countries, &c.
Ma'ple, s. a tree
Map'pery, s. the art of designing
Mar, v. a. to injure, to spoil, damage
Maranath'a, s. a form of anathematizing
Maras'mus, s. a consumption
Marau'der, s. a plundering soldier
Marau'ding, s. ranging in quest of plunder
Marave'di, s. a small Spanish copper coin
Mar'ble, s. a stone of a fine polish
Mar'ble, a. made of or like marble
Mar'ble-heart'ed, a. cruel, hard-hearted
Mar'casite, s. a hard bright fossil
Marces'cent, a. growing withered
Marces'sible, a. liable to wither or fade
March, s. the third month of the year; a
  movement of soldiers; a solemn procession
Mar'ches, s. the limits of a country
Mar'chioness, s. the wife of a marquis
March'pane, s. a kind of sweet bread

Mar'cid, a. lean, withered, faded, rotten
Mare, s. the female of a horse; a kind of tor
  por, or stagnation, called the night-mare
Mar'eschal, s. a commander of an army
Mar'garite, s. a pearl; an herb
Mar'gent, Mar'gin, s. an edge, a border
Mar'ginal, a. placed in the margin
Mar'grave, s. a German title of sovereignty
Margra'viate, s. the territory of a margrave
Margravi'ne, s. the wife of a margrave
Mar'igold, s. a yellow flower, a pot herb
Mar'inate, v. a. to preserve fish in oil
Mar'ine, a. belonging to the sea
Mari'ne, s. a sea soldier; sea affairs
Mar'iner, s. a seaman, a sailor
Mar'joram, s. a sweet-smelling herb
Mar'ish, a. moorish, fenny, boggy
Mar'ital, a. pertaining to a husband
Mar'itime, a. performed on the sea, relating
  to the sea, bordering on the sea
Mark, s. a stamp, an impression, a proof; a
  silver coin worth 13s. 4d.
Mark, v. to impress with a mark, to note
Mar'ket, s. the place for and time of sale
Mar'ketable, a. fit to be sold at market
Mar'ksman, s. a man skilful to hit a mark
Marl, s. a sort of fat clay or manure
Mar'line, s. hemp dipped in pitch
Mar'lpit, s. a pit out of which marl is dug
Mar'ly, a. abounding with marl
Mar'malade, s. quinces boiled with sugar
Marmo'rean, a. made of marble
Marmo'set, s. a small kind of monkey
Marque, s. licence for reprisals; retaliation
Marquee', s. an officer's field tent
Mar'quis, s. a title next in rank to a duke
Mar'quisate, s. dignity of a marquis
Mar'riage, s. the act of uniting for life a man
  and woman according to law
Mar'riageable, a. of age to be married
Mar'row, s. an oily substance in bones
Mar'rowfat, s. a fine large kind of pea
Mar'rowless, a. void of marrow, dry
Mar'ry, v. to join in or enter into marriage
Marsh, Ma'rish, s. a bog, a fen, a swamp
Mar'shal, s. the chief officer of arms
Mar'shal, v. a. to arrange, rank in order
Mar'shalship, s. the office of a marshal
Marshmal'low, s. the name of a plant :
Marsh'marigold, s. the name of a flower
Mar'shy, a. boggy, produced in marshes
Mart, s. a place of public traffic; a bargain
Mar'ten, s. a large weazel; a swallow
Mar'tial, a. warlike, valiant, relating to war
Mar'tialist, s. a warrior; a fighter
Mar'tingal, s. a leathern thong for a horse
Mar'tinmas, s. the feast of St. Martin
Mar'tinet, Mar'tlet, s. a kind of swallow
Mar'tyr, s. one who dies for the truth
Mar'tyrdom, s. the death of a martyr
Martyrol'ogy, s. a register of martyrs
Mar'vel, s. a wonder—v. n. to wonder at
Mar'vellous, a. astonishing; surpassing credit
Mar'vellously, ad. wonderfully, strangely
Mar'vellousness, s. wonderfulness, strange
Mas'culine, a. male, like a man, manly [n ..
Mash, s. a mixture of water, bran, &c. for
  cattle; space between the threads of a net
Mash, v. a. to break, bruise, or squeeze
Mask, s. a disguise, an entertainment
Mas'ker, s. one who revels in a mask

Ma'son, s. one who works in stone
Mason'ic, a. relating to freemasons
Ma'soury, s. the craft or work of a mason
Masquera'de, s. an assembly of maskers
Masquera'der, s. a person in a mask
Mass, s. a lump; Romish church service
Mas'sacre, s. outchery, indiscriminate murder
Mas'sacre, v. a. to butcher indiscriminately
Mas'siness, Mas'siveness, s. weight, bulk
Mas'sive, Mas'sy, a. weighty, ponderous
Mast, s. the beam of a ship to which the sail
  is fixed; the fruit of beech and oak
Mas'ter, s. a director, governor; one who
  teaches; a title in universities
Mas'ter, v. a. to rule, to govern, to conquer
Mas'terless, a. wanting a master, ungoverned
Mas'terliness, s. eminent skill
Mas'terly, a. skilful; artful; imperious
Mas'terpiece, s. a performance done with ex-
  traordinary skill; chief excellence
Mas'tership, s. power, superiority, skill
Mas'terstroke, s. a capital performance
Mas'tery, s. dominion, superiority, skill
Mastica'tion, s. the act of chewing
Mas'ticatory, s. a medicine to be chewed
Mas'tich, s. a sweet-scented gum; cement
Mas'tiff, s. a large fierce species of dog
Mas'tless, a. bearing no mast
Mas'tlin, Mes'lin, s. mixed corn
Mat, s. a texture of sedge, flags, or rushes
Mat'achin, s. an old kind of dance
Matado're, s. a term at ombre or quadrille
Match, s. a contest; an equal; marriage; a
  piece of wood dipped in brimstone
Match, v. to be equal to; suit; marry; tally
Mat'chable, a. suitable, equal, correspondent
Mat'chless, a. having no equal
Mat'chlessly, ad. in a matchless manner
Mat'chmaker, s. one who makes matches
Mate, s. a companion; second in command,
  as the *master's mate*
Mate'rial, a. important, essential; corpo-
  real, consisting of matter, not spiritual
Mate'rialist, s. one who denies the doctrine
  of spiritual substances
Material'ity, s. material existence, corporeity
Mate'rially, ad. in the state of matter, essen-
  tially, importantly, momentously
Mate'rials, s. what any thing is made of
Mater'nal, a. motherly, fond, kind
Mathemat'ic, Mathemat'ical, a., considered
  according to the doctrine of mathematics
Mathemat'ically, ad. according to the laws
  or rules of the mathematics
Mathematic'ian, s. one skilled in, or a teacher
  of, the mathematics
Mathemat'ics, s. that science which teaches
  to number and measure whatever is capa-
  ble of it, comprised under lines, numbers,
  superficies, solids, &c.
Mathe'sis, s. the doctrine of mathematics
Mat'in, a. used in the morning
Mat'ins, s. morning worship
Mat'rass, s. chemical glass vessel
Ma'trice, or Ma'trix, s. the womb; a mould,
  place where any thing is first formed
Mat'ricide, s. the murdering of a mother
Matric'ulate, v. a. to admit to a membership
  of the universities of England
Matricula'tion, s. the act of matriculating
Matrimo'nial, a. pertaining to marriage

Mat'rimony, s. marriage; nuptial state
Ma'tron, s. an elderly lady, old woman
Ma'tronly, a. elderly, ancient, motherly
Matross', s. a soldier in the artillery
Mat'ter, s. body or substance extended; affair;
  occasion; subject; purulent motion
Mat'toc, s. a pick-axe, a tool to grub weeds
Mat'tress, s. a kind of quilt made to lie on
Matura'tion, s. suppuration, ripening
Matu'rative, a. ripening, conducing to ripe-
Matu're, a. ripe, perfect, well disposed [ness
Matu'rely, ad. with counsel well digested
Matu'rity, s. ripeness, completion
Maud'lin, a. drunk, fuddled—s. a plant
Man'gre, ad. in spite of, notwithstanding
Maul, v. a. to bruise, hurt in a coarse manner
Maul, s. a heavy wooden hammer
Maund, s. a hammer with handles
Maun'der, v. n. to grumble, to murmur
Maun'dy - Thurs'day, s. Thursday before
  Good-Friday
Mausole'um, s. pompous funeral monument
Maw, s. the stomach, the craw of birds
Maw'kish, a. apt to cause a loathing
Maw'met, s. a puppet, anciently an idol
Maw'mish, a. foolish, idle, nauseous
Maw'worm, s. a worm in the stomach
Max'illary, a. pertaining to the jaw bone
Max'im, s. a general principle, an axiom
May, s. the fifth month of the year
May, v. aux. to be permitted, to have power
May'flower, s. the name of a plant
May'fly, s. an insect peculiar to May
May'game, s. a sport, diversion, play
May'lily, s. the lily of the valley
May'or, s. chief magistrate of a corporation,
  in London and York called *Lord Mayor*
May'oralty, s. the office of a mayor
May'oress, s. the wife of a mayor
May'pole, s. a pole danced round in May
May'weed, s. a species of chamomile
Maz'zard, s. a jaw, the jaw bone
Maze, s. a confusion of thought; a labyrinth
Ma'zy, a. intricate, confused, perplexed
Mea'cock, a. tame, timorous, cowardly
Mead, s. a drink made of honey and water
Mead, Mead'ow, s. pasture land
Mea'ger, a. lean, poor in flesh, hungry
Mea'gerness, s. leanness, scantiness, bareness
Meak, s. a hook with a long handle
Meal, s. edible part of corn; a repast
Mea'liness, s. a mealy quality
Mea'lman, s. one that deals in meal
Mea'ly, a. having the soft qualities of meal
Mea'lymouthed, a. bashful of speech
Mean, a. of low rank, vile, despicable
Mean, s. medium, measure, revenue
Mean, v. to intend, design, understand
Mean'der, s. a serpentine, winding maze
Mean'ing, s. a signification, intention
Mean'ly, ad. without dignity, ungenerously
Mean'ness, s. lowness of mind, sordidness
Meant, *part. pass.* of *to mean*
Mease, s. a measure of 500 herrings
Mea'sled, a. infected with the measles
Mea'sles, s. a kind of fever, attended with
  inflammation, eruptions, &c.
Meas'urable, a. capable of being measured
Meas'ure, s. that by which any thing is mea-
  sured; musical time; metre; moderation,
  not excess; limit; degree; mean to an end

Meas'ure, v. a. to compute or allot quantity
Meas'ureless, a. immense, boundless
Meas'urement, s. the act of measuring
Meas'urer, s. one that measures
Meas'ures, s. ways, means, actions, &c.
Meat, s. flesh to be eaten; food in general
Meat'ed, a. fed, foddered
Meat'offering, s. an offering to be eaten
Mechan'ic, s. a manufacturer, artificer
Mechan'ic, Mechan'ical, a. skilled in mechanics; servile: of mean occupation
Mechanic'ian, Mech'anist, s. one professing or studying the construction of machines
Mechan'ics, s. the geometry of motion
Mech'anism, s. mechanical construction
Meco'nium, s. expressed juice of poppies
Med'al, s. an ancient coin; a piece stamped in honour of some famous exploit
Medal'lion, s. a large medal or coin
Med'alist, s. one curious in medals
Med'dle, v. to interpose, to have to do
Med'dlesome, a. intermeddling
Med'dler, s. an officious busybody
Me'diate, v. to interpose as an equal friend to both parties; to be between two
Media'tion, s. an interposition, agency
Media'tor, s. an intercessor, an adviser
Media'torship, s. the office of a mediator
Media'trix, s. a female mediator
Med'icable, a. that may be healed
Med'ical, Medic'inal, a. physical
Med'ically, Medic'inally, ad. physically
Medic'ament, s. any thing used in healing
Med'icate, v. a. to impregnate with medicines
Med'icine, s. a remedy in physic
Medi'ety, s. a middle state; half
Me'diu, s. a small coin; a measure
Medioc'rity, s. a middle state; small degree
Med'itate, v. to plan, scheme, contemplate
Medita'tion, s. deep thought, contemplation
Med'itative, a. given to meditation, serious
Mediterra'nean, Mediterra'neous, a. encircled with land; remote from the sea
Me'dium, s. mean or middle state
Med'lar, s. the name of a tree and its fruit
Med'ley, s. a mixture, mingled mass
Medul'lar, Medul'lary, a. pertaining to marrow
Meed, s. a reward, recompence, gift [row
Meek, a. mild of temper, gentle, soft
Meek'ness, s. gentleness, softness, mildness
Meer, s. a lake, a boundary
Meet, v. to encounter, find, join—a. proper
Meet'ing, s. an assembly; conventicle
Meet'ly, ad. properly, fitly
Meet'ness, s. fitness, propriety
Me'grim, s. a painful disorder of the head
Mel'ancholic, Mel'ancholy, a. fanciful, gloomy, hypochondriacal, dismal
Mel'ancholy, s. sadness, pensiveness
Me'liorate, v. a. to make better, improve
Meliora'tion, Melior'ity, s. improvement
Mellif'erous, a. productive of honey
Mellifica'tion, s. the act of making honey
Mellif'luence, s. a flow of sweetness
Mellif'luent, Mellif'luous, a. flowing with honey, sweet; eloquent
Mel'low, a. soft in sound; full ripe; drunk
Mel'lowness, s. ripeness, softness by maturity
Melo'dious, a. harmonious, musical
Mel'ody, s. music, harmony of sound
Mel'on, s. a plant and its fruit

Melt, v. to make or become liquid, to dissolve
Mel'ter, s. one who melts metals
Mem'ber, s. a limb, part appendant to the body, head, clause; one of a community
Mem'brane, s. a web of many fibres
Membra'neous, a. consisting of membranes
Memen'to, s. a hint, notice, memorial
Memoi'r, s. an account of transactions familiarly written; account of any thing
Mem'orable, a. worthy of remembrance
Memoran'dum, s. a note to help memory
Memo'rial, s. a monument; hint to assist memory; a writing about public business by a public minister
Memo'rialist, s. one who writes memorials
Mem'ory, s. the power of retaining or recollecting things past; that faculty by which we call to mind any past transaction
Men, plural of Man
Men'ace, v. a. to threaten—s. a threat
Menag'e, or Mena'gerie, s. a collection of animals
Mend, v. a. to repair, correct, improve
Mendac'ity, s. a falsehood
Men'der, s. one who mends or improves
Men'dicant, a. begging—s. a beggar
Me'nial, s. a servant—a. domestic
Menol'ogy, s. a register of months
Men'trual, a. monthly, lasting a month
Men'struum, s. any liquid used in infusions
Mensurabil'ity, s. capacity of being measured
Men'surable, a. that may be measured
Men'surate, v. a. to measure any thing
Mensura'tion, s. the act of measuring
Men'tal, a. intellectual; in the mind
Men'tion, s. oral recital of any thing
Men'tion, v. a. to write or express in words
Mephit'ical, a. ill-savoured, stinking
Mer'cantile, a. trading, commercial
Mer'cat, s. the time or place of trade, a market
Mer'cenary, s. a hireling—a. venal, selfish
Mer'cer, s. one who sells silks
Mer'cery, s. the trade of mercers
Mer'chandise, s. trade, commerce, wares
Mer'chant, s. a dealer by wholesale
Mer'chantman, s. a ship of trade
Mer'ciful, a. compassionate, tender, kind
Mer'cifully, ad. tenderly, mildly, with pity
Mer'ciless, a. void of mercy, pitiless
Mercu'rial, a. consisting of mercury
Mer'cury, s. quicksilver; sprightly qualities
Mer'cy, s. clemency, pardon, mildness
Mere, a. that or this only, nothing else
Me'rely, ad. simply, only, in this manner
Meretric'ious, a. whorish, lewd, gaudy
Meretric'iously, ad. in the manner of lewd women
Merid'ian, s. mid-day; the line drawn from north to south, which the sun crosses at noon; highest point of glory and power
Merid'ional, a. southern, southerly
Mer'it, s. desert, due, reward, claim, right
Merito'rious, a. high in desert
Mer'lin, s. a sort of hawk
Mer'maid, s. a fabulous sea creature, with the upper parts described like those of a woman, and the lower like a fish
Mer'rily, ad. with gaiety, cheerfully
Mer'riment, s. cheerfulness, laughter, gaiety
Mer'ry, a. cheerful, causing laughter
Mer'ry-an'drew, s. a buffoon, a jack-pudding

Mer'rythought, *s.* a bone of a fowl
Mer'sion, *s.* the act of dipping or plunging
Mesenter'ic, *a.* relating to the mesentery
Mes'entery. *s.* that membranous part round which the guts are convolved
Mesh, *s.* space between the threads of a net
Mess, *s.* a dish or portion of food
Mess, *v. n.* to eat, to feed together
Mes'sage, *s.* an errand, advice sent
Mes'senger, *s.* one who carries a message
Messi'ah, *s.* the Saviour of the world, Christ
Mess'mate, *s.* one who eats with another
Mes'suage, *s.* a dwelling-house, &c.
Met, *pret.* and *part.* of *to meet*
Me'tage, *s.* the measuring of coals
Met'al, *s. metals* are 6 in number. viz. gold, silver, copper, tin, iron, and lead ; spirit
Metalep'tic, *a.* acting transversely
Metal'lic, *a.* pertaining to metal
Met'alline, *a.* impregnated with metal
Met'allist, *s.* one skilled in metals
Met'allurgy, *s.* the act of working metals
Metamor'phosis, *s.* a transformation
Met'aphor, *s.* the application of a word to a use to which, in its original import, it cannot be put. A *metaphor* is a simile comprised in a word
Metaphor'ical, *a.* figurative, not literal
Met'aphrase, *s.* a mere verbal translation
Metaphys'ical, *a.* relating to metaphysics
Metaphys'ics, *s.* the science which considers the general affections of things existing
Metas'tasis, *s.* a transition or removal
Metath'esis, *s.* a transposition, change
Mete, *v. a.* to reduce to measure
Metempsycho'sis, *s.* a transmigration of souls from one body to another at death
Me'teor, *s.* a body in the air or sky, that is luminous and transitory in its nature
Meteorolog'ical, *a.* relating to meteors
Meteorol'ogist, *s.* a man skilled in meteors
Meteorol'ogy, *s.* the doctrine of meteors
Me'ter, *s.* a measurer
Mete'wand. Mete'yard, *s.* a staff of a certain length, wherewith measures are taken
Metheg'lin, *s.* a drink made of honey, spices, water, &c. boiled together, and fermented
Methin'ks, *v. imp.* I think, it seems to me
Meth'od, *s.* convenient order, regularity
Method'ical, *a.* ranged in due order, exact
Method'ically, *ad.* according to method
Meth'odise, *v.a.* to bring into order, regulate
Meth'odist, *s.* a sect divided into two classes ; the one subscribes the doctrines of Calvin, the other the tenets of Arminius
Methou'ght, *pret.* of *methinks*, I thought
Meton'omy, *s.* a rhetorical figure by which one word is used for another
Metopos'copy, *s.* the study of physiognomy
Me'tre. *s.* verse, harmonic measure
Met'rical, *a.* pertaining to metre
Me'trice, *s.* a musical measure of syllables
Metrop'olis, *s.* the chief city of a country
Metropol'itan, *s.* an archbishop
Met'tle, *s.* fire, briskness, spirit, courage
Met'tled, *a.* sprightly, courageous
Met'tlesome, *a.* lively, brisk, courageous
Mew, *s.* a cage, enclosure ; a sea fowl
Mew, *v. a.* to cry as a cat ; moult ; shut up
Mewl, *v. n.* to squall as a young child
Mezzotin'to, *s.* a kind of engraving on copper

Mi'asm, *s.* such particles or atoms as are supposed to arise from distempered, putrifying, or poisonous bodies
Mice, *s. plural* of *mouse*
Mich'aelmas, *s.* the feast of St. Michael
Miche, *v. a.* to skulk, absent one's self
Mi'cher, *s.* a skulker, a lazy loiterer
Mi'crocosm, *s.* the little world ; the body of man is so called
Microm'eter, *s.* an astronomical instrument to measure small spaces
Mi'croscope, *s.* an optical instrument, by which the smallest objects are discerned
Mid, Midst, *a.* between two ; equally distant
Mid'day, *s.* noon, meridian
Mid'dle, *a.* equally distant from the two extremes ; intermediate ; intervening
Mid'dleaged, *a.* about the middle of life
Mid'dlemost, Mid'most, *a.* in the midst
Mid'dling, *a.* of middle rank ; moderate
Midge, *s.* a gnat, an insect
Midheav'en, *s.* the middle of the sky
Mid'land, *a.* surrounded by land
Mid'leg, *s.* the middle of the leg
Mid'night, *s.* twelve o'clock at night
Mid'riff, *s.* the diaphragm ; a skin separating the heart, &c. from the lower belly
Mid'shipman, *s.* a naval officer next in rank to a lieutenant
Midst, *a.* being in the middle
Mid'stream, *s.* the middle of the stream
Mid'summer, *s.* the summer solstice
Mid'way, *s.* the middle of a passage
Mid'wife, *s.* a woman who assists women in childbirth
Mid'wifery, *s.* the act of delivering women
Mid'winter, *s.* the winter solstice
Mien, *s.* air, look, manner, appearance
Might, *pret.* of *may*—*s.* power, strength
Mi'ghtily, *ad.* powerfully, efficaciously
Mi'ghtiness, *s.* power, height of dignity
Mi'ghty, *a.* powerful—*ad.* in a great degree
Mi'grate, *v. n.* to remove, to change place
Migra'tion, *s.* the act of changing residence
Milch, *a.* giving or yielding milk
Mild, *a.* kind, gentle, soft, easy, tender
Mil'dew, *s.* a dew which corrodes plants certain spots on cloth, paper, &c.
Mild'ly, *ad.* tenderly, not severely
Mild'ness, *s.* gentleness, clemency, tenderness
Mile, *s.* a land measure of 1760 yards
Mi'lestone, *s.* a stone set to mark the miles
Mil'foil, *s.* a herb with many leaves
Mil'iary, *a.* small, with millet seeds
Mil'itant, *a.* fighting ; engaged in warfare
Mil'itary, *a.* warlike, suiting a soldier
Mil'itate, *v. n.* to differ from, to oppose
Mili'tia, *s.* a national force ; tribulation
Milk, *s.* the liquor with which females feed their young from the breast or teats
Milk, *v. a.* to draw milk from a cow
Mil'ken, *a.* consisting of milk
Mil'ker, *s.* one who milks animals
Mil'kiness, *s.* softness like that of milk
Mil'kmaid, *s.* a woman employed in the dairy
Mil'ksop, *s.* a soft effeminate man
Mil'kwhite, *a.* white as milk
Mil'ky, *a.* yielding milk ; soft, gentle
Mil'ky-way', *s.* a broad white track in the heavens, caused by the combined radiance of an infinity of fixed stars ; the galaxy

Mill, *s.* an engine to grind corn, &c.

Mill, *v. a.* to grind, comminute; stamp

Mill'cog, *s.* a tooth of a wheel

Millena'rian, *s.* one who holds the doctrine of, or expects, the millennium

Mil'lenary, *a.* consisting of a thousand

Millen'nium, *s.* the space of 1000 years, during which some imagine Christ will reign on the earth after the resurrection

Mil'lepedes, *s.* woodlice with numerous feet

Mil'ler, *s.* one who attends mills; a fly

Milles'imal, *a.* a thousandth

Mil'let, *s.* the name of a fish and a plant

Mill'horse, *s.* a horse that turns a mill

Mil'liner, *s.* one who sells ribbands, bonnets, caps, and dresses for women

Mil'linery, *s.* goods sold by a milliner

Mil'lion, *s.* ten hundred thousand

Mill'pond, *s.* a bed of water near a mill

Mill'stone, *s.* a stone by which corn is ground

Mill'teeth, *s.* large teeth: the grinders

Milt, *s.* the soft roe of fishes, the spleen

Mil'ter, *s.* the male of fishes

Mim'ic, *s.* a ludicrous imitator of the gestures or voices of others, a buffoon

Mim'ic, Mim'ical, *a.* apish, imitative

Mim'icry, *s.* a burlesque imitation

Mimog'rapher, *s.* a writer of farces

Min'atory, *a.* threatening, denouncing

Mince, *v. a.* to cut very small; to clip words

Min'cingly, *ad.* in small parts, not fully

Mind, *s.* intelligent faculty; opinion

Mind, *v. a.* to mark, to attend, to remind

Mind'ed, *a.* inclined, affected, disposed

Mind'ful, *a.* regardful, attentive, heedful

Mind'fulness, *s.* attention, watchfulness

Mind'less, *a.* regardless, inattentive

Mine, *pron. posses.* belonging to me

Mine, *s.* a place where minerals are dug, a cavern under a fortification filled with gunpower—*v.* to sap or ruin by mines

Mi'ner, *s.* a person who digs mines

Min'eral, *s.* matter dug out of mines

Min'eral, *a.* consisting of fossil bodies

Min'eralist, *a.* one skilled in minerals

Mineral'ogist, *s.* one who discourses on mine.

Mineral'ogy, *s.* the doctrine of minerals [raw]

Min'gle, *v. a.* to mix, to compound, to unite

Min'gle, *s.* mixture, confused mass, medley

Min'iature, *s.* a painting very small and delicate; representation in a small compass

Min'ikin, *a.* small—*s.* a small sort of pin

Min'im, Min'um, *s.* a dwarf; a note in music

Min'imus, *s.* a being of the least size

Min'ion, *s.* a favourite; a low, unprincipled dependant; a darling

Min'ish, *v. a.* to lessen, lop, impair

Min'ister, *s.* an officer of the state, or the church; an agent; a delegate

Min'ister, *v.* to give to, supply, to attend on

Ministe'rial, *a.* pertaining to a minister of the church or state; attendant

Ministra'tion, *s.* agency, service, office

Min'istry, Min'istery, *s.* office, service; ecclesiastical function; persons employed in the affairs of a state

Min'now, *s.* a very small fish; a pink

Mi'nor, *a.* petty, smaller, inconsiderable

Mi'nor, *s.* one under age; in logic, the second proposition in the syllogism

Mi'norate, *v. a.* to diminish, to lessen

Minora'tion, *s.* the act of lessening

Minor'ity, *s.* nonage; state of being under age; the smaller number

Min'otaur, *s.* a monster, invented by the poets, half a man and half a bull

Min'ster, *s.* a monastery, a cathedral church

Min'strel, *s.* an ancient wandering musician

Min'strelsy, *s.* music; a band of musicians

Mint, *s.* a plant; place where money is coined

Min'uet, *s.* a stately regular dance

Minu'te, *a.* small, little, slender, trifling

Min'ute, *s.* the 60th part of an hour

Min'ute, *v. a.* to set down in short hints

Min'ute-book, *s.* a book of short hints

Min'ute-gun, *s.* a gun fired every minute

Minu'tely, *ad.* exactly, to a small point

Minx, *s.* a young, pert, wanton girl

Mir'acle, *s.* something above human power

Mirac'ulous, *a.* done by miracle

Mirac'ulously, *ad.* by miracle, wonderfully

Mirado'r, *s.* a balcony, a gallery

Mire, *s.* mud, dirt, filth; an ant, a pismire

Mire, *v. a.* to whelm in the mud

Mir'ror, *s.* a looking-glass, a pattern

Mir'ror-stone, *s.* a clear, transparent stone

Mirth, *s.* jollity, gaiety, laughter

Mir'thful, *a.* gay, cheerful, merry

Mi'ry, *a.* deep in mud, muddy, filthy

Misadven'ture, *s.* mischance, bad fortune

Misadvi'se, *v. a.* to give bad counsel

Misadvi'sed, *a.* ill-counselled, ill-directed

Misaim'ed, *a.* not aimed rightly

Mis'anthrope, *s.* a hater of mankind

Mixan'thropy, *s.* the hatred of mankind

Misapply', *v. a.* to apply to wrong purposes

Misapprehen'd, *v. a.* not to understand right ly, to misunderstand, to mistake

Misapprehen'sion, *s.* not right apprehension

Misassi'gn, *v. a.* to assign erroneously

Misbecom'e, *v. a.* not to become, not to suit

Misbecom'ing, *part. a.* indecent, unseemly

Misbego'tten, *part. a.* unlawfully begotten

Misbeha've, *v. n.* to act improperly or ill

Misbeha'viour, *s.* ill conduct, bad practice

Misbelie'f, *s.* a wrong faith or belief

Mis'believer, *s.* one that holds a false religion

Misca'l, *v. a.* to name improperly

Miscal'culate, *v. a.* to reckon wrong

Miscar'riage, *s.* abortion; ill success

Miscar'ry, *v. a.* to have an abortion; to fail

Miscella'neous, *a.* composed of various kinds mixed without order

Mis'cellany, *s.* a mass or mixture compounded of various kinds

Mischan'ce, *s.* ill luck, ill fortune

Mis'chief, *s.* harm, hurt, injury

Mis'chief-ma'ker, *s.* one who causes mischief

Mis'chievous, *a.* hurtful, malicious, harmful

Mis'cible, *a.* possible to be mingled

Miscita'tion, *s.* an unfair or false quotation

Misclai'm, *s.* an improper or mistaken claim

Misconcep'tion, *s.* a false opinion

Miscon'duct, *s.* ill management, ill behaviour

Misconstruc'tion, *s.* a wrong interpretation

Miscon'strue, *v. a.* to interpret wrong

Miscou'nt, *v. a.* to reckon wrong

Mis'creance, *s.* unbelief, false faith

Mis'creant, *s.* an infidel, a vile wretch

Miscrea'te, Miscrea'ted, *a.* formed unnaturally, or illegitimately, ill shaped

Misdee'd, *s.* an evil action, crime

Misdee'm, *v. a.* to judge ill of; to mistake
Misdemea'n, *v. a.* to behave ill
Misdemea'nor, *s.* an offence, ill behaviour
Misdevo'tion, *s.* mistaken piety
Misdirect', *v.a.* to direct wrong or improperly
Misdo', *v.* to do wrong, to commit faults
Misdou'bt, *v. a.* to suspect—*s.* suspicion
Misemploy', *v. a.* to use to wrong purposes
Misemploy'ment, *s.* improper application
Mi'ser, *s.* a wretch, covetous to extremity
Mis'erable, *a.* unhappy, wretched; stingy
Mis'erableness, *s.* state of misery
Mis'erably, *ad.* unhappily; meanly
Misery, *s.* wretchedness, calamity, avarice
Misfash'ion, *v. a.* to form wrong
Misfor'm, *v. a.* to form badly
Misfor'tune, *s.* calamity, evil fortune; ill luck
Misgiv'e, *v. a.* to fill with doubt
Misgov'ern, *v. a.* to rule amiss. govern ill
Misgui'de, *v. a.* to direct ill, to lead wrong
Misgui'dance, *s.* false direction
Mishap', *s.* mischance, ill luck
Misinfer'. *v. a.* to infer wrong, to mistake
Misinfor'm, *v.a.* to deceive by false accounts
Misinter'pret, *v. a.* to explain wrong
Misjoi'n, *v. a.* to join unfitly or improperly
Misjud'ge, *v. a.* to form false opinions
Mislay', *v. a.* to lay in a wrong place
Mis'le, *v. n.* to rain imperceptible drops
Mislea'd, *v. a.* to guide in a wrong way
Misli'ke. *v. a.* to disapprove, not to like
Misli'ke, *s.* disapprobation, dislike
Mis'ly, *a.* raining in very small drops
Misman'age. *v. a.* to manage ill, to misapply
Misman'agement, *s.* ill conduct
Mismat'ch, *v. a.* to match unsuitably
Misna'me, *v. a.* to call by a wrong name
Misno'mer, *s.* in law, an indictment vacated
  by a wrong name; a miscalling
Misobser've, *v. a.* not to observe accurately
Misog'ynist, *s.* a hater of women
Misog'yny, *s.* hatred of women
Misor'der. *v. a.* to manage irregularly
Mispersua'sion, *s.* a false persuasion
Mispla'ce, *v. a.* to put in a wrong place
Mispoi'nt, *v. a.* to point or divide wrong
Mispri'se, *v. a.* to mistake, slight, scorn
Mispris'ion, *s.* contempt, negligence, scorn:
  misprision of treason is the concealment of
  known treason
Misproportion, *v.* to join without symmetry
Misprou'd, *a.* viciously proud
Misquo'te, *v. a.* to quote falsely
Misreci'te, *v. a.* to recite or repeat wrong
Misreck'on, *v. a.* to compute wrong
Misrela'te, *v. a.* to relate inaccurately
Misrepor't, *v. a.* to give a false account
Misrepresen't, *v. a.* to represent not as it is,
  to falsify to disadvantage
Misru'le, *s.* tumult, disorder, revel
Miss, *s.* a young woman unmarried
Miss, *v.* not to hit, mistake, fall, omit
Mis'sal, *s.* the Romish mass book
Missha'pe, *v. a.* to shape ill, to form ill
Mis'sile, *a.* thrown by the hand
Mis'sion, *s.* a commission, legation
Mis'sionary, *s.* one sent to preach the gospel
  and propagate religion
Mis'sive, *a.* such as may be sent or flung
Mis'sive, *s.* a letter sent; a messenger
Misspea'k, *v. a.* to speak wrong

Misspel', *v. a.* to spell wrong
Misspen'd, *v. a.* to spend ill, waste, lavish
Missta'te, *v. a.* to state wrong or falsely
Mist, *s.* a low thin cloud; a fog; dimness
Mista'ke, *v.* to conceive wrong, to err
Mistea'ch, *v. a.* to teach wrong
Mister'm, *v. a.* to term erroneously
Misti'me, *v. a.* not to time right
Mis'tiness, *s.* cloudiness, being overcast
Mis'tion, *s.* the state of being mingled
Mis'tletoe, *s.* the name of a plant
Mis'tress, *s.* a woman teacher; a concubine
Mistrus't, *s.* want of confidence. suspicion
Mistrus'tful, *a.* suspicious. doubting
Mistrus'tfully. *ad.* with suspicion
Mistrus'tfulness, *s.* diffidence. doubt
Mistrus'tless, *a.* confident, not suspecting
Mis'ty, *a.* clouded, obscure, not plain
Misunderstan'd, *v. a.* to misconceive. to err
Misunderstan'ding, *s.* a misconception. error
Misu'sage, Misu'se, *s.* bad treatment. abuse
Mite, *s.* a small insect; any small thing
Mith'ridate, *s.* a medicine against poison
Mit'igate, *v. a.* to alleviate, to assuage
Mitiga'tion, *s.* the act of assuaging; abate
  ment of any thing harsh or painful
Mi'tre, *s.* a kind of episcopal crown
Mi'tred, *a.* adorned with a mitre
Mit'tens, *s.* gloves without fingers
Mit'tent, *a.* sending forth, emitting
Mit'timus, *s.* a warrant by which a justice of
  peace sends an offender to prison
Mix, *v. a.* to unite, join, mingle
Mix'ture, *s.* act of mixing, things mixed
Miz'maze, *s.* a labyrinth, a maze
Miz'zen, *s.* the mast in the stern of a ship
Mnemon'ics, *s.* the art or act of memory
Moan, *v.* to grieve, to deplore—*s.* a lamenta
Moat, *s.* a canal round a castle. &c.   [tion
Mob, *s.* a woman's cap; a crowd. rabble
Mob, *v. a.* to scold vulgarly, to riot
Mob'ble, *v. a.* to dress inelegantly
Mob'by, *s.* a drink made of potatoes
Mobil'ity, *s.* the populace; activity; fickleness
Mo'cho-stone, *s.* a stone nearly related to
  the agate kind
Mock, *v. a.* to mimic, ridicule, tantalize
Mock. *a.* false, counterfeit, not real
Mock'able, *a.* exposed to mockery
Mocka'does, *s.* a kind of woollen stuff
Mock'ery, *s.* ridicule, scorn, vain show
Mo'dal, *a.* relating to the form or mode
Modal'ity, *s.* accidental difference
Mode, *s.* form, state, method. fashion
Mod'el, *s.* a representation, copy, standard
Mod'el, *v. a.* to mould, shape. delineate
Mod'erate, *a.* temperate, mild, sober
Mod'erate, *v. a.* to regulate, to restrain
Mod'erately, *ad.* temperately, mildly
Modera'tion, *s.* calmness of mind, equani-
  mity; keeping the passions within due
  bounds; frugality in expense
Modera'tor, *s.* one who rules or restrains
Mod'ern, *a.* late, recent, not ancient. mean
Mod'ernise, *v. a.* to adapt ancient composi
  tions to modern persons or things
Mod'erns, *s.* persons of late times
Mod'est, *a.* diffident, chaste, discreet
Mod'estly, *ad.* not arrogantly, chastely
Mod'esty, *s.* chastity, decency, humility
Mod'icum, *s.* a small portion. a pittance

M

Mod'ifiable, *a.* that which may be diversified
Modifica'tion, *s.* the act of modifying
Mod'ify, *v. a.* to qualify, soften, shape
Modil'lion, *s.* a sort of bracket
Mo'dish, *a.* fashionable, tasty, gay
Mo'dishly, *ad.* in a modish manner
Mo'dishness, *s.* affectation of fashion
Mod'ulate, *v. a.* to form sounds to a certain key, or to certain notes
Modula'tion, *s.* an agreeable harmony
Modula'tor, *s.* one who forms sounds to a certain key; a tuner of instruments
Mod'ule, *s.* an empty representation
Mo'dus, *s.* a compensation in lieu of tithes
Mogul', *s.* an emperor of India
Mo'hair, *s.* a thread, or stuff made of hair
Mo'hoc, *s.* a barbarous Indian, a ruffian
Mol'dered, *a.* crazed, bewildered
Moido're, *s.* Portugal coin, value 1l. 7s.
Moi'ety, *s.* half, one of two equal parts
Moil, *v.* to daub, to toil, drudge, weary
Moist, *a.* wet, not dry, damp, juicy
Mois'ten, *v. a.* to make damp, to wet
Mois'tness, *s.* dampness, wettishness
Mois'ture, *s.* a small quantity of water, &c.
Mole, *s.* a natural spot; an animal
Mo'lecatcher, *s.* one who catches moles
Mo'lehill, *s.* a hillock made by a mole
Moles't, *v. a.* disturb, vex, disquiet
Molesta'tion. *s.* disturbance, vexation
Mole'warp, Mould'warp, *s.* a mole
Mol'lient, *a.* softening, assuaging
Mol'lifiable, *a.* that may be softened
Mollifica'tion, *s.* the act of mollifying
Mol'lify, *v. a.* to soften, assuage, pacify
Molos'ses, Molas'ses, *s.* treacle; the spume or scum of the juice of the sugar cane
Mol'ten, *part. pass.* from *to melt*
Mol'ting, or Moul'ting, *part. a.* the falling off, or change of feathers, horns, &c.
Mo'ly, *s.* a kind of wild garlic
Mome, *s.* a dull, blockish person; a post
Mo'ment, *s.* an indivisible part of time; consequence, importance, value
Mo'mentary, *a.* lasting for a moment
Momen'tous, *a.* important, weighty
Mom'mery, *s.* a farcical entertainment
Mon'achal, *a.* monastic, monkish
Mon'achism, *s.* a monastic life
Mon'ad, Mon'ade, *s.* an indivisible thing
Mon'arch, *s.* a sovereign, a king
Monar'chial, *a.* suiting a monarch, regal
Monar'chical, *a.* vested in a single ruler
Mon'archy, *s.* a kingly government; empire
Mon'astery, *s.* a convent, a cloister
Monas'tic, *a.* pertaining to a convent
Monas'tically, *ad.* reclusely
Mon'day, *s.* the second day of the week
Mon'ey, *s.* any metal coined for traffic
Mon'eyed, *a.* rich in money, wealthy
Mon'eyless, *a.* wanting money, poor
Mon'eyscrivener, *s.* one who raises money for others
Mon'ger, *s.* a trader, dealer, seller
Mon'grel, *s.* an animal of a mixed breed
Mon'ish, *v. a.* to admonish, counsel
Mon'isher, *s.* an admonisher, a monitor
Moni'tion, *s.* information, document
Mon'itor, *s.* one who warns of faults, or gives necessary hints
Mon'itory, *a.* admonishing—*s.* a warning

Monk, *s.* one who lives in a monastery
Mon'key, *s.* an ape, a baboon; silly fellow
Monk'ish, *a.* monastic; pertaining to monk
Mon'ochord, *s.* an instrument of one string
Monoc'ular, Monoc'ulous, *a.* one-eyed
Mon'ody, *s.* a poem sung by one person
Monog'amy, *s.* a marriage of one wife only
Mon'ogram, *s.* a cipher, or character, composed of many letters interwoven
Mon'ologue, *s.* a soliloquy
Monom'achy, *s.* a single combat, a duel
Monopet'alous, *a.* having but one leaf
Monop'olist, *s.* one who engrosses a trade or business entirely to himself
Monop'olize, *v. a.* to engross all of a commodity in a person's own hands
Monop'oly, *s.* the sole privilege of selling
Monop'tote, *s.* a noun but of one case
Monosyl'lable, *s.* a word of one syllable
Monos'tich, *s.* a composition of one verse
Monot'ony, *s.* a want of variety in cadence
Monsoo'n, *s.* a periodical trade wind
Mon'ster, *s.* a thing unnatural or horrible
Mon'strous, *a.* unnatural, shocking
Monte'ro, *s.* a horseman's cap
Monte'th, *s.* a vessel to wash glasses in
Month, *s.* a space of time, four weeks
Month'ly, *a.* happening every month
Mon'ument, *s.* any thing to perpetuate memory, as a tomb, pillar, statue, &c.
Monumen'tal, *a.* preserving memory
Mood, *s.* a term in grammar; disposition
Moo'dy, *a.* angry, out of humour; menta.
Moon, *s.* the great luminary of the night
Moon'beam, *s.* a ray of lunar light
Moon'calf, *s.* a monster; a stupid fellow
Moon'eyed, *a.* dim-eyed, purblind
Moon'less, *a.* not illuminated by the moon
Moon'light, *s.* light afforded by the moon
Moon'y, *a.* like the moon, lunated
Moor, *s.* a negro; a marsh, fen, bog
Moor, *v.* to fasten by anchors, to be fixed
Moor'hen, *s.* name of a water fowl
Moor'ing, *s.* a place where a ship anchors
Moor'ish, Moor'ly, *a.* marshy, fenny
Moor'land, *s.* a marsh, watery ground
Moose, *s.* a large American deer
Moot, *v. a.* to exercise in law pleadings
Moot-case, or *point*, *s.* a disputable point
Moot'ed, *a.* plucked up by the roots
Mop, *s.* a utensil to clean floors, &c.
Mope, *v. n.* to be spiritless or drowsy
Mopus, Mo'pus, *s.* a drone, a dreamer
Mop'pet, Mop'sey, *s.* a puppet, a doll
Mor'al, *a.* relating to human life, as it is virtuous or criminal, good or bad
Mor'al, *s.* the instruction of a fable, &c.
Mor'alist, *s.* one who practises morality
Moral'ity, *s.* the doctrine of the duties
Mor'alize, *v.* to write, &c. on moral subject
Mor'alizer, *s.* he who moralizes
Mor'ally, *ad.* honestly, justly; probably
Mor'als, *s.* the practice of moral duties
Morass', *s.* a fen, a bog, a moor, a swamp
Mor'bid, *a.* diseased, corrupted
Mor'bidness, *s.* the state of being diseased
Morbif'ic, *a.* causing diseases
Morbo'se, *a.* proceeding from disease
Morda'cious, *a.* biting, apt to bite
More, *a.* in greater number or degree
Morel', *s.* a kind of cherry, a plant

Moreo'ver, *ad.* more than yet mentioned

Mores'que, *s.* a sculpture or painting, consisting of imperfect figures intermixed

Morig'erous. *a.* obedient, obsequious

Mo'rion, *s.* armour for the head, a casque

Moris'co, *s.* a dancer of the morris-dance

Morn, Morn'ing, *s.* first part of the day

Moro'se, *a.* cross, peevish, surly, sour

Moro'seness, *s.* peevishness, sourness

Mer'phew, *s.* a scurf upon the face

Mor'ris-dance, *s.* an antic dance performed by men with bells on their legs, which was learned from the Moors

Mor'row, *s.* the day following the present

Morse, *s.* an animal called the sea horse

Mor'sel, *s.* a small piece, a mouthful

Mort, *s.* tune at the death of game

Mor'tal, *a.* deadly, destructive, violent

Mor'tal, *s.* a human being, man

Mortal'ity. *s.* frequency of death; power of destruction; human nature

Mor'tally, *ad.* irrecoverably; deadly

Mor'tar, *s.* a cement for building; a vessel to pound in; a bomb cannon

Mor'gage, *v. a.* to pledge lands, &c.

Mor'gagee, *s.* one who takes a mortgage

Mor'gager, *s.* one who gives a mortgage

Mortif'erous, *a.* fatal, deadly, destructive

Mortifica'tion, *s.* a gangrene; humiliation

Mor'tify, *v.* to gangrene; humble, vex

Mor'tise, *s.* a hole cut in one piece of wood to admit the tenon of another

Mor'tmain, *s.* an unalienable estate

Mor'tress, *s.* a dish of various meats

Mor'tuary, *s.* a gift left to the church

Mosa'ic, *a.* a kind of painting in pebbles, cockles, and other shells

Moscheto, *s.* a West Indian stinging gnat

Mo-que, *s.* a Mahometan church

Moss, *s.* a substance growing on trees, &c.

Mos'sy, *a.* overgrown with moss

Most, *a.* greatest in number or quantity

Most, *s.* the greatest number or value

Mos'tic, *s.* a painter's staff

Most'ly, *ad.* for the most part

Mota'tion, *s.* the act of moving

Mote, *s.* a very small particle of matter; a court of judicature

Motet'to, *s.* a kind of church music

Moth, *s.* a small insect that eats cloth

Moth'eaten, *part.* eaten by moths

Moth'er, *s.* a woman that has borne a child; familiar address to an old woman

Moth'er, *a.* native, had at the birth

Moth'erless, *a.* destitute of a mother

Moth'erly, *a.* suiting a mother, fond

Moth'ery, *a.* dreggy, feculent, mouldy

Moth'y, *a.* full of moths

Mo'tion, *s.* the act of moving; a proposal

Mo'tionless, *a.* being without motion

Mo'tive, *s.* the reason of an action

Mot'ley, *a.* mingled, of various colours

Mot'to, *s.* the sentence added to a device

Move, *v.* to change place, affect, persuade

Move'able, *a.* capable of being moved

Move'ables, *s.* personal goods, furniture

Move'less, *a.* not to be put out of the place

Move'ment, *s.* motion, manner of moving

Mov'ing, *part. a.* pathetic, touching

Mould, *s.* mouldiness, earth; cast, form

Mould, *v. a.* to knead, to model, to shape

Moul'der, *v.* to turn to dust; to crumble

Moul'dering, *part. a.* crumbling into dust

Moul'diness, *s.* the state of being mouldy

Moul'ding, *s.* ornaments, projectures in wood, stone, &c.

Moul'dy, *a.* overgrown with concretions

Moult, *v. s.* to shed, change or lose feathers

Mound, *s.* any thing raised to defend

Mount, *s.* an artificial hill, vast bulk of earth

Mount, *v.* to get on horseback; ascend

Moun'tain, *s.* vast bulk of earth

Mountaineer', *s.* a rustic, a highlander

Moun'tainous, *a.* full of mountains, hilly

Moun'tebank, *s.* a quack, a stage doctor

Moun'ter, *s.* one that mounts

Moun'ty, *s.* the rise of a hawk

Mourn, *v.* to grieve, be sorrowful, bewail

Mourn'er, *s.* one that mourns

Mourn'ful, *a.* causing sorrow, sorrowful

Mourn'fully, *ad.* sorrowfully, with sorrow

Mourn'fulness, *s.* sorrow, show of grief

Mourn'ing, *s.* the dress of sorrow, grief

Mouse, *s.* a small quadruped

Mou'ser, *s.* one that catches mice

Mou'se-trap, *s.* a trap to catch mice with

Mouth, *s.* the aperture in the head at which food is received; an entrance

Mouth, *v.* to vociferate, to grumble

Mouth'ful, *s.* what the mouth can hold

Mouth'less, *a.* being without a mouth

Mow, *s.* a heap of hay or corn

Mow, *v.* to cut with a scythe, make mows

Mow'burn, *v. n.* to ferment and heat in the mow

Mox'a, or Mox'o, *s.* an Indian moss

Moyle, *s.* a mule; a graft or scion

Much, *ad.* nearly; often; in a great degree

Much, *s.* a great deal; something strange

Mu'cid, *a.* hoary, musty, mouldy, slimy

Mu'cidness, *s.* sliminess, mustiness

Mu'cilage, *s.* a slimy or viscous body

Mucilag'inous, *a.* slimy, viscous, ropy

Muck, *s.* dung; any thing filthy

Muck, *v. a.* to manure with dung

Muck'ender, *s.* a handkerchief

Muck'hill, *s.* a dunghill, a heap of dirt

Muck'iness, *s.* nastiness, filth, dirtiness

Muck'worm, *s.* a worm bred in dung; a curmudgeon; a miser

Muck'y, *a.* nasty, filthy, dirty

Mu'cous, Mu'culent, *a.* slimy, viscous

Mu'cronated, *a.* narrowed to a point

Mu'cus, *s.* any slimy liquor or moisture

Mud, *s.* filth or mire; wet dirt

Mud'dily, *ad.* with foul mixture, dirtily

Mud'diness, *s.* state of being muddy

Mud'dle, *v. a.* to make tipsy; to foul

Mud'dy, *a.* turbid, dark, cloudy

Mud'dy, *v.* to make muddy

Mud'sucker, *s.* a sea fowl

Mud'wall, *s.* a wall built with mud

Muff, *s.* a cover or fur for the hands

Muf'fin, *s.* a kind of light spungy cake

Muf'fle, *v.* to wrap up, to blindfold, to hide

Muf'fler, *s.* a cover for the face

Muf'ti, *s.* the high priest of the Mahometans

Mug, *s.* a cup to drink out of

Mug'gish, Mug'gy, *a.* moist, damp, close

Mug'house, *s.* an alehouse

Mu'gient, *a.* lowing or bellowing

Mulat'to, *s.* one born of parents of whom the one is black and the other white

Mul'berry, s. a tree and its fruit
Mulct, v. a. to punish by fine or forfeiture—s. a penalty, a pecuniary fine
Mule, s. an animal generated between a horse and an ass, or an ass and a mare
Mulieb'rity, s. womanhood; tenderness
Mull, v. a. to heat and sweeten wine, &c.
Mul'lar, s. a grinding stone for colours
Mul'let, s. a sea fish
Mul'ligrubs, s. twisting of the guts
Mul'lock, s. dirt or rubbish
Mul'tan'gular, a. having many corners
Multicap'sular, a. divided into cells
Multifa'rious, a. having great multiplicity, &c
Multif'idous, a. divided into many parts
Mul'tiform, a. having various shapes
Multiform'ity, s. diversity of shape
Multinom'inal, a. having many names
Multip'arous, a. having many at a birth
Mul'tipede, s. an insect with many feet
Mul'tiple, s. a term in arithmetic when one number contains another several times
Multiplican'd, s. number to be multiplied
Multiplica'tion, s. the act of multiplying
Multiplica'tor, s. that which multipli
Multiplic'ious, a. manifold
Multiplic'ity, s. great variety
Mul'tiplier, s. the multiplicator
Mul'tiply, v. a. to increase in number
Multi'potent, a. having manifold powe
Multi'sonous, a. having many sounds
Mul'titude, s. many; a crowd or throng
Multitu'dinous, a. manifold
Multoc'ular, a. having many eyes
Mul'ture, s. a toll for grinding corn
Mum, interj. hush—s. a kind of ale
Mum'ble, v. to speak inwardly, to grumble
Mum'bler, s. a mutterer, a slow speaker
Mum'blingly, ad. with inarticulate utterance
Mum'mer, s. a masker, a player
Mum'mery, s. masking, buffoonery
Mum'my, s. a dead body preserved by the Egyptian art of embalming; a kind of wax
Mump, v. a. to nibble, to bite quick; to beg
Mum'per, s. a beggar
Mum'pish, a. sullen, obstinate
Mumps, s. sullenness silent an er, squinancy
Munch, Mounch, v. n. to chew eagerly
Mund, s. peace, quiet
Mun'dane, a. belonging to the world
Munda'tion, s. the act of cleansing
Mun'datory, a. having the power to cleanse
Mun'dic, s. a kind of marcasite
Mundifica'tion, s. act of cleansing
Mun'dify, v. a. to cleanse or make clean
Mundun'gus, s. stinking tobacco
Mu'nerary, a. having the nature of a gift
Mun'grel, a. of a mixed breed, base-born
Munic'ipal, a. belonging to a corporation
Munif'icence, s. liberality, bountifulness
Munif'icent, a. bountiful, liberal, generous
Munif'icently, ad. liberally, generously
Mu'niment, s. a fortification; support
Munit'ion, s. fortification; ammunition
Mu'ral, a. pertaining to a wall
Mur'der, s. the act of killing unlawfully
Mur'der, v. a. to kill unlawfully, to destroy
Mur'derer, s. one who kills unlawfully
Mur'derous, a. bloody, guilty of murder
Mure, v. a. to enclose in walls—s. a wall
Muriat'ic, a. partaking the nature of brine

Mu'ricated, a. full of sharp points
Murk, s. husks of fruit; darkness
Mur'ky, a. dark, cloudy, wanting light
Mur'mur, v. n. to grumble, to mutter inwardly
Mur'mur, s. a complaint, a grumbling
Mur'murer, s. a grumbler, a repiner
Mur'rain, s. a plague amongst cattle
Mur'rey, a. darkly red
Mus'cadine, s. sweet grapes; sweet wine
Mus'cle, s. a fleshy fibre; a shell fish
Musco'seness, Muscos'ity, s. moistness
Mus'cular, a. full of muscles, brawny
Muse, s. the power of poetry; thought
Muse, v. n. to study, to ponder, to think close
Mu'sea, or Mu'sia, s. a mosaic work
Muse'um, s. a repository of curiosities
Mush'room, s. a spungy plant; an upstart
Mu'sic, s. the science of sounds; harmony
Mu'sical, a. harmonious, sweet sounding
Music'ian, s. one skilled in harmony
Mu'sic-mas'ter, s. one who teaches music
Mu'sing, a. thinking, ruminating
Musk, s. a perfume; a flower; a grape
Musk'apple, s. a fine kind of apple
Mus'ket, s. a soldier's hand gun; a hawk
Musketee'r, Musquetee'r, s. a soldier whose weapon is his musket
Musketoo'n, s. a blunderbuss, a short gun
Musk'melon, s. a fragrant melon
Musk'rose, s. a very fragrant rose
Mus'ky, a. sweet of scent, fragrant
Mus'lin, s. fine stuff made of cotton
Mus'sack, s. a liquor much used by the Chi-
Mus'sulman, s. a Mahometan believer [nese
Must, verb imperfect, to be obliged
Must, v. to mould, to make mouldy
Musta'ches, Musta'choes, s. whiskers
Mus'tard, s. a plant, and its seed
Mus'ter, v. to assemble, to review, to collect
Mus'ter, s. a re few and register of forces
Mus'ter-mas'ter, s. one who superintends the muster to prevent frauds
Mus'ter-roll, s. a register of forces
Mus'tily, ad. mouldily, dampiy
Mus'tiness, s. mould, damp, foulness
Mus'ty, a. mouldy, spoiled with damp; dull
Mutabil'ity, s. changeableness, inconstancy
Mu'table, a. alterable, inconstant, unsettled
Mu'tableness, s. changeableness, uncertainty
Muta'tion, s. the act of changing, alteration
Mute, a. silent, dumb, not vocal
Mute, s. one that has no power of speech
Mute, v. n. to dung as birds—s. dung
Mu'tely, ad. silently, not vocally
Mu'tilate, v. a. to maim, to cut off
Mu'tilated, a. maimed, defective
Mutila'tion, s. deprivation of a limb, &c.
Mu'tine, Mutinee'r, s. a mover of sedition
Mu'tinous, a. seditious, turbulent
Mu'tiny, v. n. to rise against authority
Mu'tiny, s. sedition, revolt, insurrection
Mut'ter, v. to grumble, to utter imperfectly
Mut'ton, s. the flesh of a sheep
Mut'ton-fist, s. a hand large and red
Mu'tual, a. reciprocal, acting in return
Mutual'ity, s. reciprocation
Mu'tually, ad. reciprocally, in return
Muz'zle, s. the mouth of any thing
Muz'zle, v. to bind the mouth
Myog'raphy, s. a description of the muscles
Myol'ogy, s. the doctrine of the muscles

Myot'omy, s. the dissecting of muscles
Myr'iad, s. the number of ten thousand
Myr'midon, s. any rude ruffian
Myrrh, s. a strong aromatic gum; it is brought from Ethiopia, but the tree which produces it is wholly unknown
Myr'rhine, a. belonging to myrrh
Myr'tle, s. a fragrant kind of shrub
Mysel'f, pron. I myself, not another
Mys'tagogue, s. an interpreter of mysteries

Myste'rious, a. full of mystery, obscure
Mys'teriously, ad. enigmatically, obscurely
Mys'terize, v. a. to turn to enigmas [culty
Myste'riousness, s. obscurity, an artful diffi-
Mys'tery, s. something secret or hidden
Mys'tic, Mys'tical, a. obscure, secret, dark
Mytholog'ical, a. relating to fables
Mythol'ogist, s. an explainer of fables
Mythol'ogy, s. a system of fables; accounts of heathen deities

N.

N, s. the 18th letter of the alphabet
Nab, v. a. to catch unexpectedly
Na'dir, s. the point opposite to the zenith
Nag, s. a small or young horse
Nail, s. horn on fingers or toes; an iron spike; the 16th part of a yard; a stud
Nail'er, s. a maker of, or dealer in, nails
Na'ked, a. uncovered, bare; unarmed, defenceless; plain, evident, not hidden
Na'kedness, s. nudity, want of covering
Name, s. an appellation, fame, character
Name, v. a. to give a name to, to mention by name, to specify, to nominate, to utter
Na'mely, ad. particularly, specially
Na'mesake, s. one of the same name
Nan'keen, s. a kind of light cotton
Nap, s. a short sleep, slumber; down on cloth
Nape, s. the joint of the neck behind
Naph'tha, s. a very pure, clear, and thin mineral fluid of a very pale yellow
Nap'kin, s. a cloth to wipe the hand, &c.
Nap'less, a. threadbare. wanting nap
Nap'py, a. frothy, spumy; having a nap
Narcis'sus, s. the daffodil flower
Narcot'ic, a. causing torpor or stupefaction
Nard, s. an odorous shrub, an ointment
Nare, s. a nostril
Nar'rable, a. that which may be told
Narra'te, v. a. to relate, to tell
Narra'tion, Nar'rative, s. a history, a relation
Narra'tor, s. a relater, a teller, an historian
Nar'row, a. of small breadth; near. covetous
Nar'rowly, ad. contractedly, closely
Nar'rowminded, a. mean spirited, avaricious
Nar'rowness, s. want of breadth; meanness
Na'sal, a. belonging to the nose
Nas'tily, ad. dirtily, filthily. grossly
Nas'tiness, s. dirt, filth, obscenity. grossness
Nas'ty, a. dirty, filthy, sordid, lewd, obscene
Na'tal, a. relating to nativity, native
Natali'tious, a. relating to a birth-day
Nata'tion, s. the act of swimming
Na'tion, s. a people distinct from others
Nat'ional, a. public, general, not private
Na'tive, s. one born in any country, offspring
Na'tive, a. natural, not artificial, original
Nativ'ity, s. birth, state or place of birth
Nat'ural, a. produced by nature; tender. easy
Nat'ural, s. a fool; an ideot; native quality
Nat'uralist, s. a student in physics
Naturaliza'tion, s. the admission of a foreigner to the privileges of a native
Nat'uralize, v. a. to invest with the privileges of native subjects; to make easy
Nat'urally, ad. unaffectedly, spontaneously

Nat'uralness, s. conformity to truth and reality
Na'ture, s. the system of the world, or the assemblage of all created beings; the regular course of things; native state of any thing; disposition of mind; compass of natural existence; species; physics
Na'val, a. consisting of or relating to ships
Nave, s. part of a church or wheel
Na'vel, s. part of the body; the middle
Naught, a. bad, corrupt—s. nothing
Naug'htily, ad. wickedly, corruptly, basely
Naug'htiness, s. badness, wickedness
Naug'hty, a. bad, wicked, corrupt, vicious
Nav'igable, a. passable by ships or boats
Nav'igate, v. a. to pass by ships or boats
Naviga'tion, s. the act of passing by water; the act of conducting a ship at sea
Naviga'tor, s. a seaman, a traveller by water
Nau'machy, s. a mock sea-fight
Nau'sea, s. a propensity to vomit; disgust
Nau'seate, v. to grow squeamish, to loathe
Nau'seous, a. loathsome, disgustful
Nau'seousness, s. loathsomeness, disgust
Nau'tical, a. pertaining to ships or sailors
Nau'tilus, s. a shell fish furnished with something resembling oars and a sail
Na'vy, s. company of ships of war, a fleet
Nay, ad. no, not only so, but more
Neaf, s. a fist
Neal, v. a. to temper by a gradual heat
Neap, a. low, scanty; used only of the tide
Neap'tide, s. a low tide, a short or slack tide
Near, a. close, not distant; parsimonious
Near, Near'ly. ad. at hand; closely; meanly
Near'ness, s. closeness, niggardliness
Neat, a. elegant, clean, pure—s. oxen
Neat-herd, s. a cow-keeper
Neat'ly, ad. cleanly, trimly, artfully
Neat'ness, s. cleanliness, spruceness
Neb, s. the nose, beak, mouth, bill of a bird
Neb'ulous, a. misty, cloudy, overcast
Nec'essaries, s. things not only convenient but needful for the support of human life
Nec'essarily, ad. indispensably, inevitably
Nec'essary, a. needful, fatal, unavoidable
Necessita'rian, s. one denying free agency
Neces'sitate, v. a. to make necessary
Neces'sitous, a. pressed with poverty
Neces'situde, s. want, need, friendship
Neces'sity, s. compulsion; fatality; indispensableness; want; poverty; cogency
Neck, s. part of the body, of land, &c.
Neck'cloth, s. what men wear on their necks
Neck'lace, s. a woman's neck ornament
Nec'romancer, s. a conjurer. a wizard

M 3

Nec'romancy, s. the art of foretelling future events by communication with the dead
Nec'romantic,a.of,or relating to, necroman-
Nec'tar, s. the feigned drink of the gods [cy
Necta'reous, Nec'tarine, a. sweet as nectar
Nee'tarine, s. a fruit of the plum kind
Nec'tary, s. the honey cup, or melliferous part of a flower
Need. Need'iness, s. exigency, want
Need, v. to want, lack, to be necessitated
Need'ful, a. indispensably requisite
Nee'dle,s.a small instrument for sewing; the small steel bar which in the mariner's compass stands regularly north and south
Nee'dle-ma'ker, s. one who makes needles
Nee'dlework, s. work done with a needle
Need'less, a. unnecessary, not requisite
Needs, ad. indispensably, inevitably
Nee'dy, a. distressed by poverty
Nef, s. the body of a church
Nefa'rious, a. heinous, wicked, abominable
Nega'tion, s. denial, contrary to affirmation
Neg'ative, a. denying, not positive
Neg'ative, s. a proposition that denies
Neg'atively, ad. in the form of a denial
Neglec't, v. a. to omit by carelessness, slight
Neglec't, s. inattention, negligence
Neglec'tful. a. heedless, careless, inattentive
Neg'ligence, s. remissness, carelessness
Neg'ligent, a. neglectful, careless, heedless
Nego'tiable, a. that which may be negotiated
Nego'tiate, v. n. to traffic, to treat with
Nego'tiating, a. trading, managing
Negotia'tion, s. a treaty of business, &c.
Ne'gro, s. a blackamoor
Ne'gus,s. a mixture of wine,water,sugar,&c.
Neif, s. the fist; a bad woman
Neigh, s. the voice of a horse—v. n. to make a noise like a horse
Neigh'bour, s. one who lives near another
Neigh'bou hood,s. the people, &c. adjoining
Neigh'bourly, a. friendly, civil, kind
Nei'ther, conj. not either, no one
Nem'oral, a. pertaining to a grove
Neoter'ic, a. modern, novel, late
Nepen'the, s. an herb that drives away sad-ness; also a drug that expels all pains
Neph'ew, s. the son of a brother or sister
Nephrit'ic, a. good against the stone
Nep'otism, s. a fondness for nephews
Nerve, s. an organ of sensation
Ner'veless, a. without strength; insipid
Ner'vous, Ner'vy, a. sinewy, vigorous; also having diseased or weak nerves
Nes'cience, s. the state of not knowing
Nest, s. a bed of birds; drawers; an abode
Nest'egg, s. an egg left in the nest
Nes'tle, v. to settle, to lie close, to cherish
Nes'tling, s. a bird just hatched
Net, s. a texture for catching fish, birds, &c.
Neth'er, a. lower, not upper; infernal
Neth'ermost, a. lowest
Net'ting, s. a reticulated piece of work
Net'tle, s. a common stinging herb
Net'tle, v. a. to vex, to provoke, to irritate
Nev'er, ad. at no time, in no degree
Nevertheless', ad. notwithstanding that
Neu'ter, Neu'tral, a. of neither party
Neutral'ity, s. a state of indifference
New, a. fresh, modern, not ancient
New'el s. the upright post in a staircase

Newfan'gled, a. formed with one of novelty
Newfash'ioned, a. lately come in fashion
New'grown, part. lately grown up
New'ly, ad. lately, freshly
New'ness, s. freshness; novelty; late change
News, s. fresh accounts of transactions
News'paper, s. a paper of present transac-
Newt, s. an eft, a small lizard [tions
Next, a. nearest in place or gradation
Nib, s. the point of a pen; the bill of a bird
Nib'bed, a. having a nib
Nib'ble, v. to eat slowly; to find fault with
Nice, a. accurate, scrupulous, delicate
Ni'cely, ad. accurately, minutely, delicately
Ni'cety, s. minute accuracy, punctilious dis-crimination; effeminate softness; a dainty
Niche, s. a hollow to place a statue in
Nick, s. exact point of time; a notch; a score
Nick, v. a. to cut in notches; to hit; cozen
Nick'name, s. a name in scoff or contempt
Nick'name,v.to call by an opprobrious name
Nic'tate, v. n. to wink
Nide, s. a brood, as a brood of pheasan's
Nid'orous, a. having the smell of roast fat
Niece, s. the daughter of a brother or sister
Nig'gard, s. a sordid, greedy person
Nig'gard, Nig'gardly, a. sordid—ad. meanly
Nigh, a. near to, allied closely by blood
Nigh, Nigh'ly, ad. nearly, within a little
Night, s. time from sun-set to sun-rise
Night'cap, s. a cap worn in bed
Nigh'dew, s. dew that falls in the nigh
Night'ed, a. darkened, clouded, black
Nightfa'ring, a. travelling in the night
Night'fire, s. an ignis-fatuus, a vapour
Night'gown, s. a gown used for an undress
Night'ingale, s. a bird that sings by night
Night'ly, ad. by night, every night
Night'man, s. one who empties privies
Night'mare, s. a morbid oppression during sleep, resembling the pressure of weight upon the breast
Night'piece, s. a picture so coloured as to be supposed to be seen by candlelight
Night'rail, s. a light kind of night dress
Night'warbling, a. singing in the night
Night'watch, s. a period of night as distin-guished by change of the watch
Nigres'cent, a. growing black
Nihil'ity, s. nothingness; non-existence
Nill, v. a. not to will; to refuse, to reject
Nim, v. a. to steal, to filch
Nim'ble, a. quick, active, ready, lively
Nim'blefooted, a. active, nimble
Nim'blewitted, a. quick; eager to speak
Nim'bly, ad. quickly, speedily, with agility
Nim'ious, a. being too much, vast, huge
Nine, s. one more than eight
Nine'fold, a. nine times repeated
Nine'ty, s. nine times ten
Nin'ny,Nin'nyhammer, s. a fool, a simpleton
Ninth, a. the ordinal of nine
Nip, v. a. to pinch; to blast; to ridicule
Nip'per, s. one that nips; a satirist
Nip'pers, s. small pincers
Nip'ple, s. a teat; a dug; an orifice
Nisi-pri'us, s. a law term for civil causes
Nit, s. the egg of a louse, bug, &c.
Nit'id, a. bright, shining, luminous
Ni'tre, s. saltpetre
Ni'trous, a. impregnated with nitre

Nit'ly, a. abounding with the eggs of lice
Ni'val, a. abounding with snow
Niv'eous, a. snowy, resembling snow
Ni'zy, s. a dunce, a simpleton, a booby
No, ad. the word of denial—a. not any
Nobil'ity, s. persons of high rank; dignity
No'ble, a. illustrious, exalted, generous
No'ble, s. one of high rank; an ancient gold coin valued at 6s. 8d.
No'bleman, s. one who is ennobled
No'bleness, s. greatness, dignity, splendour
Nobless'e, s. the body of nobility; dignity
No'bly, ad. greatly, illustriously, splendidly
No'body, s. not one, not any one
No'cent, No'cive, a. criminal, hurtful
Noctam'bulist, s. one who walks in sleep
Noctid'ial, a. comprising a day and a night
Noc'tuary, s. an account of night affairs
Noc'turn, s. devotion performed by night
Noctur'nal, a. nightly—s. an instrument
Nod, v. n. to bend the head, to be drowsy
Nod'dle, s. the head, in contempt
Nod'dy, Noo'dle, s. a simpleton, an idiot
Node, s. a knob; a swelling; an intersection
No'dous, a. knotty, full of knots
Nog'gin, s. a small cup or mug
Noise, s. any sound, outcry, clamour
Noise'less, a. silent, without sound
Nol'siness, s. loudness of sound
Noi'some, a. noxious, offensive, disgusting
Noi'sy, a. sounding, turbulent
Noli'tion, s. unwillingness, reluctance
Nom'bles, s. the entrails of a deer
Nomencla'tor, s. one who gives names
Nomencla'ture, s. a vocabulary; a name
Nom'inal, a. only in name, not real
Nom'inally, ad. by name, titularly
Nom'inate, v. a. to name, entitle, appoint
Nomina'tion, s. the power of appointing
Nom'inative, s. in grammar, the first case that designates the name of any thing
Nou'age, s. minority in age, immaturity
Non-appear'ance, s. omission of due appearance in a court of judicature
Nonconfor'mist, s. one who refuses to conform to the established worship
Nondescrip't, a. not yet described
None, a. not one, not any, not another
Nonen'tity, s. non-existence, an ideal thing
None'such, s. an extraordinary person, &c.
Nonexis'tence, s. state of not existing
Nonju'ror, s. one who refuses to swear allegiance to a monarch
Nonnat'urals, s. the more immediate causes of diseases—as air, diet, sleep, &c.
Nonpare'il, s. a small printing letter; an apple of unequalled excellence
Non'plus, s. a puzzle—v. a. to confound
Nonregar'dance, s. want of due regard
Nonres'idence, s. a failure of re-idence
Nonresis'tance, s. passive obedience
Non'sense, s. unmeaning language; trifles
Nonsen'sical, a. unmeaning, foolish
Nonsolu'tion, s. a failure of solution
Non'suit, v. a. to quash a legal process
Nook, s. a corner, a covert; part of land
Noon, s. the middle of the day
Noon'day, Noon'tide, s. mid-day
Noose, v. a. to knot—s. a running knot
Nor, conj. a negative particle
Nor'mal, a. perpendicular, upright

North, s. opposite the south; the point opposite to the sun in the meridian
Nor'therly, Nor'thern, North'ward, a. being in or towards the north
North'star, s. the pole star
North'ward, ad. towards the north
Nose, s. part of the face—v. to smell
Nose'gay, s. a posy, a bunch of flowers
Nos'le, s. the extremity of any thing
Nos'tril, s. the cavity in the nose
Nos'trum, s. a medicine not made public
Not, ad. the particle of negation
Not'able, a. remarkable, memorable, bustling
Not'ableness, s. diligence, remarkableness
No'tary, s. a scrivener that takes notes, protests bills, or draws contracts
Nota'tion, s. the act of noting, signification
Notch, s. a nick, a hollow cut in any thing
Note, s. a mark; notice; written paper; stigma; sound in music; annotation; symbol
Note, v. a. to observe, to remark, set down
No'ted, part. a. remarkable; eminent
Noth'ing, s. non-existence, not any thing
No'tice, s. remark, heed, intelligence
Notifica'tion, s. the act of making known
No'tify, v. a. to declare, to make known
No'tion, s. a sentiment, opinion, thought
No'tional, a. imaginable, id al, visionary
Notori'ety, s. public knowledge or exposure
Noto'rious, a. publicly known, manifest
Noto'riously, ad. publicly, openly, evidently
Notorious'ness, s. public fame
Nott, v. a. to shear, to crop
Notwithstan'ding, conj. nevertheless
No'tus, s. the south wind
Nova'tion, s. introduction of something new
Nev'el, a. new, not ancient; unusual
Nov'el, s. a feigned story or tale
Nov'elist, s. an innovator; a writer of novels
Nov'elty, s. newness, freshness, recen'ness
Novem'ber, s. the eleventh month of the year
Nover'cal, a. pertaining to a step-mother
Nought, s. nothing, not any thing
Nov'ice, s. an unskilful person, &c.
Novit'iate, s. the state of a novice; the time in which the rudiments are learned
Nov'ity, s. newness, novelty
Noun, s. the name of any thing in grammar
Nour'ish, v. to support with food; to train
Nour'ishable, a. susceptible of nourishment
Nour'ishment, s. food, nutrition, support
Nous'el, v. a. to nurse up
Now, ad. at this time—s. present moment
Now'adays, ad. in the present age
Now'ed, a. knotted, inwreathed
No'where, ad. not in any place
No'wise, ad. not in any manner or degree
Nox'ious, a. hurtful, baneful, offensive
Nox'iousness, s. hurtfulness, insalubrity
Nub'ble, v. a. to bruise with fighting
Nubif'erous, a. bringing clouds
Nu'bilate, v. a. to cloud
Nu'bile, a. marriageable, fit for marriage
Nu'bilous, a. cloudy, overcast
Nucif'erous, a. not bearing
Nu'cleus, s. the kernel of a nut; any thing about which matter is gathered
Nu'dity, s. nakedness, a picture
Nuga'city, or Nugal'ity, s. trifling talk
Nu'gatory, a. trifling, futile, ineffectual
Null, s. a thing of no force or meaning

Nul'lity, s. want of force or existence
Numb, a. torpid, chill, benumbing
Numb, v. a. to make torpid, to stupify
Num'ber, v. a. to count, to tell, to reckon
Num'ber, s. many—pl. harmony; poetry
Num'berer, s. he who numbers
Num'berless, a. more than can be reckoned
Num'bness, s. stupefaction, torpor. deadness
Nu'merable, a. capable to be numbered
Nu'meral, a. relating to numbers
Nu'merary, a. belonging to a number
Numera'tion, s. the art of numbering
Numera'tor, s. he that numbers; that number which measures others
Numer'ical, a. denoting number, numeral
Nu'merist, s. one who deals in numbers
Nu'merous, a. containing many; musical
Num'mary, a. relating to money
Num'skull, s. a dunce, a dolt, a blockhead
Nun, s. a religious recluse woman
Nun'chion, s. food eaten between meals
Nun'cio, s. envoy from the Pope; messenger
Nuncu'pative, a. verbally pronounced
Nun'nery, s. a convent of nuns
Nup'tial, a. pertaining to marriage

Nup'tials, s. marriage or wedding
Nurse, s. a woman who has the care of ano ther's child, or of a sick person
Nurse, v. a. to bring up a child, to feed
Nur'sery, s. a place where children are nur sed and brought up; a plantation of young trees to be transplanted to another ground
Nur'sling, s. one nursed up, a foundling
Nur'ture, s. food. diet; education, institution
Nur'ture, v. a. to educate, train up
Nus'tle, v. a. to fondle, to cherish
Nut, s. a fruit; part of a wheel
Nuta'tion, s. a kind of tremulous motion
Nut'gall, s. the excrescence of an oak
Nut'meg, s. a warm Indian spice
Nutrica'tion, s. the manner of feeding
Nu'triment, s. nourishment, food, aliment
Nutrimen'tal, a. having the qualities of food
Nutri'tion, s. the quality of nourishing
Nutri'tious, Nu'tritive, a. nourishing
Nu'triture, s. the power of nourishing
Nut'tree, s. a tree that bears nuts; a hazel
Nuz'zle, v. a. to hide the head as a child does in its mother's bosom; to nurse, to foster
Nymph, s. a goddess of the woods, a lady

O.

O, s. the 14th letter of the alphabet—interj. of wishing or exclamation
Oaf, s. changeling, foolish fellow, an idiot
Oaf'ish, a. dull, stupid, doltish
Oaf'ishness, s. stupidity, doltishness
Oak, s. a tree and the wood of it
Oak'apple, s. a spungy excrescence on oak
Oak'en, a. made of or gathered from oak
Oak'um, s. cords untwisted, reduced to hemp
Oar, s. an instrument to row with—v. to row, to impel by rowing
Oat'cake, s. a cake made of oatmeal
Oat'en, a. made of, or bearing oats
Oath, s. a promise or affirmation, corroborat ed by the attestation of the Divine Being
Oathbreak'ing, s. violation of an oath
Oat'malt, s. malt made of oats
Oat'meal, s. flour made by grinding oats
Oats, s. a grain generally given to horses
Obambula'tion, s. the act of walking about
Obco'nical, a. inversely conical
Obcor'date, a. heart-shaped, with the apex downwards
Obduce', v. a. to draw over, as a covering
Obduc'tion, s. a covering or overlaying
Ob'duracy, s. hardness of heart, impenitence
Ob'durate, a. hard of heart, stubborn, rugged
Obdura'tion, Ob'durateness, s. stubbornness
Ob'durately, ad. inflexibly, stubbornly
Obe'dience, s. submission to authority
Obe'dient, a. submissive, obsequious
Obedien'tial, a. pertaining to obedience
Obe'diently, ad. with obedience
Obei'sance, s. an act of reverence. a bow
Ob'elisk, s. a pyramid; mark of reference in the margin of a book, thus (†)
Oberra'tion, s. the act of wandering about
Obe'se, a. fat, gross, laden with flesh
Obey', v. a. to pay submission to, to yield to
Ob'ject, s. that on which we are employed

Object', v. to urge against, to oppose
Objec'tion, s. an adverse argument; a charge
Objec'tive, a. relating to the object
Objec'tor, s. one who offers objec.ions
O'bit, s. funeral obsequies
Obit'uary, s. a register of the dead
Objura'tion, s. act of binding by oath
Objur'gate, v. a. to chide, rebuke, reprov
Objurga'tion, s. a chiding, reprehension
Obla'te, a. flatted at the poles
Obla'tion, s. an offering, a sacrifice
Oblecta'tion, s. recreation, delight, pleasure
Obliga'tion, s. engagement, contract, bond
Ob'ligatory, a. binding, imposing obligation
Obli'ge, v. a. to bind, to compel, to gratify
Obligee', s. one bound by a contract
Obli'ging, part. a. complaisant, binding
Obli'que, a. not direct, not perpendicular
Obli'queness, Obliq'uity, s. deviation from moral rectitude; crookedness
Oblit'erate, v. a. to efface, to destroy
Oblitera'tion, s. effacement, extinction
Obliv'ial, a. causing forgetfulness
Obliv'ion, s. forgetfulness; amnesty
Obliv'ious, a. causing forgetfulness
Ob'long, a. longer than broad
Oblong'ly, ad. in an oblong direction
Ob'loquy, s. blame, slander, disgrace
Obmutes'cence, s. loss of speech
Obnox'ious, a. accountable; liable; exposed
Obnu'bilate, v. a. to cloud, to obscure
Ob'ole, s. in pharmacy, twelve grains
Obrep'tion, s. the act of creeping on secretly
Obsce'ne, a. immodest, disgusting, offensiv
Obsce'nely, ad. in an immodest manner
Obscen'ity, s. lewdness, unchastity
Obscura'tion, s. the act of darkening
Obscu're, a. dark, gloomy, abstruse, difficult
Obscu're, v. a. to darken, to conceal; to make less visible, less intelligible, or less glorious

Obscu rely, *ad.* darkly, privately

Obscu'reness, Obscu'rity, *s.* darkness; unnoticed state, privacy; darkness of meaning

Obsecra'tion, *s.* a supplication, an entreaty

Ob'sequies, *s.* funeral solemnities

Obse'quious, *a.* compliant, obedient

Obse'quiousness, *s.* obedience, compliance

Obser'vable, *a.* remarkable, eminent

Obser'vably, *ad.* in a manner worthy of note

Obser'vance, *s.* respect, attention

Obser'vant, *a.* attentive, diligent, watchful

Observa'tion, *s.* a noting, a remark, a note

Observa'tor, Obser'ver, *s.* a remarker

Obser'vatory, *s.* a place built for making astronomical observations

Obser've, *v.* to watch; note, regard, obey

Obses'sion, *s.* the act of besieging

Ob'solete, *a.* disused, grown out of use

Ob'stacle, *s.* a let, hinderance, obstruction

Obstet'ric, *a.* doing a midwife's office

Ob'stinacy, *s.* stubbornness, peevishness

Ob'stinate, *a.* stubborn, contumacious, fixed

Ob'stinately, *ad.* stubbornly, resolutely

Ob'stinateness, *s.* stubbornness, contumacy

Obstipa'tion, *s.* act of stopping chinks, &c.

Obstrep'erous, *a.* noisy, loud, vociferous

Obstric'tion, *s.* an obligation, a bond

Obstruc't, *v. a.* to hinder, to block up, to bar

Obstruc'tion, *s.* an hinderance, an obstacle

Obstruc'tive, *a.* hindering, impelling

Ob'struent, *a.* blocking up, hindering

Obstupefac'tion, *s.* act of inducing stupidity

Obtai'n, *v.* to gain; to acquire; to prevail

Obtain'able, *a.* that which may be obtained

Obtain'ment, *s.* the act of obtaining

Obten'd, *v. a.* to oppose; to pretend; to offer

Obtenebra'tion, *s.* darkness, making dark

Obten'sion, *s.* opposition, denial, pretence

Obtes't, *v.* to beseech, to supplicate

Obtesta'tion, *s.* application, entreaty

Obtrecta'tion, *s.* slander, detraction, calumny

Obtru'de, *v. a.* to thrust into a place by force; to offer with unreasonable importunity

Obtru'sion, *s.* forcing in or upon

Obtru'sive, *a.* inclined to obtrude on others

Obtun'd, *v. a.* to blunt; to quell; to deaden

Obtu'se, *a.* not pointed, dull, obscure

Obtu'sely, *ad.* without a point, dully

Obtu'seness, *s.* bluntness, stupidity, dulness

Obtu'sion, *s.* the act of dulling

Obver'se, *a.* turned upside down

Obver't, *v. a.* to turn towards or upwards

Ob'viate, *v. a.* to prevent, to meet in the way

Ob'vious, *a.* easily discovered, plain, open

Ob'viously, *ad.* evidently, plainly, naturally

Ob'viousness, *s.* the state of being evident

Obum'brate, *v. a.* to shade, to cloud

Occa'sion, *s.* casualty, opportunity, incident

Occa'sion, *v. a.* to cause, influence, produce

Occa'sional, *a.* incidental, casual

Occa'sionally, *ad.* incidentally, casually

Occeca'tion, *s.* act of blinding or making

Oc'cident, *s.* the west—*a.* western [blind

Occiden'tal, Occid'uous, *a.* western

Oc'ciput, *s.* the hinder part of the head

Occlu'de, *v. a.* to shut up

Occlu'se, *a.* shut up, closed

Occul't, *a.* unknown, hidden, secret

Occulta'tion, *s.* the act of hiding; in astronomy, the time that a star or planet is concealed from the sight in an eclipse

Oc cupancy, *s.* the act of taking possession

Oc'cupant, *s.* he that takes possession

Oc'cupate, *v. a.* to possess, hold; take up

Occupa'tion, *s.* a taking possession; trade

Oc'cupier, *s.* a possessor, one who occupies

Oc'cupy, *v. a.* to possess; to fill or take up; to employ, to use, to expend

Occur', *v. n.* to be remembered, to appear

Occur'rence, *s.* incident, accidental event

Occur'sion, *s.* a clash, a mutual blow

O'cean, *s.* the main, any immense expanse

Ocel'lated, *a.* resembling the eyes

Och'imy, or Ock'amy, *s.* a mixed base metal

O'chre, *s.* a rough yellow or blue earth

O'chreous, *a.* consisting of ochre

Oc'tagon, *s.* a figure of eight sides and angles

Octag'onal, *a.* having eight angles and sides

Octan'gular, *a.* having eight angles

Oc'tant, *a.* is when a planet is in such position to another, that their places are only distant an eighth part of a circle

Oc'tave, *s.* the eighth day after some festival; the interval of an eighth in music

Octa'vo, *s.* sheet folded in eight leaves

Octen'nial, *a.* done or happening every eighth year; lasting eight years

Octo'ber, *s.* the tenth month of the year

Oc'ular, *a.* known by the eye

Oc'ulist, *s.* one who cures distempered eyes

Odd, *a.* not even; particular, strange

Odd'ity, *s.* a particularity, a strange person

Odd'ly, *ad.* not evenly; strangely, particularly, unaccountably, uncouthly

Odd'ness, *s.* particularity, strangeness

Odds, *s.* inequality; more than an even wager or number; advantage, superiority

Ode, *s.* a poem to be sung to music

O'dious, *a.* hateful, heinous, abominable

O'diously, *ad.* so as to cause hate

O'diousness, *s.* state of being hated

O'dium, *s.* invidiousness; hatred; blame

Odorif'erous, *a.* fragrant, perfumed, sweet

Odorif'erousness, *s.* sweetness of scent

O'dorous, *a.* fragrant, perfumed

O'dour, *s.* scent, good or bad; fragrance

Oecon'omy. See Economy

Oecumen'ical, *a.* general, universal

Oeil'iad, *s.* a wink, token of the eye

O'er, *ad.* contracted from *over*

Of, *prep.* from, out of, relating to

Off, *ad.* signifying distance; from, not toward

Of'fal, *s.* waste meat, refuse, carrion

Offen'ce, *s.* crime; injury; anger

Offen'ceful, *a.* injurious, giving displeasure

Offen'celess, *a.* unoffending, innocent

Offen'd, *v.* to make angry, injure, attack

Offen'der, *s.* one who commits an offence

Offen'sive, *a.* displeasing, injurious, hurtful

Offen'sively, *ad.* displeasingly, injuriously

Offen'siveness, *s.* injuriousness, cause of disgust

Of'fer, *v.* to present; to attempt; to sacrifice

Of'fer, *s.* a proposal; endeavour; price bid

Of'fering, *s.* sacrifice or oblation

Of'fertory, *s.* act of offering, thing offered; place where offerings are kept

Of'fice, *s.* public employment, agency

Of'ficer, *s.* a commander, one in office

Of'ficered, *a.* supplied with commanders

Offi'cial, *a.* pertaining to an office

Offi'cial, *s.* a deputy in the church court

Offi'cialty, s. the charge of an official
Offi'ciate, v. to perform another's duty
Offi'cinal, a. used in or relating to shops
Offic'ious, a. importunately forward; kind
Offic'iously, ad. with unasked kindness
Offic'iousness, s. forwardness of civility
Off'ing, s. the act of steering to a distance from the land
Off'set, s. a sprout, the shoot of a plant
Off'spring, s. propagation, children
Offus'cate, v. a. to darken; to cloud, to dim
Oft, Of'ten, Of'tentimes, Of'times, ad. frequently, many times, not rarely
Ogee'.Ogi've, s. sort of moulding in architecture, consist'ing of a round and a hollow
O'gle, v. n. to view with side glances
O'gling, s. a viewing sidely or obliquely
O'glio, s. a dish of mixed meats; a medley
Oh! interj. denoting sorrow or surprise
O l. s. the expressed juice of olives, &c.
Oil'iness, s. unctuousness, greasiness
Oil'man, s. one who trades in pickles, &c.
Oil'y, a. consisting of oil, fat, greasy
Oin'ment, s. an unguent, salve
Old, Ol'den, a. not new, ancient, long used
Oldfash'ioned, a. obsolete, out of fashion
Olea'ginous,O'leose,O'leous,a.oily,unctuous
Olfac'tory, a. having the sense of smelling
Oliba'num, s. a sweet-scented gum
Oligar'chical, a. relating to oligarchy
Ol'igarchy, s. a form of government which places the supreme power in the hands of few; an aristocracy
Olit'ory, a. belonging to a kitchen garden
Oliva'ster, a. darkly brown, tawny
Ol'ive, s. a plant; its fruit; emblem of peace
Om'bre, s. a game at cards played by three
Ome'ga, s. the last letter of the Greek alphabet,therefore metaphorically applied in the Holy Scriptures for the last
Om'elet, s. a pancake made with eggs
O'men, s. a good or bad sign, a prognostic
O'mer, s.aHebrew measure containing about three pints and a half English
Om'inate, v. to foretoken
Om'inous,a.exhibiting bad tokens of futurity
Omis'sion, Omit'tance, s. a neglect of duty
Omit', v. a. to leave out; to neglect
Omnifa'rious, a. of all kinds and sorts
Omnif'ic, a. all-creating
Om'niform, a. having every shape [sorts
Omnig'enous, a. consisting of all kinds or
Omnip'otence, Omnip'otency, s. almighty power, unlimited power
Omnip'otent, a. almigh'y, all-powerful
Omnipres'ence, s. the quality of being everywhere present; ubiquity
Omnipres'ent, a. present in every place
Omnis'cience, s. boundless knowledge
Omnis'cient, a. infinitely wise, all-knowing
Omniv'orous, a. all-devouring
Omol'ogy, s. likeness; agreeableness
On, prep. upon—ad. forward, not off
Once, ad. one time, a single time; formerly
One, a. one of two, single—s. a single person
One'eyed, a. having only one eye
Oneirocrit'ic, s. an interpreter of dreams
On'erary, a. fitted for carriage or burdens
On'erate, v. a. to load, to burden
On'erous, a. burdensome, oppressive
On'ion, s. a plant with a bulbous root

On'ly, ad. simply, barely—a. single, this only
Onomancy, s. divination by names
On'set, s. an attack; an assault; a storm
Ontol'ogy, s. metaphysics; the science of beings or ideas in general
On'ward, ad. progressively; forward
O'nyx, s. a clear, elegant, and valuable gem
Ooze, s. soft mud; slime; soft flow; spring
Ooze, v. n. to run gently, to flow by stealth
Oo'zy, a. miry, muddy, slimy
Opa'cate, v. a. to shade, to cloud, to darken
Opac'ity, s. cloudiness,want of transparency
Opa'cous, Opa'que, a. dark, not transparent
O'pal, s. a precious stone
O'pen, v. to unclose, unlock; divide; begin
O'pen, a. unclosed, plain, clear, exposed
Openey'ed, a. watchful, vigilant, attentive
Openhand'ed, a. generous, liberal, bountiful
Openheart'ed,a.generous,candid,ingenuous
Openheart'edness, s. liberality, munificence
O'pening,s. a breach, an aperture; the dawn
O'penly, ad. publicly, evidently, plainly
O'penmouthed, a. greedy, clamorous
O'penness, s. freedom from disguise
O'pera, s. a musical entertainment
Op'erant, a. active; able to produce
Op'erate, v. a. to act; to produce effects
Operat'ical, a. relating to an operation
Opera'tion, s. agency, influence, effect
Op'erative, a. having the power of acting
Opera'tor, s. one that performs any act of the hand; one who produces any effect
Oper'cle, s. a lid or covering, a term used in natural history
Opero'se, a. laborious; full of trouble
Operta'neous, a. secret; done in secret
Ophthal'mic, a. relating to the eye
Oph'thalmy, s. a disease of the eyes
O'piate, s. a medicine that causes sleep
Opin'iative, a. stubborn; imagined
Opin'ion, s. a sentiment; notion
Opin'ionative, a. fond of preconceived no
Opip'arous, a. sumptuous [tions
Opitula'tion, s. an aiding, a helping
O'pium, s. the juice of Turkish poppies
Op'pilate, v. a. to heap up obstruction
Oppila'tion, s. an obstruction, a stoppage
Op'pilative, a. obstructive, apt to obstruct
Oppo'nent, a. opposite, adverse
Oppo'nent, s. an adversary, an antagonist
Opportu'ne, a. reasonable, convenient, fit
Opportu'nity, s. fit place; time; convenience
Oppo'se, v. to act against, to insist, to hinde
Oppo'seless,a. irresistible, not to be opposed
Op'posite, a. placed in front; adverse
Op'posite, s. an adversary, an antagonist
Op'positely, ad. so as to face each other
Opposit'ion, s. hostile resistance; contrariety of interest, conduct, or meaning
Oppress', v. a. to crush by hardships, subdue
Oppres'sion, s. cruelty, severity; hardship
Oppres'sive, a. cruel, inhuman; heavy
Oppres'sor, s. one who harasses others
Opprobrious, a. reproachful, disgraceful
Oppro'briously, ad. reproachfully
Oppro'briousness, s. scurrility, abuse
Oppro'brium, s. reproach, disgrace, infamy
Oppu'gn, v. a. to oppose, attack, refute
Oppu'gnancy, s. opposition; resistance
Opsim'athy, s. late education; late education
Op'tative, a. expressing of desire

Op'tic, a. visual, relating to vision
Op'tic, s. an instrument or organ of sight
Op'tical, a. relating to the science of optics
Optic'ian, s. one skilled in optics
Op'tics, s. the science of the laws of vision
Op'timacy, s. nobility, the body of the nobles
Op'tion, s. a choice, power of choosing
Op'ulence, Op'ulency, s. wealth, affluence
Op'ulent, a. rich, wealthy, affluent
Or, conj. either—s. gold, in heraldry
Or'acle, s. something delivered by supernatural wisdom; one famed for wisdom
Orac'ular, Orac'ulous, a. uttering oracles
O'ral, a. delivered verbally, not written
Or'ange, s. a well known fruit
Oran'gery, s. a plantation of orange trees
Ora'tion, s. a public discourse; an harangue
Or'ator, s. an eloquent public speaker
Orator'ical, a. rhetorical; befitting an orator
Orato'rio, s. a kind of sacred drama
Or'atory, s. rhetorical expression; eloquence
Orb, s. a sphere; a circle; a wheel; the eye
Or'bate, a. childless, fatherless; poor
Orba'tion, s. privation of parents or children
Or'bed, a. circular, formed in a circle
Orbic'ular, a. spherical, circular
Or'bit, s. the path in which a planet moves
Or'chard, s. a garden of fruit trees
Orches'tra, or Or'chestre, s. a gallery or place for musicians to play in
Ordai'n, v. a. to appoint, establish, invest
Or'deal, s. a trial by fire or water
Or'der, s. method, a mandate, a rule
Or'der, v. a. to regulate, command, ordain
Or'derless, a. disorderly, out of rule
Or'derly, a. methodical, regular
Or'ders, s. admission to the priesthood
Or'dinable, a. such as may be appointed
Or'dinal, s. a ritual—a. noting order
Or'dinance, s. a law; rule; appointment
Or'dinary, s. a judge; a stated chaplain; a place for eating, where a certain price is paid for each meal; settled establishment
Or'dinary, a. common; usual; mean; ugly
Or'dinate, a. methodical—v. a. to appoint
Ordina'tion, s. the act of ordaining
Ord'nance, s. cannon, heavy artillery
Or'dure, s. animal dung, filth
Ore, s. metal yet in its mineral state
Or'gal, s. the lees of wine, &c.
Or'gan, s. a natural or musical instrument
Organ'ic, Organ'ical, a. instrumental
Or'ganism, s. organical structure
Or'ganist, s. one who plays on the organ
Organiza'tion, s. a due construction of parts
Or'ganize, v. a. to form organically
Or'gasm, s. a sudden vehemence
Or'gies, s. frantic revels, rites of Bacchus
Or'gillous, a. proud, haughty, lofty
O'rient, a. rising as the sun; eastern; bright
Orien'tal, a. eastern, placed in the east
Or'ifice, s. any opening or perforation
Or'igin, s. beginning, source, descent
Orig'inal, s. first copy—a. pristine
Orig'inally, ad. primarily, at first
Orig'inary, a. productive, primitive
Orig'inate, v. a. to bring into existence
Or'ison, or Or'aison, s. a prayer, verbal supplication, or oral worship
Or'lop, s. the lowest deck of a ship
Or'nament, s. decoration, embellishment

Or'nament, v. a. to adorn, to embellish
Ornamen'tal, a. serving to decorate
Ornamen'ted, a. embellished, decorated
Or'nate, a. bedecked, decorated, fine
Ornithol'ogy, s. a discourse on birds
Or'phan, s. a child bereaved of father or mother, or both—a. bereft of parents
Or'piment, s. a mineral, yellow arsenic
Or'rery, s. an instrument which represents the revolutions of the heavenly bodies
Or'ris, s. gold and silver lace; a plant
Or'thodox, a. sound in opinion or doctrine
Or'thodoxy, s. soundness in doctrine, &c.
Ortho'epy, s. the right pronunciation of words
Or'thogon, s. a rectangled figure
Orthog'rapher, s. one who spells rightly
Orthograph'ical, a. rightly spelled
Orthograph'ically, ad. according to rule
Orthog'raphy, s. the part of grammar which teaches how words should be spelled; the elevation of a building delineated
Or'tive, s. rising of a planet or star
Or'tolan, s. a delicate small bird
Orts, s. fragments, mere refuse
Oscilla'tion, s. the moving like a pendulum
Os'citancy, Oscita'tion, s. the act of yawning, unusual sleepiness; carelessness
Os'citant, a. yawning, sleepy, sluggish
Oscula'tion, s. the act of kissing
O'sier, s. a tree of the willow kind
Os'seous, a. bony, like bone; hard
Os'sicle, s. a small bone
Ossifica'tion, s. a change into bony substance
Os'sifrage, s. a kind of eagle
Os'sify, v. a. to change to bone
Ossiv'orous, a. devouring bones
Os'suary, s. a charnel-house
Ost, or Oust, s. a vessel for drying malt on
Osten'sible, a. that may be shown, apparent
Osten'sive, a. showing, betokening
Osten't, s. air, manner, show; a portent
Ostenta'tion, s. an outward vain show
Ostenta'tious, a. boastful, vain, fond of show, fond to expose to view
Ostenta'tiously, ad. vainly, boastfully
Ostenta'tiveness, s. vanity, boastfulness
Osteol'ogy, s. a description of the bones
Os'tiary, s. the mouth of a river   [inn
Os'tler, s. he who takes care of horses at an
Os'tracism, s. a passing sentence by ballot! banishment; public censure by shells
Os'trich, s. a very large African fowl
Otacou'stic, s. an instrument to facilitate o improve the sense of hearing
Oth'er, pron. not the same; not I, not he
Oth'erwise, ad. in a different manner
Ot'ter, s. an amphibious animal
Ot'toman, a. belonging to the Turks
O'val, a. oblong, shaped like an egg
Ova'rious, a. consisting of, or like, eggs
O'vary, s. the seat of eggs, or impregnation the rudiment of the fruit
Ova'tion, s. a lesser kind of Roman triumph
Ov'en, s. an arched place for baking in
O'ver, prep. and ad. above; across
Overac't, v. a. to act more than enough
Overan'xious, a. too careful
Overar'ch, v. a. to cover as with an arch
Overawe', v. a. to keep in awe, to terrify
Overbal'ance, v. a. to preponderate
Overbear', v. a. to subdue to repress

Overbid', v. a. to offer more than the value
O'verboard, ad. off or out of the ship
Overboil', v. a. to boil too much
O'verhold, a. impudent, daring, audacious
Overbur'den, v. a. to burden too much
Overcar'ry, v. a. to hurry too far
Overcast', a. clouded—v. a. to cloud
Overchar'ge, v. a. to rate too high ; to cloy ; to crowd too much ; to burthen
Overcloud'd, v. a. to cover with clouds
Overcome', v. a. to subdue, to vanquish
Overcou'nt, v. a. to rate above the true value
Overdo', v. a. to do more than enough
Overdri've, v. a. to drive too hard or fast
Overeye', v. a. to superintend ; to remark
Overfee'd, v. to feed too much, to cram, glut, stuff
Overflow', v. to be full ; to deluge
Overflow'ing, s. exuberance; copiousness
Overflow'ingly, ad. abundantly, exuberantly
Overfor'wardness, s. too great quickness
O'vergrown, part. a. grown too big
O'vergrowth, s. exuberant growth
Overha'le, v. a. to examine over again
Overhead', ad. aloft, above, in the zenith
Overhe'ar, v. to hear privately, or by chance
Overhe'at, v. a. to heat too much
O'verjoy, v. a. to transport—s. ecstacy
Overla'de, v. a. to overburden, to overload
Overle'ap, v. a. to pass over by a jump
Overla'y, v. a. to smother, to cover over
Overlo'ad, v. a. to burden with too much
Overlon'g, a. too long, too long continued
Overlook', v. a. to superintend ; view from a nigher place ; pass by indulgently ; excuse
Overmast'ed, a. having too much mast
Overmat'ch, v. to be too powerful
Overmuch', a. too much, more than enough
Overni'ght, s. night before bed time
Overpass', v. a. to omit, overlook, cross
Overpa'y, v. a. to pay more than the price
Overpee'r, v. a. to overlook ; to hover over
Overplus', s. what is left more than sufficient
Overpoi'se, v. a. to outweigh, preponderate
Overpow'er, v. a. to oppress by power
Overpress', v. a. to destroy, to overwhelm
Overpri'ze, v. a. to value or love too much
Overran'k, a. too rank, very offensive
Overra'te, v. a. to rate too high
Overrea'ch, v. to deceive ; to rise above
Overri'pen, v. to make or grow too ripe
Overroa'st, v. a. to roast too much
Overru'le, v. a. to superintend, to supersede
Overrun', v. a. to ravage; outrun; overspread
Oversee', v. a. to superintend, manage. omit
Oversee'r, s. one who overlooks; a parish officer who has the care of the poor
Overset', v. to turn the bottom upwards, to overthrow off the basis, to overturn, to subvert
Overshe'de, v. a. to cover with darkness
Overshad'ow, v. a. to shelter, cover, protect
Overshoo't, v. n. to fly beyond the mark
Oversight, s. error, superintendence
Oversi'ze, v. a. to surpass in bulk ; to plaster
Overskip', v. a. to pass by leaping ; to escape
Oversle'ep, v. n. to sleep too long
Overslip', v. a. to pass undone, to neglect
Overspread', v. a. to cover over, scatter over
Overstan'd, v. to stand too much upon terms
Overstock', v. a. to fill too full, to crowd
Overstra'in, v. to stretch too far

Oversway', v. a. to overrule, to bear down
Overswell', v. a. to rise above
O'vert, a. open, manifest, public, apparent
Overta'ke, v. a. to catch any thing by pursuit
Overthrow', v. a. to ruin, defeat, overturn
Overthwart', a. opposite, perverse, adverse
Overthwart'ness, s. pervicacity, perverseness
O'vertly, ad. openly, publicly, manifestly
Overtook', pret. and part. pass. of to overtake
Overtop', v. a. to rise above ; excel, surpass
Overtrip', v. a. to walk lightly over
O'verture, s. a disclosure, discovery, proposal ; a flourish of music before the scenes are opened in a play
Overturn', v. a. to throw down ; overpower
Overval'ue, v. a. to rate at too high a price
Overveil', v. a. to veil or cover over
Overwe'ak, a. too weak, too feeble
Overween', v. n. to think with arrogance
Overween'ingly, ad. with too much arrogance
O'verweight, s. preponderance [rance
Overwhel'm, v. to crush ; to fill too much
Overwi'se, a. wise to affectation
Overwrou'ght, part. laboured too much
Overwor'n, part. worn out, spoiled by time
Ought, s. any thing, something. This word is more properly written aught
Ought, v. imp. to be fit ; to be obliged by duty
O'viform, a. having the shape of an egg
Ovip'arous, a. bringing forth eggs
Ounce, s. a weight ; a lynx, a panther
Our, pron. poss. belonging to us
Ourselves, pron. recip. we, us, not others
Oust, v. a. to vacate ; to deprive, to eject
Out, ad. not within, not at home ; not in affairs ; to the end ; loudly ; at a loss
Outac't, v. a. to go beyond, to exceed
Outbal'ance, v. a. to overweigh, preponderate
Outbid', v. a. to bid more than another
Outbound, a. destined to a distant voyage
Outbra've, v. a. to bear down or outdo by more splendid or insolent appearance
Outbra'zen, v. a. to bear down by impudence
Outbreak, s. that which breaks forth, eruption
Outcast, s. an exile, one rejected [tion
Outcraf't, v. a. to excel in cunning
Out'cry, a cry of distress, noise ; an auction
Outda're, v. a. to venture or dare beyond
Outdo', v. a. to excel, to surpass, to go beyond
Out'er, a. that which is without, outward
Out'ermost, a. remotest from the midst
Outfa'ce, v. a. to stare down by impudence
Out'fall, s. a canal ; a fall of water ; a quarrel
Outfly', v. a. to leave behind ; to fly beyond
Out'gate, s. an outlet, a passage outward
Outgi've, v. a. to surpass in giving
Outgo', v. a. to surpass, to excel, overreach
Outgro'w, v. a. to excel in growth
Out'guard, s. the advanced guard
Outknave, v. a. to go beyond in knavery
Outland'ish, a. foreign, not native
Out'law, s. one excluded from the benefit of the law ; a plunderer, a robber, a bandit
Outlaw', v. a. to deprive of the protection of the law
Out'lawry, s. a decree by which a man is excluded from the protection of the law
Outle'ap, v. a. to excel in leaping
Out'let, s. a passage or discharge outward
Out'line, s. the line by which any figure defined ; contour ; extremity

Ou'liv'e, v. a. to survive, to live beyond
Outfac'e, v. a. to face down, to browbeat
Outlus'tre, v. a. to surpass in lustre
Outmar'ch, v. a. to leave behind in the march
Outmeas'ure, v. a. to exceed in measure
Out'most, a. remotest from the middle
Outnum'ber, v. a. to exceed in number
Outpa'ce, v. a. to outgo, to leave behind
Out'parish, s. a parish without the walls
Outpri'ze, v. a. to prize or value too highly
Out'rage, s. violence, tumultuous mischief
Out'rage, v. to injure roughly, and contume-
    liously; to commit exorbitancies
Outra'geous, a. violent, furious, atrocious
Outra'geousness, s. fury, violence
Outrea'ch, v. a. to go beyond, exceed; cheat
Outri'de, v. a. to pass by riding
Out'rider, s. a traveller for orders, servant,
    bailiff
Outri'ght, ad. immediately; completely
Outroa'r, v. a. to exceed in roaring
Outroot', v. a. to root up, to destroy, spoil
Outrun', v. a. to leave behind in running
Outsail', v. a. to leave behind in sailing
Outscorn', v. a. to bear down by contempt
Outsell', v. a. to sell for a higher price
Outshi'ne, v. a. to excel in lustre or brightness
Outshoo't, v. a. to excel in shooting
Out'side, s. external part, outer part, show
Outsit', v. a. to sit beyond the due time
Outslee'p, v. to sleep beyond proper time
Outspread', v. a. to spread open, to diffuse
Outsta're, v. a. to browbeat, to face down
Outstret'ch, v. a. to extend, to spread out
Outstrip', v. a. to outgo, to leave behind
Outswea'r, v. a. to overpower by swearing

Outtalk', v. a. to overpower by talk
Outton'gue, v. a. to bear down by noise
Outval'ue, v. a. to value or esteem too highly
Outvi'e, v. a. to exceed, to surpass, to excel
Outvo'te, v. a. to conquer by plurality of votes
Outwalk', v. a. to leave one in walking
Out'wall, s. outward part of a building
Out'ward, a. external, foreign, apparent
Out'ward, ad. to foreign or outer parts
Out'wardly, ad. in appearance, not sincerely,
    externally, opposed to inwardly
Out'wards, ad. towards the out parts
Outwea'r, v. a. to pass tediously
Outwei'gh, v. a. to exceed in weight, &c.
Outwit', v. a. to overcome by stratagem
Out'works, s. externals of a fortification
Outwor'n, part. destroyed by use or age
Owe, v. a. to be indebted; to be obliged
Owl, Owl'et, s. a bird that flies by night
Ow'ler, s. one who exports wool or other
    goods contrary to law
Own, pron. my own, his own
Own, v. a. to acknowledge, to confess
Own'er, s. one to whom a thing belongs
Own'ership, s. property, rightful possession
Owse, s. bark of young oak beaten small
Ows'er, s. bark and water mixed in a tanpit
Ox, s. pl. Ox'en, a castrated bull or bull
Ox'gang of land, s. twenty acres
Ox'lip, s. the cowslip, a vernal flower
Ox'ycrate, s. a mixture of vinegar and water
Ox'ymel, s. a mixture of vinegar and honey
O'yer, v. n. to hear—s. a court, a commission
Oyes', s. an introduction to any proclamation
    given by the public criers
Oy'ster, s. a bivalve shell-fish

P.

P, s. the 15th letter of the alphabet
Pab'ular, Pab'ulous, a. affording provender
Pa'cated, a. appeased, made placable
Pace, s. step, gait; measure of five feet
Pace, v. to move slowly; to measure by steps
Pa'cer, s. one who paces, a pacing horse
Pacif'ic, a. mild, gentle, appeasing
Pacifica'tion, s. the act of making peace
Pacifica'tor, s. a mediator, or peacemaker
Pacif'icatory, a. tending to make peace
Pac'ifier, s. one who pacifies or appeases
Pac'ify, v. a. to appease, to compose
Pack, s. a bundle tied up for carriage, a set
    of cards; a number of hounds, &c.
Pack, v. to bind or tie up goods; to sort cards
Pack'age, s. a charge, or wrapper for packing
Pack'cloth, s. cloth in which goods are tied
Pack'er, s. one who binds up bales
Pack'et, s. a small pack; a mail of letters
Pack'horse, s. a horse of burden
Pack'saddle, s. a saddle to carry burdens
Pack'thread, s. a thread used in packing
Pact, Pac'tion, s. a bargain, a covenant
Pad, s. an easy-paced horse, a foot robber
Pad, v. n. to travel gently; to rob on foot
Pad'ar, s. grouts, coarse flour
Pad'dle, v. n. to play in the water; to row
Pad'dle, s. an oar used by a single rower
Pad'dock, s. a toad or frog; a small enclosure

Pad'lock, s. a pendent or hanging lock
Pad'lock, v. a. to fasten with a padlock
Pæ'an, s. a song of triumph or praise
Pa'gan, s. a heathen—a. heathenish
Pa'ganism, s. heathenism
Page, s. one side of the leaf of a book; a young
    boy attending on a great person
Page, v. a. to mark the pages of a book
Pag'eant, s. a statue in a show; any show; a
    spectacle of entertainment
Pag'eant, a. showy, pompous, ostentatious
Pag'eantry, s. pomp, ostentation, show
Pag'inal, a. consisting of pages
Pa'god, s. an Indian idol, or its temple
Paid, pret. and part. pass. of to pay
Pail, s. a wooden vessel for water, milk, &c.
Pain, s. sensation of uneasiness, punishment
    denounced; labour; uneasiness of mind
Pain, v. a. to afflict, torment, make uneasy
Pain'ful, a. full of pain, giving pain, difficult
Pain'fully, ad. with great pain, laboriously
Pain'fulness, s. affliction, laboriousness
Pai'nim, s. an infidel, a pagan
Pain'less, a. free from pain or trouble
Pains'taker, s. a laborious person
Pains'taking, a. laborious, industrious
Paint, s. colours for painting
Paint, v. a. to represent, colour, describe
Pain'ter, s. one who professes painting

Pain'ting, s. the art of representing objects by delineation and colours ; a picture

Pair, s. two things suiting one another

Pair, v. a. to join in pairs, to suit, to unite

Pal'ace, s. a royal or splendid house

Pala'cious, a. royal, noble, magnificent

Palanquin'n, s. an Indian sedan or chair

Pal'atable, a. pleasing to the taste

Pal'ate, s. instrument of taste, mental relish

Palat'ic, a. belonging to the palate

Palat'inate, s. the country wherein is the seat of a palatine, or chief officer in the court of a sovereign prince

Pal'atine, a. possessing royal privileges

Pal'atines, s. the inhabitants of a palatinate

Pale, a. wan, whitish—s. a district, or enclosure ; a flat stake stuck in the ground ; the third and middle part of a scutcheon

Pale, v. a. to enclose with pales, encompass

Pa'lefaced, a. having the face wan, pale

Pale'ly, ad. wanly, not ruddily

Pal'endar, s. a kind of coasting vessel

Pa'leness, s. wanness, want of colour

Pa'leous, a. husky, chaffy, foul, unclean

Pal'ette, s. a light board for painters' colours

Pal'frey, s. a small horse trained for ladies

Pal'freyed, a. riding on a palfrey

Pal'ing, s. a kind of fence-work used for enclosure or defence

Pal'inode, Pal'inody, s. a recantation

Palisa'de, Palisa'do, s. pales set for enclosure

Pa'lish, a. somewhat pale, sickly

Pall, s. a cloak or mantle of state, or of an archbishop; covering thrown over the dead

Pall, v. to become insipid, to cloy ; weaken

Pal'lat, s. a nut on a watch

Pal'let, s. a small or mean bed

Pal'liament, s. a robe, a dress, a garment

Pal'liate, v. to excuse, to extenuate, ease

Pallia'tion, s. extenuation, imperfect cure

Pal'liative, a. extenuating, mitigating

Pal'lid, a. pale, not high coloured

Pallmall', s. a game with a ball and a mallet

Palm, s. a tree ; triumph ; part of the hand

Palm, v. a. to hide in the hand, cheat, impose

Pal'mar, a. relating to a hand's breadth

Pal'mer, s. a pilgrim ; deer's crown ; cheat

Palmet'to, s. a species of the palm-tree

Palmif'erous, a. bearing palms

Pal'mipede, a. webfooted, as swans, &c.

Pal'mister, s. one who deals in palmistry

Pal'mistry, s. the cheat of fortune-telling by lines in the palm of the hand

Pal'my, a. bearing or having palms

Palpabil'ity, s. quality of being palpable

Pal'pable, a. that may be felt ; plain, gross

Pal'pably, ad. plainly, evidently

Palpa'tion, s. the act of feeling

Pal'pitate, v. a. to beat as the heart, flutter

Palpita'tion, s. a throbbing of the heart

Pals'grave, s. a German title of honour

Pal'sical, Pal'sied, a. afflicted with the palsy

Pal'sy, s. a privation of the sense of feeling

Pal'ter, v. to shift, to dodge, to squander

Pal'triness, s. state of being worthless

Pal'try, a. worthless, despicable, mean

Pam, s. the knave of clubs

Pam'per, v. a. to feed luxuriously, to glut

Pam'phlet, s. a small stitched book

Pamphletee'r, s. a scribbler of books

Pan, s. a vessel of various metals, &c.

Panace'a, s. an universal medicine ; a herb

Pana'da, Pana'do, s. bread boiled in water

Pan'cake, s. a thin pudding fried in a pan

Pancrat'ical, a. excelling in all the gymnastic exercises

Pan'creas, s. the sweetbread of an animal

Pan'cy, or Pan'sy, s. a flower, kind of violet

Pan'dect, s. a complete treatise on any science

Pandemo'nium, s. chamber of devils

Pandem'ic, a. incident to a whole people

Pan'der, s. a pimp, a male bawd, a procurer

Pan'der, v. a. to minister to lust

Pandicula'tion, s. a yawning and stretching

Pan'durated, a. having furrowed stalks

Pandu'riform, a. shaped like a guitar

Pane, s. a square of glass, wainscot, &c.

Panegyr'ic, s. an eulogy, encomium, praise

Panegyr'ical, a. bestowing praise

Panegyr'ist, s. one who bestows praise

Pan'egyrize, v. to praise highly

Pan'el, s. a square of wainscot, &c. a roll of jurors' names provided by the sheriff

Pang, s. violent and sudden pain

Pan'ic, a. violently frighted without cause

Pan'ic, s. sudden consternation without rea-

Panna'de, s. the curvet of a horse [son

Pan'nel, s. a kind of rustic saddle

Pan'nier, s. a basket carried on horses

Pan'oply, s. a complete armour or harness

Pant, v. n. to beat as the heart ; wish earnestly

Pant, s. palpitation, motion of the heart

Pantaloo'n, s. a man's garment ; a buffoon

Panthe'on, s. a temple of all the heathen gods

Pan'ther, s. a spotted wild beast, a pard

Pan'tile, Pen'tile, s. a tile for gutters or roofs

Pan'tler, s. one who in a great family keeps the bread

Panto'fle, s. a slipper, an easy shoe

Pan'tomime, s. a tale exhibited only in gesture and dumb show ; a buffoon

Pan'try, s. a room for provisions

Pap, s. the nipple ; food for infants ; pulp

Papa', s. a fond name for father

Pa'pacy, s. the popedom, popish dignity

Pa'pal, a. belonging to the pope, popish

Papav'erous, a. resembling poppies

Pa'per, s. a substance made from rags

Pa'per, v. to hang a place with paper

Pa'permaker, s. one who makes paper

Pa'permill, s. a mill to make paper in

Pa'perstainer, s. one who colours paper

Papil'io, s. a moth of various colours

Papil'ionaceous, a. like the wings of a butter-

Pap'illary, Pap'illous, a. resembling paps [fly

Pa'pist, s. one who adheres to popery

Papis'tical, a. popish, adhering to popery

Pap'py, a. soft, succulent, easily divided

Par, s. a state of equality, equal value

Par'able, s. a similitude ; figurative speech

Parab'ola, s. one of the conic sections

Parabol'ical, a. expressed by a parable ; having the nature and form of a parabola

Parabol'ically, ad. allusively

Parab'olism, s. in algebra, the division of the terms of an equation by a known quantity involved or multiplied in the first term

Paracen'trical, a. deviating from circularity

Par'achronism, s. an error in chronology

Par'aclete, s. a comforter, an intercessor

Para'de, s. a military order, guard, show

Par'adise, s. the blissful regions, heaven

Paradisi'acal, *a.* suiting or making paradise
Par'adox, *s.* a tenet contrary to received opinion, an assertion contrary to appearance
Paradox'ical, *a.* inclined to new tenets
Par'adrome, *s.* an open gallery or passage
Par'agon, *s.* something supremely excellent; a model, pattern; companion, fellow
Par'agraph, *s.* a distinct part of a discourse
Parallac'tic, *a.* pertaining to a parallax
Par'allax, *s.* the distance between the true and apparent place of any star viewed from the earth
Par'allel, *s.* lines continuing their course and still preserving the same distance from each other; resemblance; conformity
Par'allel, *a.* in the same direction, equal
Par'allelism, *s.* state of being parallel
Parallel'ogram, *s.* a right-lined quadrilateral figure, of which the opposite sides are parallel and equal
Paral'ogism, Paral'ogy, *s.* false argument
Paral'ysis, *s.* a palsy
Paralyt'ic, *a.* palsied, inclined to palsy
Par'alyze, *v. a.* to weaken, to deprive of strength, as if struck with a palsy
Paramoun't, *s.* the chief—*a.* superior
Par'amour, *s.* a lover or mistress
Par'anymph, *s.* a brideman; a supporter
Par'apet, *s.* a wall breast high
Parapherna'lia, *s.* goods in a wife's disposal
Par'aphrase, *s.* an explanation in many words —*v. a.* to translate loosely [words
Par'aphrast, *s.* one who explains in many
Paraphras'tical, *a.* not literal, not verbal
Par'asang, *s.* a Persian measure of length
Par'asite, *s.* a flatterer of rich men
Parasit'ical, *a.* flattering, wheedling
Par'asol, *s.* a small canopy carried over the head to shelter from the heat of the sun
Par'boil, *v. a.* to half boil
Par'cel, *s.* a small lot, bundle, quantity
Par'cel, *v. a.* to divide into portions
Par'cenery, *s.* a joint tenure or inheritance
Parch, *v.* to burn slightly, to scorch, dry up
Par'chment, *s.* skins dressed for writing on
Pard, Par'dale, *s.* a leopard, a spotted beast
Par'don, *v. a.* to excuse, to forgive, to remit
Par'don, *s.* forgiveness, remission
Par'donable, *a.* that may be pardoned
Par'donableness, *s.* susceptibility of pardon
Par'donably, *ad.* excusably, venially
Pare, *v. a.* to cut off the surface, to cut off by little and little, to diminish
Paregor'ic, Paragor'ic, *a.* having the power in medicine to mollify, assuage, &c.
Parenchym'atous, *a.* spongy, soft
Pa'rent, *s.* a father or mother
Par'entage, *s.* birth, extraction, descent
Paren'tal, *a.* pertaining to parents
Paren'thesis, *s.* a sentence so included in another sentence, as that it may be taken out without injuring the sense of that which encloses it, commonly marked thus ( )
Parenthet'ical, *a.* relating to a parenthesis
Paren'ticide, *s.* killing a father or mother
Pa'rer, *s.* a tool to cut away the surface
Par'ergy, *s.* something unimportant
Par'get, *s.* a plaster—*v. a.* to plaster
Parhe'lion, *s.* a mock sun
Pari'etal, *a.* constituting sides or walls
Paril'ity, *s.* resemblance, proportion

Pa'ring, *s.* what is pared off; the rind
Par'ish, *s.* a district or division of land under a priest having the cure of souls
Parish'ioner, *s.* one that belongs to the parish
Parisyllab'ical, *a.* having equal syllables
Par'ity, *s.* equality, resemblance, likeness
Park, *v. a.* to enclose in a park
Park, *s.* an enclosure for beasts of chase
Par'ley, or Parle, *s.* conversation, oral treaty
Par'ley, *v. n.* to treat by word of mouth
Par'liament, *s.* the assembly of the three estates, the King, Lords, and Commons
Parliamen'tary, *a.* enacted by parliament, suiting or pertaining to parliament
Par'lour, *s.* a lower room for entertainment
Par'lous, *a.* keen, sprightly, waggish
Paro'chial, *a.* pertaining to a parish
Par'ody, *s.* change of another's words
Par'ody, *v. a.* to copy by way of parody
Paro'le, *s.* a word given as an assurance
Paron'ymous, *a.* resembling another word
Par'oquet, *s.* a small species of parrot
Parot'id, *a.* salivary; near the ears
Par'oxysm, *s.* periodical return of a fit, &c.
Parrici'dal, *a.* relating to parricide
Par'ricide, *s.* one who murders his father
Par'rot, *s.* a well-known talking bird
Par'ry, *v. n.* to put by thrusts, to ward off
Parse, *v. a.* to resolve by grammar rules
Parsimo'nious, *a.* covetous, saving, frugal
Parsimo'niously, *ad.* frugally, covetously
Parsimo'niousness, *s.* a disposition to save
Par'simony, *s.* niggardliness; covetousness
Pars'ley, *s.* a well-known herb
Pars'nip, Pars'nep, *s.* an edible root
Par'son, *s.* a clergyman, priest, minister
Par'sonage, *s.* a parson's benefice or house
Part, *v.* to separate, keep asunder, go away
Part, *s.* a portion, something less than the whole; share, concern, party, member
Part'able, *a.* divisible, such as may be parted
Part'age, *s.* division, act of sharing
Parta'ke, *v.* to participate, have part in
Parta'ker, *s.* an associate, a sharer
Parterre, *s.* a level ground; a flower garden
Par'tial, *a.* inclined antecedently to favour one party in a cause more than the other; affecting only one part
Partial'ity, *s.* an unequal judgment
Par'tialize, *v. a.* to make partial
Par'tially, *ad.* with unjust favour
Partic'ipant, *a.* having share or part
Partic'ipate, *v.* to partake, to share
Participa'tion, *s.* a sharing of something
Particip'ial, *a.* of the nature of a participle
Particip'ially, *ad.* in the sense of a participle
Par'ticiple, *s.* a word partaking at once of the qualities of a noun and a verb
Par'ticle, *s.* a small portion of a great substance; a small undeclinable word
Partic'ular, *a.* individual, singular, one
Partic'ular, *s.* a single instance or point
Particular'ity, *s.* something particular
Partic'ularize, *v. a.* to mention distinctly
Partic'ularly, *ad.* distinctly, peculiarly
Partisan', *s.* an adherent to a party; a pike
Partit'ion, *s.* the act of dividing, division
Partit'ion, *v. a.* to divide into distinct parts
Part'let, *s.* a hen; a ruff or band
Part'ly, *ad.* in part, in some measure
Part'ner, *s.* a sharer; a dancing mate, &c.

Part nership, *s.* a joint interest or property
Partoo'k, *pret.* of *to partake*
Par'tridge, *s.* a bird of game
Parts, *s.* qualities, faculties, districts
Partu'rient, *a.* about to bring forth
Parturit'ion, *s.* a parturient state
Par'ty, *s.* an assembly; cause; detachment
Par'ty-coloured, *a.* having different colours
Par'ty-jury, *s.* a jury in some trials, half foreigners and half natives
Par'vitude, Par'vity, *s.* minuteness
Pas, *s.* the right of precedence or priority
Pas'chal, *a.* relating to the passover
Pas'quin, Pasquina'de, *s.* a lampoon
Pass, *v.* to go beyond; to vanish; to enact a law; to omit; to thrust; to be current
Pass, *s.* a narrow entrance; licence to go
Pass'able, *a.* possible to be passed, tolerable
Passa'de, Passa'do, *s.* a push, a thrust
Pas'sage, *s.* act of passing; journey; incident; road; narrow street; part of a book
Pas'senger, *s.* a traveller, a wayfarer, one who hires a place in a carriage
Passibil'ity, *s.* the quality of receiving impressions from external agents
Pas'sible, *a.* that may be impressed
Pass'ing, *part. a.* supreme, eminent
Pass'ing-bell, *s.* the death-bell for a person
Pas'sion, *s.* anger, love; suffering of Christ
Pas'sion-week, *s.* the week before Easter
Pas'sionate, *a.* easily moved to anger
Pas'sionately, *ad.* with desire, angrily
Pas'sionateness, *s.* vehemence of mind
Pas'sive, *a.* unresisting, suffering
Pas'sively, *ad.* with a passive nature
Par'siveness, Passiv'ity, *s.* passibility, patience
Pass'over, *s.* a solemn festival of the Jews
Pass'port, *s.* permission in writing to pass
Past, *part. a.* not present, not to come, undergone, gone through, spent
Paste, *s.* any viscous, tenacious mixture
Paste'board, *s.* a thick kind of paper
Pas'tern, *s.* the knee of a horse, the leg
Pas'til, *s.* a roll of paste, a crayon
Pas'time, *s.* sport, amusement, diversion
Pas'tinate, *v. n.* to dig in a garden
Pas'tor, *s.* a shepherd, a clergyman who has the care of a flock
Pastoral, *a.* rural, rustic, like shepherds
Pas'toral, *s.* a rural poem; a bucolic
Pa'stry, *s.* pies or baked paste
Pa'strycook, *s.* one who makes pastry
Pas'turable, *a.* fit for pasture
Pas'turage, *s.* lands grazed by cattle
Pas'ture, *s.* land on which cattle feed; food
Pas'ture, *v. a.* to place in a pasture—*n.* graze
Pas'ty, *s.* a pie of crust raised without a dish
Pat, *a.* fit, convenient, exactly suitable
Pat, *v. a.* to strike lightly—*s.* a light blow
Patacoo'n, *s.* a Spanish coin, value 4*s.* 8*d.*
Patch, *v.* to mend, to piece, to put on patches
Patch-work, *s.* small pieces of different colours sewed interchangeably together
Pate, *s.* the head
Patefac'tion, *s.* the act or state of opening
Pat'en, *s.* a plate used for bread at the altar
Pa'tent, *a.* open to the perusal of all
Pat'ent, *s.* an exclusive right or privilege
Patentee', *s.* one who has a patent
Pater'nal, *a.* fatherly; hereditary
Paternos'ter, *s.* the Lord's prayer.

Path, Path way, *s.* way, road, track
Pathet'ic, Pathet'ical, *a.* moving the passions or affections, passionate
Pathet'ically, *ad.* in a moving manner
Path'less, *a.* untrodden, not known
Pathol'ogy, *s.* a part of physic which considers diseases, their causes, differences, and effects incident to the human body
Pa'thos, *s.* warmth, passion, feeling
Pat'ible, *a.* sufferable, tolerable
Pa'tience, *s.* calmness of mind, endurance
Pa'tient, *a.* not easily moved or provoked
Pa'tient, *s.* a diseased person under the care of another
Pa'tiently, *ad.* without rage, quietly
Pat'ine, *s.* the cover of a chalice
Pat'ly, *ad.* fitly, opportunely, suitably
Pa'triarch, *s.* a head of a family or church
Patriar'chal, *a.* pertaining to patriarchs
Patriar'chate, *s.* jurisdiction of a patriarch
Patric'ian, *a.* senatorial—*s.* a nobleman
Patrimo'nial, *a.* possessed by inheritance
Pat'rimony, *s.* an estate, &c. possessed by inheritance from a father or mother
Pa'triot, *s.* a real lover of his country
Patriot'ic, *a.* having patriotism
Pa'triotism, *s.* love or zeal for one's country
Patro'cinate, *v. a.* to patronize, to protect
Patrol', *s.* a guard to walk the streets
Pa'tron, *s.* an advocate, a supporter
Pa'tronage, *s.* protection, support, defence
Pa'tronal, *a.* protecting, supporting
Pa'troness, *s.* a female patron
Pat'ronize, *v. a.* to support, to defend
Patronym'ic, *s.* a name from father, &c.
Pat'ten, *s.* a clog shod with an iron ring
Pat'tepan, *s.* a pan to bake small pies in
Pat'ter, *v. n.* to make a noise like hail
Pat'tern, *s.* a specimen, archetype, model
Pav'an, or Pav'in, *s.* a kind of light dance
Pau'city, *s.* smallness of number, &c.
Pave, *v. a.* to floor with stones, &c.
Pa'vement, *s.* a stone or brick floor, &c.
Pa'ver, or Pa'vier, *s.* one who lays stones.
Pavil'ion, *s.* a tent, a temporary house
Paunch, *s.* the belly, abdominal regions
Pau'per, *s.* a poor person who receives a maintenance
Pau'perism, *s.* the state of poverty
Pause, *s.* a stop, break—*v. n.* to consider
Paw, *s.* the foot of a beast; hand
Paw, *v. a.* to handle roughly, fawn, flatter
Pawn, *v. a.* to pledge, to give in pledge
Pawn'broker, *s.* one who lends or pawns
Pay, *s.* wages, hire, money for services
Pay, *v. a.* to discharge a debt, reward, beat
Pay'able, *a.* due, that ought to be paid
Pay'ment, *s.* the act of payment; a reward
Pea, *s.* a well-known kind of pulse
Peace, *s.* respite from war, rest, silence
Peace, *interj.* silence, stop
Peace'able, *a.* not turbulent, free from war
Peace'ableness, *s.* a quiet disposition
Peace'ably, *ad.* without tumult or war
Peace'ful, *a.* pacific, mild, undisturbed
Peace'fully, *ad.* quietly, mildly, gently
Peace'fulness, *s.* quiet, freedom from war
Peace'maker, *s.* he who reconciles differences
Peach, *s.* a delicious fruit—*v. n.* to accuse
Peach'coloured, *a.* of a colour like a peach
Pea'chick, *s.* the chicken of a peacock
Pea'cock, *s.* a fowl of beautiful plumage

Pea'hen, s. the female of a peacock

Peak, s. the top of a hill; any thing pointed; the fore part of a head-dress

Peak, v.n. to look sickly or weakly; to sneak

Pea'king, part. a. sickly, poorly; sneaking

Peal, s. a loud sound, as of bells, cannon, &c.

Pear, s. a fruit of many different species

Pearl, s. a precious gem; a film on the eye

Pearl'ed, a. adorned or set with pearls

Pearl'y, a. abounding with, or like pearls

Pear'main, s. a kind of apple

Pear'tree, s. the tree that bears pears

Peas'ant, s. one who lives by rural labour

Peas'antry, s. peasants, country people

Pease'-cod, s. the shell or husk of peas

Peat, s. a species of turf for firing

Peb'ble, Peb'blestone, s. a sort of stone

Peb'bly, a. full of pebbles

Peccabil'ity, s. state of being subject to sin

Pec'cable, a. incident or liable to sin

Peccadil'lo, s. a small fault, a slight crime

Pec'cancy, s. bad quality

Pec'cant, a. criminal, ill disposed, bad

Pecca'vi, n. a form of asking pardon

Peck, s. the fourth part of a bushel

Peck, v. to pick up food with the beak

Peck'er, s. one that pecks; a bird

Pec'tinated, a. formed like a comb

Pec'toral, a. belonging to the breast

Pec'toral, s. a medicine proper to strengthen the stomach, &c.; a breast-plate

Pec'ulate, v. n. to defraud the public

Pecula'tion, s. theft of public money

Pecu'liar, s. the exclusive property

Pecu'liar, a. particular, single, appropriate

Peculiar'ity, s. particularity, oddness

Pecu'liarly, ad. particularly, singly

Pecu'niary, a. pertaining to money

Ped, s. a small pack-saddle, hamper, basket

Ped'agogue, s. a schoolmaster, a pedant

Pe'dal, a. pertaining to a root

Ped'als, s. the large pipes of an organ

Ped'ant, s. one awkwardly ostentatious of literature, one vain of low knowledge

Pedan'tic, a. like a pedant, conceited

Pedan'tically, ad. with boasting

Ped'antry, Pedan'ticness, s. ostentation of awkward, needless literature

Ped'dle, v. n. to busy about trifles

Pedere'ro, Patere'ro, s. a small ship gun

Ped'estal, s. the basis or foot of a statue

Pedes'trial, Pedes'trious, a. going on foot

Ped'icle, s. the footstalk of fruit, &c.

Pedic'ular, Pedic'ulous, a. lousy

Ped'igree, s. genealogy, lineage, descent

Ped'iment, s. an ornamental projection, &c.

Ped'ler, s. one who travels about the country with small commodities

Ped'lery, s. wares sold by pedlers

Ped'ling, s. trifling, or paltry dealing

Pe'dobaptism, s. infant baptism

Pedun'cle, s. the stalk by which the fruit adheres to the tree

Peel, v. a. to flay, to take the rind off; to rob

Peel, s. the rind; a board used by bakers

Peep, s. a sly look; first faint appearance

Peer, s. an equal, fellow; a nobleman

Peer, v. n. to come just in sight, to peep

Peer'age, Peer'dom, s. dignity of a peer

Peer'ess, s. wife of a peer, a lady ennobled

Peer'less, a. unequalled, having no peer

Peer'lessness, s. universal superiority

Pee'vish, a. irritable, petulant, easily offended

Pee'vishly, ad. angrily, querulously, morosely

Pee'vishness, s. irascibility, fretfulness

Peg, s. a wooden pin or fastener

Peg, v. a. to fasten with a peg

Pelf, s. money, riches, paltry stuff

Pel'ican, s. a bird said to admit its young to suck blood from its breast

Pe'lisse, s. a sort of cloak or robe

Pell, s. the skin of a beast

Pel'let, s. a little ball, a bullet

Pel'licle, s. a thin skin, a film

Pellmell', ad. confusedly, tumultuously

Pells, s. an office in the Exchequer

Pellu'cid, a. transparent, clear, not dark

Pelt, s. a skin, a hide—v. a. to throw at

Pelt'ing, part. a. throwing stones, &c.; paltry

Pelt'monger, s. a dealer in raw hides

Pen, s. an instrument for writing; a fold

Pen, v. n. to coop, to shut up; to write

Pe'nal, a. enacting punishment, vindictive

Penal'ity, s. liableness to punishment

Pen'alty, s. a punishment, forfeiture

Pen'ance, s. mortification inflicted for sin

Pence, s. the plural of penny

Pen'cil, s. a tool for drawing and painting

Pen'dant, s. an ear-ring, ornament, flag

Pen'dence, s. slopeness, inclination

Pen'dency, s. suspense, delay of decision

Pen'dent, a. hanging, jutting over

Pen'ding, a. depending, undecided

Pendulos'ity, Pen'dulousness, s. suspension

Pen'dulous, a. hanging, not supported below

Pen'dulum, s. anyweight hung to swing backwards and forwards, &c.

Penetrabil'ity, s. capacity of being pierced

Pen'etrable, a. that which may be pierced

Pen'etrail, s. interior parts, the entrails

Pen'etrant, a. having the power to pierce

Pen'etrate, v. to pierce, affect, understand

Penetra'tion, s. sagacity, a piercing through

Pen'etrative, a. piercing, acute, discerning

Pen'guin, s. a bird like a goose; a fruit

Penin'sula, s. land almost surrounded by water, but joined by a neck of land to the main continent

Pen'itence, s. repentance, sorrow for sin

Pen'itent, a. repentant, contrite for sin

Pen'itent, s. one sorrowful for sin

Peniten'tial, a. expressing penitence

Peniten'tial, s. a book directing penance

Peniten'tiary, s. a confessor, one who does penance; a place for hearing confession

Pen'knife, s. a knife used to cut pens

Pen'man, s. an author, a writer

Pen'manship, s. the act or art of writing

Pen'nated, a. having wings

Pen'nant, s. a rope to which a tackle is attached to hoist up boats, &c.; a flag

Pen'niless, a. wanting money, poor, distressed

Pen'non, s. a small flag or banner

Pen'ny, s. the 12th part of a shilling

Pen'nyweight, s. 24 grains troy weight

Pen'nyworth, s. a good purchase, &c.

Pen'sile, a. hanging, supported above ground

Pen'sion, s. a settled annual allowance

Pen'sionary, s. a magistrate in Dutch cities

Pen'sionary, a. maintained by a pension

Pen'sioner, s. one who receives a pension

Pen'sive, a. sorrowful, thoughtful, seriou-

N 3

Pen'sively, *ad.* with melancholy, sorrowfully
Pen'siveness, *s.* gloomy thoughtfulness
Pent, *part. pass.* of *to pen*, shut up
Pen'acap'sular, *a.* having five cavities
Pen'tachord, *s.* a five-stringed instrument
Pentae'drous, *a.* having five sides
Pen'tagon, *s.* a figure with five angles
Pentag'onal, *a.* having five angles
Pentam'eter, *s.* a verse of five feet
Pentan'gular, *a.* five cornered
Pentapet'alous, *a.* having five leaves
Pentap'tote, *s.* a noun that has five cases
Pen'tateuch, *s.* the five books of Moses
Pen'tecost, *s.* a feast among the Jews ; Whitsuntide
Pentecos'tal, *a.* belonging to Whitsuntide
Pent'house, *s.* sloping shed or roof
Penul'tima, *s.* the last syllable but one
Penum'bra, *s.* an imperfect shadow
Penu'rious, *a.* sordidly mean ; not plentiful
Penu'riousness, *s.* niggardliness, parsimony
Pen'ury, *s.* poverty, indigence
Peo'ple, *s.* a nation, persons in general
Peo'ple, *v. a.* to stock with inhabitants
Pepas'tic, *s.* a medicine to help digestion
Pep'per, *v.a.* to sprinkle with pepper ; to beat
Pep'per, *s.* an aromatic warm spice
Pep'percorn, *s.* any thing of trifling value
Pep'permint, *s.* mint eminently hot
Pep'tic, *a.* serving to concoct or digest
Peracu'te, *a.* very sharp, very violent
Peradven'ture, *ad.* perhaps, may be
Per'agrate, *v. a.* to wander over
Peram'bulate, *v. a.* to walk through
Perambula'tion, *s.* a wandering survey
Percei'vable, *a.* that may be perceived
Percei've, *v. a.* to discover, know, observe
Perceptibil'ity, *s.* the power of perceiving
Percep'tible, *a.* that may be observed
Percep'tibly, *ad.* in a manner to be perceived
Percep'tion, *s.* the power of perceiving, idea
Percep'tive, *a.* able or tending to perceive
Perch, *s.* a fish ; a measure of 5 yards and a half ; a bird's roost
Perch, *v.* to sit or roost as a bird
Perchan'ce, *ad.* perhaps, peradventure
Percip'ient, *a.* perceiving, having the faculty or power of perception
Per'colate, *v. a.* to strain through a sieve
Percola'tion, *s.* the act of straining
Percuss', *v. a.* to strike
Percus'sion, *s.* the act of striking ; stroke ; effect of sound in the ear
Percu'tient, *a.* striking, able to strike
Perdit'ion, *s.* destruction, ruin, death
Perdu', *ad.* closely, in ambush
Per'dulous, *a.* lost, thrown away
Perdura'tion, *s.* long continuance
Per'egrinate, *v. n.* to travel into far countries
Peregrina'tion, *s.* travel in foreign lands
Per'egrine, *a.* foreign, not domestic
Perem'pt, *v. a.* to kill, to crush
Peremp'tion, *s.* a crush, extinction ; law term
Per'emptorily, *ad.* absolutely, positively
Per'emptory, *a.* dogmatical, absolute
Peren'nial, *a.* lasting a year ; perpetual
Peren'nity, *s.* perpetuity, lastingness
Per'fect, *a.* complete, pure, immaculate
Per'fect, *v. a.* to finish, complete, instruct
Perfec'tion, *s.* the state of being perfect
Perfec'tive, *a.* conducing to perfection

Per'fectly, *ad.* totally, exactly, accurately
Per'fectness, *s.* completeness, goodness
Perfid'ious, *a.* treacherous, false to trust
Perfid'iously, *ad.* by breach of faith
Perfid'iousness, Per'fidy, *s.* treachery
Per'date, *v. a.* to blow through
Perfo'rate, *v. a.* to pierce through, to bore
Perfora'tion, *s.* the act of piercing ; a hole
Per'forator, *s.* the instrument of boring
Perfor'ce, *ad.* by force, violently
Perfor'm, *v.* to execute, to do, to achieve as undertaking, to succeed in an attempt
Perfor'mance, *s.* completion of something designed, composition, action
Perfor'mer, *s.* one who performs or plays
Per'fricate, *v. n.* to rub over
Per'fume, *s.* a sweet odour, fragrance
Perfu'me, *v. a.* to impregnate with scent
Perfu'mer, *s.* one who sells perfumes
Perfunc'tory, *a.* slight, careless, negligent
Perfu'se, *v. a.* to tincture, to overspread
Perhap's, *ad.* peradventure, it may be
Pericra'nium, *s.* the membrane that covers the skull
Perigee', Perige'um, *s.* that point of the heaven wherein the sun or any planet is nearest the centre of the earth
Perihe'lium, *s.* that point of a planet's orbit wherein it is nearest the sun
Per'il, *s.* danger, hazard ; danger denounced
Per'ilous, *a.* hazardous, dangerous
Perim'eter, *s.* circumference of a figure
Pe'riod, *s.* a circuit, epoch ; a full stop
Period'ical, *a.* regular, at stated times
Period'ically, *ad.* at stated periods
Peripatet'ic, *a.* relating to Aristotle
Periph'ery, *s.* circumference
Periph'rasis, *s.* circumlocution ; the use of many words to express the sense of one
Peripneu'mony, *s.* inflammation of the lungs
Per'ish, *v.* to die, to be destroyed, to decay
Per'ishable, *a.* liable to decay or perish
Peristal'tic, *a.* wormlike, spiral
Per'istyle, *s.* a circular range of pillars
Per'jure, *v. a.* to forswear ; to swear falsely
Per'jurer, *s.* a forsworn person
Per'jury, *s.* the act of swearing falsely
Per'iwig, *s.* a wig, covering for the head
Per'iwinkle, *s.* a kind of fish-snail
Perk, *v.* to hold up the head affectedly
Per'manence, Per'manence, *s.* duration
Per'manent, *a.* durable, unchanged
Per'manently, *ad.* durably, lastingly
Per'meable, *a.* that may be passed through
Per'meant, *a.* passing through
Permis'cible, *a.* such as may be mingled
Permis'sible, *a.* what may be permitted
Permis'sion, *s.* grant of leave or liberty
Permis'sive, *a.* granting mere liberty
Permit', *v. a.* to allow, to suffer, to give up
Per'mit, *s.* a warrant from officers of excise for the removal of tea, spirits, &c.
Permuta'tion, *s.* an exchange, a barter
Pernic'ious, *a.* destructive, very hurtful
Pernic'iously, *ad.* hurtfully, destructively
Pernic'ity, *s.* swiftness, celerity
Perora'tion, *s.* the conclusion of an oration
Perpen'd, *v. a.* to consider attentively
Perpendic'ular, *a.* that falls, hangs, or is directly downward
Perpendic'ular, *s.* a level or plumb-line

Perpen'sion, s. consideration

Per'petrate, v. a. to commit a crime

Perpetra'tion, s. the commission of a crime

Perpet'ual, a. never ceasing, continual

Perpet'ually, ad. continually, incessantly

Perpet'uate, v. a. to make perpetual

Perpetu'ity, s. duration to all futurity

Perplex', v. a. to disturb with doubts, to vex

Perplex', a. intricate, difficult

Perplex'ed, part. a. confused, difficult

Perplex'ity, s. anxiety, intricacy

Per'quisite, s. a gift free of office, &c.

Per'ry, s. wine or drink made of pears

Per'secute, v. a. to oppress, vex, trouble

Persecu'tion, s. the act of persecuting

Per'secutor, s. an oppressor

Perseve'rance, s. firmness, resolution

Perseve'rs, v. n. to be stedfast, to persist

Persis't, v. n. to persevere, to continue firm

Persis'tence, s. obstinacy, contumacy

Per'son, s. an individual; human being: the shape of the body; exterior appearance

Per'sonable, handsome, graceful

Per'sonage, s. a considerable person

Per'sonal, a. pertaining to a person

Personal'ity, s. individuality of any one

Per'sonally, ad. in person, particularly

Per'sonate, v. a. to counterfeit, to represent

Personifica'tion, s. prosopopœia, the change of things to persons

Person'ify, v. a. to change from a thing to a person

Perspec'tive, a. relating to vision, optical

Perspec'tive, s. a spying-glass, view, vista

Perspica'cious, a. quick-sighted, sharp

Perspicac'ity, s. quickness of sight, &c.

Per'spicil, s. a glass through which things are viewed; an optical glass

Perspicu'ity, s. transparency; easiness to be understood; freedom from ambiguity

Perspic'uous, a. transparent, not ambiguous

Perspic'uously, ad. clearly, not obscurely

Perspic'uousness, s. freedom from obscurity

Perspi'rable, a. emitted by the pores

Perspira'tion, s. excretion by the pores

Perspi're, v. n. to emit by the cuticular pores

Persua'de, v. a. to bring to an opinion

Persua'sible, a. that may be persuaded

Persua'sion, s. the act of persuading

Persua'sive, Persua'sory, a. fit to persuade

Persulta'tion, s. an eruption of the blood

Pert, a. brisk, lively, saucy, petulant

Pertai'n, v. n. to belong, to relate to

Pertina'cious, a. obstinate, stubborn, wilful

Pertina'ciously, ad. obstinately, stubbornly

Pertinac'ity, s. obstinacy, resolution

Per'tinence, s. fitness, appositeness

Per'tinent, a. apt, to the purpose, fit

Pertin'gent, reaching to, touching [iantly

Pert'ly, ad. briskly, smartly, saucily, pert-

Pert'ness, s. brisk folly, sauciness, petulance

Pertur'bate, v. a. to disturb, to disorder

Perturba'tion, s. a disquiet of mind

Pertur'bed, a. disturbed, disquieted

Pertu'sed, a. punched, pierced with holes

Pertu'sion, s. the act of piercing

Perva'de, v. a. to pass through, to permeate

Perva'sion, s. the act of passing through

Perv'erse, a. obstinate, stubborn, petulant

Perver'sely, ad. vexatiously, crossly

Perver'seness, s. petulance, perversion

Perver'sion, s. turning to a wrong sense

Perver'sity, s. perverseness, crossness

Perver't, v. a. to distort, corrupt, mislead

Pervert'ible, a. that may be perverted

Pervica'cious, a. spitefully obstinate

Per'vious, a. admitting passage

Per'uke, s. a cap of false hair, a wig

Per'uke-maker, s. a wig-maker

Peru'sal, s. the act of reading over

Peru'se, v. a. to read over, to observe

Pesa'de, s. motion of a horse in rearing

Pest, s. a plague, pestilence, mischief

Pes'ter, v. a. to disturb, harass, perplex

Pest'house, s. a plague-hospital

Pestif'erous, a. deadly, malignant, infectious

Pes'tilence, s. plague, contagious distemper

Pes'tilent, a. producing plagues, malignant

Pestilen'tial, a. infectious, contagious, pernicious

Pes'tle, s. a tool to beat in a mortar

Pet, s. a slight displeasure; a fondling lamb

Pet'al, s. the leaf of a flower

Petar'd, s. an engine to blow up places

Pete'chial, a. pestilentially spotted

Pe'tiole, s. the stalk of a leaf

Pet'it, a. small, little, inconsiderable

Peti'tion, s. a request, prayer, entreaty

Peti'tion, v. a. to supplicate, to solicit

Peti'tionary, a. supplicatory, petitioning

Peti'tioner, s. one who offers a petition

Petres'cent, a. becoming stone, hardening

Petrifac'tion, s. act of turning to stone

Petrifac'tive, a. able to turn to stone

Pet'rify, v. to change to or become stone

Pet'ronel, s. a pistol or small gun

Pet'ticoat, s. a woman's lower vestment

Pet'tifogger, s. a petty small-rate lawyer

Pet'tifogging, a. low, mean

Pet'tish, a. apt to be peevish, froward

Pet'tishness, s. fretfulness, peevishness

Pet'titoes, s. the feet of a sucking pig

Pet'to, s. the breast; figuratively, privacy

Pet'ty, a. small, inconsiderable, little

Pet'ulance, s. sauciness, peevishness

Pet'ulant, a. saucy, perverse, wanton

Pet'ulantly, ad. with saucy pertness

Pew, s. a seat enclosed in a church

Pew'et, s. a water-fowl, the lapwing

Pew'ter, s. a compound of metals

Pew'terer, s. one who works in pewter

Phae'ton, s. a high open carriage

Phagede'na, s. an ulcer, where the sharpness of the humours eats away the flesh

Pha'lanx, s. a troop of men closely embodied

Phan'tasm, s. vain imagination, a vision

Phan'tom, s. a spectre, a fancied vision

Pharisa'ical, a. externally religious, &c.

Pharisa'ically, ad. ostentatiously, vainly

Pharmacol'ogy, s. the knowledge of drugs

Pharmacope'ia, s. a dispensatory

Pharmacop'olist, s. an apothecary

Phar'macy, s. the trade of an apothecary

Pha'ros, s. a light-house, a watch-tower

Pha'sels, s. French beans

Pha'ses, s. appearances exhibited by any body, as the changes of the moon

Pheas'ant, s. a kind of wild cock or hen

Phe'ese, v. a. to comb, to fleece, to cut

Phe'nix, Phœ'nix, s. the bird which supposed to exist single, and to rise from its own ashes

Phenom'enon, _s._ any thing that strikes by its new or extraordinary appearance

Phi'al, _s._ a small bottle

Philan'thropy, _s._ love of mankind, kindness

Phil'ibeg, _s._ a kind of short petticoat

Philip'pic, _s._ any invective, declamation

Philol'oger, Philol'ogist, _s._ a grammarian

Philolog'ical, _a._ critical, grammatical

Philol'ogy, _s._ grammatical learning, criticism

Phi'lomath, _s._ a lover of learning

Phil'omel, _s._ the nightingale

Phil'omot, _a._ coloured like a dead leaf

Philos'opheme, _s._ a principle of reasoning

Philos'opher, _s._ a man deep in knowledge

Philos'opher's-stone, _s._ a stone dreamed of by alchymists, which they assert will, by its touch, transmute base metals into gold

Philosoph'ical, _a._ belonging to philosophy

Philos'ophy, _s._ knowledge natural or moral ; the hypothesis upon which natural effects are explained ; reasoning, argumentation

Phil'ter, _s._ something to cause love

Phiz, _s._ the face, the countenance

Phlebot'omise, _v. a._ to let blood

Phlebot'omy, _s._ the act of blood-letting

Phlegm, _s._ a watery humour of the body

Phlegmat'ic, _a._ troubled with phlegm, dull

Phleg'mon, _s._ a tumour, an inflammation

Phleg'monous, _a._ inflammatory, burning

Phleme, _s._ an instrument to bleed cattle

Phlogis'tic, _a._ inflammatory, hot, burning

Phlogis'ton, _s._ chymical liquor very inflammable ; the inflammable part of the body

Pho'nics, _s._ the doctrine of sounds

Phonocam'ptic, _a._ able to alter sounds

Phos'phorus, _s._ a chymical substance which, exposed to air, takes fire ; morning star

Phrase, _s._ an idiom or mode of speech

Phraseol'ogy, _s._ style, diction, phrase-book

Phrenet'ic, _a._ inflamed in the brain, frantic

Phreni'tis, _s._ inflammation of the brain

Phren'sy, _s._ madness, franticness

Phthis'ic, _s._ a consumption of the body

Phthis'ical, _a._ wasting by disease

Phylac'tery, _s._ a bandage on which was inscribed some memorable sentence

Phys'ic, _s._ the art of curing diseases ; medicines, remedies, a purge

Phys'ical, _a._ relating to natural philosophy, not moral ; medicinal

Physic'ian, _s._ one who professes physic

Phys'ics, _s._ natural philosophy

Physiog'nomist, _s._ a judge of faces

Physiog'nomy, _s._ the art of discovering the temper, &c. by the features of the face ; the face, the cast of the look

Physiolog'ical, _a._ relating to physiology

Physiol'ogy, _s._ the doctrine of nature

Phytiv'orous, _a._ that eats grass or vegetables

Phytol'ogy, _s._ the doctrine of plants

Pi'acle, _s._ an enormous crime

Piac'ular, _a._ expiatory, criminal

Pi a-ma'ter, _s._ a skin covering the brain

Pi'anet, _s._ a magpie ; the lesser woodpecker

Pias'ter, _s._ a foreign coin, value about 5s.

Piaz'za, _s._ a walk under a roof supported by pillars

Pi'ca, _s._ a kind of printing letter

Picaroo'n, _s._ a robber, a plunderer

Pick, _v._ to choose, take up, select, gather, clean, peck, rob, open a lock, eat slowly

Pick'apack, _ad._ in manner of a pack

Pick'axe, _s._ an axe with a sharp point

Pick'back, _a._ on the back

Pick'ed, or Pi'ked, _a._ sharp, smart, pointed

Pickee'r, _v._ to pirate, pillage, rob; to skirmish

Pick'er, _s._ one who picks, a pickaxe

Pick'et, _s._ a guard ; a sharp stake

Pic'kle, _s._ a salt liquor, a thing pickled

Pic'kle, _v. a._ to preserve in pickle, season

Pic'kle-her'ring, _s._ a jack-pudding, a zany

Pick'lock, _s._ a tool to pick locks with

Pick'pocket, _s._ one that steals from pockets

Pick'thank, _s._ an officious person, a flatterer

Picto'rial, _a._ produced by a painter

Pic'ture, _s._ resemblance of things in colours

Pictures'que, _a._ like a picture

Pid'dle, _v. n._ to feed squeamishly, to trifle

Pie, _s._ a crust baked with something in it

Pie'bald, _a._ of various colours, diversified

Piece, _s._ a patch, a fragment, gun, coin, &c.

Piece, _v._ to enlarge, to join, to unite

Piece'meal, _a._ separate—_ad._ in pieces

Pi'ed, _a._ party-coloured, speckled, spotted

Pier, _s._ the column or support of an arch

Pierce, _v._ to penetrate, to bore ; to affect

Pier'cer, _s._ who or what pierceth

Pier'cingly, _ad._ sharply, keenly, acutely

Pi'etism, _s._ an affectation of piety

Pi'ety, _s._ discharge of duty to God

Pig, _s._ a young sow or boar, an oblong mass of metal

Pig'eon, _s._ a well-known bird

Pig'eon-liv'ered, _a._ mild, soft, gentle

Pig'gin, _s._ a small wooden vessel

Pig'ment, _s._ a paint, colours for painting

Pig'my, _s._ a very little person, a dwarf

Pignora'tion, _s._ the act of pledging

Pig'nut, _s._ an earth-nut

Pike, _s._ a fish, a lance used by soldiers

Pi'kestaff, _s._ the wooden handle of a pike

Pilas'ter, _s._ a small square column

Pil'chard, Pil'cher, _s._ a fish resembling a herring

Pil'cher, _s._ a cloak lined with fur

Pile, _s._ a heap, an edifice, piece of wood

Pile, _v._ to heap or lay upon

Pil'fer, _v. a._ to steal, practise petty thefts

Pil'ferer, _s._ one who steals petty things

Pil'grim, _s._ a traveller, a wanderer, one who travels to sacred places for devotion

Pil'grimage, _s._ a journey for devotion

Pill, _s._ a small round ball of physic

Pil'lage, _s._ plunder—_v. a._ to plunder, spoil

Pil'lar, _s._ a column, supporter, maintainer

Pil'lared, _a._ supported by or like pillars

Pil'lion, _s._ a woman's saddle, a pad

Pil'lory, _s._ an instrument of punishment

Pil'low, _s._ a bag of feathers to sleep on

Pil'lowbeer, _s._ the cover of a pillow

Pilos'ity, _s._ hairiness, roughness

Pi'lot, _v. a._ to direct the course of a ship

Pi'lot, _s._ one who directs a ship's course

Pi'lotage, _s._ the pay or office of a pilot

Pimen'ta, _s._ allspice, Jamaica pepper

Pimp, _s._ a procurer, a pander

Pimp'ing, _a._ little, small, petty

Pim'ple, _s._ a small red pustule on the skin

Pin, _s._ a short pointed wire, a peg, a bolt

Pin'cers, _s._ an instrument to draw nails, &c.

Pinch, _v._ to squeeze, gripe, be frugal

Pinch, _s._ a painful squeeze with the fingers

Pinch'beck, _s._ kind of yellow metal

Pin'cushion, _s._ a stuffed bag to stick pins in

Pine, v. to languish, grieve for—s. a tree
Pi'neapple, s. a fruit, the anana
Pin'fold, s. a place to pen cattle in
Pin'guid, a. fat, unctuous, greasy, plump
Pin'ion, s. the wing of a fowl; fetters
Pin'ion, v. a. to bind the wings, to shackle
Pink, s. a flower, a stamp, a ship, a fish; any
 thing supremely eminent; colour used by
Pink, v. to pierce in small holes [painters
Pin'maker, s. one who makes pins
Pin'money, s. a wife's pocket money
Pin'nace, s. a man of war's boat
Pin'nacle, s. a turret, a high spiring point
Pin'ner, s. a part of a head-dress; a pinmaker
Pint, s. half a quart
Pionee'r, s. a soldier to level roads, &c.
Pi'ous, a. devout, godly, religious
Pi'ously, ad. religiously, devoutly, holily
Pip, s. a spot on cards; a disease of fowls
Pip, v. n. to chirp or cry as a bird
Pipe, s. a musical instrument; a tube; a li-
 quid measure containing two hogsheads;
 the key of the voice, &c.
Pipe, v. n. to play on a pipe, to whine
Pi'per, s. one who plays on a pipe
Pi'ping, a. weak, sickly, feeble; hot
Pip'kin, s. a small earthen boiler
Pip'pin, s. a small apple
Piq'uant, a. stimulating, sharp, pungent
Pique, s. ill-will, petty malice, grudge
Pique, v. a. to offend, to irritate
Piquet', s. a game at cards
Pi'racy, s. the act of robbing on the sea
Pi'rate, s. a sea robber; a plagiary
Pirat'ical, a. predatory, robbing
Pis'cary, s. a privilege of fishing
Pisca'tion, s. the act or practice of fishing
Pis'catory, a. relating to fish or fishing
Pisciv'orous, a. fish-eating, living on fish
Push! interj. of slighting or contemning
Pis'mire, s. an ant or emmet
Pista'chio, s. a fragrant Syrian nut
Pis'tol, s. the smallest of fire-arms
Pisto'le, s. a foreign coin. value 17s.
Pis'ton, s. a part of a pump, or a syringe
Pit, s. a hole; abyss; the grave; hollow part
Pit'apat, s. a flutter, a palpitation
Pitch, s. the resin of the pine; size; rate
Pitch, v. to fix; light; smear with pitch
Pitch'er, s. an earthen vessel; an iron bar
Pitch'fork, s. a fork to load dung, &c.
Pitch'y, a. black, dark, dismal; smeared
Pit'coal, s. a fossile coal
Pit'eous, a. sorrowful; exciting pity; mean
Pit'eously, ad. after a piteous manner
Pit'eousness, s. sorrowfulness, tenderness
Pit'fall, s. a pit dug and covered over
Pith, s. the marrow of a plant; energy
Pith'ily, ad. with strength, or force
Pith'iness, s. energy, force, strength
Pith'less, a. wanting pith, wanting energy
Pith'y, a. consisting of pith; forcible
Pit'iable, a. deserving pity
Pit'iful, a. tender, melancholy; mean, paltry
Pit'ifully, ad. mournfully, despicably
Pit'iless, a. wanting compassion, merciless
Pit'man, s. a person who works in pits
Pit'saw, s. a large saw for two men
Pit'tance, s. an allowance, a small portion
Pitu'itous, a. consisting of phlegm
Pit'y, s. sympathy with misery or pain

Pit'y, v. a. to compassionate misery
Piv'ot, s. a pin on which any thing turns
Pix, s. the box for the consecrated host
Pla'cable, a. that which may be appeased
Placar'd, Placar't, s. an edict, a manifesto
Pla'cate, v. a. to appease, to reconcile
Place, s. locality, space in general, a man-
 sion, existence, rank, priority, office
Place, v. a. to put in a place, fix, settle
Plac'id, a. gentle, quiet, kind, soft
Plac'idness, s. peaceableness, quietness
Plac'it, s. decree, determination
Plack'et, s. a petticoat
Pla'giarism, s. literary theft, adoption of the
 thoughts or works of another
Pla'giary, Pla'giarist, s. a thief in literature
Plague, s. a pestilence, trouble, vexation
Plague, v. a. to infect with pestilence; tease
Pla'guily, ad. vexatiously, horribly
Pla'guy, a. vexatious, troublesome, harassing
Plaice, s. a common kind of flat fish
Plaid, s. a variegated stuff, a Scotch dress
Plain, a. smooth, artless, clear, simple
Plain, Plain'ly, ad. sincerely, flatly, fairly
Plaindea'ling, a. acting without art
Plain'ness, s. levelness, want of show
Plaint, s. a lamentation, a complaint
Plain'tiff, s. he that commences a suit
Plain'tive, a. expressive of sorrow, lamenting
Plain'work, s. common needle-work
Plais'ter, s. a salve spread on linen
Plait, s. a fold, a double—v. a. to fold
Plan, s. a scheme, form, draught, model
Plan, v. a. to scheme, to form in design
Plan'ched, a. made of boards
Plan'cher, s. a board, a plank, a floor of wood
Plane, s. a level, a tool—v. to level
Plan'et, s. an erratic or wandering star
Plan'etary, a. pertaining to the planets
Plan'etstruck, a. blasted, amazed
Plan'ish, v. a. to polish, to smooth
Plan'isphere, s. a sphere projected on a plane
Plank, s. a board—v. a. to lay with planks
Planoco'nical, a. level on one side and coni-
 cal on the other [vex on the other
Planocon'vex, a. flat on the one side and con-
Plant, s. any vegetable production
Plant, v. a. to set, cultivate, fix, settle
Plan'tain, s. a herb, a tree and its fruit
Plan'tal, a. pertaining to plants
Planta'tion, s. a colony, a place planted
Plan'ted, a. settled, established
Plan'ter, s. one who sows or cultivates
Plash, s. a small puddle of water [branches
Plash, v. a. to dash with water; to interweave
Plash'y, a. watery, filled with puddles
Plasm, s. a mould, a matrix for metals
Plas'ter, s. lime to cover walls; a salve
Plas'ter, v. a. to cover with plaster, &c.
Plas'terer, s. one who plasters walls, &c.
Plas'tic, a. having power to give form
Plas'tron, s. a piece of stuffed leather
Plat, s. a piece of ground—v. to interweave
Plate, s. wrought metal, a dish to eat on
Plat'en, s. a part of a printing press
Plat'form, s. a horizontal plane, a level
Plat'ina, s. a metal heavier than gold
Platon'ic, a. relating to Plato, pure
Platoo'n, s. a square body of musqueteers
Plat'ter, s. a large earthen or wooden dish
Plau'dit, s. applause, approbation

Plau'ditory, *a.* praising, commending
Plausibil'ity, *s.* appearance of right
Plau'sible, *a.* superficially pleasing, specious
Plau'sibleness, *s.* show of right
Plau'sibly, *ad.* speciously, seemingly fair
Plau'sive, *a.* applauding, plausible
Play, *s.* amusement, sport, game, drama
Play, *v.* to sport, game, trifle, perform
Play'er, *s.* one who plays or performs
Play'fellow, *s.* a companion in youth
Play'ful, *a.* sportive, full of levity
Play'game, *s.* play of children
Play'house, *s.* a house for acting plays in
Play'some, *a.* wanton, full of levity
Play'thing, *s.* a toy, a thing to play with
Play'wright, *s.* a maker or writer of plays
Plea, *s.* a form of pleading, an apology
Plead, *v. a.* to defend, to discuss, to argue
Plea'dable, *a.* that which may be discussed
Plea'der, *s.* one who speaks for or against
Plea'ding, *s.* the act or form of arguing
Pleas'ant, *a.* delightful, cheerful, merry
Pleas'antly, *ad.* merrily, in good humour
Pleas'antness, *s.* delightfulness, gaiety
Pleas'antry, *s.* gaiety, merriment
Please, *v.* to delight, content, like, choose
Pleas'ingly, *ad.* so as to give delight
Pleas'urable, *a.* delightful, full of pleasure
Plea'sure, *s.* delight, gratification, choice
Plebe'ian, *a.* popular, vulgar, low, common
Plebe'ian, *s.* one of the lower people
Pled'ge, *s.* a pawn—*v. a.* to invite to drink
Pled'get, *s.* a small mass of lint
Plei'ades, *s.* a northern constellation
Plen'arily, *ad.* fully, entirely, perfectly
Plen'ary, *a.* full, entire, perfect
Plenilu'nary, *a.* relating to the full moon
Plenip'otence, *s.* fulness of power
Plenip'otent, *a.* invested with full power
Plenipoten'tiary, *s.* a negotiator for a prince
  or state, invested with power to treat, &c.
Ple'nist, *s.* a philosopher who holds all space
  to be full of matter
Plen'itude, *s.* fulness, repletion, abundance
Plen'teous, *a.* copious, abundant, fruitful
Plen'teously, *ad.* copiously, abundantly
Plen'tiful, *a.* copious, exuberant, fruitful
Plen'tifully, *ad.* copiously, abundantly
Plen'ty, *s.* abundance, fruitfulness
Ple'onasm, *s.* a redundancy of words
Pleth'ora, Pleth'ory, *s.* a fulness of blood
Plev'in, *s.* in law, a warrant or assurance
Pleu'ra, *s.* a skin that covers the chest
Pleu'risy, *s.* an inflammation of the pleura
Pleurit'ic, *a.* diseased with a pleurisy
Pli'able, *a.* flexible, apt to bend
Pli'ableness, *s.* easiness to be bent
Pli'ant, *a.* flexible; easily persuaded
Pli'antness, *s.* flexibility, toughness
Pli'ers, *s.* a kind of small pincers
Plight, *s.* condition, state, good case, gage
Plight, *v. a.* to pledge, give as surety, weave
Plinth, *s.* the lowermost part of a pillar
Plod, *v. n.* to toil, to drudge, to study closely
Plod'der, *s.* a dull, heavy, laborious man
Plod'ding, *s.* close drudgery, or study
Plot, *s.* a small extent of ground, a scheme,
  conspiracy, stratagem, contrivance
Plot, *v.* to scheme mischief, plan, contrive
Plov'er, *s.* the name of a bird, a lapwing
Plough, *s.* an instrument of husbandry

Plough, *v. a.* to turn up with a plough
Plough'man, *s.* one that attends the plough
Plough'share, *s.* the iron of a plough
Pluck, *s.* a pull; the liver and lights, &c.
Pluck, *v. a.* to snatch, draw, strip feathers
Plug, *s.* a stopple—*v. a.* to stop with a plug
Plum, *s.* a fruit; dried grapes; 100,000 *L.*
Plu'mage, *s.* feathers, a suit of feathers
Plumb, *s.* a leaden weight on a line
Plumb, *v. a.* to sound, to regulate by a plumb
Plumb, *ad.* perpendicularly to the horizon
Plumb'er, *s.* one who works upon lead
Plume, *s.* a feather; pride, towering mien
Plume, *v. a.* to pick and adjust feathers, to
  adorn, to make proud; to strip
Plumig'erous, *a.* having feathers; feathered
Plum'met, *s.* a leaden weight or pencil
Plu'mous, *a.* feathery, resembling feathers
Plump, *a.* somewhat fat, not lean, sleek
Plump, *v.* to fall like a stone in water; to fat-
  ten, to swell, to make large
Plump'er, *s.* sudden stroke, what plumps out
Plump'ness, *s.* fulness, comeliness
Plumpud'ding, *s.* pudding made with plums
Plu'my, *a.* covered with feathers
Plun'der, *s.* pillage, spoils gotten in war
Plun'der, *v. a.* to pillage, to rob by force
Plun'derer, *s.* a hostile pillager, a thief
Plunge, *v.* to put or sink suddenly under wa-
  ter; to fall into any hazard or distress
Plunge, *s.* the act of putting under water
Plunk'et, *s.* a kind of blue colour
Plu'ral, *a.* implying more than one
Plu'ralist, *s.* a clergyman who holds more
  benefices than one, with cure of souls
Plural'ity, *s.* a number more than one
Plush, *s.* a kind of shaggy cloth
Plu'vial, Plu'vious, *a.* rainy, wet
Plu'vial, *s.* a priest's vestment or cope
Ply, *v.* to work closely; to solicit; to bend
Ply, *s.* bent, turn, form, bias, fold
Pneumat'ic, *a.* relative to wind
Pneumat'ics, *s.* the doctrine of the air
Pneumatol'ogy, *s.* the doctrine of spiritual
  existence
Poach, *v.* to boil slightly; to steal game
Poach'er, *s.* one who steals game
Poach'y, *a.* damp, marshy, moist
Pock, *s.* a pustule of the small pox
Pock'et, *s.* a small bag inserted into clothes
  —*v. a.* to put in the pocket
Pock'et-glass, *s.* a glass for the pocket
Pock'hole, *s.* a scar made by the small-pox
Poc'ulent, *a.* fit for drink, drinkable
Pod, *s.* the husk or shell of pulse, seeds, &c.
Pod'der, *s.* a gatherer of peasecods
Podge, *s.* a puddle, a plash, a watery place
Po'em, *s.* a composition in verse
Po'esy, *s.* the art of writing poems
Po'et, *s.* a writer of poems, an inventor
Poetas'ter, *s.* a vile petty poet
Po'etess, Po'etress, *s.* a female poet
Poet'ical, *a.* pertaining to poetry
Poet'ically, *ad.* by the fiction of poetry
Po'etry, *s.* metrical composition, poems
Poig'nancy, *s.* sharpness, asperity
Poig'nant, *a.* sharp, irritating, satirical
Point, *s.* a sharp end; indivisible part of time
  or space; punctilio; degree; aim; in-
  stance; a cape; a stop; a single position
Point, *v.* to sharpen, direct, note, level

Point'ed, part. a. sharp, epigrammatical
Point'edly, ad. in a pointed manner
Point'el, s. any thing on a point
Point'er, s. any thing that points; a dog
Point'less, a. blunt, not sharp, obtuse
Poise, s. a weight, balance, equipoise
Poise, v. a. to balance, to weigh mentally
Poi'son, s. what destroys life, venom
Poi'son, v. a. to infect with poison, corrupt
Poi'sonous, a. venomous, destructive
Poi'trel, s. a graving tool, a breast-plate
Poke, s. a small bag or pocket
Poke, v. a. to feel in the dark, search out
Po'ker, s. an iron bar used to stir the fire
Po'lar, a. relating to the poles
Polar'ity, s. tendency to the pole
Pole, s. either extremity of the axis of the
    earth; a staff; a measure of five yards and
    a half; a piece of timber erected
Pole'axe, s. an axe fixed to a long pole
Pole'cat, s. a stinking animal, the fitchew
Pole'davy, s. a sort of coarse canvas
Polem'ic, s. a disputant, a controvertist
Polem'ic, a. controversial, disputative
Pole'star, s. a star near the pole; any guide
Poli'ce, s. the regulation of a city, &c.
Pol'icy, s. art of government, prudence
Pol'ish, s. artificial gloss, elegance
Pol'ish, v. to smooth, brighten; to civilize
Pol'isher, s. what refines or polishes
Poli'te, a. elegant of manners, glossy
Poli'teness, s. gentility, good breeding
Pol'itic, Polit'ical, a. relating to politics,
    prudent, cunning, artful, skilful
Polit'ically, ad. with policy, artfully
Politic'ian, s. one skilled in politics
Pol'itics, s. the science of government
Pol'iture, s. the gloss given by polishing
Pol'ity, s. form of government of any city or
    commonwealth, civil constitution
Poll, s. the head, list of those that vote
Poll, v. a. to lop the tops of trees; to mow;
    take a list of voters; to shear, clip short
Pol'lard, s. a tree lopped, a fine sort of bran
Pol'len, s. the prolific powder of flowers
Pol'lenger, s. brushwood
Pollu'te, v. a. to defile, to taint, to corrupt
Pollu'tion, s. act of defiling, defilement
Poltroon', s. a coward, dastard, scoundrel
Polyacou'stic, a. multiplying sound
Polyan'thus, s. the name of a flower
Polycar'pous, a. bearing much fruit
Polye'drous, a. having many sides
Polyg'amy, s. a plurality of wives
Pol'yglot, a. that is in many languages
Pol'ygon, s. a figure of many angles
Polyg'onal, a. having many angles
Pol'ygram, s. a figure of many lines
Polyg'raphy, s. art of writing in ciphers
Polyph'onism, s. a multiplicity of sounds
Pol'ypus, s. a sea animal with many feet; a
    disease or swelling in the nostrils
Polysyl'lable, s. a word of many syllables
Pol'ytheism, s. a belief of a plurality of gods
Poma'ceous, a. consisting of apples
Poma'de, s. a fragrant ointment
Poma'tum, s. an ointment made of hog's lard,
    sheep-suet, &c.
Poman'der, s. a perfumed ball or powder
Pome'granate, s. a tree and its fruit
Pom'eroy, s. a large kind of apple

Pomif'erous, a. bearing apples
Pom'mel, s. a knob on a sword or saddle
Pom'mel, v. a. to beat, to bruise, to punch
Pomp, s. splendour, pride, ostentation
Pom'pion, Pump'kin, s. a kind of melon
Pompos'ity, s. ostentatiousness
Pom'pous, a. stately, magnificent, grand
Pom'pously, ad. magnificently, splendidly
Pom'pousness, s. magnificence, splendour
Pond, s. a small pool or lake of water
Pon'der, v. to weigh mentally, to muse
Pon'derable, a. capable to be weighed
Pon'deral, a. estimated by weight
Ponderos'ity, s. weight, gravity, heaviness
Pon'derous, a. heavy, momentous, forcible
Po'nent, a. western
Pon'iard, s. a small pointed dagger
Pon'tage, s. bridge duties for repairs
Pon'tiff, s. a high-priest, the Pope
Pontif'ical, a. belonging to a high-priest
Pontif'ical, s. a book of ecclesiastical rites
Pontif'icate, s. papacy, the popedom
Pon'tifice, s. bridge work, edifice of a bridge
Ponto'n, s. a floating bridge of boats
Po'ny, s. a small horse
Pool, s. a standing water; a term at cards
Poop, s. the hindmost part of a ship
Poor, a. not rich; trifling; mean; dejected
Poor'ly, ad. without spirit, indifferently
Pop, s. a small, smart, quick sound
Pop, v. to move or enter quickly or silly
Pope, s. the bishop of Rome; a fish
Pope'dom, s. jurisdiction of the Pope
Po'pery, Pa'pistry, s. the Popish religion
Pop'eseye, s. a part of the thigh
Pop'gun, Pot'gun, s. a child's gun
Popina'tion, s. a frequenting of taverns
Pop'injay, s. a parrot, a woodpecker; a fop
Po'pish, a. taught by the Pope, Romish
Pop'lar, s. a tree
Pop'py, s. the name of a plant
Pop'ulace, s. the multitude of the vulgar
Pop'ular, a. pleasing to the people, vulgar
Popular'ity, s. the favour of the people
Pop'ulate, v. n. to breed people
Popula'tion, s. the number of people
Pop'ulous, a. full of people, well inhabited
Por'celain, s. China ware; an herb
Porch, s. a portico, an entrance with a roof
Por'cupine, s. a sort of large hedgehog
Pore, v. n. to examine with great attention,
    to look close to   [spiration
Pore, s. spiracle of the skin; passage for per-
Pore'blind, a. near-sighted, short-sighted
Po'rism, s. a general theorem, a general rule
Pork, s. swine's flesh unsalted
Pork'er, Pork'ling, s. a young pig
Poros'ity, s. quality of having pores
Po'rous, Po'ry, a. full of pores
Por'poise, Por'pus, s. the sea hog
Porra'ceous, a. greenish, like a leek
Por'ret, s. a scallion, a leek
Por'ridge, Pot'tage, s. a kind of broth or milk
Por'ringer, s. a vessel for spoon meat
Port, s. a harbour, aperture; air, mien
Port'able, a. that which may be carried
Port'age, s. price of carriage, a porthole
Port'al, s. a gate, the arch of a gate
Port'ance, s. air, mien, port, demeanour
Portcul'lis, s. a sort of drawbridge
Porte, s. the court of the Turkish emperor

Por'ten ed, a. borne in a regular order
Porten'd, v. a. to forebode, to foreshow
Porten'sion, s. the act of foretokening
Porten't, s. an omen, or foretokening of ill
 a ten tous, a. prodigious, ominous
Por'ter, s. one who has charge of a gate; a
 carrier; a kind of strong beer
Por'terage, s. the hire of a porter
Portfo'lio,s.a case to keep papers or prints in
Port'glaive, Port'glave, s. a sword-bearer
Port'hole, s. a hole to point cannon through
Por'tico, s. a covered walk, a piazza
Por'tion, s. part, allotment; wife's fortune
Port'liness, s. grandeur of mien
Port'ly, a. majestical, grand of demeanour
Portman'teau, s. a bag to carry clothes in
Por'trait, s. a picture drawn from the life
Portra'y, v. a. to paint; to adorn
Por'tress, s. the female guardian of a gate
Pose, v. a. to puzzle, oppose, interrogate
Pos'ited, a. placed, ranged, put
Posit'ion, s. a situation, an assertion
Posit'ional, a. respecting position
Pos'itive, a. absolute, assured, certain
Pos'itively, ad. certainly, peremptorily
Pos'se, s. an armed power, a large body
Possess', v.a. to have as an owner, to obtain
Posses'sion, s. having in one's power
Pos'sessive, Pos'sessory,a. having possession
Posses'sor, s. an owner, master, proprietor
Pos'set, s. milk curdled with wine, &c.
Possibil'ity, s. the power of being or doing
Pos'sible, a. having the power to be or do
Pos'sibly, ad. by any power; perhaps
Post, s. a messenger, piece of timber, office
Post, v. to travel with speed, to place, to fix
Po'stage, s. money paid for a letter
Postchai'se, s. a light body-carriage
Postda'te, v.a. to date later than the real time
Postdilu'vian, a. posterior to the flood
Po'ster, s. a courier, one who travels hastily
Poste'rior, a. happening after, backward
Posterior'ity, s. the state of being after
Poste'riors, s. the hinder part; the breech
Poster'ity, s. succeeding generations
Pos'tern, s. a small gate, a little door
Postexis'tence, s. a future existence
Postha'ste, s. haste like that of a courier
Po'sthouse, s. a house to take in letters
Pos'thumous,a.done, had, or published after
 one's decease
Postil'lion,s. one who guides a chaise,or the
 first pair of a set of six horses in a coach
Postmerid'ian, a. being in the afternoon
Po'st-office, s. a post-house, place for letters
Postpo'ne, v. a. to put off, delay, undervalue
Po'script, s. a writing added to a letter
Pos'tulate, s. a position assumed or supposed
 without proof—v. a. to assume
Postula'tion, s. a supposing without proof
Postula'tum, s. an assumed position
Pos'ture, s. position, place, disposition
Pos'ture-mas'ter, s. one who teaches or
 practises artificial contortions of the body
Po'sy, s. a motto on a ring; a nosegay
Pot, s. a vessel to hold liquids or meats
Pot, v. a. to preserve seasoned in pots
Po'table, Po'tulent, a. fit to drink
Pot'ash, s. ashes from burnt vegetables
Pota'tion, s. drinking-bout, a draught
Pota'to, s. an esculent root

Pot'bellied, a. having a swoln paunch
Potch, v. a. to thrust, to push, to poach
Pot'companion, s. a fellow-drinker
Po'tency, s. power, influence, efficacy
Po'tent, a. powerful, efficacious, mighty
Po'tentate, s. a monarch, sovereign, prince
Poten'tial, a. existing in possibility, not in
 act; powerful, efficacious
Po'tently, ad. powerfully, forcibly
Poth'er, s. a bustle, stir, tumult
Pot'hook, s. a hook to hang pots, &c. on
Po'tion, s. a draught, commonly in physic
Pot'sherd, s. a fragment of a broken pot
Pot'ter, s. a maker of earthen vessels
Pot'tery, s. the work, &c. of a potter
Pot'tle, s. a measure of four pints
Potval'iant, a. heated to courage by liquor
Pouch, s. a small bag, pocket, purse
Pov'erty, s. indigence, meanness, defect
Poult, s. a young chicken
Poul'terer, s. one who sells fowls
Poul'tice, s. a mollifying application
Poul'try, all kinds of domestic fowls
Pounce, s. the talon of a bird of prey; the
 powder of gum-sandarach for paper
Pound, s. a weight; 20 shillings; a pinfold
Pound, v. a. to beat with a pestle
Pound'age,s. an allowance of so much in the
 pound; payment rated by weight; fee
 paid to the keeper of a pound
Pound'er, s. a cannon of a certain bore
Pour, v. to empty liquids out of any vessel,
 to flow, to rush tumultuously
Pout, s. a kind of fish; a kind of bird
Pout, v. n. to look sullen, to frown
Pow'der, s.dust; dust of starch; gunpowder
Pow'der, v. a. to reduce to dust, to salt
Pow'der-box, s. a box for hair-powder
Pow'der-horn, s. a horn for gunpowder
Pow'dering-tub, s. a vessel for salting meat
Pow'der-mill, s. a mill in which gunpowder
Pow'dery, a. dusty, friable, soft [is made
Pow'er, s. command, authority, ability,
 strength, force, influence, military force
Pow'erful, a. forcible, mighty, efficacious
Pow'erfully, ad. potently, efficaciously
Pow'erfulness, s. power, efficacy, force
Pow'erless, a. weak, impotent, helpless
Poy, s. a rope-dancer's or waterman's pole
Prac'ticable, a. performable, assailable
Prac'tical, a. relating to action, &c.
Prac'tically, ad. by practice, in real fact
Prac'tice, s. habit, use, dexterity, method
Practise, v. a. to do, to exercise, to transact
Practit'ioner, s. one engaged in any art
Prae'cipe, s. a writ, a command
Praecog'nita, s. things previously known
Pragmat'ical, a. meddling, impertinent
Praise, s. renown, laud, commendation
Praise, v.a. to commend, applaud, celebrate
Praise'worthy, a. deserving praise
Prame, s. a flat-bottomed boat
Prance, v. n. to spring or bound
Prank, s. a frolic, trick, wicked act
Prate, v. n. to talk carelessly, to chatter
Pra'tingly, ad. with loquacity
Pra'tique,s. a licence for a ship to traffic, up-
 on certificate that the place from whence
 she sailed is not annoyed with any infec-
 tious disease
Prattle, v. n. to talk lightly, to chatte

s. a trifling talker, a chatterer
Prav'ity, *s.* corruption, badness, malignity
Prawn, *s.* a shell-fish like a shrimp
Pray, *v.* to entreat, to supplicate, to implore
Pray'er, *s.* a petition to heaven ; entreaty
Pray'erbook, *s.* a book of prayer
Preach,*v.n.* to pronounce a public discourse on religious subjects—*s.* a discourse
Prea'cher, *s.* one who preaches, a minister
Pre amble, *s.* an introduction, a preface
Preb'end, *s.* a stipend in cathedrals
Preben'dary, *s.* a stipendiary of a cathedral
Preca'rious, *a.* dependant, uncertain
Preca'riously, *ad.* uncertainly, by dependance ; dependantly on the will of others
Precau'tion, *s.* preservative caution
Preceda'neous, *a.* previous, antecedent
Prece'de, *v. a.* to go before in rank or time
Prece'dence, *s.* priority, the foremost place
Prece'dent, *a.* going before ; former
Prec'edent, *s.* example, thing done before
Prece'dently, *ad.* beforehand
Precen'tor, *s.* he that leads the choir
Pre'cept, *s.* a command, injunction, mandate
Precep'tial, *a.* consisting of precepts
Precep'tive, *a.* containing or giving precepts
Precep'tor, *s.* a teacher, a tutor
Preces'sion, *s.* the act of going before
Pre'cinct, *s.* an outward limit, a boundary
Prec'ious, *a.* valuable, costly, of great price
Prec'iously, *ad.* valuably
Prec'ipice, *s.* a perpendicular declivity
Precip'itance, *s.* rash haste, headlong hurry
Precip'itant, *a.* falling headlong, hasty
Precip'itantness, *s.* hastiness, rashness
Precip'itate,*s.*corrosive mercurial medicine
Precip'itate, *v.* to throw headlong ; to hurry
Precip'itate, *a.* headlong, hasty, violent
Precip'itately, *ad.* headlong ; in blind fury
Precipita'tion, *s.* hurry; blind, rash haste ; a
Precip'itous, *a.* headlong, rash, heady [fall
Preci'se, *a.* formal, affected, finical, exact
Preci'sely, *ad.* exactly, nicely, accurately
Precis'ion, Preci'seness, *s.* nicety
Preci'sive, *a.* exactly limiting
Preclu'de, *v.a.* to shut out by some anticipa-
Preco'cious, *a.* ripe before the time [tion
Precoc'ity, *s.* ripeness before the time
Precogita'tion, *s.* previous consideration
Precognit'ion, *s.* antecedent examination
Preconce'it, *s.* opinion antecedently formed
Preconce'ive,*v.a.*to form an opinion beforehand ; to imagine beforehand
Preconcep'tion,*s.*opinion previously formed
Preconcer't, *v.* to concert or settle before-
Precon'tract, *s.* a previous contract [hand
Precur'se, *s.* a forerunning ; going before
Precur'sor, *s.* a forerunner, a harbinger
Preda'ceous, *a.* living by prey or plunder
Pre'dal, *a.* robbing; practising robbery
Preda'tion, *s.* the act of plundering
Preda'tious, *a.* plundering, rapacious
Pred'atory, *a.* practising rapine ; rapacious
Predeces'sor, *s.* one going before
Predestina'rian, Predestina'tor, *s.* one who maintains the doctrine of predestination
Predes'tinate, *v.* to decree beforehand
Predestina'tion, *s.* fatal decree ; pre-ordina-
tion ; pre-established necessity
Predes'tine, *v. a.* to decree beforehand
Predetermina'tion,*s.*previous determination

Pre'dial, *a.* consisting of farms
Pred'icable, *s.* a logical term of affirmation
Pred'icable, *a.* such as may be affirmed
Predic'ament, *s.* a class, arrangement, kind
Pred'icant, *s.* one that affirms any thing
Pred'icate, *s.* what is affirmed of a subject
Pred'icate, *v. a.* to affirm or declare
Predica'tion, *s.* affirmation, declaration
Predic't, *v. a.* to foretel ; to foreshow
Predic'tion, *s.* a prophecy ; a foretelling
Predic'tor, *s.*one who foretells or prophesies
Predilec'tion, *s.* prepossession in favour of any particular person or thing
Predispo'se, *v. a.* to dispose beforehand
Predisposit'ion, *s.* previous adaptation
Predom'inance, *s.* prevalence, superiority
Predom'inant, *a.* prevalent, ascendant
Predom'inate, *v. n.* to prevail in or over
Pre-elec't, *v.a.*to choose by previous decision
Pre-em'inence, *s.* superiority, precedence
Pre-em'inent, *a.* excellent above others
Pre-emp'tion,*s.*right of buying before others
Preen, *v.* to dress, clean, trim, compose
Pre-enga'ge, *v. a.* to engage beforehand
Pre-enga'gement, *s.* precedent obligation
Pre-estab'lish, *v. a.* to settle beforehand .
Pre-exis't, *v. n.* to exist beforehand
Pre-exis'tence, *s.* existence beforehand
Pre-exis'tent, *a.* preceding in existence
Pref'ace, *s.* an introduction to a book, &c.
Pref'ace, *v.* to say something introductory
Pref'atory, *a.* introductory
Pre'fect, *s.* a governor, a commander
Pref'ecture, *s.* the office of government
Prefer', *v.a.* to regard more ; advance, raise
Pref'erable,*a.*eligible before something else
Pref'erence, *s.* estimation before another
Prefer'ment, *s.* advancement, preference
Prefigura'tion, *s.* antecedent representation
Prefig'ure, *v. a.* to exhibit beforehand
Prefi'ne, *v. a.* to limit beforehand
Prefix', *v. a.* to appoint beforehand ; settle
Pre'fix, *s.* a particle placed before a word
Prefor'm, *v. a.* to form beforehand
Preg'nancy, *s.* the state of being with young; fertility ; power ; acuteness
Preg'nant, *a.* breeding, teeming, fruitful
Pregusta'tion, *s.* the act of tasting first
Preju'dge, *v.a.*to judge beforehand; generally, to condemn beforehand
Preju'dicate, *v.* formed by prejudice
Prejudica'tion, *s.* a judging beforehand
Prej'udice, *s.* prepossession, mischief, hurt
Prej'udice, *v.* to fill with prejudice ; hurt
Prejudic'ial, *a.* hurtful, injurious; opposite
Prel'acy, *s.* the dignity or office of a prelate
Prel'ate, *s.* a bishop, a high ecclesiastic
Prelat'ical, *a.* relating to prelates or prelacy
Prela'tion, *s.* a preference ; a setting above
Prelec'tion, *s.* reading ; lecture
Prelim'inary, *a.* previous, introductory, antecedently preparatory
Prel'ude, *s.* a flourish of music before a full concert ; something introductory
Prel'ude, *v. n.* to serve as an introduction
Prelu'sive, *a.* introductory, proemial
Prematu're, *a.* ripe too soon ; too soon said or done ; too early ; too hasty
Prematu'rely, *ad.* too early ; too soon
Premed'itate, *v. a.* to think befo ehand
Premedita'tion, *s.* a meditating beforehand

O

Premer'it, v. a. to deserve before another
Pre'mier, a. first, chief, principal
Pre'mier, s. a chief person ; a first minister
Premi'se, v. a. to explain previously
Prem'ises, s. lands, &c. before mentioned in a lease, &c. ; in logic, the two first propositions of a syllogism ; in law, houses, &c.
Prem'iss, s. an antecedent proposition
Pre'mium, s. something given to invite a loan or a bargain
Premon'ish, v. a. to warn beforehand
Premonit'ion, s. previous intelligence
Premon'itory, a. previously advising
Premon'strate, v. a. to show beforehand
Premuni're, s. a writ, a penalty, a distress
Prenom'inate, v. a. to forename
Preno'tion, s. prescience, foreknowledge
Prenuncia'tion, s. act of telling before [sion
Preoccupa'tion, s. anticipation, prepossession
Preoc'cupancy, s. taking possession before
Preoc'cupate, v. a. to anticipate, prepossess
Preoc'cupy, v. a. to seize before another
Preopin'ion, s. prepossession, prejudice
Preordai'n, v. a. to ordain beforehand
Preor'dinance, s. antecedent decree
Prepara'tion, s. act of preparing any thing to any purpose; previous measures; anything made by process ; accomplishment
Prepar'ative, a. serving to prepare
P epar'atory, a. introductory, antecedent
Prepa're, v. a. to make ready, qualify, form
Prepen'se, a. forethought, preconceived
Prepon'der, Prepon'derate, v. a. to outweigh; to exceed in influence
Prepon'derance, s. superiority of weight
Preposit'ion, s. in grammar, a particle set before a noun, and governing a case
Prepossess', v. a. to prejudice, to bias
Preposses'sion, s. first possession; prejudice; preconceived opinion
Prepos'terous, a. wrong, absurd, perverted
Prepos'terously, ad. absurdly, strangely, &c.
Prepo'tency, s. predominance ; superiority
Pre'puce, s. that which covers the glands
Prerequi're, v. a. to demand beforehand
Prereq'uisite, a. that is previously necessary
Prerog'ative, s. exclusive privilege or right
Prerog'atived, a. having an exclusive privilege or right ; having prerogative
Presa'ge, Presa'gement, s. a foretoken
Presa'ge, v. a. to forebode, to foreshow
Pres'byter, s. a priest, a presbyterian
Presbyte'rial, a. pertaining to a presbyter
Presbyte'rian, s. a follower of Calvin
Pres'bytery, s. eldership ; priesthood ; also church government by lay elders
Pre'science, s. knowledge of futurity
Pre'scient, a. foreknowing, prophetic
Prescin'd, v. a. to cut off, to abstract
Prescin'dent, a. abstracting ; cutting off
Prescri'be, v. to order ; to direct medically
Pre'script, s. a direction, precept, order
Prescrip'tion, s. a rule produced and authorised by long custom till it has the force of law ; a medical receipt
Pres'ence, s. state of being present ; mien ; demeanour, quickness at expedients
Pres'ent, a. not absent ; not past ; ready
Pres'ent, s. a gift ; a donation ; a mandate
Present', v. a. to exhibit, to give, to prefer, to offer, to favour with gifts

Present'able, a. what may be presented
Presenta'neous, a. ready, immediate, quick
Presenta'tion, s. the gift of a benefice
Presentee', s. one presented to a benefice
Presen'tial, a. supposing actual presence
Presential'ity, s. state of being present
Presen'timent, s. previous idea ; notion previously formed
Pres'ently, ad. at present, soon after
Present'ment, s. the act of presenting
Preserva'tion, s. the act of preserving
Preser'vative, s. that has power to preserve
Preser've, v. to save, keep, season fruits, &c.
Preser've, s. fruit preserved in sugar
Preser'ver, s. one who preserves or keeps
Presi'de, v. n. to be set over, direct, manage
Pres'idency, s. superintendence
Pres'ident, s. one at the head of a society
Presid'ial, a. of or belonging to a garrison
Press, v. to squeeze ; distress ; urge, force
Press, s. an instrument for pressing; a crowd, case for clothes ; instrument for printing ; act of forcing men into service
Press'gang, s. a gang of sailors that go about to press men into naval service
Press'ing, part. a. very urgent; squeezing
Press'ingly, ad. with force ; closely
Press'man, s. a printer who works at press ; one who forces away
Press'money, s. money for pressed soldiers
Press'ure, s. force; affliction ; an impression
Prest, a. ready—part. pressed—s. a loan
Presu'mable, a. that may be presumed
Presu'mably, ad. without examination
Presu'me, v. a. to suppose, affirm ; venture
Presu'ming, part. a. supposing ; confident
Presump'tion, s. conjecture ; a strong probability ; supposition previously formed ; arrogance ; pride
Presump'tive, a. presumed; supposed, as the *presumptive heir* ; confident, arrogant
Presump'tuous, a. haughty ; irreverent
Presump'tuously, ad. haughtily, proudly
Presump'tuousness, s. arrogance, pride, irreverence
Presuppo'sal, s. supposal previously formed
Presuppo'se, v. a. to suppose beforehand
Presurmi'se, s. surmise previously formed
Preten'ce, s. a pretext ; an assumption
Preten'd, v. to allege falsely ; to shew hypocritically ; to claim ; to presume
Preten'der, s. one who claims or arrogates to himself what does not belong to him
Preten'sion, s. a claim ; a false appearance
Preterimper'fect, a. in grammar, denotes the tense not perfectly past
Pret'erite, a. belonging to the past tense
Preterlap'sed, a. past and gone
Pretermis'sion, s. the act of omitting
Pretermit', v. a. to pass by, omit, neglect
Preternat'ural, a. not natural ; irregular
Preternat'urally, ad. miraculously
Preterper'fect, a. absolutely past
Preterplu'perfect, a. time relatively past, or past before some other past time
Pretext', s. a pretence, false allegation
Pre'tor, s. a Roman judge ; a mayor
Preto'rian, a. judicial ; exercised by a pretor
Pret'tily, ad. neatly, elegantly, agreeably
Pret'tiness, s. beauty without dignity
Pret'ty, a. neat, elegant, handsome

Pret ty, *ad.* in some degree, nearly

Prevail'l, *v. a.* to be in force, overcome, persuade, to have influence, to have power

Prevail'ing, *a.* having most influence

Prev'alent, *a.* powerful, predominant

Prev'alently, *ad.* powerfully, forcibly

Prevar'icate, *v. n.* to cavil; to quibble

Prevarica'tion, *s.* double dealing; shuffle

Prevarica'tor, *s.* a caviller; a shuffler

Preve'nient, *a.* preceding; preventive

Preven't, *v.* to hinder, to obstruct; to guide

Preven'tion, *s.* act of going before; anticipation, hinderance, prejudice

Preven'tive, *a.* preservative, hindering

Pre'vious, *a.* antecedent; going before

Pre'viously, *ad.* beforehand; antecedently

Pre'viousness, *s.* antecedence

Prey, *s.* something to be devoured; spoil

Prey, *v.* to feed by violence; plunder; corrode

Pri'apism, *s.* a preternatural tension

Price, *s.* value; estimation; rate; reward

Prick, *v.* to pierce, to spur—*s.* a puncture

Pric'ket, *s.* a buck in his 2nd year; a basket

Pric'kle, *s.* a small sharp point; a thorn

Pric'kly, *a.* full of sharp points

Pride, *s.* inordinate self-esteem; haughtiness; insolent exultation; ostentation

Pride, *v. a.* to rate himself high; make proud

Priest, *s.* one who officiates at the altar

Priest'craft, *s.* religious fraud

Priest'ess, *s.* a female priest

Priest'hood, *s.* the office or order of priests

Priest'liness, *s.* the manner, &c. of a priest

Priest'ly, *a.* belonging to a priest; sacerdotal

Priest'ridden, *a.* managed by priests

Prig, *s.* a pert, conceited little fellow

Prim, *a.* formal, precise, affectedly nice

Pri'macy, *s.* dignity or office of a primate

Pri'mage, *s.* a duty paid to a master of a ship for the use of his stores, &c.

Pri'marily, *ad.* in the first intention

Pri'mary, *a.* first in order, chief, principal

Pri'mate, *s.* the chief ecclesiastic

Prime, Pri'mal, *a.* early; first rate; first

Prime, *s.* the dawn, the morning; best part; spring of life; the flower or choice; height of health, beauty, or perfection

Prime, *v. a.* to put powder into the touch-pan or hole of a gun, &c.; to lay the first colours on a painting

Prime'ly, *ad.* originally, excellently, well

Prime'ness, *s.* the state of being first; excellence

Pri'mateship, *s.* dignity, &c. of a primate

Prim'er, *s.* a small book for children

Prime'ro, *s.* an ancient game at cards

Pri'mest, *a.* best, most excellent

Prime'val, *a.* original; such as was at first

Prim'itive, *a.* ancient, original, formal

Prim'itively, *ad.* originally, not derivatively

Prim'ness, *s.* formality, demureness

Primoge'nial, *a.* first-born; original

Primogen'iture, *s.* state of being first born

Primor'dial, *a.* existing from the beginning

Primor'dial, *s.* origin, first principle

Prim'rose, *s.* the name of a flower

Prince, *s.* a sovereign; a king's son; chief

Prin'cedom, *s.* the rank, estate, or power of the prince; sovereignty

Prin'celike, *a.* becoming a prince [prince

Prin'celiness, *s.* the manner or dignity of a

Prin'cely, *a.* royal, august, generous

Prin'cess, *s.* a sovereign lady; the daughter of a king; a prince's consort

Prin'cipal, *a.* chief, capital, essential

Prin'cipal, *s.* a head, a chief, one primarily engaged; a sum placed out at interest

Principal'ity, *s.* a prince's domain

Prin'cipally, *ad.* chiefly; above the rest

Principia'tion, *s.* analysis into constituent or elemental parts

Prin'ciple, *s.* primordial substance; constituent part; original cause, motive; opinion

Print, *s.* mark made by impression; form, size, &c. of the types used in printing; formal method—*v.* to mark by impression

Print'er, *s.* one who prints books, &c.

Print'less, *a.* that leaves no impression

Pri'or, *a.* former, antecedent, anterior

Pri'or, *s.* the head of a priory of monks

Pri'oress, *s.* superior of a convent of nuns

Prior'ity, *s.* precedence in time or place

Pri'orship, *s.* office or dignity of a prior

Pri'ory, *s.* a convent inferior to an abbey

Pri'sage, *s.* a duty of a 10th upon lawful prizes

Prism, *s.* an optical glass used in experiments on light and colours

Prismat'ic, *a.* formed like a prism

Prismat'ically, *ad.* in the form of a prism

Pris'moid, *s.* a solid body like a prism

Pris'on, *s.* a gaol, place of confinement

Pris'oned, *part.* shut up in prison

Pris'oner, *s.* a captive, one under arrest

Pris'tine, *a.* first, ancient, original

Pri'thee, *abbreviation* for I pray thee

Pri'vacy, *s.* secrecy, retreat, taciturnity

Priva'do, *s.* a secret or intimate friend

Pri'vate, *a.* secret, alone, particular, not relating to the public, not open

Privatee'r, *s.* a private ship of war

Pri'vately, *ad.* secretly, not openly

Pri'vateness, *s.* secrecy, privacy, obscurity

Priva'tion, *s.* absence or loss of any thing; obstruction; degradation from office

Priv'ative, *a.* causing privation, negative

Priv'ilege, *s.* immunity, public right

Priv'ilege, *v. a.* to grant a privilege, exempt

Priv'ily, *ad.* privately, secretly

Priv'ity, *s.* private concurrence

Priv'y, *a.* private, secret, acquainted with

Prize, *s.* a reward gained, booty

Prize, *v. a.* to rate, to esteem, value highly

Probabil'ity, *s.* likelihood, appearance of truth, evidence of argument

Prob'able, *a.* likely, or like to be

Prob'ably, *ad.* likely, in all likelihood

Pro'bat, Pro'bate, *s.* the proof of wills, &c. in the spiritual court

Proba'tion, *s.* a proof, trial, noviciate

Proba'tioner, *s.* one upon trial; a novice

Probe, *s.* a surgeon's instrument

Probe, *v. a.* to search, to try with a probe

Prob'ity, *s.* uprightness, honesty, veracity

Prob'lem, *s.* a question proposed for solution

Problemat'ical, *a.* uncertain, disputable

Probos'cis, *s.* the trunk of an elephant, &c.

Procac'ity, *s.* sauciness, petulance

Proce'dic, *a.* going before, antecedent

Proceed, *v.* proceeding

Proceed, *s.* issue from; to

Procedure; to advance

Process, *s.* a legal process

Procerity, *s.* tallness, height of stature
Process, *s.* course of law; order of things
Procession, *s.* a train marching in solemnity
Prochronism, *s.* an error in chronology
Proclaim, *v.* to publish solemnly, to tell openly, to outlaw by public denunciation
Proclamation, *s.* a public notice given by authority, a declaration of the king's will
Proclivity, *s.* propensity, readiness
Proclivous, *a.* inclined downward
Proconsul, *s.* a Roman governor
Procrastinate, *v.* to defer, delay, put off
Procrastination, *s.* delay, dilatoriness
Procreant, *a.* productive, pregnant
Procreate, *v. a.* to generate, to produce
Procreation, *s.* generation, production
Procreative, *a.* generative, productive
Procreator, *s.* a generator, begetter
Proctor, *s.* a manager of another man's affairs; an attorney in the spiritual court; the magistrate of the university
Proctorship, *s.* the office of a proctor
Procumbent, *a.* lying down, prone
Procurable, *a.* obtainable, acquirable
Procurator, *s.* a manager, agent, factor
Procure, *v.* to obtain, to manage, to pimp
Procurer, *s.* an obtainer, pimp, pander
Procuress, *s.* a bawd, a seducing woman
Prodigal, *a.* profuse, wasteful, lavish
Prodigal, *s.* a spendthrift, a waster
Prodigality, *s.* extravagance, profusion
Prodigally, *ad.* profusely, wastefully
Prodigious, *a.* amazing, monstrous, vast
Prodigiously, *ad.* amazingly, enormously
Prodigy, *s.* a preternatural thing; a monster; any thing astonishing
Prodition, *s.* treason, treachery
Produce, *v.* to bring forth, yield, cause
Produce, *s.* amount, profit, product
Producent, *s.* one who exhibits or offers
Product, *s.* the thing produced, work, effect
Production, *s.* whatever is produced
Productive, *a.* fertile, generative, efficient
Proem, *s.* a preface, an introduction
Profanation, *s.* the act of profaning, polluting, or violating any thing sacred
Profane, *a.* not sacred; irreverent; polluted
Profane, *v. a.* to violate, to pollute, to put to wrong use, to misapply
Profanely, *ad.* irreverently, wickedly
Profaneness, *s.* irreverence, impiety
Profaner, *s.* one who profanes or pollutes
Profess, *v.* to declare openly and plainly
Professedly, *ad.* openly, avowedly
Profession, *s.* a vocation, known employment, calling; declaration, opinion
Professional, *a.* relating to a particular profession or calling
Professor, *s.* a public teacher of some art
Professorship, *s.* the office of a public teacher
Proffer, *v. a.* to propose, offer, attempt
Proffer, *s.* an offer made, essay, attempt
Proficience, Proficiency, *s.* advancement in any thing, improvement gained
Proficient, *s.* one who has made good advancement in any study or business
Profile, *s.* the side face, a half face
Profit, *s.* gain, advantage, improvement
Profit, *v.* to gain advantage, improve
Profitable, *a.* lucrative, beneficial
Profitableness, *s.* gainfulness, usefulness

Profitably, *ad.* advantageously, gainfully
Profitless, *a.* void of gain or advantage
Profligacy, *s.* profligate behaviour
Profligate, *a.* wicked, abandoned, debauched, lost to virtue and decency, shameless
Profligate, *s.* an abandoned wretch
Profligately, *ad.* shamelessly, wickedly
Profligateness, *s.* want of virtue and decency
Profluence, *s.* progress, course
Profluent, *a.* flowing forward, or plentifully
Profound, *a.* deep, learned, humble, lowly
Profoundly, *ad.* deeply; with deep insight
Profundity, *s.* depth of place or knowledge
Profuse, *a.* lavish, wasteful, overabounding
Profusely, *ad.* lavishly, with exuberance
Profuseness, *s.* lavishness, prodigality
Profusion, *s.* prodigality, exuberance, plenty
Prog, *s.* victuals, provisions of any kind
Prog, *v. n.* to shift meanly for provisions
Progenitor, *s.* an ancestor in a direct line
Progeny, *s.* offspring, issue, generation
Prognostic, *s.* a prediction, a token forerunning—a. foretokening
Prognosticate, *v. a.* to foretel, to foreshow
Prognostication, *s.* the act of foretelling
Prognosticator, *s.* one who foretels
Progress, *s.* a course; improvement
Progression, *s.* regular advance, course
Progressional, *a.* advancing, increasing
Progressive, *a.* going forward, advancing
Progressively, *ad.* by a regular course
Prohibit, *v. a.* to forbid, debar, hinder
Prohibition, *s.* an interdiction, &c.
Prohibitory, *a.* implying prohibition
Project, *s.* a scheme, contrivance, design
Project, *v.* to scheme, contrive; jut out
Projectile, *s.* a body put in motion
Projection, *s.* act of shooting forwards; delineation; scheme, plan
Projector, *s.* one who forms schemes, &c.
Projecture, *s.* a jutting out
Prolapse, *v. a.* to extend out too much
Prolate, *v. a.* to pronounce, to utter
Prolate, *a.* oblate, flat
Prolation, *s.* pronunciation, delay
Prolepsis, *s.* an anticipation of objections
Proleptical, *a.* previous, antecedent
Proletarian, *a.* wretched, vile, vulgar
Prolific, Prolifical, *a.* fruitful, generative
Prolifically, *ad.* fruitfully, pregnantly
Prolix, *a.* tedious, not concise, dilatory
Prolixity, *s.* tediousness, want of brevity
Prolocutor, *s.* the speaker of a convocation
Prolocutorship, *s.* the office of prolocutor
Prologue, *s.* a speech before a stage play
Prolong, *v. a.* to lengthen out, to put off
Prolongation, *s.* a delay to a longer time
Prolusion, *s.* a prelude, a diverting performance
Promenade, *s.* a walk, walking
Prominence, *s.* a jutting out, protuberance
Prominent, *a.* jutting or standing out
Promiscuous, *a.* mingled, confused
Promiscuously, *ad.* with confused mixture
Promise, *v.* to give one's word, to assure
Promiser, *s.* one who promises
Promising, *part. a.* giving hopes
Promissory, *a.* containing a promise
Promontory, *s.* a headland, a cape
Promote, *v. a.* to forward, exalt, advance
Promoter, *s.* an advancer, encourager
Promotion, *s.* advancement, preferment

Promove, v. a. to forward, to promote
Prompt, a. quick, ready, propense, acute
Prompt, v. a. to assist, to incite, remind
Promp'ter, s. one who helps a public speaker
Promptly, ad. quickly, readily
Prom'ptitude, Promp'tness, s. readiness, quickness
Prom'ptuary, s. a magazine, a repository
Promul'gate. Promul'ge, v. a. to publish, to teach openly
Promulga'tion, s. publication, exhibition
Promulga'tor, s. a publisher, open teacher
Prone, a. bending downward, inclined
Pro'neness s. an inclination; a descent
Prong, s. a fork, a pitch-fork
Pronom'inal, a. belonging to a pronoun
Pro'noun, s. a word used for a noun
Pronoun'ce, v. to speak, to utter, to pass judgment, to utter sentence
Pronoun'cer, s. one who pronounces
Pronuncia'tion, s. the mode of utterance
Proof, s. trial, test, evidence; impenetrability; a rough sheet of print to be corrected
Proof, a. impenetrable, able to resist
Proof'less, a. wanting evidence, not proved
Prop, s. a support, that which holds up
Prop, v. a. to support, to sustain, to keep up
Prop'agate, v. to generate, increase, extend
Propaga'tion, s. a generation, production
Propaga'tor, s. spreader, promoter
Propel', v. a. to drive forward
Propen'd. v. n. to incline to any part or side
Propen'dency, s. inclination or tendency of desire
Propen'se, a. inclined, disposed, prone to
Propen'sity, s. inclination, tendency
Prop'er, a. peculiar, fit, exact; one's own
Prop'erly, ad. fitly; in a strict sense
Prop'erty, s. peculiar quality; possession
Proph'ecy, s. a prediction, declaration
Proph'esy, v. to predict, foretel, prognosticate
Proph'et, s. a foreteller of future events
Proph'etess, s. a female prophet
Prophet'ic, a. foretelling future events
Prophylac'tic, a. preventive, preservative
Propin'quity, s. proximity, kindred
Propi'tiate, v. a. to induce to favour, to gain
Propitia'tion, s. an atonement for a crime
Propi'tiatory, a. serving to propitiate
Propi'tious, a. favourable, kind, merciful
Propi'tiously, ad. favourably, kindly
Pro'plasm, s. a mould, a matrix
Propo'nent, s. one who makes a proposal
Propor'tion, s. an equal part, ratio, size
Propor'tion, v. a. to adjust parts, to fit
Propor'tionable, a. adjusted, such as is fit
Propor'tional, a. having due proportion
Propor'tional, s. a quantity in proportion
Propor'tionally, ad. in a stated degree
Propor'tionate, a. adjusted to something else that is according to a certain rate
Propo'sal, s. a proposition or design propounded to consideration or acceptance
Propo'se, v. a. to offer to the consideration
Propo'ser, s. one who offers to consideration
Proposi'tion, s. a thing proposed; a sentence in which any thing is affirmed or decreed
Proposi'tional, a. considered as a proposition
Propoun'd, v. a. to propose, offer, exhibit
Propri'etary, a. belonging to a certain owner
Propri'etary, s. an owner in his own right

Propri'etor, s. a possessor in his own right
Proprie'ty, s. exclusive right; justness, accuracy
Propu'gn, v. a. to defend, to vindicate
Propul'sion, s. the act of driving forward
Prore, s. the prow or fore part of a ship
Proroga'tion, s. a prolongation, continuance
Proro'gue, v. a. to protract, put off, delay
Prorup'tion, s. the act of bursting out
Prosa'ic, a. belonging to or like prose
Proscri'be, v. a. to doom to destruction
Proscrip'tion, s. doom to death or confiscation
Prose, s. the usual way of speaking or writing, in opposition to verse
Pros'ecute, v. a. to pursue, continue, sue
Prosecu'tion, s. a pursuit; a criminal suit
Pros'ecutor, s. one who pursues any purpose or sues another by law, in a criminal cause
Pros'elyte, s. a convert to a new opinion
Prosemina'tion, s. propagation by seed
Proso'dian, Pros'odist, s. one skilled in prosody or metre
Pros'ody, s. that part of grammar that teaches the sound and quantity of syllables, and the measure of verse
Prosopopœ'ia, s. a figure in rhetoric, by which things are made persons; personification
Pros'pect, s. a view, an object of view
Prospec'tive, a. viewing at a distance
Prospec'tus, s. a summary account of a new plan or publication
Pros'per, v. n. to be successful, to thrive
Prosper'ity, s. good success, good fortune
Pros'perous, a. successful, fortunate
Pros'perously, ad. fortunately, successfully
Prosterna'tion, s. dejection, depression
Pros'titute, v. a. to expose upon vile terms
Pros'titute, a. vicious for hire
Pros'titute, s. a public strumpet, a hireling
Prostitu'tion, s. the act of prostituting
Pros'trate, a. laid flat along, lying at mercy
Pros'trate, v. a. to throw down, to lay flat, to cast one's self at the feet of another
Prostra'tion, s. the act of falling down in adoration; dejection, depression
Protect', v. a. to defend, to save, to shield
Protec'tion, s. a defence, a shelter
Protec'tive, a. defensive, sheltering
Protec'tor, s. a defender, supporter, regent
Proten'd, v. a. to hold out, to stretch forth
Protest', v. to give a solemn declaration of opinion or resolution
Pro'test, s. a declaration against a thing
Prot'estant, s. one of the reformed religion who protests against popery
Protesta'tion, s. solemn declaration, a vow
Prothon'otary, s. a head register or notary
Pro'tocol, s. the original copy of a writing
Protomar'tyr, s. the first martyr, St. Stephen
Pro'totype, s. the original of a copy
Protract', v. a. to draw out, delay, lengthen
Protrac'tion, s. a delay, a lengthening out
Protrac'tive, a. dilatory, delaying
Protru'de, v. to thrust forward
Protru'sion, s. the act of thrusting forward
Protu'berance, s. a swelling above the rest
Protu'berant, a. prominent, swelling
Proud, a. elated, arrogant, lofty, grand
Proud'ly, ad. arrogantly, ostentatiously
Prove, v. to evince; to try; to experience
Prove'able, a. that may be proved

O S

Proved'itor, Provedo're, s. one who undertakes to procure supplies for an army

Prov'ender, s. food for brutes, hay, corn, &c.

Prov'erb, s. a maxim; a common saying

Prover'bial, a. mentioned in a proverb

Prover'bially, ad. in a proverb

Provi'de, v. to prepare; supply; stipulate

Prov'idence, s. divine care and superintendence; prudence, frugality, foresight

Prov'ident, a. forecasting; cautious; prudent

Providen'tial, a. effected by Providence

Providen'tially, ad. by the care of Providence

Prov'idently, ad. with careful precaution

Prov'ince, s. a conquered country; office; business; a region; tract

Provin'cial, a. relating to a province; rude

Provin'cial, s. a spiritual or chief governor

Provin'ciate, v. a. to turn to a province

Provis'ion, s. a providing beforehand; victuals, food; measures taken; terms settled

Provis'ional, a. temporarily established

Provis'ionally, ad. conditionally

Provi'so, s. a stipulation; a caution

Provo'cation, s. a cause of anger

Provo'cative, s. any thing which revives a decayed or cloyed appetite

Provo'ke, v. a. to rouse, enrage, challenge

Provo'kingly, ad. so as to raise anger

Prov'ost, s. the chief of any corporate body; a military executioner

Prow, s. the head or fore part of a ship

Prow'ess, s. bravery, military courage

Prowl, v. to rove over; wander for prey

Prowl'er, s. one who roves about for prey

Prox'imate, Prox'ime, a. next, near; immedi-

Proxim'ity, s. nearness, neighbourhood [ate

Prox'y, s. a substitute or agent for another

Pruce, s. Prussian leather

Prude, s. a woman over-nice and scrupulous

Pru'dence, s. wisdom applied to practice

Pru'dent, a. practically wise, cautious

Pruden'tial, a. upon principles of prudence

Pruden'tially, ad. according to prudence

Pruden'tials, s. maxims of prudence

Pru'dently, ad. wisely, discreetly

Pru'dery, s. overmuch nicety in conduct

Pru'dish, a. affectedly grave

Prune, s. a dried plum—v. to lop trees, &c.

Prunel'lo, s. a kind of silken stuff; a plum

Pru'rience, s. an itching or great desire

Pru'rient, a. itching, hot, eager

Pry, v. n. to inspect officiously, &c.

Psalm, s. a holy song, a sacred hymn

Psal'mist, s. a writer, &c. of psalms

Psal'mody, s. a singing of psalms

Psal'ter, s. a psalm book, book of psalms

Psal'tery, s. a kind of harp for psalms

Pseu'do, a. false, counterfeit, pretended

Pseudol'ogy, s. false speaking, lying

Pshaw, interj. expressing contempt, &c.

Ptisan', s. a cooling medical drink made of barley, decocted with raisins, &c.

Pu'berty, Pubes'cence, s. ripeness of age, time of life in which the two sexes begin first to be acquainted

Pubes'cent, a. arriving at puberty

Pub'lic, a. common, not private, manifest

Pub'lic, s. the body of the nation; the people

Pub'lican, s. a toll-gatherer; a victualler

Publica'tion, s. the act of publishing

Pub'licly, ad. openly in full view

Pub'licness, s. state of being public

Pub'lish, v. a. to make known, to set forth

Pub'lisher, s. one who publishes a book

Pu'celage, s. a state of virginity

Puck, s. a supposed sprite or fairy

Puck'er, v. a. to gather into plaits or folds

Pud'der, s. a noise, bustle, tumult

Pud'ding, s. a sort of food; a gut

Pud'dle, s. a small dirty lake, a dirty plash

Pud'dly, a. muddy, dirty, miry

Pu'dency, Pudic'ity, s. modesty, chastity

Pu'erile, a. childish, boyish, trifling

Pueril'ity, s. childishness, boyishness

Puerp'eral, a. belonging to child-bearing

Pu'et, s. a kind of water fowl

Puff, s. a blast of wind; an utensil for powdering the hair; undeserved praise

Puff, v. a. to swell with wind; to pant

Puff'in, s. a water fowl; a fish

Puff'ingly, ad. with shortness of breath

Puff'y, a. windy; flatulent; tumid; turgid

Pug, s. a small Dutch dog, a monkey

Pugh, interj. denoting contempt

Pu'gil, s. a small handful, a champion, fighter

Puis'ne, a. young, younger; later in time; petty, small, inconsiderable, puny

Pu'issance, s. power, force, might

Pu'issant, a. powerful, mighty, forcible

Puke, Pu'ker, s. a medicine causing a vomit

Pul'chritude, s. beauty, grace, comeliness

Pule, v. a. to whine, to cry, to whimper

Pulkha', s. a Laplander's travelling sledge

Pull, s. the act of pulling, a pluck

Pull, v. a. to draw violently, to pluck, to tear

Pul'let, s. a young hen

Pul'ley, s. a small wheel for a running cord

Pul'lulate, v. n. to germinate; to bud [lungs

Pul'monary, Pulmon'ic, a. pertaining to the

Pulp, s. any soft mass, soft part of fruit

Pul'pit, s. an exalted place to speak in

Pul'py, a. soft, pappy, full of pulp

Pulsa'tion, s. act of beating or moving with quick strokes against any thing opposing; also the beating of the pulse or arteries

Pulse, s. motion of the blood perceived by the touch; all sorts of grain contained in pods

Pul'sion, s. the act of forcing forward

Pul'verize, v. a. to reduce to powder or dust

Pulver'ulent, a. dusty

Pul'vil, s. sweet scents—v. a. to perfume

Pu'mice, s. a spungy stone full of pores

Pump, s. a water engine; a sort of shoe

Pump, v. to work a pump, to throw out water by a pump; to examine artfully

Pun, s. an equivocation, a quibble

Pun, v. n. to quibble, to play upon words

Punch, s. an instrument; a buffoon; liquor

Punch, v. a. to make a hole with a punch

Punch'bowl, s. a bowl to make punch in

Punch'eon, s. a tool; a cask of 84 gallons

Punchinel'lo, s. a buffoon; a puppet

Punctil'io, s. a trifling nicety of behaviour

Punctil'ious, a. exact, nice, ceremonious

Punc'to, s. ceremony; the point in fencing

Punc'tual, a. exact, nice, punctilious

Punctual'ity, Punc'tualness, s. exactness

Punc'tually, ad. exactly, scrupulously

Punctua'tion, s. the method of pointing

Punc'tulate, v. to mark with small spots

Punc'ture, s. a hole made with a sharp point

Pun'dle, s. a short and fat woman, a dowdy

Pun'gency, s. power of pricking; acridness
Pun'gent, a. pricking, sharp, acrimonious
Pu'niness, s. smallness, tenderness
Pun'ish, v. a. to chastise, to correct, to afflict
Pun'ishable, a. worthy of punishment
Pun'ishment, s. any infliction imposed in vengeance of a crime; chastisement
Punit'ion, s. punishment
Punk, s. a strumpet; a prostitute
Pun'ster, s. one who is fond of puns
Punt, v. n. to play at basset or ombre
Pu'ny, a. young; inferior; peaking; weakly
Pup, v. n. to bring forth puppies
Pu'pil, s. the apple of the eye; a scholar
Pu'pilage, s. minority; wardship; the state of being a scholar
Pu'pilary, a. pertaining to a pupil
Pup'pet, s. a small doll; a wooden image
Pup'petshow, s. a mock play by images
Pup'py, s. a whelp; a saucy ignorant fellow
Pur'blind, a. short-sighted, near-sighted
Pur'chase, s. any thing bought for a price
Pur'chase, v. a. to buy, to acquire by paying a price, to expiate by a fine, &c.
Pur'chaser, s. one who makes a purchase
Pure, a. not sullied; chaste; unmingled
Pu'rely, ad. in a pure manner; merely
Purga'tion, s. the act of cleansing, &c.
Pur'gative, a. cleansing downwards
Pur'gatory, s. a place in which the Papists suppose that souls are purged by fire from carnal impurities, before they are received into heaven
Purge, s. a medicine causing stools
Purge, v. to cleanse, clear, evacuate by stool
Pur'ging, s. cleansing; a looseness
Purifica'tion, s. the act of purifying, &c.
Pu'rifier, s. a cleanser, a refiner
Pu'rify, v. to make or grow pure; to clear
Pu'ritan, s. a sectary pretending to eminent sanctity of religion
Puritan'ical, a. relating to puritans
Pu'ritanism, s. the doctrine of the Puritans
Pu'rity, s. cleanness, chastity, innocence
Purl, s. a kind of lace; a bitter malt liquor
Purl, v. n. to flow with a gentle noise
Pur'lieu, s. an enclosure, district, border
Pur'ling, part. a. running with a gentle noise
Pur'lins, s. inside braces to rafters
Purloi'n, v. a. to steal, to pilfer, to filch
Pur'party, s. a share, a part of a division
Pur'ple, a. red tinctured with blue
Pur'ples, s. purple spots in a fever
Pur'plish, a. somewhat purple; like purple
Pur'port, s. a design, tendency, meaning
Pur'port, v. a. to intend, to tend to show
Pur'pose, s. intention, design, effect
Pur'pose, v. a. to design, intend, resolve

Purr, v. a. to murmur, as a cat or leopard
Purse, s. a small bag to contain money, &c.
Pur'ser, s. an officer on board a ship who has the care of the provisions, &c.
Pursu'able, a. what may be pursued
Pursu'ance, s. prosecution; process
Pursu'ant, a. done in consequence or prosecution of any thing
Pursu'e, v. to chase, to continue, to proceed
Pursui't, s. the act of following; the chase
Pur'suivant, s. an attendant on heralds
Pur'sy, a. short-breathed and fat
Pur'tenance, s. the pluck of an animal
Purvey', v. to buy in provisions; to procure
Purvey'ance, s. providing victuals, corn, &c.
Purvey'or, s. one who provides victuals
Pur'view, s. a proviso; a providing clause
Pu'rulence, s. generation of pus or matter
Pu'rulent, a. full of corrupt matter or pus
Pus, s. corruption, or thick matter issuing from a wound or sore
Push, v. to thrust, to push forward, to urge
Push, s. a thrust; attack; trial; pimple
Push'ing, a. enterprising; vigorous
Pusillanim'ity, s. timidity, cowardice
Pusillan'imous, a. mean spirited, cowardly
Puss, s. the term for a hare or cat
Pus'tule, s. a little pimple or wheal; a push
Pus'tulous, a. full of pustules, pimply
Put, v. to lay, place; repose; urge; state unite; propose; form; regulate
Put, s. a rustic, a clown; a game at cards
Pu'tative, a. supposed; reputed
Pu'tid, a. mean, low, worthless
Put'log, s. a log used in bricklayer's scaffold
Putrefac'tion, s. rottenness
Putrefac'tive, a. making rotten
Pu'trefy, v. to rot, to make rotten
Putres'cent, a. growing rotten
Pu'trid, a. rotten, corrupt, offensive
Put'tock, s. a bird, the buzzard
Put'ty, s. a cement used by glaziers
Puz'zle, v. a. to embarrass, to perplex
Pygme'an, a. small, little, belonging to a dwarf
Pyg'my, s. a dwarf; a fabulous person
Pyr'amid, s. an angular pillar ending in a point   [a pyramid
Pyram'idal, Pyramid'ical, a. in the form of
Pyre, s. a pile on which the dead are burnt
Pyret'ics, s. medicines which cure fevers
Pyri'tes, s. a marcasite; a firestone
Py'romancy, s. a divination by fire
Pyrotech'nical, a. relating to fireworks
Pyr'otechny, s. the art of making fireworks
Pyr'rhonism, s. scepticism; universal doubt
Py'talism, s. an effusion of spittle
Pyx, s. the box in which the Roman Catholics keep the host

Q.

Q, s. the 16th letter of the alphabet
Quack, v. n. to cry like a duck; to brag
Quack, s. a tricking practitioner in physic
Quack'ery, s. mean or bad acts in physic
Quadrages'imal, a. pertaining to Lent
Quad'rangle, s. a figure that has four right sides, and as many angles

Quadran'gular, a. having four right angles
Qua'drant, s. the fourth part; an instrument with which altitudes are taken
Quadran'tal, a. in the fourth part of a circle
Qua'drate, a. having four equal sides
Quadrat'ic, a. belonging to a square
Quadren'nial, a. comprising four years

Quad'rible, *a.* that may be squared
Quad'rifid, *a.* cloven into four divisions
Quadrilat'eral, *a.* having four sides
Quadrill'e, *s.* a game at cards
Quadrip'artite, *a.* divided into four parts
Quad'ruped, *s.* a four-footed animal
Quad'ruple, *a.* fourfold, four times told
Quaff, *v.* to drink luxuriously or largely
Quag'gy, *a.* boggy, soft, not solid
Quag'mire, *s.* a shaking marsh, a bog
Quail, *s.* a bird of game
Quail'pipe, *s.* a pipe to allure quails with
Quaint, *a.* nice, superfluously exact
Quaint'ly, *ad.* nicely, exactly; artfully
Quaint'ness, *s.* petty elegance
Quake, *v. n.* to shake with cold or fear
Qualifica'tion, *s.* an accomplishment, &c.
Qual'ify, *v. a.* to make fit; soften, modify
Qual'ity, *s.* nature relatively considered; property; temper; rank; qualification
Qualm, *s.* a sudden fit of sickness; a temporary rising of the conscience
Qualm'ish, *a.* seized with sickly languor
Quanda'ry, *s.* a doubt, a difficulty
Quan'tity, *s.* bulk; weight; portion; measure of time in pronouncing syllables
Quan'tum, *s.* the quantity, the amount
Quaranti'ne, *s.* the space of 40 days, during which a ship suspected of infection is obliged to forbear intercourse or commerce
Quar'rel, *s.* a brawl, scuffle, contest
Quar'rel, *v. n.* to debate; scuffle; find fault
Quar'relsome, *a.* inclined to quarrels
Quar'relsomeness, *s.* cholericness
Quar'ry, *s.* an arrow; game; stone mine
Quar'ry, *v. n.* to prey upon, to feed on
Quart, *s.* the fourth part of a gallon
Quar'tan-ague, *s.* an ague, of which the fit returns every fourth day
Quarta'tion, *s.* a chymical operation
Quar'ter, *s.* a fourth part; mercy; station; region; a measure of eight bushels
Quar'ter, *v. a.* to divide into four parts; to station soldiers; diet; to bear as an appendage to the hereditary arms
Quar'terage, *s.* a quarterly allowance
Quar'terdeck, *s.* the short upper deck
Quar'terly, *a.* once in a quarter of a year
Quar'termaster, *s.* an officer who regulates the quarters for soldiers
Quar'tern, *s.* the fourth part of a pint or peck
Quar'terstaff, *s.* an ancient staff of defence
Quar'to, *s.* a book, of which every leaf is a quarter of a sheet
Quartz, *s.* a metallic stone
Quash, *v.* to crush; to squeeze; to subdue suddenly; to annul, to make void
Quash, *s.* a pompion, a kind of melon
Quas'sia, *s.* a bitter drug
Quater'nary, Quater'nion, Quater'nity, *s.* the number four
Qua'train, *s.* four lines rhyming alternately
Qua'ver, *v.* to shake the voice; to vibrate
Quay, *s.* a key for landing goods
Quean, *s.* a worthless woman, a strumpet
Quea'sy, *a.* fastidious, squeamish, sick
Queck, *v. n.* to shrink; to show pain
Queen, *s.* the wife of a king
Queer, *a.* odd, strange; original; awkward
Queer'ly, *ad.* particularly; oddly; strangely
Quell, *v.* to crush; subdue; appease; kill

Quench, *v.* to extinguish fire, allay, cool
Quench'able, *a.* that may be quenched
Quench'less, *a.* unextinguishable
Quer'ele, *s.* a complaint to a court
Querimo'nious, *a.* peevish, complaining
Querimo'niousness, *s.* a complaining temper
Que'rist, *s.* an asker of questions
Quer'po, *s.* a dress close to the body
Quer'ulous, *a.* habitually complaining
Quer'ulousness, *s.* habit of complaining
Quer'ulously, *ad.* in a complaining manner
Que'ry, *s.* a question, an inquiry
Quest, *s.* a search; an empanneled jury
Ques'tion, *s.* interrogatory, dispute, doubt
Ques'tion, *v.* to inquire, examine, doubt
Ques'tionable, *a.* doubtful, suspicious
Ques'tionar., *a.* inquiring, asking questions
Ques'tionless, *ad.* without doubt, certainly
Quest'man, *s.* a starter of lawsuits; an inquirer into misdemeanors. &c.
Ques'tor, *s.* a Roman public treasurer
Ques'tuary, *a.* studious of profit, greedy
Quib, *s.* a sarcasm, bitter taunt
Quib'ble, *v. n.* to equivocate, to pun
Quib'bler, *s.* a punster, an equivocator
Quick, *a.* living; swift, speedy, ready
Quick, *s.* living flesh; any sensible part
Quick'en, *v.* to make or become alive; excite
Quick'lime, *s.* lime unslaked
Quick'ly, *ad.* speedily, actively, nimbly
Quick'ness, *s.* speed, activity, sharpness
Quick'sand, *s.* a shifting or shaking sand
Quick'set, *s.* a sort of thorn of which hedges are made; a living plant set to grow
Quicksight'ed, *a.* having a sharp sight
Quick'silver, *s.* mercury, a fluid mineral
Quid'dany, *s.* marmalade, a confection of quinces
Quid'dity, *s.* a quirk, cavil; essence
Quies'cence, Quies'cency, *s.* rest, repose
Quies'cent, *a.* resting, lying at repose
Qui'et, *a.* still, smooth—*s.* rest, repose
Qui'et, *v. a.* to calm, pacify, put to rest
Qui'etist, *s.* one who places religion in quiet
Qui'etism, *s.* tranquillity of mind
Qui'etly, *ad.* calmly, peaceably, at rest
Qui'etness, *s.* mildness of temper, coolness
Qui'etude, *s.* rest, repose, tranquillity
Quie'tus, *s.* a full discharge; rest, death
Quill, *s.* the strong feather of the wing
Quil'let, *s.* a subtilty; nicety; quibble
Quilt, *s.* the cover of a bed—*v. a.* to stitch one cloth upon another with something soft between them
Quince, *s.* a tree and its fruit
Quin'cunx, *s.* a plantation; a measure
Quinqui'na, *s.* the drug Jesuit's bark
Quin'sy, *s.* a disease in the throat
Quint, *s.* a set or sequence of five
Quin'tal, *s.* a hundred pound weight
Quin'tescence, *s.* the spirit, chief force, or virtue of any thing; a fifth being
Quin'tuple, *a.* five-fold, five times told
Quip, *s.* a jest, taunt—*v. a.* to rally
Quire, *s.* twenty-four sheets of paper
Quire, *v. n.* to sing in concert
Quir'ister, *s.* one who sings in concert, chorister
Quirk, *s.* a subtilty; pun, smart taunt
Quit, *v. a.* to discharge, requite, give
Quite, *ad.* completely, perfectly
Quit'rent, *s.* a small reserved rent

Quits, ad. even in bet, upon equal terms
Quit'tance, s. a receipt, a recompence
Quiv'er, s. a case for arrows—v. n. to quake
Quod'libet, s. a subtilty ; a nice point
Quoif, Quoif'fure, s. a cap, a head dress
Quoin, s. a corner ; wedge ; instrument
Quoit, s. an iron to pitch at a mark
Quo'rum, s. a special commission of justices of the peace, &c. before whom all matters of importance must be transacted

Quon'dam, a. having been formerly
Quo'ta, s. a share, rate, proportion
Quota'tion, s. a citation, a passage quoted
Quote, v. to cite an author, to adduce the words of another
Quoth. v. imperf. for say or said
Quotid'ian, a. daily, happening every day
Quo'tient, s. in arithmetic, is the number produced by the division of the two given numbers the one by the other

R.

R, s. the 17th letter of the alphabet
Raba'te, v. n. to recover a hawk to the fist
Rab'bet, s. a joint in carpentry. a groove
Rab'bi, or Rab'bin, s. a Jewish doctor
Rabbin'ical, a. relating to rabbies
Rab'bit, s. a fourfooted furry animal
Rab'ble, s. an assemblage of low people
Rab'id, a. mad, furious, raging
Race, s. a family, generation ; particular breed ; running match, course ; train
Race-mif'erous, a. cluster-bearing
Ra'ciness, s. the state of being racy
Rack, s. an engine to torture with ; extreme pain ; a frame for hay, bottles, &c.
Rack, v. a. to torment, harass ; defecate
Rack'rent, s. rent raised to the utmost
Rack'et, s. a noise, a thing to strike a ball
Racoo'n, s. an American animal
Ra'cy, a. strong, flavorous ; also what by age has lost its luscious quality
Ra'diance, s. a sparkling lustre, glitter
Ra'diant, a. shining, brightly sparkling
Ra'diate, v. n. to emit rays ; to shine
Ra'diated, a. adorned with rays
Radia'tion, s. an emission of rays
Rad'ical, a. primitive ; implanted by nature
Rad'ically, ad. originally, primitively
Rad'icate, v. a. to root, plant deeply and firmly
Rad'ish, s. a root which is eaten raw
Ra'dius, s. the semidiameter of a circle
Raff, v. a. to sweep, to huddle
Raf'fle, v. n. to cast dice for a prize
Raf'fle, s. a casting dice for prizes
Raft, s. a float of timber
Raf'ter, s. the roof timber of a house
Rag, s. worn-out clothes, a tatter
Ragamuf'fin, s. a paltry mean fellow
Rage, s. violent anger, fury, passion
Rag'ged, a. rent into or drest in rags ; rugged
Ra'gingly, ad. with vehement fury
Ragou't, s. meat stewed and high seasoned
Rail, s. a sort of wooden or iron fence
Rail, v. to enclose with rails ; to insult
Rail'lery, s. slight satire, satirical mirth
Rai'ment, s. vesture, garment, dress
Rain, s. water falling from the clouds
Rain'bow, s. an arch of various colours which appears in showery weather, formed by the refraction of the sun-beams
Rain'deer, s. a large northern deer
Rai'ny, a. showery, wet
Raise, v. a. to lift, to erect, to exalt, to levy
Rai'sin, s. a dried grape
Rake, v. to gather or clear with a rake ; to scour to heap together ; to search

Rake, s. a tool with teeth ; a loose man
Ra'ker, s. one who rakes, a scavenger
Ra'kish, a. loose, lewd, dissolute
Ra'kehell, s. a wild, worthless, dissolute, debauched, sorry fellow
Ral'ly, v. to treat with satirical merriment ; to put disordered forces into order
Ram, s. a male sheep ; Aries, the vernal sign
Ram, v. a. to drive with violence
Ram'ble, s. an irregular excursion
Ram'ble, v. n. to rove loosely, to wander
Ram'bler, s. a rover, a wanderer
Ram'bling, s. the act of roving or wandering
Ramifica'tion, s. a division or separation into branches ; a branching out
Ram'ify, v. to separate into branches
Ram'mer, s. an instrument to force the charge into a gun, or drive piles, &c. into the ground
Ra'mous, a. consisting of full of branches
Ramp, s. a leap, spring
Ramp, v. n. to climb ; to leap about
Ram'pant, a. exuberant, frisky, wanton
Ram'part, Ram'pire, s. the wall round fortified places ; platform behind the parapet
Ran, pret. of to run
Ran'cid, a. strong scented, stinking
Ran'corous, a. malignant, malicious in the utmost degree
Ran'cour, s. inveterate malignity
Rand, s. a border ; the seam of a shoe
Ran'dom, a. done by chance, without plan
Ran'dom, s. want of direction, rule, or method ; chance, hazard, roving motion
Rang, pret. of to ring
Range, s. a rank ; excursion ; kitchen grate
Range, v. a. to place in order or ranks; to rove
Ra'nger, s. a rover, a forest officer
Rank, a. rancid ; coarse ; high grown
Rank, s. a line of men ; class ; dignity
Rank, v. to place in a row, to arrange
Ran'kle, v. n. to fester, to be inflamed
Ran'sack, v. a. to plunder, to search
Ran'som, s. a price paid for liberty
Rant, s. an extravagant flight of words
Rant, v. n. to rave in high sounding language
Ran'tipole, a. wild, roving, rakish
Ranun'culus, s. the flower crowfoot
Rap, v. a. to rap with a quick smart blow
Rap, s. a quick smart blow
Rapa'cious, a. seizing by violence, greedy
Rapa'ciously, ad. by violent robbery
Rapac'ity, s. addictedness to plunder
Rape, s. a violent defloration of chastity ; snatching away ; a plant

Rap'id, *a.* quick, swift, violent
Rapid'ity, *s.* celerity, velocity, swiftness
Rapid'ly, *ad.* swiftly, with quick motion
Ra'pier, *s.* a small sword for thrusting
Ra'pier-fish, *s.* the sword fish
Rap'ine, *s.* act of plundering, violence
Rapt, *v. n.* to ravish, to put in ecstacy
Rap'ture, *s.* ecstacy, transport, rapidity
Rap'turous, *a.* ecstatic, transporting
Rare, *a.* scarce; excellent; subtle; raw
Ra'reeshow, *s.* a snow carried in a box
Rarefac'tion, *s.* an extension of the parts of any body, that makes it take up more room
Rar'efy, *v. a.* to make or become thin
Ra'rely, *ad.* seldom; finely; accurately
Ra'reness, Ra'rity, *s.* uncommonness
Ras'cal, *s.* a mean fellow, a scoundrel
Rascal'lion, *s.* one of the lowest people
Rascal'ity, *s.* the scum of the people
Ras'cally, *a.* mean, worthless
Rase, *v. a.* to skin, to root up, destroy, erase
Rash, *a.* precipitate—*s.* a breaking out
Rash'er, *s.* a thin slice of bacon
Rash'ly, *ad.* violently, without thought
Rash'ness, *s.* a foolish contempt of danger
Rasp, *s.* a berry; a large rough file
Rasp, *v. a.* to rub or file with a rasp
Ras'patory, *s.* a surgeon's rasp
Ras'pberry, *s.* a berry of a pleasant flavour
Ra'sure, *s.* a scraping out of writing
Rat, *s.* an animal of the mouse kind
Ra'table, *a.* set at a certain value
Ratafi'a, *s.* a delicious cordial liquor
Ratan', *s.* a small Indian cane
Rate, *s.* a price; degree; quota; parish tax
Rate, *v. a.* to value; to chide hastily
Rath, *a.* early, before the time—*s.* a hill
Rath'er, *ad.* more willingly; in preference to
Ratifica'tion, *s.* a confirmation
Rat'ify, *v. a.* to confirm, settle, establish
Ra'tio, *s.* a proportion, a rate
Ra'tocina'tion, *s.* act of reasoning, a debate
Rat'ional, *a.* having the power of reasoning, agreeable to reason, wise, judicious
Rational'ity, *s.* the power of reasoning
Ra'tionally, *ad.* reasonably, with reason
Rat'sbane, *s.* arsenic, poison for rats
Rat'tle, *s.* empty talk; a child's plaything
Rat'tle, *v.* to rail, to scold, to make a noise
Rat'tleheaded, *a.* giddy, not steady
Rat'tlesnake, *s.* a kind of serpent
Rattoo'n, *s.* a West Indian fox
Rav'age, *v. a.* to lay waste, ransack, pillage
Rav'age, *s.* spoil, ruin, waste
Rau'city, *s.* hoarseness, a harsh voice
Rave, *v. n.* to be delirious; to be very fond
Rav'el, *v. a.* to entangle; to untwist
Rav'elin, *s.* a half moon in fortification
Ra'ven, *s.* a large black carrion fowl
Rav'enous, *a.* voracious, hungry to rage
Rav'enously, *ad.* with hungry voracity
Rav'enousness, *s.* rage for prey, furious vora-
Rav'in, *s.* prey, rapine, rapaciousness [city
Ravi'ne, *s.* a deep hollow pass
Ra'vingly, *ad.* with distraction or frenzy
Rav'ish, *v. a.* to violate, to deflower by force; to delight, to rapture, to transport
Rav'isher, *s.* he who ravishes
Rav'ishment, *s.* violation, ecstacy, transport
Raw, *a.* not subdued by fire; sore; chill; immature; unripe; unconcocted

Raw'boned, *a.* having strong or large bones
Raw'ness, *s.* state of being raw, unskilfulness
Ray, *s.* a beam of light; a fish; a herb
Raze, *s.* a root of ginger
Raze, *v. a.* to subvert; efface; extirpate
Ra'zor, *s.* a tool used in shaving
Ra'zure, *s.* the act of erasing
Reaccess', *s.* readmittance
Reach, *s.* power, ability, extent, fetch
Reach, *v.* to arrive at, to extend to; vomit
Reac'tion, *s.* the reciprocation of any impulse or force impressed
Read, *v.* to peruse, to learn, to know fully
Readep'tion, *s.* act of regaining, recovery
Rea'der, *s.* one who reads; a studious man
Read'ily, *ad.* with speed; expeditely
Read'iness, *s.* promptitude; facility
Read'ing, *s.* study, a lecture, a public reading; prelection; variation of copies
Readmis'sion, *s.* the act of admitting again
Readmit', *v. a.* to admit or let in again
Read'y, *a.* prompt, willing; near at hand
Reaffir'mance, *s.* a second confirmation
Re'al, *a.* true, certain, genuine
Real'ity, *s.* truth, verity, real existence
Re'alize, *v. a.* to bring into being or act
Re'ally, *ad.* with actual existence, truly
Realm, *s.* a kingdom, a state
Ream, *s.* twenty quires of paper
Rean'imate, *v. a.* to restore to life
Reannex', *v. a.* to annex or join again
Reap, *v. a.* to cut down corn; to obtain
Rea'per, *s.* one who reaps and gathers corn
Rear, *s.* the hinder troop, last class
Rear, *v. a.* to raise up, to elevate, to rouse
Rear-ad'miral, *s.* the admiral who carries his flag at the mizen topmast head
Rear'mouse, Ra'remouse, *s.* a bat
Reascen'd, *v.* to climb or mount up again
Rea'son, *s.* that power by which man deduces consequences from premises; motive, principle, cause
Rea'son, *v.* to argue or examine rationally
Rea'sonable, *a.* endued with reason; just
Rea'sonably, *ad.* agreeably to reason, moderately
Rea'sonableness, *s.* moderation, fairness, equity
Rea'soning, *s.* argument
Reassem'ble, *v. a.* to collect anew
Reassu'me, *v. a.* to resume, to take again
Reassump'tion, *s.* the act of reassuming
Reassu're, *v. a.* to restore from terror
Reave, *v. a.* to take by stealth or violence
Rebap'tize, *v. a.* to baptize again
Reba'te, *v. a.* to blunt; lessen—*s.* discount
Re'bec, *s.* a three-stringed fiddle
Reb'el, *s.* one who opposes lawful authority
Rebel', *v.* to oppose lawful authority
Rebel'lion, *s.* an insurrection or taking up arms against lawful authority
Rebel'lious, *a.* opposing lawful authority
Rebel'tion, *s.* the return of a bellowing sound
Reboun'd, *v.* to spring back, to reverberate
Rebuff', *s.* a quick and sudden resistance
Rebuff', *v. a.* to beat back, to disencourage
Rebuil'd, *v. a.* to build again; to repair
Rebu'ke, *v. a.* to reprehend; to chide
Re'bus, *s.* a word represented by a picture, a kind of riddle
Recal', *v. n.* to call back, to revoke
Recal', *s.* a calling

Recan't, v. a. to retract an opinion
Recanta'tion, s. a retracting an opinion
Recapit'ulate, v. a. to repeat again distinctly
Recapitula'tion, s. a detail repeated
Recap'tion, s. a second distress or seizure
Rece'de, v. n. to fall back, retreat, desist
Recei'pt, s. a reception; an acquittance
Recei'vable, a. capable of being received
Recei've, v. a. to take, to admit, to allow, to entertain; to embrace intellectually
Recei'ver, s. one who receives
.tecen'sion, s. an enumeration, review
Re'cent, a. new, late, not long passed
Re'cently, ad. newly, freshly, lately
Re'centness, s. newness, freshness
Recep'tacle, s. a place to receive things in
Recep'tary, s. the thing received
Receptibil'ity, s. possibility of receiving
Recep'tion, s. act of receiving, admission; treatment; welcome; entertainment
Recep'tive, a. capable of receiving
Recess', s. retirement; departure; privacy
Reces'sion, s. the act of retreating
Recha'nge, v. a. to change again
Rechar'ge, v. a. to accuse in return, reattack
Rechea't, s. recalling hounds by winding a horn when they are on a wrong scent
Rec'ipe, s. a medical prescription
Recip'ient, s. a receiver; a vessel to receive
Recip'rocal, a. mutual, alternate [ness
Recip'rocalness, s. mutual return, alternate-
Recip'rocate, v. n. to act interchangeably
Reciproca'tion, s. action interchanged
Recis'ion, s. cutting off, a making void
Reci'tal, Recita'tion, s. rehearsal, repetition
Recitati've, Recitati'vo, s. a kind of tuneful pronunciation, more musical than common speech, and less than song
Reci'te, v. a. to repeat, to enumerate
Reck, v. to heed, to mind, to care for
Reck'less, a. heedless, careless, mindless
Reck'on, v. to number, to esteem; compute
Reck'oning, s. an estimation, calculation
Recla'im, v. a. to reform, correct, recal
Recli'ne, v. n. to lean sideways or back
Reclo'se, v. a. to close again
Reclu'de, v. a. to open, unlock
Reclu'se, a. shut up, retired
Recoagula'tion, s. a second coagulation
Recog'nisance, s. a bond of record; a badge
Rec'ognise, v. a. to acknowledge; to review
Recognit'ion, s. acknowledgment, review
Recoil', v. n. to rush back, to shrink back, fail
Recoi'nage, s. the act of coining anew
Recollec't, v. a. to recover to memory, &c.
Recollec'tion, s. recovery of notion; revival in the memory of former ideas
Recommen'ce, v. to begin anew
Recommen'd, v. a. to commend to another
Recommenda'tion, s. the act of recommending; the terms used to recommend
Recommen'datory, a. recommending
Recommit', v. a. to commit anew
Rec'ompence, s. a requital, an amends
Rec'ompense, v. a. to repay, to requite
Recompi'lement, s. a new compilat on
Recompo'se, v. a. to settle or adjust anew
Rec'oncile, v. a. to make things agree. &c
Rec'oncileable, a. that may be reconciled
Reconci'lement, s. a reconciliation
Reconcilia'tion, s. renewal of friendship

Reconcil'iatory, a. tending to reconcile
Reconden'se, v. a. to condense anew
Rec'ondite, a. profound, abstruse; secret
Recon'ditory, s. a store-house, a repository
Reconduc't, v. a. to conduct back again
Reconnoi'tre, v. a. to view, to examine
Recon'quer, v. a. to conquer again
Reconve'ne, v. a. to assemble anew
Recor'd, v. a. to register; to celebrate
Rec'ord, s. an authentic memorial, register
Recor'der, s. a law officer; a sort of flute
Recov'er, v. to regain; to grow well again
Recov'erable, a. that may be restored, &c.
Recov'ery, s. a restoration from sickness
Recou'nt, v. a. to relate in detail
Recou'rse, s. an application for help. &c.
Rec'reant, a. cowardly, mean-spirited
Rec'reate, v. a. to refresh, delight, revive
Recrea'tion, s. relief after toil, diversion
Rec'rement, s. dross, filth, spume
Recremen'tal, Recrementit'ious, a. drossy
Recrim'inate, v. a. to accuse in return
Recrimina'tion, s. an accusation retorted
Recrudes'cent, a. growing painful again
Recru'it, v. a. to repair, replace, supply
Recru'it, s. a new enlisted soldier; supply
Rec'tangle, s. a right angle made by the falling of one line perpendicularly upon another, and which consists of 90 degrees
Rectan'gular, a. having right angles
Rec'tifiable, a. capable of being set right
Rec'tifier, s. one who rectifies
Rec'tify, v. a. to make right, reform; to exalt and improve by repeated distillation
Rectilin'ear, a. consisting of right lines
Rec'titude, s. straightness; uprightness
Rec'tor, s. a minister of a parish; a ruler
Rec'torship, s. the office of a rector
Rec'tory, s. a parish church, or spiritual living, with all its rights, glebes, &c.
Recuba'tion, Recum'bency, s. the posture of lying or loaning; rest, repose
Recum'bent, a. lying, leaning, listless
Recur', v. to have recourse to, to come back
Recur'rence, Recur'sion, s. a return
Recur'rent, a. returning from time to time
Recurva'tion, s. a bending backwards
Rec'usant, s. one who refuses any terms of communion or society
Recu'se, v. a. to refuse, deny, reject, oppose
Recus'sion, s. the act of beating back
Red. a. of the colour of blood
Red'breast, s. a small bird with a red breast
Red'den, v. to make or grow red, to blush
Red'dishness, s. a tendency to redness
Reddit'ion, s. restitution
Red'dle, s. a sort of mineral; red chalk
Rede, s. counsel, advice—v. a. to advise
Redee'm, v. a. to ransom, to relieve from any thing by paying a price; to recover, to atone for, to recompense
Redee'mable, a. capable of redemption
Redee'mer, s. one who ransoms or redeems; in particular, the Saviour of the world
Redeli'ver, v. a. to deliver or give back
Redem'ption, s. a ransom, the purchase of God's favour by the death of Christ
Redem'ptory, a. paid for ransom
Red'lead, s. calcined lead, minium
Red'olence, Red'olency, s. a sweet scent
Red'olent, a. sweet of scent, fragrant

Redoub'le, v. a. to become twice as much
Redou'bt, s. the outwork of a fortification
Redou'btable, a. formidable, much feared
Redou'nd, v. n. to be sent back by reaction
Redress', v. a. to set aright, amend, relieve
Redress', s. reformation; relief; remedy
Red'streak, s. a sort of apple and cider
Redu'ce, v. a. to make less; degrade, subdue
Redu'cement, s. a subduing; a diminishing
Redu'cible, a. possible to be reduced
Reduc'tion, s. the act of reducing
Reduc'tive, a. having the power to reduce
Redun'dance, Redun'dancy, s. a superfluity, superabundance, &c.
Redun'dant, a. overflowing, superfluous
Redu'plicate, v. a. to double over again
Reduplica'tion, s. the act of doubling
Redu'plicative, a. doubling again, two fold
Ree, v. a. to sift, to riddle—s. a small coin
Reed, s. a hollow stalk; a pipe; an arrow
Reed'ify, v. a. to rebuild, to build again
Ree'dy, a. abounding with reeds
Reef, v. a. to reduce the sails of a ship
Reek, s. smoke, vapour—v. n. to smoke
Reel, s. a frame on which yarn is wound
Reel, v. to wind on a reel; to stagger
Reelec'tion, s. a new or repeated election
Reembar'k, v. to take shipping again
Reenfor'ce, v. a. to send fresh forces
Reenfor'cement, s. fresh assistance
Reenjo'y, v. a. to enjoy again or anew
Reen'ter, v. a. to enter again or anew
Reestab'lish, v. a. to establish anew
Reeve, or Reve, s. a steward
Reexam'ine, v. a. to examine anew
Refec'tion, s. refreshment after hunger, &c.
Refec'tory, s. a room for refreshment
Refel', v. a. to refute, to repress
Refer', v. a. to yield to another's judgment
Ref'erence, s. relation; view toward; allusion to; arbitration; mark referring to the bottom of a page
Refi'ne, v. a. to purify, to clear from dross
Refi'nement, s. an improvement in purity, &c.
Refi'ner, s. a purifier, one who refines
Refit', v. a. to repair, to fit up again
Reflec't, v. a. to throw back, to reproach
Reflec'tion, s. attentive consideration; censure; the act of throwing back
Reflec'tive, a. considering things past
Reflec'tor, s. one who reflects
Re'flex, s. reflection—a. directed backward
Reflexibil'ity, s. quality of being reflexible
Reflex'ible, a. capable of being thrown back
Reflex'ive, a. respecting something past
Reflour'ish, v. n. to flourish anew
Reflow', v. n. to flow back, to flow again
Ref'luent, a. reflowing, flowing back
Re'flux, s. flowing back, ebb of the tide
Refor'm, v. to change from worse to better
Refor'm, s. a reformation, change for the better [ter
Reforma'tion, s. change from worse to bet-
Refrac't, v. a. to break the course of rays
Refrac'tion, s. variation of a ray of light
Refrac'tive, a. having power of refraction
Refrac'toriness, s. a sullen obstinacy
Refrac'tory, a. obstinate, contumacious
Ref'ragable, a. capable of confutation, &c.
Refra'in, v. to hold back, forbear, abstain
Refrau'gible, a. capable of refraction

Refresh', v. a. to recreate, improve, cool
Refresh'ment, s. food, rest, relief after pain
Refrig'erant, a. cooling, refreshing
Refrig'erate, v. a. to cool, to mitigate heat
Refrig'erative, a. able to make cool
Ref'uge, s. shelter from danger or distress
Refugee', s. one who flies for protection
Reful'gence, s. splendour, brightness
Reful'gent, a. bright, splendid, glittering
Refun'd, v. a. to pour back, repay, restore
Refu'sal, s. a denial; right of choice; option
Refu'se, v. to deny, to reject, not to accept
Ref'use, s. worthless remains; dross
Refu'ser, s. he who refuses or rejects
Refuta'tion, s. the act of refuting an assertion
Refu'te, v. a. to prove false or erroneous
Regai'n, v. a. to recover, to gain anew
Re'gal, a. royal, kingly
Rega'le, v. a. to refresh, to gratify, to feast
Rega'lement, s. entertainment, refreshment
Rega'lia, s. the ensigns of royalty
Regal'ity, s. royalty, sovereignty, kingship
Regard', v. a. to value, to observe, to esteem
Regard', s. attention, respect, veneration
Regard'ful, a. attentive, taking notice of
Regard'less, a. negligent, inattentive
Regard'lessness, s. heedlessness, negligence
Re'gency, s. the government of a kingdom during the minority, &c. of a prince
Regen'erate, v. a. to reproduce, to produce anew, to make to be born anew
Regen'erate, a. born anew by grace
Regenera'tion, s. a new birth by grace
Regen'erateness, s. state of being regenerate
Re'gent, s. a governor, a deputed ruler
Re'gent, a. governing, ruling
Regermina'tion, s. act of budding out again
Reg'icide, s. the murderer or murder of a.
Reg'imen, s. a diet in time of sickness [king
Reg'iment, s. a body of soldiers; rule, polity
Regimen'tal, a. belonging to a regiment
Re'gion, s. a country; tract of land; space; place, rank; part of the body
Reg'ister, s. a list, a record
Reg'ister, v. a. to record in a register, enrol
Reg'nant, a. predominant, prevalent
Regor'ge, v. a. to vomit up, to swallow back
Regra'de, v. n. to retire
Regra'te, v. a. to stock; engross, forestal
Re'gress, s. passage back; power of return
Regress', v. n. to go back, to return
Regres'sion, s. a returning or going back
Regret', v. a. to repent, to be sorry for
Regret', s. vexation at something past
Reg'ular, a. orderly, agreeable to rule
Regular'ity, s. a certain order; a method
Reg'ularly, ad. constantly, methodically
Reg'ulate, v. a. to adjust by rule, to direct
Regula'tion, s. method; order, rule
Reg'ulator, s. that part of a machine which makes the motion equal
Reg'ulus, s. the finest part of metals
Regur'gitate, v. to throw or be poured back
Rehea'r, v. a. to hear again
Rehear'sal, s. repetition, previous recital
Rehear'se, v. a. to recite previously, to tell
Reject', v. a. to refuse, to discard, to cast off
Rejec'tion, s. the act of casting off or aside
Reign, s. the time of a king's government
Reign, v. n. to rule as a king; to prevail
Reimbod'y, v. to embody again

Reimbur'se, v.n. to pay back again, to repair
Reimpres'sion, s. a repeated impression
Rein, s. part of a bridle—v. a. to curb
Reins, s. the kidneys ; the lower back
Reinser't, v. a. to insert a second time
Reinspi're, v. a. to inspire anew
Reinstal', v. a. to put again in possession
Reinsta'te. v. a. to restore to its former state
Reinves't, v. a. to invest anew
Rejoi'ce, v. to be glad, exult ; make joyful
Rejoi'n, v. to join again ; to meet one again ; to answer to a reply
Rejoi'nder, s. a reply to an answer. reply
Reit'erate, v. a. to repeat again and again
Reitera'tion, s. a repetition
Rejud'ge, v. a. to re-examine, to review
Rekin'dle, v. a. to set on fire again
Relap'se, v. n. to fall back into sickness, &c.
Relap'se, s. a fall into vice or error, &c. once forsaken ; regression from a state of recovery to sickness
Rela'te, v. to recite ; to have reference
Rela'tion, s. a narration ; kindred ; reference
Rel'ative, s. a relation ; a kinsman
Rel'ative, a. having relation ; respecting
Rel'atively, ad. as it respects something else
Relax', v. to be remiss, to slacken, to remit
Relaxa'tion, s. remission, diminution
Relay', s. horses placed to relieve others
Relea'se, v. a. to set free from restraint, &c.
Rel'egate, v. a. to banish, to exile
Relega'tion, s. exile, judicial banishment
Relen't, v. to feel compassion, to mollify
Relen'tless, a. unpitying, unmerciful, cruel
Rel'evant, a. relieving ; relative
Reli'ance, s. trust, dependence, confidence
Rel'ics, s. remains, the remains of bodies
Rel'ict, s. a widow
Relie'f, s. succour, alleviation
Relie've, v.a. to succour ; to change a guard
Relie'vo, s. the prominence of a figure, &c.
Relig'ion, s. a system of faith and worship
Relig'ionist, s. a bigot to any religion
Relig'ious, a. pious, devout, holy, exact
Relig'iously, ad. piously, reverently, exactly
Relin'quish, v.a. to forsake, quit, depart from, give up
Relin'quishment, s. the act of forsaking
Rel'ish, s. taste ; liking ; delight
Rel'ish, v. to season, to have a flavour
Relu'cent, a. shining, transparent
Reluc'tance, s. unwillingness, repugnance
Reluc'tant. a. unwilling, averse to
Relu'me, Relu'mine, v. a. to light anew
Rely', v. a. to put trust in, to depend upon
Remai'n, v. to continue ; await ; to be left
Remai'nder, s. what is left, remains
Remai'ns, s. relics ; a dead body
Reman'd, v. a. to send or call back
Remar'k, s. observation. notice
Remar'k, v. a. to note, distinguish, mark
Remar'kable, a. observable, worthy of note
Remar'kably, ad. observably, uncommonly
Reme'diable, a. capable of remedy
Rem'ediless, v. not admitting remedy
Rem'edy, s. medicine ; reparation ; cure
Rem'edy, v. a. to cure, to heal ; to repair
Remem'ber, v. a. to bear in or call to mind
Remem'berer, s. one who remembers
Remem'brance, s. retention in the memory
Remem'brancer, s. one who reminds

Rem'igrate, v. n. to remove back again
Remigra'tion, s. a removal back again
Remi'nd, v. a. to put in mind
Reminis'cence, s. recovery of ideas
Remiss', a. not vigorous, slack, careless, slothful
Remiss'ible, a. admitting forgiveness
Remis'sion, s. abatement, forgiveness, pardon
Remiss'ly, ad. carelessly, negligently
Remit', v. to relax ; pardon a fault ; send money to a distant place ; slacken. abate
Remit'tance, s. a sum sent to a distant place
Rem'nant, s. a residue ; what is left
Remon'strance, s. a strong representation
Remon'strate, v. a. to show reason against
Rem'ora, s. an obstacle ; a let ; a fish
Remor'se, s. a pain of guilt, tenderness
Remor'seful, a. tender, compassionate
Remor'seless, a. cruel, savage, unpitying
Remo'te, a. distant in time, place, or kin ; foreign ; not closely connected ; alien
Remote'ly, ad. not nearly, at a distance
Remo'teness, s. distance, not nearness
Remo'tion, s. the act of removing
Remo'vable, a. such as may be removed
Remo'val, s. a dismission from a post. &c.
Remo've, v. to put from its place, to change place ; to place at a distance ; to go from one place to another
Remou'nt, v. to mount again
Remu'nerable, a. fit to be rewarded
Remu'nerate, v. a. to reward. requite. repay
Remu'nerative, a. exercised in giving reward
Remunera'tion, s. reward. requital
Remur'mur, v. n. to utter back in murmurs
Ren'ard, s. the name of a fox ; a sly person
Renas'cent, a. rising or springing anew
Renas'cible, a. possible to be produced again
Rencoun'ter, s. a personal opposition ; sudden combat ; casual engagement
Rend. v. a. to tear with violence : lacerate
Ren'der, v. a. to return, repay ; to translate
Ren'dezvous, s. a meeting appointed
Rendi'tion, s. the act of yielding
Ren'egade, Renega'do, s. an apostate
Renew', v.a. to renovate, repeat. begin again
Renew'able, a. capable to be renewed
Renew'al, s. act of renewing, renovation
Reni'tency, s. resistance, opposition
Reni'tent, a. resisting, opposing, repelling
Ren'net, s. a kind of apple ; juice of a calf's maw
Ren'ovate, v. a. to renew. to restore
Renova'tion, s. the act of renewing
Renou'nce, s. to disown ; to abnegate
Renow'n, s. fame, celebrity, merit
Renow'ned, part. a. famous, eminent
Rent, s. a laceration ; annual payment
Rent, v. a. to tear, to hold by paying rent
Rent'al, s. a schedule or account of rent
Rent'charge, s. a charge on an estate
Rent'er, s. he that holds by paying rent
Renu'merate, v. a. to pay back ; to recount
Renuncia'tion, s. the act of renouncing
Reorda'in, v. a. to ordain again or anew
Reordina'tion, s. a being ordained again
Repai'r, v. to amend, to refit—v.n. to go unto
Repai'r, s. a reparation, a supply of loss
Repai'rable, or Rep'arable, a. capable of being amended or retrieved
Repan'dous, a. bent upwards
Repara'tion, s. the act of repairing
Repartee', s. a smart or witty reply

Repass', v. a. to pass again, to pass back
Repas't, s. the act of taking food ; a meal
Repay', v. a. to recompense, to requite
Repe al, v. a. to recal, to abrogate, to revoke
Repe'al, s. revocation, recal from exile
Repea't, v. a. to recite, to do again
Repea'tedly, ad. over and over, frequently
Repea'ter, s. one who repeats ; a watch
Repel', v. a. to drive back ; to act with force
Repel'lent, s. an application that has a repelling power
Repen't, v. n. to feel sorrow for what is past
Repen'tance, s. sincere sorrow for sins
Repen'tant, a. sorrowful for sins
Repercuss', v. a. to beat or drive back
Repercus'sion, s. the act of driving back
Repercus'sive, a. rebounding, driven back
Repertit'ious, a. found, gained by finding
Rep'ertory, s. a book of records ; a treasury
Repetit'ion, s. a recital ; repeating
Repi'ne, v. n. to fret, to be discontented
Repi'ner, s. one that frets or murmurs
Repla'ce, v. a. to put again in place
Replan't, v. a. to plant anew
Replen'ish, v. a. to stock, to fill ; to finish
Reple'te, a. full, completely filled
Reple'tion, s. the state of being too full
Replev'iable, a. what may be replevied
Replev'in, Replev'y, v. a. to set at liberty any thing seized, upon security given
Replica'tion, s. a repercussion ; a reply
Reply', v. a. to answer, to rejoin
Reply', s. an answer, return to an answer
Repol'ish, v. a. to polish again
Repor't, s. a rumour, account ; loud noise
Repor't, v. a. to tell, relate, noise abroad
Repo'se, s. rest, sleep, quiet, peace
Repo'se, v. to lay to rest, to lodge, to lay up
Repos'ite, v. a. to lodge in a place of safety
Reposit'ion, s. the act of replacing
Repos'itory, s. a storehouse or place where any thing is safely laid up ; a warehouse
Repossess', v. a. to possess again
Reprehen'd, v. a. to reprove, to blame, chide
Reprehen'sible, a. blameable, censurable, culpable
Reprehen'sion, s. reproof, open blame [pable
Reprehen'sive, a. given to reproof
Represen't, v. a. to exhibit ; describe; appear for another ; tell respectfully
Representa'tion, s. an image ; description
Represen'tative, s. a substitute in power
Represen'tment, s. an image ; a likeness
Rep'ress, Repres'sion, s. the act of crushing
Repress', v. a. to crush, subdue, compress
Repres'sive, a. able or tending to repress
Reprie've, s. a respite after sentence of death
Reprie've, v. a. to respite from punishment
Repriman'd, s. a reproof, reprehension
Repriman'd, v. a. to chide, check, reprove
Reprin't, v. a. to print a new edition
Repri'sal, s. seizure by way of retaliation
Repro'ach, v. a. to censure, to upbraid
Repro'ach, s. censure, infamy, disgrace
Repro'achable, a. worthy of reproach
Repro'achful, a. scurrilous, shameful, vile
Rep'robate, a. lost to virtue, abandoned
Rep'robate, s. one abandoned to wickedness; a man lost to virtue
Rep'robate, v. a. to disallow, to reject
Reproba'tion, s. the act of reprobating
Reprodu'ce, v. a. to produce again or anew

Reproduc'tion, s. the act of producing anew
Reproo'f, s. blame to one's face ; rebuke
Repro'vable, a. worthy of reproof or blame
Repro've, v. a. to blame, to chide, to check
Repru'ne, v. a. to prune a second time
Rep'tile, s. a creeping thing ; a mean person
Repub'lic, s. a commonwealth ; the public
Repub'lican, s. one who thinks a common wealth without monarchy the best government [the people
Repub'lican, a. placing the government in
Repu'diate, v. a. to divorce, to put away
Repudia'tion, s. a divorce, rejection
Repug'nance, s. reluctance ; contrariety
Repug'nant, a. disobedient ; contrary
Repug'nantly, ad. contradictorily
Repul'lulate, v. n. to bud again or anew
Repul'se, s. a being driven off, rejection
Repul'se, v. a. to beat back, to drive off
Repul'sion, s. act of driving off from itself
Repul'sive, Repul'sory, a. having power to
Repur'chase, v. a. to buy again [beat back
Rep'utable, a. honourable ; of good repute
Reputa'tion, s. honour ; character of good
Repu'te, v. a. to account, to think, to hold
Repu'te, s. character ; reputation, credit
Reques't, s. an entreaty, demand ; repute
Reques't, v. a. to ask, solicit, entreat
Re'quiem, s. a hymn or prayer for the dead
Requi're, v. a. to demand, to ask a thing as of right ; to make necessary ; to need
Req'uisite, a. necessary, needful, proper
Req'uisite, s. any thing necessary
Req'uisitely, ad. necessarily
Requisit'ion, s. a request, demand, claim
Requi'tal, s. a retaliation, a recompence
Requi'te, v. a. to repay, to recompense
Rere'ward, s. the last troop of an army
Re'sale, s. the second or subsequent sale
Resalu'te, v. a. to salute or greet anew
Rescin'd, v. a. to cut off ; to abrogate a law
Rescis'sion, s. an abrogation, a cutting off
Rescri'be, v. a. to write back or over again
Re'script, s. the edict of an emperor
Res'cue, v. a. to set free from danger, violence, or confinement ; to release
Res'cue, s. a deliverance from restraint, &c.
Resear'ch, s. an inquiry, strict search
Resem'blance, s. a similitude, a likeness
Resem'ble, v. a. to be like ; to compare
Resen't, v. a. to take as an affront, &c.
Resen'tful, a. malignant, easily provoked
Resen'tment, s. a deep sense of injury
Reserva'tion, s. something kept back
Reser've, s. a store untouched ; an exception
Reser've, v. a. to keep in store, retain, lay up
Reser'ved, a. modest, sullen, not frank [ness
Reser'vedness, s. closeness, want of frank-
Res'ervoir, s. a conservatory of water; a store
Reset'tlement, s. the act of settling again
Resi'de, v. n. to live in a place ; to subside
Res'idence, Res'iance, s. place of abode
Res'ident, Res'iant, a. dwelling in a place
Res'ident, s. an agent, a public minister
Residen'tiary, a. holding residence
Resid'ual, a. relating to the residue
Resid'uary, a. entitled to the residue of property, as, a residuary legatee
Res'idue, s. the remaining part, what is left
Resi'gn, v. a. to give or yield up, to submit
Resigna'tion, s. a resigning ; patience

Resi'gnment, *s.* the act of resigning
Res'liah, *s.* an ancient patriarchal coin
Resil'ieuce, *s.* a starting or leaping back
Resil'ient, *a.* starting or springing back
Res'in, or Ros'in, *s.* the fat sulphureous part
    of some vegetable, &c.
Res'inous, *a.* containing resin, or like resin
Resis't, *v. a.* to oppose, to act against
Resis'ance, *s.* the act of resisting, opposition
Resis'tible, *a.* that which may be resisted
Resis'tless, *a.* that cannot be resisted
Resolv'able, *a.* that may be analyzed
Res'oluble, *a.* that which may be melted
Resol've, *v.* to inform; to solve; to melt; to
    analyze; to determine; to confirm
Resol've, *s.* fixed determination, resolution
Resol'vedly, *ad.* with firmness and constancy
Resol'vent, *a.* having power to dissolve
Res'olute, *a.* determined, firm, steady
Resolu'tion, *s.* a fixed determination; con-
    stancy; act of clearing difficulties
Res'onant, *a.* resounding, echoing
Resor'b, *v.* to suck back, to swallow up again
Resor't, *v. n.* to have recourse; to repair
Resor't, *s.* a meeting, assembly, concourse
Resou'nd, *v. a.* to echo, sound, ring, celebrate
Reso'urce, *s.* a resort, an expedient
Respec't, *v. a.* to regard; to have relation to
Respec't, *s.* regard, reverence; relation
Respec'table, *a.* meriting regard
Respec'tful, *a.* full of outward civility
Respec'tfully, *ad.* with a degree of reverence
Respec'tive, *a.* particular, relative
Respec'tively, *ad.* particularly, relatively
Resper'sion, *s.* the act of sprinkling
Respira'tion, *s.* the act of breathing; relief
Respi're, *v. n.* to breathe, to rest from toil
Res'pite, *s.* a reprieve, pause, interval
Resplen'dence, *s.* lustre, brightness
Resplen'dent, *a.* bright, shining
Resplen'dently, *ad.* brightly, splendidly
Respon'd, *v. n.* to correspond, to answer
Respon'dent, *s.* one who answers in a suit
Respon'se, *s.* an alternate answer, a reply
Respon'sible, *a.* answerable, accountable
Respon'sion, *s.* the act of answering
Respon'sive, Respon'sory, *a.* answering
Rest, *s.* sleep, repose, quiet, peace; support
Rest, *a.* others, those not included
Rest, *v.* to sleep; die; be still; lean; remain
Restag'nant, *a.* remaining without flow
Restag'nate, *v. n.* to stand without flow
Restaura'tion, *s.* the act of recovering to the
    former state; restoration
Restem', *v. a.* to force against the current
Res'tiff, Res'tive, Res'ty, *a.* unwilling to stir
Res'tifness, *s.* obstinate reluctance
Restitu'tion, *s.* the act of restoring
Res'tless, *a.* without sleep, unquiet, unsettled
Res'tlessness, *s.* want of sleep, want of rest
Resto'rable, *a.* what may be restored
Restora'tion, *s.* replacing in a former state
Resto'rative, *a.* able to recruit life, &c.
Resto're, *v. a.* to relieve; to give back
Restrai'n, *v. a.* to withhold, repress, limit
Restrai'nable, *a.* capable to be restrained
Restrai'nt, *s.* an abridgement of liberty, &c.
Restric't, *v. a.* to limit, to confine
Restric'tion, *s.* confinement, limitation
Restric'tive, *a.* expressing limitation
Restrin'gent, *a.* having power to bind

Resul't, *v.* to fly back; to arise from
Resul't, *s.* act of flying back, consequence
Resu'mable, *a.* what may be taken back
Resu'me, *v. a.* to take back; to begin again
Resum'ption, *s.* the act of resuming
Resum'ptive, *a.* taking back
Resurrec'tion, *s.* return from the grave
Resur'vey, *v.* to review or survey again
Resus'citate, *v. a.* to raise up again; renew
Resuscita'tion, *s.* the act of raising up again
    from either sleep or death, &c.
Retai'l, *v. a.* to divide into, or sell, in small
    quantities, or at second hand—*s.* sale by
    small quantities
Retai'ler, *s.* one who sells by small quantities
Retai'n, *v.* to keep, to hire, to continue
Reta'ke, *v. a.* to take again
Retal'iate, *v. a.* to return, to repay, requite
Retalia'tion, *s.* return of like for like
Retar'd, *v.* to hinder. to delay, to stay back
Retarda'tion, *s.* hinderance; act of delaying
Retch, *v. n.* to strain, to vomit
Reten'tion, *s.* act of retaining, memory
Reten'tive, *a.* having power to retain
Retic'ular, Ret'iform, *a.* in form of a net
Ratic'ulated, *a.* made of net-work
Ret'inue, *s.* a train of attendants
Reti're, *v.* to retreat, to withdraw
Reti'red, *part. a.* secret, solitary, private
Reti'rement, *s.* a private abode or habitation
Reto'ld, *part.* related or told again
Retor't, *s.* a glass vessel; a censure returned
Retor't, *v. a.* to throw back; to return
Retoss', *v. a.* to toss or throw back again
Retouch', *v. a.* to improve by new touches
Retra'ce, *v. a.* to trace back or over again
Retrac't, *v. a.* to recal, recant, resume
Retracta'tion, *s.* change of opinion declared
Retrac'tion, *s.* a withdrawing a question
Retrea't, *s.* a place of retirement or security
Retrea't, *v. n.* to retire, to take shelter
Retren'ch, *v.* to cut off, confine, reduce
Retren'chment, *s.* a reduction of expenses, &c.
Retrib'ute, *v. a.* to pay back, make payment
Retribu'tion, *s.* a repayment, a requital
Retrie've, *v. a.* to recover, repair, regain
Retrie'vable, *a.* that may be recovered
Retroces'sion, *s.* the act of going back
Retroduc'tion, *s.* a leading back, &c.
Ret'rograde, *a.* going backwards; contrary
Retrogres'sion, *s.* the act of going back
Ret'rospect, *s.* a looking on things past
Retrospec'tion, *s.* a looking backwards
Retrospec'tive, *a.* looking backwards
Retun'd, *v. a.* to blunt, to turn the edge
Retur'n, *v.* to come or go back; to retort; to
    repay; to send back, to transmit
Retur'n, *s.* the act of coming back; profit,
    repayment, restitution, relapse
Retur'nable, *a.* allowed to be returned
Revea'l, *v. a.* to disclose, lay open, impart
Rev'el, *v. a.* to carouse—*s.* a noisy feast
Revel', *v. a.* to retract, to draw back
Revela'tion, *s.* a communication of sacred
    truths, &c. by a teacher from heaven
Rev'eller, *s.* one who feasts with jollity
Rev'elrout, *s.* a mob, an unlawful assembly
Rev'elry, *s.* loose jollity, festive mirth
Reven'ge, *s.* return of an injury or affront
Reven'ge, *v. a.* to return an injury, &c.
Reven'geful, *a.* vindictive, given to revenge

Rev'enue, s. an income ; annual profits
Raver'b, v. a. to reverberate, to resound
Mever'berate, v. to beat back, to be driven back ; to bound back ; to resound
Reverbera'tion, s. a beating or driving back
Raver'beratory, a. returning ; beating back
Reve're, v. a. to reverence, to venerate, to honour with an awful respect
Rev'erence, s. veneration, respect ; a bow
Rev'erence, v. a. to regard with respect
Rev'erend, a. venerable ; deserving reverence—s. the honorary title of the clergy
Rev'erent, a. humble ; testifying veneration
Rev'erently, ad. respectfully, with awe
Reveren'tial, a. expressive reverence
Reverie', Rev'ery, s. loose or irregular thought
Rever'sal, s. a change of sentence
Rever'se, v. a. to subvert, repeal, contradict
Rever'se, s. the opposite side, vicissitude
Rever'sible, a. capable of being reversed
Rever'sion, s. succession, right of succession
Rever'sionary, a. to be enjoyed in success on
Rever't, v. to change, to return ; to reverbe-
Rever'tible, a. that may be returned [rate
Reves't, v. a. to clothe again, to reinvest
Reves'tiary, s. a place for vestments
Revi'brate, v. n. to vibrate back
Revic'tual, v. a. to stock with victuals again
Review', v. a. to look back, survey, examine
Review', s. a survey, reexamination
Review'er, s. one who reviews
Revi'le, v. a. to reproach, to abuse, to vilify
Revi'ler, s. one who reviles
Revi'sal, Revis'ion, s. a reexamination
Revi'se, v. a. to review, to overlook
Revi'se, s. a proof of a sheet corrected
Revis'it, v. a. to visit again
Revi'val, s. recal from obscurity, &c.
Revi've, v. to return to life ; renew ; rouse
Revivifi'cate, Reviv'ify, v. a. to recal to life
Revi'ving, part. comforting, recovering
Reu'nion, s. reuniting ; a rejoining ; cohesion
Reuni'te, v. a. to join again ; to reconcile
Rev'ocable, a. that may be recalled
Rev'ocate, v. to recal, to call back
Revoca'tion, s. act of recalling ; a repeal
Revo'ke, v. a. to repeal, reverse, draw back
Revol't, v. n. to fall off from one to another, to rise against a prince or state
Revol've, v. to perform a revolution ; to consider, to meditate on
Revolu'tion, s. a returning motion ; a change of government in a state or country
Revul'sion, s. the turning of a flux of humours from one part of the body to another
Rewar'd, v. a. to recompense, to repay
Rewar'd, s. a recompense given for good
Rewor'd, v. a. to repeat in the same words
Rhab'domancy, s. divination by a wand
Rhap'sodist, s. one who writes rhapsodies
Rhap'sody, s. irregular writings, &c.
Rhet'oric, s. oratory, the art of speaking
Rhetor'ical, a. pertaining to rhetoric
Rhetor'ically, ad. figuratively ; like an orator
Rhetori'cian, s. one who teaches rhetoric
Rheum, s. a thin watery humour, chiefly oozing out of the glands from the mouth
Rheumat'ic, a. relating to the rheumatism
Rheu'matism, s. a painful distemper
Rheu'my, a. full of sharp moisture

Rhinoc'eros, s. a large beast in the East Indies, armed with a horn on his nose
Rhomb, s. a quadrangular figure
Rhom'bic, a. shaped like a rhomb
Rhom'boid, s. a figure approaching to rhomb ; a kind of muscle fish
Rhu'barb, s. medicinal, purgative root
Rhumb, s. a kind of spiral line
Rhyme, s. the consonance of verses, poetry
Rhyme, v. n. to agree in sound ; make verses
Rhyth'mical, a. harmonical, musical
Rib, s. a bone, a piece of timber in ships
Rib'ald, s. a loose, rough, brutal wretch
Rib'aldry, s. mean, lewd, brutal language
Rib'and, or Rib'bon. s. a fillet of silk
Rice, s. a foreign esculent grain
Rich, a. wealthy ; valuable ; fertile ; copious
Rich'es, s. money or possessions ; splendour
Rich'ly, ad. wealthily, splendidly
Rich'ness, s. opulence, splendour ; fertility
Rick, s. a pile or heap of corn, hay, &c.
Rick'ets, s. a distemper in children
Rick'ety, a. diseased with the rickets
Rid, v. a. to set free, clear, drive away
Rid'dance, s. a deliverance, disencumbrance
Rid'dle, s. an enigma, any thing puzzling, a dark problem ; a coarse or open sieve
Rid'dle, v. to solve, to sift by a coarse sieve
Ride, v. to travel on horseback, &c.
Ri'der, s. one who rides a horse, &c.
Ridge, s. the upper part of a slope, &c.
Rid'gel, Rid'geling, s. a ram half castrated
Rid'gy, a. rising in a ridge
Rid'icule, s. a wit that provokes laughter
Rid'icule, v. a. to expose to laughter
Ridic'ulous, a. exciting laughter
Ridic'ulously, ad. in a ridiculous manner
Ri'ding, s. a district visited by an officer
Ri'dinghood, s. a woman's riding coat
Ridot'to, s. an entertainment of music,
Rife, a. prevalent ; abounding
Ri'fle, v. a. to rob, to plunder, to pillage
Rift, s. a cleft, a breach—v. to split
Rig, v. a. to dress ; to fit with tackling
Rigadoo'n, s. a kind of French dance
Rig'ging, s. the tackling, &c. of a ship
Rig'gish, a. wanton, lewd, whorish
Right, a. fit, suitable ; straight ; true
Right, ad. properly, justly, in truth, very
Right, s. justice ; just claim ; privilege
Right, v. a. to relieve from wrong
Right'eous, a. just, virtuous, equitable
Right'eousness, s. justice, honesty, virtue, piety
Right'ful, a. having a just claim ; honest
Right'ly, ad. honestly, uprightly, exactly
Rig'id, a. stiff ; severe, sharp, cruel
Rigid'ity, s. stiffness, want of easy elegance
Rig'idly, ad. stiffly, unpliantly
Rig'idness, s. severity, inflexibility
Rig'let, s. a flat thin piece of wood commonly used by printers
Rig'our, s. cold ; severity, strictness ; rage
Rig'orous, ad. severely, without mitigation
Rill, Ril'let, s. a small brook or stream
Rim, s. a border, a margin, an edge
Rime, s. a hoar frost ; a hole, a chink
Ri'my, a. steamy, foggy, full of frozen mist
Rind, s. bark, husk—v. n. to husk, to bark
Rin'dle, s. a small watercourse or gutter
Ring, s. a circle ; a sound, as of a bell
Ring, v. a. to strike bells, &c.; to fit with rings

Ring'dove, s. a kind of pigeon
Ring'er, s. one who rings
Ring'leader, s. the head of a mob or riot
Ring'let, s. a small ring ; a circle ; a curl
Ring'streaked, a. circularly streaked
Ring'tail, s. a kind of kite with a whitish tail
Ring'worm, s. a circular tetter ; a disease
Rinse, v. a. to cleanse by washing, &c.
Ri'ot, s. an uproar, sedition, tumult
Ri'ot, v. n. to revel, to raise an uproar
Ri'oter, s. one who raises an uproar
Ri'otous, a. licentious, festive, turbulent
Rip, v. a. to tear, to lacerate ; to disclose
Ripe, a. complete, mature, finished
Ripe, Ri'pen, v. n. to grow ripe ; be matured
Ri'peness, s. maturity, perfection, fitness
Rip'ple, v. n. to lave or wash lightly over
Rise, v. n. to get up, ascend ; grow ; increase
Rise, s. a beginning ; ascent ; increase
Risibil'ity, s. the quality of laughing
Ris'ible, a. exciting laughter ; ridiculous
Risk, s. hazard, danger, chance of harm
Risk, v. a. to hazard, to put to chance
Rite, s. a solemn act of religion
Rit'ual, s. a book of religious ceremonies
Rit'ual, a. solemnly ceremonious
Ri'val, s. a competitor, opponent
Ri'val, v. a. to emulate ; to oppose
Ri'valry, s. competition, emulation
Rive, v. to split, to cleave, to be divided
Riv'el, v. a. to contract into wrinkles
Riv'er, s. a land current of water bigger than
Riv'erdragon, s. a crocodile   [a brook
Riv'ergod, s. the tutelar deity of a river
Riv'erhorse, s. the hippopotamus
Riv'et, s. a fastening pin clenched at both ends
Riv'et, v. a. to fasten strongly with rivets
Riv'ulet, s. a small river, a brook
Rixdol'lar, s. a German coin, value 4s. 6d.
Roach, s. the name of a fish
Road, s. a large way for travelling ; path
Roam, v. to wander, ramble, rove
Roan, a. bay, sorrel, or black spotted
Roar, v. n. to make a loud noise
Roar, s. the cry of a wild beast, &c.
Roast, v. a. to dress meat ; to banter
Roast, s. any thing roasted
Rob, v. a. to steal, to plunder, deprive unlaw-
Rob'ber, s. a thief, a plunderer   [fully
Rob'bery, s. theft by force or with privity
Robe, s. a dress of dignity
Robe, v. a. to dress pompously ; to invest
Robust', a. strong, sinewy, vigorous, violent
Roc'ambole, s. a kind of wild garlic
Rocheal'um, s. a pure sort of alum
Roch'et, s. a surplice ; a fish
Rock, s. a vast mass of stone ; a defence
Rock, v. to shake ; to move a cradle
Rock'et, s. an artificial firework ; a plant
Rockru'by, s. a sort of garnet
Rock'salt, s. a mineral salt
Rock'work, s. a building imitating rocks
Rock'y, a. full of rocks ; hard, stony
Rod, s. a twig, instrument of correction
Rode, pret. of to ride
Rodomonta'de, s. an empty noisy bluster
Roe, s. the female of the hart ; eggs of fish
Roga'tion, s. the litany ; supplication
Roga'tion-week, s. the week preceding
    Whitsunday
Rogue, s. a vagrant, a knave, a wag

Ro'guery, s. knavish tricks, waggery
Ro'guish, a. fraudulent, knavish, waggish
Roist, v. n. to act at discretion ; to bluster
Roll, v. to move in a circle ; to enwrap
Roll, s. the act of rolling ; a mass made round ;
    a register ; a catalogue ; a warrant
Roll'er, s. any thing turning on its own axis ;
    a bandage ; a fillet
Roll'ingpin, s. a round, smooth, tapered piece
    of wood to mould paste, &c.
Roll'ingpress, s. a press for printing from
    copper-plates, &c.
Rom'age, s. a tumult, a bustle
Roman'ce, s. a fable, a fiction, a lie
Roman'cer, s. a forger of tales, a liar
Ro'manist, s. one who professes popery
Ro'manize, v. a. to latinize. to write latin
Roman'tic, a. wild, improbable, fanciful
Ro'mish, a. Popish, belonging to Rome
Romp, s. a rude untaught girl ; rude play
Romp, v. n. to play rudely and noisily
Rom'ping, s. rude noisy play
Rondeau', s. a fable of ancient poetry ; a
    name applied to all songs and tunes which
    end with the first part or strain repeated
Ron'ion, s. a fat bulky woman
Ront, s. an animal stinted in growth
Rood, s. the fourth part of an acre, a pole,
    an old name for a holy cross
Roof, s. the cover of a house ; the inside of
    the arch that covers a building ; the palate
    or upper part of the mouth
Roof, v. a. to cover with a roof
Rook, s. a bird ; a cheat ; a piece at chess
Rook, v. n. to rob, to cheat, to deceive
Rook'ery, s. a nursery of rooks
Room, s. space, extent ; stead ; chamber
Room'age, s. space, place
Room'y, a. spacious, wide, large
Roost, s. that on which a bird sits to sleep
Roost, v. n. to sleep as a bird ; to lodge
Root, s. that part of the plant which rests in
    the ground, and supplies the stems with
    nourishment ; the first cause ; bottom
Root, v. to take root ; radicate ; destroy
Root'ed, a. fixed, deep, radical
Root'edly, ad. deeply, strongly
Rope, s. a thick hempen cord, string, halter
Rope, v. n. to concrete into filaments
Ro'pedancer, s. one who dances on ropes
Ro'pemaker, s. one who makes ropes
Ro'pewalk, s. a place where ropes are made
Ro'piness, s. viscosity, glutinousness
Ro'py, a. viscous, glutinous, tenacious
Roq'uelaure, Roq'uelo, s. a man's cloak
Ro'sary, s. a set of beads on which Romanists
    number their prayers
Ros'cid, a. abounding with dew
Rose, s. a fragrant flower
Ro'seate, a. rosy, blooming, fragrant
Ro'semary, s. a plant
Ro'set, s. a red colour used by painters
Ro'sewater, s. water distilled from roses
Ros'in, s. inspissated turpentine
Ros'trum, s. the beak of a bird ; a pulpit
Ro'sy, a. like a rose in bloom, fragrant, &c.
Rot, v. to putrefy, to make putrid
Rot, s. a distemper in sheep ; putrefaction
Ro'tary, Rota'tory, a. whirling as a wheel
Ro'tated, a. whirled round
Rota'tion, s. a turning round   succession

Rote, s. words uttered by mere memory; a harp, lyre—v. a. to fix in the memory
Rot'ten, a. putrid, not firm, not sound
Rotun'd, a. round, circular, spherical
Rotun'dity, s. roundness, circularity
Rotund'o, Rotond'o, s. a round building
Rove, v. to ramble, to range, to wander
Ro'ver, s. a wanderer, pirate; fickle person
Rouge, s. a red paint
Rough, a. not smooth, harsh, severe, stormy
Rough'cast, s. a form in its first rudiments
Rough'draw, v. a. to draw or trace coarsely
Rough'en, v. to make or grow rough
Rough'ly, ad. rudely, severely, boisterously
Rough'ness, s. unevenness, harshness
Roun'ceval, s. a kind of pea
Round, a. circular; plain; smooth; brisk
Round, s. a circle, sphere, district; rundle
Roun'dabout, a. ample; indirect; loose
Roun'delay, s. a kind of ancient poetry
Roun'dhouse, s. the constable's prison
Roun'dly, ad. in a round form, plainly
Rouse, v. to wake from slumber; excite
Rout, s. a multitude, a rabble; tumultuous crowd; the confusion of an army defeated
Rout, v. to defeat, assemble in crowds
Route, s. a road, way; march, journey
Row, s. a range of men or things
Row, v. to impel a vessel in the water with oars
Row'el, s. the point of a spur; an issue
Row'er, s. one who manages an oar
Roy'al, a. kingly, becoming a king, regal
Roy'alist, s. an adherent to a king
Roy'ally, ad. in a kingly manner, regally
Roy'alty, s. the office or state of a king
Rub, v. to scour, polish; fret; get through
Rub, s. friction; hinderance; difficulty
Rub'ber, s. one that rubs; a coarse file; two games out of three; a whetstone
Rub'bish, s. ruins of buildings; refuse
Ru'bify, v. a. to make red
Ru'bric, s. directions printed in prayer books and books of law
Ru'by, s. a precious red stone; a blotch
Ructa'tion, s. breaking wind upwards
Rud'der, s. the part that steers a ship
Rud'diness, s. approaching to redness
Rud'dy, a. approaching to red, yellow
Rude, a. rough, harsh; ignorant, artless
Ru'dely, ad. in a rough manner, violently
Ru'deness, s. incivility, boisterousness
Ru'diment, s. the first elements of a science; the first part of education
Rudimen'tal, a. relating to first principles
Rue, v. a. to grieve for, lament—s. an herb
Rue'ful, a. mournful, woful, sorrowful
Rue'fulness, s. sorrowfulness, mournfulness
Ruell'e, s. an assembly at a private house; a circle; a street
Ruff, s. a puckered linen ornament; a fish
Ruff, v. a. to trump at cards
Ruf'fian, a. brutal, savage, boisterous
Ruf'fian, s. a brutal fellow, a robber
Ruf'fle, v. to disorder, to fret; to plait
Ruf'fle, s. an ornament for the wrists
Rug, s. a coarse, nappy, woollen cloth
Rug'ged, a. rough; brutal; surly; shaggy

Rug'gedly, ad. in a rugged manner
Rug'gedness, s. roughness; asperity
Ru'gine, s. a surgeon's rasp
Rugo'se, a. full of wrinkles
Ru'in, s. fall, destruction, overthrow
Ru'in, v. to subvert, destroy, impoverish
Ru'inate, v. a. to bring to poverty, &c.
Ruina'tion, s. subversion; demolition
Ru'inous, a. fallen to ruin; mischievous
Ru'inously, ad. with ruin, destructively
Rule, s. government; sway; regularity
Rule, v. to govern, to control, to settle
Ru'ler, s. a governor; an instrument by the direction of which lines are drawn
Rum, s. a spirit drawn from sugar
Rum'ble, v. n. to make a hoarse low noise
Ru'minant, a. chewing the cud
Ru'minate, v. to chew the cud; to muse
Rumina'tion, s. a chewing the cud; meditation, reflection
Rum'mage, v. to search places, to plunder
Rum'mer, s. a large glass, a drinking cup
Ru'mour, s. flying or popular report
Ru'mour, v. a. to report abroad; to bruit
Rump, s. the buttock, end of the back bone
Rum'ple, s. a rough plait; a wrinkle
Run, v. to move swiftly, flee, go away, vanish; melt; smuggle
Run, s. cadence; course, continued success
Run'agate, s. a fugitive, a coward
Ruu'ciate, a. shaped like a saw, with teeth on each side
Run'dle, s. the step of a ladder; a round
Run'dlet, or Run'let, s. a small barrel
Rung, pret. and part. of to ring
Run'nel, s. a rivulet, a small brook
Run'ner, s. one who runs; a shoot
Run'nion, s. a paltry, scurvy wretch
Runt, s. a dwarf animal; a small cow
Rupee', s. an Indian coin, value about 2s. 3d.
Rup'tion, s. breach, solution of continuity
Rup'ture, s. a breach of peace; eruption
Ru'ral, a. belonging to the country
Rush, s. a plant; a worthless thing
Rush, v. n. to enter or move with violence
Rush'light, s. a candle with a rush wick
Rusk, s. a kind of biscuit or hard bread
Rus'set, a. reddishly brown; coarse; rustic —s. a country dress
Rus'seting, s. a rough kind of apple
Rust, s. a red rust grown upon iron, &c.
Rus'tic, a. rural, rude, simple, plain
Rus'tical, a. rough, savage, brutal, rude
Rus'ticate, v. to banish into the country
Rustic'ity, s. rural appearance, simplicity
Rus'tily, ad. in a rusty manner; shabbily
Rus'tle, v. n. to make a low rattling noise
Rus'ty, a. covered with rust, impaired
Rut, s. the track of a cart wheel, &c.; the copulation of deer, wild boars, &c.
Ruth, s. mercy, pity, tenderness
Ruth'ful, a. rueful, woful, compassionate
Ruth'less, a. cruel, pitiless, barbarous
Rut'tish, a. wanton, libidinous, lustful
Ry'al, s. a Spanish coin worth sixpence three farthings
Rye, s. a coarse kind of bread corn
Rye'grass, s. a kind of strong grass

S.

S, s. the 18th letter of the alphabet
Saba'oth, s. hosts or armies
Sab'bath, s. the day of rest and worship
Sabbat'ical, a. resembling the Sabbath
Sa'ble, s. a dark fur—a. black, dark
Sa'bre, s. a cimeter, short broadsword
Sabulos'ity, s. grittiness, sandiness
Sab'ulous, a. gritty, sandy, gravelly
Sac'charine, a. having the taste, &c. of sugar
Sacerdo'tal, a. belonging to the priesthood
Sa'chel, s. a small leathern bag [tribe
Sa'chem, s. a prince, the chief of an Indian
Sack, v. a. to take by storm; pillage, plunder; to put in bags
Sack, s. a bag containing 3 bushels; woman's loose robe; plunder; pillage; Canary wine
Sack'but, s. a kind of pipe
Sack'cloth, s. a cloth for sacks
Sackpos'set, s. a posset made of milk, &c.
Sac'rament, s. an oath, the Lord's supper
Sacramen'tal, a. constituting a sacrament
Sa'cred, a. holy, consecrated, inviolable
Sa'credness, s. holiness, sanctity
Sac'rifice, v. a. to offer up; destroy, devote
Sac'rifice, s. an offering made to God; any thing destroyed or finally quitted
Sacrific'ial, a. pertaining to sacrifice
Sac'rilege, s. the robbery of a church
Sacrile'gious, a. violating things sacred
Sacrile'giously, ad. with sacrilege
Sa'cring-bell, s. a bell rung before the host
Sa'crist, Sac'ristan, s. a sexton; a vestry-keeper; a church-officer
Sac'risty, s. the vestry of a church
Sad, a. sorrowful, heavy, gloomy; bad
Sad'den, v. a. to make sad and gloomy
Sad'dle, s. a seat to put on a horse's back
Sad'dle, v. a. to put on a saddle; to load
Sad'dler, s. one who makes saddles
Sad'ly, ad. sorrowfully, miserably
Sad'ness, s. mournfulness, melancholy
Safe, a. free from danger—s. a buttery
Safecon'duct, s. a convoy, passport, guard
Sa'feguard, s. a defence, convoy, passport
Sa'fely, ad. without danger, without hurt
Sa'fety, s. freedom from danger, custody
Saf'fron, s. a plant—a. yellow
Sag, v. to hang heavy; to load, to burthen
Saga'cious, a. quick of thought or scent
Sagac'ity, s. acuteness, keenness
Sage, s. a plant; a man of wisdom—a. wise
Sa'gely, ad. wisely, prudently
Sag'ittary, s. a centaur
Sa'go, s. a nourishing sort of grain, a drug
Sail, s. a canvas sheet; ship; wing
Sail, v. to move with sails; pass by sea
Sai'lor, s. a seaman, one used to the sea
Sail'yard, s. a pole to extend a sail with
Saim, s. hog's lard, the fat or grease of swine
Sain'foin, s. a sort of herb, trefoil
Saint, s. a person eminent for piety, &c.
Saint, v. to canonize; to appear very pious
Saint'ed, a. holy, pious; canonized
Saint'ly, Saint'like, a. holy, devout
Sake, s. final cause; purpose; account

Sa'ker, s. a kind of cannon; a hawk
Sala'cious, a. lustful, lecherous, wanton
Sala'city, s. lechery, wantonness
Sal'ad, s. food composed of raw herbs
Sal'amander, s. an animal like a lizard
Sal'ary, s. annual or periodical payment
Sale, s. the act of selling, vent, market
Sa'leable, a. fit for sale, marketable
Sa'lesman, s. one who sells made clothes
Sa'lework, s. work for sale; careless work
Sal'ient, a. leaping; panting; springing
Sal'ine, Sali'nous, a. consisting of salt, brinish
Sal'iva, s. spittle separated by the glands
Sal'ivate, v. a. to cause a spitting, &c.
Saliva'tion, s. a curing by spitting
Sal'low, a. sickly; yellow—s. a willow
Sal'ly, s. a frolic; flight; an eruption
Sal'ly, v. n. to make an eruption; issue out
Sal'lyport, s. a port to make sallies from
Salmagun'di, s. a mixture of chopped meat, pickled herrings, oil, onions, vinegar, &c.
Sal'mon, s. a delicious well-known fish
Salmontrou't, s. a trout of the salmon kind
Saloo'n, s. an elegant, lofty h
Salt, s. a well-known seasoning
Salt, a. having the taste of salt
Sal'tant, a. jumping, dancing
Salt'cellar, s. a sort of cup to hold salt
Salt'er, s. one who salts or sells salt
Salt'ern, s. a place where salt is made
Salt'ish, a. somewhat salt, brinish
Saltpe'tre, s. a mineral salt, nitre
Salvabil'ity, s. possibility to be saved
Sal'vable, a. possible to be saved
Sal'vage, s. a reward allowed for saving goods out of a wreck—a. wild; cruel
Salva'tion, s. reception into the happiness of heaven, preservation from eternal death
Sal'vatory, s. a place where any thing is preserved, a repository
Salu'brious, a. wholesome, promoting health
Salu'brity, s. wholesomeness, healthfulness
Salve, s. an emplaster; remedy, cure
Sal'ver, s. a piece of plate with a foot
Sal'vo, s. an exception; reservation; excuse
Sal'utary, a. wholesome, healthful; safe
Saluta'tion, s. act of saluting, greeting
Salu'te, v. a. to greet, to hail, to kiss
Salu'te, s. a salutation, greeting; a kiss
Salutif'erous, a. bringing health, healthy
Same, a. identical, of the like kind, &c.
Sa'meness, s. identity, not different
Sam'let, s. a little salmon
Sam'phire, s. a plant preserved in pickle
Sam'ple, s. a specimen; part of a whole
Sam'pler, s. a piece of girl's needle work
San'able, a. remediable, curable
San'ative, a. of a healing quality, &c.
Sanctifica'tion, s. the act of making holy
Sanc'tify, v. a. to make holy or virtuous
Sanctimo'nious, a. saintly, appearing holy
Sanc'timony, s. holiness, devoutness
Sanc'tion, s. ratification, confirmation
Sanc'titude, Sanc'tity, s. holiness, goodness
Sanc'tuary, s. a holy place, an asylum

Sand, s. gravelly earth ; barren land

San'dal, s. a sort of slipper or loose shoe

San'ders, s. a precious kind of Indian wood

Sand'stone, s. a stone easily crumbled

San'dy, a. full of sand, gritty ; unsolid

Sane, a. sound in mind ; healthy

Sanguif'erous, a. conveying blood

Sanguifica'tion, s. production of blood ; conversion of the chyle into blood

San'guifier, s. a producer of blood

Sanguif'luous, a. flowing with blood

San'guinary, a. bloody, cruel, murderous

San'guine, a. blood red ; warm, ardent

Sanguin'eous, a. full of blood

Sanguin'ity, s. ardour, heat, confidence

San'hedrim, s. the chief council among the Jews, consisting of 70 elders

Sa'nies, s. a watery matter, serous excretion

Sa'nious, a. running with thin matter

San'ity, s. soundness of mind

Sank, pret. of to sink

Sap, s. the vital juice of plants

Sap, v. to undermine, subvert, destroy

Sap'id, a. tasteful, palatable, savoury

Sa'pience, s. wisdom, knowledge, sageness

Sa'pient, a. wise, sage, prudent

Sap'less, a. wanting sap ; dry ; old ; husky

Sap'ling, s. a young tree, a young plan.

Sapona'ceous, Sap'onary, a. soapy, like soap

Sa'por, s. taste ; a stimulating quality

Sapph'ire, s. a precious blue stone

Sapph'irine, a. made of, or like sapphire

Sap'piness, s. succulence ; simpleness

Sap'py, a. juicy, succulent ; young, not firm

Sar'aband, s. a Spanish dance

Sar'casm, s. a keen reproach, taunt, gibe

Sarcas'tic, Sarcas'tical, a. keen, taunting

Sarcas'tically, ad. tauntingly, severely

Sar'cenet, s. a fine thin woven silk

Sar'cle, v. a. to weed corn

Sarcoph'agous, a. eating or feeding on flesh

Sarcoph'agus, s. a tomb

Sarcot'ic, s. a medicine producing new flesh

Sar'dine, Sar'donyx, s. a precious stone

Sarsaparil'la, s. the name of a plant

Sarse, s. a sort of fine lawn sieve

Sash, s. a silk belt ; a window that lets up and down by pulleys

Sashoo'n, s. a leather stuffing in a boot

Sas'safras, s. a tree used in physic

Sat, pret. of to sit

Sa'tan, s. the prince of hell, the devil

Satan'ic, Satan'ical, a. devilish, infernal

Sat'chel, s. a small bag used by schoolboys

Sate, Sa'tiate, v. a. to glut, to satisfy, to pall

Sat'ellite, s. a small or secondary planet revolving round a larger

Satelli'tious, a. consisting of satellites

Sa'tiate, a. glutted, full of satiety

Sati'ety, s. the state of being filled, fulness

Sat'in, s. a soft, close, and shining silk

Sa'tire, s. a poem censuring vice, folly, &c.

Satir'ic, Satir'ical, a. belonging to satire

Satir'ically, ad. with a design to vilify

Sat'irist, s. one who writes satires

Sat'irize, v. a. to censure as in a satire

Satisfac'tion, s. the state of being pleased or satisfied ; atonement, amends

Satisfac'tive, a. giving satisfaction

Satisfac'torily, ad. to give satisfaction

Satisfac'tory, a. giving satisfaction

Satisfac'toriness, s. power of giving content

Sat'isfy, v. to content, please ; convince

Sat'urant, a. impregnating to the fill

Sat'urate, v. a. to impregnate till no more can be received or imbibed

Sat'urday, s. the last day in the week

Satu'rity, s. fulness, repletion

Sa'turn, s. a planet ; in chymistry, lead

Saturn'ian, a. happy ; golden

Sat'urnine, a. gloomy, grave ; severe

Sa'tyr, s. a sylvan god ; a lustful man

Sav'age, a. wild, cruel, uncivilized, brutal

Sav'age, s. a barbarian, a man uncivilized

Sav'agely, ad. barbarously, cruelly

Sav'ageness, s. barbarousness, cruelty

Savan'na, s. an open meadow without wood

Sauce, s. something to give relish to food

Sauce'box, s. a petulant fellow

Sauce'pan, s. a pan to make sauce, &c. in

Sau'cer, s. a small plate for a teacup, &c.

Sau'cily, ad. impudently, petulantly

Sau'ciness, s. impudence, impertinence

Sau'cy, a. pert, petulant, impudent

Save, v. to preserve from danger or ruin ; to keep frugally—ad. except

Sa'veall, s. a pan to save candle ends on

Sa'ving, a. frugal—ad. excepting

Sa'vingly, ad. with parsimony

Sa'vingness, s. parsimony, frugality

Sa'viour, s. the Redeemer ; he who saves

Saun'ter, v. n. to wander about idly, loiter

Sa'vory, s. the name of a plant

Sa'vour, s. a scent, odour, taste

Sa'vour, v. to have a smell or taste ; to like

Sa'vouriness, s. pleasing taste or smell

Sa'voury, a. pleasing to the smell or taste

Savoy', s. a sort of colewort

Sau'sage, s. a composition of meat, spice,&c.

Saw, s. an instrument with teeth, for cutting boards or timber ; a saying, a proverb

Saw, v. a. to cut timber, &c. with a saw

Saw'dust, s. a dust arising from sawing

Saw'pit, s. a pit where wood is sawed

Saw'yer, s. one who saws timber

Sax'ifrage, s. a plant good against the stone

Saxif'ragous, a. dissolvent of the stone

Say, v. to speak, utter, allege, tell

Say'ing, s. an expression ; an opinion

Scab, s. an incrustation over a sore

Scab'bard, s. the sheath of a sword

Scab'biness, s. the state of being scabby

Scab'by, a. diseased with scabs

Sca'brous, a. rough, rugged, harsh

Scaf'fold, s. a temporary gallery ; the gallery raised for the execution of malefactors ; a kind of stage erected on certain occasions

Scaf'folding, s. a support for workmen

Scala'de, Scala'do, s. storming a place by raising ladders against the walls

Scald, s. a burn with liquids ; scurf on the head

Scald, v. a. to burn with hot liquor

Scale, s. a balance ; part of the covering of a fish ; a ladder ; means of ascent ; line of distances ; the gamut

Scale, v. a. to mount ; scrape off scales

Sca'led, a. having scales like a fish; squamous

Sca'liness, s. the state of being scaly

Scall, s. a leprosy ; morbid baldness

Scal'lion, s. a kind of onion

Scal'lop, s. a shellfish ; an indentation

Scal'lop, v. a. to indent the edge, &c.

Scalp, *s.* the skull; integuments of the head
—*v.* to cut the flesh off the skull
Sea'ly, *a.* covered with scales
Scam'ble, *v.* to scramble; shift awkwardly
Scam'mony, *s.* a concreted resinous juice
Scam'per, *v. n.* to run with fear and speed
Scan, *v. a.* to examine nicely; to canvas
Scan'dal, *s.* a reproachful assertion, infamy
Scan'dalize, *v. a.* to offend by some action; to disgrace, reproach, defame
Scan'dalous, *a.* opprobrious, shameful, vile
Scan dalously, *ad.* shamefully, censoriously
Scan'dalousness, *s.* public shamefulness
Scan'dent, *a.* climbing, creeping
Scan'ning, *s.* in poetry, the measuring of a verse, to ascertain its number of feet
Scant, *a.* parsimonious; scarce, not enough
Scan'tily, *ad.* narrowly, sparingly
Scan'tiness, *s.* want of space, compass, &c.
Scan'tlet, *s.* a small quantity or piece
Scan'tling, *s.* timber cut to a small size
Scan'ty, *a.* narrow, small; poor, niggardly
Scape, *v.* to escape—*s.* a flight, evasion
Scap'ular, *a.* relating to the shoulders
Scar, *s.* the mark of a cut; a cicatrix
Scar'amouch, *s.* a buffoon in motley dress
Scarce, *a.* not plentiful, rare, uncommon
Scarce, Sca'rcely, *ad.* hardly, scantily
Sca'rceness, Sca'rcity, *s.* want of plenty
Scare, *v. a.* to frighten, affright, terrify
Sca'recrow, *s.* an image set to frighten birds
Scarf, *s.* a loose covering for the shoulders
Scarf'skin, *s.* the outer skin of the body
Scarifica'tion, *s.* an incision of the skin
Scar'ify, *v. a.* to lance or cut the skin
Scar'iose, *a.* dry and sonorous to the touch
Scar'let, *s.* a deep red colour
Scar'let, *a.* of the colour of scarlet
Scarlethe'an, *s.* a garden plant
Scarp, *s.* the slope on that side of a ditch which is next to a fortified place
Scate, *s.* an iron to slide with; a flat fish
Scath, *v. a.* to waste, damage, destroy
Scath'ful, *a.* mischievous, destructive
Scat'ter, *v.* to spread thinly, to disperse
Scav'enger, *s.* a cleaner of the streets
Scel'erat, *s.* a villain, a wicked wretch
Scene, *s.* a part of a play; an appearance
Sce'nery, *s.* imagery; representation
Scen'ic, *a.* dramatic, theatrical
Sceneog'raphy, *s.* the art of perspective
Scent, *s.* smell, odour, chase by smell
Scep'tic, *s.* one who doubts of all things
Scep'tical, *a.* doubting every thing
Scep'ticism, *s.* universal doubt
Scep'tre, *s.* the ensign of royalty borne in
Scep'tred, *a.* bearing a sceptre [the hand
Sched'ule, *s.* a small scroll; an inventory
Scheme, *s.* a plan, project, design
Sche'mer, *s.* a projector, a contriver
Schirros'ity, *s.* an induration of the glands
Schirr'ous, *a.* having an indurated gland
Schism, *s.* a division in the church
Schis'matic, *s.* one guilty of schism
Schismat'ical, *a.* implying schism
Schismat'ically, *ad.* in a schismatical manner
Schol'ar, *s.* a disciple, a man of learning
Schol'arship, *s.* learning, literature
Scholas'tic, *a.* pertaining to the schools
Scholas'tically, *ad.* according to the schools
Scho'liast, *s.* a writer of explanatory notes

Scho'lium, *s.* an explanatory note
Scho'ly, *v. n.* to write expositions
School, *s.* a place for education
School'fellow, *s.* a fellow student
School'man, *s.* one skilled in the niceties of academical disputation, and in divinity
School'master, *s.* he who teaches in a school
School'mistress, *s.* she who keeps a school
Sciag'raphy, *s.* the section of a building to show the inside thereof; the art of dialling
Sciather'ic, *a.* belonging to a sun-dial
Sciat'ical, *a.* troubled with the hip-gout [art
Sci'ence, *s.* knowledge, deep learning, skill,
Sciences, *s. pl.* grammar, logic, arithmetic, rhetoric, geometry, astronomy, and music
Scien'tial, *a.* of, or pertaining to, science
Scientif'ic, *a.* what promotes knowledge, &c.
Scim'itar, *s.* a sword with a convex edge
Scin'tillate, *v. n.* to sparkle, to emit sparks
Scintilla'tion, *s.* the act of sparkling
Sci'olist, *s.* one of superficial knowledge
Sci'olous, *a.* knowing superficially
Sciom'achy, *s.* battle with a shadow
Sci'on, *s.* a small twig or shoot; a graft
Scis'sars, *s.* a small pair of shears
Scis'sible, Scis'sile, *a.* that may be divided
Scis'sion, *s.* the act of cutting
Scis'sure, *s.* a crack, rent; fissure; chap
Sclerot'ic, *a.* hard; rough
Scoat, *v. n.* to stop the wheel of a carriage
Scoff, *v. n.* to deride or mock, to ridicule
Scoff'ingly, *ad.* in contempt, in ridicule
Scold, *v. n.* to chide; quarrel clamorously
Scol'lop, *s.* a fish; an indenting
Sconce, *s.* a branched candlestick; a small fort; a bulwark; the head
Sconce, *v. a.* to mulct, to fine
Scoop, *s.* a large ladle; a sweep
Scoop, *v. a.* to lade out; to cut hollow
Scope, *s.* intention; drift, aim; space
Scorbu'tic, *a.* diseased with the scurvy
Scorch, *v.* to burn, to be dried up
Score, *s.* a long incision; line drawn; account; motive; the number twenty
Sco'rious, *a.* drossy, foul, worthless
Scorn, *s.* contempt—*v.* to scoff, to despise
Scorn'ful, *a.* contemptuous, insolent, proud
Scorn'fully, *ad.* contemptuously, insolently
Scor'pion, *s.* a reptile with a very venomous sting, a sign of the zodiac
Scot, *s.* a Scotchman; shot; payment
Scotch, *v. a.* to cut slightly
Scotch, Scot'tish, *a.* relating to Scotland
Scot'free, *a.* excused from paying his scot
Scot'omy, *s.* a dizziness in the head
Scot'ticism, *s.* a Scotch mode of speech
Sco'vel, *s.* a mop for sweeping an oven
Scoun'drel, *s.* a mean rascal, a villain
Scour, *v.* to cleanse, scamper; purge
Scour'er, *s.* one who scours; a purger
Scourge, *s.* a whip, a lash; punishment
Scourge, *v. a.* to whip, punish, chastise
Scout, *s.* one who is sent privily to observe the motions of an enemy
Scout, *v. n.* to go out privately to observe
Scowl, *v. n.* to frown, to look angry or sullen
Scrag, *s.* any thing lean or thin; the neck
Scrag'gy, *a.* lean, thin, rough, rugged
Scram'ble, *v. n.* to catch at eagerly; to climb
Scram'ble, *s.* eager contest for any thing
Scranch, *v. a.* to grind between the teeth

Scran'nel, *a.* vile, worthless, grating
Scrap, *s.* a small particle, fragment, bit
Scrape, *v. a.* to pare lightly; erase; shave
Scrape, *s.* difficulty, perplexity, distress
Scra'per, *s.* an iron utensil; a vile fiddler
Scratch, *v. a.* to tear with the nails; to wound slightly; to draw awkwardly
Scrat'ches. *s.* a disease in horses
Scraw, *s.* the surface or scurf
Scrawl, *v. a.* to draw or write badly
Screak, *v. n.* to make a loud, shrill noise
Scream, *v. n.* to cry out as in terror, &c.
Screech, *v. n.* to shriek, to cry as an owl
Screech'owl, *s.* an owl that hoots by night
Screen, *v. a.* to shelter, conceal; sift, riddle
Screw, *s.* one of the mechanical powers
Scrib'ble, *s.* very careless bad writing
Scrib'bler, *s.* a petty author, a bad writer
Scribe, *s.* a writer; secretary; public notary
Scrine, *s.* a repository for writings
Scrip, *s.* a small bag; schedule; small writing
Scrip'tory, *a.* written; not delivered orally
Scrip'tural, *a.* contained in the Bible, holy
Scrip'ture, *s.* the Bible, the sacred writings
Scriv'ener, *s.* one who draws contracts, &c.
Scrof'ula. *s.* the disease called the king's-evil
Scrof'ulous, *a.* troubled with sores, ulcers, &c
Scroll, *s.* a writing rolled up
Scro'tum, *s.* the membrane which contains the seminal organs
Scrub, *s.* a mean fellow—*v. a.* to rub hard
Scrub'bed, Scrub'by, *a.* mean, vile, sorry
Scru'ple, *s.* a doubt, a weight of 20 grains
Scru'ple, *v. n.* to doubt, to hesitate, question
Scrupulos'ity, *s.* tenderness of conscience
Scru'pulous, *a.* nicely doubtful; vigilant
Scru'pulousness, *s.* state of being scrupulous
Scru'pulously, *ad.* carefully, nicely, anxiously
Scru'table, *a.* that may be searched
Scrutinee'r, *s.* an examiner, an inquirer'
Scru'tinize, *v. a.* to examine thoroughly
Scru'tinous, *a.* captious; full of inquiries
Scru'tiny, *s.* a strict search; careful inquiry
Scruto'ire, *s.* a case of drawers for writings
Scud, *v. n.* to sail before a hard gale, &c.
Scuf'fle, *s.* confused quarrel or broil
Scuf'fle, *v. n.* to fight confusedly
Sculk, *v. n.* to lurk secretly; to lie close
Scull, *s.* the brain pan; a small oar
Scul'ler, *s.* a small boat with one rower
Scul'lery, *s.* a place to clean and keep dishes
Scul'lion, *s.* a kitchen drudge
Sculp, *v.* to carve, to engrave—*s.* a cut, a print
Sculp'tile, *a.* made by carving or engraving
Sculp'tor, *s.* a carver or engraver
Sculp'ture, *s.* art of carving, carved work
Scum, *s.* what rises to the top of any liquor
Scum, *v. a.* to clear off the scum; to skim
Scurf, *s.* a dry scab; scale; adherent stain
Scur'finess, *s.* the state of being scurfy
Scurf'fy, *a.* full of or having scurf or scabs
Scurril'ity, *s.* grossness of reproach, opprobrious language, lewdness of jocularity
Scur'rilousness, *s.* baseness of manners
Scur'vily, *ad.* vilely, basely, coarsely
Scur'viness, *s.* meanness, sorriness, baseness
Scur'vy, *s.* a disease—*a.* scabbed, vile
Scur'vygrass, *s.* a plant; spoonwort
Scut, *s.* the tail of a hare or rabbit, &c.
Scut'tle, *s.* a wide shallow basket for coals; a small grate; a quick pace

Scut'cheon, *s.* the field or ground on which a coat of arms is painted; a piece of brass placed before a lock
Scythe, *s.* an instrument for mowing grass, &c
Sea, *s.* the ocean, a large lake
Sea'beat, *a.* dashed by the waves of the sea
Sea'born, *a.* produced by the sea
Sea'boy, *s.* a boy employed on shipboard
Sea'beach, *s.* the sea shore
Sea'calf, *s.* the seal, a sea animal
Sea'chart, *s.* a map of the sea coast
Sea'coal, *s.* pit-coal brought by sea
Sea'compass, *s.* the mariner's compass
Sea'faring, *a.* employed or living at sea
Sea'girt, *a.* encircled by the sea
Sea'gull, *s.* a waterfowl
Seal, *s.* the seacalf; a stamp; a confirmation
Seal, *v.* to fasten with a seal, ratify, close
Seal'ing-wax, *s.* wax used to seal letters, &c.
Seam, *s.* what joins two pieces together; a measure of eight bushels; a scar; tallow
Seam, *v. a.* to join together; mark, scar
Sea'maid, *s.* the mermaid
Sea'man, *s.* a sailor, mariner, merman
Sea'mew, *s.* a fowl that frequents the sea
Seam'less, *a.* having no seam
Seam'stress, *s.* one who lives by sewing
Seau, or Seine, *s.* a kind of large fishing net
Sea'nymph, *s.* a goddess of the sea
Sea'piece, *s.* representation of anything at sea
Sea'port, *s.* a harbour or port for ships
Sear, *v. a.* to burn—*a.* dry; no longer green
Searce, *v. a.* to sift finely—*s.* a fine sieve
Search, *s.* an inquiry quest, pursuit
Search, *v.* to examine, inquire, to seek
Sear'cloth, *s.* a large strengthening plaster
Sea'shore, *s.* the coast of the sea
Sea'sick, *a.* sick by the motion of the sea
Sea'son, *s.* one of the four parts of the year, spring, summer, autumn, winter; a fit time; a time not very long
Sea'son, *v.* to give a relish to; to mature
Sea'sonable, *a.* opportune, proper as to time
Sea'soning, *s.* that which gives relish to
Seat, *s.* a chair; mansion; situation
Seat, *v. a.* to place on seats; fix; place firm
Sea'ward, *ad.* towards the sea
Se'cant, *a.* dividing into two parts—*s.* a line
Sece'de, *v. a.* to withdraw from; to leave
Seces'sion, *s.* the act of withdrawing from
Seclu'de, *v.* to shut up apart, to exclude
Seclu'sion, *s.* act or state of being shut up
Sec'ond, *a.* next to the first; inferior
Sec'ond, *s.* one who accompanies another in a duel; supporter; 60th part of a minute
Sec'ond, *v. a.* to support; to follow next
Sec'ondarily, *ad.* in the second order or degree; not primarily or originally
Sec'ondary, *a.* not primary—*s.* a deputy
Sec'ondhand, *a.* not original; not primary
Sec'ondly, *ad.* in the second place
Se'crecy, *s.* privacy, solitude, close silence
Se'cret, *a.* concealed, private, unknown
Se'cret, *s.* a thing unknown, privacy
Sec'retaryship, *s.* the office of a secretary
Sec'retary, *s.* one who writes for another
Secre'te, *v. a.* to hide, conceal; separate
Secre'tion, *s.* a separation of animal fluids
Secreti'tious, *a.* parted by animal secretion
Se'cretly, *ad.* privately, in secret
Se'cretness, *s.* quality of keeping a secret

Secre'tory, a. performing the office of secre-
sect, s. men united in certain tenets [tion
Sect'ary, s. a follower of a particular sect
Secta'tor, s. a follower ; an imitator
Sec'tion, s. a distinct part of a writing or
 book ; act of cutting ; the part divided
Sec'tor. s. a geometrical instrument, part
Sec'ular. a. not bound by rules, worldly
Sec'ularize, v. a. to convert to common use
Sec'ularity, s. worldliness, carefulness
Sec'undine, s. the afterbirth
Secu're, a. free from fear or danger, safe
Secu're. v. a. to make certain, protect, insure
Secu'rely, ad. without danger ; care essly
Secu'rity, s. protection, defence, pledge
Sedan', s. a neat close chair for carriage
Seda'te, a. calm, quiet, still, serene
Seda'tely, ad. calmly, without disturbance
Seda'teness, s. calmness, tranquillity
Sed'entary, a. inactive, sitting much
Sedge, s. a growth of narrow flags
Sed'gy. a. overgrown with narrow flags
Sed'iment, s. what settles at the bottom
Sedit'ion, s. a tumu t, an insurrection
Sedit'ious, a. factious, mutinous, tu hulent
Sedit'iously, ad. factiously, mutinously
Sedu'ce, v. a. to tempt, corrupt, mislead
Sedu'cement, s. the act of seducing
Sedu'cible, a. capable of being deceived
Seduc'tion, s. the act or practice of seducing
Seduc'tive, a. apt to mislead or seduce
Sedu'lity, s. assiduity, application, industry
Sed'ulous, a. assiduous, industrious ; painful
Sed'ulously, ad. diligently, industriously
Sed'ulousness, s. assiduity, industry
See, s. the diocese of a bishop
See, v. to perceive by the eye, to descry, to
 behold, to attend ; to converse with
Seed, s. the organised particle produced by
 plants and animals, from which new ones
 are generated ; original ; race
Seed, v. n. to bring forth seed
Seed'cake, s. a kind of sweet seedy cake
Seed'ling, s. a plant just risen from the seed
Seed'p arl, s. small grains of pearl
Seeds'man, s. a sower, he who sells seed
Seed'time, s. the season for sowing
Seed'y, a. abounding with seed
See'ing, s. sight ; vision—ad. since that
Seek, v. to look for ; solicit ; go to find
Seel, v. to close the eyes
Seem, v. n. to appear, to have semblance
Seem'ing, s. appearance, show, opinion
Seem'ingly, ad. in appearance, in semblance
Seem'liness, s. decency, comeliness, beauty
Seem'ly, a. decent, becoming, proper, fit
Seer, s. one who foresees events ; a prophet
See'saw, s. a reciprocating motion
Seeth, v. to boil ; to stew ; decoct in hot liquor
Seg'ment, s. a part of a circle comprehended
 between an arch and a chord thereof
Seg'regate, v. a. to separate, or to set apart
Segrega'tion, s. a separation from others
Seigneu'rial, a. invested with large powers
Seign'ior, s. an Italian title for lord
Seign'iory, s. a lordship ; a jurisdiction
Sei'ner, s. a fisher with nets
Sei'zable, a. liable to be seized
Seize... .. ta take by force; fasten on
Sei'zin, s. the act of taking possession
Sei'zure, s. act of seizing, the thing seized

Sel'dom, ad. rarely, not frequently
Selec't, v. a. to choose in preference to others
Selec't, a. nicely chosen ; culled out
Selec'tion, s. the act of choosing
Selenog'raphy, s. a description of the moon
Self, pron. one's self, the individual
Sel'fish, a. void of regard for others
Self'same, s. numerically the same
Sel'lion, s. a ridge of land between furrows
Sell. v. a. to give for a price, to vend
Sel'lander. s. a scab in a horse's pastern
Sel'ler, v. one who sells, a vender
Sel'vage, s. the edge of cloth, &c.
Selves, s. the plural of self
Sem'blance, s. resemblance, appearance
Sem'ble, v. n. to represent, to make a likeness
Sem'i, a. in composition, signifies half
Semian'nular, a. half round
Sem'ibreve, s. a note in music, relating to time
Sem'icircle, s. half a circle
Semicir'cular, a. half round
Semico'lon, s. a point made thus [;]
Semidiam'eter, s. half a diameter
Semidiaphane'ity, Semidiaph'anous, s. im
 perfect transparency
Semiflu'id, a. imperfectly fluid
Semilu'nar, a. like the form of a half moon
Sem'inal, a. belonging to seed ; radical
Seminal'ity, s. the nature of seed
Sem'inary, s. a seed plot ; original ; school
Semina'tion, s. the act of sowing
Seminif'ic, a. produc ive of seed
Semipa'cous, s. half dark, cloudy, dull
Semior'dinate, s. in conic sections, a line
 drawn at right angles to and bisected by
 the axis, and reaching from one side of
 the section to the other
Semipellu'cid, a. imperfectly clear
Sem'iquaver, s. in music, a note containing
 half the quantity of a quaver
Sem'itone, s. half a tone or note in music
Sem'ivowel, s. a consonant which makes an
 imperfect sound. Semivowels are six in
 number, f, l, m, n, r, s
Sempiter'nal, a. everlasting, perpetual
Sempiter'nity, s. future duration without end
Sen'ary, a. containing the number of six
Sen'ate, s. an assembly of counsellors set
 apart to consult for the public good
Sen'ator, s. a member of the senate
Send. v. a. to despatch ; to commission
Senec'tude, s. old age, ancientness
Senes'cence, s. a growing old ; decay
Sen'eschal, s. a steward ; high bailiff
Se'nile, a. relating to old age
Se'nior, a. one older than another
Senior'ity, s. priority of birth, eldership
Sen'na, s. a physical purge
Sensa'tion, s. perception by the senses
Sense, s. faculty of perceiving ; meaning
Sen'seless, a. wanting sense, stupid, dull
Sensibil'ity, s. quickness of sensation
Sen'sible, a. having quick intellectual feeling;
 convinced, persuaded ; of good sense
Sen'sibly, ad. with sense ; judiciously
Sen'sitive, a. having sense, but not reason
Sen'sual, a. pleasing to the senses ; carnal
Senso'rium, Sen'sory, s. the seat of sense, the
 organ of sensation
Sensual'ity, s. addiction to carnal pleasure
Sen'sualist, s. a person given to sens

Sen'sualize, v. a. to render sensual
Sen'sually, ad. in a sensual manner
Sen'tence, s. a determination; a period
Sen'tence, v. a. to condemn, to judge
Senten'tious, a. short and energetic
Senten'tiously, ad. with striking brevity
Senten'tiousness, s. brevity joined to strength
Sen'tient, a. perceiving—s. one perceiving
Sen'timent, s. thought, notion, opinion
Sentimen'tal, a. reflecting, thoughtful
Sen'tinel, Sen'try, s. a soldier on guard
Sep'arable, a. that may be separated
Sep'arate, v. a. to break, disunite
Sep'arate, a. divided, disunited from
Sep'arately, ad. apart, singly, distinctly
Separa'tion, s. a disjunction, divorce
Se'poy, s. an Indian foot soldier
Sept, s. a clan, race, generation
Septem'ber, s. the ninth month of the year
Sep'tenary, a. consisting of seven
Septen'nial, a. lasting seven years
Septen'trion, s. the north; Charles's-wain
Septen'trional, a. relating to the north
Septen'trionally, ad. towards the north
Septen'trionate, v. n. to tend northerly
Sep'tic, a. tending to produce putrefaction
Septilat'eral, a. having seven sides
Septuagen'ary, a. consisting of seventy
Sep'tuagint, s. the old Greek version of the Old Testament, so called, as being supposed the work of 72 interpreters
Sep'tuple, a. seven times as much
Sepul'chral, a. relating to burial, or the grave
Sep'ulchre, s. a tomb, grave, monument
Sep'ulture, s. interment, burial
Sequa'cious, a. following; attendant; ductile
Sequac'ity, s. ductility; toughness
Se'quel, s. a conclusion; consequence
Se'quence, s. a following order
Se'quent, a. following; consequential
Seques'ter, v. a. to put aside; deprive of
Seques'trable, a. that may be separated
Sequestra'tion, s. deprivation of profits
Sequestra'tor, s. he into whose custody the thing in dispute is committed
Seragl'io, s. the apartments of Mahometan women secluded from the rest
Ser'aph, s. one of the orders of angels
Seraph'ic, a. angelic, angelical, pure
Ser'aphim, s. one of the orders of angels
Sere, Seer, a. withered; no longer green
Serena'de, s. music by lovers in the night
Sere'ne, a. calm, placid, quiet, unruffled
Sere'nely, ad. calmly, quietly, coolly
Sere'neness, Seren'ity, s. calmness, peace
Seren'itude, s. calmness, coolness of mind
Serf, s. a slave employed in husbandry
Serge, s. a kind of thin woollen cloth
Ser'geant, s. a petty officer in the army; a degree in law below a judge
Se'ries, s. sequence, succession, order
Se'rious, a. grave, solemn, weighty, important
Se'riously, ad. gravely, solemnly, in earnest
Se'riousness, s. gravity, solemnity
Ser'mon, s. a pious instructive discourse
Ser'monize, v. n. to preach a sermon
Seros'ity, s. thin watery part of the blood
Se'rous, a. thin, watery, adapted to serum
Ser'pent, s. a snake; a musical instrument
Ser'pentine, a. winding like a serpent
Serpig'inous, a. diseased with a serpigo

Serpi'go, s. a kind of tetter
Ser'rate, Ser'rated, Ser'rulated, a. jagged like a saw
Ser'vant, s. one who serves another
Serve, v. to attend at command, assist, obey
Ser'vice, s. an office; obedience, use, favor
Ser'viceable, a. active, diligent, beneficial
Ser'vile, a. slavish, dependant, cringing
Ser'vilely, ad. meanly, slavishly, pitifully
Servil'ity, Ser'vileness, s. slavishness, baseness
Ser'vingman, s. a menial servant
Ser'vitor, s. the lowest order in a university
Ser'vitude, s. slavery, dependance
Se'rum, s. the watery part of the blood
Sesquial'teral, a. one and a half more
Sess, s. a rate, a tax; cess charged
Ses'sion, s. a sitting of magistrates
Set, v. to place, to fix, to frame, to plant
Set, part. a. regular, in a formal manner
Set, s. a complete suit or assortment
Seta'ceous, a. bristly, set with strong hairs
Se'ton, s. an issue or rowel
Settee', s. a large long seat with a back
Set'ter, s. one who sets; a kind of dog
Set'tle, s. a seat, a bench with a seat
Set'tle, v. to fix, confirm, determine, subside
Set'tled, a. confirmed, determined
Set'tlement, s. act of settling; legal possession; subsidence; a colony; a jointure
Sev'en, a. four and three, one more than six
Sev'enfold, a. repeated seven times
Sev'ennight, or Sen'night, s. a week
Sev'enteen, a. ten and seven
Sev'enthly, ad. in the seventh place
Sev'enty, a. seven times ten
Sev'er, v. to force asunder, divide, disjoin
Sev'eral, a. divers, many, distinct
Sev'erally, ad. distinctly, separately
Seve're, a. sharp, austere, cruel, painful
Seve'rely, ad. painfully, afflictively, horridly
Sever'ity, s. cruel treatment, rigour
Sew, v. a. to join with a needle and thread
Sew'er, s. an officer; passage for water
Sex, s. the distinction of male and female
Sexag'enary, a. aged sixty years
Sexages'ima, s. second Sunday before Lent
Sexages'imal, a. numbered by sixties
Sexan'gular, a. having six angles
Sexen'nial, a. lasting six years
Sex'tant, s. the sixth part of a circle
Sex'tile, s. the distance of 60 degrees
Sex'ton, s. an under officer of the church
Sex'tonship, s. the office of a sexton
Sex'tuple, a. sixfold, six times told
Shab'bily, ad. meanly, reproachfully
Shab'biness, s. meanness, paltriness
Shab'by, a. ragged, mean, slovenly, paltry
Shac'kle, v. a. to chain, to fetter, to limit
Shac'kles, s. fetters, chains, gyves
Shade, s. a shadow; screen, shelter
Shade, v. a. to cover from light or heat
Sha'diness, s. the state of being shady
Shad'ow, s. a shade, faint representation
Shad'ow, v. a. to cloud, darken; represent
Shad'owy, a. full of shade; gloomy
Sha'dy, a. secure from light or heat; cool
Shaft, s. an arrow; narrow deep pit; a spire
Shag, s. rough hair; rough cloth; a bird
Shag'ged, Shag'gy, a. rough, rugged, hairy
Shagreen, s. a fish skin, remarkably rough
Shagree'n, v. a. to provoke, to irritate
Shake, v. to tremble, to totter, to be agitated

Shake, *s.* a vibratory motion; concussion
Shall, *v. defective,* it has no tenses but *shall* future, and *should* imperfect
Shalloo'n, *s.* a light woollen stuff
Shal'lop, or Shalloo'p, *s.* a small vessel
Shal'low, *a.* not deep; futile; silly
Shal'low, *s.* a sand; a flat; a shoal
Shal'lowness, *s.* a want of depth or thought
Shalot', *s.* a kind of small onion
Shalt, second person of *shalt*
Sham, *v. n.* to counterfeit, trick, cheat
Sham, *s.* a fraud, trick, delusion
Sham, *a.* false, counterfeit, fictitious
Sham'bles, *s.* a butchery, place to sell meat
Sham'bling, *a.* moving awkwardly
Shame, *s.* reproach, ignominy, disgrace
Shame, *v.* to make ashamed, to disgrace
Sha'mefaced, *a.* modest, bashful, sheepish
Sha'meful, *a.* disgraceful, ignominious
Sha'mefully, *ad.* disgracefully, infamously
Sha'meless, *a.* impudent, audacious
Sham'ois, or Cham'ois, *s.* a wild goat
Sham'rock, *s.* a three-leaved Irish grass
Shank, *s.* middle joint of the leg; the handle
Shape, *v. a.* to form, mould, image, create
Shape, *s.* a form, make, proportion
Sha'peless, *a.* wanting regularity of form
Sha'peliness, *s.* beauty of proportion or form
Sha'pely, *a.* well formed, symmetrical
Shard, *s.* a piece of a pot; plant; fish; frith
Shard'ed, *a.* inhabiting or like shards
Share, *s.* a portion; dividend; plough blade
Share, *v. a.* to divide, partake of, cut
Sha'rer, *s.* one who divides; a partaker
Shark, *s.* a voracious sea fish; a sharper
Sharp, *a.* keen, piercing, acute, sour
Sharp'en, *v. a.* to make keen; make quick
Sharp'er, *s.* a cheating, tricking fellow
Sharp'ly, *ad.* severely, keenly, afflictively
Sharp'ness, *s.* keenness; ingenuity; severity
Sharp'set, *a.* eager, hungry, ravenous
Sharpsight'ed, *a.* having quick sight
Shat'ter, *v.* to break into pieces; to impair
Shat'terbrained, *a.* inattentive, giddy
Shave, *v. a.* to pare close with a razor
Sha'ver, *s.* one who shaves; a sharp dealer
Sha'ving, *s.* a thin slice pared off any thing
Shaw, *s.* a thicket, a small wood [mates
Shawl, *s.* a kind of cloak usually worn by fe-
Sheaf, *s.* a bundle of new cut corn; a heap
Shear, *v. a.* to strip or cut off with shears
Shear'er, *s.* one that shears sheep
Shears, *s.* an instrument with two blades
Shear'man, *s.* he that shears
Sheath, *s.* a scabbard, the case of any thing
Sheath, or Sheathe, *v. a.* to put into a sheath
Shea'thy, *a.* forming a sheath
Shed, *s.* a shelter made of boards, &c.
Shed, *v.* to spill, to scatter, to let fall
Sheen, *s.* brightness, splendour—*a.* bright
Sheep, *s.* a well-known animal
Sheep'cot, Sheep'fold, *s.* an inclosure to pen sheep in
Sheep'ish, *a.* over-modest, bashful, timorous
Sheep'ishness, *s.* bashfulness, mean diffidence
Sheep'shearing, *s.* the time of shearing sheep; a feast made when sheep are shorn
Sheep's-eye, *s.* a loving, sly look
Sheep'walk, *s.* a pasture for sheep
Sheer, *a.* clear, pure, unmingled
Sheet, *s.* linen for a bed; sail; paper, &c.

Sheetan'chor, *s.* the largest anchor
She'kel, *s.* a Jewish coin, value *vs.* 6*d.*
Shelf, *s.* a board fastened against a wall, &c. to place things on; a sand bank in the sea; a rock under shallow water
Shell, *s.* the hard covering of any thing, &c.
Shell, *v.* to strip off or cast the shell
Shell'fish, *s.* a fish covered with a shell
Shel'ly, *a.* abounding with shells
Shel'ter, *s.* a cover from injury; protection
Shel'ter, *v.* to defend, protect, give shelter
Shel'ving, *a.* sloping, slanting, inclining
Shel'vy, *a.* shallow; full of banks; rocky
Shep'herd, *s.* one who tends sheep
Shep'herdess, *s.* a lass that tends sheep
Shep'herdy, *s.* the work of a shepherd
Sherbet', *s.* mixture of acid, water, and sugar
Sher'iff, *s.* a chief annual officer for a county
Sher'iffalty, *s.* the office of the sheriff
Sher'ry, *s.* a kind of Spanish white wine
Shield, *v. a.* to cover, to defend, to secure
Shield, *s.* a buckler, defence, protection
Shift, *s.* an evasion; a woman's body linen
Shift, *v.* to change, alter, practise evasions
Shift'er, *s.* an artful person, a trickster
Shift'less, *a.* wanting expedients to act, &c.
Shil'ling, *s.* a silver coin, value 12 pence
Shil'lishalli, *ad.* in a wavering manner
Shi'ly, *ad.* not frankly, not familiarly
Shin, *s.* the fore part of the leg
Shine, *v. n.* to glisten, to glitter, to be conspicuous; to be glossy, gay, splendid
Shine, *s.* fair weather; lustre, splendour
Shin'gles, *s.* a disease; a kind of tetter; thin boards, &c. to cover houses
Shi'ny, *a.* bright, luminous, splendid
Ship, *s.* a large vessel to sail on the sea
Ship, *v. a.* to put on board a ship
Ship'board, *ad.* on board or in a ship
Ship'man, *s.* a sailor, a seafaring man
Ship'ping, *s.* vessels for navigation
Ship'wreck, *s.* the loss of a ship by rocks, &c.
Ship'wright, *s.* a ship carpenter or builder
Shire, *s.* a division of the kingdom, a county
Shirt, *s.* a man's under linen garment
Shirt'less, *a.* wanting a shirt
Shit'tim, *s.* a very precious Arabian wood
Shit'tlecock, *s.* a plaything for children
Shive, *s.* a slice of bread; a thick splinter
Shiv'er, *v.* to quake, to tremble, to shatter
Shoal, *s.* a crowd; shallow; sand bank
Shoa'ly, *a.* full of shoals or shallows
Shoar, Shore, *v. a.* to underprop
Shock, *s.* a conflict, a concussion; an offence
Shock, *v.* to shake violently; to disgust; to offend, to be offensive
Shocking, *a.* disgusting, dreadful, violent
Shoe, *s.* the outer cover of the foot
Shoe'boy, *s.* a boy that cleans shoes
Shoe'inghorn, *s.* a horn to draw on shoes
Shoe'maker, *s.* one who makes shoes
Shoe'string, *s.* a riband, &c. to tie the shoes
Shoot, *v.* to discharge a gun, &c.; to germinate; to push forward; to jet out; to move swiftly; to feel a quick pain
Shoot'er, *s.* one that shoots, an archer
Shop, *s.* a place for sale or for work
Shop'board, *s.* a bench or table to work on
Shop'keeper, *s.* one who sells in a shop
Shoplif'ter, *s.* one who steals goods out of a
Shop'man, *s.* a foreman, &c. in a shop [shop

Q

Shore, Shorn, *pret.* and *part.* of to *shear*
Shore, *s.* the coast of the sea; a drain; buttress
Sho'reless, *a.* having no shore
Short, *a.* not long; scanty; brittle
Short'en, *v.* to make short, contract, lop
Short'hand, *s.* a compendious mode of writing
Short'lived, *a.* not living or lasting long
Short'ly, *ad.* quickly, soon; concisely, briefly
Short'ness, *s.* the quality of being short
Shortsight'ed, *a.* defective in the sight
Shot, *s.* balls for guns, &c.; a reckoning
Shot'free, *a.* clear of the reckoning
Shot'ten, *a.* having ejected the spawn
Shove, *v.* to push by main strength, to push
Shove, *s.* the act of shoving, a push
Shov'el, *s.* an instrument for digging, &c.
Shov'elboard, *s.* a game and table to play on
Shough, *s.* a species of shaggy dog
Should, *v.* *auxiliary* in *sub. mood*
Shoul'der, *s.* the joint that connects the arm
    to the body; a prominence
Shoul'der, *v.a.* to put on the shoulder; jostle
Shoul'derbelt, *s.* a belt for the shoulder
Shoul'derknot, *s.* a knot of lace, &c. worn on
    the shoulders of footmen, &c.
Shout, *s.* a loud cry of triumph, &c.
Shout, *v. n.* to cry in triumph or exultation
Show, *v.* to exhibit; prove; direct; teach
Show, *s.* a spectacle; semblance; pomp
Show'er, *s.* rain, moderate or violent
Show'er, *v. a.* to wet; scatter with liberality
Show'ery, *a.* rainy, inclinable to showers
Sho'wy, *a.* splendid, gaudy, ostentatious
Shred, *s.* a small piece, a fragment
Shrew, *s.* a peevish, clamorous woman
Shrewd, *a.* cunning, smart, turbulent
Shrewd'ly, *ad.* cunningly, wittily, slily, with
    strong suspicion, vexatiously
Shriek, *v. n.* to scream—*s.* an inarticulate
    cry of horror or anguish
Shrift, *s.* confession to a priest
Shrill, *a.* sounding with a piercing, tremu
    lous, or vibratory sound
Shrill'ness, *s.* sharpness of sound
Shrimp, *s.* a small shellfish; a dwarf
Shrine, *s.* a cabinet or case to hold relics, &c.
Shrink, *v.* to contract itself; to express fear,
    pain, or horror, by contracting the body
Shriv'el, *v. a.* to contract into wrinkles
Shroud, *s.* dress of the dead; a shelter, cover
Shroud, *v.* to shelter, to conceal, to harbour
Shrouds, *s.* large ropes extended from the
    mast-head to the sides of a ship, to support
    the masts, and enable them to carry sail
Shro'vetide, *s.* the Tuesday before Lent
Shrub, *s.* a bush; spirit with acid and sugar
Shrub'by, *a.* full of or like shrubs
Shrug, *v. a.* to contract or draw up
Shrug, *s.* a contracting of the shoulders to
    signify contempt, pity, or aversion
Shud'der, *v. n.* to quake with fear, &c.
Shuf'fle, *v.* to dodge; to shift; to play mean
    tricks; to change the position of the cards;
    to move with an irregular gait
Shuf'fle, *s.* a disordering of things; a trick
Shuf'flecap, *s.* a kind of play or game
Shuf'fler, *s.* he who plays tricks or shuffles
Shun, *v. a.* to avoid, to endeavour to escape
Shut, *v.* to close, confine, exclude, contract
Shut'ter, *s.* a cover for a window, &c.
Shut'tle, *s.* an instrument used in weaving

Shy, *a.* reserved, cautious, suspicious, war
Shy'ness, *s.* reservedness, coyness, back
Sib'ilant, *a.* hissing   [wardness
Sibila'tion, *s.* a hissing sound
Sicca'tion, *s.* the act of drying
Siccif'tic, *a.* causing dryness
Sic'city, *s.* dryness; want of moisture
Sice, *s.* the number *six* at dice
Sick, *a.* afflicted with disease; disgusted
Sick'en, *v.* to make sick; disgust; decay
Sic'kle, *s.* a hook for reaping corn
Sick'ly, *a.* not healthy, faint, weakly
Sick'ness, *s.* a disease, disorder of the body
Side, *s.* the rib part of animals; the edge
Side, *a.* not direct—*v. n.* to join with
Si'deboard, *s.* a side table on which conve
    niences are placed
Si'delong, *a.* lateral, oblique, not direct
Sid'eral, Side'real, Side'rean, *a.* starry
Sid'erated, *a.* planet-struck; blasted
Sidera'tion, *s.* a mortification; a blast
Si'desaddle, *s.* a woman's seat on horseback
Si'desman, *s.* an assistant to a churchwarden
Si'deways, Si'dewise, *ad.* on one side   [tion
Si'dle, *v. n.* to move slowly in a lateral direc-
Siege, *s.* the besieging a fortified place
Sieve, *s.* hair or lawn strained on a hoop
Sift, *v. a.* to put through a sieve; to examine
Sif'ter, *s.* he who sifts; a sieve
Sigh, *s.* a mournful breathing, a sob
Sight, *s.* the sense of seeing; a show
Sight'less, *a.* blind, not sightly; offensive
Sight'liness, *s.* handsomeness, seemliness
Sight'ly, *a.* comely, pleasing to the eye
Sig'il, *s.* a seal; a kind of charm
Sign, *s.* a token, mirace, symbol, device
Sign, *v. a.* to mark, to ratify by writing
Sig'nal, *s.* a sign that gives notice, mark
Sig'nal, *a.* memorable, remarkable
Sig'nalize, *v. a.* to make remarkable
Sig'nally, *ad.* remarkably, memorably
Sig'nature, *s.* a mark, sign; among printers,
    a letter to distinguish different sheets
Sig'net, *s.* a seal, especially the king's
Signif'icancy, *s.* meaning, force, energy
Signif'icant, *a.* expressive, important
Signif'icantly, *ad.* with force of expression
Significa'tion, *s.* a meaning by sign or word
Signif'icative, *a.* strongly expressive
Sig'nify, *v.* to declare, to mean, to import
Si'gnior, Si'gniory. See Seignor, Seignory
Si'lence, *s.* stillness, taciturnity, secrecy
Si'lence, *interj.* commanding silence
Si'lent, *a.* mute, still, quiet, not speaking
Si'lently, *ad.* without speech or noise
Silic'ious, *a.* made of hair; flinty
Sil'iqua, *s.* a pod
Sil'iquose, Sil'iquous, *a.* having a pod
Silk, *s.* a fine soft thread, spun by silk worms;
    any thing made of it
Silk'en, *a.* made of silk; soft; tender
Silk'mercer, *s.* a dealer in silk
Silk'weaver, *s.* a weaver of silken stuffs
Silk'worm, *s.* the worm that spins silk
Silk'y, *a.* made of silk, soft, pliant
Sill, *s.* the foot of a door-case, &c.
Sil'labub, or Sil'libub, *s.* a liquor made of
    milk, cider or wine, sugar, &c.
Sil'liness, *s.* simplicity; harmless folly
Sil'ly, *a.* harmless, weak, simple, foolish
Sil'van, Syl'van, *a.* woody, full of woods

Sil'ver, s. a white hard metal
Sil'ver, a. made of or like silver
Sil'very, a. besprinkled with silver
Sil'versmith, s. one who works in silver, &c.
Simar', or Sima're, s. a woman's loose robe
Sim'ilar, a. of a like form or quality
Similar'ity, s. likeness, resemblance
Sim'ile, s. a comparison for illustration
Simil'itude, s. likeness, comparison
Sim'mer, v. n. to boil gently or slowly
Sim'nel, s. a kind of sweet bread or cake
Sim'ony, s. the crime of buying or selling church preferments
Si'mous, a. having a flat or snubbed nose
Sim'per, v. n. to smile, or look pleasantly
Sim'per, s. a kind of pleasant smile
Sim'ple, a. plain, artless; unmingled; silly
Sim'ple, s. a single ingredient; an herb, &c.
Sim'ple, v. n. to gather simples
Sim'pler, Sim'plist, s. an herbalist
Sim'pleton, s. a silly or simple person
Simplic'ity, s. plainness, weakness
Sim'ply, ad. without art, foolishly
Sim'ular, s. one that counterfeits
Simula'tion, s. a dissembling, feigning
Simulta'neous, a. acting together
Sin, s. a violation of the laws of God
Sin, v. n. to violate the laws of God
Since, ad. because that, before this; ago
Since're, a. pure, honest, uncorrupt
Sincer'ity, s. purity of mind, honesty
Sin'don, s. a fold, a wrapper
Sine, s. a kind of geometrical line
Si'necure, s. an office which has revenue without any employment
Sin'ew, s. a tendon, muscle, or nerve
Sin'ewed, a. furnished with sinews, strong
Sin'ewy, a. nervous, strong, forcible
Sin'ful, a. not holy; wicked, profane
Sing, v. to form the voice to melody; to ce'ebrate; give praises to; to recite in poetry
Singe, v. a. to scorch, to burn slightly
Sing'er, s. one skilled in singing
Sin'gle, a. alone, unmarried, individual
Sin'gleness, s. not duplicity; sincerity
Sin'gly, ad. individually, only, by himself
Sin'gular, a. only one; particular; rare
Singular'ity, s. any thing remarkable; a curiosity; a distinguished charac er
Sin'gularly, ad. particularly; strangely
Sin'guit, s. a sigh
Sin'ister, a. on the left hand; bad; unlucky
Sink, v. to fall gradually, settle, decline
Sink, s. a drain, jakes, place of filth
Sin'less, a. exempt from sin, innocent
Sin'ner, s. an offender, a criminal
Sin'offering, s. an expiation for sin
Sin'oper, Sin'ople, s. a kind of red earth
Sin'uous, a. bending in and out
Si'nus, s. a bay of the sea; gulf; opening
Sip, v. to drink by small draughts
Sip, s. a small draught, small mouthful
Si'phon, Sy'phon, s. a pipe to draw off liquors
Sip'pet, s. a small sop
Sir, s. a word of respect to men; a title
Sire, s. a father; a male
Si'ren, Sy'ren, s. a goddess who enticed men by singing, and then devoured them
Sir'ius, s. the great dog-star
Sir'name, s. the family name
Siroc'co, s. the south east or Syrian wind

Sir'rah, s. a name of reproach and insult
Sir'up, Syr'up, s. a vegetable juice boiled with sugar
Sis'ter, s. a woman born of one's parents
Sis'terhood, s. women of the same society
Sis'terly, a. like or becoming a sister
Sit, v. to repose on a seat; to incubate
Site, s. a situation, local position
Sith, ad. since; seeing that
Sit'ting, s. the act of resting on a seat
Sit'uate, Sit'uated, a. placed; lying
Situa'tion, s. a position; condition; state
Six, a. twice three, one more than five
Six'fold, a. six times told
Six'pence, s. half a shilling
Sixtee'n, a. six and ten
Sixth, a. the next after the fifth
Sixth'ly, ad. in the sixth place
Six'tieth, a. the tenth six times repeated
Six'ty, a. six times ten
Si'zable, a. reasonably bulky
Size, s. bulk; a glutinous substance
Si'zer, s. the lowest rank of students in a college
Si'zy, a. glutinous, viscous, ropy
Skate, s. a flat seafish; a sliding shoe
Skate, v. n. to slide on ice with skates
Skean, s. a short sword; a knife
Skein, s. a hank of silk, thread, &c.
Skel'eton, s. the bones of the body preserved as in their natural situation
Skel'lum, s. a villain, a scoundrel
Sketch, s. an outline; rough draught
Sketch, v. n. to trace the outlines; to plan
Skew, v. n. to squint; to look disdainfully
Skew'er, s. a sort of pin to truss meat
Skiff, s. a small light boat
Skil'ful, a. knowing, experienced
Skil'fully, ad. with skill, dexterously
Skil'fulness, s. art, dexterity
Skill, s. knowledge, experience, dexterity
Skil'led, a. knowing, acquainted with
Skil'let, s. a small kettle or boiler
Skim, v. to take off the scum; pass lightly
Skim'mer, s. a ladle to take off the scum
Skim'milk, s. milk deprived of its cream
Skin, s. the hide, pelt; rind of fruit
Skin, v. a. to flay; to uncover; to heal
Skin'ker, s. one that serves drink
Skin'ner, s. a dealer in skins or pelts
Skin'ny, a. wanting flesh, thin, lean
Skip, v. to pass by quick leaps; to miss
Skip, s. a light leap or bound
Skip'jack, s. an upstart; a lackey
Skip'per, s. a ship-master; or ship-boy
Skir'mish, s. a slight fight, a contest
Skirt, s. the edge, margin, extreme part
Skit, s. a whim; lampoon; insinuation
Skit'tish, a. easily frighted; wanton; fickle
Skreen, s. a coarse sieve; a shelter
Skreen, v. a. to sift; to shade; to shelter
Skue, a. oblique, sidelong
Skulk, v. n. to hide; lurk in fear or malice
Skull, s. the bone that incloses the head
Sky, s. the heavens, the firmament
Sky'lark, s. a bird that soars and sings
Sky'light, s. a window in the roof
Sky'rocket, s. a kind of rising firework
Slab, s. a plane of stone; a puddle
Slab, a. thick, viscous, glutinous
Slab'ber, v. to drivel, to shed; to spill
Slab'by, a. plashy, dirty, thick, viscous

Slank, a. not tense, loose, remiss, relaxed
Slack, Slack'en, v. to be remiss, abate, flag
Slack, s. coal broken into small parts
Slack'ness, s. looseness ; negligence
Slag, s. the dross or recrement of metals
Slain, part. pass. of to slay
Slake, v. to quench, extinguish, be relaxed
Slam, s. winning all the tricks at cards
Slam, v. a. to crush ; to shut a door violently
Slan'der, s. false invective ; reproach
Slan'der, v. a. to backbite, to censure falsely
Slan'derer, s. one who belies another
Slan'derous, a. falsely abusive, calumnious
Slant, v. to cast obliquely or sideways
Slant, Slan'ting, a. oblique, sloping
Slap, v. a. to strike with the open hand
Slap'dash, ad. all at once, suddenly
Slash, v. to cut ; lash ; strike at random
Slash, s. a wound ; cut in cloth, &c.
Slate, s. a grey fossil stone
Slate, v. a. to cover the roof
Sla'ter, s. one who covers with slates
Slat'tern, s. a negligent, careless woman
Slave, s. one deprived of freedom
Slave, v. n. to drudge, to moil, to toil
Slav'er, s. to emit or smear with spittle
Sla'very, s. the condition, &c. of a slave
Slaugh'ter, s. destruction with a sword
Slaugh'ter, v. a. to massacre, to slay
Slaugh'terhouse, s. a house in which beasts
   are killed by the butcher
Slaugh'terman, s. one employed in killing
Slaugh'terous, a. destructive, murderous
Sla'vish, a. servile, mean, base, dependant
Sla'vishly, ad. servilely, meanly
Sla'vishness, s. servility, meanness
Slay, v. a. to kill, butcher, put to death
Sleaz'y, a. thin, slight, wanting substance
Sled, or Siedge, s. a carriage without wheels
   a smith's large hammer
Sleek, Sleek'y, a. smooth, glossy, delicate
Sleek'ly, ad. smoothly, glossily
Sleek'ness, s. smoothness, glossiness
Sleep, s. repose, rest, slumber—v. n. to rest
Sleep'ily, ad. drowsily, dully, stupidly
Sleep'ing, s. the act of taking rest in sleep
Sleep'iness, s. drowsiness, heaviness
Sleep'less, a. without sleep ; always awake
Sleep'y, a. drowsy, sluggish, causing sleep
Sleet, s. a kind of smooth, small snow
Sleet'y, a. bringing sleet
Sleeve, s. the dress covering the arm
Sleeve'button, s. a button for the sleeve
Sleeve'less, a. having no sleeves
Sleight, s. dexterous practice, art, trick
Slen'der, a. thin, small, not bulky ; sparing
Slen'derly, ad. without bulk, meanly
Slen'derness, s. thinness, want of strength
Slice, v. to cut into thin pieces, to divide
Slide, v. to glide on ice ; pass unnoticed
Slide, s. a frozen place to slide on
Slight, a. small ; worthless ; not strong
Slight, s. neglect ; contempt ; artifice ; scorn
Slight, v. a. to neglect, to disregard
Slight'ingly, ad. with disdain, negligently
Slight'ly, ad. negligently ; scornfully ; weakly
Slight'ness, s. weakness ; negligence
Slim, a. slender, thin of shape
Slime, s. any glutinous substance, mud
Sli'miness, s. viscosity, glutinous matter
Slim'ness, s. slenderness, thinness of shape

Sli'my, a. viscous, glutinous, ropy
Sling, s. a missive weapon for stones; a stroke
Sling, v. a. to throw by a sling, &c.
Slink, v. to sneak away ; to cast its young
Slip, v. to slide ; fall into error ; fall out of
   the memory ; convey secretly
Slip, s. a false step ; mistake ; twig ; escape
Slip'board, s. a board sliding in grooves
Slip'knot, s. a bow knot, a knot easily untied
Slip'per, s. a morning shoe, a loose shoe
Slip'periness, s. the state of being slippery
Slip'pery, Slip'py, a. glib ; uncertain
Slip'shod, a. not having the shoe pulled up
Slip'slop, s. bad or insipid liquor
Slit, v. a. to cut any thing length wise
Slit, s. a long cut or narrow opening
Sli'ver, v. a. to split—s. a branch torn off
Sloats, s. the under parts of a cart
Slob'ber, v. to slaver, to wet with spittle
Sloe, s. the fruit of the blackthorn
Sloop, s. a small sea vessel
Slop, v. a. to dash with water ; drink hastily
Slope, s. a declivity, an oblique direction
Slope, a. oblique, not perpendicular
Slope, Slo'pewise, Slo'pingly, ad. obliquely
Slop'py, a. miry and wet, plashy
Sloth, s. slowness, idleness ; an animal
Sloth'ful, a. idle, lazy, sluggish, inactive
Sloth'fully, ad. with sloth, inactively, lazily
Slouch, s. a downcast look ; a man who looks
   heavy and clownish
Slou'ching, a. walking awkwardly
Slov'en, s. one dirtily or carelessly dressed
Slov'enly, a. negligent, not neat ; dirty
Slov'enly, ad. in a coarse inelegant manner
Slough, s. a deep miry place ; the skin which
   a serpent throws off periodically
Slough'y, a. miry, boggy, muddy
Slow, a. not swift ; late ; dull ; tardy
Slow'ly, ad. not speedily, not rashly
Slow'ness, s. want of velocity, deliberation
Slow'worm, s. a small worm or viper
Slub'ber, v. a. to do a thing lazily ; to daub
Slubberdegul'lion, s. a mean dirty wretch
Sludge, s. mire, dirt mixed with water
Slug, s. an idler, a drone ; a slow snail
Slug'gard, s. a drone ; an idle, lazy fellow
Slug'gish, a. dull, drowsy, lazy, slothful
Slug'gishly, ad. dully, not nimbly, idly
Sluice, s. a water-gate, a flood-gate
Sluice, v. a. to emit by flood-gates
Slum'ber, v. to sleep lightly, to doze
Slum'ber, s. light sleep, repose
Slum'berous, a. causing sleep, sleepy
Slung, pret. and part. of to sling
Slur, s. a slight disgrace—v. a. to sully, soil
Slut, s. a dirty woman ; a word of contempt
Slut'tish, a. nasty, not cleanly, dirty
Slut'tishness, s. nastiness ; dirtiness
Sly, a. meanly artful, secretly insidious
Smack, s. taste, savour ; a loud kiss
Small, a. little, slender ; minute ; petty
Small'coal, s. small wood coals used in light
   ing fires
Small'craft, s. vessels less than ships
Small'ness, s. minuteness ; weakness
Small'pox, s. an eruptive malignant distem-
   per, very contagious
Smalt, s. a beautiful blue substan
Smarag'dine, a. made of or lik
Smart, a. pungent, quick, acute

Smart, *v. n.* to feel quick lively pain	Snatch'block, *s.* a kind of pulley in a ship
Smart'ly, *ad.* sharply, briskly, wittily	Snatch'er, *s.* one who snatches hastily
Smart'ness, *s.* quickness; liveliness; vigour	Sneak, *v. n.* to creep silly. to crouch
Smatch, *s.* a taste; tincture; a bird	Snea'ker, *s.* a large vessel of drink
Smat'ter, *s.* superficial knowledge	Snea'king, *a.* servile, mean, niggardly
Smat'tering, *s.* a slight knowledge	Snea'kingly, *ad.* servilely, meanly
Smear, *v. a.* to soil, to daub, to contaminate	Snea'kup, *s.* a cowardly creeping scoundrel
Smea'ry, *a.* dauby; adhesive	Sneap, *s.* a reprimand—*v. a.* to check; nip
Smeeth, *v. a.* to blacken with smoke	Sneck, *s.* a latch, or fastening to a door
Smell, *v.* to perceive by the nose, &c.	Sneer, *s.* contempt—*v. n.* to show contempt
Smell, *s.* the power of smelling. scent	Sneeze, *s.* emission of wind audibly by the
Smelt, *pret.* and *part. pass.* of *to smell*	nose—*v. n.* to emit wind by the nose
Smelt, *s.* a small sea fish	Snib, Sneb, Snub, *v. a.* to check, to repri-
Smelt, *v. a.* to extract metal from ore	mand, to chide
Smel'ter, *s.* one who melts ore	Snick and Snee, *s.* a combat with knives
Smerk, *v. n.* to smile amorously, &c.	Snick'er, *v. n.* to laugh wantonly or silly
Smerk, Smirk, *a.* nice, smart, jaunty, gay	Sniff, *v. n.* to draw breath by the nose
Smick'et, *s.* a woman's under garment	Snig'gle, *v. n.* to fish for eels with a bait
Smile, *v. n.* to look gay, &c.; be propitious	Snip, *v. n.* to cut at once with scissars, &c.
Smile, *s.* a look of pleasure or of kindness	Snip, *s.* a single cut
Smi'lingly, *ad.* with a look of pleasure	Snipe, *s.* a small fen-fowl; a fool
Smit, Smit'ten, *part. pass.* of *to smite*	Snip'pet, *s.* a small part; a share
Smite, *v.* to strike; kill; destroy; blast	Snip'snap, *s.* tart dialogue
Smith, *s.* one who works in metals	Sniv'el, *v. n.* to run at the nose; cry childishly
Smith'ery, Smith'y, *s.* a smith's shop	Sniv'elling, *a.* peaking, whining, pitiful
Smock, *s.* the under garment of a woman	Snore, *s.* a noise through the nose in sleep
Smock'faced, *a.* beardless, maidenly, pale	Snort, *v. n.* to blow through the nose as a
Smoke, *s.* a sooty exhalation; a steam	high-mettled horse
Smoke, *v.* to emit smoke; to burn; discover;	Snout, *s.* the nose of a beast, the nose
use tobacco; dry in smoke; sneer or ridi-	Snow, *s.* water frozen in flakes; a small ship
cule; smell out, find out	Snow'ball, *s.* a lump of congealed snow
Smo'kedry, *v. a.* to dry in the smoke	Snow'drop, *s.* a small white spring flower
Smo'ky, *a.* emitting or full of smoke, fumed	Snow'y, *a.* white as snow, full of snow
Smooth, *a.* even; plain; bland; mild	Snub, *s.* a knot in wood; a jag, a snag
Smooth, *v. a.* to level; to make easy; soften	Snuff, *s.* the burnt wick of a candle; powder
Smoo'then, *v. a.* to make even and smooth	ed tobacco taken up the nose
Smoo'thly, *ad.* evenly; easily; calmly	Snuff, *v.* to crop; to scent; to draw breath
Smoo'thness, *s.* evenness of surface; mildness	Snuff'box, *s.* a box in which snuff is carried
Smote, *pret.* of *to smite*	Snuff'ers, *s.* an instrument for snuffing can
Smoth'er, *v.* to suffocate; to suppress	Snuf'fle, *v. a.* to speak through the nose [dles
Smoth'er, *s.* a smoke, thick dust; suppression	Snug, *a.* close, hidden, concealed, sly
Smug, *a.* nice, spruce, neat	Snug'gle, *v. n.* to lie close; to lie warm
Smug'gle, *v. a.* to import or export goods	So, *ad.* in like manner; thus; provided that
without paying the customs	Soak, *v.* to steep in any liquid; to imbibe; to
Smug'gler, *s.* one who cheats the revenue	drain; to exhaust
Smug'ly, *ad.* neatly, sprucely, nicely	Soap, *s.* a substance used in washing
Smug'ness, *s.* spruceness, neatness	Soap'boiler, *s.* one who makes soap
Smut, *s.* spot with soot; mildew; obscenity	Soar, *v. n.* to fly aloft, to rise high, to aim
Smutch, *v. a.* to black with smoke	high, to be aspiring
Smut'tily, *ad.* smokily, blackly; obscenely	Sob, *v. n.* to sigh convulsively in weeping,
Smut'ty, *a.* black with smoke; obscene	&c.—*s.* a convulsive sigh
Snack, *s.* a share, a part taken by compact	So'ber, *a.* temperate, regular, serious
Snaf'fle, *s.* a bridle that crosses the nose	So'ber, *v. a.* to make sober
Snag, *s.* a jag; a protuberance; a tooth	So'berly, *ad.* temperately, moderately, cool-
Snag'ged, Snag'gy, *a.* full of jags	ly, calmly; gravely, seriously
Snail, *s.* a testaceous animal; a drone	So'berness, Sobri'ety, *s.* temperance in drink,
Snake, *s.* a serpent of the oviparous kind	calmness, freedom from enthusiasm
Sna'keroot, *s.* the name of a medicinal root	Soc'cage, *s.* an ancient tenure of lands
Sna'ky, *a.* serpentine; having serpents	So'ciable, *a.* inclined to company; familiar
Snap, *v.* to break at once, bres' snort; bite	So'ciableness, *s.* inclination to company, &c.
Snap'dragon, *s.* a plant; a kind of play	So'ciably, *ad.* conversably, as a companion
Snap'per, *s.* one who snaps	So'cial, *a.* familiar, fit for society
Snap'pish, *a.* eager to bite, surly, cross	So'cialness, *s.* the quality of being social
Snap'pishly, *ad.* crossly, peevishly, tartly	Soci'ety, *s.* fraternity; company; partnership
Snap'sack, *s.* a soldier's bag, a knapsack	Socin'ian, *s.* a follower of Socinus
Snare, *s.* a gin, net, trap, snare	Socin'ianism, *s.* the doctrines of Socinus
Snare, *v. a.* to entrap, to entangle	Sock, *s.* something put between the shoe and
Snarl, *v.* to growl like a dog, &c.; to speak	stocking; the shoe of the ancient actors
roughly; to entangle	Sock'et, *s.* any hollow that receives something
Snar'ler, *s.* a surly captious fellow	inserted; the receptacle of the eye
Snatch, *v.* to seize hastily—*s.* a hasty catch	Sod, *s.* a turf, a clod

Q 3

Sodal'ity, s. fellowship, society, fraternity
Sod'den, part. pass. of to seeth; boiled
So'der, or Sol'der, s. a metallic cement
Sod'omite, s. one guilty of sodomy
Sod'omy, s. a very unnatural crime
So'fa, s. a splendid covered seat
Soft, a. not hard or rough; simple, gentle
Soft, interj. hold! stop! not so fast!
Soft'en, v. to make soft or easy, to mollify
Soft'ly, ad. gently, slowly, mildly, tenderly
Soft'ness, s. quality of being soft; effeminacy
Soho'! interj. form of calling to one far off
Soil, s. dung; compost; dirt, land, earth
Soil, v. a. to pollute, stain, sully
So'journ, v. n. to dwell awhile in some place
So'journer, s. a temporary dweller
Sol'ace, s. comfort, pleasure, alleviation
Sol'ace. v. a. to comfort, to cheer
So'lar, Sol'ary, a. pertaining to the sun
Sold, pret. and part. pass. of to sell
Sol'dan, s. a Mahometan prince, or sultan
Sol'dier, s. one who fights for pay, a warrior
Sol'diery, s. a body of soldiers, soldiership
Sole, s. the bottom of the foot or shoe; a fish
Sole, v. a. to furnish shoes with new soles
Sole, a. single, alone; in law, unmarried
Sol'ecism, s. an impropriety of speech
Sole'ly, ad. singly; only; separately
Sol'emn, a. awful; religiously grave; serious
Solem'nity, s. a ceremony; affected gravity
Solemniza'tion, s. the act of celebration
Sol'emnize, v. a. to dignify by formalities
Sol'emnly, ad. in a solemn manner
Solic'it, v. a. to excite; implore, ask
Solicita'tion, s. an importunity, an entreaty
Solic'iter, s. one who acts for another
Solic'itous, a. anxious; careful; concerned
Solic'itously, ad. anxiously, carefully
Solic'itress, s. a woman who solicits
Solic'itude, s. anxiety; carefulness
Sol'id, a. not fluid, firm, true, compact
Solid'ity, s. fulness of matter, firmness
Solifid'ian, s. one who holds faith only, not
   works, necessary to salvation
Solil'oquy, s. a discourse, &c. to one's self
Sol'itaire, s. a neck ornament; a hermit
Sol'itary, a. retired, gloomy; single
Sol'itude, s. a lonely life or place; a desart
So'lo, s. a tune played by one person
Sol'stice, s. the tropical point of the sun
Solstit'ial, a. belonging to the solstice
Solv'able, a. possible to be cleared
Sol'uble, a. capable of dissolution
Solubil'ity, s. susceptiveness of separation
Solve, v. a. to clear, explain, resolve
Sol'vency, s. an ability to pay debts
Sol'vent, a. able to pay debts; dissolving
Solu'te, a. loosened; disengaged; fluent
Solu'tion, s. a separation; explanation
Solu'tive, a. laxative, causing relaxation
Somatol'ogy. s. the doctrine of bodies
Som'bre, Somb'rous, a. dark, gloomy
Some. a. more or less; certain persons
Some'body, s. an indiscriminate person
Som'erset, Sum'merset, s. a leap by which
   the jumper throws his heels over his head
Some'how, ad. one way or other
Some'thing, s. not nothing, part
Some'time, ad. once, formerly
Some'times, ad. now and then, not never
Some'what, s. something, more or less

Some'where, ad. in one place or other
Soranif'erous, Somnif'ic, a. causing sleep
Somnif'ugous, a. driving away sleep
Som'nolency, s. sleepiness, inclination to sleep
Son, s. a male child, native, descendant
Son-in-law, s. one married to one's daughter
Sonn'ta, s. a tune for instruments only
Song, s. a composition in verse to be sung
Song'ster, s. a singer of songs
Song'stress, s. a female singer
Sonif'erous. a. giving or bringing sound
Son'net, s. a short poem of 14 lines
Sonnetee'r, s. a small poet, in contempt
Sonorif'ic, Sonorif'erous, a. giving sound
Sono'rous, a. loud, or high sounding
Soon, ad. before long, early, readily
Soot, s. condensed or embodied smoke
Soot'ed, a. smeared or covered with soot
Sooth, s. truth, reality—a. pleasing
Soothe, v. a. to flatter, to calm, to gratify
Sooth'say, v. n. to predict, foretel
Sooth'sayer, s. a foreteller, a predictor
Sooth'saying, s. foretelling future events
Soo'ty, a. smeared with soot, black, dark
Sop, s. any thing steeped in liquor
Sop, v. a. to steep in liquor
Soph, s. an under graduate of two years
So'phi, s. the emperor of Persia
Soph'ism, s. a fallacious argument
Soph'ist, s. a subtle disputer; philosopher
Soph'ister, s. a disputant fallaciously subtle
Sophis'tical, a. fallacious, deceitful
Sophis'tically, ad. with fallacious subtilty
Sophis'ticate, v. a. to adulterate, to debase
Soph'istry, s. fallacious ratiocination
Soporif'erous, Soporif'ic, a. causing sleep
Sor'cerer, s. a conjurer, magician, wizard
Sor'ceress, s. a female magician, enchantress
Sor'cery, s. magic, enchantment, conjuration
Sord, s. turf, grassy ground
Sordes, s. foulness, dregs
Sor'did, a. foul, dirty, base, mean, covetous
Sor'didly, ad. meanly, poorly, covetously
Sore, a. a place tender and painful, an ulcer
Sor'el, s. a buck of the third year
Sore'ly, ad. with great pain or vehemence
Sor'rel, s. an acid plant; a reddish colour
Sor'rily, ad. meanly, poorly, despicably
Sor'row, s. grief, sadness, mourning
Sor'rowful, a. mournful, grieving, sad
Sor'ry, a. grieved; vile, worthless
Sort, s. a kind, species, manner; class; de-
   gree of any quality; lot; set; suit
Sort, v. to separate, cull; suit; conjoin; fit
Sort'ance, s. suitableness, agreement
Sort'ilege, s. the act of drawing lots
Sort'ment, s. a distribution, a parcel sorted
Soss, v. n. to fall plump into; to sit lazily
Sot, s. a drunkard; dolt, blockhead
Sot'tish, a. addicted to liquor; stupid
sov'ereign, a. supreme in power or efficacy
   —s. a monarch, a king, supreme lord
Sov'ereignty, s. state, &c. of a sovereign
   prince; supremacy, highest place
Soul, s. the immaterial, immortal spirit of
   man; spirit; essence; vital principle
Sound, a. healthy; right; stout, hearty
Sound, s. any thing audible; a shallow sea
Sound, v. to try depth with a plummet; exa
   mine; celebrate by sound; make a noise
Sound'ing, a. of a loud or magnificent sound

Sound'ings, *s.* places fathomable at sea	Spear, *s.* a long pointed weapon, a lance
Sound'ly, *ad.* heartily; stoutly; rightly	Spear'mint, *s.* a plant, a species of mint
Sound'ness, *s.* health, rectitude, solidity	Spec'ial, *a.* particular; uncommon; chief
Soup, *s.* decoction of flesh for the table	Spe'cies, *s.* a kind, sort; class of nature
Sour, *a.* acid; austere; painful; cross	Specif'ic, *a.* that which distinguishes one sort
Source, *s.* a spring; head; original cause	from another; a particular quality
Sour'ish, *a.* somewhat sour	Specif'ic, *s.* a remedy for one disease
Sour'ly, *ad.* with acidity or acrimony	Specif'ically, *ad.* according to the species
Sous, *s.* a small French coin	Spec'ify, *v. a.* to particularize, to express in
Souse, *s.* a pickle made of salt and water	particular, to mention in express terms
Souse, *ad.* all at once, with sudden violence	Spec'imen, *s.* an example, pattern; essay
Souse, *v.* to steep in pickle; to plunge into	Spe'cious, *a.* showy; plausible; striking
water; to fall, as a bird on its prey	Spe'ciously, *ad.* with fair appearance
South, *s.* the part where the sun is to us at	Speck, *s.* a spot of dirt, &c.—*v. a.* to spot
noon;the southern regions; the south wind	Speck'le, *v. a.* to mark with small spots
South, *a.* southern—*ad.* toward the south	Speck'led, *a.* full of small spots
South'ing, *a.* approaching to the south	Spec'tacle, *s.* a show, an exhibition
South'erly, *a.* from or toward the south	Spec'tacles, *s.* glasses to assist the sight
South'ernwood, *s.* a plant	Specta'tor, *s.* a looker-on, a beholder
South'ward, *ad.* toward the south	Specta'torship, *s.* the act of beholding
Sow, *s.* a female pig; a large mass of lead	Spec'tre, *s.* a frightful apparition, a ghost
Sow, *v.* to scatter, to spread; to propagate	Spec'ulate, *v.* to meditate, to contemplate
Sow'ins, *s.* flummery; oatmeal soured	Specula'tion, *s.* view; contemplation; a men
Space, *s.* extension; quantity of time	tal scheme not reduced to practice
Spa'cious, *a.* wide, extensive, roomy	Spec'ulative, *a.* contemplative; ideal
Spa'ciously, *ad.* widely, extensively	Spec'ulator, *s.* one who forms theories
Spa'ciousness, *s.* roominess, wide extension	Spec'ulum, *s.* a mirror, a looking-glass
Spade, *s.* a sort of shovel; suit of cards	Speech, *s.* articulate utterance, talk
Spadic'eous, *a.* of a light red colour	Speech'less, *a.* deprived of speech, dumb
Spadill'e, *s.* ace of spades at quadrille, &c.	Speed, *s.* quickness, celerity, haste—*v.* to
Spagyr'ic, Spagyr'ical, *a.* chymical	make haste; to have success; to hasten
Spag'yrist, *s.* one who professes chymistry	Speed'ily, *ad.* with haste, readily
Spall, *s.* the shoulder	Speed'y, *a.* quick, swift, nimble, ready
Span, *s.* nine inches; any short duration	Spell, *s.* a charm; a turn at work
Span, *v. a.* to measure with the hand extended	Spell, *v.* to form words of letters; to charm
Span'gle, *s.* a small plate of shining metal	Spel'ter, *s.* a kind of semi-metal
Span'gle, *v. a.* to besprinkle with spangles	Spend, *v.* to consume, to expend, to waste
Span'iel, *s.* a dog for sport; a sycophant	Spend'thrift, *s.* a prodigal, a lavisher
Spank, *v. a.* to slap with the open hand	Sperm, *s.* the seed of animals
Spank'er, *s.* a small coin	Spermace'ti, *s.* an unctuous substance drawn
Spank'ing, *a.* large; jolly; strong; fine	from the oil of large whales
Span'ner, *s.* the lock of a fusee or carabine	Spermat'ic, *a.* seminal, consisting of seed
Spar, *s.* marcasite; a small beam; a bar	Spew, *v.* to vomit, to eject, to cast forth
Spar, *v.* to shut close; fight; quarrel	Sphac'elus, *s.* a mortification, a gangrene
Spar'able, *s.* a small nail used in shoe heels	Sphere, *s.* a globe, orb; circuit, province
Spare, *v.* to be frugal; to forbear, to forgive	Spher'ic, Spher'ical, *a.* round, globular
Spare, *a.* scanty; lean; superfluous	Spher'icalness, Spheric'ity, *s.* rotundity
Spa'rerib, *s.* ribs of pork with little flesh	Spher'oid, *s.* a body approaching to the form
Spa'ring, *a.* frugal, scanty, parsimonious	of a sphere, but not exactly round
Spa'ringly, *ad.* not abundantly; cautiously	Spheroi'dical, *a.* of the form of a spheroid
Spark, *s.* a small particle of fire; a gay man	Spher'ule, *s.* a small globe or sphere
Spar'kle, *s.* a small particle of fire or light	Spice, *s.* an aromatic substance, as nutmegs,
Spar'kle, *v. n.* to emit sparks, shine, glitter	mace, pepper, ginger, &c.
Spar'row, *s.* a small kind of bird	Spi'cery, *s.* a repository of spices
Spar'rowhawk, *s.* a kind of small hawk	Spick and Span, *ad.* quite fresh, very new
Spasm, *s.* a convulsion; violent contraction	Spi'cy, *a.* producing spice, aromatic
Spasmod'ic, Spasmod'ical, *a.* convulsive	Spi'der, *s.* a well-known spinning insect
Spat, *s.* the young of shellfish	Spig'ot, *s.* a peg put into the faucet
Spa'tiate, *v. n.* to rove, to ramble at large	Spike, *s.* an ear of corn; a great nail
Spat'ter, *v.* to sprinkle; asperse; spit	Spike, *v. a.* to fasten or set with spikes
Spat'terdashes, *s.* covering for the legs	Spi'kenard, *s.* a fragrant Indian plant
Spat'ula, *s.* an instrument used by apotheca-	Spill, *s.* a small quantity; thin bar, &c.
ries for spreading plasters	Spill, *v.* to shed, destroy, waste, lavish
Spav'in, *s.* a disease in horses	Spil'ler, *s.* a kind of fishing line
Spaw, *s.* a well or spring of mineral water	Spin, *v.* to form threads by drawing out and
Spawl, *s.* spittle, saliva	twisting any filamentous matter; to pro-
Spawn, *s.* the eggs of fish, &c.; an offspring	tract tediously;exercise the art of spinnin
Spay, *v. a.* to castrate female animals	Spin'ach, or Spin'age, *s.* a garden plant
Speak, *v.* to talk; celebrate; pronounce	Spi'nal, *a.* belonging to the backbone
Speak'able, *a.* having power, or fit to speak	Spin'dle, *s.* an instrument used in spinnin
Speak'er, *s.* one who speaks or proclaims	any thing long and slender

Spin'dle-shanked, a. having slender legs
Spine, s. the backbone ; a thorn
Spin'et, s. a small harpsichord
Spinif'erous, a. bearing thorns, thorny
Spin'ner, s. one that spins, a spider
Spinos'ity, s. crabbedness, thorny perplexity
Spi'nous, a. thorny, full of thorns
Spin'ster, s. a woman that has not been married, a woman that spins
Spi'ny, a. thorny, briary ; perplexed
Spir'acle, s. a breathing hole, a vent
Spi'ral, a. turning round like a screw
Spi'rally, ad. in a spiral form
Spire, s. a curve line ; a wreath ; a steeple
Spire, v. n. to shoot out pyramidically
Spir'it, s. the soul ; a ghost ; ardour ; genius
Spir'it, v. a. to animate, excite
Spir'ited, a. lively, vivacious, full of fire
Spir'itedness, Spir'itfulness, s. liveliness
Spir'its, s. inflammable liquors, as brandy, rum, &c. ; liveliness, gaiety
Spir'itless, a. dejected, depressed, low
Spir'itous, a. refined, fine, ardent, active
Spir'itual, a. incorporeal ; ecclesiastical
Spirituai'ity, s. incorporeity ; devotion
Spiritualiza'tion, s. the act of spiritualizing
Spir'itualize, v. a. to apply to a religious sense
Spir'itualty, s. ecclesiastical body
Spir'itually, ad. without corporeal grossness
Spir'ituous, a. vivid, airy, gay ; distilled
Spirt, v. to stream ; to throw out in a jet
Spi'ry, a. pyramidical ; wreathed, curled
Spis'sated, a. thickened, firm, gross
Spis'situde, s. grossness; thickness; firmness
Spit, s. a utensil to roast meat with
Spit, v. to put upon a spit ; to thrust through ; to eject from the mouth
Spitch'cock, s. an eel cut up and roasted
Spite, s. malice, rancour, malignity, hatred
Spite, v. a. to mischief, to vex, to offend
Spite'ful, a. malicious, malignant, cross
Spite'fully, ad. maliciously, malignantly
Spite'fulness, s. malice, desire of vexing
Spit'tle, s. the moisture of the mouth
Splash, v. a. to daub with water or dirt
Splash'y, a. wet ; dirty, apt to daub
Splay'foot, a. having the foot turned inward
Spleen, s. the milt ; spite, ill humour
Spleen'ed, a. deprived of the spleen
Spleen'ful, a. angry, fretful, peevish
Splen'dent, a. shining, glossy
Splen'did, a. showy, magnificent, sumptuous
Splen'didly, ad. sumptuously, pompously
Splen'dour, s. lustre, magnificence, pomp
Splen'etic, a. fretful, peevish, angry
Splen'itive, a. hot, fiery, passionate
Splice, v. a. to join ropes without a knot
Splint, s. a thin wood used by surgeons
Splin'ter, s. a thin piece of wood, bone, &c.
Split, v. a. to cleave, divide, part ; crack
Splut'ter, s. bustle, tumult
Spoil, s. pillage, plunder, booty
Spoil, v. to rob, to plunder, to corrupt
Spoil'er, s. a robber, plunderer, a pillager
Spoke, s. the bar of a wheel—pret. of to speak
Spo'kesman, s. one who speaks for another
Spolia'tion, s. act of robbery or privation
Spon'dee, s. a foot of two long syllables
Spon'sal, a. relating to marriage
Spon'sion, s. becoming surety for another
Spon'sor, s. a surety ; godfather, proxy

Sponta'neous, a. voluntary, not compelled
Sponta'neously, ad. voluntarily, freely
Sponta'neousness, s. freedom of will
Spool, s. weaver's quill—v. to wind yarn, &c.
Spoom, v. n. to pass swiftly
Spoon, s. a vessel used in eating liquids, &c.
Spoon'ing, s. scudding ; a sea phrase
Spoon'ful, s. as much as a spoon can hold
Sport, s. diversion of the field, as hunting, &c. ; merriment, mock, mirth, play
Sport, v. to divert, frolic, game, trifle
Sport'ful, a. merry, ludicrous, done in jest
Sport'fulness, s. play, frolic
Spor'tive, a. gay, merry, playful, wanton
Sports'man, s. one who loves hunting, &c.
Spot, s. a blot ; taint, disgrace ; certain place
Spot, v. a. to corrupt, disgrace ; maculate
Spot'less, a. pure, holy, immaculate
Spou'sal, a. nuptial, bridal, conjugal
Spouse, s. a husband or wife, married person
Spout, s. a wooden gutter, pipe, cataract
Spout, v. to pour or issue out with force
Sprain, s. a violent extension of the ligaments without dislocation of the joint
Sprat, s. a small sea-fish
Sprawl, v. n. to struggle ; to tumble, or creep
Spray, s. the extremity of a branch ; foam of the sea
Spread, v. to extend ; cover over ; stretch ; disseminate, divulge
Spread, s. extent, compass ; expansion
Sprent, part. sprinkled, scattered, besprinkled
Sprig, s. a small branch or spray
Spright, s. spirit, shade, apparition ; arrow
Spright'liness, s. liveliness, brightness, viva-
Spright'ly, a. gay, lively, vivacious   [city
Spring, v. to grow ; start ; bound ; fire a mine
Spring, s. a season of the year ; elastic force ; bound ; fountain ; cause ; original
Springe, s. a gin, a noose to catch by a jerk
Spring'halt, s. a lameness by which a horse twitches up his legs
Sprin'gle, s. a springe, an elastic noose
Spring'tide, s. a high tide at the new moon, &c
Sprin'kle, v. to scatter in small drops, a scatter in small masses, to wash, to wet
Sprit, s. a shoot, a sprout
Sprite, s. a spirit, an incorporeal agent
Sprit'sail, s. the sail on a ship's bowspr'
Sprout, v. n. to shoot by vegetation
Sprout, s. a shoot of a vegetable
Spruce, a. neat, trim—s. a kind of fir
Sprucebee'r, s. a kind of physical beer
Spru'ceness, s. neatness without elegance
Spud, s. a short knife
Spume, s. foam, froth—v. a. to foam
Spu'mous, Spu'my, a. frothy, foamy
Spunge, s. a soft porous substance, remarkable for sucking up water
Spun'ging-house, s. a bailiff's house
Spun'gy, a. soft and porous like a spunge
Spunk, s. touchwood, rotten wood
Spur, v. to prick with a spur ; to incite
Spur, s. a sharp point fixed to the heel ; stimulus, incitement, instigation
Spur'galled, a. hurt with a spur
Spu'rious, a. counterfeit, not legitimate
Spur'ling, s. a small sea-fish
Spurn, v. to kick ; reject, put away with contempt—s. kick, insolent treatment
Spur'rier, s. one who makes spurs

spurt, _v. n._ to fly out with a quick stream
Spurt, _s._ a start or sudden fit, a hurry
Sputa'tion, _s._ the act of spitting
Sput'ter, _v._ to speak hastily ; to spit much
Spy, _s._ one who watches another's motions
Spy, _v._ to discover at a distance ; search
Spy'boat, _s._ a boat sent out for intelligence
Squab, _s._ a kind of sofa or couch
Squab, _a._ unfeathered ; thick and short
Squab'bish, Squab'by, _a._ heavy ; fleshy
Squab'ble, _v. n._ to quarrel, wrangle, fight
Squab'ble, _s._ a low brawl, a petty quarrel
Squad'ron, _s._ a part of an army or fleet
Squal'id, _a._ foul, nasty, filthy ; ill favoured
Squall, _s._ sudden gust of wind ; loud scream
Squall, Squeal, _v. n._ to scream suddenly
Squall'y, _a._ windy, gusty, stormy
Squa'mose, Squa'mous, _a._ scaly ; rough
Squan'der, _v. a._ to spend profusely ; scatter
Square, _a._ having right angles, cornered ;
    well set, stout ; equal ; exact, fair, &c.
Square, _s._ a regular figure ; an instrument
Square, _v._ to form with right angles ; fit
Squash, _s._ any thing soft ; a sudden fall
Squat, _v. n._ to sit close to the ground
Squat, _a._ cowering down ; thick and short
Squeak, _v. n._ to make a shrill noise, cry out
Squeak, _s._ a shrill, quick cry
Squea'mish, _a._ weak-stomached ; nice
Squeeze, _v. a._ to press, crush, oppress
Squelch, _s._ a sudden and heavy fall
Squib, _s._ a small paper pipe, with wild-fire
Squill, _s._ a sea-onion ; a fish ; an insect
Squin'ancy, _s._ inflammation in the throat
Squint, _v. n._ to look obliquely or awry
Squint, _a._ looking obliquely or asquint
Squire, _v. n._ to conduct a person—_s_ a title
Squir'rel, _s._ a small active animal
Squirt, _s._ a pipe to eject liquor
Squirt, _v._ to throw out in a quick stream
Stab, _v. a._ to pierce with a pointed weapon ;
    to wound the mind by calumny
Stab, _s._ a wound with a sharp weapon ; a blow
Stabil'ity, _s._ steadiness, fixedness, firmness
Sta'ble, _a._ fixed, constant ; strong, firm
Sta'ble, _s._ a house for horses, &c.
Stack, _s._ a pile of hay, corn, or wood ; a row
    of chimneys or funnels
Sta'dle, _s._ a staff ; a crutch ; a young tree
Stadt'holder, _s._ the chief magistrate of the
    united provinces of Holland
Staff, _s._ a stick ; a prop ; an ensign of office
Stag, _s._ a red male deer, five years old
Stage, _s._ a theatre, place where any thing
    public is exhibited ; a resting-place on a
    journey ; a single step of gradual process
Sta'gecoach, _s._ a coach that travels by stages
Stag'gard, _s._ a four-year-old stag
Stag'ger, _v._ to reel ; faint ; hesitate ; alarm
Stag'gers, _s._ a vertigo in horses ; madness
Stag'nant, _a._ not flowing or agitated
Stag'nate, _v. n._ to have no course or stream
Stagna'tion, _s._ a stop of course or motion
Staid, _part. a._ sober, grave, regular
Stain, _v. a._ to blot, maculate ; disgrace
Stain, _s._ a blot, taint of guilt, shame
Stair, _s._ a step to ascend a house, &c. by
Stair'case, _s._ a whole set of stairs
Stake, _s._ a post ; a wager ; pledge ; hazard
Stake, _v. a._ to defend with stakes ; wager
Stalac'tites, _s._ spar in the form of icicles

Stalac'tical, _a._ resembling an icicle
Stale, _a._ not fresh, old, worn out of notice
Stale, _v. n._ to make water
Sta'leness, _s._ oldness, not freshness
Stalk, _v. n._ to walk stately—_s._ a stem
Stalk'inghorse, _s._ a horse used by fowlers to
    conceal themselves from the game
Stall, _s._ a crib for horses, &c. ; a booth
Stal'lion, _s._ a horse not castrated
Stam'ina, _s._ first principles of any thing ;
    solids of a human body, threads of plants
Stamin'eous, _a._ consisting of threads
Stam'mer, _v. n._ to falter in one's speech
Stam'mering, _s._ an impediment in speech
Stamp, _s._ any instrument to make an im-
    pression ; character, good or bad ; a mark
    set upon things that pay customs
Stamp, _v._ to strike with the foot ; to mark
Stanch, _a._ sound, firm ; trusty ; hearty
Stanch, _v. a._ to stop blood, &c. from running
Stan'chion, _s._ a prop, a support
Stan'chless, _a._ that cannot be stopped
Stand, _v._ to be upon the feet, remain erect,
    halt ; offer as a candidate ; persist ; abide
Stand, _s._ a station, post ; halt ; perplexity
Stan'dard, _s._ an ensign in war ; a fixed
    weight ; a measure ; undoubted authority
Stan'del, _s._ a tree of long standing
Stan'ding, _s._ continuance ; station ; rank
Stan'ding, _part. a._ established, settled, last-
    ing ; stagnant ; not transitory
Stan'dish, _s._ a case for pen and ink
Stang, _s._ a measure of land, a perch
Stan'nary, _s._ the mines and places where tin
    is digged and refined
Stan'za, _s._ a set of verses
Sta'ple, _s._ a settled mart, an established em-
    porium ; a loop of iron
Sta'ple, _a._ settled, established in commerce
Star, _s._ a luminous globe in the heavens
Star'board, _s._ the right side of a ship
Starch, _s._ a kind of viscous substance made
    of flour or potatoes, to stiffen linen with
Starch, _v. a._ to stiffen with starch
Starch'ed, _a._ stiffened with starch ; formal
Starch'ly, _ad._ stiffly, precisely
Stare, _v. n._ to look with wonder, &c.
Star'gazer, _s._ an astronomer or astrologer
Stark, _a._ stiff ; strong ; full ; simple ; plain
Stark'ly, _ad._ stiffly, strongly
Star'less, _a._ having no light of stars
Star'light, _s._ lustre of the stars
Star'like, _a._ stellated, bright, illustrious
Star'ling, _s._ a small singing bird ; a defence
    to the piers of bridges in a river
Star'red, _a._ decorated with stars
Star'ry, _a._ consisting of or like stars
Start, _v._ to rise or move suddenly ; propose
Start, _s._ a motion of terror, quick spring
Start'er, _s._ one that shrinks from his purpose
Star'tish, Star'tlish, _a._ apt to start
Star'tle, _v._ to start by surprise or fright ; to
    fright, shock, impress with sudden terror
Starve, _v._ to kill with hunger or cold
Star'ving, _part._ dying with hunger
Star'veling, _s._ a lean meagre person
Sta'tary, _a._ fixed, settled, determined
State, _s._ condition, dignity ; a republic
State, _v. a._ to settle, separate, represent
Sta'teliness, _s._ grandeur, dignity, pride
Sta'tely, _a._ pompous, august, elevated

Sta'tely, *ad.* majestically, proudly
Sta'tement, *s.* the act of stating ; a history or
   account
Sta'tesman, *s.* one employed in public affairs,
   one versed in the arts of government
Stat'ic, Stat'ical, *a.* relating to weighing
Stat'ics, *s.* the science of weighing bodies
Sta'tion, *s.* act of standing, post, rank
Sta'tion, *v. a.* to place in a certain post, &c.
Sta'tionary, *a.* fixed ; not progressive
Sta'tioner, *s.* a dealer in paper, &c.
Sta'tionery, *s.* wares sold by a stationer
Sta'tist, *s.* a statesman, a politician
Statis'tical, *a.* political   [ment
Statis'tics, *s.* the science of political govern-
Stat'uary, *s.* a carver of images
Stat'ue, *s.* an image of wood, metal, &c.
Stat'ure, *s.* the height of any animal
Stat'utable, *a.* acting according to statute
Stat'ute, *s.* an act of parliament, law, edict
Stave, *v.* to break in pieces : push off ; fight
Staves, *s.* the *plural of staff*
Stay, *v.* to continue in a place ; stop ; prop
Stay, *s.* continuance in a place ; stop ; prop
Stay'ed, *a.* settled, fixed, serious, grave
Stays, *s.* bodice for women ; any support
Stead, *s.* place, room ; use ; help ; frame
Stead, *v. a.* to help, to support, to assist
Stead'fast, *a.* firm, fixed, constant, resolute
Stead'fastly, *ad.* firmly, constantly
Stead'fastness, *s.* fixedness, firmness
Stead'iness, *s.* firmness, unvaried conduct
Stead'y, *a.* firm, not fickle, not wavering
Steak, Stake, *s.* a slice of flesh, a collop
Steal, *v.* to take by theft, to pass silently
Stealth, *s.* the act of stealing, secret act
Steam, *s.* the vapour of hot liquor, &c.
Steed, *s.* a horse ; horse for state, war, &c.
Steel, *s.* iron refined by fire ; a weapon
Steel, *v. a.* to point with steel ; to harden
Steel'y, *a.* made of steel, hard, firm
Steel'yard, *s.* a kind of balance for weighing
Steen, *s.* a fictitious vessel of clay or stone
Steep, *a.* rising or descending with great
   inclination, of a difficult ascent
Steep, *s.* a precipice—*v. a.* to soak in liquor
Stee'ple, *s.* a turret of a church, a spire
Steep'ly, *a.* steep, perpendicular, inclining
Steer, *s.* a young ox—*v.* to guide a ship
Steer'age, *s.* the act of steering ; an apart-
   ment before the great cabin of a ship,
   from which it is separated by a partition
Steers'man, *s.* he who steers a ship
Steganog'raphy, *s.* the art of secret writing
Stegnot'ic, *a.* binding, making costive
Stel'lar, Stel'lary, *a.* relating to the stars
Stel'late, Stel'lated, *a.* pointed as a star
Stellif'erous, *a.* having stars
Stel'lion, *s.* a newt ; a spotted lizard
Stem, *s.* a stalk, twig ; family, race, gene-
   ration ; prow or fore part of a ship
Stem, *v. a.* to oppose a current, to stop
Stench, *s.* a stink, a bad smell
Stenog'raphy, *s.* short-hand writing
Stento'rian, *a.* loud, uncommonly loud [ing
Stentorophon'ic, *s.* loudly speaking or sound-
Step, *v. n.* to move with the feet, to walk
Step, *s.* footstep ; action ; round of a ladder
Step'dame, Step'mother, *s.* a mother-in-law
Step'daughter, *s.* a daughter-in-law
Stercora'tion, *s.* the act of dunging

Stereog'raphy, *s.* the art of drawing the
   forms of solids upon a plane
Stereom'etry, *s.* the art of measuring al
   sorts of solid bodies
Stereo'type, *s.* a type-metal plate, to print
   from at the letter-press
Ster'il, *a.* barren, unfruitful, dry
Steril'ity, *s.* barrenness, unfruitfulness
Ster'ilize, *v. a.* to make barren
Ster'ling, *s.* English coin ; standing rate
Ster'ling, *a.* genuine ; lawful English coin
Stern, *a.* severe of look or manners, harsh
Stern, *s.* the hindermost part of a ship
Stern'ly, *ad.* severely, harshly, rigidly
Stern'ness, *s.* severity of look, harshness
Ster'non, or Ster'num, *s.* the breast bone
Sternuta'tion, *s.* the act of sneezing
Sternu'tative, *a.* apt to cause sneezing
Stew, *v.* to seeth slowly—*s.* a hot-house
Stew'ard, *s.* a manager of another's affairs
Stew'ardship, *s.* the office of a steward
Stib'ial, *a.* antimonial
Stick, *s.* a small piece of wood, a staff
Stick, *v.* to fasten on ; adhere ; scruple ; stab
Stic'kle, *v. n.* to contend with obstinacy
Stic'kler, *s.* a busy-body ; a second to a duel-
   list ; an obstinate contender
Stic'ky, *a.* viscous, adhesive, glutinous
Stiff, *a.* inflexible, harsh, formal, strong
Stiff'en, *v.* to make or grow stiff, he harden-
   ed, grow obstinate, become unpliant
Stiff'ly, *ad.* rigidly, inflexibly, stubbornly
Stiff'necked, *a.* stubborn, contumacious
Stiff'ness, *s.* rigidity, tension, obstinacy
Sti'fle, *v.* to suffocate, suppress, extinguish
Stig'ma, *s.* a brand, a mark of infamy
Stig'matize, *v. a.* to mark with infamy
Sti'lar, *a.* belonging to the stile of a dial
Stile, *s.* steps in a field ; a pin of a sun-dial
Stilet'to, *s.* a small dagger or tuck
Still, *v. a.* to silence, quiet, appease, distil
Still, *a.* silent, calm—*ad.* nevertheless
Still, *s.* a vessel for distillation ; silence
Stillatit'ious, *a.* drawn by a still
Stil'latory, *s.* a still ; a laboratory
Still'born, *a.* dead in the birth, born lifeless
Still'ness, *s.* calmness, quietness, silence
Stilts, *s.* walking supports used by boys
Stim'ulate, *v. a.* to excite, urge, spur on
Stimula'tion, *s.* an excitement, pungency
Sting, *v. a.* to pierce or wound with a sting
Sting, *s.* a sharp point with which some ani-
   mals are armed ; any thing that gives pain ;
   the point in the last verse
Stin'giness, *s.* covetousness, niggardliness
Stin'go, *s.* a fine old strong beer
Stin'gy, *a.* covetous, niggardly, avaricious
Stink, *s.* an offensive smell, a stench
Stink'pot, *s.* a kind of hand grenade, filled
   with a stinking composition
Stint, *v. a.* to bound, to limit, to restrain
Sti'pend, *s.* wages, salary, settled pay
Stipen'diary, *s.* one who serves for a stipend
Stip'tic, *a.* apt to stop blood ; astringent
Stip'ulate, *v. n.* to contract, to settle terms
Stipula'tion, *s.* a bargain, a contract
Stipula'tor, *s.* one who bargains
Stir, *v.* to move, agitate, incite, rise
Stir, *s.* tumult, bustle, commotion
Stir'ious, *a.* resembling icicles
Stir'rer, *s.* one in motion ; an early riser

Stir'rup, s. an iron for a horseman's foot
Stitch, v. to sew with a needle; join, unite
Stitch, s. a sharp pain in the side
Stive, v. a. to put up close; to make hot
Stocca'do, s. a thrust with a rapier
Stock, v. a. to store, to lay in store
Stock, s. the trunk or body of a plant; a log; linen for the neck; lineage; quantity; fund of money; frame of a gun, &c.
Stock'dove, s. a kind of wild pigeon
Stock'fish, s. a cod dried without salt
Stock'ing, s. a covering for the leg
Stock'jobber, s. one who deals in stock
Stock'lock, s. a lock fixed in wood
Stocks, s. a prison for the legs; a frame of timber, &c. on which ships are built
Sto'ic, s. a philosopher of the sect of Zeno
Stole, s. a long vest, a royal robe
Stom'ach, s. the ventricles of digestion; appetite; anger; sullenness; pride
Stom'ach, v. to resent, to be violently angry
Stom'acher, s. an ornament for the breast
Stomach'ic, a. relating to the stomach
Stone, s. a mineral not ductile or malleable; a gem; a concretion in the bladder or kidneys; a weight of 14lb. &c.; the case which contains the seeds of some fruits
Stone, a. made of or like stone
Stone, v. a. to pelt or kill with stones
Sto'nefruit, s. plums, apricots, peaches, &c.
Sto'nehorse, s. a horse not castrated
Sto'nepit, s. a quarry where stones are dug
Sto'nepitch, s. hard, inspissated pitch
Sto'ny, a. made of or full of stones, hard
Stool, s. a seat without a back; an evacuation
Stool'ball, s. a kind of game with balls
Stoop, v. n. to bend, to yield, to submit
Stoop, s. a measure of two quarts
Stop, v. a. to hinder, to close up, to obstruct
Stop, s. a pause or stand; prohibition; point in writing; regulation in music, &c.
Stop'cock, s. a pipe made to let out liquor, stopped by turning a cock
Stop'page, s. an obstruction, hindrance
Stop'ple, or Stop'per, s. that by which the mouth or hole of a vessel is stopped
Sto'rax, s. the name of a tree, and its gum
Store, s. plenty, abundance; a warehouse
Store, v. to furnish, replenish, lay up
Sto'rehouse, s. a magazine, a treasury
Stork, s. a bird of passage
Storm, s. a tempest; assault; sedition
Storm, v. to attack by open force, to rage
Stor'my, a. violent, tempestuous
Sto'ry, s. a narrative, a tale; flight of rooms
Stove, s. a hot-house; a place to make fire in
Stout, a. strong, brave, firm, intrepid, lusty
Stout'ly, ad. boldly, lustily, obstinately
Stout'ness, s. strength, fortitude, obstinacy
Stow, v. a. to lay up in order, and close
Stow'age, s. place where goods may be stowed or laid up; a being laid up
Stra'bism, s. squinting; act of looking asquint
Strad'dle, v. n. to walk wide and awkwardly
Strag'gle, v. n. to wander dispersedly, to rove, to ramble; to exuberate
Straight, a. not crooked; right; narrow
Straight, Straight'ways, ad. immediately
Straight'en, v. a. to make straight
Strain, v. to squeeze through something; sprain; make; turn force, constrain

Strain, s. style of speaking; song; note, rank; character; turn; tendency
Strain'er, s. an instrument for filtration
Strait, a. narrow, close, difficult, not wide
Strait, s. a narrow pass or frith; difficulty
Strait'en, v. a. to make narrow, to confine
Strait'ly, ad. narrowly, strictly, rigorously
Strait'ness, s. narrowness, rigour, distress
Strake, s. a plate of iron; seam; breadth
Strand, s. the sea-beach, verge of any river
Strand, v. to drive or force on the shallows
Strange, a. foreign, wonderful, irregular, odd
Strange, interj. an expression of wonder
Stra'ngely, ad. wonderfully, uncommonly
Stra'nger, s. a foreigner, one unacquainted
Stran'gle, v. a. to choke, suffocate, suppress
Stran'gles, s. a disease in horses
Stran'gury, s. difficulty of urine with pain
Strap, s. a long narrow slip of leather
Strappa'do, s. chastisement with a strap
Strap'ping, a. large, vast, bulky
Stra'ta, s. beds or layers of different matter
Strat'agem, s. an artifice in war; a trick
Stra'tum, s. a bed or layer of any matter
Straw, s. the stalk on which corn grows
Straw'berry, s. a fine summer fruit
Straw'coloured, a. of a light yellow colour
Stray, v. n. to wander, rove, err, deviate
Stray, s. any creature, &c. lost by wandering
Streak, s. a line of colour, stripe, track
Streak, v. a. to stripe, variegate, dapple
Strea'ky, a. striped, variegated by hues
Stream, s. a running water, a current
Stream, v. to flow, issue continually, streak
Stream'er, s. an ensign, flag, pennon
Stream'let, s. a little stream, a rivulet
Street, s. a paved way between houses
Strength, s. force, vigour, armament
Strength'en, v. to make strong, to confirm
Strength'ener, s. that which makes strong
Stren'uous, a. bold, active, brave, zealous
Stren'uously, ad. vigorously, zealously
Strep'ent, a. making a loud hoarse noise
Strep'erous, a. loud, noisy, jarring, hoarse
Stress, s. importance, violence, force
Stretch, v. a. to extend, expand, draw out
Stretch, s. extension, reach, struggle
Stret'cher, s. any thing used for extension; the wood against which rowers set their feet; one who stretches; a support
Strew, v. n. to spread by scattering
Striæ, s. small channels in cockle-shells, &c.
Stri'ate, Stri'ated, a. formed in channels
Strick'en, part. beaten, smitten, advanced
Strick'le, s. that which strikes the corn in a measure to level it
Strict, a. exact, rigorous, severe, confined
Strict'ly, ad. exactly, rigorously, accurately
Stric'ture, s. a contraction; a slight touch
Stride, s. a long step—v. to make long steps
Strife, s. contention, contest, discord
Strig'ment, s. scrapings, dross, filth
Strike, v. to hit with a blow; impress; stamp, lower; make a bargain; be stranded
Strike, s. a bushel; a dry measure
Stri'king, part. a. affecting, surprising
String, s. a slender rope; cord; series
String, v. a. to furnish with strings; to tie
String'ed, a. having or produced by strings
Strin'gent, a. binding, contracting
String'halt, s. a disorder in horses

String'y, a. fibrous, consisting of threads
Strip, v. a. to make naked, to rob, to divest
Strip, s. a narrow shred, a slip
Stripe, s. a streak in silk, cloth, &c.; a lash
 with a whip; a blow—v. a. to variegate
 with lines of different colours
Strip'ling, s. a youth
Strive, v. n. to struggle, labour, contend, vie
Stroke, s. a blow, knock; sound of a clock
Stroke, v. a. to rub gently or tenderly
Stroll, v. n. to wander, to rove, to gad idly
Stroll'er, s. a vagrant, wanderer, vagabond
Strong, a. vigorous, hale, potent, cogent
Strong'ly, ad. powerfully, vehemently
Stro'phe, s. the first stanza of a poem
Struc'ture, s. an edifice, building; form
Strug'gle, v.n. to labour, to strive, to contest
Strug'gle, s. labour, effort, contest, agony
Stru'mous, a. having swellings in the glands;
 relating to the king's evil
Strum'pet, s. a prostitute, a harlot
Strut, v. n. to walk affectedly, to swell
Stub, s. a log, a block—v. a. to root up
Stub'bed, a. short and thick; truncated
Stub'ble, s. stalks of corn after reaping
Stub'born, a. obstinate, inflexible; rugged
Stub'bornly, ad. obstinately, contumaciously
Stub'bornness, s. obstinacy, contumacy
Stub'nail, s. a nail broken off
Stuc'co, s. a fine plaster for walls
Stud, s. a stock of breeding mares; a button
Stu'dent, s. a scholar, a bookish man
Stud'ied, a. learned, versed in any study
Stu'dious, a. diligent, contemplative
Stu'diously, ad. diligently, carefully
Stu'diousness, s. addiction to study
Stud'y, s. application to books and learning;
 deep thought; an apartment for books
Stud'y, v. to muse, to contrive, to consider
Stuff, s. furniture, goods; medicine; cloth
Stuff, v. to fill, to swell, to feed gluttonously
Stuf'fing, s. that by which any thing is filled;
 relishing ingredients put into meat
Stultil'oquence, s. foolish talk
Stul'tify, v. a. to make foolish
Stum, s. new wines used to raise fermenta-
 tion in dead and vapid wines
Stum'ble, v. to trip in walking, to err, to slip
Stum'bler, s. one that stumbles or mistakes
Stum'blingblock, s. cause of offence
Stump, s. the part of any solid body remain-
 ing after the rest is taken away
Stum'py, a. full of stumps, hard, strong
Stun, v.a. to render stupid by a noise or a blow
Stunt, v. a. to hinder from growth
Stupe, s. warm medicaments for a sore, &c.
Stupe, v. a. to foment; to dress with stupes
Stupefac'tion, s. insensibility, stupidness
Stupefac'tive, a. causing insensibility
Stupen'dous, a. wonderful, astonishing
Stu'pid, a. dull, heavy, sluggish
Stupid'ity, s. heaviness of mind, dulness
Stu'pidly, ad. dully, without apprehension
Stu'pify, v. a. to make stupid, to benumb
Stu'por, s. a suspension of sensibility
Stu'prate, v. a. to violate, to ravish, deflour
Stupra'tion, s. rape, violence, ruin
Stur'diness, s. stoutness; brutal strength
Stur'dy, a. hardy, obstinate, strong, stout
Stur'geon, s. the name of a fish
Sturk, s. a young ox or heifer

Stut'ter, v. n. to stammer, to speak badly
Stut'terer, s. one that stutters
Sty, s. a hovel for hogs [Styx
Styg'ian, a. hellish, pertaining to the river
Style, s. manner of writing or speaking; ti-
 tle; method of reckoning the year, &c.
Style, v. to call, to term, to name
Styp'tic, s. an astringent medicine or lotio-
Styp'tic, a. astringent; able to stop blood
Stypticity, s. the power of stopping blood
Sua'sible, a. easy to be persuaded
Sua'sive, a. having power to persuade
Suav'ity, s. sweetness, pleasantness
Subac'id, a. sour in a small degree
Subac'rid, a. pungent in a small degree
Subac'tion, s. the act of reducing
Sub'altern, a. subordinate, inferior
Sub'altern, s. an inferior officer or judge
Subalter'nate, a. succeeding by turns
Subchan'ter, s. the deputy of a precentor
Subcla'vian, a. lying under the arm-pit
Subcuta'neous, a. lying under the skin
Subdea'con, s. the deacon's servant
Subdea'n, s. the vicegerent of a dean
Subdec'uple, a. containing one part of ten
Subdiver'sify, v. a. to diversify over again
Subdivi'de, v. a. to divide again
Sub'dolous, a. cunning, artful, sly
Subdu'ce, Subduc't, v. a. to withdraw, to take
 away, to subtract by arithmetic
Subduc'tion, s. the act of taking away
Subdue', v. a. to conquer, to crush, to tame
Subdue'ment, s. the act of subduing
Subdu'ple, Subdu'plicate, a. half, one in two
Subja'cent, a. lying under
Subjec't, v. a. to reduce to submission, to
 enslave, to make liable, to expose
Sub'ject, a. placed under; liable, apt
Sub'ject, s. one who is under the dominion
 of another; the matter treated of
Subjec'tion, s. state of being under a supe-
 rior; the act of subduing
Subjec'tive, a. relating to the subject
Subingres'sion, s. secret entrance
Subjo'in, v. a. to add to the end, or after
Subita'neous, a. sudden, hasty
Sub'jugate, v. a. to conquer, to subdue
Subjuga'tion, s. the act of subduing or hum-
Subjunc'tion, s. the act of subjoining [bling
Subjunc'tive, a. subjoined to something else
Sublap'sary, a. done after the fall of man
Subla'tion, s. the act of taking away
Subli'mable, a. possible to be sublimed
Sub'limate, s. quicksilver sublimed
Sublima'tion, s. a chymical operation which
 raises bodies in the vessel by force of fire
Subli'me, v. a. to raise by chymical fire; to
 exalt
Subli'me, s. the grand or lofty style
Subli'me, a. high in place or style, lofty
Subli'mely, ad. in a lofty manner, grandly
Sublim'ity, s. height of place, style or excel-
 lence; loftiness of style or sentimen.
Sublin'gual, a. placed under the tongue
Sublu'nar, Sub'lunary, a. under the orb of the
 moon, terrestrial, earthly
Submari'ne, a. lying or acting under the sea
Submer'sion, s. the act of drowning
Submiss', Submis'sive, a. humble, obsequious
Submis'sion, s. a yielding to, obedience
Submis'sively, ad. humbly, obsequiously

Submis'siveness, s. confession of inferiority
Submit', v. to refer to judgment; to yield; to resign to authority; to let down; to sink
Sub'multiple, s. an even part
Subnas'cent, a. growing out underneath
Suboc'tave, Suboc'tuple, a. one part of eight
Subor'dinacy, Subor'dinancy, s. the state of being subject; series of subordination
Subor'dinate, a. inferior in order, subject
Subor'dinately, ad. in a series regularly descending; in an inferior degree
ubordina'tion, s. a state of being inferior
Subor'n, v. a. to procure by secret collusion
Suborna'tion, s. the crime of procuring any one to do a bad action
Subpœ'na, s. a writ commanding attendance in a court, under a penalty
Subquad'ruple, a. containing a fourth part
Subquin'tuple, a. containing a fifth part
Subreptit'ious, a. fraudulently obtained
Subscri'be, v. to sign, to attest, to consent to
Subscri'ber, s. one who subscribes, &c.
Subscrip'tion, s. any thing underwritten; attestation or consent by underwriting the name; money, &c. subscribed for carrying on any undertaking; submission
Subsec'utive, a. following in train
Sub'sequence, s. the state of following
Sub'sequent, a. following, not preceding
Sub'sequently, ad. so as to follow in train
Subserve, v. a. to promote, to help forward
Subser'vience, s. instrumental fitness or use
Subser'vient, a. instrumental, serviceable
Subsi'de, v. n. to sink or tend downwards
Subsi'dency, s. tendency downwards
Subs'diary, a. assistant, brought in aid
Sub'sidy, s. an aid, tax, or tribute
Subsi'gn, v. a. to sign under
Subsis't, v. n. to endure, have means of living
Subsis'tence, s. real being; competence
Subsis'tent, a. having real being, existent
Sub'stance, s. something existing; essential part; something real; body; wealth
Substan'tial, a. real, solid, corporeal, strong
Substantial'ity, s. corporeity, materiality
Substan'tialize, v. a. to reduce to reality
Substan'tially, ad. strongly, solidly, really
Substan'tiate, v. a. to make to exist
Sub'stantive, s. a noun betokening a thing
Sub'stantive, a. solid; denoting existence
Sub'stitute, v. a. to put in the place of another
Sub'stitute, s. one acting for another
Substra'tum, s. a layer of earth or any other thing that lies under another
Substruc'tion, s. an under building
Subsul'tive, Sub'sultory, a. moving by starts
Subten'd, v. a. to extend underneath
Subten'se, s. the chord of an arch
Subter'fluent, a. running under
Sub'terfuge, s. an evasion, shift, trick
Subterra'nean, Subterra'neous, a. lying under the earth, placed below the surface
Subterran'ity, s. a place under ground
Sub'tile, a. thin, nice, acute, cunning
Sub'tilely, ad. finely, artfully, cunningly
Sub'tileness, s. fineness, rareness; cunning
Subtil'iate, v. a. to make thin
Subtilia'tion, s. the act of making thin
Sub'tility, s. thinness; cunningness, slyness
Sub'tilize, v. to make thin, to refine
Subtiliza'tion, s. superfluous acuteness

Sub'tle, a. sly, artful, cunning
Subtrac't, v. a. to take away part
Subtrac'tion, s. a taking part from the whole
Subven'tion, s. a supply, aid, relief
Subver'sion, s. overthrow, ruin, destruction
Subver'sive, a. tending to overturn
Subver't, v. n. to overturn, ruin
Sub'urbs, s. buildings, &c. belonging to a city, but without the walls
Succeda'neous, a. in the room of another
Succeda'neum, s. that which is put to serve for something else
Succee'd, v. to follow in order, to prosper
Success', s. happy termination of any affair
Success'ful, a. prosperous, fortunate
Success'fully, ad. prosperously, luckily
Succes'sion, s. a series of things or persons following one another; lineage; inheritance; order of descendants
Success've, a. following in order
Success'ively, ad. in an uninterrupted order
Success'or, s. one who succeeds to another
Succin'ct, a. tucked up; concise, brief
Succin'ctly, ad. briefly, concisely
Suc'cory, s. a plant, wild endive
Suc'cour, v. a. to relieve, assist in distress
Suc'cour, s. aid, assistance, relief
Suc'culent, a. juicy, moist, full of juice
Succumb', v. n. to sink under difficulty, yield
Succus'sion, s. the act of shaking
Such, prom. of that, or the like kind
Suck, v. to draw in; to extract moisture
Suck'er, s. any thing that draws; part of a pump; a young twig or shoot
Suck'et, s. a sweetmeat, a con erve
Suc'kle, v. a. to nurse at the breast
Suck'ling s. a sucking child, lamb, &c.
Suc'tion, s. the act of sucking up
Suda'tion, s. act of sweating
Su'datory, a. sweating—s. a sweating bath
Sud'den, a. without notice, hasty, violent
Sud'den, s. any unexpected occurrence
Sud'denly, ad. in an unexpected manner
Sudorif'ic, a. provoking or causing sweat
Suds, s. a lixivium of soap and water
Sue, v. to prosecute by law; beg, entreat
Su'et, s. fat, hard fat about the kidneys
Su'ety, a. consisting of or like suet
Suf'fer, v. to bear, endure, permit, undergo
Suf'ferable, a. that may be borne
Suf'ferance, s. pain, patience, permission
Suf'ferer, s. one who endures or suffers
Suf'fering, s. pain suffered
Suffi'ce, v. to be enough or sufficient
Suffi'ciency, s. a being sufficient, competency, supply equal to want
Suffi'cient, a. equal to; qualified for
Suffi'ciently, ad. enough; tolerably
Suf'focate, v. a. to smother, stifle, choke
Suffoca'tion, s. the act of choking
Suf'fragan, s. a term applied to a bishop, as subject to his metropolitan
Suf'frage, s. a vote, voice, approbation
Suffu'migate, v. a. to smoke underneath
Suffumiga'tion, s. fume raised by fire
Suffu'mige, s. a medical fume
Suffu'se, v. a. to spread over with a tincture
Suffu'sion, s. a spreading over; a dimness
Sug'ar, s. the native salt of the sugar-cane
Sug'arplum, s. a kind of sweetmeat
Sug'ary a. sweet, tasting of sugar

Suggest'. v. a. to hint, to prompt, to put in one's mind, to inform secretly

Sugges'tion, s. hint, intimation, notice

Sug'gilate, v. a. to beat black and blue

Sui'cide, s. self-murder; a self-murderer

Sui'llage, s. a drain of filth [securkm

Sui'ing, s. the act of soaking through; a pro-

Suit, s. a petition; set; courtship; retinue

Suit. v. to fit, to become, to agree, to accord

Suit'able. a. agreeable to, according with

Suit'ably, ad. agreeably, according to

Suit'er, Suit'or, s. a petitioner; a wooer

Suit'ress, s. a female petitioner

Sul'ky, a. sullen, sour, morose, gloomy

Sul'len, a. gloomy, dismal; obstinate

Sul'lenly, ad. gloomily, angrily, intractably

Sul'lenness, s. moroseness, malignity

Sul'ly, v. a. to soil, to tarnish, to dirt, to spot

Sul'phur, s. brimstone, a fat unctuous mineral substance, inflammable by fire

Sulphu'reous, a. containing or like sulphur

Sul'phury, a. partaking of sulphur

Sul'tan, s. the Turkish emperor

Sulta'na, Sul'taness, s. the queen of an eastern emperor

Sul'try, a. hot and close, hot and cloudy

Sum, s. the whole of any thing; a ce tain quantity of money; a compendium

Sum. v. a. to compute, to comprise; collect

Sum'less, a. not to be computed

Sum'marily, ad. briefly, the shortest way

Sum'mary, a. concise—s. an abridgment

Sum'mer, s. the second season

Sum'mer-house, s. a pleasure house or arbour in a garden, used in the summer

Sum'merset, s. a leap heels over head

Sum'mit, s. the top, the utmost height

Sum'mon, v. a. to call with authority, cite

Sum'moner, s. one who summons or cites

Sum'mons, s. a call of authority, citation

Sump'ter, s. a horse of state; a packhorse

Sump'tion, s. the act of taking

Sump'tuary, a. of or pertaining to expenses

Sump'tuous, a. costly, expensive, splendid

Sump'tuously, ad. expensively, splendidly

Sump'tuousness, s. expensiveness

Sun, s. the luminary that makes the day

Sun'beam, s. a ray of the sun

Sun'burnt, a. tanned by the sun

Sun'day, s. the Christian sabbath

Sun'der, v. a. to divide or part asunder

Sun'dial, s. a marked plate on which the shadow points the hour

Sun'dry, a. several, various, more than one

Sun'flower, s. a large yellow flower

Sun'less, a. wanting sun, wanting warmth

Sun'ny, a. bright, clear, exposed to the sun

Sun'rise, s. the beginning of the morning

Sun'set, s. the close of the day, evening

Sun'shine, s. the radiant light of the sun

Sun'shiny, a. bright with or like the sun

Sup, v. to drink by sups; to eat supper

Sup, s. a small draught of liquor

Su'perable, a. that may be conquered

Superabou'nd. v. n. to be exuberant

Superabun'dance. s. more than enough

Superabun'dant, a. being more than enough

Superadd', v. n. to add over and above

Superaddi'tion, s. act of adding to something

Superadve'nient, a. coming unexpected

Superan'nuate, v. to impair by age, &c

Superan'nuated, a. disqualified by age

Superb', a. grand, pompous, stately

Superb'ly, ad. in a superb manner, proudly

Supercar'go, s. a sea officer to manage trac

Superceles'tial, a. above the firmament

Supercil'ious, a. proud, haughty; arbitra

Supercil'iously, ad. contemptuously

Supercil'iousness, s. haughtiness, pride

Superem'inence, s. superior excellence

Superem'inent, a. eminent in a high degr

Superer'ogate, v. n. to do more than duty

Supereroga'tion, s. doing more than duty

Superex'cellent, a. uncommonly excellent

Su'perfice, s. the surface, the outside

Superfic'ial, a. lying on the surface; contrived to cover something; shallow

Superfic'ially, ad. without penetration

Superfic'ialness, s. slight knowledge

Superfic'ies, s. the outside, or surface

Superfi'ne, a. eminently fine

Superflu'itant, a. floating on the top

Superflu'ity, s. more than enough

Super'fluous, a. exuberant, unnecessary

Su'perflux, s. what is more than is wanted

Superincum'bent, a. lying or leaning on the top of something else

Superindu'ce, v. a. to bring in as an addition

Superinten'd, v. a. to oversee; to manage

Superinten'dency, s. the act of overseeing

Superinten'dent, s. a chief overseer

Superior'ity, s. a being greater or higher, &c.

Supe'rior, a. higher, greater, preferable

Superla'tion, s. an exaggeration, excess

Super'lative, a. implying the highest degree

Super'latively, ad. in the highest degree

Superlu'nar, a. placed above the moon

Super'nal, a. coming from above, celestial

Superna'tant, a. swimming above

Supernat'ural, a. above nature; miraculous

Supernat'urally, ad. in a manner contrary to nature

Supernu'merary, a. above a stated number

Superscri'be, v. a. to inscribe on the top or outside of a letter, deed, writing, &c.

Superscrip'tion, s. a writing on the outside

Superse'de, v. a. to make void; to suspend

Superstit'ion, s. false devotion or religiou

Superstit'ious, a. addicted to superstition

Superstit'iously, ad. with erroneous religion

Superstrai'n, v. a. to overstrain

Superstruc't, v. a. to build upon any thing

Superstruc'tion, s. edifice raised on any thing

Superstruc'ture, s. what is built on another

Supervaca'neous, a. needless; superfluous

Superve'ne, v. n. to come unexpected

Superve'nient, a. added, additional

Superven'tion, s. a coming on a sudden

Supervi'se, v. a. to overlook, to oversee

Supervi'sor, s. an overseer, an inspector

Supi'ne, a. lying with the face upwards

Supi'ne, s. a verbal noun, in grammar

Supi'nely, ad. drowsily, indolently

Supi'neness, s. drowsiness, indolence

Sup'per, s. evening repast, last meal of the day

Sup'perless, a. without a supper

Supplan't, v. a. to displace by stratagem

Sup'ple, a. pliant, yielding, fawning

Sup'plement, s. an addition to supply defects

Supplemen'tal, Supplemen'tary, a. additional, that may supply the place of what is lost

Sup'pleness, s. pliantness, flexibility, facility

Sup'pletory, s. what fills up deficiencies
Sup'pliant, a. entreating, submi-sive
Sup'pliant, Sup'plicant, s. a petitioner
Sup'plicate, v. n. to implore, to entreat
Supplica'tion, s. a petition humbly delivered
Supply', v. a. to relieve, serve instead of
Supply', s. a relief of want, aid, support
Suppor't, v. a. to sustain, endure, maintain
Suppor't, s. a prop, maintenance, supply
Suppor'table, a. tolerable; moderate
Suppor'ter, s. one that supports; a prop
Suppo'se, v. a. to imagine or believe without examination; to believe without proof; to admit without proof
Supposit'ion, s. position laid down; hypothesis; imagination yet unproved
Supposit'ious, a. counterfeit, imaginary
Supposit'iousness, s. a being counterfeit
Suppos'itory, s. a kind of solid clyster
Suppress', v. a. to crush, to subdue; conceal
Suppres'sion, s. the act of suppressing
Sup'purate, v. a. to generate pus or matter
Suppura'tion, s. ripening of a humour to pus
Sup'purative, a. digestive, generating matter
Suppu'ta'tion, s. a reckoning, calculation
Suppu'te, v. a. to reckon, to calculate
Supramun'dane, a. above the world
Suprem'acy, s. the highest place or authority
Supre'me, a. highest in dignity, &c.
Supre'mely, ad. in the highest degree
Su'ral, a. being in the calf of the leg
Su'rance, s. a warrant, a security
Surcea'se, v. to stop, to cease, to leave off
Surchar'ge, v. a. to overburden, &c.
Sur'cingle, s. a girth; a girdle of a cassock
Sur'cle, s. a shoot, a twig, a sucker
Sur'coat, s. a short coat worn over the dress
Surd, a. deaf, unheard; incommensurable
Sur'dity, s. deafness; dulnes s, heaviness
Sure, a. certain, confident: safe, firm
Sure, Su'rely, ad. certainly, undoubtedly
Su'rety, s. certainty, security, hostage, bail
Sur'face, s. the superficies; the out ide
Sur'feit, v. to make sick with eating, &c.
Surge, s. a swelling sea—v. n. to rise high
Sur'geon, s. one who professes surgery
Sur'gery, s. curing by manual operation
Sur'gy, a. rising in billows; swelling
Sur'liness, s. gloomy moroseness, sour anger
Sur'ly, a. morose, rough, uncivil, sour
Surmi'se, s. an imperfect notion, a suspicion
Surmou'nt, v. a. to rise above; to conquer, to overcome, to surpass, to exceed
Surmou'ntable, a. conquerable; superable
Sur'name, s. a family name, appellation
Surpass', v. a. to excel, exceed, go beyond
Surpass'ing, part. excelling—ad. exceeding
Sur'plice, s. a clergyman's white garment
Sur'plus, s. an overplus, a remainder
Surpri'se, s. a sudden confusion or perplexity
Surpri'se, v. a. to take unawares, astonish
Surpri'sing, part. a. wonderful, astonishing
Surren'der, v. to yield, to give one's self up
Surren'der, s. the act of yielding, or resigning
Surrep'tion, s. a surprise, sudden invasion
Surreptit'ious, a. done by stealth or fraud
Sur'rogate, s. a deputy; a delegate
Surrou'nd, v. a. to encompass, to enclose
Sursol'id, s. the fourth power of any root
Surtou't, s. a large upper coat, a great coat
Surve'ne, v. a. to supervene, to be added

Survey', v. a. to overlook, to oversee, view
Sur'vey, s. a view, a prospect; a measure
Survey'or, s. an overseer; a measurer
Survi've, v. to live after, to remain alive
Survi'ver, Survi'vor, s. the longest liver
Survi'vorship, s. the state of a survivor
Susceptibil'ity, s. the quality of admitting
Suscep'tible, Suscep'tive, a. apt to take an impression; capable of admitting
Suscep'tion, s. the act of taking or admitting
Suscip'iancy, s. reception, admission
Suscip'ient, s. one who admits or receives
Sus'citate, v. n. to rouse, to excite
Suspec't, v. to fear, mistrust, think guilty
Suspen'd, v. a. to hang, to delay, to put off, to debar, to make, to stop for a time
Suspen'se, s. an uncertainty, doubt; stop
Suspen'sion, s. a hanging up; a being suspended from an office; ceasing for a time
Suspen'sory, a. suspended, hanging by
Suspic'ion, s. the act of suspecting
Suspic'ious, a. inclined to suspect, liable to suspicion; giving reason to imagine ill
Suspira'tion, s. a sigh, a breathing deep
Suspi're, v. n. to sigh, to breathe hard or deep
Susta'in, v. a. to bear, to support, to maintain, to help; to defend a position
Sus'tenance, s. maintenance; victuals
Susur'rate, v. n. to whisper, to speak low
Susurra'tion, s. a whisper, a soft murmur
Sut'ler, s. one who sells victuals, liquors, &c
Sut'tle, s. the neat weight of commodities
Su'ture, s. a sewing of wounds; a joining
Swab, s. a kind of mop—v. a. to mop
Swab'ber, s. a cleaner of a ship's deck, &c.
Swad'dle, v. a. to swathe, to bind in clothes
Swad'dle, s. clothes bound round the body
Swag, v. n. to sink down by its weight
Swag'ger, v. n. to bluster, to bully, to brag
Swain, s. a country servant, a clown
Swal'low, s. a small bird; the throat
Swal'low, v. a. to take down the throat
Swamp, s. a marsh, a fen, watery ground
Swam'py, s. boggy, fenny, marshy
Swan, s. the name of a large water-fowl
Swan'skin, s. a kind of fine soft flannel
Swap, ad. hastily—v. to exchange
Sward, s. a green turf, the skin of bacon
Swarm, s. a great number of bees, &c., a crowd—v. n. to breed multitudes
Swar'thy, a. dark of complexion, tawny
Swash, v. a. to make a clutter or great noise
Swathe, v. a. to bind with rollers or bands
Sway, v. to bias, to govern, to have weight
Sway, s. power, rule, influence, direction
Swe al, Swale, v. n. to waste away, to melt
Swear, v. to utter an oath, declare upon oath
Sweat, v. to emit moisture; toil, labour
Sweat'y, a. moist with sweat, toilsome
Sweep, v. to clean with a besom; to carry with pomp; to carry off with violence
Sweep, s. the compass of any motion
Sweep'ings, s. what is swept away
Sweep'net, s. a large kind of net
Sweep'stake, s. a man that wins all
Sweet, a. luscious to the taste, mild, soft, grateful, not stale, pleasing to any sense
Sweet, s. sweetness, a word of endearment
Sweet'bread, s. the pancreas of a calf
Sweet'brier, s. a fragrant shrub
Sweet'en, v. to make or grow sweet

Sweet'ener, s. one who palliates, &c.

Sweet'heart, s. a lover or mistress

Sweet'in:, s. a word of endearment

Sweet'ish. a. somewhat sweet

Sweet'ly. ad. lusciously, mildly, gratefully

Sweet'meat,s.fruits,&c.preserved with sugar

Sweet'scented, a. having a sweet smell

Sweetwil'liam, s. a garden flower

Sweetwil'low, s. gale or Dutch myrtle

Swell, v. to grow bigger, look big; heighten

Swell, s. extension of bulk; anger

Swell'ing, s. protuberance, prominence

Swel'ter. v. to be pained or dried with heat

Swel'try, a. suffocating with heat

Swerve, v. n. to wander, to rove, to deviate

Swift, a. quick, nimble, ready, prompt

Swift'ness, s. speed, rapidity. quickness

Swig, v. to drink by large draughts

Swill, v. to drink luxuriously, inebriate

Swim, v. to float on water, to glide along

Swim'ming, s. moving on water; dizziness

Swim'mingly, ad. smoothly, unobstructedly

Swin'dler, s. one who lives by defrauding, a

Swine, s. a hog, a pig [cheat

Swi'neherd, s. a keeper of hogs

Swing, v. to wave loose y in the air

Swing, s. motion of any thing hanging loose-

ly; unrestrained liberty

Swinge, v. a. to whip, bastinade, punish

Swinge'ing, a. great, huge

Swin'gle, v. n. to dangle, swing; beat flax

Swi'nish, a. resembling swine; gross

Switch, s. a small flexible twig

Swiv'el, s. a thing to run upon; a gun

Swob'her, s. a sweeper of a ship's deck

Swoon, v. n. to faint—s. a fainting fit

Swoop, v. a. to fly down hastily, like a hawk

on its prey; prey upon, catch up

Swop, Swap, v. a. to exchange

Sword, s. a well-known military weapon

Sword'cutler, s. one who deals in swords

Sword'law, s. violence, force

Sword'man, s. a soldier, a fighting man

Sword'player, s. a gladiator, a fencer

Syc'ophant, s. a parasite, a flatterer

Sycophan'tic, a. flattering. wheedling

Syllab'ic,Syllab'ical,a.consisting of syllables

Syl'lable, s. as much of a word as is uttered

by the help of one vowel, or one articula-

tion; any thing proverbially concise

Syl'labus, s. the heads of a dis....

Syl'logism, s. an argument of three propo-

sitions; as, every man thinks, Peter is a

man, therefore Peter thinks

Syllogist'ical, a. consisting of a syllogism

Sylphs, s. a kind of fairy nymphs, elves, &c.

Syl'van, (better Silvan), a. woody, shady

Syl'van, s. a wood god, a satyr

Sym'bol, s. an abstract; compendium, type

Symbol'ical, a. representative, typical

Sym'bolize, v. to represent, to resemble

Symmet'rian, s. one studious of proportion

Symmet'rical. Sym'metral, a. proportionate

Sym'metry. s. a due proportion or relation

of parts to the whole; harmony

Sympathet'ic, a. having mutual sensation

Sym'pathize. v. n. to feel with or for another

Sym'pathy, s. mutual sensibility, fellow-

feeling, compassion

Sympho'nious, a. harmonious, musical

Sym'phony, s. harmony of mingled sounds

Symp'tom, s. a sign, a token, an indication

Symptomat'ic, a. happening concurrently

Syn'agogue, s. a place of Jewish worship

Synale'pha, s. a contraction, &c. of a syllable

Syn'chronism, s. a concurrence of events

Syn'cope, s. a fainting fit. a contraction

Syn'copist, s. a contractor of words

Syn'dic, s. a deputy; magistrate, alderman

Syn'dicate, v. n. to pass sentence on, to judge

Syn'drome, s. a concurrent action

Synec'doche, s. a figure of rhetoric, by which

a part is taken for the whole, or the whole

for a part

Syn'od, s. an ecclesiastical assembly

Synod'ical, a. pertaining to a synod

Synon'ymous, a. of the same signification

Synop'sis, s. a general view; all the parts

brought under one view

Syn'tax, s. a system; that part of grammar

which teaches the construction of words

Syn'thesis, s. the act of joining or com-

pounding

Sy'ringe, s. a pipe to squirt liquor with

Syr'tis, s. a quicksand, a bog

Sy'stem, s. a method, theory, science

Systemat'ic, s. one who observes system

System'ical, a. methodical, connected

Sys'tole, s. the contraction of the heart; the

shortening of a long syllable

T

T, s. the 19th letter of the alphabet

Tab'ard, Tab'erd, s. a herald's coat

Tab'by, s. a kind of waved silk—a. brindled;

varied with different colours

Tab'efy, v. n. to waste; be extenuated

Tab'ernacle, s. a sacred place, a place of

worship; temporary habitation

Tab'id, a. consumptive, wasted by disease

Tab'lature, s. painting on walls or ceilings

Ta'ble, s. any flat surface; a syllabus; index

Ta'ble, v. to board; to set down regularly

Ta'blecloth, s. linen spread on a table

Ta'bleman, s. a man at draughts

Tab'let, s. a small table; a small level sur-

face; a medicine in a square form

Ta'bour,s.a small drum; a drum beaten with

one stick, to accompany a pipe

Tab'ular, a. formed in squares or laminæ

Tab'ulated, a. having a flat surface

Tache, s. a button, a loop, a catch

Tachyg'raphy, s. the art of quick writing

Tac'it, a. silent; implied, or meant, though

not expressed by words

Tac'itly, ad. silently; without oral expression

Tacitur'nity, s. habitual silence

Tack, v. to join, to unite; to turn a ship

Tack, s. a small nail; rope; turn of a ship

Tac'kle, s. ropes of a ship; an arrow

Tack'ling, s. ropes and furniture of ships

instruments of action

Tac'tic, *a.* relating to the art of war

Tac'tics, *s.* the art of ranging forces in the field of battle

Tac'tile, *a.* that which may be felt

Tad'pole, *s.* a young shapeless frog

Taf'feta, or Taf'fety, *s.* a sort of thin silk

Tag, *s.* a metal at the end of a lace, &c.

Tag, *v. a.* to fix on a tag ; to join together

Tail, *s.* the hinder or lower part, end

Tai'lor, *s.* one who makes men's clothes

Taint, *v.* to stain, sully, infect, corrupt

Taint, *s.* a tincture, stain, soil, infection

Tain'ture, *s.* tinge, taint, defilement

Take, *v.* to receive ; seize ; surprise ; catch ; exact ; procure ; suppose ; captivate

Ta'king, *s.* seizure ; distress, calamity

Tal'bot, *s.* a kind of spotted dog for hunting

Tale, *s.* a story, narrative, fable ; reckoning

Ta'lebearer, *s.* a malignant officious telltale

Tal'ent, *s.* a certain weight or sum ; faculty, gift of nature, quality, disposition

Tul'isman, *s.* a magical character

Talk, *v. n.* to speak, prattle, reason ; confer

Talk'ative, *a.* full of prate ; loquacious

Talk'ativeness, *s.* loquacity ; garrulity

Talk'er, *s.* a prattler, a loquacious fellow

Talk'ing, *s.* the act or power of speaking

Tall, *a.* high in stature, lofty ; lusty

Tall'ness, *s.* height of stature ; procerity

Tal'low, *s.* the fat of beasts melted, suet

Tal'lowchandler, *s.* one who makes and sells tallow candles

Tal'lowish, *a.* having the nature of tallow

Tal'ly, *s.* two sticks equally notched

Tal'ly, *.* to fit ; to conform, to be suitable

Tal'lyman, *s.* one who sells clothes, &c. to be paid for by weekly payments

Tal'mud, Thal'mud, *s.* the book containing the Jewish traditions

Tal'on, *s.* the claw of a bird of prey

Tam'arind, *s.* an acid Indian fruit

Tam'barine, Tam'bour, *s.* a small drum ; a fine sieve

Tame, *a.* not wild ; depressed, spiritless

Tame, *v. a.* to subdue ; make gentle ; crush

Ta'mely, *ad.* not wildly ; meanly

Ta'meness. *s.* gentleness, want of spirit

Tam'my. Tam'iny, *s.* a sort of worsted stuff

Tam'per, *v. a.* to meddle with ; to practise

Tan, *v.* to prepare skins ; become tawny

Tang, *s.* a strong taste, relish ; sound, tone

Tan'gent, *s.* a line perpendicular to a radius

Tan'gible, *a.* perceptible to the touch

Tan'gle, *v.* to knit together ; entrap, embroil, embarrass, ensnare

Tank, *s.* a reservoir of water ; a large basin

Tan'kard, *s.* a drinking vessel with a lid

Tan'ner, *s.* one who tans hides for leather

Tan'pit, *s.* a pit for tanner's work

Tan'sy, *s.* the name of a plant

Tan'talise, *v. a.* to torment with false hopes

Tan'tamount, *a.* equivalent, worth as much

Tantiv'y, *ad.* with haste, with full speed

Tap, *s.* a gentle blow ; a small pipe

Tap, *v. a.* to touch lightly, to pierce, broach

Tape, *s.* a narrow linen fillet or band

Ta'per, *s.* a wax candle—*a.* sloping, conical

Ta'per, *v. n.* to grow gradually smaller

Ta'perness, *s.* a tapering quality

Tap'estry, *s.* cloth woven with figures

Tap'ster, *s.* one whose trade is to draw beer

Tar, *s.* the juice of pines or firs ; a sailor

Taran'tula, *s.* a venomous insect, whose bite is cured only by music

Tardig'radous, *a.* moving slowly

Tar'dily, *ad.* slowly, sluggishly, heavily

Tar'diness, *s.* slowness, sluggishness

Tar'dy, *a.* slow ; late ; unwary ; criminal

Tare, *s.* a weed ; an allowance in weight

Tar'get, *s.* a kind of buckler or shield

Tar'iff, *s.* a cartel of commerce

Tar'nish, *v.* to sully, soil, lose brightness

Tarpawl'ing, *s.* tarred canvas, a sailor

Tar'riance, *s.* stay, delay ; sojourn

Tar'rier, *s.* one who tarries ; a small dog

Tar'ry, *v.* to stay, to loiter, to wait for

Tart, *a.* sour, severe—*s.* a small fruit pie

Tar'tan, *s.* a kind of woollen stuff

Tar'tane, *s.* a small single-masted ship

Tar'tar, *s.* a native of Tartary ; wine lees

Tarta'rean, *a.* hellish, infernal

Tarta'reous, *a.* consisting of tartar ; hellish

Tart'ly, *ad.* sharply, sourly, severely

Tart'ness, *s.* sharpness, acidity ; ill nature

Task, *s.* employment ; business imposed

Tas'sel, *s.* an ornamental bunch of silk, &c. ; a male hawk ; an herb

Tas'ses, Ta'ces, *s.* armour for the thighs

Taste, *v.* to try the relish ; to feel ; to enjoy

Taste, *s.* the act of tasting ; discernment ; experiment ; intellectual discernment

Ta'steless, *a.* insipid ; having no taste

Ta'stelessness, *s.* insipidity, want of taste

Ta'ster, *s.* one who tastes ; a dram cup

Tat'ter, *v. a.* to tear, to rend—*s.* a rag

Tatterdema'lion, *s.* a ragged fellow

Tat'tle, *v. n.* to prate, to talk idly

Tat'tler, *s.* an idle talker, a prater

Tattoo', *s.* a beat of drum by which soldiers are warned to quarters

Tav'ern, *s.* a house where wine is sold

Taunt, *v. a.* to reproach, insult, revile

Taunt, *s.* an insult, scoff, reproach

Taunt'ingly, *ad.* in a reproachful manner

Tautolog'ical, *a.* repeating the same thing

Tautol'ogy, *s.* a repetition of the same words

Taw, *v.* to dress white leather—*s.* a marble

Taw'dry, *a.* ridiculously or meanly showy

Taw'ny, *a.* yellow, like things tanned

Tax, *s.* an impost, tribute, charge ; censure

Tax, *v.* to lay a tax ; censure ; charge

Tax'able, *a.* liable to be taxed

Taxa'tion, *s.* the act of loading with taxes

Tea, *s.* a Chinese shrub, liquor made thereof

Tea'board, *s.* a board for tea cups, &c.

Teach, *v.* to instruct, inform, show, tell

Tea'chable, *a.* susceptive of instruction

Tea'cher, *s.* an instructor ; a preacher

Tea'cup, *s.* a small cup to drink tea from

Tead, or Tede, *s.* a torch, a flambeau

Teague, *s.* name of contempt for an Irishman

Teal, *s.* a wild fowl of the duck kind

Team, *s.* a farmer's waggon ; flock, number

Tear, *s.* water from the eye ; fissure

Tear, *v.* to rend in pieces ; to rave, to fume

Tear'ful, *a.* weeping, full of tears

Tease, *v. a.* to comb wool ; to scratch ; vex

Tea'sel, *s.* a plant used in dressing cloth

Teat, *s.* the dug of an animal

Tech'nical, *a.* of or belonging to arts sciences

Tech'y, or Tetch'y, *a.* peevish, captious

R 3

Tuston'ic, *a.* pertaining to building
Ted, *v. a.* to lay newly mown grass in rows
Te i e'um, *s.* a hymn used in the liturgy
Te'dious, *a.* wearisome, irksome, slow
Te'diously, *ad.* in a manner to weary
Teem, *v.* to bring forth young, to abound
Teem'ful, *a.* pregnant, prolific, brimful
Teem'less, untruitful, not prolific
Teens, *s.* the years between 12 and 20
Teeth, *plural of tooth—v. n.* to breed teeth
Teg'ument, *s.* a cover, the outward part
Teint, *s.* colour, shade, touch of a pencil
Tel'ary, *a.* spinning webs
Tel'egraph, *s.* a machine for the speedy conveyance of intelligence by signals
Tel'escope, *s.* a glass used for distant views
Tell, *v.* to utter, relate, count, betray
Tell'er, *s.* one who tells or counts, or relates
Tell'tale, *s.* an officious talebearer
Temera'rious, *a.* rash, careless, heedless
Temer'ity, *s.* rashness, unadvisedness, unreasonable contempt of danger
Tem'per, *s.* calmness of mind, moderation; due mixture of contrary qualities
Tem'per, *v. a.* to soften, to mingle, ma' e fit
Tem'perament, *s.* constitution, a medium
Tem'perance, *s.* moderation, patience
Tem'perate, *a.* moderate, calm, not excessive
Tem'perately, *ad.* moderately, calmly
Tem'perature, *s.* constitution of nature; moderation, mediocrity, temperament
Tem'pest, *s.* the utmost violence of the wind
Tem'pest-tost, *a.* driven about by storms
Tempes'tuous, *a.* stormy, boisterous
Tem'plar, *s.* a student in the law
Tem'ple, *s.* a church; the side of the head
Tem'poral, *a.* measured by time; not eternal, secular, not spiritual; name of an arte y
Tem'porally, *ad.* with respect to this life
Tem'porally, *s.* the laity, secular possessions
Tem'porary, *a.* lasting only for a time
Tem'porize, *v. n.* to delay, to procrastinate; to comply with the times or occasions
Tempt, *v.* to entice to ill, to provoke
Tempta'tion, *s.* the act of tempting to ill
Tempt'er, *s.* one who tempts, an enticer
Tem'ulent, *a.* intoxicated, inebriated
Ten, *s.* the decimal number, twice five
Ten'able, *a.* that which may be held or kept
Tena'cious, *a.* retentive, cohesive, not willing to let go an opinion or privilege
Tena'ciously, *ad.* in a tenacious manner
Tenac'ity, *s.* a stiffness in opinion
Ten'ancy, *s.* any temporary possession of what belongs to another
Ten'ant, *s.* one who holds of another
Ten'antable, *a.* fit to be inhabited
Ten'antless, *a.* unoccupied, unpossessed
Tench, *s.* a river or pond fish
Tend, *v.* to watch, move towards, to aim at
Ten'dance, *s.* attendance, a waiting upon
Ten'dence, Ten'dency, *s.* a course, a drift
Ten'der, *a.* soft; easily pained; kind
Ten'der, *v. a.* to offer, to exhibit; to esteem
Ten'der, *s.* a proposal for acceptance
Ten'derhearted, *a.* compassionate, kind
Ten'derling, *s.* the first horns of a deer
Ten'derly, *ad.* gently, mildly, kindly
Ten'derness, *s.* susceptibility of impression; kind attention; scrupulousness, caution
Ten'dinous, *a.* sinewy, containing tendons

Ten'don, *s.* sinew, a ligature of joints
Ten'dril, *s.* the clasper of a vine, &c.
Tene'brious, *a.* dark, gloomy
Ten'ement, *s.* any thing held by a tenant
Tenes'mus, *s.* continual need to go to stool
Ten'et, *s.* a position, principle, opinion
Ten'nis, *s.* a play with a racket and ball
Ten'on, *s.* a term in carpentry
Ten'or, or Ten'our, *s.* continuity of state; sense contained; purport; sound in music
Tense, *s.* a variation of the verb to signify time—*a.* stretched, not lax
Tense'ness, *s.* contraction, tension
Ten'sible, Ten'sile, *a.* capable of extensie
Ten'sion, *s.* the act of stretching, not laxity
Ten'sive, *a.* giving a sensation of stiffness
Tent, *s.* a pavilion, movable habitation; roll of lint put into a sore; a red wine
Tenta'tion, *s.* trial, temptation
Ten'tative, *a.* essaying, experimental
Ten'ted, *a.* covered with tents
Ten'ter, *s.* an iron hook to stretch things on
Tenth, *s.* a yearly tribute from clergymen to the king, ecclesiastical tithes
Tenu'ity, *s.* thinness, slenderness
Ten'uous, *a.* thin, small, minute
Te'nure, *s.* the manner or condition whereby tenements are holden
Tep'id, *a.* lukewarm, warm in a small degree, not zealous
Terce, *s.* a vessel containing 42 gallons
Tercema'ior, *s.* a sequence of three best cards
Tergem'inous, *a.* threefold
Tergiversa'tion, *s.* a shift, evasion, change
Term, *s.* a boundary, limit, a limited or set time; the word by which any thing is expressed, stipulation, time for seats of justice, and exercises at a university
Term, *v. a.* to name, to call
Ter'magant, *s.* a scolding brawling woman
Ter'minable, *a.* admitting of bounds or limits
Ter'minate, *v.* to bound, to limit, to end
Termina'tion, *s.* a limit, bound, conclusion
Ter'miner, *s.* a trial for malefactors
Term'less, *a.* boundless, unlimited, undefined
Ter'race, *s.* a raised walk; a flat roof
Terra'queous, *a.* composed of land and water
Terre'ne, Terres'trial, *a.* earthly; worldly
Ter'reous, Terres'trious, *a.* earthy
Ter'rible, *a.* dreadful, formidable, frightful
Ter'ribly, *ad.* dreadfully, violently
Ter'rier, *s.* a survey of lands; a dog; auger
Terrif'ic, *a.* dreadful, causing terror
Ter'rify, *v. a.* to fright, to make afraid
Territo'rial, *a.* belonging to a territory
Ter'ritory, *s.* land, country, dominion
Ter'ror, *s.* great fear, dread, cause of fear
Terse, *a.* smooth, cleanly written; neat
Ter'tian, *a.* returning every third day
Tes'selated, *a.* variegated by squares
Test, *s.* a vessel to try metals; examination
Testa'ceous, *a.* consisting of shells
Tes'tament, *s.* a will; each of the volumes of the scriptures, as, the old and new Testament
Testamen'tary, *a.* relating to a will
Tes'tate, *a.* having made a will
Testa'tor, *s.* one who leaves a will
Testa'trix, *s.* a woman who leaves a will
Tes'ted, *a.* tried by a test, witnessed
Tes'ter, *s.* a sixpence; the cover of a bed

Tes'ticle, s. a stone
Testifica'tion, s. the act of witnessing
Tes'tifier, s. one who testifies
Tes'tify, v. to witness, to certify, to prove
Tes'tily, ad. fretfully, peevishly, morosely
Testimo'nial, s. a certificate or attestation
Tes'timony, s. evidence, proof, profession
Tes'tiness, s. moroseness, peevishness
Tes'ty, a. fretful, peevish, apt to be angry
Tete, s. a woman's false hair for the head
Tete-a-tete, s. face to face; a private conversation between two
Teth'er, s. a restraint for horses at pasture
Tet'ragon, s. a square, a four-sided square
Te'trarch, s. a Roman governor
Tetrar'chate, s. a fourth part of a province
Tetras'tic, s. an epigram or stanza of 4 verses
Tet'rical, a. forward, perverse, sour
Tet'ter, s. a scab, a scurf; a ring-worm
Tew'el, s. a pipe at the back of a forge
Tew'taw, or Tow'tow, v. a. to beat, break
Text, s. that on which a comment is written; a sentence of scripture
Text'hand, s. a large kind of writing
Tex'tile, a. woven, that may be woven
Tex'tuary, s. a divine well versed in scripture; one ready in the text of scripture
Tex'ture, s. a web; manner of weaving
Than, ad. a particle used in comparison
Thane, s. an old title of honour
Thank, v. a. to return acknowledgments for any favour or kindness
Thank'ful, a. full of gratitude, grateful
Thank'less, a. ungrateful, unthankful
Thanks, s. acknowledgment paid for favours
Thanksgiv'ing, s. a celebration of mercy
That, pron. which; who; the thing—conj. because
Thatch, s. straw, &c. laid on the tops of houses, to keep out the weather
Thatch, v. a. to cover a house, &c. with straw
That'cher, s. one who covers with straw
Thaw, v. to melt, to dissolve
Thaw, s. the dissolution of a frost
The, article, denoting a particular thing
The'atre, s. a place in which shows are exhibited; a playhouse
Theat'ric, Theat'rical, a. suiting a theatre
Thee, the oblique case singular of thou
Theft, s. the act of stealing; thing stolen
The'ism, The'ist, s. a deist
Their, pron. poss. of they
Theme, s. a subject, short dissertation, talk
Themsel'ves, pron. pl. these very persons
Then, ad. at that time, in that case
Thence, ad. from that place, for that reason
Thence'forth, ad. from that time
Thencefor'ward, ad. on from that time
Theoc'racy, s. divine government
Theocrat'ical, a. relating to theocracy
Theod'olite, s. a mathematical instrument used in surveying, taking heights, &c.
Theog'ony, s. the generation of the gods
Theolo'gian, s. a professor of divinity
Theolog'ical, a. relating to theology
Theol'ogist, The'ologue, s. a divine
Theol'ogy, s. the science of divinity
Theor'bo, s. a large lute used by the Italians
The'orem, s. a position laid down as an established truth; a given principle
Theoret'ic, Theoret'ical, a. speculative

The'orist, s. one given to speculation
The'ory, s. a speculation, a scheme, a plan
Therapeu'tic, a. teaching the cure of diseases
There, ad. in that place; at that time
Thereabout', ad. near that place, nearly
Thereaf'ter, ad. according to that
Thereat', ad. at that place, at that
Thereby', ad. by that, by means of that
There'fore, ad. for this reason, in consequence; in recompence for this or that
Therefrom', ad. from that, from this
Therein', ad. in that, in this
Thereinto', ad. into that, into this
Thereof', ad. of that, of this
Thereon', Thereupon', ad. on that, on this
Thereto', Thereunto', ad. to that or this
Therewith', ad. with that, immediately
Therewithal', ad. over and above, also
Theri'acal, a. medicinal, physical
Thermom'eter, s. an instrument for measuring the heat of the air, &c.
These, pron. pl. of this
The'sis, s. a position, proposition, subject
The'urgy, s. the power of doing supernatural things by lawful means
They, pron. men, women, persons
Thick, a. not thin; gross, muddy, close
Thick, ad. frequently, closely, deeply
Thick'en, v. to make or grow thick; to concrete, to condense, to be consolidated
Thick'et, s. a close knot or tuft of trees
Thick'ish, a. somewhat thick, dull
Thick'ness, s. density, closeness, dulness
Thick'set, a. close planted
Thief, s. one who steals another's property
Thief'catcher, s. one who takes thieves
Thieve, v. n. to steal, to practise theft
Thie'very, s. the practice of stealing
Thie'vish, a. given to stealing; secret, sly
Thigh, s. a limb of the body, including all between the groin and the knee
Thill, s. the shafts of a waggon or cart
Thill'horse, s. a horse between the shafts
Thim'ble, s. a cap for the needle-finger
Thin, a. not thick, lean, slim, rare, small
Thine, pron. relating to thee
Thing, s. whatever is; not a person
Think, v. to have ideas, to fancy, to muse
Think'ing, s. imagination, judgment
Thin'ly, ad. not thickly, not numerously
Thin'ness, s. tenuity, scarcity, rareness
Third, a. the next after the second
Third'ly, ad. in the third place
Thirl, v. a. to pierce, to perforate
Thirst, s. the pain suffered for want of drink, eagerness, vehement desire, drought
Thirst, v. to feel want of drink, to be dry
Thir'sty, a. suffering want of drink
Thir'stiness, s. the state of being thirsty
Thir'teen, a. ten and three added
Thir'teenth, a. the third after the tenth
Thir'ty, a. thrice ten, twenty and ten
This, pron. that which is present
This'tle, s. a prickly weed growing in fields
This'tly, a. overgrown with thistles
Thith'er, ad. to that place, point, or end
Thith'erto, ad. to that end, so far
Thith'erward, ad. toward that place
Thole, v. n. to wait a while; to endure
Thong, s. a strap or string of leather
Thorac'ic, a. belonging to the breast

Tho'ral, a. relating to the bed
Tho'rax, s. the inward part of the breast
Thorn, s. a prickly tree, a difficult point
Thorn'back, or Thorn'butt, s. a sea fish
Thorn'y, a. full of thorns, perplexing
Thor'ough, a. complete, passing through
Thor'oughfare, s. a passage through a place
Thor'oughly, ad. completely, fully
Thor'oughpaced, a. perfect, complete
Thor'oughstitch, ad. completely, fully
Thorp, s. a village, a small country town
Those, pr. plural of that
Thou, the second pronoun personal
Though, conj. although, however
Thought, s. the act of thinking; idea, sentiment, reflection, solicitude, concern
Thought'ful, a. contemplative, careful
Thought'less, a. airy, gay, careless; dull
Thought'sick, a. uneasy with reflection
Thou'sand, s. or a. the number ten hundred
Thowl, s. a place or pin for oars to turn in
Thral'dom, s. slavery, servitude
Thrall. s. a slave, bondage
Thrap'ple, s. the windpipe of any animal
Thrash, v. to beat corn, to beat or drub
Thrash'er, s. one who thrashes; a fish
Thrason'ical, a. boastful, bragging
Thread, s. a small line or twist of silk, flax, &c. any thing continued in a course
Thread, v. a. to pass through with a thread
Thread'bare, a. deprived of the nap; trite
Thread'en, a. made of thread
Threap, v. a. to argue much, to contend
Threat, s. a menace, denunciation of ill
Threat'en, v. a. to menace, to denounce evil
Threat'ening, s. a denunciation of ill
Three, a. two and one added
Three'cornered, a. having three corners
Three'fold, a. thrice repeated
Three'penny, a. vulgar, mean
Three'pile, s. an old name for good velvet
Three'score, a. thrice twenty, sixty
Thren'ody, s. a song of lamentation
Thresh'old, s. an entrance, a gate, a door
Thrice, ad. three times, at three times
Thrift, s. profit, gain, parsimony
Thrif'tily, ad. frugally, parsimoniously
Thrif'tiness, s. frugality, husbandry
Thrif'tless, a. profuse, extravagant
Thrif'ty, a. frugal, sparing, not profuse
Thrill, v. to pierce, to penetrate, to tingle
Thrive, v. n. to prosper, to grow rich
Throat, s. the fore part of the neck
Throb, v. n. to heave, to beat, to palpitate
Throe, s. the pain of travail, &c.
Throne, s. the seat of a king or bishop
Throng, s. a multitude, a crowd
Throng. v. n. to crowd, press close together
Thros'tle, s. the thrush, a singing bird
Throt'tle, s. the windpipe
Throt'tle, v. a. to choke, to suffocate
Through. prep. from end to end
Throughout'. ad. quite through, in every part
Throw, v. to fling, to cast, to toss; repose
Throw'ster. s. one who twists or winds silk
Thrum, s. the end of a weaver's thread
Thrum, v. a. to grate, to play coarsely
Thrush, s. a singing bird, a disorder
Thrust, v. to push, intrude, drive, stab
Thrust. s. an assault, hostile attack, a push
Thir'yfallow, v. a. to plough a third time

Thumb, s. the first finger of the hand
Thumb, v. n. to handle awkwardly
Thumb's'all, s. a cover for the thumb; thimble
Thump, s. a dull, hard, heavy blow
Thum'per, s. the person, &c. who thumps
Thum'ping, s. beating—a. large
Thun'der, s. a loud noise in the air, &c.
Thun'der, v. to emit with noise and terror, to make thunder, to publish any threat
Thun'derbolt, s. lightning, fulmination
Thun'derclap, s. an explosion of thunder
Thun'derer, s. the power that thunders
Thun'dering, a. loud, noisy, terrible
Thun'derstruck, a. hurt or blasted by lightning; amazed, suddenly alarmed
Thurif'erous, a. bearing frankincense
Thurs'day, s. the fifth day of the week
Thus, ad. in this manner, to this degree
Thwack, v. a. to strike, to thrash, to bang
Thwack, s. a heavy hard blow
Thwart, a. transverse, perverse, inconvenient
Thwart, v. a. to cross, traverse, oppose
Thy, pr. of thee; belonging to thee
Thyself', pr. recip. belonging to thee only
Thyme, s. a fragrant plant
Ti'ar, Tia'ra, s. a diadem, dress for the head
Tib'ial, a. relating to a pipe or the shin
Tice, v. a. to draw, to allow, to tempt
Tick, s. a score, account, trust; bed-case
Tick'en, Tick'ing, s. a cloth for bed-cases
Tick'et, s. a token of right, on the delivery of which admission is granted, or a claim acknowledged; a voucher
Tick'le, v. to cause to laugh by titillation
Tick'lish, a. easily tickled, unfixed, nice
Tick'tack, s. a game at tables, a noise
Tid, a. tender, soft, nice, delicate
Tid'dle, v. a. to use tenderly, to fondle
Tide, s. ebb and flow of the sea; season
Ti'dewaiter, s. a custom-house officer
Ti'dily, ad. neatly, readily
Ti'diness, s. neatness, readiness, spruceness
Ti'dings, s. news, intelligence, information
Ti'dy, a. seasonable, neat, clever, spruce
Tie, s. a knot, fastening, obligation
Tie, v. to bind, to fasten, to hinder
Tier, s. a row or rank; a set
Tierce, s. a third part of a pipe, a thrust
Tiff, s. liquor, drink; a pet, a quarrel
Tif'fany, s. a very thin kind of silk
Ti'ger, s. a fierce beast of the lion kind
Tight, a. tense, close, not loose
Tight'en, v. a. to straiten, to make close
Tight'ly, ad. closely, not idly, neatly
Tight'ness, s. closeness, not looseness
Ti'gress, s. the female of the tiger
Tike, s. a clown's name, a dog, a bullock
Tile, s. burnt clay to cover houses with
Ti'ler, s. one whose trade is to cover houses with tiles; a freemason's porter
Ti'ling, s. the roof covered with tiles
Till, s. the money-box in a shop
Till, conj. to the time, to the degree that
Till, prep. to the time of
Till, v. a. to cultivate, to plough, husband
Til'lable, a. arable, fit for the plough
Til'lage, s. the art of ploughing or culture
Til'ler, s. a ploughman; handle of a rudder
Tilt, s. a cover of a boat, a military game
Tilt, v. to cover, turn up, fight, lift up
Tim'ber, s. wood fit for building

Tim'bered, a. built, formed, contrived

Tim'ber-yard, s. a place for timber

Tim'brel, s. a kind of musical instrument

Time, s. the measure of duration, an age

Time, v. a. to regulate, to measure, to adapt

Ti'meful, a. seasonable, timely, early

Ti'mekeeper, Ti'mepiece, s. a clock or watch

Ti'meless, a. unseasonable, immature

Ti'mely, a. early, soon

Ti'mely, ad. seasonably, sufficiently early

Ti'meserving, a. meanly complying with present power, mean, servile, obsequious

Ti'meserver, s. a changeling, a turncoat

Tim'id, a. fearful, wanting courage

Timid'ity, Tim'orousness, s. fearfulness

Tim'orous, a. fearful, bashful, nice

Tim'orously, ad. fearfully, with much fear

Tin, s. a kind of common white metal

Tin'cal, Tin'car, s. a kind of mineral

Tinct, s. a colour, stain, spot, dye

Tinc'ture, s. a colour; extract of drugs

Tinc'ture, v. a. to imbue, tinge, colour

Tin'der, s. any thing very inflammable

Tine, s. the tooth of a harrow, trouble

Tine, v. to kindle, to rage, to fight

Ti'neman, s. a night officer of a forest

Tinge, v. a. to impregnate with a colour

Tin'gent, a. able to tinge or colour

Tin'gle, v. n. to feel a sharp pain, tinkle

Tin'ker, s. a mender of old brass, &c.

Tin'kle, v. n. to make a sharp, quick noise

Tin'kling, s. a kind of sharp, quick noise

Tin'man, s. a manufacturer of tin

Tin'ner, s. one who works in tin mines

Tin'sel, s. a sort of shining silk or cloth, &c.

Tint, s. a dye, hue, colour, stain

Ti'ny, a. little, small, puny, diminutive

Tip, s. the top, end, point, extremity

Tip, v. a. to cover on the end, to top

Tip'pet, s. something worn about the neck

Tip'ple, v. to drink in luxury or excess

Tip'pler, s. a sottish drunkard

Tip'pling, s. frequent drinking, muddling

Tip'staff, s. an officer and his staff of justice

Tip'sy, a. drunk, fuddled, muddled

Tip'toe, s. the end of the toe

Tire, s. a rank, row; furniture; apparatus

Tire, v. to fatigue, to harass, to dress

Ti'resome, a. wearisome, fatiguing

Ti'rewoman, s. a woman whose business is to make dresses for the stage

Ti'ring-room, s. the room in which players dress for the stage

Tis'sue, s. cloth interwoven with gold, &c.

Tit, s. a small horse, a woman, a bird

Tit'bit, s. a nice bit, nice food, delicate morsel

Tithe, s. the tenth part; the part assigned to the maintenance of the ministry

Ti'theable, a. subject to payment of tithes

Ti'ther, s. one who gathers or collects tithes

Ti'thing, s. a part of a parish, a district

Ti'thingman, s. a petty peace officer

Tit'illate, v. n. to tickle

Titilla'tion, s. the act of tickling

Ti'tle, s. an appellation, claim of right; the first page of a book, telling its name and its subject; name of honour

Ti'tle, v. a. to name, to entitle, to call

Ti'tlepage, s. the page containing the title of a book

Tit'mouse, or Tit, s. a small species of bird

Tit'ter, v. n. to laugh with restraint

Tit'tle, s. a small particle, a point, a dot

Tit'tletattle, s. idle talk, prattle, gabble

Tituba'tion, s. the act of stumbling

Tit'ular, a. nominal, having only the name

Tiv'y, ad. with great haste or speed

To, prep. noting motion towards, &c.

Toad, s. an animal resembling a frog, but the frog leaps, the toad crawls

Toad'stone, s. a concretion supposed to be found in the head of a toad

Toad'stool, s. a plant like a mushroom

Toast, v. s. to dry at the fire, propose a health

Toast, s. bread toasted, a health proposed; a celebrated woman whose health is often drank

Toa'ster, s. he who toasts, an utensil

Tobac'co, s. a plant used for smoking

Tobac'conist, s. a vender of tobacco

Tod, s. a bush, a weight of 28lb. of wool

Toes, s. the fingers of the feet

Toft, s. a place where a messuage has stood

Togeth'er, ad. not apart, in company

Toil, v. to labour, to work at, to weary

Toil'et, s. a dressing-table

Toil'some, a. laborious, weary, heavy

Toil'someness, s. weariness, laboriousness

Tokay', s. an esteemed wine

To'ken, s. a mark, a sign, a remembrance

Tole, v. to train up, to draw by degrees

Tol'erable, a. supportable, not excellent

Tol'erableness, s. the state of being tolerable

Tol'erably, ad. supportably; neither well nor ill; passably, moderately well

Tol'erance, s. the act or power of enduring

Tol'erate, v. a. to allow, permit, suffer

Tolera'tion, s. sufferance, permission

Toll, v. to pay toll, to sound a bell, to annul —s. an excise of goods

Toll'booth, s. a market, a prison

Toluta'tion, s. the act of ambling or pacing

Tom'ahawk, s. an Indian hatchet

Tomb, s. a sepulchre for the dead, a vault

Tomb'less, a. wanting a tomb, unburied

Tom'boy, s. a romping girl, a mad fellow

Tomb'stone, s. a stone laid over the dead

Tome, s. one volume of many; a book

Tom'tit, s. a titmouse, a small bird

Ton, s. a weight of two thousand pounds

Tone, s. a note, accent, whine, elasticity

Tong, s. the catch of a buckle

Tongs, s. an utensil to take up fire, &c.

Tongue, s. the organ of speech; language

Tongue'tied, a. having defect in speech

Ton'ic, a. elastic; relating to sounds

Ton'nage, s. a duty upon every ton

Ton'sils, s. two round glands placed on the sides of the basis of the tongue

Ton'sure, s. act of clipping or shaving hair

Tonti'ne, s. a raising of money upon annuities

Too, ad. overmuch, more than enough; also

Tool, s. any instrument; a hireling

Tooth, s. a bone in the jaw; taste; prong

Tooth'ach, s. a pain in the teeth

Tooth'less, a. wanting or deprived of teeth

Tooth'pick, s. an instrument for cleaning the teeth

Tooth'some, a. palatable; grateful

Top, s. the highest part or place

Top, v. to rise above, to tip, to

To'paz, s. a precious yellow

Tope, v. n. to drink hard or to excess
To'per, s. a hard drinker, a sot, a drunkard
Top'ful, a. full to the brim or top
Topgal'lant, s. the highest mast and sail
Topha'ceous, a. gritty, stony, sandy
Topheav'y, a. having the upper part too weighty for the lower; drunk
Top'ic, s. a general head something to which other things are referred
Top'ical, a. local, confined to some place
Top'knot, s. a knot worn on the head
Top'most, a. uppermost, highest
Topog'raphy, s. a description of particular places, as of a parish, town, manor, &c.
Top'ping, a. fine, noble, gallant, wealthy
Top'ple, v. to tumble down, to fall forward
Top'sail, s. the sail below the topgallant sail
Topsytur'vy, ad. with the bottom upwards
Tor, s. a tower, turret, high pointed wall
Torch, s. a wax light larger than a candle
Torment', v. a. to put to pain, vex, harass
Tor'ment, s. misery, anguish, torture
Tormen'ter, s. one who gives pain to others
Torna'do, s. a hurricane, a whirlwind
Torpe'do, s. a fish whose touch benumbs
Tor'pent, a. motionless, not active, numbed
Tor'pid, a. numbed, sluggish, inactive
Tor'pidness, s. the state of being numbed
Tor'por, s. dulness, inability to move
Torrefac'tion, s. the act of drying by fire
Tor'refy, v. a. to dry by fire, to scorch
Tor'rent, s. a rapid stream, violent current
Tor'rid, a. violently hot, parched
Tor'sel, s. any thing in a twisted form
Tort, s. mischief, injury, wrong, calamity
Tor'tile, Tor'tive, a. twisted, wreathed
Tor'toise, s. an animal covered with a hard
Tortuos'ity, s. a wreath, a flexure [shell
Tor'tuous, a. twisted, winding; injurious
Tor'ture, s. pain, judicial torments, anguish
To'ry, s. one who adheres to the ancient constitution of the state, and the apostolical hierarchy of the church of England
Toss, v. a. to throw, to agitate, to fling
Toss'pot, s. a toper, a drunken fellow
To'tal, a. complete—s. the whole
To'tally, ad. wholly, fully, completely
Tot'ter, v. n. to shake so as to threaten a fall
Touch, v. to join; to affect; mark out; try
Touch, s. the sense of feeling; test, proof
Touch'hole, s. a small hole in fire-arms
Touch'stone, s. a stone to prove metals, a test
Touch'wood, s. rotten wood that easily fires
Touch'y, a. peevish, irritable, cross
Tough, a. stiff; not brittle; viscous, ropy
Tough'en, v. n. to grow tough
Toupee', Toupet', s. a kind of peruke, an artificial lock of hair; a curl
Tour, s. a journey, travel; a revolution
Tour'nament, s. a tilt, a mock encounter
Tour'niquet, s. a bandage used in amputation
Touse, v. a. to haul, to drag, to pull, to tear
Tow, s. combed flax or hemp
Tow, v. a. to draw by a rope, particularly through the water
To'ward, a. ready to do, not froward
To'ward, ad. near; in a state of preparation
To'wards, prep. in a direction to; regarding
Tow'el, s. a cloth to wipe hands, &c. on
Tow'er, s. a high building; a fortress
Tow'er, v. n. to soar, to fly or rise high

Tow'ery, a. adorned or guarded with towers
Town, s. any large collection of houses
Town'clerk, s. an officer who manages the public business of a corporate town
Town'house, s. a hall for public business
Towns'man, s. one of the same town
Tox'ical, a. poisonous, containing poison
Toy, s. a plaything, a bauble; folly, sport
Toy, v. n. to play, trifle; dally amorously
Toy'shop, s. a shop where toys are sold
Trace, v. a. to follow by the footsteps; to mark out; to follow with exactness
Tra'ces, s. the harness of draught animals
Track, s. a mark left; a road; beaten path
Track'less, a. untrodden, not marked out
Tract, s. a region, quantity of land, continuity, course, treatise, small book
Trac'table, a. manageable, docile [able
Trac'tableness, s. quality of being manage-
Trac'tate, s. a small book, treatise, tract
Trac'tile, a. that may be drawn out, ductile
Trade, s. traffic, commerce, occupation
Trade, v. to traffic, to deal, to sell
Tra'der, s. a merchant, a dealer
Tra'desman, s. a shopkeeper, a dealer
Tra'dewind, s. the monsoon; the periodical wind between the tropics, which at certain times blows regularly one way at sea
Tradi'tion, s. oral account from age to age
Tradi'tional, Tradi'tionary, a. descending by oral communication; unwritten
Tradu'ce, v. a. to censure, to condemn, to calumniate, to represent as blameable
Tradu'cement, s. obloquy, censure, scandal
Tradu'cent, a. traducing, censuring
Tradu'cer, s. a slanderer, a calumniator
Tradu'cible, a. such as may be derived
Tradu'cingly, ad. slightingly, slanderously
Traduc'tion, s. derivation, tradition
Traf'fic, s. commerce, merchandise
Trag'acanth, s. a sort of plant or gum
Trage'dian, s. a writer or actor of tragedy
Trag'edy, s. a dramatic representation of any serious action; any dreadful event
Trag'ic, Trag'ical, a. mournful, sorrowful
Tragicom'edy, s. a drama compounded of serious and humorous events
Tragicom'ical, a. relating to tragicomedy
Traject', v. a. to cast through, to throw
Traj'ect, s. a ferry, a passage over
Trajec'tion, s. the act of darting through
Trail, v. to draw along, to hunt by track
Trail, s. any thing drawn behind, or to a length; the track of a hunter
Train, v. a. to educate, entice, breed, draw
Train, s. the tail of a bird; a retinue; a series; a procession; part of a garment that drags behind on the ground; a line of gunpowder
Trainban'ds, s. the militia; the part of a community instructed in martial exercises
Train'oil, s. oil drawn from fat of wales
Traipse, Trapes, s. a sluttish woman, a slut
Trait, s. a stroke, a touch, the outline [tor
Trai'tor, s. one who betrays his trust
Trai'torly, Trai'torous, a. perfidious, faithless
Trai'torously, ad. perfidiously
Trai'tress, s. a woman who betrays
Tralin'eate, v. n. to deviate, to turn aside
Tram'mel, s. any kind of net; shackles for a horse; an iron to hang pots on

Tram'mel, *v. a.* to catch, to intercept
Tram'ple, *v. a.* to tread under foot, &c.
Trana'tion, *s.* the act of swimming over
Trance, Transe, *s.* an ecstasy, a rapture
Tran'ced, *a.* lying in a trance or ecstasy
Tran'quil, *a.* quiet, undisturbed
Tranquil'lity, *s.* peace of mind, stillness
Tran'quillize, *v.* to quiet, calm, harmonize
Transac't, *v. a.* to manage, to conduct, to negotiate, to perform, to carry on
Transac'tion, *s.* negotiation; dealing between man and man; affairs in hand
Transcen'd, *v.* to exceed, to outgo, to excel
Transcen'dence, Transcen'dency, *s.* unusual excellence, supereminence
Transcen'dent, *a.* supremely excellent
Transcen'dently, *ad.* supereminently
Transcri'be, *v. a.* to write from an exemplar
Tran'script, *s.* a copy from an original
Transcrip'tion, *s.* the act of copying
Transcur'sion, *s.* a ramble, passage through
Tran-fer', *v. a.* to make over, to convey, to move, to transport
Transfigura'tion, *s.* change of form; the miraculous change of our blessed Saviour's appearance on the Mount
Transfig'ure, *v. a.* to change the figure
Transfix', *v. a.* to pierce through
Trans'forate, *v. a.* to make a hole through
Transfor'm, *v.* to metamorphose, to change
Transforma'tion, *s.* change of form, &c.
Transfreta'tion, *s.* a passage over the sea
Transfu'se, *v. a.* to pour into another
Transgress', *v.* to violate; pass over; offend
Transgres'sion, *s.* a violation, crime, fault
Transgres'sor, *s.* an offender, a law-breaker
Tran'sient, *a.* not lasting, momentary
Transil'ience, *s.* a leap from thing to thing
Tran'sit, *s.* the passing of a planet, &c.
Transi'tion, *s.* a removal; change, passage
Tran'sitory, *a.* passing away speedily
Transla'te, *v.* to remove, explain, interpret
Transla'tion, *s.* removal, change, version
Transla'tor, *s.* one that turns any thing out of one language into another
Translu'cency, *s.* transparency, clearness
Translu'cent, Translu'cid, *a.* diaphanous
Transmari'ne, *a.* lying beyond sea, foreign
Trans'migrate, *v. n.* to pass from one place or country to another, to travel
Transmigra'tion, *s.* passage from one state, or place, or body, into another
Transmis'sion, *s.* the act of transmitting
Transmis'sive, *a.* transmitted, sent
Transmit', *v. a.* to convey, to make over to another, to send from one person or place to another
Transmit'tal, *s.* the act of transmitting
Transmu'table, *a.* capable of being changed
Transmuta'tion, *s.* the changing of metals, &c. into another nature or substance
Transmu'te, *v. a.* to change from one nature or substance to another
Tran'som, *s.* a beam over a door or window
Transpa'rency, *s.* translucence, clearness
Transpa'rent, *a.* clear, pellucid, pervious to the light; translucent; not opaque
Transpic'uous, *a.* pervious to the sight
Transpie'rce, *v. a.* to pierce through
Transpi're, *v.* to emit in vapour; to escape from secrecy to notice

Transpla'ce, *v. a.* to remove to another place
Transplan't, *v. a.* to plant in a new place
Transpo'rt, *v. a.* to banish; put into ecstasy
Tran'sport, *s.* a vessel of carriage; rapture, ecstasy; conveyance, transportation
Transpor'tance, *s.* conveyance, carriage
Transporta'tion, *s.* removal, conveyance; banishment for felony
Transpo'rter, *s.* one that transports
Transpo'sal, *s.* a misplacing, a changing
Transpo'se, *v. a.* to put out of place, to change as to order
Transposit'ion, *s.* the act of misplacing
Transubstan'tiate, *v. a.* to change substance
Transubstantia'tion, *s.* change of substance
Transu'de, *v. n.* to pass through in vapour
Transver'sal, *s.* running crosswise
Tran'sverse, *a.* being in a cross direction
Trap, *s.* a snare, ambush, plaything, play
Trap, *v. a.* to ensnare, to catch, to adorn
Trapdoo'r, *s.* a door in the floor or roof
Trap'pings, *s.* ornament, dress, finery
Trap'stick, *s.* a boy's plaything, a small leg
Trash, *s.* dross; dregs; a worthless thing, &c.
Trav'ail, *v.* to toil, to be in labour, to harass
Trav'ail, *s.* labour, toil, labour in childbirth
Trav'el, *v. n.* to make journeys, go, move
Trav'el, *s.* a journey, labour, toil
Trav'eller, *s.* one who goes journeys
Trav'erse, *ad.* and *prep.* athwart, crosswise
Trav'erse, *a.* lying across, athwart
Trav'erse, *v.* to sail across, wander over; to use a posture of opposition, to examine
Trav'esty, *a.* ludicrous, burlesqued
Traumat'ic, *a.* useful to wounds; vulnerary
Tray, *s.* a shallow trough of wood
Tray'trip, *s.* a kind of game, play, pastime
Treach'erous, *a.* faithless, perfidious, false
Treach'erously, *ad.* faithlessly, perfidiously
Treach'ery, *s.* perfidy, a breach of faith
Trea'cle, *s.* a sort of medicine; molasses
Tread, *s.* a step with the foot; track, way
Tread, *v.* to set the foot; walk; cover; beat
Trea'dles, *s.* pieces of wood belonging to looms, &c. moved with the feet
Trea'son, *s.* disloyalty, treachery, rebellion
Trea'sonable, *a.* of the nature of treason
Treas'ure, *s.* hoarded wealth, riches
Treas'ure, *v. a.* to hoard, to lay up
Treas'urer, *s.* one who has charge of the money of a prince, state, corporation, &c.
Treas'ury, *s.* a place where riches are kept
Treat, *v.* to handle, negotiate, maintain
Treat, *s.* an entertainment given; pleasure
Trea'tise, *s.* a discourse, a written discourse
Treat'ment, *s.* usage, good or bad
Trea'ty, *s.* a negotiation, contract of parties
Treb'le, *a.* threefold—*s.* a sharp sound
Tree, *s.* a large vegetable, arising with one woody stem, to a considerable height
Tree'n, *s.* trees—*a.* made of wood
Tre'foil, *s.* a three-leaved grass, clover
Trel'lage, *s.* pales to support espaliers
Trel'lis, *s.* a lattice work of wood, &c.
Trem'ble, *v. n.* to shake quick, shudder
Tremen'dous, *n.* dreadful, awful, horrible
Tre'mor, *s.* a quivering or shaking motion
Trem'ulous, *a.* fearful, trembling, vibrating
Tren, *s.* a spear to strike fish with
Trench, *s.* a ditch; a defence for soldiers
Tren'chant, *a.* sharp, cutting, keen

Tren'cher, s. a wooden platter
Tren'tals, s. thirty masses for the dead
Trepan', s. a snare, a surgeon's instrument
Trepan', v. a. to cut with a trepan; to perforate, to catch, to ensnare
Trephi'ne, s. a small trepan for one hand
Trep'id, a. fearful, trembling, quaking
Trepida'tion, s. the state of trembling
Tres'pass, s. a sin, offence, unlawful entry
Tress'es, s. knots or curls of hair
Tres'tle, Tres'sel, s. a frame to support any thing
Tret, s. an allowance in weight for waste
Trev'et, s. an iron stand with three legs
Trey, s. the three at cards or dice
Tri'able, a. capable of trial or examination
Tri'ad, s. three united, the number three
Tri'al, s. a test of virtue; examination
Tri'angle, Tri'gon, s. a figure of three angles
Trian'gular, a. having three angles
Tribe, s. a certain division of the people
Trib'let, s. a tool for making rings with
Tribula'tion, s. vexation, distress, persecution
Tribu'nal, s. a court of justice, judge's seat
Trib'une, s. a Roman magistrate
Trib'utary, a. paying tribute, subject unto
Trib'ute, s. a payment made in acknowledgment of subjection, a tax
Trice, s. a short time, moment, instant
Trick, v. a. to deceive, cheat; dress, adorn
Trick'ing, s. dress, ornaments, a cheating
Tric'kle, v. n. to run down in drops
Tride, a. short, ready, swift, quick
Tri'dent, s. a three-forked sceptre, a curve
Trien'nial, a. happening every three years
Tri'fallow, v. a. to plough the land three times
Tri'fle, v. n. to act with levity, be foolish
Tri'fle, s. a thing of no moment or value
Tri'fler, s. one who acts or talks foolishly
Tri'fling, a. worthless, mean, shuffling
Tri'form, a. having a triple form or shape
Trig'ger, s. a catch of a wheel or gun
Trigonomet'rical, a. relating or pertaining to trigonometry, or measuring triangles
Trigonom'etry, s. the art of measuring triangles, either plain or spherical
Trilat'eral, a. having three sides
Trill, s. a quaver—v. n. to quaver, to trickle
Tril'lion, s. a million of millions of millions
Trim, a. nice, neatly dressed up, spruce
Trim, v. a. to dress, shave; balance, &c.
Trim, s. dress, condition, ornaments
Trim'ly, ad. nicely, neatly, sprucely
Trim'mer, s. a turncoat; a piece of wood
Trim'ming, s. lace, &c. on clothes
Trine, a. belonging to the number three
Trine, s. an aspect of two planets, supposed by astrologers to be eminently benign
Trin'ity, s. the three persons in the Godhead
Trin'ket, s. a toy, thing of small value
Tri'o, s. a musical performance by 3 voices
Trip, v. to supplant, err, stumble, detect
Trip, s. a stumble; error; short voyage
Trip'artite, a. divided into three parts
Tripe, s. the intestines, the guts
Triph'thong, s. a coalition of three vowels
Trip'le, a. treble, three times repeated
Trip'let, s. three of a kind, three lines
Trip'licate, a. thrice as much, trebled
Triplic'ity, s. state of being threefold
Tri'pod, s. a seat or stool with three feet

Trip'oly, s. sharp cutting sand or stone
Trip'ping, a. nimble, passing quickly
Trip'tote, s. a noun used only in three cases
Tripu'diary, a. performed by dancing
Trisec'tion, s. division into three equal parts
Tris'tful, a. sad, melancholy, gloomy
Trisyl'lable, a. consisting of three syllables
Trite, a. stale, worn out, common
Tri'theism, s. the worship of three gods
Trit'urable, a. possible to be pounded, &c.
Tritura'tion, s. a rubbing to powder
Triv'ial, a. inconsiderable, worthless
Tri'umph, s. public joy, for success, victory, conquest, state of being victorious
Tri'umph, v. n. to be insolent; to rejoice for victory, obtain victory, celebrate a victory with pomp
Trium'phal, a. used in celebrating victory
Trium'phant, a. celebrating victory
Trium'vir, s. one of three in the same office
Trium'virate, s. a government by three men
Tri'une, a. at once, three in one
Troat, v. n. to cry like rutting bucks
Tro'car, s. a chirurgical instrument
Trocha'ic, a. consisting of trochees
Trochee', s. a foot used in Latin poetry, consisting of a long and short syllable
Tro'chings, s. branches on a deer's head
Tro'chisch, Tro'kisk, s. a kind of lozenge
Trod, Trod'den, part. pass. of to tread
Troll, v. to move circularly, roll; to fish for pike, barbel, &c. with a rod which has a pulley near the bottom
Trol'lop, s. a slattern, a slovenly woman
Troop, s. a body of soldiers, a company
Troop, v. n. to march in a body or in haste
Troop'er, s. a horse-soldier, a horseman
Trope, s. a figure in speech, turn, change
Tro'phied, a. adorned with trophies
Tro'phy, s. something taken in battle
Trop'ic, s. an astronomical line of the sun
Trop'ical, a. figurative, near the tropics
Trot, v. a. to ride in a trot, to walk fast
Froth, s. truth, faithfulness; a petty oath
Troth'plight, a. betrothed, espoused
Trou'ble, v. a. to perplex, to afflict, to sue
Trou'ble, s. disturbance, calamity, affliction
Trou'blesome, a. vexatious, tiresome
Trou'blesomely, ad. vexatiously, wearisomely
Trou'blesomeness, s. vexatiousness [ly
Tro'ver, s. an action for goods found, and not delivered to the owner on demand
Trough, s. any long thing hollowed
Troul, v. n. to move or utter quickly
Trounce, v. n. to punish, beat, sue, cheat
Trou'sers, s. breeches, hose, sailors' breeches
Trout, s. a fish; an honest silly fellow
Trow, v. n. to imagine, to think, to trust
Trow, interj. denoting inquiry
Trow'el, s. a tool used by bricklayers
Troy'weight, s. a weight of 19 oz. to the lb.
Tru'ant, s. an absenter from school, &c.
Tru'ant, a. idle, lazy, loitering, careless
Truce, s. a temporary cessation of war
Trucida'tion, s. the act of killing
Truck, s. traffic by exchange
Truck, v. a. to give in exchange
Truc'kle, v. n. to be in subjection, to cringe
Truc'klebed, s. a bed with wheels to run under another; a bed for children
Truc'ulent, a. savage, terrible of aspect

Trudge, *v. n.* to jog on heavily, to labour
True, *a.* not false, certain, steady
Trueheart'ed, *a.* honest, faithful, just
Trueloveknot', *s.* a particular kind of knot
True'ness, *s.* sincerity, faithfulness
True'penny, *s.* a worthy honest fellow
Truf'fie, *s.* a subterraneous mushroom
Trug, *s.* a tray, hod, ancient measure
Tru'ism, *s.* an undoubted truth; a certainty
Trull, *s.* a va rant dirty strumpet
Tru'ly, *ad.* certainly, exactly, really
Trump, *s.* a trumpet; the trump turn-card
Trump, *v. a.* to win with a trump, devise
Trum'pery, *s.* trifles, trash; idle talk
Trum'pet, *s.* a kind of musical instrument
Trum'pet, *v. a.* to publish by sound of trumpet, to proclaim
Trum'peter, *s.* one who sounds a trumpet
Trun'cate, *v. a.* to cut short, to maim
Trun'cheon, *s.* a staff of command, a cudgel
Trun'cheon, *v. a.* to beat with a truncheon
Trun'dle, *v. n.* to roll, to bowl along
Trun'dle, *s.* any round rolling thing
Trun'dietail, *s.* a round-tailed dog
Trunk, *s.* the body of any thing; a sort of chest; the proboscis of an elephant, &c.
Trunk'hose, *s.* a kind of large breeches
Trun'nions, *s.* the knobs on cannon, by which they are supported on carriages
Truss, *s.* a bandage for ruptures; a bundle of hay or straw
Truss, *v. a.* to pack close together
Trust, *s.* confidence, care, charge, credit
Trust, *v.* to place confidence in, to believe
Trustee', *s.* one entrusted with any thing
Trus'ty, *a.* honest, true, faithful, strong
Truth, *s.* honesty, reality, faithfulness
Try, *v.* to examine, to essay, to attempt
Tub, *s.* a vessel of wood of various sizes
Tube, *s.* a pipe, a siphon, a long hollow body
Tu'bercle, *s.* a small swelling, a pimple
Tu'berose, *s.* a sweet-smelling flower
Tu'berous, *a.* full of knobs or swellings
Tu'bular, Tu'bulated, Tu'bulous, *a.* long and hollow, like a cylinder; fistular
Tuck, *s.* a long narrow sword, a net
Tuck, *v. a.* to lay close, to inclose under
Tuck'er, *s.* a small piece of linen that shades the breast of a woman
Tuck'et, *s.* a voluntary in music
Tues'day, *s.* the third day of the week
Tuft, *s.* a cluster of grass, hair, &c.
Tuftaf'fety, *s.* a shaggy kind of si k
Tuf'ty, *a.* adorned with or having tufts
Tug, *v.* to pull along, to draw, to contend
Tug, *s.* a pull with force, a great effort
Tui'tion, *s.* guardianship, care of a tutor
Tu'lip, *s.* the name of a flower
Tum'ble, *s.* a fall, downfal, accident
Tum'bler, *s.* one who shows feats of activity
Tum'brel, *s.* h dunghill, a dungcart
Tumefac'tion, *s.* a swelling
Tu'mefy, *v. a.* to swell, to make to swell
Tu'mid, *a.* puffed up, swelled, pompous
Tu'mour, *s.* morbid swelling; affected pomp
Tu'morous, *a.* swelling, falsely magnificent
Tu'mult, *s.* a riot, bustle, wild commotion
Tumul'tuarily, *ad.* in a riotous manner
Tumul'tuariness, *s.* turbulence, riotousness
Tumul'tuary, *a.* disorderly, restless
Tumul'tuous, *a.* turbulent, full of riot

Tumul'tuously, *ad.* with confusion and
Tun, *s.* a cask of four hogsheads, two pi e
Tu'nable, *a.* harmonious, musical, sweet
Tun'bellied, *a.* having a large be y, fat
Tune, *s.* harmony, an air, order, fit temper
Tune, *v. a.* to put into a musical state
Tu'neful, *a.* musical, harmonious, pleasing
Tune'less, *a.* unharmonious, untuneful
Tu'ner, *s.* one who sings, one who tunes
Tu'nic, *s.* a child's upper garment
Tu'nicle, *s.* a cover, integument, skin
Tun'nage, *s.* contents of a vessel measured by the tun, a duty of so much per tun
Tun'nel, *s.* the shaft of a c imney, a vessel to bottle liquor, net to catch partridges
Tun'ny, *s.* the name of a sea-fish
Tup, *s.* a ram—*v.* to butt like a ram
Tur'ban, *s.* a cover made of fine linen, worn by the Turks about their heads
Tur'bary, *s.* a right of digging turf
Tur'bid, *a.* thick, muddy, not clear
Tur'binated, *a.* twisted, spiral
Tur'bith, *s.* yellow precipitate; an herb
Tur'bot, *s.* the name of a delicious fish
Tur'bulence, *s.* tumult, confusion
Tur'bulent, *a.* tumultuous, violent
Tur'bulently, *ad.* with confusion
Turf, *s.* a clod covered with grass
Turf'y, *a.* full of or like turfs; green
Tur'gent, *a.* swelling, protuberant, tumid
Tur'gid, *a.* tumid, swelled, bloated
Turk, *s.* a native or inhabitant of Turkey
Tur'key, *s.* a large fowl well known
Turkois', or Tur'cois, *s.* a kind of blue stone
Tur'meric, *s.* an Indian root which makes a yellow dye
Turmoil, *v. a.* to labour hard, toil, weary
Turn, *v.* to transform, to change, to alter
Turn, *s.* the act of moving about, change
Turn'coat, *s.* a renegade, an apostate
Tur'ner, *s.* one who turns in a lathe
Tur'ning, *s.* a winding, bending, curling
Tur'nip, *s.* a well-known esculent root
Turn'pike, *s.* a toll gate on a road
Turn'spit, *s.* one who turns a spit, a dog
Turn'stile, *s.* a kind of whirling stile
Tur'pentine, *s.* a gum from the pine, &c.
Tur'pitude, *s.* inherent vileness, badness
Tur'ret, *s.* a small tower or eminence
Tur'tle, *s.* the turtle-dove; a tortoise
Tur'tledove, *s.* a species of dove or pigeon
Tush, Tut, *interj.* expressing contempt
Tusk, *s.* a fish, fang, very large tooth
Tu'telage, *s.* guardianship, protection, care
Tu'telar, Tu'telary, *a.* guarding, protecting, defend, g; having guardianship
Tu'tor, *s.* one who instructs, a preceptor
Tu'torage, *s.* the office of a tutor, education
Tu'toress, *s.* a governess, an instructress
Tut'ty, *s.* a sublimate of zinc or calamine collected in the furnace
Tuz, or Tuzz, *s.* a lock or tuft of hair
Twain, *a.* two, both—*ad.* in two, asunder
Twang, *s.* a sharp quick sound, an accent
Twang, *v. n.* to make to sound sharply
Twat'tle, *v. n.* to prate, to gabble, to chatter
Tweak, *v. a.* to pinch, to squeeze
Twee'dle, *v. a.* to handle lightly or softly
Twee'zers, *s.* nippers, small pincers
Twelfth, *a.* the second after the tenth
Twelfth'tide, *s.* the Epiphany or twelfth day

twelve, a. two and ten, twice six
twe've'month, s. a year of solar months
twen'ty. a. twice ten, a proverbial number
Twi'bill, s. a halbert, a pavior's tool
Twice, ad. two times, doubly
Twid'dle, v. a. to touch lightly
Twig, s. a small branch, switch, sprout
Twi'light, s. the dubious or faint light before
  sun rise, and after sun-set
Tw''git, a. deeply shaded, obscure
Twin, s. one of two produced togethe
Twin'bo.n, a. born at the same birth
Twine, v. to twist, wrap about, wind
Twine, s. a twisted thread; embrace
Twinge, v. a. to pinch, weak, torment
Twin'kle, v. n. to open and shut the eye
Twin'kling, s. a motion of the eye, a light
  that seems every moment in and out
Twin'ling, s. the name of a twin lamb
Twirl, v. a. to turn round quick
Twirl, s. circular motion, rotation, twist
Twist, v. n. to form by complication
Twist, s. a thread made by forming two to-
  gether, a single string of cord, twitch, twig

Twit, v. a. to reproach, to upbraid, to sneer
Twitch, v. a. to snatch, to pluck forcibly
Twit'ter, v. a. to make a noise like swallows
Twit'ter, s. a disorder of passion, laughter
Two'fold, a. double—ad. doubly, twice
Two'handed, a. big, bulky, enormous
Two'pence, s. a penny twice told, small coin
Tym'bal, s. a kind of kettle-drum
Tym'pan, s. a printer's frame, a pannel
Tym'panum, s. a drum, part of the ear
Tym'pany, s. a dry windy dropsy
Type, s. an emblem, printing letter, stamp
Typ'ical, a. emblematical, figurative
Typ'ically, ad. in a typical manner
Typog'rapher, s. a printer, one who prints
Typograph'ical, a. belonging to printing
Typog'raphy, s. the art of printing
Tyran'nic, Tyran'nical, a. like a tyrant
Tyran'nicide, s. the act of killing a tyrant
Tyr'annise, v. a. to play or act the tyrant
Tyr'annous, a. arbitrary, cruel, despotic
Tyr'anny, s. cruel government, severity
Ty'rant, s. a cruel despotic ruler or master
Ty'ro, s. a beginner, student, novice

U. & V.

U, s. the fifth vowel, and the 20th letter of the
  alphabet—V, the consonant of U
Va'cancy, s. empty space, vacuity
Va'cant, a. empty, free, disengaged
Va'cate, v. a. to make vacant, to annul
Vaca'tion, s. leisure, intermission, a recess
Vac'cinate, v. a. to inoculate with vaccine
  matter for the cow-pox
Vaccina'tion, s. inoculation for the cow-pox
Vac'cine, a. of or belonging to a cow
Vacua'tion, s. an emptying, an evacuation
Vacu'ity, s. an emptiness, space unfilled
Vac'uous, a. empty, void, unfilled, hollow
Vac'uum, s. space unoccupied by matter
Va'de-me'cum, s. the title of a book
Vag'abond, s. a vagrant, a wanderer
Vaga'ry, s. a wild sudden frolic, a freak
Va'grant, s. an idle strolling person
Va'grant, a. wandering, unsettled, vagabond
Va'gue, a. wandering, unmeaning, unsettled
Vail, s. a covering, a perquisite
Vail, v. to cover, to let fall, to yield
Vain, a. fruitless, meanly proud, idle
Vainglo'rious, a. vain without merit
Vainglo'ry, s. empty pride, vanity, folly
Vain'ly, ad. without effect, foolishly
Val'ance, s. the hanging of a bed tester
Vale, s. a valley; money given to servants
Val'entine, s. a choice on Valentine's day
Vale'rian, s. the name of a plant
Val'et, s. a waiting servant, a footman
Valetudina'rian, s. a weak sickly person
Val'iant, a. brave, stout, courageous, bold
Val'iantly, ad. with personal strength
Val'iantness, s. valour, personal bravery
Val'id, a. conclusive, prevalent, efficacious
Valid'ity, s. certainty, value, force
Val'ley, s. a low ground between two hills
Val'our, s. personal bravery, prowess
Val'orous, a. brave, stout, valiant, heroic
Val'orously, ad. in a brave manner

Val'uable, a. precious, worthy of value
Valua'tion, s. an estimate of the value of a
  thing, high rate, price, worth
Val'ue, s. a price, worth, rate, high rate
Val'ue, v. a. to fix a price, to apprai se
Valve, s. any thing that opens over the
  mouth of a tube, &c.; a folding door
Vamp, s. the upper leather of a shoe, &c.
Vamp, v. a. to mend old things, to piece
Vam'pire, s. a kind of bat
Van, s. the front line of an army; a fan
Vane, s. a plate turned with the wind
Van'guard, s. the front line of an army
Vanil'la, s. the name of a plant and nut
Van'ish, v. n. to disappear, to pass away
Van'ity, s. emptiness, arrogance, falsehood
Van'quish, v. a. to conquer, to subdue
Van'quisher, s. a conqueror, a subduer
Van'tage, s. gain, profit, superiority, parti
  cular convenience, opportunity, &c.
Vant'brass, s. armour for the arms
Vap'id, a. spiritless, dead, flat, mawkish
Va'porous, a. full of vapours, windy; funny
Va'pour, s. fume, spleen, wind, steam
Va'pours, s. hysteric fits, fits, whims
Va'riable, a. changeable, inconstant, fickle
Va'riableness, s. changeableness, inconstan
Va'riably, ad. inconstantly, changeably
Va'riance, s. disagreement, dissension
Varia'tion, s. a change, difference, deviation
Va'riegate, v. a. to diversify with colours
Variega'tion, s. a diversity of colours
Va'riety, s. an intermixture, change
Va'rious, a. different, manifold, changeable
Var'let, s. a rascal, anciently a footman
Var'nish, s. a shining liquid substance
Var'nish, v. a. to set a gloss, to palliate
Var'nisher, s. one whose trade is to varnish
Va'ry, v. to diversify, to deviate, to change
Vas'cular, a. consisting of vessels
Vase, s. a vessel with a foot; an ornament

Vas'sal, s. a subject, dependant, slave
Vas'salage, s. the state of a vassal, slavery
Vast, Vas'ty, a. very great, enormous
Vast. s. an empty waste, an empty space
Vast'ly. ad. to a great degree, greatly
Vast'ness, s. immensity, enormous greatness
Vat, s. a brewer's working tub, a fat
Vat'icide, s. a murderer of poets or prophets
Vati'cinate, v. n. to prophesy, to foretel
Vav'asour, s. a lord next in rank to a baron
Vault, s. a cellar, an arch, a cave, a grave
Vault, v. to leap, to jump, to tumble ; to arch
Vault'age. s. an arched cellar, &c.
Vault'ed, Vault'y, a. arched, like an arch
Vaun'mure, s. a false wall, breastwork
Vaunt, v. to boast, to brag, to talk largely
Vaunt, s. a boast, vain ostentation
U'berty, s. abundance, fruitfulness
Ubica'tion, Ubi'ety, s. a relation to place
Ubiq'uity, s. a being in all places
Ud'der, s. the dugs of a cow
Veal, s. the flesh of a calf killed
Vec'ture, s. carriage, conveyance, removal
Veer, v. to turn about, to turn, to change
Veg'etable, s. all sorts of plants
Veg'etate, v. n. to grow as plants
Vegeta'tion, s. the growth of plants
Veg'etative, a. growing without life
Vege'te, a. sprightly, active, vigorous
Ve'hemence, s. violence, eagerness, ardour
Ve'hement, a. forcible, eager, earnest
Ve'hemently, ad. forcibly, eagerly
Ve'hicle, s. a carriage, a conveyance
Veil, v. a. to cover, invest, hide, conceal
Veil, s. a cover to conceal the face ; disguise
Vein, s. a tube in the flesh ; course of metal
in mines ; a current ; turn of mind
Velle'ity, s. the lowest degree of desire
Vel'licate, v. a. to twitch, pluck, stimulate
Vellica'tion, s. a twitching or stimulating
Vel'lum, s. a fine kind of parchment
Veloc'ity, s. speed, quick motion
Vel'vet, s. a silk with a fur or pile upon it
Vel'vet, a. made of velvet, soft, delicate
Ve'nal, a. mercenary, base ; in the veins
Venal'ity, s. sordidness, prostitution
Venat'ic, a. relating to hunting or chasing
Vend, v. a. to sell, to set, or offer to sale
Vendee', s. one to whom any thing is sold
Ven'der, s. one who sells or puts off goods
Ven'dible, a. saleable. marketable
Vend'ibleness, s. saleable state or quality
Vendit'ion, s. sale, the act of selling
Veneer', v. a. to cover with thin wood, &c.
Venefic'ial, a. poisonous ; bewitching
Venefic'iously, ad. by poison or witchcraft
Ven'emous, a. poisonous ; malignant
Vene'nate, v. a. to poison, to kill by poison
Ven'erable, a. worthy of reverence
Ven'erate, v. a. to regard with awe
Venera'tion, s. a reverend or awful regard
Vene'real, a. relating to love, &c.
Ven'ery, s. the sport of hunting ; the plea-
sures of the bed
Venesec'tion, s. a bleeding ; blood-letting
Ve'ney, s. a bout, turn, push, thrust
Venge, v. a. to avenge. punish, chastise
Ven'geance, s. punishment, revenge
Venge'ful, a. vindictive, revengeful, spiteful
Ve'niable, Ve'nial, a. pardonable, allowed
Ven'ison, s. a beast of chase ; flesh of

Ven'om, s. poison, poisonous matter
Ven'omous. See Ven'emous
Vent, s. a hole, passage ; sale ; dischar
Vent, v. a. to publish, emit, let off, sell
Ven'tiduct, s. a passa e for the wind
Ven'tilate, v. a. to fan ; examine, discuss
Ventila'tion, s. the act of fanning or cool-
ing ; vent, utterance. refrigeration
Ventila'tor, s. an engine to supply air with
Ven'tricle, s. the stomach ; any small cavity
in an animal body. or of the heart
Ventril'oquist, s. one who speaks so as that
the sound seems to issue from his belly
Ven'ture, v. to dare, hazard, send on a venture
Ven'ture, s. a hazard, hap, chance
Ven'turesome, Ven'turous, a. daring. bold
Ven'turously, Ven'turesomely, ad. daringly
Verac'ity, s. honesty of report, truth
Verb, s. one of the parts of speech which
signifies being. doing, or suffering
Ver'bal, a. spoken, oral ; verbose, literal
Ver'bally, ad. orally, in words
Verba'tim, ad. word for word, literally
Ver'berate, v. a. to beat. strike, chastise
Verbera'tion, s. the act of beating, blows
Verbo'se, a. prolix, tedious
Verbos'ity, s. much empty talk
Ver'dant, a. green, flourishing ; beautiful
Ver'derer, Ver'deror, s. a forest officer
Ver'dict, s. a determination by a jury, &c.
Ver'digris, s. the green rust of brass
Ver'diture, s. a kind of pale-green colour
Ver'dure, s. a green colour, greenness
Verid'ical, a. telling truth
Verge, s. a rod ; a dean's mace ; brink
Verge, v. n. to tend, to bend downwards
Ver'ger, s. a mace-bearer in cathedrals, &c.
Ver'ify, v. a. to justify, confirm, prove true
Ver'ily, ad. in truth, certainly, really
Verisim'ilar, a. probable. likely
Verisimil'itude, Verisimil'ity, s. probability
Ver'itable, a. agreeable to fact, true
Ver'ity, s. truth, certainty, a true assertion
Ver'juice, s. the liquor of crab apples
Vermicel'li, s. a paste spun like threads
Vermic'ular, a. acting like a worm ; spiral
Vermic'ulate, v. a. to chequer; to inlay wood,
Ver'micule, s. a little grub or worm [&c.
Vermic'ulous, a. full of worms or grubs
Vermil'ion, s. a beautiful red colour
Ver'min. s. any noxious animal
Ver'minate, v. n. to breed vermin
Vermina'tion, s. a breeding vermin
Ver'minous, a. tending to vermin
Vernac'ular, a. of one's own country
Ver'nal, a. belonging to the spring
Vernil'ity, s. fawning behaviour. meanness
Ver'satile, a. turning round, variable
Versatil'ity, s. the quality of being versatile
Verse, s. a piece of poetry ; lays ; a paragraph
Ver'sed, a. skilled. well practised
Versifica'tion, s. the art of making verses
Ver'sifier, s. a maker of verses
Ver'sify, v. to make or relate in verse
Ver'sion, s. the act of translating, translation
Vert, s. every green tree in a forest
Ver'tebral, a. relating to the backbone
Ver'tebre, s. a joint in the back
Ver'tex, s. the zenith; the point over the head;
the top of a hill ; the top of any tning
Ver'tible, a. capable of being turned

Ver'tical, a. placed in the zenith, perpendicu-
Vortic'ity, s. the act of turning about [lar
Vertig'inous, a. turning round, giddy
Verti'go, s. a giddiness; a whirling motion
Ver'vain, s. the name of a plant
Ver'vel, s. a label tied to a hawk
Ver'y, a. real, true—ad. in a great degree
Ves'icate, v. a. to blister; to puff up; to swell
Vesic'atory, s. a blistering medicine
Ves'icle, s. a small circle inflated; a blister
Ves'per, s. the evening star; the evening
Ves'pers, s. evening service or prayers
Ves'sel, s. any utensil made to contain li-
    quors; a ship, bark, &c.; a pipe for the
    blood or humours in any animal body
Vest, s. an outer garment, a kind of coat
Vest, v. a. to dress, deck, invest, admit
Ves'tal, s. a pure virgin, a sacred virgin
Ves'tal, a. denoting pure virginity
Ves'tibule, s. the entrance of a house
Ves'tige, s. a footstep, trace, mark, sign
Ves'tment, s. a garment, part of dress
Ves'try, s. a room adjoining to a church; peo-
    ple legally assembled in it; meeting
Ves'ture, s. a garment, habit, dress
Vetch, s. a leguminous plant; a kind of pea
Vet'eran, s. old soldier; man long practised
Veterina'rian, s. one skilled in the diseases
    of cattle
Vex, v. a. to plague, to disquiet, to torment
Vexa'tion, s. the act or cause of plaguing
Vexa'tious, a. afflictive, troublesome
Vexa'tiously, ad. troublesomely
Vexa'tiousness, s. troublesomeness
Ug'liness, s. deformity, moral depravity
Ug'ly, a. deformed, offensive to the sight
Vi'al, s. a small bottle—v. a. to bottle up
Vi'and, s. meat dressed, meat, food
Viat'ic, a. relating to a journey
Viat'icum, s. provision for a journey; a rite
Vi'brate, v. to brandish, quiver, move to
    and fro
Vibra'tion, s. a moving with quick return
Vic'ar, s. a minister of a parish where the
    tithes are impropriated; a substitute
Vic'arage, s. the benefice of a vicar
Vica'rial, a. belonging to a vicar; small
Vica'rious, a. deputed, delegated
Vice, s. wickedness, offence; an iron press
Vice, *in composition*, signifies *second in rank*
Vice-ad'miral, s. the second in command
Vice-a'gent, s. one who acts for another
Vicege'rency, s. the office of a vicegerent
Vicege'rent, s. one who is entrusted with the
    power of the superior; a lieutenant
Vicechan'cellor, s. a second magistrate in the
    universities of Oxford and Cambridge
Vi'ceroy, s. one who governs a tributary king-
    dom with regal authority, and is account-
    able only to the king his master
Vic'inage, s. neighbourhood, a place adjoin-
Vici'nal, Vici'ne, a. near, adjoining to [ing
Vicin'ity, s. neighbourhood, nearness
Vic'ious, a. addicted to vice, wicked, base
Vicis'situde, s. change, revolution
Vic'tim, s. a sacrifice; something destroyed
Vic'tor, s. a conqueror, a vanquisher
Victo'rious, a. conquering, vanquishing,
    having obtained conquest
Victo'riously, ad. triumphantly, with victory
Vic'tory, s. conquest, success, triumph

Vict'ual, v. a. to provide with food
Vict'ualler, s. a provider of victuals, &c.
Vict'uals, s. provision of food, meat, stores
Videl'icet, ad. to wit; that is. Frequently
    written viz.
Vie, v. n. to contend, contest, strive with
View, v. a. to survey, to examine, to see
View, s. a prospect, sight, show, survey
Vig'il, s. the eve of a holiday; watch
Vig'ilance, Vig'ilancy, s. watchfulness
Vig'ilant, a. watchful, circumspect, diligent
Vig'ilantly, ad. watchfully, attentively
Vignette', s. a wreath or picture of leaves
    and flowers
Vig'orous, a. full of strength and life
Vig'orously, ad. with strength, forcibly
Vig'orousness, s. force, strength
Vig'our, s. force, strength, energy, efficacy
Vile, a. sordid, wicked, worthless, mean
Vi'lely, ad. shamefully, meanly, basely
Vile'ness, s. baseness, worthlessness
Vil'ify, v. a. to debase, to defame, to abuse
Vill, or Vil'la, s. a country seat, a village
Vil'lage, s. a small collection of houses
Vil'lager, s. an inhabitant of a village
Vil'lain, s. a wicked wretch; a servant
Vil'lanous, a. base, vile, wicked, sorry
Vil'lanously, ad. wickedly, basely
Vil'lany, s. wickedness, baseness, a crime
Vil'lous, a. shaggy, rough, hairy
Vimin'eous, a. made of or like twigs
Vin'cible, a. conquerable, tameable
Vin'dicate, v. a. to justify, to revenge, clear
Vindica'tion, s. a defence, justification
Vin'dicative, a. revengeful, malicious
Vindic'ative, a. revengeful, given to revenge
Vindic'tively, ad. revengefully, maliciously
Vine, s. the name of a tree bearing grapes
Vin'egar, s. any real or metaphorical sour
Vin'eyard, s. a ground planted with vines
Vi'nous, a. having the quality of wine
Vin'tage, s. the time of making wine
Vin'tager, s. one who gathers the vintage
Vint'ner, s. one who sells wine, &c.
Vint'ry, s. the place of selling wine
Vi'ol, s. a stringed musical instrument
Vi'olable, a. that may be violated or hurt
Viola'ceous, a. resembling or like violets
Vi'olate, v. a. to injure, to infringe, ravish
Viola'tion, s. infringement; a deflowering
Vi'olence, s. force, outrage, injury
Vi'olent, a. forcible, extorted, outrageous
Vi'olently, ad. forcibly, outrageously
Vi'olet, s. the name of a sweet flower
Vi'olin, s. a fiddle, a musical instrument
Vi'olist, s. a player on the viol or violin
Violoncel'lo, s. a musical instrument
Vi'per, s. a serpent, a mischievous person
Vira'go, s. a bold, resolute woman
Vi'rent, a. green, not faded, unfaded
Virge, s. a dean's mace, mace, rod
Vir'gin, s. a maid, a woman not a mother
Vir'gin, a. befitting a virgin, maidenly
Vir'ginal, s. a stringed musical instrument
Vir'ginal, a. maidenly, pertaining to a maiden
Virgin'ity, s. maidenhood, purity
Vi'rile, a. manly, bold, courageous
Viril'ity, s. character of manhood; the power
    of procreating the species
Vir'tual, s. effectual, powerful, prevalent
Vir'tually, ad. effectually, not formally

Vir'tuate, v. a. to make efficacious
Vir'tue, s. moral goodness, valour, efficacy
Virtuo'so, s. one skilled in curiosities, &c.
Vir'tuous, a. morally good, efficacious, devout, having medicinal qualities
Vir'ulence, s. poison, venom, malignity, acrimony of temper, bitterness
Vir'ulent, a. malignant, poisonous, venomous
Vi'rus, s. stinking matter from ulcers
Vis'age, s. the face, countenance, look
Vis'cerate, v. a. to take out the bowels
Viscos'ity, s. glutinousness, tenacity
Vi'scount, s. degree of nobility next an earl
Vi'scountess, s. the lady of a viscount
Vis'cous, a. clammy, glutinous, ropy, sticky
Visibil'ity, Vis'ibleness, s. a visible state
Vis'ible, a. apparent, open, conspicuous
Vis'ibly, ad. openly, conspicuously, clearly
Vis'ion, s. sight, a dream, a phantom
Vis'ionary, a. imaginary, seen in a dream
Vis'ionary, s. one disturbed in thought
Vis'it, s. the act of going to see another
Vis'itant, s. one who visits another
Visita'tion, s. a judicial visit; the act of visiting; a judgment from heaven
Vis'iter, Vis'itor, s. one who visits a neighbour or friend; an occasional judge
Visne, s. a kind of brandy or wine
Vis'or, s. a mask, disguise, concealment
Vis'ta, or Vis'to, s. a long view or prospect between two rows of trees, an avenue
Vis'ual, a. used in sight, exercising sight
Vi'tal, a. necessary to life, essential
Vital'ity, s. the power of subsisting in life
Vi'tals, s. parts essential to life, essence
Vit'iate, v. a. to deprave; spoil, corrupt
Vitia'tion, s. depravation, corruption
Vit'ious, a. corrupt, wicked, depraved
Vit'reous, a. glassy, resembling glass
Vit'rify, v. to change into or become glass
Vit'riol, s. a kind of medicinal salt
Vit'riolate, a. impregnated with vitriol
Vitriol'ic, a. containing or resembling vitriol
Vitu'perate, v. a. to censure, to blame
Vitupera'tion, s. blame, censure, dispraise
Viva'cious, a. sprightly, gay, active
Vivac'ity, s. sprightliness, liveliness
Viv'ency, s. manner of supporting life
Vives, s. a distemper among horses
Viv'id, a. quick, active, lively, sprightly
Viv'idness, s. life, liveliness, sprightliness
Vivif'ic, a. giving life, making alive
Viv'ify, v. a. to make alive, to animate
Vivip'arous, a. bringing the young alive
Vix'en, s. a she fox, a scolding woman
Viz. ad. to wit, that is. See Videlicet
Viz'ard, s. a mask to cover the face
Viz'ier, s. the Ottoman prime minister
Ul'cer, s. a dangerous running sore
Ulcera'tion, s. a breaking into sores
Ul'cerous, a. afflicted with sores
Ul'cered, a. grown to be an ulcer
Ulig'inous, a. slimy, muddy, fenny
Ul'terior, a. farther, lying farther or beyond
Ul'timate, a. the very last, final, ending
Ul'timately, ad. in the last consequence
Ultima'tum, s. the final resolution
Ultramari'ne, s. a very fine blue
Ultramari'ne, a. foreign, beyond the sea
Um'ber, s. a yellow colour, a fish
Um'bles, s. the entrails of a deer

Um'bo, s. the point or top of a buckler
Um'brage, s. shadow, offence, resentment
Umbra'geous, Umbro'se, a. shady
Umbrel'la, s. a cover from the sun or rain
Um'pire, s. one who decides disputes
Unaba'sed, a. not humbled, not abased
Unabash'ed, a. not ashamed, undaunted
Una'ble, a. not able, weak, impotent
Unabol'ished, a. remaining still in force
Unaccep'table, a. disagreeable, unpleasing
Unaccept'ed, a. not accepted, not received
Unaccom'panied, a. not attended, alone
Unaccom'plished, a. unfinished, awkward
Unaccount'able, a. not to be accounted for, not reducible to rule, not explicable
Unaccount'ably, ad. strangely, oddly
Unac'curate, a. not exact, incorrect
Unaccus'tomed, a. new, not usual, strange
Unacquaint'ed, a. not known, unusual
Unadmi'red, a. not regarded with honour
Unado'red, a. not worshipped; neglected
Unadvi'sed, a. indiscreet, imprudent
Unaf'fable, a. insociable, stern, haughty
Unaffect'ed, a. not moved, open, real
Unaid'ed, a. not assisted, not helped
Una'lienable, a. that cannot be alienated
Unalli'ed, a. having no powerful relation
Unal'terable, a. that cannot be altered
Unamu'sing, a. unpleasing, uninstructive
Unanim'ity, s. agreement in mind, &c.
Unan'imous, a. being of one mind
Unan'swerable, a. not to be refuted
Unappall'ed, a. not daunted, not dismayed
Unappeas'able, a. not to be pacified
Unapt', a. unfit, unsuitable, improper, dull
Unar'gued, a. not disputed, not censured
Unarm'ed, a. having no armour or weapons
Unart'ful, a. wanting skill or cunning
Unask'ed, a. not asked, not desired
Unaspi'ring, a. not ambitious, humble
Unassail'able, a. not to be assaulted
Unassist'ed, a. not assisted, not helped
Unattain'able, a. not to be gained or attained
Unattempt'ed, a. untried, not essayed
Unattend'ed, a. having no retinue, alone
Unavail'able, Unavail'ing, a. useless, vain
Unavoid'able, a. inevitable, not to be shunned
Unau'thorised, a. without authority
Unawa're, or Unawa'res, ad. suddenly
Unaw'ed, a. having no fear or dread
Unbar', v. a. to unbolt, to remove a bar
Unbar'bed, a. unshaved, bare; relieved
Unbat'tered, a. not injured by blows
Unbeat'en, a. not trodden, not beaten
Unbecom'ing, a. indecent, unsuitable
Unbefit'ting, a. unbecoming, unsuitable
Unbegot'ten, a. not generated, eternal
Unbelief', s. infidelity, incredulity, irreligion
Unbeliev'er, s. an infidel, a wicked person
Unbenefic'ed, a. not enjoying a benefice
Unbenev'olent, a. not kind, unmerciful
Unbenign', a. malevolent, malignant
Unbent', a. relaxed, unshrunk, unsubdued
Unbeseem'ing, a. unbecoming, unfit
Unbewail'ed, a. not lamented
Unbi'as, v. a. to remove prejudice
Unbid'den, a. uninvited, not bidden
Unbig'oted, a. free from bigotry
Unbind', v. a. to loose, untie, separate
Unbla'mable, a. not blamable, innocent
Unblem'ished, a. free from reproach

S 3

Unblest', *a.* wretched, unhappy, accurst
Unblown', *a.* not yet blown, unopened
Unbod'ied, *a.* freed from the body, incorpo-
Unbolt', *v. a.* to open or remove bolts [real
Unbolt'ed, *a.* coarse, not refined or sifted
Unbon'neted, *a.* having no hat or bonnet
Unborn', *a.* not yet brought into life
Unbor'rowed, *a.* not borrowed, genuine
Unbos'om, *v. a.* to reveal in confidence
Unbou'ght, *a.* obtained without money
Unbou'nd, *a.* wanting a cover, not bound
Unbou'nded, *a.* unlimited, unrestrained
Unbra'ce, *v. a.* to loose, relax, unfold
Unbred', *v.* not taught, ill-educated
Unbri'dled, *a.* not restrained, licentious
Unbro'ke, *a.* not tamed or subdued
Unbroth'erly, *a.* not like a brother
Unbuc'kle, *v. a.* to loose a buckle
Unbuild', *v. a.* to raze, destroy, pull down
Unbuilt', *a.* not yet erected, unfinished
Unbur'ied, *a.* not put into a grave, not inter-
Unbur'nt, *a.* not consumed by fire [red
Unbur'then, *v. a.* to rid of a load, throw off
Unbut'ton, *v. a.* to loose any thing buttoned
Unca'non'ical, *a.* not canonical
Uncase, *v. a.* to uncover; take out; flay
Uncau'ght, *a.* not yet catched, not taken
Uncer'tain, *a.* not certain, doubtful
Uncer'tainty, *s.* dubiousness, contingency
Unchain', *v. a.* to free from chains
Uncha'ngeable, *a.* not to be changed, fixed
Unchar'itable, *a.* having no mercy or charity
Unchar'itableness, *s.* want of charity
Uncha'ste, *a.* lewd, lustful, impure
Unchas'tity, *s.* lewdness, incontinence
Unchew'ed, *a.* not chewed, not eaten
Uncir'cumcised, *a.* not circumcised
Uncircumcis'ion, *s.* want of circumcision
Uncir'cumspect, *a.* not cautious, careless
Uncircumstan'tial, *a.* not important
Unciv'il, *a.* unpolite, rude, unkind
Unciv'ility, *ad.* unpolitely, not complaisantly
Unciv'ilized, *a.* barbarous; indecent, rude
Unclar'ified, *a.* not purified, not refined
Unclas'sic, Unclas'sical, *a.* not classical
Un'cle, *s.* a father's or mother's brother
Unclea'n, *a.* not clean; wicked, lewd
Unclean'liness, *s.* want of cleanness; sin
Unclean'ly, *a.* filthy, dirty, unchaste
Unclean'sed, *a.* not cleansed or purified
Unclen'ch, *v. a.* to open the hand
Unclog', *v. a.* to disencumber, exonerate
Unclo'se, *v. a.* to open, set open, disclose
Unclo'the, *v. a.* to strip, to make naked
Uncloud'ed, *a.* free from clouds, not darkened
Unclut'ch, *v. a.* to open the closed hand
Uncoil', *v. a.* to unfold, unravel, open
Uncollect'ed, *a.* not collected, not gathered
Unco'mbed, *a.* not parted with a comb
Uncome'ly, *a.* not comely, not graceful, ugly
Uncome'liness, *s.* want of beauty or grace
Uncom'fortable, *a.* dismal, gloomy
Uncom'fortableness, *s.* want of cheerfulness
Uncom'mon, *a.* not frequent, unusual
Uncompac't, *a.* not compact, not close
Uncommu'nicated, *a.* not communicated
Uncompel'led, *a.* not forced, not obliged
Uncompound'ed, *a.* not mixed, not intricate
Uncompres'sed, *a.* not compressed, loose
Unconcei'vable, *a.* not to be understood
Unconcei'ved, *a.* not thought, not imagined

Unconcer'n, *s.* negligence, indifference
Unconcern'ed, *a.* not anxious; easy
Unconfor'm, *a.* not conformable, unlike
Uncon'scionable, *a.* very unreasonable
Uncon'scionably, *ad.* unreasonably
Uncontrol'lable, *a.* not to be controlled
Uncou'ple, *v. a.* to separate, to let loose
Uncour'teous, *a.* uncivil, unpolite, rude
Uncourt'ly, *a.* unpolished, awkward, rough
Uncou'th, *a.* strange, unusual, odd
Uncrea'te, *a.* not created; everlasting
Uncrea'ted, *a.* not yet created, not yet born
Uncrop'ped, *a.* not cropped, not gathered
Uncrowd'ed, *a.* not crowded; at liberty
Uncrown', *v. a.* to deprive of a crown
Unc't.on, *s.* an ointment; an anointing
Unc'tuous, *a.* fat, oily, clammy, greasy
Uncul'led, *a.* not gathered, not selected
Uncul'pable, *a.* not deserving blame
Uncul'tivated, *a.* not cultivated, not civilized
Uncum'bered, *a.* not cumbered, not harassed
Uncurb'ed, *a.* not restrained, licentious
Uncurl', *v. a.* to destroy curls, to strip off
Uncurtail'ed, *a.* not curtailed, not shortened
Uncut', *a.* not cut, whole, entire
Udam', *v. a.* to open banks; to loose
Undaunt'ed, *a.* not daunted, fearless, bold
Undaunt'edly, *ad.* very boldly, without fear
Undaz'zled, *a.* not dimmed by splendour
Undebauch'ed, *a.* not corrupted, pure
Undec'agon, *s.* a figure of eleven sides
Undecay'ed, *a.* not decayed, not worn
Undece've, *v. a.* to inform justly; set right
Undecei'vable, *a.* not to be deceived
Undeci'ded, *a.* not determined, not settled
Undeck', *v. a.* to undress, strip, divest of
Undefa'ced, *a.* not disfigured, not blotted out
Undefea'sible, *a.* not a-feasible, true
Undefi'led, *a.* not polluted, pure; not vitia:ed
Undefi'nable, *a.* not to be marked out
Undefi'ned, *a.* not defined, unlimited
Undelib'erated, *a.* not carefully considered
Undelight'ed, *a.* not pleased, unfeeling
Undeni'able, *a.* that cannot be denied
Undeplo'red, *a.* not lamented or bewailed
Undepra'ved, *a.* not corrupted, innocent
Un'der, *ad.* and *prep.* beneath, below
Underbid', *v. a.* to offer less than the worth
Underdo', *v. a.* to do less than is requisite
Undergo', *v. a.* to suffer, to endure, to bear
Undergrou'nd, *s.* a subterraneous place
Un'derhand, *a.* secret, clandestine, sly
Underi'ved, *a.* not borrowed, original
Underla'bourer, *s.* a petty workman
Underlay', *v. a.* to lay under; to support
Underli'ne, *v. a.* to draw a line under
Un'derling, *s.* an inferior agent; sorry fellow
Undermi'ne, *v. a.* to sap; to injure secretly
Un'dermost, *a.* lowest, meanest, basest
Undernea'th, *ad.* below, beneath
Underog'atory, *a.* not derogatory [part
Un'derpart, *s.* subordinate, or unessential
Un'derplot, *s.* a series of events proceeding
collaterally with the main story of a dra-
matic representation, and subservient to
it; a clandestine scheme
Underra'te, *v. a.* to rate or value too low
Un'derrate, *s.* a price less than the value
Undersell', *v. a.* to sell cheaper than another
Un'dersong, *s.* chorus, burden of a song
Understand', *v.* to comprehend fully

Understand'ing, s. intellectual powers; skill
Understand'ing, a. knowing, skilful
Un'derstrapper, s. an inferior agent
Underta'ke, v. to engage, to promise
Underta'ker, s. one who engages in projects and affairs; a manager; one who manages funerals
Underta'king, s. an enterprise; business
Underten'ant, s. a secondary tenant
Underval'ue, v. a. to rate too low
Un'derwood, s. bushes under timber trees
Un'derwork, s. petty affairs, a base design
Underwri'te, v. a. to write under another
Underwri'ter, s. an insurer, a subscriber
Undescri'bed, a. not described, confused
Undescri'ed, a. undiscovered, not seen
Undeser'ved, a. not merited, not incurred
Undeser'ving, a. not deserving, worthless
Undesi'gned, a. not designed, not intended
Undesi'gning, a. sincere, honest, upright
Undestroy'ed, a. not destroyed, not wasted
Undeter'mined, a. unsettled, undecided
Undevo'ted, a. not devoted, not given up
Undiaph'onous, a. dull, not transparent
Undigest'ed, a. not concocted, not digested
Undimin'ished, a. not lessened, entire
Undip'ped, a. not dipped; not plunged; dry
Undirect'ed, a. not directed, not set right
Undiscern'ed, a. not discerned, unseen
Undiscern'ible, a. not to be discerned
Undiscern'ing, a. injudicious, silly
Undis'ciplined, a. uninstructed, untaught
Undiscov'erable, a. not to be found out
Undiscov'ered, a. not seen, unknown
Undisgui'sed, a. open, artless, sincere
Undistur'bed, a. not disturbed, quiet
Undo', v. a. to ruin; to take to pieces
Undone', a. ruined, destroyed, not performed
Undoubt'edly, ad. without question or doubt
Undress', v. a. to take off the clothes
Un'dulate, v. a. to roll or move as a wave
Undula'tion, s. a motion like waves
Undu'tiful, a. not obedient, not reverent
Unea'siness, s. trouble, care, perplexity
Unea'sy, a. not easy, disturbed, painful
Unea'ten, a. not devoured or eaten
Uned'ifying, a. not improving
Unelect'ed, a. not elected, not chosen
Unel'igible, a. not proper to be chosen
Unemploy'ed, a. not employed in work
Unendow'ed, a. not endowed, not graced
Unenjoy'ed, a. not enjoyed, not possessed
Unenlar'ged, a. not enlarged, contracted
Unenlight'ened, a. not illuminated
Unentertain'ing, a. giving no delight
Unen'vied, a. exempt from envy
Une'qual, a. not even; not equal; partial
Uneq'uitable, a. not just, partial, unfair
Unequiv'ocal, a. not equivocal, plain
Unerr'ing, a. certain, not mistaking
Unessen'tial, a. not essential; void of life
Unestab'lished, a. not established, uncertain
Une'ven, a. not level, not even, not equal
Une'venness, s. inequality, changeableness
Unexact'ed, a. not exacted, not forced
Unexam'ined, a. not examined, not tried
Unexam'pled, a. without example
Unexcep'tionable, a. not liable to objection
Unex'ecuted, a. not performed, not executed
Unexem'plified, a. not known by example
Unexem'pt, a. not privileged, not free

Unex'orcised, a. not exorcised, not cast out
Unexpand'ed, a. not spread out; confused
Unexpect'ed, a. not expected; sudden
Unexpe'rienced, a. not versed or experienced
Unexpe'dient, a. not fit, inconvenient
Unexpert', a. wanting skill, awkward
Unexplo'red, a. not searched out, not tried
Unexpress'ible, a. unutterable, ineffable
Unextend'ed, a. having no dimensions
Unextin'guishable, a. not to be put out
Unextin'guished, a. not quenched or put out
Unextir'pated, a. not rooted out
Unfa'ded, a. not withered, not decayed
Unfa'ding, a. not liable to change colour
Unfa'ir, a. not fair, dishonest, disingenuous
Unfaith'ful, a. treacherous, dishonest
Unfaith'fully, ad. treacherously, perfidiously
Unfaith'fulness, s. treachery, perfidiousness
Unfal'lowed, a. not fallowed
Unfash'ionable, a. not modish, obsolete
Unfash'ioned, a. not fashioned by art
Unfas'ten, v. a. to unloose, unfix, open
Unfath'omable, a. not to be sounded
Unfath'omed, a. not fathomed, not sounded
Unfati'gued, a. not fatigued, unwearied
Unfa'vourable, a. not favourable, unkind
Unfear'ed, a. not feared; despised
Unfeas'ible, a. impracticable, not to be done
Unfeath'ered, a. naked of feathers, bare
Unfea'tured, a. wanting regular features
Unfed', a. not supplied with food
Unfeel'ing, a. insensible, without feeling
Unfeign'ed, a. real, sincere, not pretended
Unfelt', a. not felt; not perceived
Unfer'tile, a. not fruitful, barren, bare
Unfet'ter, v. a. to free from shackles
Unfil'ial, a. unsuitable to a son, disobedient
Unfil'led, a. not filled, not supplied
Unfin'ished, a. wanting the last hand
Unfir'm, a. infirm, weak, not stable
Unfit', a. improper, unqualified, unsuitable
Unfix', v. a. to loosen, separate, make fluid
Unfix'ed, a. wandering, not settled, vagrant
Unfled'ged, a. not covered with feathers
Unfoil'ed, a. not subdued, not conquered
Unfo'ld, v. a. to expand, discover, display
Unforbid'den, a. not forbidden, allowed
Unforebo'ding, a. giving no omens or signs
Unfor'ced, a. not compelled, not feigned
Unforesee'n, a. not seen or known before
Unfor'feited, a. not forfeited; preserved
Unforgi'ving, a. implacable, inexorable
Unform'ed, a. shapeless, not modified
Unforsa'ken, a. not deserted; supported
Unfor'tified, a. not fortified, defenceless
Unfor'tunate, a. unprosperous, unlucky
Unfor'tunately, ad. without good luck
Unfou'ght, a. not fought; not determined
Unfou'nd, a. not found, not met with
Unfra'med, a. not framed, not fashioned
Unfre'quent, a. not common, unusual
Unfrequent'ed, a. forsaken, rarely visited
Unfrien'd'ed, a. wanting friends, destitute
Unfrien'd'ly, a. not benevolent, not kind
Unfro'zen, a. not frozen, not congealed
Unfruit'ful, a. not fruitful, barren, waste
Unfurl', v. a. to expand, unfold, spread
Unfur'nish, v. a. to deprive, strip, divest
Unfur'nished, a. without furniture, &c.
Ungain', Ungain'ly, a. awkward, uncouth
Ungar'nished, a. not garnished, unadorned

Ungar'tered. *a.* without garte s ; slovenly
Ougath'ered, *a.* not picked, not pulled
Ungen'erative. *a.* begetting nothing
Ungen'erous, *a.* niggardly, mean. not liberal
Unge'nial. *a.* not favourable to nature
Ungenteel', *a.* not genteel ; unbecoming
Ungen'tle. *a.* harsh, rude, rugged
Ungen'tlemanlike, *a.* mean, illiberal
Ungen'tleness, *s.* incivility ; harshness
Ungen'tly, *ad.* harshly, rudely, severely
Ungeomet'rical, *a.* not geometrical
Ungild'ed, *a.* not overlaid with gold
Ungird', *v. a.* to loose a girdle or girth
Ungirt', *a.* loosely dressed, loose, free
Unglo'rified. *a.* not honoured, not praised
Ungod'lily, *a.* wickedly, impiously
Ungod'liness. *s.* impiety, profaneness
Ungod'ly. *ad.* wicked, irreligious, profane
Ungor'ged, *a.* not filled, not sated
Ungov'ernable, *a.* not to be ruled, wild
Ungov'erned, *a.* licentious, unbridled, loose
Ungra'ceful, *a.* wanting beauty or air
Ungra'cious. *a.* wicked, unacceptable
Ungra'teful, *a.* unthankful, unpleasing
Ungra'tefully, *ad.* with ingratitude
Unground'ed, *a.* having no foundation
Unguard'ed, *a.* careless, negligent
Un'guent, *s.* an ointment ; a liquid salve
Unhand'some, *a.* ungraceful, illiberal
Unhand'y, *a.* awkward, not dexterous
Unhap'py, *a.* unfortunate, miserable
Unhar'med, *a.* unhurt, uninjured. safe
Unharmo'nious, *a.* unmusical, harsh
Unhar'ness, *v. a.* to untrace, to se' loose
Unhat'ched, *a.* not yet brought forth
Unhealth'ful, Unhealth'y, *a.* sickly, morbid
Unhe'ard, *a.* not heard, unknown
Unheed'ed, *a.* disregarded, not minded
Unheed'ful, *a.* careless, inattentive, giddy
Unhewn', *a.* not hewn, not shaped
Unhin'ge, *v. a.* to throw from the hinges
Unho'liness, *s.* profaneness, wickedness
Unho'ly, *a.* profane, impious, wicked
Unhon'oured, *a.* not treated with respect
Unhoo'p, *v. a.* to divest or strip of hoops
Unho'peful, *a.* giving no room to hope
Unhor'se, *v. a.* to throw from a horse
Unhos'pitable, *a.* not kind to strangers
Unhou'se, *v. a.* to drive out of habitation
Unhou'sed, *a.* homeless, driven out
Unhou'seled, *a.* without the sacrament
Unhum'bled, *a.* not humbled, haughty
Unhurt', *a.* not hurt, free from harm
Unhurt'ful, *a.* doing no harm ; innocent
Unhurt'fully, *ad.* without any harm
Unhusk', *v. a.* to take off the husk
U'nicorn, *s.* a beast, whether real or fabulous, with only one horn
U'niform, *a.* similar to itself ; regular
Unifor'mity, *s.* regularity ; similitude
U'niformly, *ad.* in an uniform manner
Unimag'inable. *a.* not to be imagined
Unim'itable, *a.* not to be imitated
Unimmor'tal, *a.* not immortal : frail
Unimpair'able, *a.* not liable to be impaired
Unimpea'ched, *a.* not impeached, not accused
Unimpor'tant, *a.* not important, trifling
Unimportu'ned, *a.* not solicited, not asked
Unimpro'ved, *a.* not taught, not improved
Uninfla'med, *a.* not set on fire, not burnt
Uninfor'med, *a.* uninstructed, ignorant

Uningen'uous, *a.* illiberal, no honest
Uninhab'itable, *a.* not fit to be inhabited
Uninhab'ited, *a.* not inhabited, empty
Unin'jured, *a.* not injured, unhurt, safe
Uninspi'red, *a.* not canonical ; not inspired
Uninstruc'ted, *a.* not instructed, not taught
Uninstruc'tive, *a.* not edifying
Unintel'ligent, *a.* not knowing, not skilful
Unintel'ligible, *a.* not to be understood
Uninten'tional, *a.* not designed or intended
Unin'terested, *a.* not having interest
Unintermix'ed, *a.* not mingled, separate
Uninterrup'ed, *a.* not interrupted
Unintren'ched, *a.* not intrenched, exposed
Uninves'tigable, *a.* not to be searched out
Uninvi'ted, *a.* not invited, not asked
Unjoint'ed, *a.* disjointed, having no joint
U'nion, *s.* the act of joining ; concord
U'nique. *a.* sole, without an equal
U'nison, *a.* sounding alone or the same
U'nison, *s.* a string of the same sound
U'nit, *s.* one ; the least number
Uni'te, *v.* to join ; agree ; grow into one
Uni'tedly, *ad.* with union or consent
Uni'tion, *s.* the act or power of uniting
U'nity, *s.* the being in concord ; tenour
Unjud'ged. *a.* not judicially determined
Univer'sal, *a.* general, total, all—*s.* the whole
Universal'ity, *s.* an universal state; generality
Univer'sally, *ad.* without exception
U'niverse. *s.* the general system of things
Univer'sity, *s.* a general school of liberal arts
Unjust', *a.* partial, contrary to justice
Unjus'tifiable, *a.* not to be justified
Unken'nel, *v. a.* to drive from a kennel
Un ept', *a.* not kept, not observed
Unki'nd, *a.* not kind, not obliging
Unkind'ly, *ad.* without kindness, &c.
Unkind'ly, *a.* unnatural, unfavourable
Unkind'ness, *s.* malignity ; ill will
Unknight'ly, *a.* not becoming a knight
Unknit', *v. a.* to unweave ; open ; separate
Unknot', *v. a.* to free from knots, to unite
Unknow'ing, *a.* ignorant, not qualified
Unknown', *a.* not discovered, not known
Unla'boured. *a.* not considered; spontaneous
Unla'ce, *v. a.* to loose a thing laced up
Unla'de. *v. a.* to unload, empty, put out
Unlaid', *a.* not placed, not fixed
Unlamen'ted, *a.* not lamented
Unlat'ch, *v. a.* to open a latch, to lift up
Unlaw'ful. *a.* contrary to law, unjust
Unlaw'fully, *ad.* in an unlawful manner
Unlear'ned, *a.* ignorant, not learned
Unlea'vened. *a.* not fermented, not leavened
Unless', *conj.* except ; if not ; but
Unles'soned, *a.* not instructed, not taught
Unlet'tered, *a.* unlearned, ignorant
Unlev'elled, *a.* not cut or made even
Unlibid'inous, *a.* not lustful, chaste, pure
Unli'censed, *a.* having no licence or leave
Unlick'ed, *a.* not licked ; shapeless
Unli'ke, *a.* improbable, unlikely, not like,
Unli'kelihood, Unli'keliness, *s.* improbability
Unli'kely, *a.* improbable—*ad.* improbably
Unlim'ited, *a.* having no bounds, unconfined
Unlink', *v. a.* to untwist ; open : break
Unload', *v. a.* to disburden, to exonerate
Unlock', *v. a.* to open a lock ; to solve
Unlook'ed-for, *a.* not expected, not foreseen
Unloo'se, *v.* to set loose ; to fall in pieces

Unlove'liness, s. unamiableness; ugliness
Unlove'ly, a. unable to excite love
Unluck'ily, ad. unfortunately, by ill luck
Unluck'y, a. unfortunate; mischievous
Unma'de, a. not created, deprived of form
Unmai'med, a. complete, not maimed
Unma'ke, v. a. to deprive of qualities
Unman', v. to deject; to act unbecomingly
Unman'ageable, a. not manageable, rude
Unman'aged, a. not broken, not tutored
Unman'ly, a. unbecoming a man, effeminate
Unman'nered, a. rude, gross, uncivil, brutal
Unman'nerly, a. ill bred, uncivil
Unmanu'red, a. not cultivated; poor
Unmark'ed, a. ot regarded, unobserved
Unmar'ried, a. not yet married, single
Unmask', v. to take or put off a mask
Unmask'ed, a. not masked, open to view
Unmas'tered, a. not conquered, not subdued
Unmatch'ed, a. having no equal, matchless
Unmean'ing, a. having no meaning
Unmeas'urable, a. unbounded, infinite
Unmeas'ured, a. not measured; plentiful
Unmeet', a. not worthy, unfit, improper
Unmel'ted, a. not melted, not dissolved
Unmer'ciful, a. cruel, unconscionable
Unmer'cifully, ad. without mercy
Unmer'itable, a. having no merit, worthless
Unmer'ited, a. not deserved, unjust, cruel
Unmind'ed, a. not heeded, disregarded
Unmind'ful, a. negligent, inattentive
Unmin'gled, a. not mixed, pure, separate
Unmix'ed, a. pure, not mingled with anything
Unmoan'ed, a. not lamented
Unmoles'ted, a. free from disturbance
Unmoor', v. a. to heave up an anchor
Unmort'gaged, a. not mortgaged; clear
Unmo'veable, a. not to be removed, fixed
Unmo'ved, a. not moved, not affected
Unmourn'ed, a. not mourned for
Unmuf'fle, v. a. to take off a covering
Unmu'sical, a. not harmonious; harsh
Unmuz'zle, v. a. to take off a muzzle
Unna'med, a. not mentioned, not spoken of
Unnat'ural, a. forced, contrary to nature
Unnat'urally, ad. in opposition to nature
Unnav'igable, a. not to be navigated
Unne'cessarily, ad. without necessity
Unne'cessary, a. needless, useless, trifling
Unneigh'bourly, a. not neighbourly
Unner'vate, Unner'ved, a. weak, feeble
Unner've, v. a. to weaken, to enfeeble
Unnum'bered, a. innumerable, not number-
Unobey'ed, a. not obeyed; resisted   [ed
Unobnox'ious, a. not liable, not exposed
Unobser'vable, a. not to be observed
Unobser'vant, a. inattentive, not obsequious
Unobser'ved, a. not regarded, not attended to
Unobstruc'ted, a. not hindered, not stopped
Unobtai'ned, a. not acquired, not gained
Unoc'cupied, a. not inhabited, unpossessed
Unoffen'ding, a. harmless, innocent
Uno'pened, a. not opened, closely shut
Unop'erative, a. producing no effect
Unoppo'sed, a. not opposed, not withstood
Unor'ganised, a. without organs or parts
    proper or instrumental to nourish the rest
Unor'thodox, a. not holding pure doctrine
Unpack', v. a. to open things packed up
Unpack'ed, a. not packed, not collected
Unpaid', a. not paid, not discharged

Unpain'ful, a. not painful, giving no pain
Unpal'atable, a. nauseous, disgusting
Unpar'agoned, v. unequalled, unmatched
Unpar'alleled, a. having no equal, &c.
Unpar'donable, a. not to be forgiven
Unpar'donably, ad. beyond forgiveness
Unpar'doned, a. not forgiven; not discharged
Unparliamen'tary, a. contrary to the estab-
    lished regulation of a parliament
Unpass'able, a. admitting no passage
Unpawn'ed, a. not laid in pawn
Unpeace'able, a. quarrelsome, troublesome
Unpeg', v. a. to pull or let out a peg
Unpen'sioned, a. not pensioned; neglected
Unpeo'ple, v. a. to deprive of inhabitants
Unperceiv'able, a. that cannot be perceived
Unpercei'ved, a. not observed, not seen
Unper'fect, a. incomplete, imperfect
Unperform'ed, a. not performed, not done
Unper'ishable, a. lasting, not perishable
Unper'jured, a. free from perjury
Unperplex'ed, a. not embarrassed, easy
Unpet'rified, a. not turned to stone
Unphilosoph'ical, a. not conformable to the
    rules of philosophy or right reason
Unpier'ced, a. not pierced; sound, whole
Unpil'lowed, a. wanting a pillow
Unpin', v. a. to open what is pinned or shut
Unpink'ed, a. not pinked, not set off
Unpit'ied, a. not pitied, not lamented
Unpit'ying, a. having no compassion
Unpleas'ant, a. not pleasant, uneasy
Unpleas'antly, ad. uneasily, uncivilly
Unplea'sed, a. not pleased, not delighted
Unplea'sing, a. offensive, not pleasing
Unpli'ant, a. not bending to another
Unplough'ed, a. not ploughed, not prepared
Unpoet'ical, a. not according to the rules of
    poetry; not becoming a poet
Unpol'ished, a. uncivilized; not smoothed
Unpoli'te, a. not elegant, unrefined, not civil
Unpollu'ted, a. not defiled or corrupted
Unpop'ular, a. not popular, disliked, hated
Unprac'tised, a. not skilled by use
Unprai'sed, a. not celebrated, not praised
Unprec'edented, a. not having a precedent
Unprefer'red, a. not advanced or promoted
Unprejn'dicate, a. not prepossessed
Unprej'udiced, a. free from prejudice
Unprela'tical, a. not becoming a prelate
Unpremed'itated, a. not studied beforehand
Unprepa'red, a. not prepared, not fitted
Unprepossess'ed, a. not prepossessed
Unpress'ed, a. not pressed, not forced
Unpreten'ding, a. not claiming distinction
Unpreven'ted, a. not previously hindered
Unprevai'ling, a. being of no force, vain
Unprin'cely, a. unsuitable to a prince
Unprin'cipled, a. not instructed; wicked
Unprin'ted, a. not printed, not published
Unpri'sable, a. of little value or estimation
Unpris'oned, a. set free from confinement
Unpri'zed, a. not prized, not valued
Unproclai'med, a. not publicly declared
Unprofa'ned, a. not profaned or violated
Unprof'itable, a. serving no purpose, useless
Unprof'itably, ad. uselessly, to no purpose
Unprohib'ited, a. not forbidden, lawful
Unprolif'ic, a. not fruitful, barren
Unpronoun'ced, a. not spoken, not uttered
Unpropi'tious, a. not favourable, inauspicious

Unpropor'tioned, a. not proportioned
Unprop'ped, a. not supported by props
Unpros'perous, a. unsuccessful, unfortunate
Unprotec'ted, a. not protected, unsupported
Unprovi'ded, a. not secured ; not furnished
Unprovo'ked, a. not provoked or incited
Unpub'lished, a. not yet given to the public
Unpun'ished, a. not punished ; free
Unpu'rified, a. not cleansed, not purified
Unpursu'ed, a. not pursued, not followed
Unqual'ified, a. not qualified, unfit
Unqual'ify, v. a. to divest of qualification
Unquell'ed, a. not quelled, not subdued
Unquench'able, a. not to be quenched
Unquench'ed, a. not extinguished
Unques'tionable, a. not to be doubted
Unques'tionably, ad. without doubt
Unques'tioned, a. not asked, not doubted
Unqui'et, a. disturbed, reckless, dissatisfied
Unrack'ed, a. not poured off the lees
Unra'kal, a. not thrown together
Unran'sacked, a. not plundered or pillaged
Unrav'el, v. a. to disentangle ; to explain
Unra'zored, a. unshaven ; rough ; filthy
Unrea'ched, a. not reached, not attained to
Unread', a. not read, unlearned, untaught
Unread'y, a. ungainly ; awkward ; not fit
Unre'al, a. not real, unsubstantial
Unrea'sonable, a. exorbitant, immoderate
Unrea'sonably, ad. not reasonably
Unrea've, v. a. to disentangle, to let loose
Unreba'ted, a. not blunted ; continued
Unrebu'kable, a. not blameable, innocent
Unrecei'ved, a. not received, not admitted
Unreclaim'ed, a. not reformed, not tamed
Unrec'ompensed, a. not recompensed
Unrec'onciled, a. not reconciled
Unrecor'ded, a. not recorded or registered
Unrecoun'ted, a. not related, not told
Unrecrui'table, a. not to be recruited ; lost
Unredeem'ed, a. not redeemed
Unredu'ced, a. not reduced, not lessened
Unrefrac'ted, a. not refracted, not broken
Unrefresh'ed, a. not cheered or relieved
Unregar'ded, a. not heeded, not respected
Unregen'erate, a. not regenerate ; wicked
Unrein'ed, a. not restrained by the bridle
Unrelent'ing, a. cruel, feeling no pity
Unrelie'ved, a. not succoured, not eased
Unreme'diable, a. admitting of no remedy
Unremit'ted, a. not remitted, not abated
Unrepen'ted, a. not repented of
Unrepen'ting, a. not penitent
Unreplen'ished, a. not filled again
Unreproach'ed, a. not censured or upbraided
Unrepro'ved, a. not censured, not blamed
Unreques'ted, a. not asked, not desired
Unrequi'table, a. not to be requited
Unresen'ted, a. not resented, forgiven
Unreser'ved, a. frank, open, free
Unresis'ted, a. not opposed ; obeyed
Unresis'ting, a. not making resistance
Unresol'ved, a. not determined, not solved
Unrespec'tive, a. taking little notice
Unrest', s. disquiet, want of tranquillity
Unresto'red, a. not restored, kept
Unrestrai'ned, a. not confined, loose
Unreveal'ed, a. not revealed, not told
Unreven'ged, a. not revenged, forgiven
Unrev'erend, a. irreverent, disrespectful
Unrever'sed, a. not reversed ; not repealed

Unrevo'ked, a. not revoked, not recalled
Unrewar'ded, a. not rewarded, unpaid
Unrid'dle, v. a. to solve a difficulty
Unrig', v. a. to strip off the tackle
Unright'eous, a. unjust, wicked
Unright'ful, a. not just or right, unjust
Unrip', v. a. to cut open, to rip open
Unri'pe, a. too early ; not ripe ; sour
Unri'valed, a. having no rival or equal
Unriv'et, v. a. to free from rivets, to loosen
Unroll', v. a. to open or unfurl a roll
Unroman'tic, a. not romantic
Unroof', v. a. to strip off the roofs of houses
Unroot', v. a. to tear from the root ; extirpate
Unroun'ded, a. not made round ; uneven
Unruf'fle, v. n. to cease from commotion
Unru'ly, a. ungovernable, licentious
Unsa'fe, a. not safe, hazardous, dangerous
Unsa'fely, ad. dangerously, hazardously
Unsaid', a. not uttered, not mentioned
Unsal'ted, a. not pickled or seasoned with salt
Unsanc'tified, a. unholy, not consecrated
Unsat'isfied, a. not contented, not filled
Unsa'tiable, a. not to be satisfied or pleased
Unsatisfac'tory, a. not giving satisfaction
Unsa'voury, a. tasteless, disgustful, insipid
Unsay', v. a. to retract, to recal, to recant
Unscholas'tic, a. not bred to literature
Unschool'ed, a. not learned, uneducated
Unscor'ched, a. not touched by fire
Unscreen'ed, a. not protected, not covered
Unscrew', v. a. to turn back a screw
Unseal', v. a. to open any thing sealed
Unseal'ed, a. not sealed, wanting a seal
Unseam', v. a. to cut or rip open a seam
Unsea'sonable, a. untimely, unfit, late
Unsea'sonableness, s. unfitness
Unsea'soned, a. ill-timed ; not salted
Unsec'onded, a. not supported ; left alone
Unsecu're, a. not secure, not safe
Unseem'ly, a. indecent, uncomely
Unseen', a. not seen, invisible ; unskilled
Unser'viceable, a. of no advantage or use
Unset'tle, v. a. to make uncertain
Unset'tled, a. not steady, not fixed
Unset'tledness, s. irresolution, want of fixity
Unsev'ered, a. not divided, not parted
Unshac'kle, v. a. to loose from chains
Unsha'kable, a. firm, not to be shaken
Unsha'ken, a. not moved, not agitated
Unsha'pen, a. deformed, misshapen, ugly
Unshea'th, v. a. to draw from a scabbard
Unshel'tered, a. wanting protection
Unship', v. a. to take out of a ship
Unshock'ed, a. not frighted, unshaken
Unshod', a. having no shoes, barefoot
Unshorn', a. not shaven, not clipped
Unshow'ered, a. not watered by showers
Unsif'ted, a. not tried ; not parted by a sieve
Unsight'liness, s. disagreeableness, deformity
Unsight'ly, a. disagreeable to the sight
Unsin'ew, v. a. to deprive of strength
Unsin'ning, a. having no sin ; perfect
Unskil'ful, a. wanting art or knowledge
Unskil'fulness, s. want of art or knowledge
Unskil'led, a. wanting skill or knowledge
Unsla'ked, a. not quenched, not put out
Unso'ciable, a. not sociable, not kind
Unsoil'ed, a. not polluted, not stained
Unsol'd, a. not sold, not disposed of
Unsol'dierlike, a. unbecoming a soldier

Unsolic'itous, *a.* not solicitous, not anxious
Unsol'id, *a.* not coherent or firm
Unsophis'ticated, *a.* not adulterated
Unsort'ed, *a.* not properly separated
Unsought', *a.* not seen; not searched
Unsound', *a.* not sound; rotten; dishonest; erroneous; not true; sickly
Unsound'ed, *a.* not tried by the plummet
Unsour'ed, *a.* not made sour, not morose
Unsown'. *a.* not sown, having no seed
Unspeak'able, *a.* not to be expressed
Unspeak'ably, *ad.* inexpressibly, ineffably
Unspec'ified, *a.* not particularly mentioned
Unspec'ulative, *a.* not theoretical, plain
Unspent', *a.* not wasted, not diminished
Unsphe're, *v. a.* to remove from its orb
Unspilt', *a.* not spilt, not shed; preserved
Unspoil'ed, *a.* not plundered, not marred
Unspot'ted, *a.* not stained or spotted
Unsta'ble, *a.* inconstant, not fixed
Unstaid', *a.* not steady, changeable
Unstain'ed, *a.* not stained, not dyed
Unstat'utable, *a.* contrary to some statute
Unstaunch'ed, *a.* not staunched or stopp'd
Unstrait'ened, *a.* not straitened, unconfined
Unstead'ily, *ad.* inconstantly, inconsistently
Unstead'y, *a.* irresolute, variable, inconstant
Unsted'fast, *a.* not fixed, not firm, not sure
Unstin'ted, *a.* not limited, not confined
Unstir'red, *a.* not stirred, not shaken
Unstrain'ed, *a.* easy, not forced; natural
Unstring', *v. a.* to untie, to relax strings
Unstud'ied, *a.* not studied, not laboured
Unstuff'ed, *a.* unfilled, unfurnished
Unsubdu'ed, *a.* not subdued, not conquered
Unsubstan'tial, *a.* not solid, not real
Unsuccess'ful, *a.* not successful, unlucky
Unsug'ared, *a.* not sweetened with sugar
Unsuit'able, *a.* not fit, not proportionate
Unsuit'ableness, *s.* unfitness, incongruity
Unsuit'ing, *a.* not fitting, not becoming
Unsul'lied, *a.* not fouled, not dis'raced
Unsung', *a.* not recited in verse or song
Unsun'ned, *a.* not exposed to the sun
Unsuper'fluous, *a.* not more than enough
Unsupplan'ted, *a.* not defeated by stratagem
Unsupport'ed, *a.* not sustained, not assisted
Unsuscep'tible, *a.* not liable to admit
Unsuspec'ted, *a.* not doubted or suspected
Unsuspec'ting, *a.* not suspecting
Unsuspic'ious, *a.* having no suspicion
Unsustain'ed, *a.* not supported or propped
Unsway'ed, *a.* not wielded, not swayed
Unswear', *v. n.* to recant any thing sworn
Unswor'n. *a.* not bound by an oath
Untain'ted, *a.* not sullied, not tainted
Unta'med, *a.* not tamed, not subdued
Untan'gle, *v. a.* to loose from intricacy
Untas'ted, *a.* not tried by the palate, &c.
Untaught', *a.* not taught, uninstructed
Untem'pered, *a.* not tempered or hardened
Unte'nable, *a.* not capable of defence, &c.
Unten'anted, *a.* having no tenant, empty
Unten'ded, *a.* without attendance, alone
Unter'rified, *a.* not terrified, dauntless
Unthank'ful, *a.* ungrateful; displeasing
Unthank'fully, *ad.* without thanks
Unthaw'ed, *a.* not thawed, not dissolved
Unthink'ing, *a.* thoughtless, careless
Unthor'ny, *a.* not obstructed by prickes
Unthought-of, *a.* not regarded, not heeded

Unthreat'ened, *a.* not threatened or menaced
Unthrift', *s.* a prodigal—*a.* wasteful
Unthrift'y, *a.* extravagant, lavish
Unthri'ving, *a.* not thriving, not prospering
Untie', *v. a.* to unbind, to loosen
Untied, *a.* not bound, not fastened
Until'. *ad.* to the time, place, or degree
Untill'ed, *a.* not tilled, not cultivated
Unti'mely, *a.* happening before proper time
Unti'me'y, *ad.* before the natural time
Untin'ged, *a.* not stained, not infected
Untir'ed, *a.* fresh, not tired, not made weary
Unti'tled, *a.* having no title
Un'to, *prep.* the old word for *to*
Unto'ld, *a.* not related, not revealed
Untouch'ed, *a.* not touched, not affected
Unto'ward, *a.* froward; perverse; vexatious
Unto'wardly, *ad.* awkwardly, peevishly
Untra'ceable, *a.* not to be traced
Untrain'ed, *a.* not educated, not instructed
Untranspa'rent, *a.* not transparent, opaque
Untrav'elled, *a.* never trodden by passengers
Untri'ed, *a.* not attempted, not tried
Untrim'med, *a.* not trimmed, plain
Untrod', *a.* not trodden down by the foot
Untroub'led, *a.* not disturbed; clear
Untrue', *a.* not true, false, not faithful
Untru'ly, *ad.* falsely, not according to truth
Untru'stiness, *s.* unfaithfulness, deceitfulness
Un'truth, *s.* a falsehood, a false assertion
Untu'nable, *a.* not musical, unharmonious
Unturn'ed, *a.* not turned, not changed
Untu'tored, *a.* uninstructed, untaught
Untwi'ne, Untwis't, *v. a.* to separate things involved; to open what is wrapped
Unvail', *v. a.* to throw off a vail, uncover
Unval'ued, *a.* not prized, neglected
Unvan'quished, *a.* not conquered or overcome
Unva'ried, *a.* not changed, not varied
Unvar'nished, *a.* not overlaid with varnish
Unveil', *v. a.* to disclose, show, discover
Unver'itable, *a.* not true, false, deceitful
Unver'sed, *a.* unacquainted, unskilled
Unvi'olated, *a.* not injured, not broken
Unvis'ited, *a.* not visited, not resorted to
Unu'sed, *a.* not put to use, unemployed
Unu'seful, *a.* useless, serving no purpose
Unu'sual, *a.* not common, rare, unfrequent
Unut'terable, *a.* inexpressible, ineffable
Unwall'ed, *a.* not having walls; open, bare
Unwa'rily, *ad.* without caution, carelessly
Unwa'riness, *s.* want of caution, carelessness
Unwar'like, *a.* not like or fit for war
Unwar'ned, *a.* not warned, not cautioned
Unwar'rantable, *a.* not defensible, not allowed
Unwar'ranted, *a.* not ascertained, uncertain
Unwa'ry, *a.* wanting caution; precipitate
Unwash'ed, *a.* not washed; unclean
Unwas'ted, *a.* not diminished, not lessened
Unwea'ried, *a.* not tired, indefatigable
Unwea'ry, *v. a.* to refresh after weariness
Unwedge'able, *a.* not to be cloven
Unweigh'ed, *a.* not weighed; not considered
Unwel'come, *a.* not pleasing, ungrateful
Unwell', *a.* disordered, sick, afflicted
Unwept', *a.* not lamented or grieved for
Unwhipt', *a.* not whipped, not corrected
Unwho'lesome, *a.* corrupt, not wholesome
Unwiel'dy, *a.* unmanageable; bulky
Unwill'ing, *a.* not willing, loth, not inclined
Unwind', *v. a.* to untwist, to untwine

Unwi'se, a. defective in wisdom, weak
Unwit', v. a. to deprive of understanding
Unwit'tingly, ad. willingly, ignorantly
Unwit'ty, a. destitute of wit; coarse
Unwon'ted, a. uncommon, unusual
Unwor'thily, ad. without due regard
Unwor'thy, a. not deserving; mean
Unwrea'th, v. a. to untwine, to untwist
Unwrit'ten, a. not written; traditional
Unwrou'ght, a. not manufactured
Unwrung', a. not wrung, not pinched
Unyiel'ded, a. not yielded, not given up
Unyo'ke, v. a. to loose from a yoke [book
Vocab'ulary, s. a small dictionary or word-
Vo'cal, a. of or belonging to the voice
Vo'cally, ad. articulately; in words
Voca'tion, s. a summons; employment
Voc'ative, s. the case of nouns in grammar
  used in calling or speaking to
Vocif'erate, s. to shout, bawl, make a noise
Vocifera'tion, s. clamour, outcry
Vocif'erous, a. clamorous, noisy, loud
Vogue, s. fashion, mode; esteem, repute
Voice, s. a vote; suffrage; sound emitted by
  the mouth; opinion expressed; language
Void, a. empty, vain; null; unoccupied
Void, s. an empty space, emptiness
Void, v. a. to quit, emit, evacuate, annul
Vo'lant, a. flying, active, passing through air
Vol'atile, a. flying, evaporating, lively
Vol'atileness, Volatil'ity, s. the quality of fly-
  ing away by evaporation; airiness
Volca'no, s. a burning mountain
Vole, s. a deal at quadrille, that draws the
  whole tricks to one party
Vol'ery, or Vol'ary, s. a flight of birds
Voli'ta'tion, s. the act and power of flying
Voli'tion, s. the act of willing; the power of
  choice exerted
Vol'ley, s. a burst of shot—v. n. to throw out
Volt, s. a certain tread of a horse; a round
Volubil'ity, s. fluency of speech; mutability
Vol'uble, a. fluent in words; active, nimble
Vol'ume, s. a book; any compact matter
Volu'minous, a. consisting of many volumes
Vol'untarily, ad. of one's own accord
Vol'untary, a. acting by choice, willing
Vol'untary, s. music played at will; volunteer
Volunteer', s. a soldier of his own accord
Volup'tuary, s. one given up to luxury
Volup'tuous, a. luxuriant, extravagant
Vom'it, v. a. to cast out of the stomach
Vom'it, s. a medicine to cause to vomit
Vomi'tion, s. the act or power of vomiting
Vora'cious, a. ravenous, greedy to eat
Vora'ciousness, Vorac'ity, s. ravenousness
Vor'tex, s. a whirlpool; a whirlwind
Vor'tical, a. having a whirling motion
Vo'taress, Vo'tress, s. a female votary
Vo'tary, s. one devoted to any service, &c.
Vote, v. a. to choose or give by vote
Vo'ter, s. one who has a right to vote
Vo'tive, a. given or done by vote; vowed
Vouch, v. to bear witness, to attest; to war-
  rant; to maintain; to appear as a witness
Vouch, s. a warrant, attestation
Vou'cher, s. who or what witnesseth
Vouchsa'fe, v. to condescend, to grant
Vow, s. a solemn and religious promise
Vow, v. to make a vow; to protest
Vow'el, s. a letter utterable by itself

Voy'age, s. a travel by sea; a course; attemp
Voy'ager, s. one who travels by sea
Up, ad. aloft; out of bed; above; not down
Up, prep. from a lower to a higher part
Upbraid', v. a. to chide, reproach, charge
Upbraid'ingly, ad. by way of reproach
Upheld', part. maintained, sustained
Up'hill, a. difficult, laborious, troublesome
Uphold', v. a. to lift on high, to support
Uphold'er, s. a supporter; an undertaker
Uphol'sterer, s. one who furnishes houses
Up'land, s. higher ground—a. higher
Up'ay, v. a. to lay up, hoard up, preserve
Uplift', v. a. to raise aloft, lift up on high
Up'most, a. highest, topmost, uppermost
Upon', prep. not under; with respect to
Up'per, a. higher in place, superior to
Up'permost, a. highest in place, power. &c.
Uprai'se, v. a. to raise up, exalt, advance
Up'right, a. straight up, erected; honest
Up'rightly, ad. perpendicularly; honestly
Up'rightness, s. straight erection, honest
Upri'se, v. n. to raise from a seat, to ascend
Up'roar, s. tumult, confusion, hustle
Uproo't, v. a. to tear up by the roots
Up'shot, s. a conclusion, end, event
Up'side, s. the upper side, upper part
Up'start, s. one suddenly raised to wealth
Up'start, v. n. to spring up suddenly
Up'ward, a. directed higher; more than
Urban'ity, s. civility, elegance, politeness
Ur'chin, s. a hedgehog, a brat, a child
Ure'thra, s. the passage of the urine
Urge, v. a. to incite, to provoke, to press
Ur'gency, s. a pressure of difficulty
Ur'gent, a. pressing, earnest, importunate
Ur'gently, ad. cogently, violently, vehemently
Ur'ger, s. one who urges, one who incites
U'rinal, s. a bottle to keep urine for inspection
U'rinary, a. relating or belonging to urine
U'rine, s. water coming from animals
Urn, s. a vessel used for the ashes of the
  dead; a Roman measure of 4 gallons
Uros'copy, s. an examination of urine
Us, the oblique case of we
U'sage, s. treatment, custom, fashion
U'sance, s. use, usury, interest for money
Use, s. usage, habit, custom, advantage
Use, v. to employ, to frequent, to treat
Use'ful, a. convenient, serviceable, profitable
Use'fulness, s. conduciveness to some end
Use'fully, ad. conveniently, profitably
Use'less, a. answering no end or purpose
Use'lessly, ad. without answering any pur-
Use'lessness, s. unfitness to any end [pose
Ush'er, s. an under-teacher; an introducer
Usquebau'gh, s. an Irish compound distilled
  spirit, drawn from aromatics; the High-
  land sort, by corruption, they call whisky
Us'tion, s. in surgery, the act of searing
  with a hot iron; state of being burnt
Usto'rious, a. having the quality of burning
U'sual, a. common, customary, frequent
U'sually, ad. commonly, customarily
Usufruc't, s. temporary enjoyment of profits
U'surer, s. one who practises usury
Usu'rious, a. exorbitantly greedy, griping
Usurp', v. a. to hold without right
Usurpa'tion, s. an illegal possession
Usurp'er, s. one who is in possession of any
  thing that is another's right

U'sury, s. money paid for the use of money
Uten'sil, s. an instrument for any use
U'terine, a. belonging to the womb
Util'ity, s. usefulness, profit, convenience
Ut'most, a. highest, extreme
Uto'pian, a. chimerical, imaginary
Ut'ter, v. a. to speak ; to vend, to publish
Ut'terable, a. that may be uttered or told
Ut'terance, s. pronunciation ; an extremity
Ut'terly, ad. perfectly, completely. fully
Ut'termost, a. extreme, most remote
Ut'hermost, s. the greatest degree or part
Vul'gar, a. mean, low. common, ordinary
Vul'gar, s. the common or lower people
Vul'garism, s. grossness, vulgarity

Vulgar'ity, s. meanness, rudeness
Vul'garly, ad. among the common people
Vul'gate, s. a Latin version of the Bible au
  thorised by the church of Rome
Vul'nerable, a. that which may be wounded
Vul'nerary, a. useful in curing wounds
Vul'pinary, a. cunning. crafty, sly. subtle
Vul'pine, a. belonging to a fox, crafty
Vul'ture, s. the name of a bird of prey
Vul'turous, a. voracious ; like a vulture
U'vula, s. a piece of flesh suspended from the
  palate, to cover the entrance of the wind-
  pipe
Uxo'rious, a. submissively fond of a wife
Uxo'riousness, s. connubial dotage

W.

W, s. the 21st letter of the alphabet
Wab'ble, v. n. to move from side to side
Wab'blingly, ad. totteringly
Wad, s. paper, tow. &c. to stop a gun charge ;
  a bundle of straw,&c. thrust close together
Wad'ding, s. a coarse woollen stuff
Wad'dle, v. n. to walk like a duck
Wade, v. n. to walk through water, &c.
Wa'fer, s. a thin dried paste for several uses
Waft, v. to beckon ; to carry over ; to float
Wag, s. a merry droll fellow ; a low wit
Wage, v. a. to lay a wager, to engage in
Wa'ger, s. a bet ; offer upon oath—v. to bet
Wa'ges, s. hire or reward given for service
Wag'gery, s. wantonness, merry pranks
Wag'gish, a. frolicsome. sportive, merry
Wag'gle, v. n. to move up and down
Wag'gon. Wag'on,s. a four-wheeled carriage
Wag'goner, s. one who drives a waggon
Wag'tail, s. the name of a small bird
Waif, s. goods found, but unclaimed
Wail, v. to lament, to bewail, to grieve
Wail, Wail'ing, s. lamentation. grief
Wail'ful, a. mournful, sorrowful
Wain, s. a sort of cart or waggon
Wain'scot, s. a lining for rooms
Waist, s. the middle part of the body
Wais'tcoat, s. a part of a man's dress
Wait, v. to expect, attend, stay, watch
Wait'er, s. an attendant, one in waiting
Waits, s. nightly musicians, nightly music
Wake, v. to watch, not sleep, rouse
Wake, s. a watch ; merriment : track
Wa'keful, a. not sleeping. watchful
Wa'ken, v. to wake, to rouse from sleep
Wale, s. a rising part in cloth, &c.; the outer
  timber in the sides of a ship
Walk, v. n. to go on foot, to pass, to travel
Walk, s. the act of walking ; gait ; path
Walk'er, s. one that walks ; an officer
Walk'ingstick, s. a staff to walk with
Walk'mill, s. a fulling-mill
Wall, s. a partition of brick or stone, &c.
Wall, v. a. to enclose with a wall
Wal'let, s. a bag. knapsack, double pouch
Wall'eyed, a. having white eyes
Wal'lop, v. n. to boil, to boil violently
Wal'low, v. n. to roll in the mire, &c.
Wal'nut, s. a large kind of nut
Wal'trop, s. the sea-horse ; the morse

Wam'ble, v. n. to roll with sickness
Wan, a. pale, sickly. languid of look
Wand, s. a small stick, a long slender staff
Wan'der, v. to rove, to go astray, to ramble
Wan'derer, s. a rover, rambler, traveller
Wane, v. n. to diminish, to decrease
Want, v. to be without, to need ; to fail
Want, s. lack, need, deficiency ; poverty
Wan'ton, a. licentious. sportive, jocund
Wan'ton, s. a strumpet, a lascivious person
Wan'ton, v. n. to play lasciviously ; to revel
Wan'tonly, ad. in a lascivious manner
Wan'ty, s. a surcingle ; a leathern girth
Wa'ped, a. dejected, crushed, borne down
Wap'entake, s. a division of a county, the
  same as a hundred
War, s. hostility, fighting, combat
War, v. to make or carry on war
War'ble, v. to quaver any sound ; to sing
War'bler, s. a songster, a singing bird
Ward, s. a garrison ; district of a town ; cus-
  tody ; one under a guardian, &c.
Ward, v. to act on the defensive ; guard
War'den, s. a head officer ; guardian
War'der, s. a keeper, guard, beadle
Ward'more, s. a ward meeting
Ward'robe, s. a place where apparel is kep'
Ward'ship, s. guardianship, pupilage
Wa'rehouse, s. a house for merchandise
Wares, s. goods or property to be sold
War'fare, s. military service and life
Wa'rily, ad. cautiously, with wise forethought
War'like, a. military, fit for war
Warm, a. a little hot, zealous, furious
Warm, v. a. to heat moderately
War'mingpan, s. a pan to warm a bed
Warmth, s. gentle heat, zeal, passion
Warn, v. a. to caution, to give notice, to tell
War'ning, s. previous notice. caution
Warp, s. the thread that crosses the woof
War'rant, s. a writ of caption, authority
War'rant, v. n. to justify ; authorise ; attest
War'rantable, a. justifiable. defensible
War'ranty, s. a deed of security for the per
  formance of a contract ; authority
War'ren, s. a park or inclosure for rabbits
War'rener, s. a keeper of a warren
War'rior, s. a soldier, a military man
Wart, s. a corneous excrescence ; a small
  protuberance on the flesh

T

War'ty, a. grown over with or like warts
War'worn, a. worn with war, battered
Wa'ry, a. cautious, scrupulous, nice
Wash, v. a. to cleanse with water
Wash, s. the act of washing linen; dish-water, &c. given to hogs; a watery place
Wash'ball, s. a ball made of soap, &c.
Wash'erwoman, s. a woman who washes
Wash'y, a. watery, damp, weak
Wasp, s. a brisk stinging insect like a bee
Was'pish, a. peevish, cross, touchy, fretful
Wax'sail, s. a drink made of roasted apples, sugar, and ale; a drunken bout
Was'sailer, s. a toper, a drunkard
Waste, v. to diminish, spend, dwindle
Waste, a. desolate, uncultivated, ruined
Waste, s. a desolate uncultivated ground
Wa'steful, a. destructive, lavish, profligate
Watch, s. a night-guard; a pocket-clock; the time a seaman, &c. is upon guard
Watch, v. to keep guard, to observe
Watch'et, a. blue, pale blue
Watch'ful, a. attentive, careful, cautious
Watch'house, s. a place where the night-watch is set; a place of confinement
Watch'maker, s. one who makes watches
Watch'man, s. a night guard, a sentinel
Watch'word, s. a sentinel's night-word
Wa'ter, s. one of the elements; urine; lustre of a diamond; gloss on dyed silk
Wa'ter, v. to supply with water; to take in water; to shed or supply moisture
Wa'terage, s. money paid for a journey taken by water or for water carriage
Wa'tercolours, s. colours of a soft consistence used with gum-water
Wa'tercourse, s. a channel for water
Wa'tercresses, s. a plant of five species
Wa'terfall, s. a cascade, a cataract
Wa'terfowl, s. a fowl that swims in the water, and lives or breeds near it
Watergru'el, s. food of oatmeal and water
Wa'terman, s. a boatman, a ferryman
Wa'termark, s. the mark of the flood
Wa'termill, s. a mill turned by water [stone
Wa'tersapph'ire, s. a kind of blue precious
Wa'terwork, s. an hydraulic performance
Wa'tery, a. thin; abounding with water
Wat'tle, v. a. to bind or make firm with twigs
Wat'tles, s. hurdles made of willows; the barbs, or red flesh below a cock's bill
Wave, v. to play loosely; put off; beckon
Wave, s. a billow at sea; inequality
Wa'ved, a. moved loosely; variegated
Wa'ver, v. n. to be unsettled, to move loosely
Wa'vy, a. rising in waves, undulating
Wax, s. a thick tenacious substance extracted from the honeycomb of bees
Wax, v. to smear with wax; to grow [ger
Wax'ed, Wax'en, a. made of wax; become high-
Way, s. a road, passage; means, method
Way'farer, s. a passenger, a traveller
Waylay', v. a. to beset by ambush
Way'ward, a. froward, unruly; peevish
Weak, a. feeble, pliant, unfortified
Weak'en, v. a. to make weak, to enfeeble
Weak'ness, s. a defect, feebleness, failing
Weal, s. the republic or state; happiness, prosperity; public interest; mark of a stripe
Wealth, s. riches, money, goods, possessions
Weal'thy, a. opulent, rich, abundant

Wean, v. a. to deprive of the breast, &c.
Weap'on, s. an instrument of offence
Wear, v. to waste, to have on, to hold out
Wear, s. the act of wearing; a dam of water
Wear'er, s. one who wears any thing
Wea'riness, s. fatigue, lassitude, tediousness
Wear'ing, s. clothes, the act of wasting
Wea'risome, a. tedious, tiresome
Wea'ry, v. a. to tire, to harass—a. tired
Wea'sand, Wea'son, s. the windpipe
Wea'sel, s. the name of a small animal
Weath'er, s. the state of the air; a storm
Weath'er, v. a. to pass with difficulty
Weath'erbeaten, a. grown rough or tarnished, or harassed by bad weather
Weath'ercock, s. a vane on a spire
Weath'ergage, s. the advantage of the wind; a thing that shows the weather
Weath'erglass, s. a glass to show the weather
Weath'erwise, a. foretelling the weather
Weave, v. a. to form by texture; to insert
Wea'ver, s. one who weaves cloth, &c.
Web, s. any thing woven; a film on the eye
Web'footed, a. palmipedous; having films between the toes, as swans or geese
Web'ster, s. a weaver, one who weaves
Wed, v. a. to marry, to join in marriage
Wed'ded, a. married, attached to
Wed'ding, s. the marriage ceremony
Wedge, s. a body with a sharp edge
Wedge, v. a. to fasten with wedges
Wed'lock, s. the marriage state, matrimony
Wee, a. little, small, diminutive, puny
Wedn'esday, s. the fourth day of the week
Weed, s. a wild herb; a mourning habit
Wee'der, s. one who weeds or takes away
Weed'hook, s. a hook to root up weeds
Wee'dy, a. abounding with weeds
Week, s. the space of seven days
Week'day, s. any day except Sunday
Week'ly, a. done, &c. every week
Weel, s. a whirlpool; a kind of trap for fish
Ween, v. n. to think, to suppose, to imagine
Weep, v. to shed tears, to bewail, lament
Wee'per, s. a mourner; a white border of linen on the sleeve of a mourning dress
Wee'rish, a. insipid, watery, sour, surly
Weet, v. n. to know, to be sensible of
Wee'vil, s. a grub injurious to corn
Weft, s. a thing woven; the woof of cloth; goods which have no owner; gentle blast
Wef'tage, s. a texture; the thing woven
Weigh, v. to try the weight of any thing; to heave up, to examine nicely, to judge
Weigh, Wey, s. a measure, weight, way
Weigh'ed, a. examined by weight, &c.
Weight, s. ponderous mass; heaviness, gravity; importance; a standard by which other bodies are weighed; pressure, burden
Weight'ily, ad. heavily, solidly, importantly
Weight'iness, s. heaviness, importance, force
Weight'less, a. light, having no gravity
Weight'y, a. heavy, important, strong
Weird, a. fatal, predicting, witchlike
Wel'come, a. received with gladness
Wel'come, s. kind reception—v. a. to receive
Wel'come, interj. used to a visitor
Wel'comeness, s. the act of making welcome, a kind reception, gratefulness
Wel'comer, s. one who bids welcome
Weld, Would, s. a dyer's weed for yellow

Weal, v. a. to beat one mass into another
Wel'fare, s. happiness, prosperity, success
Wel'kin, s. the visible regions of the air
Wel'king, a. clouding, weak, languishing
Well, s. a spring, a source; a cavity
Well, a. not sick, happy, convenient
Well, ad. not amiss, rightly, properly
Well'aday, interj. denoting grief, pity, &c.
Wellbe'ing, s. prosperity, happiness
Wellborn', a. not meanly born or descended
Wellbred', a. polite, elegant of manners
Welldone', interj. denoting praise, &c.
Wellfa'voured, a. beautiful, handsome
Wellmet', interj. denoting salutation, &c.
Wellni'gh, ad. almost, nearly, adjacent
Wellset', a. well-made, stout built
Well'spent, a. spent with virtue
Well'spring, s. spring, fountain, source
Wellwil'ler, s. one who means well
Wellwish', s. a wish of happiness, &c.
Wellwish'er, s. one who wishes good
Welt, s. a border, a selvage, an edging
Wel'ter, v. n. to roll in blood, mire, &c.
Wem, s. a spot, scar, fault, the belly
Wem'less, a. unspotted, innocent
Wen, s. a dangerous fleshy excrescence
Wench, s. a young woman, a strumpet
Wen'cher, s. a fornicator
Wen'ching, s. following of bad women
Wend, v. n. to go, turn round, to pass from
Wen'ny, a. having the nature of a wen
Went, pret. and part. of to go
Were, pret. of the verb to be
West, s. the region where the sun sets
West, ad. to the west of any place
Wes'tering, a. tending towards the west
Wes'terly, a. towards the west
Wes'tern, a. westerly, from the west
Wes'tward, ad. towards the west
Wet, a. rainy, moist—s. water, rain
Wet, v. a. to moisten; to make to drink
Weth'er, s. a ram that is castrated
Wet'ness, s. the state of being wet, rain
Wet'tish, a. rather wet, rather moist
Wex, v. a. to grow, increase, grow large
Whale, s. the largest of all fish
Wharf, s. a place to land goods at
Whar'fage, s. rates for landing at a wharf
Whar'finger, s. a keeper of a wharf
What, pron. that which; which part
Whatev'er, Whatsoev'er, pron. this or that
Wheal, s. a pustule; body of matter; insect
Wheat, s. bread corn, the finest of grains
Wheat'ear, s. the name of a small bird
Wheat'en, a. made of wheat corn
Whee'dle, v. a. to entice by soft words
Wheel, s. a circular body that turns round its
    axis; engine for torture; revolution
Wheel, v. to move on wheels; to turn round
Wheel'barrow, s. a carriage of one wheel
Wheel'wright, s. a maker of wheels
Wheeze, v. n. to breathe with a noise
Whelk, s. a protuberance; a shellfish
Whelm, v. a. to cover, turn down, bury
Whelp, s. the young of a dog, lion, &c.
When, ad. at the time that, &c.
Whence, ad. from what place, &c.
Whence'soever, ad. from what place soever
Whenev'er, ad. at whatsoever time
Where, ad. at which place, at what place
Where'abouts, ad. near what place

Whereas', ad. when on the contrary; at
    which place; the thing being so that
Whereat', ad. at which
Whereby', ad. by which
Wherev'er, ad. at whatever place
Where'fore, ad. for what or which reason
Wherein', ad. in which
Whereinto', ad. into which
Whereof', ad. of which, concerning which
Wheresoev'er, ad. in what place soever
Whereunto', ad. to or unto which
Whereupon', ad. on or upon which
Wherewithal', ad. with which, with what
Wher'ret, v. a. to hurry, to tease, &c.
Wher'ry, s. a light river boat
Wher'ry, v. a. to convey over in a boat
Whet, v. a. to sharpen, to edge, to provoke
Whet, s. the act of sharpening
Wheth'er, pron. which of the two
Whet'stone, s. a sharpening stone
Whet'ter, s. a sharpener of knives, &c.
Whey, s. the serous part of milk
Whey'ey, Whey'ish, a. like whey; waterish
Which, pron. rel. that, whether of two things
Whichev'er, Whichsoev'er, pron. one or the
Whiff, s. a puff, blast, breath   [other
Whif'fle, v. a. to prevaricate, shuffle, play
Whif'fler, s. a shuffler, fifer, marcher
Whig, s. a partyman opposed to a tory
Whig'gish, a. inclined to whiggism
Whig'gism, s. the principles of the whigs
While, s. time; a space of time
While, Whiles, Whilst, ad. as long as
Whilere', ad. a little while ago
Whi'lom, ad. formerly, since, of old
Whim, Whimsey, s. an odd fancy, caprice
Whim'per, v. n. to cry lowly as a child
Whim'pled, a. distorted with crying
Whim'sical, a. capricious, freakish, fanciful
Whim'wham, s. a gewgaw, toy, trifle
Whin, s. furze, a shrub, a prickly bush
Whine, v. n. to lament in low murmurs; to
    moan effeminately
Whin'ny, n. n. to make a noise like a horse
Whin'yard, s. a large crooked sword
Whip, s. an instrument of correction
Whip, v. to cut with a whip, to lash, &c.
Whip'cord, s. a cord for whiplashes
Whip'hand, s. an advantage over another
Whip'lash, s. the small end of a whip
Whip'saw, s. a large saw for two persons
Whip'ster, s. a nimble fellow; a sharper
Whirl, v. to turn or run round rapidly
Whirl, s. a rapid turning or circumvolution
Whirl'igig, s. a whirling plaything
Whirl'pool, s. water moving circularly
Whirl'wind, s. a storm moving circularly
Whir'ring, s. a noise made by a bird's wing
Whisk, s. a small besom; a child's tippet
Whisk, v. a. to brush with a whisk, to run
Whis'ker, s. hair on the lips; a mustachio
Whis'ky, s. a spirituous liquor procured
    from barley
Whis'king, part. a. brushing, passing quick
Whis'per, v. n. to speak with a low voice
Whis'per, s. a low voice, a speaking softly
Whis'perer, s. one who whispers low
Whist, s. a game at cards—a. silent, still
Whis'tle, v. to form a kind of musical mo
    dulation of the breath; to blow a whistle
Whis'tle, s. an inarticulate musical sound

Whit, s. a point, jot, tittle
White, a. snowy, pale; pure—s. a colour
Whit'elivered, a. envious, malicious
Whi'ten, v. to make or grow white
Whi'teness, s. the state of being white
Whit'epot, s. a kind of food from milk, eggs, white bread, sugar, spice, &c.
Whit'ethorn, s. a species of thorn
Whi'tewash, v. a. to make white; clear
Whi'tewash, s. a kind of liquid plaster to whiten the walls of houses; a wash to make the skin seem fair
Whith'er, ad. to what place or degree
Whi'ting, s. a small fish, a soft chalk
Whi'tish, a. somewhat or rather white
Whit'leather, s. leather drest with alum
Whit'low, s. a swelling at the finger's end
Whit'ster, s. a bleacher of linen, &c.
Whit'suntide, s. the feast of Pentecost
Whit'tle, s. a knife; a blanket
Whiz, v. n. to make a loud humming noise
Who, pron. rel. which person
Whoev'er, pron. any one; whatever person
Whole, s. a solid, the total, all of a thing
Whole, a. all, total; restored to health
Who'lesale, s. a sale in the gross or by the lump; not in small parcels
Who'lesome, a. contributing to health
Whom, accus. sing. and plur. of who
Whomsoev'er, pron. any person whatever
Whoop, s. a shout of pursuit; a bird
Whore, s. a prostitute; a fornicatress
Who'redom, s. playing the whore, adultery
Who'remaster, s. one who keeps whores
Who'reson, s. a bastard—a. spurious
Who'rish, a. unchaste, incontinent, loose
Whor'tleberry, Whurt, s. a bilberry, a plant
Whose, pron. poss. of who and which
Whosoev'er, pron. any without exception
Why, ad. for what reason or cause
Wick, s. the cotton of a candle or lamp
Wick'ed, a. given to vice, cursed
Wick'edly, ad. in a wicked manner
Wick'edness, s. guilt, moral ill, vice
Wick'er, a. made of small willows or sticks
Wick'et, s. a small door; a small gate
Wide, a. broad, remote, extended
Wide. Wi'dely, ad. remotely, at a distance
Wi'den, v. to make or grow wide
Wid'geon, s. the name of a water fowl
Wid'ow, s. a woman whose husband is dead
Wid'ower, s. a man whose wife is dead
Wid'owhood, s. the state of a widow
Width, s. breadth or wideness
Wield, v. a. to use with full power
Wiel'dy, a. capable of being managed
Wi'ery, Wi'ry, a. made or drawn into wire
Wife, s. a woman that is married
Wig, s. a light cake; a periwig
Wight, s. a man or woman—a. swift
Wig'wam, s. an Indian cabin
Wild, a. not tame; desart; savage, uncouth
Wild, s. a desart, an uninhabited country
Wil'der, v. a. to lose in a wilderness, &c.
Wil'derness, s. a wild uninhabited tract of land; a savage country; a desart
Wild'fire, s. gunpowder rolled up wet
Wild'goosechase, s. a vain foolish pursuit
Wild'ing, s. the name of a wild sour apple
Wild'ness, s. ferocity, savageness, fury
Wile, s. a deceit, fraud, trick. shift

Wil'ful, a. stubborn, tenacious, designed
Wil'fully, ad. obstinately, on purpose
Wil'fulness, s. obstinacy, perverseness
Will, s. a choice, command, bequest
Will, v. a. to command, direct, desire
Will'ing, a. inclined to any thing; desirous
Wil'low, s. the name of a tree
Will-with-a-wisp, s. a fiery vapour appearing in the night; an ignis fatuus
Wi'ly, a. sly, cunning, full of stratagem
Wim'ble, s. a tool for boring holes—a. active
Wim'ple, s. a hood, a veil—v. a. to draw over
Win, v. to gain by conquest or play
Wince, or Winch, v. n. to shrink from pain
Winch, s. a handle to turn a mill or screw
Wind, s. a flowing wave of air; breath
Wind'egg, s. an imperfect egg
Wind'er, s. who or what winds; a plant
Wind'fall, s. fruit blown down by the wind, an advantage coming unexpectedly
Wind'flower, s. a flower; the anemone
Wind'gun, s. a gun to discharge a bullet, by letting loose the air pent within
Wi'nding, s. a turning about; a following
Wi'nding-sheet, s. a sheet in which the dead are enwrapped, serving for a shroud
Wind'lass, s. a machine for raising weights
Win'dle, s. a spindle, reel, machine
Wind'mill, s. a mill turned by the wind
Win'dow, s. an opening in a house for light and air; the glass it contains
Wind'pipe, s. the passage for the breath
Wind'ward, ad. towards the wind
Win'dy, a. breeding wind; swelled; stormy
Wine, s. the fermented juice of grapes, &c.
Wing, s. that part of a bird used in flying the side of an army; any side-piece
Wing, v. to furnish with wings; to fly
Wing'ed, a. having wings; swift; wounded
Wink, v. n. to shut the eyes; connive, hint
Wink, s. a hint by motion of the eye
Win'ner, s. one who wins, one who gains
Win'ning, a. attractive—s. the sum won
Win'now, v. to fan, to sift, to examine
Win'ter, s. the cold season of the year
Win'ter, v. to pass or feed in the winter
Win'terly, Win'try, a. suitable to winter
Wi'ny, a. having the taste of or like wine
Wipe, v. a. to cleanse by rubbing; to clear
Wipe, s. an act of cleansing; a blow; a reproof, a rub; a stroke; a bird
Wire, s. a metal drawn out into threads
Wi'redrawer, s. one who makes wire
Wis, v. n. wist—pret. to know—ad. verily truly
Wis'dom, s. knowledge and judgment conducted by discretion
Wise, a. judging right; prudent, grave
Wise, s. manner; way of being or acting
Wi'seacre, s. a fool; dunce, simpleton
Wi'sely, ad. judiciously, prudently. gravely
Wish, s. a longing desire, a thing desired
Wish, v. to have a strong desire, to long for
Wish'er, s. one who longs or wishes
Wish'ful, a. showing desire, longing, eager
Wish'fully, ad. earnestly, with longing
Wis'ket, or Whis'ket, s. a basket, a scuttle
Wisp, s. a small bundle of straw or hay
Wist, pret. and part. of to wis
Wist'ful, a. attentive, full of thought
Wist'fully, Wist'ly, ad. attentively

Vit, s. quickness of fancy, a man of genius;
  understanding, judgment, sense
To Wit, ad. namely, or that is
Witch, s. a woman given to unlawful arts
Witch'craft, s. the practice of witches
Wit'craft, s. invention, contrivance
Withal', ad. along with the rest; besides
Withdraw', v. to draw back, retire, retreat
Withdraw'ing-room, s. a room near another
  to retire to, usually called a drawing-room
Withe, s. a willow twig; a band of twigs
With'er, v. to fade, cause to fade; pine, &c.
With'ers, s. the joint uniting the neck and
  shoulders of a horse
Withhold', v. a. to keep back, to refuse
Within', prep. not within compass of
Within'side, ad. in the inward parts
Without', prep. not within compass of
Withstand', v. a. to oppose, resist, re-train
With'y, s. a willow, the shoot of a willow
Wit'less, a. wanting understanding
Wit'ling, s. a petty pretender to wit
Wit'ness, s. testimony; an evidence
Wit'ness, v. to bear testimony, to attest
Wit'ness, interj. denoting an exclamation
Wit'ticism, s. a mean attempt at wit
Wit'tily, ad. ingeniously, cunningly, artfully
Wit'tingly, ad. knowingly, by design
Wit'tol, Wit'hal, s. a contented cuckold
Wit'tol'y, a. cuckoldly, low, despicable
Wit'ty, a. ingenious, sarcastic, smart
Wive, v. to marry, to take a wife
Wives, s. plur. of wife
Wiz'ard, s. a conjurer, a cunning man
Woe, s. grief, sorrow, misery, calamity
Woad, s. a plant used in dyeing blue
Wo'ful, a. sorrowful, calamitous
Wold, s. a plain open country; a down
Wolf, s. a fierce beast; an eating ulcer
Wolf'dog, s. a large dog to guard sheep
Wolf'ish, or Wolv'ish, a. fierce like a wolf
Wolfs'bane, s. a poisonous plant
Wo'man, s. the female of the human race
Wo'manhater, s. one who hates women
Wom'anhood, s. the qualities of a woman
Wom'anish, a. suitable to a woman
Wom'ankind, s. female sex; race of women
Wom'anly, a. becoming a woman, not girlish
Womb, s. place of generation—v. a. to enclose
Wom'en, s. plur. of woman
Won, pret. and part. pass. of to win
Won'der, v. n. to be astonished
Won'der, s. amazement, admiration
Won'derful, a. admirable, strange
Won'derfully, ad. in a wonderful manner
Won'derstruck, a. amazed, astonished
Won'drous, a. marvellous, strange, surprising
Won'drously, ad. in a strange manner
Wont, v. n. to be accustomed or used to
Wont'ed, part. a. accustomed, usual, used
Woo, v. to court, to make love, to sue
Wood, s. a forest; a place filled with timber-
  trees; the substance of trees
Wood'ashes, s. ashes of burnt wood
Wood'bine, s. the honeysuckle
Wood'cock, s. a bird of passage
Wood'ed, a. supplied or thick with wood
Wood'en, a. made of wood; clumsy
Wood'hole, s. a place where wood is laid
Wood'land, s. land covered with wood
Wood'louse, s. vermin about old wood

Wood'man, s. a sportsman, a hunter, &c.
Wood'note, s. a wild note; wild music
Wood'nymph, s. a nymph of the woods
Wood'offering, s. wood burnt on the altar
Wood'pecker, s. the name of a bird
Wood'pigeon, s. a wild pigeon
Wood'sare, s. the froth on herbs
Wood'y, a. abounding with wood; ligneous
Woo'er, s. one who courts women
Woof, s. the set of threads that crosses the
  warp; the weft; texture; cloth
Wool, s. the fleece of sheep, short hair
Wool'fel, s. a skin with the wool on
Wool'len, a. made or consisting of wool
Wool'lendraper, s. a dealer in woollen goods
Wool'pack, s. a bag or pack of wool
Wool'ly, a. composed of or resembling wool
Wool'stapler, s. one who deals in wool
Word, s. a single part of speech; promise
Word, v. to express properly; to dispute
Word'y, a. verbose, full of words
Wore, pret. of to wear
Work, v. to labour; be agitated; raise, &c.
Work, s. labour, deed, employment; a book
Work'house, s. a receptacle for parish poor
Work'ing-day, s. day for work
Work'man, s. an artificer, a labourer
Work'manlike, a. like a workman, skilful
Work'manship, s. manufacture, skill, art
Work'shop, s. a shop to work in
Work'woman, s. one skilled in needlework
World, s. the earth; mankind; universal
  empire
World'ling, s. one who idolizes his money
World'ly, a. human; bent upon this world
Worm, v. to act slowly and secretly
Worm, s. an insect, any spiral thing
Worm'eaten, a. gnawed by worms; old
Worm'wood, s. the name of a bitter herb
Worm'y, a. full of worms, having worms
Worn, part. pass. of to wear
Wor'ril, s. a maggot; a worm in cows
Wor'ry, v. a. to tear, to mangle, to harass
Worse, a. more bad, more ill
Wor'ship, s. dignity, eminence; term of ho-
  nour; religious reverence; adoration
Wor'shipful, a. respected for dignity, &c.
Werst, a. most bad, most ill, most wicked
Worst, s. most calamitous or wicked state
Wors'ted, s. woollen yarn; wool spun
Wort, s. an herb; ale or beer not fermented
Worth, a. deserving of, equal in value to
Worth, s. price, value, importance
Wor'thily, ad. suitably, justly, deservedly
Wor'thiness, s. worth, desert, excellence
Worth'less, a. undeserving, unworthy
Worth'lessness, s. want of worth or value
Wor'thy, a. deserving, valuable, noble
Wor'thy, s. a man deserving praise
Wot, v. n. to know, to be aware of
Wove, pret. and part. of to weave
Would, pret. of to will
Wound, s. a hurt—v. a. to hurt by violence
Wound, pret. of to wind
Wrack, s. ruin, destruction—v. a. to tor-
  ture; to destroy in the water; to wreck
Wrack, s. See Wreck.
Wran'gle, s. a perverse dispute; a quarrel
Wran'gle, v. n. to dispute peevishly
Wran'gler, s. a peevish disputative person
Wrap, v. a. to roll together; to contain

T 3

Wrap'per, s. a cloth or paper cover, &c.
Wrath, s. extreme anger, vengeance
Wrath'ful, a. angry, raging, furious
Wrath'fully, ad. furiously, passionately
Wrath'less, a. free from anger, meek
Wreak, v. a. to revenge; to execute
Wreak, s. revenge, vengeance, passion
Wreak'ful, a. revengeful, malicious
Wreak'less, a. unrevenging, impotent
Wreath, s. a garland; any thing twisted
Wreath, v. a. to turn, to twist, to curl
Wreath'y, a. spiral, twisted, curling
Wreck, s. a shipwreck; destruction, ruin
Wreck, v. to suffer wreck or loss, destroy, ruin
Wren, s. the name of a very small bird
Wrench, v. a. to pull by force, to wrest
Wrench, s. a sprain, violent twist; a trap
Wrest, v. a. to twist by violence, to writhe
Wrest, s. a distortion, a violence
Wres'tle, v. n. to struggle for a fall
Wres'tler, s. one skilled in wrestling
Wres'tling, s. the exercise of wrestling
Wretch, s. a miserable or worthless person
Wret'ched. ad. miserable, despicable
Wret'chedly, ad. despicably, meanly
Wret'chedness, s. misery, despicableness
Wrig'gle, v. n. to move to and fro
Wright, s. a workman; an artificer in wood

Wring, v. to twist, to squeeze, press, harass, torture, extort, force, to turn round by violence; to writhe
Wrin'kle, s. a crease in cloth, &c.
Wrin'kle, v. n. to cause creases or wrinkles
Wrist, s. the joint of the hand to the arm
Wrist'band, s. the fastening about the wrist
Writ, s. scripture; a legal process, &c.
Writ. pret. of to write
Write, v. to express in writing, engrave
Wri'ter, s. an author; one who writes
Writhe, v. to distort, to twist, to wrest
Wri'ting, s. any thing written with pen and ink; the art or act of writing
Wri'tingmaster, s. one who teaches to write
Wri'tings, s. legal conveyances, &c.
Writ'ten, part. pass. of to write
Wriz'zled, a. wrinkled, withered, shrunk
Wrong, s. injury, injustice; an error
Wrong, a. not right, unfit—v. a. to injure
Wrong, Wrong'ly, ad. amiss, improperly
Wrong'ful, a. unjust, dishonest, injurious
Wrong'fully, ad. unjustly, injuriously
Wrote, pret. part. of to write
Wroth. a. angry, enraged, provoked
Wrought, part. performed; manufactured
Wrung, pret. and part. of to wring
Wry, a. crooked, distorted, wrested

X.

X, s. the 22d letter of the alphabet. Though found in Saxon words it begins no word in the English language
Xe'rif, s. the title of a prince of Barbary

Xe'beck, s. a small vessel
Xero'collyrium, s. a plaster for sore eyes
Xeroph'agy, s. dry victuals; a fast
Xy'stus, s. a very spacious portico

Y.

Y, s. the 23d letter of the alphabet
Yacht, or Yatch, s. a small ship with one deck, richly adorned, and contrived for swiftness and pleasure
Yam, s. an Indian vegetable, somewhat resembling a potato, but much larger, and having a thick coat or rind
Yard, s. ground enclosed adjoining to a house; a measure of three feet; supports for a vessel's sails
Yard'ward, s. a measure of a yard
Yarn, s. spun wool; woollen thread
Yawl, s. a ship's boat—v. n. to bawl
Yawn, v. n. to gape; oscitate; open wide
Yawn'ing, a. sleepy, slumbering
Yclad', a. clad, clothed, adorned
Yclep'ed, a. called, named, denominated
Ye, nominative plural of thou
Yea, ad. yes, surely, certainly, truly
Yean, v. n. to bring forth young, as sheep
Yean'ling, s. the young of a sheep
Year, s. the term of twelve calendar months
Year'ling, a. being a year old
Year'ly, ad. once a year—a. lasting a year
Yearn, v. n. to feel great uneasiness
Yearn'ing, s. an emotion of tenderness
Yelk or Yolk, s. the yellow part of an egg

Yell, v. n. to make a howling noise
Yell, s. a cry of horror or distress
Yel'low, a. of a bright glaring colour, as gold
Yel'low-ham'mer, s. a small bird
Yel'lowish, a. approaching to yellow
Yel'lows, s. a disease in horses
Yelp, v. a. to bark as a beagle hound
Yeo'man, s. a gentleman farmer; a free holder; an officer in the king's court
Yeo'manry, s. a collective body of yeomen
Yerk, v. a. to throw out a horse's hind leg
Yes, ad. a term of affirmation; yea, truly
Yest, or Yeast, s. the froth in the working of new ale or beer; spume on a troubled sea
Yes'terday, s. the day last past
Yes'ternight, ad. on the night last past
Yes'ty, Yeas'ty, a. frothy; smeared with yest
Yet, conj. nevertheless, notwithstanding
Yet, ad. beside, still, at least, after all
Yew, s. a tree of tough wood
Yew'en, a. made of or resembling yew
Yield, v. to produce, to afford; to give up
Yoke, s. a bandage for the neck; a mark of servitude; a chain; bond; couple, pair
Yoke, v. a. to couple together; to enslave
Yo'kefellow, s. a companion in labour
Yon, Yon'der, a. being within view

Yore, *ad.* of long time past, of old time
You, *pron. oblique case* of ye
Young, *a.* youthful, not old; tender
Young, *s.* the offspring of any creature
Youn'ger, *a.* more young, not so old
Youn'gest, *a.* the most young of all
Young'ster, Yon'ker, *s.* a young person

Your, *pron.* belonging to you
Yourself, *pron.* even you, you *elly*
Youth, *s.* one past childhood; tender age
Youth'ful. *a.* young, frolicsome, vigorous
Youth'ly, Youth'y, *a.* young, youthful, eary
Yule, *s.* the time of Christmas
Yux, Yex, *s.* the hiccough

Z.

Z, *s.* the 24th letter of the alphabet
Zac'cho, *s.* in architecture, the lowest part of the pedestal of a column
Zaf'far, Zaf'fir, *s.* a hard composition mistaken for a native mineral
Za'ny, *s.* buffoon, silly fellow, merry andrew
Zar'nich, *s.* a solid substance in which orpiment is found
Zeal. *s.* a passionate ardour; warmth
Zeal'ot, *s.* one passionately ardent in any cause
Zeal'ous, *a.* ardently passionate in any cause
Zeal'ously, *ad.* with passionate ardour
Zeal'ousness, *s.* the quality of being zealous
Zech'in, *s.* a Venetian gold coin of 9s.
Ze'doary, *s.* a spicy plant, like ginger
Zena'na, *s.* the apartments of the women in the house of an eastern potentate
Ze'nith, *s.* that point in the heavens directly over our heads, opposite the Nadir
Zeph'yr, Zeph'yrus, *s.* the west wind
Zest, *s.* the peel of an orange squeezed into wine; a relish; a taste added
Zest, *v. a.* to heighten by added relish
Ze'ta, *s.* a Greek letter: a dining room
Zetet'ic, *a.* proceeding by inquiry; seeking
Zeug'ma, *s.* a figure in grammar, when a verb agreeing with divers nouns, or an adjective with divers substantives, is referred to one expressly, and to the other by supple-

ment, as, lust overcame shame, boldness fear, and madness reason
Zig'zag, *a.* turning short; winding
Zinc, or Zink, *s.* a kind of fossil substance
Zo'cle, *s.* a small sort of stand or pedestal, being a low square piece or member, and to support a busto, statue, &c.
Zo'diac, *s.* a great circle of the sphere, containing the twelve signs
Zodi'acal, *a.* relating to the zodiac
Zone, *s.* a girdle, a division of the earth, a space contained between two parallels
Zoog'rapher, *s.* one who describes the nature, properties, and forms of animals
Zoog'raphy, *s.* a description of the forms, natures, and properties of animals
Zool'ogist, *s.* one who treats of animals
Zool'ogy, *s.* a treatise on living creatures
Zo'ophites, *s.* certain substances or vegetables which partake of the nature both of vegetables and animals
Zoophor'ic, *s.* a statuary column, or a column supporting the figure of an animal
Zooph'orus, *s.* a part between the architraves and cornice, so called on account of the ornaments carved on it, among which are the figures of animals
Zoot'omist, *s.* one who dissects brute beasts
Zoot'omy, *s.* a dissection of the bodies beasts

MYTHOLOGY

Is a term compounded of two Greek words, and, in its original import, it signifies any kind of fabulous doctrine. In its more appropriated sense, it means those fabulous details concerning the objects of worship which were invented and propagated by men who lived in the early ages of the world; and by them transmitted to succeeding generations, either by written records or by oral tradition.

The *Pantheon* is the Temple of the Gods, which the folly of men hath feigned either through the grossest ignorance or contempt of the true and only God.

The Pagan priests, especially in Egypt, were probably the first who reduced Mythology to a kind of system. Egypt was the land of graven images; allegory and mythology were the veil which concealed religion from the eyes of the vulgar: fable was the groundwork of that impenetrable covering.

The worship of brute animals, and of certain vegetables, universal among the Egyptians, was another exuberant source of mythological adventures. After these objects, animate or inanimate, were consecrated as the visible symptoms of the Deities, it soon became fashionable to make use of their figures to represent those Deities to which they were consecrated. Hence Jupiter Ammon was represented under the figure of a Ram, Apis under that of a Cow, Osiris of a Bull, Pan of a Goat, Thol or Mercury of an Ibis, Bubastis or Diana of a Cat, &c. It was likewise a common practice among the deluded people to dignify these objects, by giving them the names of those Deities which they represented. From these two sources are derived the fabulous transformation of the Gods, so generally celebrated in the Egyptian Mythology, and from it imported into Greece and Italy. In consequence of this practice, their mythological system was rendered at once enormous and unintelligible.

The adventures of Jupiter, Juno, Mercury, Apollo, Diana, Mars, Minerva or Pallas, Venus, Bacchus, Ceres, Proserpine, Pluto, Neptune, and the other descendants and coadjutors of the ambitious family of the Titans, furnish by far the greatest part of the Mythology of Greece. They left Phenicia, about the age of Moses; they settled in Crete, a large island: from this region they made their way into Greece; which, according to the most authentic accounts, was at that time inhabited by a race of savages. The arts and inventions which they communicated to the natives; the mysteries

of religion which they inculcated; the laws, customs, policy, and good order, which they established; in short, the blessings of humanity and civilization which they every where disseminated, in process of time inspired the unpolished inhabitants with a kind of divine admiration. Those ambitious mortals improved this admiration into divine homage and admiration.

The greatest part of that worship, which had been formerly addressed to the luminaries of Heaven, was now transferred to those illustrious personages. They claimed and obtained divine honours from the deluded rabble of enthusiastic Greeks. Hence sprung an inexhaustible fund of the most inconsistent and irreconcileable fictions. The foibles and frailties of the deified mortals were transmitted to posterity, incorporated as it were with the pompous attributes of supreme divinity. Hence the heterogeneous mixture of the mighty and the mean which chequers the characters of the heroes of the Iliad and Odyssey.

The labours of Hercules originated in Egypt, and evidently relate to the annual progress of the Sun in the Zodiac, though the vain-glorious Greeks accommodated them to a hero of their own, the reputed son of Jupiter and Alcmena. The expedition of Osiris they borrowed from the Egyptians, and transformed to their Bacchus. The transformations and wanderings of Io are evidently transcribed from the Egyptian romance of the travels of Isis in quest of the body of Osiris, or of the Phenician Astarte, drawn from Sanchoniathon. The fable of the conflagration occasioned by Phaeton, is clearly of Oriental extraction, and alludes to an excessive drought, which, in the early period of time, scorched Ethiopia and the adjacent countries. The rape of Proserpine, and the wanderings of Ceres; the Eleusinian Mysteries; the Orgia, or sacred rites of Bacchus; the rites and worship of the Cabiri; were imported from Egypt and Phenicia, but strangely garbled and disfigured by the Hierophants of Greece. In short, the groundwork of the Grecian Mythology is to be traced in the East. The Roman Mythology was borrowed from the Greeks. They had indeed gleaned a few fables from the Pelasgi and Hetruscans, which, however, are of such little consequence, that they are not worth the transcribing. Besides, we hope it will be remembered that the narrowness of the limits prescribed us would scarce admit of a more copious det.

AJA

ARI

AB'ARIS, a Scythian, priest of Apollo
Abeo'na, a goddess of voyages, &c.
Abreta'nus, a surname of Jupiter
A'hron, a Grecian given to sensuality
Aby'la, a famous mountain in Africa
Acan'tha, a nymph beloved by Apollo
Acas'tus, the name of a famous hunter
Ace'tus, one of the priests of Bacchus
Achæ'menes, the first king of Persia
Acha'tes, the faithful friend of Æneas
Ach'eron, a son of Sol and Terra, metamorphosed into a river of hell for assisting the Titans in their war against Jupiter
Achil'les, son of Peleus king of Thrace, and Thetis, a goddess of the sea, who was invulnerable in every part except the right heel. He signalized himself at the siege of Troy, for his valour, as well as cruelty
Acida'lia and Arma'ta, names of Venus
Acid'alus, a famous fountain of Bœotia
A'cis, a Sicilian shepherd, killed by Polyphemus
Ac'mon, a famous king of the Titans
Acra'tus, the genius of drunkards at Athens
Ac'teon, a celebrated hunter, who accidentally discovered Diana bathing, and was by her turned into a stag, and devoured by his own hounds
Adme'tus, a king of Thessaly
Ado'nis, a remarkably beautiful youth, beloved by Venus and Proserpine
Adras'tea, the goddess Nemesis
Æ'acus, one of the infernal judges
Æ'ga, Jupiter's nurse, daughter of Olenus
Æge'us, a king of Attica, giving name to the Ægean sea by drowning himself in it
Ægi'na, a particular favourite of Jupiter
Æ'gis, a Gorgon killed by Pallas
Æg'le, one of the three Hesperides
Æ'gon, a wrestler famous for strength
Ægyp'tus, son of Neptune and Lybia
Æl'lo, one of the three Harpies
Æne'as, son of Anchises and Venus
Æ'olus, the god of the winds
Æo'us, one of the four horses of the sun
Æscula'nus, a Roman god of riches
Æscula'pius, the god of physic
Æthal'ides, a son of Mercury
Æthon, one of the four horses of the sun
Ætnæ'us, a title of Vulcan
Æto'lus, son of Endymion and Diana
Agamem'non, generalissimo of the Grecian army at the siege of Troy
Aganip'pe, daughter of the river Permessus which flows from mount Helicon
Age'nor, the first king of Argos
Ageno'ra, a. the goddess of industry
Agelas'tus and Agesila'us, names of Pluto
Agla'ia, one of the three Graces
A'jax, a famous hero at the siege of Troy

Albu'nea, a famous sybil of Tripoli
Alci'des, a title of Hercules
Alcin'ous, a king of Corcyra
Alci'oneus, a giant killed by Hercules
Alci'ope, a favourite mistress of Neptune
Alcme'na, the wife of Amphytrion
Alec'to, one of the three Furies
Alec'tryon or Gal'lus, a favourite of Mars
Al'mus and Alum'nus, titles of Jupiter
Alo'a, a festival of Bacchus and Ceres
Alœ'us, a giant who warred with Jupiter
Amalthæ'a, the goat that suckled Jupiter
Ambarva'lia, a spring sacrifice to Ceres
Ambro'sia, the food of the gods
Am'mon, a title of Jupiter
Amphiara'us, descended from Apollo and Hypermnestra, and a famous augur
Amphim'edon, one of the suitors of Penelope
Amphi'on, a famous musician
Amphitri'te, the wife of Neptune
Amyn'tor, a king of Epirus
Anac'reon, an eminent lyric poet of Greece
Anai'tis, the goddess of prostitution
Ancæ'us, a king of Arcadia
Andro'geus, the son of Minos
Androm'ache, the wife of Hector
Androm'eda, the daughter of Cepheus and Cassiope, who was bound to a rock, and exposed to be devoured by a sea monster, but Perseus rescued and married her
Angero'na, the goddess of silence
Au'na, the sister of Pygmalion and Dido
Antæ'us, a giant, son of Neptune and Terra; he was squeezed to death by Hercules
An'teros, one of the names of Cupid
Antever'ta, a goddess of women in labour
An'thia and Argi'va, titles of Juno
Anu'bis, an Egyptian god with a dog's head
Aoni'des, a name of the Muses
Apatu'ria and Aphro'dites, names of Venus
A'pis, son of Jupiter and Niobe; called also Serapis and Osiris
Arach'ne, a princess, changed into a spider for presuming to vie with Minerva at spinning
Arethu'sa, the daughter of Nereus; a river
Argenti'nus and Æscula'nus, gods of wealth
Ar'go, the ship that conveyed Jason to Colchis; said to have been the first ship of war
Ar'gonauts, the companions of Jason
Ar'gus, son of Aristor, had 100 eyes; also an architect, who built the ship Argo
Ariad'ne, daughter of Minos, who assisted Theseus out of the Cretan labyrinth; being afterwards deserted by him, she married Bacchus, and became his priestess
Arimas'pi, a warlike people of Scythia
Ari'on, a lyric poet of Methymna
Aristæ'us, son of Apollo and Cyrene
Aristo'menes a cruel Titan

Artemis, the Delphic sibyl; also Diana
Asole'pia, festivals of Æsculapius
Asco'lia, Bacchanalian festivals in Attica
Aste'ria, a daughter of Ceus
Astrapœ'us and Atahy'rus, names of Jupiter
Astræ'a, the goddess of Justice
Astrol'ogus, a title of Hercules
Asty'anax, the only son of Hector
Astypalæ'a, daughter of Phœnix
A'te, the goddess of revenge
Atlan'tes, a savage people of Æthiopia
At'las, a king of Mauritania
At'ropos, one of the three Fates
Aver'nus, a lake on the borders of hell
Averun'cus, a god of the Romans
Auge'as, a king of Elis, whose stable of 3000
    oxen was not cleansed for 30 years, yet
    was cleansed by Hercules in one day
A'stuper, a title of Priapus
Aut'rea, a name of Fortuna
Auro'ra, the goddess of the morning
Auto'leon, a general of the Crotonians
Autum'nus, the god of fruits

BAC'CHUS, the god of wine
Bap'ta, the goddess of shame
Barba'ta, a name of Venus and Fortuna
Bas'nareus, a name of Bacchus
Bat'tus, a herdsman, tranformed by Mer-
    cury into a loadstone
Bau'cis, an old woman, who, with her hus-
    band Philemon, entertained Jupiter and
    Mercury in their travels through Phrygia
Beller'ophon, son of Glaucus king of Ephyra
Bello'na, the goddess of war
Berecyn'thia Ma'ter, a name of Cybele
Beren'ice, a Grecian lady, the only woman
    ever permitted to see the Olympic games
Ber'gion, a giant, slain by Jupiter
Bib'lia, the wife of Duillius, the first who in-
    stituted a triumph for a naval victory
Bi'ceps and Bi'frons, names of Janus
Bisul'tor, a name of Mars
Bi'thon, a remarkably strong Grecian
Boli'na, a nymph rendered immortal for her
    modesty and resistance of Apollo
Bo'na De'a, a title of Cybele and Fortuna
Bo'nus Dæ'mon, a title of Priapus
Bo'reas, son of Æstraeus and Heribaia, gene-
    rally put for the north wind
Bre'vis, a title of Fortuna
Bria'reus, a giant, son of Titan and Terra;
    said to have had 100 arms and 50 heads
Bri'mo and Bubas'tis, names of Hecate
Brise'is, daughter of Brises, priest of Jupiter,
    given to Achilles, on the taking of Lyrnes-
    sus, a city of Troas, by the Greeks
Bron'tes, a maker of Jupiter's thunder
Bro'theus, a son of Vulcan, flung himself in-
    to Ætna, on account of his deformity
Bruma'lia, feasts of Bacchus
Bubo'na, the goddess of oxen
Busi'ris, son of Neptune, a most cruel tyrant
Byb'lis, the daughter of Miletus

CABAR'NI, priests of Ceres
Cabi'ri, priests of Cybele
Cabi'rus, a god of the Phaselitæ
Ca'cus, a son of Vulcan, slain by Hercules
Cad'mus, son of Agenor and Telephessa,
    built the city of Thebes, and invented 16
    letters of the Greek alphabet

Cadu'ceus, Mercury's golden rod or wand
Cæ'ca and Conserva'trix, titles of Fortune
Cæc'ulus, a robber, son of Vulcan
Cæ'neus, a title of Jupiter
Cal'chas, a famous Greek soothsayer
Calis'to, the daughter of Lycaon
Calli'ope, the muse of heroic poetry
Calyp'so, daughter of Oceanus and Theti
    who reigned in the island of Ogygia, wher
    she entertained and became enamoura
    of Ulysses, in his return from Troy
Cam'bles, a gluttonous king of Lydia
Camby'ses, the son of Cyrus, and king of th
    Medes and Persians
Camœ'næ and Car'na, goddess of infants
Ca'nes, a name of the Furies
Cano'pus, an Egyptian god
Car'dua, a household goddess
Carmen'ta, a name of Themis
Car'na, a Roman goddess
Carya'tis, a title of Diana
Cas'pii, people of Hyrcania, reputed to starve
    their parents to death when 70 years old,
    and to train up dogs for war
Cassan'dra, a daughter of Priam, endowed
    with the gift of prophecy by Apollo
Castal'ides, the Muses, from the fountain
    Castalius, at the foot of Parnassus
Cas'tor, son of Jupiter and Leda, who, with
    his brother Pollux, shared alternately the
    privileges of immortality
Ca'tius, a tutelar god to grown persons
Ce'crops, the first king of Athens
Celœ'no, one of the three Harpies
Cen'taurs, children of Ixion, half men, half
    horses, inhabiting Thessaly
Ceph'alus, the son of Mercury and Hersa
Ce'pheus, a prince of Arcadia and Æthiopia
Cerau'nius, a title of Jupiter
Cer'berus, a dog who guarded the gates of
    hell, with three heads and necks
Cerea'lia, festivals in honour of Ceres
Ce'res, the goddess of agriculture
Ce'rus, or Se'rus, the god of opportunity
Chal'ora, festivals in honour of Vulcan
Char'ites, a name of the Graces
Cha'ron, the ferryman of hell
Chime'ra, a strange monster of Lycia, which
    was slain by Bellerophon
Chi'ron, the preceptor of Achilles
Chiro'mis, a cruel son of Hercules
Chrysao'rius, a surname of Jupiter
Chry'sis, a priestess of Juno at Argos
Cir'ce, a famous enchantress
Cir'rha, a cavern near Delphi, whence the
    winds issued which caused a divine rage,
    and produced oracular responses
Cithœ'rides, a title of the Muses
Claust'ra, a name of Venus
Clau'sius, or Clu'sius, a name of Janus
Cleome'des, a famous wrestler
Cli'o, the muse who presides over history
Clo'tho, one of the three Fates
Clytemnes'tra, daughter of Jupiter, slain by
    Orestes, for her adultery with Ægisthus
Co'cytus, a river in hell, flowing from Styx
Colli'na, the goddess of hills
Compita'lia, games of the household gods
Co'mus, the god of festivals and merriment
Concor'dia, the goddess of peace
Conserva'tor and Cus'tos, titles of Jupiter

Con'sus, a title of Neptune
Corti'na, the covering of Apollo's tripos
Coryban'tes and Cure'tes, priests of Cybele
Cre'on, a king of Thebes
Cri'nis, a priest of Apollo
Crinis'sus, an amorous Trojan prince
Crœ'sus, a rich king of Lydia
Cro'nia, festivals in honour of Saturn
Ctes'ibus, a famous Athenian parasite
Cu'nia, the goddess of new-born infants
Cu'pid, son of Mars and Venus, the god of
  love, smiles, &c.
Cy'clops, Vulcan's workmen, with only one
  eye in the middle of their forehead
Cyb'ele, the wife of Saturn
Cyc'nus, a king of Lyguria; also a son of
  Neptune, who was invulnerable
Cylle'nius and Camil'lus, names of Mercury
Cynoceph'ali, a people of India, said to have
  heads resembling those of dogs
Cyn'thia and Cyn'thius, Diana and Apollo
Cyparissæ'a, a title of Minerva
Cyp'ria, Cythere'a, titles of Venus

DÆDA'LION, the son of Lucifer
Dæd'alus, an ingenious artificer of Athens,
  who formed the Cretan labyrinth, and invented the auger, axe, glue, plumb-line,
  saw, and masts and sails for ships
Da'mon, the faithful friend of Pythias
Dæ'mon Bo'nus, Dithyram'bus, and Dio-
  nys'ius, titles of Bacchus
Da'nae, the daughter of Acrisius, king of
  Argos, seduced by Jupiter
Dana'ides, the 50 daughters of Danaus, king
  of Argos, all of whom, except Hypermnes-
  tra, killed their husbands on the wedding-
  night, and were doomed to draw water out
  of deep wells with buckets full of holes
Daph'ne, a nymph beloved by Apollo
Dar'danus, the founder of Troy
Da'res, a very ancient historian, who wrote
  an account of the Trojan war
De a Syr'ia, a title of Venus
De'cima, a title of Lachesis
Dejani'ra, the wife of Hercules
Deida'mia, daughter of Lycomedes, king of
  Scyros, by whom Achilles had Pyrrhus,
  whilst he was disguised in women's ap-
  parel, in the court of her father
Delope'a, a beautiful attendant on Juno
Deiph'obe, the Cumean sybil
Deiph'obus, a son of Priam and Hecuba
De'lia, De'lius, Diana and Apollo
De'los, the island where Apollo was born
Del'phi, a city of Phocis, famous for a tem-
  ple and an oracle of Apollo
Del'phicus, Didymæ'us, titles of Apollo
Dem'ades, an Athenian orator
Der'bices, a people near the Caspian sea,
  who punished all crimes with death
Deuca'lion, son of Prometheus, who, with
  his wife Pyrrha, was preserved from the
  general deluge, and re-peopled the world
  by throwing stones behind them
Dever'ra, the goddess of breeding women
Diag'oras, a Rhodian, who died for joy, be-
  cause his three sons had on the same day
  gained prizes at the Olympic games
Dia'na, the goddess of hunting, &c.
Di'do, daughter of Belus and queen of

Carthage, who burnt herself through de-
  spair, because Æneas left her
Di'es and Dies'piter, titles of Jupiter
Din'dyme, Dindyme'ne, titles of Cybele
Diome des, a king of Ætolia, who, assisted
  by Ulysses, carried off the Palladium,
  Troy; also, a tyrant of Thrace
Dio'ne, one of Jupiter's mistresses
Dionys'a, feasts in honour of Bacchus
Dioscu'ri, a title of Castor and Pollux
Di'ræ, a title of the Furies
Dis, a title of Pluto
Discor'dia, the goddess of contention
Domidu'ca, a title of Juno
Domidu'cus and Domit'ius, nuptial
Dom'ina, a title of Proserpine
Dry'ades, nymphs of the woods and forests

ECHI'ON, a companion of Cadmus
Ec'ho, daughter of Aer and Tellus, who
  pined away for the love of Narcissus
Edon'ides, priestesses of Bacchus
Edu'ca, a goddess of new-born infants
Ege'ria, a title of Juno; also, a goddess
Elec'tra, a daughter of Agamemnon and
  Clytemnestra, who incited Orestes to re-
  venge their father's death on their mother
  and her adulterer Ægysthus
E'leus and Eleuthe'rius, titles of Bacchus
Eleusin'ia, feasts in honour of Ceres
Flo'ides, nymphs of Bacchus
Empu'sæ, a name of the Gorgons
Endym'ion, a shepherd of Caria, who, for
  his solicitation of Juno, was condemned
  to a sleep of 30 years; Diana visited him
  by night in a cave of Mount Latmus
Enia'lius, a title of Mars
Eny o, the same as Bellona
Epe'us, the artist of the Trojan horse
Epig ones, the sons of the seven worthies
  who besieged Thebes a second time
Epilæ'nea, sacrifices to Bacchus
Epistro phia and Eryci'na, titles of Venus
Epizeph'rii, a people of Locris, who pun-
  ished those with death that drank more
  wine than the physicians prescribed
Era'to, the muse of love-poetry
Er'ebus, an infernal deity, son of Chaos and
  Nox; also, a river of hell
Er'gane, a river whose waters inebriated
Eric'thonius, a king of Athens, who being
  lame, and deformed in his feet, invented
  coaches to conceal his lameness
Erin'nis, a common name of the Furies
E'ros, one of the names of Cupid
Eros'tratus, he who, to perpetuate his name,
  set fire to the temple of Diana at Ephesus
Ete'ocles and Polyni'ces, sons of Oedipus,
  who hated, and, at last, killed each other
Evad'ne, daughter of Mars and Thebe, who,
  out of affection, threw herself on the fu-
  neral pile of her husband Catenus
Euc'rates, a person distinguished for shuf-
  fling, duplicity, and dissimulation
Rumen'ides, a name of the Furies
Euphros'yne, one of the three Graces
Eu'ropa, daughter of Agenor, who was car-
  ried away by Jupiter, in the form of a bull
Eury'ale, one of the three Gorgons
Euryd'ice, the wife of Orpheus
Eurym'one, an infernal deity

Euter'pe, the muse presiding over music
Euthy'mus, a very famous wrestler

FAB'ULA, the goddess of lies
Fabuli'nus, a god of infants
Fa'ma, the goddess of report, &c.
Fas'cinum, a title of Priapus
Fates, the three daughters of Nox and Erebus; Clothos, Lachesis, and Atropos, entrusted with the lives of mortals
Fau'na and Fat'ua, names of Cybele
Fau'nus, the father of the Fauns
Feb'rua, Flor'ida, Fluo'nia, titles of Juno
Feb'rua, a goddess of purification
Feb'ruus, a title of Pluto
Felic'itas, the goddess of happiness
Fer'culus, a household god
Fere'trius and Fulmina'tor, titles of Jupiter
Fero'nia, a goddess of woods
Fesso'nia, a goddess of wearied persons
Fid'ius, the god of treaties
Flam'ines, priests of Jupiter, Mars, &c.
Flo'ra, the goddess of flowers
Fluvia'les, or Potam'ides, nymphs of rivers
For'nax, a goddess of corn and bakers
Fortu'na, or Fortune, the goddess of happiness and misery, said to be blind
Fu'ries, the 3 daughters of Nox and Acheron; Alecto, Megæra, and Tisiphone, armed with snakes and lighted torches

GALAN'THUS, a servant of Alcmena, turned into a weasel for deceiving Juno
Galate'a, daughter of Nereus and Doris, passionately beloved by Polyphemus
Gal'li, castrated priests of Cybele
Gal'lus, or Alectryon, a favourite of Mars
Gan'ymede, the cup-bearer of Jupiter
Gelasi'nus, the god of mirth and smiles
Gelo'ni, a people of Scythia, who painted themselves to terrify their enemies
Ge'nii, guardian angels
Ge'nius, a name of Priapus
Ge'ryon, a king of Spain who had three heads, and fed his oxen with human flesh
Glauco'pis, a name of Minerva
Glau'cus, a fisherman, made a sea-god by eating a certain herb; also, the son of Hippolochus, who exchanged his arms of gold for the brazen ones of Diomede
Gnos'sis, a name of Ariadne
Gor'dius, a husbandman, afterwards king of Phrygia; he tied a knot in so very intricate a manner that Alexander, unable to unravel it, cut it in pieces
Gor'gons, the three daughters of Phorcys and Ce'a; Medusa, Euryale, and Stheno, who could change into stones those whom they looked on; Perseus slew Medusa
Gorgoph'orus, a title of Pallas
Gra'ces, the daughters of Jupiter and Eurynome; Aglaia, Thalia, and Euphrosyne, attendants on Venus and the Muses
Gradi'vus, a title of Mars
Gy'ges, a rich king of Lydia; also, a shepherd, who, by means of a ring, could render himself invisible

HA'DES, a title of Pluto
Hamaxo'bii, a people of Scythia, who lived in carts, and removed from place to place

Harmo'nia, a famous artist of Troy
Harpal'yce, a very beautiful maid of Argos
Har'pies, three monsters, Aello, Celæno, and Occypete; with female faces, bodies of vultures, and hands armed with large claws
Harpoc'rates, the Egyptian god of si ence
He'be, the goddess of youth
He'brus, a river in Thrace
Heca'bus, a title given to Jupiter by Theseus
Hec'ate, Diana's name in hell
Hec'tor, a son of Priam and Hecuba, and the most valiant of all the Trojans
Hec'uba, the wife of Priam
Hege'sias, a philosopher of Cyrene, who drew such a gloomy picture of the miseries of human life, that many of his auditors killed themselves through despair
Hel'ena, wife of Menelaus, the most beautiful woman in the world, whose flight with Paris occasioned the Trojan war
Hel'enus, a son of Priam and Hecuba
Hel'icon, a famous mountain of Bœotia, dedicated to Apollo and the Muses
Hera'ia, sacrifices to Juno
Her'cules, the son of Jupiter and Alcmena, remarkable for his numerous exploits
Herbe'ia, the wife of Astreus
Her'mæ, statues of Mercury
Her'mes, a name of Mercury
Hermi'one, a daughter of Mars and Venus, married to Cadmus; also, a daughter of Menelaus and Helena, married to Pyrrhus
He'ro, a beautiful woman of Sestos, in Thrace; Leander, of Abydos, loved her so tenderly that he swam over the Hellespont every night to see her
Herod'otus, a very famous historian
Heroph'ila, the Erythræan sibyl
Hersi'lia, the wife of Romulus
Hes'perus, or Ves'per, the evening star
Hesper'ides, daughters of Hesperus; Ægle, Arethusa, and Hesperethusa, who had a garden bearing golden apples, watched by a dragon, which Hercules slew
He'sus, a name of Mars among the Gauls
Hip'pias, a philosopher of Elis
Hippocam'pi, Neptune's horses
Hip'pocrene, a fountain at the bottom of mount Helicon, dedicated to Apollo
Hippol'ytus, the son of Theseus and Antiope, or Hippolyte. He was restored to life by Æsculapius, at the request of Diana
Hippom'enes, a Grecian prince, married to Atalanta, and changed into a lion
Hippo'na, the goddess of horses and stables
Histo'ria, the goddess of history
Horten'sis, a name of Venus
Ho'rus, a title of the sun
Hostili'na, a goddess of corn
Hy'ades, the seven daughters of Atlas and Æthra; Ambrosia, Eudora, Coronis, Pasithoo, Plexaris, Pytho, and Tyche. They were changed by Jupiter into 7 stars
Hy'bla, a mountain in Sicily, universally famous for its thyme and bees
Hy'dra, a serpent which had seven heads, slain by Hercules in the lake Lerna
Hyge'ia, the goddess of health
Hyl'lus, the son of Hercules and Dejanira
Hy'men, the god of marriage
Hype'rion, a son of Cœlus and Terra

Hypsip'yle, a queen of Lemnos, who was banished for preserving her father, Thoas, when all the other men of the island were murdered by their kindred

IAC'CHUS, a name of Bacchus

Jan'itor and Juno'nius, titles of Janus

,an the, the beautiful wife of Iphis

Ja'nus, the first king of Italy, son of Apollo

Iap'etus, a son of Cœlum and Terra

Iar'bas, a cruel king of Mauritania

Ja'son, a Thessalian prince, son of Æon, who brought the golden fleece from Colchis

Ica'rius, the son of Oebalus, who, having made some shepherds drunk with wine, which they thought poison, they threw him into a well

Ic'arus, son of Dædalus, who, flying with his father out of Crete into Sicily, and soaring too high, melted the wax of his wings and fell into the sea, thence called the Icarian sea

I'da, a mountain near Troy, where Paris judged between Venus, Juno, and Pallas

Idæ'a Ma'ter, a name of Cybele

Idæ'i Dac'tyli, priests of Cybele

Ida'lia, a name of Venus

Id'mon, a famous soothsayer

Ido'thea, Jupiter's nurse

Ili'one, the eldest daughter of Priam

Ilis'sus, a river in Attica

I'lus, the son of Tros and Callirrhoe, from whom Troy was called Ilium

Impera'tor, a name of Jupiter

In'achis and I'sis, names of Io

I'no, daughter of Cadmus and Hermione

Interci'dona, a goddess of breeding women

Interdu'ca and Ju'ga, names of Juno

In'uus, and Inc'ubus, names of Pan

I'o, daughter of Inachus, who was worshipped as a goddess by the Egyptians, under the name of Isis

Jocas'ta, the daughter of Creon, who unwittingly married her own son Oedipus

Iph'iclus, the twin brother of Hercules

Iphige'nia, daughter of Agamemnon and Clytemnestra, who, when prepared to be sacrificed to Diana, was, by her, transformed into a white hart, and made her priestess

I'phis, a prince of Cyprus, who hanged himself for love; also a daughter of Lygdus

Iph'itus, son of Praxonides, who instituted Olympic games in honour of Hercules

I'ris, companion and messenger of Juno, who turned her into a rainbow

I'tys, the son of Tereus and Progne, murdered and served up by his mother at a banquet, for having defloured her sister

Ju'no, the sister and wife of Jupiter

Ju'no Infer'na, a title of Proserpine

Juno'nes, guardian angels of women

Ju'piter, a son of Saturn and Ops, the supreme deity of the heathens

Ju'piter Secun'dus, a name of Neptune

Ju'piter Ter'tius, Infer'nus, or Sty'gius, veral names of Pluto

Juven'ta, a goddess of youths

Ix'ion, the son of Phlegias, who was fastened in hell to a wheel always turning round, for boasting that he had lain with Juno

LA'CHESIS, one of the three Fates

Lacin'ia and Lucil'ia, titles of Juno

Lactu'la, or Lactuci'na, a goddess of corn

Lastrig'ones, cannibals of Italy, who roasted and ate the companions of Ulysses

La'ius, a king of Thebes, killed unwittingly by his own son Oedipus

La'miæ, a name of the Gorgons

Laoc'oon, a son of Priam, and priest of Apollo; he and his 2 sons were killed by serpents

La'pis, or Lapid'eus, titles of Jupiter

La'res, sons of Mercury and Lara, worshipped as household gods

Latera'nus, a household god

Laver'ne, a goddess of thieves

Lean'der. See Hero

Le'da, daughter of Thespius, and wife of Tyndarus, seduced by Jupiter

Lemoni'ades, nymphs of meadows, &c.

Le'næ, priestesses of Bacchus

Ler'na, a marsh of Argos, famous for a hydra, killed there by Hercules

Le'the, a river of hell, whose waters caused a total forgetfulness of things past

Leva'na, a goddess of new-born infants

Libiti'na, the goddess of funerals

Li'nus, son of Apollo and Terpsichore

Luben'tia, the goddess of pleasure

Lu'cifer, son of Jupiter and Aurora, made the morning star

Lu'na, Diana's name in heaven

Luperca'lia, feasts in honour of Pan

Luper'ci, priests of Pan

Lyca'on, king of Arcadia, turned into a wolf

MA'IA, loved by Jupiter, and by him changed into a star, to avoid Juno's rage

Mantu'ra, a goddess of corn

Mantur'na and Me'na, nuptial goddesses

Mari'na, Mel'anis, Mer'etrix, Migoni'tis, and Mur'cia, titles of Venus

Mars, the god of war

Mauso'lus, king of Caria, who had a magnificent tomb erected by his wife Artemisia

Mede'a, a famous sorceress, by whose assistance Jason obtained the golden fleece

Menitri'na, a goddess of grown persons

Medu'sa, the chief of the three Gorgons

Megæ'ra, one of the three Furies

Megalen'sia, festivals in honour of Cybele

Mega'ra, the wife of Hercules

Melani'ra, a name of Venus

Me'lia, nymphs of the fields

Me'lius, a name of Hercules

Melo'na, the goddess of honey

Melpom'ene, the muse of tragedy

Mem'non, a king of Abydos

Menela'us, a famous Centaur

Menela'us, the husband of Helen

Men'tha, a mistress of Pluto

Men'tor, the governor of Telemachus

Mer'cury, the messenger of the gods, inventor of letters, and god of eloquence, merchandise, and robbers

Mer'ope, one of the seven Pleiades

Mi'das, a king of Phrygia, who had the power given him, by Bacchus, of converting whatever he touched into gold

Mi'lo, a wrestler of remarkable strength

Mimal'lones, attendants on Bacchus

Miner'va, the goddess of wisdom

U

Mi'nos, a king of Crete, appointed, for his extraordinary justice, a judge of hell

Min'otaur, a monster, half man, half beast

Min'yæ, a name of the Argonauts

Mnemos'yne, the goddess of memory

Mo'mus, the god of raillery, wit, &c.

Mors, the goddess of death

Mul'ciber, a title of Vulcan

Mu'ses, nine daughters of Jupiter and Mnemosyne, mistresses of all the sciences, presidents of musicians and poets, and governesses of the feasts of the gods; Calliope, Clio, Erato, Euterpe, Melpomene, Polyhymnia, Terpsichore, Thalia, and Urania

Mu'ta, the goddess of silence

NÆ'NIA, the goddess of funeral songs

Na'iades, nymphs of rivers, &c.

Narcis'sus, a very beautiful youth, who, falling in love with his own shadow in the water, pined away into a daffodil

Na'tio and Nundi'na, goddesses of infants

Nemæ'a, a country of Elis, famed for a terrible lion killed by Hercules

Nem'esis, the goddess of revenge

Nep'tune, the god of the sea

Nere'ides, sea nymphs

Ne'rio, the wife of Mars

Niceph'orus, a title of Jupiter

Ni'nus, the first king of the Assyrians

Ni'obe, the wife of Amphion, who had her 14 children killed by Diana and Apollo, and wept herself into a statue

No'mius, a name of Apollo

Nox, the most ancient of all the deities; she was even reckoned older than Chaos

OB'SEQUENS, a title of Fortuna

Occa'tor, the god of harrowing

Oce'anus, an ancient sea god

Ocyp'ete, one of the three Harpies

Oed'ipus, son of Laius and Jocasta, and king of Thebes, who solved the riddle of the Sphinx, unwittingly killed his father, married his mother, and at last ran mad, and tore out his eyes

O ym'pus, the residence of the gods

Om'phale, a queen of Lydia, with whom Hercules was so enamoured, that she made him submit to spinning

Oper'tus, a name of Pluto

Opi'gena, a name of Juno

Ops, a name of Cybele

Orho'na, a goddess of grown persons

Ores'tes, son of Agamemnon

Ori'on, a great and mighty hunter

Orithy'a, a queen of the Amazons

Or'pheus, son of Jupiter and Calliope, who had great skill in music, and was torn in pieces by the Mœnades, for his dislike to women after the death of his wife Eurydice

PAC'TOLUS, a river of Lydia, with golden sands and medicinal waters

Pæ'an and Phœ'bus, names of Apollo

Pa'les, the goddess of shepherds

Palli'lia, feasts in honour of Pales

Palla'dium, a statue of Minerva, which the Trojans imagined fell from heaven

Pal'las and Py'lotis, names of Minerva

Pan, the god of shepherds

Pando'ra, the first woman made by Vulcan, endued with gifts by all the deities; Jupiter gave her a box containing all manner of evils, with Hope at the bottom

Pan'ope, one of the Nereides

Pa'phia, a title of Venus

Par'cæ, a name of the Fates

Par'is, or Alexander, son of Priam and Hecuba, a beautiful youth, who ran away with Helena, and occasioned the Trojan war

Parnas'sus, a mountain in Phocis, famous for a temple of Apollo, and being the favourite seat of the Muses

Partun'da, a nuptial goddess

Pastoph'ori, priests of Isis

Pat'areus, a title of Apollo

Patel'na, a goddess of corn

Patula'cius, a name of Janus

Patule'ius, a name of Jupiter

Paven'tia and Poli'na, goddesses of infants

Peg'asus, a winged horse belonging to Apollo and the Muses

Pello'nia, the goddess of grown persons

Pena'tes, small statues of household gods

Penel'ope, daughter of Icarus, celebrated for her chastity and fidelity to Ulysses

Per'seus, son of Jupiter and Danaë, who performed many extraordinary exploits by means of Medusa's head

Phæcasia'ni, ancient gods of Greece

Phae'ton, son of Sol and Clymene, who had the guidance of his father's chariot for one day, to prove his divine descent; but, unable to manage the horses, he set the world on fire

Phal'lica, feasts of Bacchus

Philam'mon, a skilful musician

Philome'la, daughter of Pandion king of Athens, ravished by her brother-in-law Tereus, and was changed into a nightingale

Phi'neas, son of Agenor; also, a king of Thrace

Phleg'ethon, a boiling river of hell

Phle'gon, one of the four horses of Sol

Phleg'yæ, a people of Bœotia, destroyed by Neptune for their piracies and crimes

Phœ'bas, the priestess of Apollo

Phœ'bus, a title of Apollo

Phœ'nix, son of Amyntor, who had his eyes torn out, but was cured by Chiron

Pieum'nus, a rural god

Pilum'nus, a god of breeding women

Pin'dus, a mountain of Thessaly

Pi'tho, a goddess of eloquence

Ple'iades, the seven daughters of Atlas and Pleione; Maia, Electra, Taigete, Asterope, Merope, Halcyone, and Celæno

Plu'to, the god of Hell

Plu'tus, the god of riches

Pol'lux, brother of Castor, which see

Poly'damas, a famous wrestler

Polyd'lus, a famous prophet and physician

Polyphe'mus, a monstrous giant, with but one eye in the middle of his forehead

Pomo'na, the goddess of fruit and autumn

Pose'idon, a name of Neptune

Prænesti'na, a name of Fortuna

Præs'tes, a title of Jupiter and Minerva

Praxit'eles, a famous statuary

Pri'am, son of Laomedon, and father of Paris, Hector, &c.; the last king of Troy

Prog'ne, wife of Tereus, king of Thrace

Prome'theus, son of Iapetus, who animated with fire a man that he had formed of clay; he was chained by Jupiter to mount Caucasus, with a vulture preying on his liver

Propylæ's, a name of Hecate

Pros'erpine, the wife of Pluto

Pro'teus, a sea god who could transform himself into any shape

Psy'che, the goddess of pleasure

Pyl'ades, the constant friend of Orestes

Pyr'amus and This'be, two lovers of Babylon, who killed themselves under a mulberry-tree, which turned its berries from white to red

Pyræ'tis, one of the four horses of the Sun

Pyr'rhus, son of Achilles, remarkable for his cruelty at the siege of Troy

Py'thon, a serpent produced from the mud of the deluge, killed by Apollo, who, in memory thereof, instituted the Pythian games

Pythonis'sa, the priestess of Apollo

QUAD'RIFRONS, a title of Janus

Qui'es, a goddess of grown persons

Quieta'lis and Qule'tus, names of Pluto

Quinqua'tria, feasts of Pallas

REC'TUS, a title of Bacchus

Re'dux and Re'gia, titles of Fortune

Regi'na, a title of Juno

Rhadaman'thus, one of the infernal judges

Rhe'a, a title of Cybele

Rhe'a Syl'via, the mother of Romulus

Robi'gus, a god of corn

Rom'ulus, the first king of Rome

Ru'mina, a goddess of new-born infants

Runci'na, the goddess of weeding

Rusi'na, a rural deity

SABA'ZIA, feasts of Proserpine

Sa'lii, the 12 frantic priests of Mars

Salmone'us, a king of Elis, struck by a thunderbolt for imitating Jupiter's thunder

Sa'lus, the goddess of health

Sanc'us, a god of the Sabines

Sa'tor and Sorri'tor, rural gods

Saturna'lia, feasts of Saturn

Satur'nus, or Sa'turn, the son of Cœlum and Terra

Sat'yrs, the attendants of Bacchus, horned monsters, half men, half goats

Scy'ron, a famous robber of Attica

Se'ia and Sege'tia, goddesses of corn

Sel'li, priests of Jupiter

Senta, a goddess of married women

Sile'nus, the foster-father and companion of Bacchus, who was drunk every day

Si'mis, a famous robber, killed by Hercules

Sis'yphus, the son of Æolus, killed by Theseus, and doomed, for his perfidy, to roll incessantly a huge stone up a mountain

Sol, a name of Apollo

Som'nus, the god of sleep

Sphinx, a monster born of Syphon and Echidna, who destroyed herself because Oedipus solved the enigma she proposed

Sta'ta, a goddess of grown persons

Sten'tor, a Grecian whose voice was as loud as the voices of 50 men together

Sthe'no, one of the three Gorgons

Styx, a river of hell

Sua'da, a nuptial goddess

Summa'nus, a name of Pluto

Sylva'nus, a god of woods and forests

Sy'rens, sea monsters

TA'CITA, a goddess of silence

Tan'talus, a king of Paphlagonia, doomed to everlasting thirst for his barbarity

Tar'tarus, the place of the wicked in hell

Tau'rus, the bull under whose form Jupiter carried away Europa

Telchi'nes, priests of Cybele

Telem'achus, the only son of Ulysses

Tem'pe, a most beautiful valley in Thessaly, the resort of the gods

Ter'minus, the god of boundaries

Terpsich'ore, the muse of music, &c.

Ter'ror, the god of dread and fear

Tha'lia, the muse of comedy

Thes'pis, the first tragic poet

Phe'tis, the goddess of laws, oracles, &c.

Thyr'sus, the rod of Bacchus

Ti'phys, the pilot of the ship Argo

Tisiph'one, one of the three Furies

Ti'tan, elder brother of Saturnus, or Saturn

Tma'rius, a title of Jupiter

Tri'ton, Neptune's trumpeter

Trito'nia, a name of Minerva

Tro'ilus, a son of Priam and Hecuba

Troy, a city of Phrygia, which held out a siege of ten years against the Greeks, but at last captured and destroyed by them.

Tuteli'na, a goddess of corn

Ty'ro, one of the Nereides

VACU'NA, the goddess of idle persons

Vagita'nus, a god of little infants

Vallo'nia, a goddess of valleys

Venil'ia, a wife of Neptune

Ve'nus, the goddess of love, beauty, &c.

Vergil'iæ, a name of the Pleiades

Verticor'dia, a name of Venus

Vertum'nus, the god of the spring

Ves'ta, the goddess of fire

Via'les, deities of the highways

Vibil'ia, the goddess of wanderers

Virgine'sis, a nuptial goddess

Vir'go, a name of Astrea and Fortune

Viri'lis and Visca'ta, titles of Fortune

Vit'nia, the goddess of mirth

Ulys'ses, son of Laertes and Anticlea, and king of Ithaca, who, by his talents, was eminently serviceable in the Trojan war

Volu'sia, a goddess of corn

Ura'nia, the muse of astronomy

Vul'can, the god of subterraneous fire

XAN'THUS, one of the horses of Achilles also, a river near Troy, called also Scamander

ZA'GREUS, a title of Bacchus

Zeph'yrus, son of Æolus and Aurora, who passionately loved the goddess Flora, and is put for the west wind

Ze'tes and Cal'ais, sons of Boreas and Orithya, who accompanied the Argonauts

Ze'tus, the son of Jupiter and Antiope, very expert in music

Ze'us, a title of Jupiter

N. B. The dates denote the time when the following writers died—but when that event cannot be correctly ascertained, the period in which they flourished is signified by fl. The names in *italics* are those who have given the best English translations.

B.C.

907 HOMER, the first profane writer and Greek poet, supposed to have flourished—*Chapman, Pope, Cowper*

Hesiod, the Greek poet, supposed to have lived near the time of Homer—*Cooke, Elton*

884 Lycurgus, the Spartan lawgiver

600 Sappho, the Greek lyric poetess, fl.—*Fawkes*

558 Solon, lawgiver of Athens

556 Æsop, the first Greek fabulist—*Croxall*

548 Thales, the first Greek astronomer and geographer

497 Pythagoras, founder of the Pythagorean philosophy in Greece—*Rowe*

474 Anacreon, the Greek lyric poet—*Addison, Fawkes, Moore*

456 Æschylus, the first Greek tragic poet—*Potter*

435 Pindar, the Greek lyric poet—*West*

413 Herodotus, of Greece, the first writer of profane history—*Littlebury*

407 Aristophanes, the Greek comic poet, fl. —*White, Mitchell*

407 Euripides, the Greek tragic poet—*Woodhull, Potter*

406 Sophocles, ditto—*Franklin, Potter*

406 Confucius, the Chinese philosopher, fl.

400 Socrates, the founder of moral philosophy in Greece

391 Thucydides, the Greek historian—*Smith, Hobbes*

361 Hippocrates, the Greek physician—*Clifton*

361 Democritus, the Greek philosopher

359 Xenophon, the Greek philosopher and historian—*Smith, Spelman, Ashby, Fielding*

348 Plato, the Greek philosopher, and disciple of Socrates—*Sydenham*

396 Isocrates, the Greek orator—*Dimsdale*

332 Aristotle, the Greek philosopher, and disciple of Plato—*Hobbes, Taylor*

318 Demosthenes, the Athenian orator, poisoned himself—*Leland, Francis*

288 Theophrastus, the Greek philosopher, and disciple of Aristotle—*Budgel*

285 Theocritus, the first Greek pastoral poet, fl.—*Fawkes*

277 Euclid, of Alexandria, in Egypt, the mathematician, fl.—*R. Simson, Leslie*

270 Epicurus, founder of the Epicurean philosophy in Greece—*Digby*

264 Xeno, founder of the Stoic philosophy in Greece

214 Callimachus, the Greek elegiac poet

206 Archimedes, the Greek geometrician

B.C.

184 Plautus, the Roman comic poet — *Thornton*

159 Terence, of Carthage, the Latin comic poet—*Colman*

155 Diogenes, of Babylon, the Stoic philosopher

124 Polybius, of Greece, the Greek and Roman historian—*Hampton*

54 Lucretius, the Roman poet—*Creech*

44 Julius Cæsar, the Roman historian and commentator, killed—*Duncan*

44 Diodorus Siculus, of Greece, the universal historian, fl.—*Booth*

44 Vitruvius, the Roman architect, fl.

43 Cicero, the Roman orator and philosopher, put to death—*Guthrie, Melmoth*

43 Cornelius Nepos, the Roman biographer, fl.—*Rowe*

34 Sallust, the Roman historian—*Gordon, Rowe*

30 Dionysius, of Halicarnassus, the Roman historian—*Spelman*

19 Virgil, the Roman epic poet—*Dryden, Pitt, Warton*

11 Catullus, Tibullus, and Propertius, Roman poets—*Grainger, Dart*

8 Horace, the Roman lyric and satiric poet—*Francis*

A.C.

17 Livy, the Roman historian—*Ray, Baker*

19 Ovid, the Roman elegiac poet—*Garth*

20 Celsus, the Roman philosopher and physician, fl.—*Grieve*

25 Strabo, the Greek geographer

33 Phædrus, the Roman fabulist—*Smart*

45 Paterculus, the Roman historian, fl.—*Newcombe*

62 Perseus, the Roman satiric poet—*Brewster*

61 Quintus Curtius, a Roman, historian of Alexander the Great, fl.—*Digby*

61 Seneca, of Spain, the philosopher and tragic poet, put to death—*L'Estrange*

65 Lucan, the Roman epic poet, ditto—*Rowe*

79 Pliny the elder, the Roman natural historian—*Holland*

93 Josephus, the Jewish historian—*Whiston*

94 Epictetus, the Greek Stoic philosopher, fl.—*Mrs. Carter*

95 Quinctilian, the Roman orator and advocate—*Guthrie*

96 Statius, the Roman epic poet—*Lewis*

96 Lucius Florus, of Spain, the Roman historian, fl.

99 Tacitus, the Roman historian —*Gordon*

A.C.

104 Martial, of Spain, the epigrammatic poet—*Hay*

104 Valerius Flaccus, the Roman epic poet

116 Pliny the younger, historical letters—*Melmoth, Orrery*

117 Suetonius, the Roman historian—*Hughes*

119 Plutarch of Greece, the biographer—*Dryden, Langhorne*

128 Juvenal, the Roman satiric poet—*Dryden, Gifford*

140 Ptolemy, the Egyptian geographer, mathematician, and astronomer, fl.

150 Justin, the Roman historian, fl.—*Turnbul*

161 Arrian, the Roman historian and philosopher, fl.—*Rooke*

167 Justin, of Samaria, the oldest Christian author after the apostles

180 Lucian, the Roman philologer—*Lansdale, Dryden, Franklin, Carr*

180 Marcus Aur. Antoninus, Roman emperor and philosopher—*Collier. Elphinstone*

193 Galen, the Greek philosopher and physician

200 Diogenes Laertius, the Greek biographer, fl.

229 Dion Cassius, of Greece, the Roman historian, fl.

254 Origen, a Christian father of Alexandria

254 Herodian, of Alexandria, the Roman historian, fl.—*Hart*

258 Cyprian, of Carthage, suffered martyrdom—*Marshal*

273 Longinus, the Greek critic, put to death by Aurelian—*Smith*

320 Lactantius, a father of the church, fl.

336 Arius, a priest of Alexandria, founder of the sect of Arius

342 Eusebius, the ecclesiastical historian and chronologer—*Hanmer*

379 Bazil, bishop of Cæsarea

389 Gregory Nazianzen, bishop of Constantinople

397 Ambrose, bishop of Milan

415 Macrobius, the Roman grammarian

428 Eutropius, the Roman historian

524 Boethius, the Roman poet, and Platonic philosopher—*Bellamy. Preston*

539 Procopius, of Cæsarea, the Roman historian—*Holcroft*

[Here ends the illustrious list of Ancients, or, as they are styled, Classic authors; but it will ever be regretted that a small part only of their writings have come to our hands.

The invention of printing in the sixteenth century, forms a memorable period in the annals of learning; and a race of men have sprung up in a new soil. France, Germany, and Britain; who, if they do not exceed, at least equal the greatest geniuses of antiquity. Of these, our own countrymen have the reputation of the first rank, with whose names we shall finish our list.]

731 Bede, a priest of Northumberland; history of the Saxons, Scots, &c.

901 King Alfred; history, philosophy, and poetry

A.C.

1259 Matthew Paris, monk of St. Alban's; history of England

1292 Roger Bacon, Somersetshire; natural philosophy

1308 John Fordun, a priest of Mearnshire history of Scotland

1400 Geoffrey Chaucer, London; the father of English poetry

1402 John Gower, Wales; the poet

1535 Sir Thomas More, London; history, politics, divinity

1552 John Leland, London; lives and antiquities

1568 Roger Ascham, Yorkshire; philosophy and polite literature

1572 Rev. John Knox, the Scotch reformer; history of the church of Scotland

1582 George Buchanan, Dumbartonshire; history of Scotland, psalms of David, politics, &c.

1598 Edmund Spencer, London; Fairy Queen, and other poems

1615-25 Beaumont and Fletcher, 53 dramatic pieces

1616 William Shakspeare, Stratford; 37 tragedies and comedies

1622 John Napier, of Marcheston, Scotland; discoverer of logarithms

1623 William Cambden, London; history and antiquities

1626 Lord Chancellor Bacon, London; natural philosophy, literature in general

1634 Lord Chief Justice Coke, Norfolk; laws of England

1634 Ben Jonson, London; 53 dramatic pieces

1641 Sir Henry Spelman, Norfolk; laws and antiquities

1654 John Spelden, Sussex; antiquities and laws

1657 Dr. William Harvey, Kent; discovered the circulation of the blood

1667 Abraham Cowley, London; miscellaneous poetry

1674 John Milton, London; Paradise Lost, Paradise Regained, and various other pieces in verse and prose

1674 Hyde, earl of Clarendon, Wiltshire; history of the civil wars in England

1675 James Gregory, Aberdeen; mathematics, geometry, and optics

1677 Rev. Dr. Isaac Barrow, London; natural philosophy, mathematics, and sermons

1680 Samuel Butler, Worcestershire; Hudibras, a burlesque poem

1685 Thomas Otway, London; 10 tragedies and comedies, with other poems

1687 Edmund Waller, Bucks; poems, letters, speeches, &c.

1688 Dr. Ralph Cudworth, Somersetshire intellectual system

1689 Dr. Thomas Sydenham, Dorsetshire history of physic

1690 Nathaniel Lee, London; 11 tragedies

1690 Robert Barclay, Urie; apology for Quakers

1691 Hon. Robert Boyle, natural and experimental philosophy and theology

U 3

A.C.

1691 Sir George M'Kenzie, Dundee; antiquities and laws of Scotland

1694 John Tillotson, archbishop of Canterbury, Halifax; 254 sermons

1697 Sir William Temple, London; politics and polite literature

1701 John Dryden, Northamptonshire; 27 tragedies and comedies, Virgil, satiric poems

1704 John Locke, Somersetshire; philosophy, government, and theology

1705 John Ray, Essex; botany, natural philosophy, and divinity

1707 George Farquhar, Londonderry; 8 comedies

1713 Ant. Ash. Cowper, earl of Shaftesbury; characteristics

1714 Gilbert Burnet, Edinburgh, bishop of Salisbury; history, biography, divinity, &c

1718 Nicholas Rowe, Devons.: 7 tragedies, translation of Lucan's Pharsalia

1719 Rev. John Flamstead, Derbyshire; mathematics and astronomy

1719 Joseph Addison, Wiltshire; Spectator, Guardian, poems, politics

719 Dr. John Keil, Edinburgh; mathematics and astronomy

721 Matthew Prior, London; poems and politics

1724 William Wollaston, Staffordshire; Religion of Nature delineated

1727 Sir I. Newton, Lincolnshire; mathematics, geometry, optics, astronomy

1720 Rev. Dr. Samuel Clarke, Norwich; mathematics, divinity, &c.

729 Sir Richard Steele, Dublin; 4 comedies, papers in Tatler, &c.

729 William Congreve, Staffordshire; 7 dramatic pieces

732 John Gay, Exeter; poems, fables, and 11 dramatic pieces

731 Dr. John Arbuthnot, Mearnshire; medicine, coins, politics

1739 Dr. Edmund Halley; natural philosophy, astronomy, navigation

1739 Dr. Richard Bentley, Yorkshire; classical learning, criticism

1744 Alexander Pope, London: poems, letters, translation of Homer

1745 Rev. Dr. Jonathan Swift, Dublin; politics, poems, and letters

1746 Colin M'Laurin, Argyleshire; algebra, View of Newton's Philosophy

1748 James Thomson, Roxburghshire; Seasons, and other poems. 5 tragedies

1749 Rev. Dr. Isaac Watts, Southampton; logic, philosophy, psalms, hymns, sermons, &c.

1.6 Dr. Francis Hutcheson, Ayrshire; system of moral philosophy

50 Rev. D. Conyers Middleton, Yorkshire; life of Cicero, &c.

750 Andrew Baxter, Old Aberdeen; metaphysics and natural philosophy

61 Henry St. John, lord Bolingbroke, Surrey; philosophy, metaphysics, and ethics

Alexander Monro, Edinburgh; of the hu   body

A.C.

1754 Dr. Richard Mead, London; on poison, plague, small-pox, medicine, precepts

1754 Henry Fielding, Somersetshire; Tom Jones, Joseph Andrews, &c.

1757 Colley Cibber, London; 25 tragedies and comedies

1761 Thomas Sherlock, bishop of London; 69 sermons, &c.

1761 Benjamin Hoadley, bishop of Winchester; sermons and controversy

1761 Samuel Richardson, London; Grandison. Clarissa, Pamela

1761 Rev. Dr. Leland, Lancashire; answer to Deistical writers

1765 Rev. Dr. Edw. Young; Night Thoughts, and other poems, 8 tragedies

1765 Robert Simson, Glasgow; conic sections, Euclid, Apollonius

1768 Rev. L. Sterne; 45 sermons, Tristram Shandy, Sentimental Journey

1769 Robert Smith, Lincolnshire; harmonics and optics

1770 Rev. Dr. Jortin; life of Erasmus, ecclesiastical history, and sermons

1770 Dr. Mark Akenside, Newcastle-upon-Tyne; poems

1770 Dr. Tobias Smollet, Dumbartons.: history of England, novels, translations

1771 Thomas Gray, Professor of Modern History, Cambridge; poems

1773 Philip Dormer Stanhope, earl of Chesterfield; letters

1773 George lord Lyttleton, Worcestershire; history of England

1774 Oliver Goldsmith; poems, essays, and other pieces

1774 Zachary Pearce, bishop of Rochester: annotations on the New Testament

1775 Dr. John Hawkesworth; essays

1776 David Hume, Merse; history of England, essays

1776 James Ferguson, Aberdeenshire; astronomy

1777 Samuel Foote, Cornwall; plays

1779 David Garrick, Hereford; plays, &c.

1779 William Warburton, bishop of Gloucester; divine legation of Moses, and various other works

1780 Sir William Blackstone, judge of the court of Common Pleas, London; commentaries on the laws of England

1780 Dr. John Fothergill, Yorkshire; philosophy and medicine

1780 James Harris; Hermes, philological inquiries, and philosophical arrangements

1782 Thomas Newton, bishop of Bristol, Litchfield; discourses on the prophecies, and other works

1782 Sir John Pringle, bart. Roxburghshire, diseases of the army

1783 Henry Home, lord Kaimes, Scotland; elements of criticism, sketches of the history of man

1783 Dr. W. Hunter, Lanarkshire; anatomy

1783 Dr. Benjamin Kennicot; Hebrew version of the Bible, theological tracts

1784 Dr. Thomas Morell; editor of Ainsworth's dictionary, Hederieus's lexicon, and some Greek tragedies

A.C.

1784 Dr. Samuel Johnson, Litchfield; English dictionary. biography, essays. poetry. Died December 18, aged 71

1785 Wm. Whitehead, poet laureat; poems and plays. Died April 14

1785 Rev. Richard Burn, LL. D.; author of the Justice of Peace. ecclesiastical law, &c. Died November 20

1785 Richard Glover, esq.; Leonidas, Medea, &c. Died November 25

1786 Jonas Hanway, esq.; travels, miscellanies. Died September 5, aged 74

1787 Dr. Robert Lowth, bishop of London; criticism, divinity, grammar. Died Nov. 3

1787 Soame Jenyns, esq.; internal evidence of the Christian religion, and other pieces. Died December 18

1788 James Stuart, esq. celebrated by the name of "Athenian Stuart." Died Feb. 1

1788 Thomas Gainsborough, esq. the celebrated painter. Died August 2

1788 Thomas Sheridan, esq.; English Dictionary, works on education, elocution, &c. Died August 14

1788 William Julius Mickle, esq. translator of the Lusiad. Died Oct. 25

1789 Dr. William Cullen; practice of physic, materia medica, &c. Died Feb. 5

1790 Dr. Benjamin Franklin, Boston, New England; electricity, natural philosophy. miscellanies. Died April 17

1790 Rev. Thomas Warton, B.D. history of English poetry, and poems. Died April 21

1790 Dr. Adam Smith. Scotland; moral sentiments, inquiry into the wealth of nations

1790 John Howard. esq. Middlesex; account of prisons and lazarettos. &c.

1791 Rev. Dr. Richard Price, Glamorganshire; morals, providence. civil liberties, annuities, reversionary payments. sermons, &c. Died Feb. 19, aged 68

1791 Dr. Thomas Blacklock, Annandale. poems, consolations from natural and revealed religion. Died July. aged 70

1792 Sir Joshua Reynolds, Devonshire; discourses on painting, delivered before the academy led Feb. 23 ~ed 66

1792 John Smeaton. orkshire, civil engineer; mechanics, Eddystone lighthouse, Ramsgate harbour, and other public works of utility

1792 Rev. Dr. William Robertson; history of Scotland, of the reign of Charles V. history of America, and historical disquisition concerning India. Died June 11, aged 72

1793 J. Hunter, esq.; anatomy. Died Aug. 16

1793 James Beattie; poetry, criticism, &c.

1794 Edward Gibbon. esq.; history of the Roman empire, &c. Died Jan. 16

1794 James Bruce. esq. of Kinnaird; travels into Abyssinia

1794 Sir William Jones; law, Arabic and Persian literature, &c. Died April 7

1795 Josiah Wedgwood. esq.; potteries of Staffordshire. Died Jan. 3

1795 James Boswell, esq.; life of Dr. Johnson. &c. Died May 19

1795 Dr. Andrew Kippis; biography and divinity. Died Oct. 8

1796 James Macpherson, esq.; Ossian, state papers, &c. Died Feb. 17

1796 Dr. George Campbell. Aberdeen; philosophy of rhetoric, new translation of the Gospels, &c. Died April 6

1796 Dr. Thomas Reid, Glasgow; metaphysics. Died Oct. 7

1797 The right hon. Horace Walpole, earl of Orford; royal and noble authors, anecdotes of painting, and miscellaneous writings. Died March 2

1797 Rev. William Mason; poetry, and memoirs of Gray. Died April 5

1797 Edmund Burke, esq.; statesman, orator, and political writer. Died July 8

1797 Joseph Wright, esq. Derby; painter. Died Aug. 29

1797 Dr. William Enfield; theological, miscellaneous, &c. Died Nov. 2

1797 Dr. Richard Brocklesby, physician. Died Dec. 12

1797 John Wilkes, esq.; politics. Died Dec. 28

1798 Thomas Sandby, esq.; architecture. Died July 25

1798 Dr. Richard Farmer; literary and topographical antiquities, commentator on Shakspeare. &c. Died Sept. 8

1798 Thomas Pennant, esq.; natural history and antiquities. Died Dec. 16

1798 Wm. Wales, esq.; mathematics. Died Dec. 29

1799 George Stevens, F.R. and A.S.S.; commentator on Shakspeare. Died Jan. 22

1799 John Strange, LL.D., F.R.S. and F.S.A. several papers in the Archæologia. Died March 19

1799 Hon. Daines Barrington, F.R. and A.S.S. observations on the statutes. Died March 17

1799 J. Norbury, Fellow of Eton College; translation into Greek verse of Gray's Elegy

1799 Sir Francis Buller, bart. one of the judges of the court of common pleas; nisi prius. Died June 5

1799 William Cruikshanks. Glasgow; surgery. Died June

1799 John Tweddel; classical compositions. Died July 25

1799 Dr. Matthew Young, bishop of Clonfert; divinity and philosophy. Died November

1799 Dr. Hugh Blair, Edinburgh; rhetoric and belles lettres. Died December

1799 Sir G. Staunton, F.R.S.; history of the embassy to China. Died Dec. 30

1801 William Drake. M.A. and F.R.S.; antiquary. Died May 13

1801 Dr. Wm. Heberden. F.R.S. and S.A.; literary and medical subjects. Died May 17

1801 Gilbert Wakefield; theology, classics, etus, &c. Died Sept. 9

A.C.

1801 Mrs. H. Chapone; education and poetry. Died Dec. 25

1801 Sir Grey Cooper; politics. Died July 20

1802 Rev. Alex. Geddes, LL.D.; biblical and classical subjects. Died Feb. 26

1802 Lord Kenyon; chief justice of the court of King's Bench

1802 Dr. John Moore; Zeluco, travels in France, Italy, &c. Died Feb. 26

1802 Francis, duke of Bedford; politics, agriculture, &c. Died March 2

1802 The earl of Clare, lord high chancellor of Ireland; politics. Died March 27

1802 Dr. Fordyce; physic and chemistry

1802 Dr. Darwin; botany. Died April 28

1802 Dr. Garnett; natural philosophy

1805 Dr. William Paley; theology and moral philosophy. Died May 25

1808 Theophilus Lindsey; divinity. Died Nov. 3

A.C.

1808 Holcroft; plays and novels. Died March 23

1809 Beilby Porteus; divinity and poems. Died May

1811 Richard Cumberland; dramatic pieces, essays, and epic poetry

1812 John Horne Tooke, politics, &c.

1816 Richard Watson, bishop of Llandaff theology, chemistry, &c.

1816 Richard Brinsley Sheridan; dramatic pieces

1819 John Wolcot (called Peter Pindar); satirical poetry

1819 Professor Playfair, Scotland; outlines of natural philosophy, miscellanies

1820 Sir Joseph Banks, naturalist. Died June 19

1824 The right hon. lord Byron; poetry

1825 Rev. Abraham Rees, D.D. editor of the New Cyclopædia, &c. Died June 9

EXPLANATION OF THE MOST COMMON ABBREVIATIONS OF WORDS.

A. B. Artium Baccalaureus, *Bachelor of Arts.*
Abp. *Archbishop.*
A. C. Anno Christi, *In the year of Christ.*
Acct. *Accompt.*
A. D. Anno Domini, *In the year of our Lord.*
A. M. or M. A. Artium Magister, *Master of Arts.*
A. M. Anno Mundi, *In the year of the world;* Ante Meridiem, *Forenoon.*
B. A. *Bachelor of Arts.*
Bart. or Bt. *Baronet.*
B. C. *Before Christ.*
B. D. *Bachelor of Divinity.*
Bp. *Bishop.*
B. L. *Bachelor of Laws.*
C. or Cent. *for* Centum, *A hundred.*
Cr. *Creditor.*
Cwt. *A hundred weight.*
D. D. *Doctor in Divinity.*
d. *for* Denarium, *A penny.*
Dec. or 10ber. *December.*
Dr. *Doctor and Debtor.*
e. g. Exempli gratia, *For example.*
Exr. *Executor.*
F. *Fellow;* as,
F. R. S. *Fellow of the Royal Society.*
G. R. Georgius Rex, *George the King.*
n. e. Hoc est, *That is.*
H. M. S. *His Majesty's Ship.*
Id. Idem, *The same.*
i. e. Id est, *That is.*
J. H. S. Jesus Hominum Salvator, *Jesus the Saviour of Mankind.*
K. B. *Knight of the Bath.*
K. C. *Knight of the Crescent.*
Kt. or Knt. *Knight.*
L. and Lib. Libræ, *Pounds.*
L. D. *Lady Day.*
LL. D. Legum Doctor, *Doctor of Laws.*
L. S. Locus Sigilli, *The place of the Seal.*
M. Mille, *A thousand.*
M. B. Medicinæ Baccalaureus, *Bachelor of Physic.*
M. D. Medicinæ Doctor, *Doctor of Physic.*
Messrs. *Gentlemen.*

Mr. Master (*Magister*).
Mrs. Mistress (*Magistra*).
M. S. Memoriæ Sacrorum, *Sacred to the Memory.*
Ms. *Manuscript.*
MSS. *Manuscripts.*
N. *North* and *Note.*
N. B. Nota Bene, *Mark well.*
n. l. Non liquet, *It appears not.*
No. *Number.*
Nov. or 9ber. *November.*
N. S. *New Style.*
Oct. or 8ber. *October.*
O. S. *Old Style.*
Per cent. Per centum, *By the hundred.*
P. M. Post Meridiem, *Afternoon.*
P. S. *Postscript.*
q. Quadrans, *A farthing.*
q. d. Quasi dicat, *As if he should say;* and Quasi dictum, *As if it were said.*
q. e. d. Quod erat demonstrandum, *Which was to be demonstrated.*
q. l. Quantum libet, *As much as you will.*
q. s. Quantum sufficit, *A sufficient quantity.*
Qy. *Query.*
Reg. Prof. Regius Professor, *King's Professor.*
Rev. *Reverend.*
Rt. Wpful. *Right Worshipful.*
Rt. Hon. *Right Honourable.*
S. *South;* and Solidus, *A shilling.*
S. or St. *Saint.*
S. A. Secundum artem, *According to the rules of art.*
Sept. or 7ber. *September.*
Servt. *Servant.*
ss. Semissis, *Half a pound.*
S. T. P. Sacro-sanctæ Theologiæ Professor, *Professor of Divinity.*
v. Vide. *See;* and *Verse.*
viz. Videlicet, *To wit.*
Wp. *Worship.*
Xmas. *Christmas.*
&. et, *and.*
&c. et cætera, *and the rest; and so forth.*

DIRECTIONS

FOR ADDRESSING PERSONS OF EVERY RANK AND DENOMINATION;

1. In Writing or Conversation ;—2. In the Super criptions of Letters.

THE ROYAL FAMILY.

The KING—
1. *Sire*, or *Sir*; *Most Gracious Sovereign*; *May it please your Majesty.*
2. *To the King's Most Excellent Majesty.*

The QUEEN—
1. *Madam*; *Most Gracious Sovereign*; *May it please your Majesty.*
2. *To the Queen's Most Excellent Majesty.*

The Sons and Daughters, Brothers and Sisters, of Sovereigns—
1. *Sir*, or *Madam*; *May it please your Royal Highness.*
2. *To his Royal Highness the Duke of Clarence*; *To her Royal Highness the Duchess of Clarence.*

Other branches of the Royal Family—
1. *Sir*, or *Madam*; *May it please your Highness.*
2. *To his Highness the Duke of Gloucester*; or, *To her Highness the Princess Sophia of Gloucester.*

THE NOBILITY.

A Duke or Duchess—
1. *My Lord*, or *My Lady*; *May it please your Grace.*
2. *To his Grace the Duke* (or, *To her Grace the Duchess*) *of Wellington.*

A Marquis or Marchioness—
1. *My Lord*, or *My Lady*; *May it please your Lordship*, or, *May it please your Ladyship.*
2. *To the Most Noble the Marquis* (or *Marchioness*) *of Lansdown.*

An Earl or Countess—The same:
To the Right Honourable the Earl (*Countess*) *of Harrowby.*

A Viscount or Viscountess—
1. *My Lord*, or *My Lady*; *May it please your Lordship*, or *May it please your Ladyship.*
2. *To the Right Honourable Viscount* (or *Viscountess*) *Goderich.*

Baron or Baroness—The same:
To the Right Honourable Baron (or *Baroness*) *De Tabley.*

The Widow of a Nobleman is addressed in the same style, with the introduction of the word *Dowager*—
To the Right Honourable the Dowager Lady Byron.

The Sons of Dukes and Marquisses, and the eldest Sons of Earls, have, by courtesy, the titles of *Lord* and *Right Honourable*; and all the Daughters have those of *Lady* and *Right Honourable.*

The younger Sons of Earls, and the Sons and Daughters of Viscounts and Barons, are styled *Honourable.*

OFFICIAL MEMBERS OF THE STATE.

A Member of his Majesty's most Honourable Privy Council—
1. *Sir*, or *My Lord*; *Right Honourable Sir*, or *My Lord*; as the case may require.
2. *To the Right Honourable John, Lord Lyndhurst, Lord High Chancellor of England.*
To the Right Honourable George Canning, First Commissioner of his Majesty's Treasury, &c.
To the Right Honourable Viscount Dudley and Ward, his Majesty's Principal Secretary of State for Foreign Affairs.

The whole Privy Council, taken together, are styled *Most Honourable.*

Ambassadors and Governors under his Majesty—
1. *Sir*, or *My Lord*, as the case may be; *May it please your Excellency.*
2. *To his Excellency the American* (or *Russian*, or other) *Ambassador.*
To his Excellency the Honourable David Erskine, His Majesty's Minister to the United States of America.
To his Excellency Richard Colley, Marquis Wellesley, Lieutenant General and General Governor of that part of the United Kingdom called Ireland.

Judges—
1. *My Lord*; *May it please your Lordship.*
2. *To the Right Honourable Lord Tenterden, Lord Chief Justice of England.*

The Lord Mayor of London, York, or Dublin; and the Lord Provost of Edinburgh, during office—
1. *My Lord*; *May it please your Lordship.*
2. *To the Right Honourable A. Brown, Lord Mayor of London*; *To the Right Honourable Sir James Fettes, Bart. Lord Provost of Edinburgh.*

The Mayors of all Corporations, (excepting the preceding Lord Mayors,) and the Sheriffs, Recorder, and Aldermen of London, are addressed *Right Worshipful*; and the Aldermen and Recorders of other Corporations, and Justices of the Peace, *Worshipful.*

THE PARLIAMENT.

House of Peers—
1. *My Lords*; *May it please your Lordships.*
2. *To the Right Honourable the Lords Spiritual and Temporal, in Parliament assembled.*

House of Commons—
1. *May it please your Honours.*
2. *To the Honourable the Knights, Citizens, and Burgesses, in Parliament assembled.*

The Speaker of Ditto—
1. *Sir,* or *Mr. Speaker.*
2. *To the Right Honourable Charles Manners Sutton, Speaker of the House of Commons.*

A Member of the House of Commons, not ennobled—
1. *Sir.*
2. *To John Dent, Esq. M. P. Clapham, Surry.*

THE CLERGY.
An Archbishop—
1. *My Lord; May it please your Grace.*
2. *To his Grace the Archbishop of Canterbury;* or, *To the most Reverend Father in God, Charles Lord Archbishop of Canterbury.*

A Bishop—
1. *My Lord; May it please your Lordship.*
2. *To the Right Reverend Father in God, Thomas Lord Bishop of Salisbury.*

A Dean—
1. *Sir,* or *Mr. Dean; Reverend Doctor.*
2. *To the Reverend Doctor Isaac Milner, Dean of Carlisle, Queen's College, Cambridge.*

Archdeacons and Chancellors are addressed in the same manner.

The rest of the Clergy—
1. *Sir; Reverend Sir.*
2. *To the Reverend Josiah Pratt, Doughty-street, London.*

If ennobled, to be addressed as follows—
2. *To the Right Honourable and Reverend William Earl Nelson, D.D. &c.*

INCORPORATED BODIES.
Some have the title *Honourable* conferred upon them—
1. *Honoured Sirs; May it please your Honours.*
2. *To the Honourable the Court of Directors of the United Company of Merchants of England trading to the East Indies.*
To the Honourable the Governor, Deputy-Governor, and Directors of the Bank of England.
To the Honourable the Governor and Company of the Plate-Glass Manufacturers.

N. B. Where any Nobleman, having the title *Right Honourable,* is at the head of an incorporated Body, that addition must be used, as in the following instance; the *Right Honourable Henry William, Marquis of Anglesey,* being Master-General of the Ordnance.

To the Right Honourable and Honourable the Board of Ordnance.

THE ARMY AND NAVY.
A Nobleman is addressed according to his particular title, to which is added that which his commission confers upon him—
To the Right Honourable Cuthbert Lord Collingwood, Commander in Chief of his Majesty's Ships and Vessels in the Mediterranean.

Generals, Admirals, Colonels, Field-Officers, and all other Officers, have the title of their commission set first in the superscription of letter—
To Major-General Sir John Doyle, Bart. and K. C. Colonel of his Majesty's 81th Regiment of Foot.
To Major A. A. Campbell, of his Majesty's 42d Regiment of Foot; or, *To Captain Horton, of his Majesty's Ship Gloucester;*—and at the beginning of letters, *Sir;* or, when addressed by a person of very inferior station, *Honoured Sir;* or *May it please your Honour.*

BARONETS AND KNIGHTS.
1. *Sir.*
2. *To Sir Francis Burdett, Bart. St. James's Place.*
To Sir J. T. Duckworth, K. B.
To Sir William Ouseley.
Their Ladies are addressed by the title of *Lady.*

GENTRY.
Gentlemen of property, and Gentlemen in the profession of the Law, are universally addressed by the title of *Esquire.*

Gentlemen in the profession of Physic have the title of *Doctor* prefixed—
To Dr. George Birkbeck, Broad-street, Bishopsgate.

PERSONS IN TRADE,
Carrying on business singly, are addressed *Sir,* and have *Mr.* (for *Magister* or *Master*) prefixed to their names in the superscription of letters.

In partnership, they are styled *Gentlemen,* and have *Messrs.* (for *Messieurs*) prefixed to their names.

LATIN AND FRENCH QUOTATIONS AND PHRASES.

LATIN

AB initio, *from the beginning*
Ab urbe condita, *from the building of the city*
Ac etiam, *and also* [city]
Ad captandum vulgus, *to catch the vulgar*
Ad extremum, *at the worst*
Adficietur malo, *he shall suffer for it*
Ad infinitum, *to infinity*
Ad libitum, *at pleasure*
Ad quod damnum, *to what damage*
Ad referendum, *to be further considered*
Ad scriptus glebæ, *attached to the soil*
Ad valorem, *according to the value*
A fortiori, *with stronger reason*
Agere gratias, *to give thanks*
Alias, *otherwise*
Alibi, *elsewhere* [fry]
Aliud mihi est agendum, *I have other fish to*
Alma mater, *a benign mother; University*
Alternis horis, *every other hour*
Amicus humani generis, *a friend of the human race*
Amicus certus in re incerta cernitur, *a friend in need is a friend indeed*
Amicus curiæ, *a friend of the court*
Amor patriæ, *the love of our country*
Anglice, *in English*
Anguis in herba, *a snake in the grass*
Animo furandi, *with the intention of stealing*
Anno domini, *the year of our Lord* [ing]
Annus mirabilis, *the year of wonders*
Ante hos sex menses, *six months ago*
A posteriori, *from the latter; from behind*
A priori, *from the former; from before*
Arcanum, *a secret*
Arcana imperii, *state secrets*
Ardentia verba, *glowing words*
Ardentem facem, *a lighted brand*
Argumentum ad hominem, *an argument; fist argument, strong from personal application*
Assumpsit, *he took upon him to pay* [bold]
Audentes fortuna juvat, *fortune favours the*
Audi alteram partem, *hear the other party*
Audita querela, *the complaint being heard*
Aurea mediocritas, *the golden mean*
Auri sacra fames, *the accursed thirst of gold*
Aut Cæsar, aut nullus, *he will be Cæsar or nobody; he will reach the first station or not exist* [of marriage]
A vinculo matrimonii, *from the chain or tie*

Beneficiis maleficia pensare, *to do good for evil*
Bona fide, *in good faith; in reality* [evil]
Bonus, *good, happy*
Brutum fulmen, *a harmless thunderbolt*

Cacoethes carpendi, *a rage for collecting*
Cacoethes loquendi, *a rage for speaking*
Cacoethes scribendi, *an itch for writing*
Cadit questio, *the question falls, or drops to the ground*

Caput mortuum, dead residuum; the worthless remains
Cede Deo, *yield to Providence*
Certum pete finem, *aim at a sure end*
Cæteris paribus, *the rest being alike, or other things being equal*
Commune bonum, *a common good*
Compos mentis, *a man of a sound and composed mind*
Concordia discors, *a jarring concord*
Contra bonos mores, *against good manners*
Cor unum, via una, *one heart, one way*
Credenda, *things to be believed*
Credula res amor est, *love is credulous*
Crux, *any thing vexatious or difficult*
Cui bono? *to what good will it tend?*
Cui malo? *to what evil?*
Cura facit canos, *care will kill a cat*
Currente calamo, *with great expedition*
Custos rotulorum, *the keeper of the rolls*

Data, *things granted*
Deceptio visus, *a visual illusion*
De facto, *from the fact; in reality*
De jure, *from the law*
De mortuis nil nisi bonum, *of the dead let nothing be said but what is favourable*
Desunt cætera, *the remainder is wanting*
Dicto tempore, *at the appointed time*
Dii penates, *household gods*
Divide et impera, *divide and govern*
Domus, *home*
Domus amica, domus optima, *home is home, be it never so homely*
Ducit amor patriæ, *the love of my country leads me*
Dum spiro, spero, *whilst I breath I hope*
Dum vivimus vivamus, *whilst we live let us live*
Durante bene placito, *during good pleasure*
Durante vita, *during life* [weapon]
Durum telum necessitas, *necessity is a hard*

Ecce homo, *behold the man*
Ego de alliis loquor, tu de cepis respondes, *I talk of chalk, and you talk of cheese*
Esto perpetuo, *be thou perpetual*
Et cætera, *and the rest*
Et decus et pretium recti, *the ornament and the reward of virtue*
Et sic de similibus, *and so of the like*
Ex cathedra, *from the chair*
Excerpta, *extracts from a work* [case
Ex necessitate rei, *from the necessity of the*
Ex intervallo, *at some distance*
Ex nihilo nihil fiat, *nothing can come of nothing*
Ex officio, Ex officiis, *by virtue of office or offices*
Ex parte, *on one side only*
Ex tempore, off hand, without loss of time

Fac simile, *an exact copy*
Fata obstant, *the fates oppose it*
Favete linguis, *be attentive*   [*naille*
Fæx populi, *the dregs of the people; the ca-*
Fecit, *made it, or did it*
Felicitas multos habet amicos, *prosperity has many friends*
Felix qui nihil debet, *happy is the man who owes nothing*
Felo de se, *self-murder*
Feræ naturæ, *of a wild nature*
Fiat, *let it be done*
Fiat justitia ruat cœlum, *let justice be done though the heavens should fall*
Fiat lux, *let there be light*
Fide et amore, *by faith and love*
Fidus et audax, *faithful and intrepid*
Fide et fortitudine, *by faith and fortitude*
Finem respice, *look to the end*
Flagrante bello, *during hostilities*
Flecti non frangi, *to bend, not to break*
Fortes fortuna juvat, *fortune favours the bold*
Forti et fideli nil difficile, *nothing is difficult to the brave and faithful*
Fortuna favet fatuis, *fools have fortune*
Fortuna sequatur, *let fortune follow*
Fortunæ filius, *a son of fortune*
Furor loquendi, *an eagerness for speaking*
Furor scribendi, *an itch for writing*

Gratis, *for nothing*
Gratis dictum, *said for nothing*
Gravis ira regum semper, *the anger of kings is always severe*

Haud passibus æquis, *not with equal steps*
Hic et ubique, *here and there, and every where*
Hominis est errare, *it is human to err*
Homo multarum literarum, *a learned man*
Hortus siccus, *leaves of plants in a dried*
Hypogastrium, *the bottom of the belly* [*state*

Ignis fatuus, *wildfire*
Ignoramus, *an uninformed person*
Ignorantia facti excusat, *ignorance of the fact excuses*
Ignorantia non excusat legem, *ignorance does not prevent the operation of the law*
Illud satius est quod satis est, *enough is as good as a feast*
Impromptu, *a witticism made off hand*
In angustiis amici apparent, *adversity trieth friends*
In cœlo quies, *there is rest in heaven*
In loco, *in this place*
In propria persona, *in his own person*
In puris naturalibus, *stark naked*
Interdum stultus bene loquitur, *a fool speaks well at times*
Inter nos, *between ourselves*
In terrorem, *in terror*
In transitu, *on the passage*
In utroque fidelis, *faithful in both*   [*cuse*
nventa est caussa, *you have found an ex-*
n vino veritas, *there is truth in wine*
.pse dixit, *on his sole assertion*
Ipso facto, *by the fact it self*
Ipso jure, *by the law it self*
Ita est, *it is even so*

Jure humano, *by human law*
Jure divino, *by divine law*
Jus civile, *the civil law*
Jus gentium, *the law of nations*
Jus sanguinis, *the right of blood*

Lapsus linguæ, *a slip of the tongue*
Latet anguis in herba, *there is a snake in the grass*
Laus Deo, *praise be to God*
Lex talionis, *the law of retaliation*
Lex terræ, *the law of the land*
Libidini indulget, *he gives way to his humour*
Locum tenens, *a deputy or substitute*
Ludere cum sacris, *to jest profanely*

Magna charta, *the great charter*
Maximus in minimis, *great in little things*
Memento mori, *remember death*
Memorabilia, *matters deserving of record*
Mens conscia recti, *a mind conscious of rectitude*
Mens sana in corpore sano, *a sound mind in a sound body*
Meum et tuum, *mine and thine*
Minutiæ, *matters of nice distinction; trifles*
Mirabile dictu, *wonderful to tell*
Mittimus, *a writ to send one to prison*
Multum in parvo, *much in little*

Ne cede malis, *yield not to misfortunes*
Necessitas non habet legem, *necessity has no law*   [*fearfully*
Nec temere nec timide, *neither rashly nor*
Nec timeo nec sperno, *I neither fear nor despise*
Nemine contradicente, [nem. con.] *no e opposing, without opposition*
Nemine dissentiente, [nem. dis.] *no e dis-agreeing*
Ne plus ultra, *nothing more beyond*
Nolle prosequi, *unwilling to proceed*
Non compos mentis, *not of sound mind*
Non constat, *it does not appear*
Non obstante, *notwithstanding*
Non omnia possumus omnes, *man can of do every thing*   [*his country*
Non sibi sed patriæ, *not for himself, but for*
Non sum qualis eram, *I am not what I was*
Nosce teipsum, *know thyself*   [*been*
Noscitur ex sociis, *he is known by his com-*
Nudum pactum, *a simple agreement (pany*
Nunc aut nunquam, *now or never*
Nunquam non paratus, *always ready*

Obiter dictum, *a thing said by the way*
Odi profanum vulgus, *I hate the profane vulgar*
Omnia vincit amor, *love conquers all things*
Onus probandi, *the burden of proving*
O bonos mores! *O good manners!*
Operæ pretium est, *it is worth while*
Ora et labora, *pray and labour*
Ore tenus, *from the mouth*
O si sic omnia! *O had he thus always conducted himself!*
O tempora! O mores! *how are the times changed! and the manners debased!*
Otium cum dignitate, *ease and respect*
Otium sine dignitate, *leisure without respect*

Par nobile fratrum, (ironically) a noble pair of associates

Pari passu, with an equa. pace

Parvum parva decent, little things little men

Passim, everywhere

Patriis virtutibus, by hereditary virth.

Pater patriæ, the father of his country

Peccavi, I have sinned

Pendente lite, whilst the suit is depending

Per fas et nefas, through right and wrong

Permitte cætera divis, leave the rest to Providence

Per se, by itself

Pluries, at several times

Poeta nascitur non fit, a poet is born a poet

Posse comitatus, the power of the country

Postulata, things required

Prima facie, on the first view

Primæ viæ, the first passages

Primum mobile, the main spring

Principiis obsta, oppose mischief in the bud

Pro aris et focis, for our religion and firesides

Pro bono publico, for the good of the public

Pro et con, for and against

Pro tempore, for the time

Quid nunc, what now? applied to a person who makes news his principal pursuit

Quid pro quo, what for what; a mutual consideration; tit for tat

Quo animo, with what intention

Quod avertat Deus, which God forbid

Quod satis est, that which is enough

Quo jure, by what right

Quot homines tot sententiæ, so many men, so many opinions

Rara avis in terris, a rare bird on the earth; a prodigy

Rara fides, good faith

Recte et suaviter, justly and mildly

Requiescat in pace, may he rest in peace

Res facta, matter of fact

Res publica, the commonwealth

Salus populi, the welfare of the people

Salvo jure, saving the right

Scio tanquam ungues digitosque, I have it at my fingers' ends

Scire facias, cause it to be known

Sculpsit, engraved it

Semper idem, semper eadem, always the same

Semper paratus, always ready

Seriatim, in order, or in a series

Sibi quisque caveat oportet, every tub must stand on its own bottom

Sic donec, thus, until

Sic passim, so everywhere

Sic transit gloria mundi, such are the fluctuations of worldly splendour

Sicut ante, as before

Sine die, indefinitely

Sine joco, without jesting

Sine omni periculo, without any danger

Sine qua non, a thing without which another cannot be; an indispensable condition

Spes mea in Deo, my hope is in God

Spero meliora, I hope for better things

Status quo, or, status quo ante bellum, the condition of both parties before a war

Stratum super stratum, one layer upon another

Suaviter in modo, fortiter in re, gentle in manner, but rigorous in deed

Sub pœna, under a penalty

Sub silentio, in silence; without any notice

Si fortuna juvat, if fortune favour

Sui generis, of its own kind

Succedaneum, a substitute

Summum bonum, the chief good

Summum jus summa injuria, strict law is sometimes the greatest injustice

Supersedeas, you may remove or set aside

Tabula rasa, a smooth tablet

Tanto melius, all the better

Tempus edax rerum, time devours all things

Tuum est, it is your own

Ubi supra, where above mentioned, a refer

Ult. Ultimus, the last

Utile dulci, the useful with the pleasant

Uti possidetis, as you possess

Vade mecum, constant companion

Veni, vidi, vici, I came, I saw, I conquered

Ventis secundis, with prosperous winds; with uniform success

Veritas vincit, truth conquers

Vice versa, the terms exchanged, the reverse

Versus, against

Vide, or Vide ut supra, see, or see as above

Vide et crede, see and believe

Vide ut supra, see what has been said above or before

Vi et armis, by force and arms; illegally

Vincit amor patriæ, the love of my country overcomes

Vincit veritas, truth conquers

Vis inertiæ, the force of indolence

Vitiis nemo sine nascitur, no man is without his faults

Viva voce, by the living voice; orally

Vox et præterea nihil, a voice and nothing more

Vox populi vox Dei, the voice of the people is the voice of God

FRENCH.

A tion proces, action at law

A dieu pour jamais, farewell for ever

Affaire d'honneur, a business of honour

A faire de cœur, love affair; an amour

Affranchir une lettre, to frank a letter

Aimé, loved, beloved

A la bonne heure, well timed

A-la-hate, in haste

A-la-mode, in the fashion

Alègre, cheerful, merry

A l'improviste, unawares

Allez vous coucher, go to bed

Amende honorable, to recompense

A votre santé, to a wonder

Apres demain, *the day after to-morrow*
Apropos, *to the purpose; opportunely*
Argent comptant, *ready money*
Avancer de l'argent, *to advance money*
Avant-courier, *a harbinger*
Avec le temps, *in process of time*
Au commencement, *in the beginning*
Au pis aller, *at the worst*
Autant de tetes, autant d'opinions, *so many men, so many minds*
Autre affaire, *another affair*
Autre chose, *another thing*

Beau monde, *the gay world*
Beaux esprits, *men of wit*
Bien dit, *well spoken*
Bon avocat mauvais voisin, *a good lawyer, a bad neighbour*
Bon gre, mal gre, *whether the party will it or not*
Bon jour, *good morrow*
Bon jour, bonne œuvre, *the better day, the better deed*
Bon mot, *a jest, a quibble*
Bonne bouche, *a delicate morsel*
Bonne et belle assez, *good and handsome enough*
Bou ton, *high fashion*
Bourreau d'argent, *a spendthrift*

Carte blanche, *unlimited powers, or one's own terms*
C'est fait de lui, *it is all over with him*
C'est une autre chose, *it is quite a different thing*
C'est un vrai panier perce, *his money burns in his pocket*
Chacun a son gout, *every man to his taste*
Chasse cousin, *bad cheer given to offend poor relations*
Chef d'œuvre, *a master-piece*
Chevaux de frize, *stakes sharpened at each end, used to stop the progress of cavalry*
Comme dit l'autre, *as the saying is*
Comme il faut, *as it should be; handsomely*
Comme le temps passe! *how the time passes away!*
Comment vous en va? *how is it with you?*
Congé d'elire, *a leave to elect*
Corden, *a line*
Corps diplomatique, *the diplomatic body*
Coup de main, *a sudden or bold enterprise*
Coup d'œil, *a quick glance of the eye*
Coup de grace, *a stroke of mercy*
Courage sans peur, *courage without fear*
Coute qui coute, *let it cost what it may*
Cul de sac, *the bottom of a bag*

D'accord, *agreed*
De gaiete de cœur, *out of wantonness*
De haute lutte, *by main force*
De mal en pis, *from bad to worse*
Depot, *a store or magazine*
Dernier resort, *the last resource*
Detour, *a circuitous march*
De tout mon cœur, *with all my heart*
Dieu aidant! *by God's help*
Dieu defend le droit, *God defends the right*
Dieu et mon droit, *God and my right*
Dieu vous benisse, *God bless you*
Diseur de bons mots, *a sayer of good things*
Dos d'ane, *a thing rising to a ridge*
Double entendre, *a double meaning*

Doux yeux, *soft glances*
Droit des gens, *the law of nations*
Droit et avant, *right and forward*
Du fort au foible, *from the strong to the weak*

En abrege, *in short, in few words*
En avant, *forward*
En belle humeur, *in fine spirits*
En bon point, *in good plight; in good condition*
En conscience, *upon my conscience*
En detail, *by retail*
En Dieu est ma fiance, *in God is my trust*
Enfans perdus, *the forlorn hope of an army*
Enfant gate, *a spoiled child*
Enfant trouve, *a foundling*
En gros, *in a lump*
En la rose je fleurie, *I flourish in the rose*
En masse, *in a body*
En passant, *in passing*
En suivant la verite, *in following truth*
Entre deux vins, *half tipsy*
Entre-deux, *so so, indifferently*
Entre nous, *between ourselves*
Esperance en Dieu, *hope in God*
Esperance et Dieu, *hope and God*

Facon de parler, *a manner of speaking*
Faire mon devoir, *to do my duty*
Faire sans dire, *to act without ostentation*
Femme couverte, *a married woman*
Femme sole, *an unmarried woman*
Ferme ornee, *a decorated farm*
Fete champetre, *a rural feast in the open air*
Fidelite est de Dieu, *fidelity is of God*
Fille de chambre, *a chambermaid*
Fort bien, *very well*
Fort juste, *very right*
Foy en tout, *faith in every thing*
Foy pour devoir, *faith for duty*

Gaiete de cœur, *wantonness, mere mischief*
Gardez bien, *take care*
Gardez la foy, *keep faith*
Gibier de potence, *game for the gallows*
Gorge, *a narrow pass*
Goutte a goutte, *drop by drop*
Grisette jolie, *a plain girl*
Grossierete, *rudeness in conversation or manners*
Guerre a mort, *war till death*
Guerre a outrance, *war to extermination*

Haro, *hue and cry*
Haut et bon, *great and good*
Haut gout, *high flavour*
Hauteur, *haughtiness*
Honi soit qui mal y pense, *evil be to him that evil thinks*
Hors de combat, *disabled*

Il aboye tout le monde, *he snarls at every one [mighty enterprise*
Il a la mer a boire, *he has entered on a*
Il a le vin mauvais, *he is quarrelsome in his cups*
Il a seme des fleures sur un terrain aride, *he has planted flowers on a barren soil*
Il a tort, *he is in the wrong*
Il conduit bien sa barque, *he knows how to make his way through the world*

Il en fait ses choux gras, *he thereby makes ais cabbage fat*

Il est comme l'oiseau sur la branche, *he is like the bird on the branch; he has no settled state*

Il faut avoir des ailes avant que de voler, *you must learn to creep before you go*

Il faut souffrir patiemmement ce qui est inevitable. *what cannot be cured, must be endured*

Il n'a pas invente la poudre, *he is no conjuror*

Il n'a ni bouche ni eperon, *he has neither wit nor courage*

Il ne fait bien ni mal, *he is like a chip in porridge*

Il ne sait plus de quel bois faire fleche, *he is put to his last shift*

Il ne sait sur quel pied danser, *he knows not which way to turn him*

Il n'est sauce que d'appetit, *hunger is the best sauce*

Il se port forte mal, *he is very ill*

Il vaut mieux faire envie que pitie, *it is better to be envied than pitied*

J'ai bonne cause, *I have a good cause*

Jamais arriere, *never behind*

Je le tiens, *I hold it*

Je ne cherche qu'un. *I seek but for one*

Je ne le sais pas, *I don't know*

Je n'oublierai jamais, *I shall never forget*

J'en suis ravin, *I am ravished with it*

Je pense, *I think*

Je serai bien aise de vous voir, *I shall be very glad to see you*

Je suis pret, *I am ready*

Je vous en conjure, *I entreat you*

Je vous remercie, *I thank you*

Je vous rend mille graces, *I render you a thousand thanks*

Je vous souhaite une bonne annee! *a happy new year to you!*

Jeu de mots, *a play on words, a pun*

Jeu d'esprit, *a pun; a witticism*

Jeu de theatre, *stage-trick; attitude,* &c.

Jour de ma vie, *the day of my life*

La beaute passe promptment, *beauty soon fades*

La faim chasse le loup hors du bois, *famine drives the wolf from the wood*

La langue des femmes est leur epee, et elles ne la laissent pas rouiller, *a woman's tongue is her sword, which she does not suffer to rust*

L'amour de la justice, *the love of justice*

L'amour propre, *self-love*

La pauvrete est un glaive bien acere, *poverty is a sharp weapon*

Langage des halles, *the language of the markets; low abuse*

La sante est preferable aut richesses, *health is preferable to riches*

Le beau monde, *the gay or fashionable world*

Le bonheur, *good fortune*

Le bon temps viendra, *the good time will come* [cards

De desseus de cartes, *the lower face of the*

Le diable est aux vaches, *there is the devil to pay*

Le grand œuvre, *philosopher's stone*

Le malheur, *bad fortune*

Le mal tombera sur vous, *the mischief will light upon your own head*

Le monde est le livre des femmes, *the world is the book of women*

L'enfance est le temps le plus henreux de la vie, *childhood is the happiest time of life*

L'ennui, *disgust*

Le roi le veut, *the king wills it*

Le roi et l'etat, *the king and state*

Le sage entend a demi mot, *the wise man understands half a word*

Les bons comptes font les bon amis, *short reckonings make long friends*

Le scavoir faire, *address*

Le scavoir vivre, *the knowledge of the world*

Les doux yeux, *soft or amorous glances*

Les eaux sont basses chez lui, *his resources are exhausted*

Les mœurs, *manners or morals* [ears

Les murailles ont des oreilles, *walls have*

Les petits ruisseaux font les grandes rivieres, *many drops make a shower, or many a little makes a mickle*

Les savans, *the learned*

Le vent du bureau est bon, *things take a favourable turn*

Le vrai moyen, *the sure mode*

L'experience est la maitresse des fous, *experience is the mistress of fools*

L'horlage avance, *the clock goes too fast*

Liberte toute entiere, *liberty complete*

L'impiete perd les jeunes esprits, *irreligion is the ruin of youth*

Loyaute n'a honte, *loyalty has no shame*

Loyaute m'oblige, *loyalty binds me*

Ma chere madame, *my dear madam*

Maintien le droit. *maintain the right*

Maison de ville, *the town-house*

Maitre d'hotel, *a house steward*

Mal-a-propos, *untimely, ill-suited*

Marchand qui perd ne peut rire, *let him laugh that wins*

Mauvaise honte, *false shame, bashfulness*

Mieux vaut un tenez, que deux vous l'aurez, *one bird in the hand is worth two in the bush*

Mine relevee, *a noble look*

Mon cher ami, *my dear friend*

Mot du guet, *a watch-word*

Mots d'usage, *phrases in common use*

Ne nous contredisons pas, *let us be consistent with ourselves* [other

Ni l'un ni l'autre, *neither the one nor the*

Ni plus ni moins, *neither more nor less*

Nom de guerre. *a traveller's title*

N'oubliez, *do not forget*

On dit. *it is said*

On doit respecter la vieillesse, *we should respect old age*

On est assez riche quand on a le necessaire, *enough is as good as a feast*

Oublier je ne puis, *I can never forget*

Ouvrage de longue haleine, *a long-winded business*

Papier mache, *mashed paper*

Par accident, *casually, by chance*
Par astuce, *by craft*
Pardonnez moi, *excuse me*
Par exemple, *for instance*
Par meprise, *through mistake*
Pas a pas, on va bien loin, *fair and softly goes far*
Pense a bien, *think for the best*
Permettez moi, *permit me*
Petite garcon, *a young boy*
Petites maisons, *a mad-house*
Peu de bien, peu de soin, *little wealth, little care*
Pierre qui roule n'amasse point de mousse, *a rolling stone gathers no moss*
Plus on boit, plus on veut boire, *ever drunk, ever dry*
Point du tout, *not at all*
Pour bien desirer, *to desire good*
Pour passez le temps, *in order to pass time*
Pour le moins, *at the very least*
Pour tuer le temps, *in order to kill time*
Pour y parvenir, *to attain the object*
Prend moi tel que je suis, *take me such as I am*
Prendre la lune avec les dents, *to aim at impossibilities*
Prenez garde, *take care*
Presque la meme chose, *almost the same thing*

Quand les larrons s'entrebattent, les larcins se decouvrent, *when rogues fall out, honest men come by their own*
Querelle d'allemand, *a hasty quarrel about nothing*
Qui fait bien trouve bien, *well do, well have*
Qui se sent morveux se mouche, *if the cap fit, let him wear it*
Qu'il fait chaud, *how warm it is*
Qui m'aime, aime mon chien, *love me, love my dog*
Qui pense, *who thinks*
Qui perd peche, *the unsuccessful is generally held in the wrong*
Qui vive, *who goes there? on the* qui vive, *i. e. on the alert*

Regle, *a rule, custom, practice*
Rengainez votre compliment, *forbear those compliments*
Rien moins, *nothing else*
Ruse de guerre, *a stratagem*
Ruse contre ruse, *trick upon trick*

Sang froid, *cold blood; indifference*

Sans changer, *without changing*
Sans Dieu rien, *nothing without God*
Sans doute, *without doubt; certainly*
Sauve qui peut, *save himself who can*
Sens devant derriere, *the wrong way*
Si je puis, *if I can*
Si vous lui laissez prendre un pied, il en prendra quatre, *if you give him an inch, he will take an ell*
Soi-disant, *self-called, self-styled*
Soyez ferme, *be firm, persevere*
Suivez raison, *follow reason*
Surement, *to be sure*
Sur mon honneur, *upon my honour*
Sur ma vie, *upon my life*

Tache sans tache, *a work without a stain*
Taisez-vous, *hold your tongue*
Tant mieux, *so much the better*
Tant pis, *so much the worse*
Tel maitre, tel valet, *like master, like man*
Tete-a-tete, *face to face; cheek by jowl*
Toujours pret, *always ready*
Tout bien ou rien, *the whole or nothing*
Tout le monde, *every body*

Un bel esprit, *a wit*
Un cœur contrit, *a broken heart*
Un esprit fort, *a free thinker*
Un homme prevoyant donne peu au hasard, *a prudent man depends little on chance*
Un homme d'esprit, *a witty or ingenious man*
Un homme timide ne reçut jamais aupres des belles, *faint heart never won fair lady*
Un sot a triple etage, *an egregious block head*
Un tout seul, *one alone*

Vent d'aval, *a westerly wind*
Verite sans peur, *truth without fear*
Vis-a-vis, *over against, opposite*
Vive l'amour, *success to love*
Vive la bagatelle, *success to trifling*
Vive le roi, *God save the king*
Vivre au jour la journee, *to live from hand to mouth*
Voila, *there is*
Voila une autre chose, *there you see is another thing*
Vous avez bonne mine, *you look well*
Vous avez bien rencontre, *you hit the right nail on the head*
Vous y perdrez vos pas, *you will there lose your labour*

A LIST

OF THE CITIES, BOROUGHS, and MARKET TOWNS,

IN ENGLAND AND WALES;

The Days on which the MARKETS are held, and how far distant from
London in measured Miles.

Corrected from Gray's New Book of Roads, 1827.

BAS	BRA
ABBOTSBURY, Dorsetsh. Thursday ..127	BATH. Somer. Wednesday, Saturday....106
Aberconway, Caern. Friday........226	Battle, Sussex, Thursday 56
Aberford, Yorkshire, Wednesday 186	Bawtry. Yorkshire, Wednesday 153
Abergavenny, Monm. Tuesday 147	Beaconsfield, Bucks, Thursday. 23
Abergeley, Denbighshire, Saturday 224	Beaminster, Dorsetsh. Thursday........138
Aberystwith, Card. Monday............207	Beaumaris, B. Anglesey. Wednesday....250
Abingdon, B. Berks, Monday. Friday....56	Beccles. Suffolk, Saturday 109
St. Albans. B. Hertfordshire, Saturday ..21	Bedale, Yorksh. Tuesday 223
Alcester, Warwickshire, Tuesday........97	Bedford, Bedfordsh. Tuesday, Saturday ..50
Aldborough, B. Suffolk, Saturday........94	Bedwin, B. Wiltsh. Tuesday 70
Aldborough. B. Yorkshire, Saturday....207	Bellingham, Northumb.Tuesday, Saturd. 285
Alford, Lincolnshire, Tuesday..........196	Belper, Derbysh. Saturday..............134
Alfreton, Derbyshire, Monday..........140	Bere Regis. Dorsetsh. Wednesday 112
Alnwick, Northumberland. Saturday....308	Berkeley. Gloucestersh. Wednesday 113
Alresford, Hants, Thursday..............57	Berkhampstead, Hertfordsh. Saturday....26
Alston Moor, Cumberland, Saturday....307	Berwick, Northumberland, Saturday....338
Alton, Hants, Saturday 47	Betley, Staffordshire, Tuesday..........157
Altringham. Cheshire, Tuesday 183	Beverley, B. Yorks.Wednesday. Saturday 179
Ambleside, Westmoreland, Wednesday..278	Bewdley, B. Worcestersh. Saturday 122
Amersham, B. Bucks, Tuesday 26	Bicester, Oxfordsh. Friday 55
Amesbury, Wiltshire, Friday 77	Biddeford, Devonsh. Tuesday 197
Ampthill, Bedfordshire, Thursday........50	Biggleswade. Bedfordsh. Tuesday........45
Andover. B. Hants, Saturday 63	Billericay, Essex, Tuesday 23
Appleby. B. Westmoreland, Saturday....270	Billesdon, Leicestersh. Friday 93
Appledore, Kent, Saturday 60	Bilston, Suffolk, Wednesday 63
Arundel, B. Sussex, Wednesday, Saturday 55	Binbrook, Lincolnsh. Wednesday 157
ST. ASAPH, Flint. Saturday 217	Bingham, Nottinghamshire. Thursday ..127
Ashborn, Derbyshire, Saturday 140	Birmingham. Warwicksh. Thursday 109
Ashburton. B. Devon. Tuesday.Saturday 183	Bishop's Auckland, Durham, Thursday..249
Ashby de la Zouch, Leic. Saturday......115	Bishop's Castle, B. Salop, Friday........159
Ashford, Kent, Saturday 54	Bishop's Stortford, Herts. Thursday......30
Askrigg, Yorkshire, Thursday..........246	Bisley, Gloucestershire, Thursday........96
Atherstone, Warwickshire, Tuesday 107	Bitford, Warwickshire, Friday..........101
Attleborough, Norfolk. Thursday........94	Blackburn, Lancashire. Monday........212
Auburn, Wiltshire. Tuesday 73	Blandford, Dorsetshire, Saturday 103
St. Austle, Cornwall, Friday 73	Bletchingly, B. Surrey 21
Axbridge, Somersetshire. Thursday 129	Blythe, Nottinghamshire, Thursday 151
Axminster, Devonshire, Saturday 147	Bodmin, B. Cornwall, Saturday 234
Aylesbury, B. Bucks, Saturday 39	Bolingbroke, Lincolnshire. Tuesday 129
Aylsham. Norfolk, Saturday............126	Bolsover, Derbyshire, Friday 145
Bakewell, Derbyshire, Monday 152	Bolton, Lancash. Monday 199
Bala, Merion. Saturday 194	Bootle, Cumberland. Wednesday........271
Baldock, Hertfordshire, Thursday........37	Boroughbridge, B. Yorksh. Saturday....206
Bampton, Oxford. Wednesday............71	Bosscastle, Cornwall, Thursday 19C
Bampton, Devonshire. Saturday........162	Bossiney, B. Cornwall 234
Banbury. B. Oxfordshire, Thursday......69	Boston, B. Lincolnsh. Wed. Saturday....112
BANGOR. Caern. Wednesday 236	Bosworth, Leicestersh. Wednesday 106
Barking, Essex, Saturday 7	Botisdale, Suffolk, Wednesday 86
Barkway, Herts, Saturday 34	Bourn, Lincolnsh. Saturday 93
Barnard-Castle. Durham, Wednesday..244	Bow, Devonsh. Thursday 179
Barnet, Herts, Monday..................11	Brackley, B. Northamptonsh. Wed.......63
Barnsley, Yorkshire, Wednesday 176	Bradfield, Essex, Thursday 47
Barnstaple, B. Devonshire. Friday......189	Bradford, Wiltsh. Monday..............109
Barton, Lincolnshire. Monday..........163	Bradford. Yorksh. Thursday............205
Basingstoke, Hants, Wednesday..........45	Bradninch, Devonsh. Saturday 172

Wotton Basset, B. Wiltsh. Thursday 66	Yarmouth, B. Hants, Friday	
Wrexham, Denbighsh. Mond. Thursd. ..152	Yarmouth, B. Norfolk...................	
Wrington, Somersetsh. Tuesday 129	Yarm, Yorkshire, Thursday	
Wrotham, Kent, Tuesday.................24	Yaxley, Suffolk............... 81	
Wycomb, High, B. Bucks, Friday........29	Yeovil, Somersetsh. Friday 1.2	
Wye, Kent, Thursday.....................55	YORK, Yorksh. Thursday, Saturday. . ..199	
Wyndham, Norfolk, Friday 100		

TABLES
OF
IMPERIAL WEIGHTS AND MEASURES.

TROY WEIGHT.

4 Grains make ....1 Carat
24 Grains or 6 Carats....1 Pennyweight
20 Pennyweights ......1 Ounce
12 Ounces ....1 Pound

Note.—A Pound Avoirdupois contains 14 Ounces, 11 Pennyweights, 16 Grains Troy.

AVOIRDUPOIS WEIGHT.

16 Drams make ....1 Ounce
16 Ounces ....1 Pound
14 Pounds ....1 Stone
28 Pounds ....1 Quarter
4 Quarters or 112 lbs. ..1 Hundred weight
20 Hundred weights ....1 Ton

Note.—The Imperial Pound Avoirdupois is lighter than the old one, about half a grain Troy.

APOTHECARIES' WEIGHT.

20 Grains make ....1 Scruple
3 Scruples ....1 Drachm
8 Drachms ....1 Ounce
12 Ounces ....1 Pound

Note.—The Apothecaries' Grain, Ounce, and Pound, are the same as the Troy, but differing in their divisions and subdivisions.

LONG MEASURE.

3 Barley-corns make ..1 Inch
4 Inches ....1 Hand
12 Inches, or 3 Hands ..1 Foot
3 Feet ....1 Yard
6 Feet or 2 Yards ......1 Fathom
5 Yards and a Half ....1 Rod, pole or per.
40 Poles or Perches ....1 Furlong
8 Furlongs or 1760 yds. 1 Mile
3 Miles ....1 League
60 Geographical or 69 &
  a Half Statute Miles 1 Degree
360 Degrees ....A Circle, or the circumference of the Earth

Note.—The degree of longitude is different in different latitudes.—The height of horses is measured by the Hand; and depths are ascertained by the Fathom.

SQUARE MEASURE.

144 Inches make........1 Foot
9 Feet ....1 Yard

272 Feet and a Quarter..1 Rod, pole or p
16 Poles or Perches....1 Chain
40 Poles or Perches....1 Rood
4 Roods or 4840 Yards 1 Acre
640 Acres ....1 Mile

CUBIC OR SOLID MEASURE.

1728 Inches make ......1 Foot
27 Feet ....1 Yard
40 Ft. of rough timber 1 Ton or
50 Ft. of hewn timber 1 Ton or

CLOTH MEASURE.

2 Inches and a qr. make 1 nail
4 Nails ....1 Quarter of a y
3 Quarters ....1 Flemish Ell
4 Quarters ....1 Yard
5 Quarters ....1 English Ell
6 Quarters ....1 French Ell

Note.—The Yard in Cloth Measure is the same as in Long, but differs in its divisions and subdivisions.

BEER MEASURE.

4 Gills make ....1 Pint
2 Pints ....1 Quart
4 Quarts ....1 Gallon
9 Gallons ....1 Firkin
2 Firkins or 18 Gallons 1 Kilderkin
36 Gallons ....1 Barrel
54 Galls. or 1 Bar. & half 1 Hogshead
72 Gallons ....1 Puncheon
2 Hogshds. or 108 Galls. 1 Butt

Note.—The Imperial Ale and Beer Measures are about one-sixtieth part less than the old measure.

WINE MEASURE.

4 Gills make ....1 Pint
2 Pints ....1 Quart
4 Quarts ....1 Gallon
10 Gallons ....1 Anker
18 Gallons ....1 Runlet
31 Gallons and a Half....Half a Hogsh
42 Gallons ....1 Tierce
63 Gallons ....1 Hogshead
84 Gallons ....1 Puncheon
2 Hogshds. or 126 Galls. 1 Pipe or Bu
2 Pipes or 252 Gallons..1 Tun

Note.—The Imperial Wine Mea about one fifth larger than the o

IMPERIAL WEIGHTS AND MEASURES.

DRY MEASURE.

4 Gills make 1	Pint
2 Pints 1	Quart
2 Quarts 1	Pottle
2 Pottles or 4 Quarts 1	Gallon
2 Gallons 1	Peck
4 Pecks or 8 Gallons 1	Bushel
2 Bushels 1	Strike
4 Bushels 1	Coomb
2 Coombs or 8 Bushels ..1	Quarter
4 Quarters 1	Chaldron
5 Quarters or 40 Bushels 1	Wey
2 Weys 1	Last

Note.—The Imperial Dry Measures are about 1-32d part larger than the old—and cause an increase of three farthings in every two shillings.

COAL MEASURE.

4 Pecks make..........1	Bushel
8 Bushels 1	Sack
9 Bushels 1	Vat or Strike
12 Sacks or 36 Bushels ..1	Chaldron
5 Chaldrons and a Qtr. 1	Room
Chaldrons 1	Score

HAY AND STRAW.

36 lbs. make 1	Truss of Straw
56 lbs. 1	Truss of old Hay
60 lbs. 1	Trs. of new Hay
36 Trusses 1	Load

WOOL WEIGHT.

7 Pounds make 1	Clove
2 Cloves or 14 lbs......1	Stone
2 Stones or 28 lbs......1	Tod
6 Tods and a Half......1	Wey
2 Weys or 364 lbs.......1	Sack
12 Sacks 1	Last

Note.—The Stone varies according to the Goods and Places of purchase and sale.

MISCELLANEOUS.

	lbs.
A Fother of Lead is 19 cwt. & a half or	2184
A Puncheon of Prunes..................	1120
A Barrel of Soap......................	256
A Chest of Candles	144
A Faggot of Steel.....................	120

	lbs.
A Barrel of Raisins....................	112
A Quintal	100
A Chest of Tea, about	84
A Firkin of Soap	64
A Firkin of Butter	56
A Bushel of Salt	56
A Stone of Hemp	32
A Stone of Cheese	16
A Peck of Salt	14
A Stone of Iron Shots, or Horseman's weight...............	14
A Gallon of Oil, old measure ......7 & a hf.	
Imperial ditto ....9 & a qr.	
A Stone of Butcher's Meat	8
A Stone of Glass	5

MISCELLANEOUS FRACTIONS.

960 Furthings 1	Pound Sterling
7000 Grains 1	lb. Avoirdupois
5760 Grains 1	lb. Troy
5760 Grains 1	lb. Apothecaries
1792 Ounces 1	Cwt.
63360 Inches 1	Mile
525960 Minutes 1	Julian Year
525948 Minutes 1	Solar Year

VALUE OF ANCIENT COINS.

	s.	d.
A Moidore	27	0
A Jacobus	25	0
A Carolus.......................	23	0
A Mark	13	4
An Angel	10	0
A Noble	6	8

WEIGHT OF ENGLISH CURRENT COIN.

GOLD.	dwt.	gr.
A Sovereign 5	2 & a half	
Half Sovereign..........2	13 & a quarter	

SILVER.	dwt.	gr.
A Crown 18	4 & 4-11ths	
Half a Crown 9	2 & 2-11ths	
A Shilling 3	15 & 3-11ths	
Sixpence 1	19 & 7-11ths	

Note.—The standard for Silver Coin is 11 oz. 2 dwt. of silver and 18 dwt. of copper melted together; for Gold Coin 22 carats of fine gold and 2 of copper.

BILL AND RECEIPT STAMPS.

BILLS, DRAFTS, &c.

	Not exceed.	Exc.
	2 months.	2 m.
If L2 & not above L5 5s...0	1 0...0	1 6
Above 5 5s......... 20 0...0	1 6...0	2 0
20 0 .... 30 0...0	2 0...0	2 6
30 0 .... 50 0...0	2 6...0	3 6
50 0 .... 100 0...0	3 6...0	4 6
100 0 .... 200 0...0	4 6...0	5 0
200 0 .... 300 0...0	5 0...0	6 0
300 0 .... 500 0...0	6 0...0	8 6
1000 0...0	8 6...0	12 0
0 0	15 0	

RECEIPTS.

If L2 & under L5	two-pence
5	10 three-pence
10	20 sixpence
20	50 one shilling
50	100 one shilling & sixpence
100	200 two shillings & sixpence
200	300 four shillings
300	500 five shillings
500	1000 seven shillings & sixpence
1000 or upwards ten shillings	

Receipts in full of all demands...ten shillings
The stamp to be paid

DRY MEASURE.

4 Gills make ....1 Pint
2 Pints ....1 Quart
2 Quarts...............1 Pottle
2 Pottles or 4 Quarts ....1 Gallon
2 Gallons ....1 Peck
4 Pecks or 8 Gallons ....1 Bushel
2 Bushels ....1 Strike
4 Bushels ....1 Coo...
2 Coombs or 8 Bushels ..1 Q...
4 Quarters.............1 C...
5 Quarters or 40 Bushels 1 ...
2 Weys ....

Note.—The Imperia'
about 1-3rd part lar...
cause an increase of
two shillings.

CO...

4 Pecks ma'
8 Bushels
9 Bushe'
12 Sack'
5 Ch...
erland, 1 C...
n Colfie'
f ham, N
sea, G'
don, V 86 lb.
aster. 56 lb:
worth 60 lb...
ing, 86 Tr
rsh
itor

7 P...
2 Cl...
2 St...
6 To
2 W
12 Sa...

Not.
Goods

A Foth
A Pur...
A Ba...
A Che
A Fag...

B...

If 1
Above
...
...
5
b
10
20...
80...
50...
100
200
800

Lightning Source UK Ltd.
Milton Keynes UK
UKOW06n2301130716

278240UK00017B/109/P

9 781297 621826